# Information Security Management Handbook

## Sixth Edition

## Volume 4

# Information Security Management Handbook

## Sixth Edition

## Volume 4

Edited by

Harold F. Tipton, CISSP · Micki Krause, CISSP

CRC Press
Taylor & Francis Group
Boca Raton London New York

CRC Press is an imprint of the
Taylor & Francis Group, an **informa** business

AN AUERBACH BOOK

CRC Press
Taylor & Francis Group
6000 Broken Sound Parkway NW, Suite 300
Boca Raton, FL 33487-2742

First issued in paperback 2019

© 2010 by Taylor & Francis Group, LLC
CRC Press is an imprint of Taylor & Francis Group, an Informa business

No claim to original U.S. Government works

ISBN-13: 978-1-4398-1902-9 (hbk)
ISBN-13: 978-0-367-38388-6 (pbk)

### Library of Congress Cataloging-in-Publication Data

Tipton, Harold F.
    Information security management handbook / Harold F. Tipton, Micki Krause. --6th ed.
        p. cm. ((ISC) 2 Press ; 27)
    Includes bibliographical references and index.
    ISBN 978-1-4398-1902-9
    1. Computer security--Management--Handbooks, manuals, etc. 2. Data protection--Handbooks, manuals, etc. I. Krause, Micki. II. Title.

QA76.9.A25154165 2006
005.8--dc22
                                                                        2006048504

**Visit the Taylor & Francis Web site at**
**http://www.taylorandfrancis.com**

**and the CRC Press Web site at**
**http://www.crcpress.com**

# Contents

## *Policies, Standards, Procedures, and Guidelines*

## *Risk Management*

# DOMAIN 4: APPLICATION SECURITY
## *System Development Controls*

# DOMAIN 5: CRYPTOGRAPHY
## *Crypto Concepts, Methodologies, and Practices*

# Preface

The days of wringing hands and warning of "fear, uncertainty, and doubt" have given way to thoughtful and intelligent approaches to protecting information. This is due, in great part, to the adoption of comprehensive and far-reaching standards that foster the practice of integrating security into the business.

So, although some may still be "atwitter" with loud and dramatic cries for enhanced, strengthened, and enforced security, many organizations are realizing the benefits of embedding appropriate controls into ongoing operations, thereby yielding effective and efficient safeguards.

Enter the *Information Security Management Handbook*, which for over a decade has offered a virtual toolset of essays and dissertations addressing people, processes, and technologies. The information herein is practical, useful, and hands-on. The chapters are written by dedicated and committed authors who seek to share their "been there, done that" stories with those who may benefit from them. Within each of the chapters, you will find personal histories and problem solving that each author has been gracious enough to share. We thank them.

Further, the handbook's mission is to be used by a wide audience. Yes, the chapters are of substantial value to the security professional; however, they also address issues applicable to managers, executives, attorneys, risk managers, technology operators, and beyond. So, read hearty. If you learn one thing or find one idea to apply, we have succeeded.

As always, we wish you the best.

**Harold F. Tipton**
**Micki Krause Nozaki**

# Editors

**Harold F. Tipton**, currently an independent consultant, was a past president of the International Information System Security Certification Consortium and a director of computer security for Rockwell International Corporation, Seal Beach California for about 15 years. He initiated the Rockwell computer and data security program in 1977 and then continued to administer, develop, enhance, and expand the program to accommodate the control needs produced by technological advances until his retirement from Rockwell in 1994.

Tipton has been a member of the Information Systems Security Association (ISSA) since 1982. He was the president of the Los Angeles Chapter in 1984, and the president of the national organization of ISSA (1987–1989). He was added to the ISSA Hall of Fame and the ISSA Honor Role in 2000.

Tipton was a member of the National Institute for Standards and Technology (NIST), the Computer and Telecommunications Security Council, and the National Research Council Secure Systems Study Committee (for the National Academy of Science). He received his BS in engineering from the U.S. Naval Academy and his MA in personnel administration from George Washington University, Washington, District of Columbia; he also received his certificate in computer science from the University of California, Irvine, California. He is a certified information system security professional (CISSP), ISSAP, and ISSMP.

He has published several papers on information security issues for

Auerbach Publishers—*Handbook of Information Security Management*
*Data Security Management*
*Information Security Journal*
National Academy of Sciences—*Computers at Risk*
Data Pro Reports
Elsevier
ISSA "Access" Magazine

He has been a speaker at all the major information security conferences including the following: Computer Security Institute, the ISSA Annual Working Conference, the Computer Security Workshop, MIS Conferences, AIS Security for Space Operations, DOE Computer Security Conference, National Computer Security Conference, IIA Security Conference, EDPAA, UCCEL Security & Audit Users Conference, and Industrial Security Awareness Conference.

He has conducted/participated in information security seminars for (ISC)²®, Frost & Sullivan, UCI, CSULB, System Exchange Seminars, and the Institute for International Research.

He participated in the Ernst & Young video "Protecting Information Assets." He is currently serving as the editor of the *Handbook of Information Security Management* (Auerbach). He chairs the (ISC)² CBK Committees and the QA Committee. He received the Computer Security Institute's Lifetime Achievement Award in 1994 and the (ISC)²'s Hal Tipton Award in 2001.

**Micki Krause Nozaki**, MBA, CISSP, has held positions in the information security profession for the past 20 years. Krause was named one of the 25 most influential women in the field of information security by industry peers and *Information Security* magazine as part of their recognition of Women of Vision in the field of information technology (IT) security. She received the Harold F. Tipton Award in recognition of sustained career excellence and outstanding contributions to the profession.

She has held several leadership roles in industry-influential groups, including the Information Systems Security Information (ISSA) and the International Information Systems Security Certification Consortium (ISC)², and is a passionate advocate for professional security leadership.

She is also a reputed speaker, published author, and coeditor of the *Information Security Management Handbook* series.

# ACCESS CONTROL

## *Access Control Administration*

# Chapter 1

# Back to the Future

Paul A. Henry

## Contents

Network security appears (at least to the author), in some respects, to have come full circle. Many of today's so-called innovations in network security can in fact, at least in part, be traced back to having originally been implemented in one form or another in the decades-old Orange Book standards. The author, having worked with a firewall vendor that in the early 1990s had developed the first (and only) firewall to achieve an Orange Book "B Level" certification, gained a perhaps unique—firsthand perspective—of the security benefits of the components of an Orange Book–compliant security implementation.

Ironically, many of the features of Orange Book that were shunned in the commercial marketplace decades ago are now being embraced in one form or another in security implementations as the only sensible solutions to the environment we find ourselves in today. Perhaps Orange Book requirements were simply decades ahead of their time.

In our efforts to solve the most pressing issues that we face in network security today, perhaps a trip "Back to the Future" and a reexamination of the security provisions of the decades-old Orange Book are in order.

## Revisiting Orange Book

In the late 1980s–early 1990s, the methodologies that were core components of trusted computer systems often referred to as Orange Book–based security were adopted by a small number of network security product vendors. While no one can argue that adopting Orange Book security did not provide for a higher level of attainable security, the commercial marketplace literally shunned them as overkill, administratively burdensome, and relegated it as old technology.

For those of us working for security product vendors at that time, it was widely felt that anything above an Orange Book B1 level was simply not achievable and sustainable in a commercial security product. See Figure 1.1.

## Official Overview of Orange Book Classes

*Class* (D): *Minimal protection*
This class is reserved for those systems that have been evaluated but that fail to meet the requirements for a higher evaluation class.

*Class* (C1): *Discretionary security protection*
The Trusted Computing Base (TCB) of a class (C1) system nominally satisfies the discretionary security requirements by providing separation of users and data. It incorporates some form of credible controls capable of enforcing access limitations on an individual basis, that is, ostensibly suitable for allowing users to be able to protect project or private information and to keep other users from accidentally reading or destroying their data. The class (C1) environment is expected to be one of cooperating users processing data at the same level(s) of sensitivity.

*Class* (C2): *Controlled access protection*
Systems in this class enforce a more finely grained discretionary access control than (C1) systems, making users individually accountable for their actions through login procedures, auditing of security-relevant events, and resource isolation.

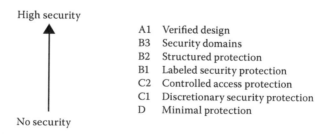

**Figure 1.1 Orange Book Security Classes. (From Department of Defense, *Trusted Computer System Evaluation Criteria,* DOD 5200.28-STD, December 1985, Appendix C, pp. 88–89.)**

*Class* (B1): *Labeled security protection*
Class (B1) systems require all the features required for class (C2). In addition, an informal statement of the security policy model, data labeling, and mandatory access control over named subjects and objects must be present. The capability must exist for accurately labeling exported information. Any flaws identified by testing must be removed.

*Class* (B2): *Structured protection*
In class (B2) systems, the TCB is based on a clearly defined and documented formal security policy model that requires the discretionary and mandatory access control enforcement found in class (B1) systems to be extended to all subjects and objects in the ADP system. In addition, covert channels are addressed. The TCB must be carefully structured into protection-critical and non-protection-critical elements. The TCB interface is well defined and the TCB design and implementation enable it to be subjected to more thorough testing and more complete review. Authentication mechanisms are strengthened, trusted facility management is provided in the form of support for system administrator and operator functions, and stringent configuration management controls are imposed. The system is relatively resistant to penetration.

*Class* (B3): *Security domains*
The class (B3) TCB must satisfy the reference monitor requirements that it mediate all accesses of subjects to objects, be tamperproof, and be small enough to be subjected to analysis and tests. To this end, the TCB is structured to exclude code not essential to security policy enforcement, with significant system engineering during TCB design and implementation directed toward minimizing its complexity. A security administrator is supported, audit mechanisms are expanded to signal security-relevant events, and system recovery procedures are required. The system is highly resistant to penetration.

*Class* (A1): *Verified design*
Systems in class (A1) are functionally equivalent to those in class (B3) in that no additional architectural features or policy requirements are added. The distinguishing feature of systems in this class is the analysis derived from formal design specification and verification techniques and the resulting high degree of assurance that the TCB is correctly implemented. This assurance is developmental in nature, starting with a formal model of the security policy and a formal top-level specification (FTLS) of the design. In keeping with extensive design and development analysis of the TCB required of systems in class (A1), more stringent configuration management is required and procedures are established for securely distributing the system to sites. A system security administrator is supported.

# Security Architecture Models in the Era of Orange Book

1. Bell–La Padula
   The Bell–La Padula confidentiality model provides the "mandatory" component of a mandatory access control system with the following mandatory access control parameters:
   a. Top Secret level subjects
      i. Top secret level subject can create as well as write only top secret level objects
      ii. Can read top secret level objects as well as lower sensitivity level objects—secret and confidential
      iii. Cannot write "down" to lower sensitivity level object—secret and confidential

b. Secret level subjects
   i. Secret level subject can create as well as write secret level objects and top secret level objects
   ii. Cannot read "up" in top secret level objects
   iii. Can read secret level objects as well as lower sensitivity level objects — confidential
   iv. Cannot write "down" to lower sensitivity level object—confidential

c. Confidential level subjects
   a. Confidential level subject can create as well as write confidential level objects as well as secret and top secret level objects
   b. Can read only confidential level objects
   c. Cannot read "up" in top secret or secret level objects

*A common theme among applications of mandatory access control is the "No read up—No write down" policy applied to each subject's sensitivity level. This is the "mandatory" part of mandatory access control.*

*It is the implementation of the Bell–La Padula security model:*

i. *Simple security property*
   *The subject cannot read information from an object with a higher sensitivity level than the subject's*

ii. *Star property*
   *The subject cannot write information to an object with a sensitivity level that is lower than the subject's*

2. Biba
   The Biba formal model was written by K.J. Biba in 1977 and is the basis for the "integrity": aspects of the mandatory access control model. The Biba formal model provides for three primary rules:
   a. An access control subject cannot access an access control object that has a lower integrity level
   b. An access control subject cannot modify an access control object that has a higher integrity level
   c. An access control subject cannot request services from an access control object that has a higher integrity level

3. Clark–Wilson
   The Clark–Wilson formal model was written by Dr. David D. Clark and David R. Wilson in 1987, was updated in 1989, and like the Biba formal model, it addresses integrity. However, unlike the Biba formal model, the Clark–Wilson formal model extends beyond limiting access to the access control object by adding integrity considerations to the processes that occur while using the access control object.
   *The Clark–Wilson formal model effectively provides for the integrity of the access control object by controlling the process that can create or modify the access control object.*
   Further, the Clark–Wilson formal model also provides for the separation of duties. This aspect of the Clark–Wilson formal model establishes guidelines that require that no single person should perform a task from beginning to end and that the task should be accomplished by two or more people to mitigate the potential for fraud in one person performing the task alone.

Other considerations of Clark–Wilson:

a. Well-formed transaction
   The well-formed transaction is the basis of the Clark–Wilson model and provides for integrity through the use of rules and certifications applied to data as it is processed through various states. A well-formed transaction also employs the use of separation of duties whereby the implementer of a transaction and the certifier of a transaction must be separate entities.
b. Access Triple
   Historically, the Clark–Wilson Triple referred to the relationship between an authenticated user, the programs that operate on the data items, and the data itself. Similarly, an Access Triple refers to an authenticated user having permission to use a given program upon a specific set of data.

4. Brewer–Nash—Chinese Wall
   The Chinese Wall adds an additional element—the interrelationships of data to other models. In an example of the addition of a Chinese Wall to the Bell–La Padula, not only would a given user be restricted to only accessing a specific set of data, but a further consideration of what other data sets the user had previously accessed would be examined before permitting access to the data. In an example of Clark–Wilson augmented with a Chinese Wall, not only is access to data restricted to a given process, but consideration is also given to which other data the processes had been used upon.

## An Unofficial View of Orange Book Classes

C1, C2—Simple enhancement of existing systems that did not break applications
B1—Relatively simple enhancement of existing systems that will break some applications
B2—Relatively major enhancement of existing systems that will break many applications
B3—Systems that failed A1 certification
A1—Complete top-down design and implementation of a new system from scratch

While originally written for military system usage, the security classifications that were at the very core of Orange Book are today, decades later, being adopted and being used within current generation network security products. A few, perhaps "overly simplified," examples we will discuss in this chapter are

- Positive security model
- Mandatory protection
- Use of data classification labeling
- Covert channels

### Driven by the changing threat environment
If we look back at 1988, only a single advisory was published by CERT for the entire year. In 2000, for the first time in history, BugTraq reported that the number of new vulnerabilities reported monthly had exceeded 100 (Figure 1.2). By 2006, the number of annual vulnerabilities cataloged unofficially by CERT had grown to 8064 (Figure 1.3). By 2007, obfuscation of malware had become a common practice, and by 2009, due to the use of obfuscation, the number of unique samples of malware found in the wild exceeded 5,500,000 samples annually (Figure 1.4).

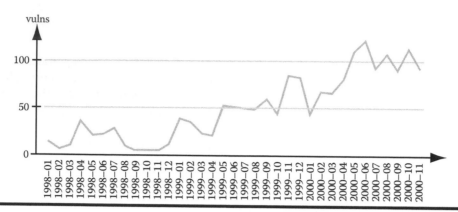

**Figure 1.2    In 2000, BugTraq reported that the number of new vulnerabilities reported monthly had exceeded 100.**

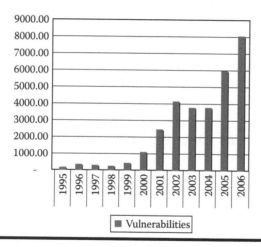

**Figure 1.3    By 2006, the number of annual vulnerabilities recorded by CERT had grown to 8064.**

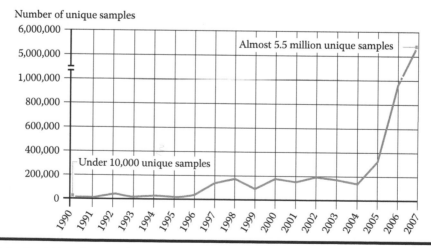

**Figure 1.4    By 2007, the number of unique samples of malware found in the wild exceeded 5,500,000 samples annually.**

## Positive Security Model

In a positive security model–based defense, the security administrator must first configure the security product (such as a firewall) to match the business needs of the organization.

Denied by default—simply put if not configured as "known good," is determined to be necessary to meet the business needs of the organization and is explicitly allowed to pass by formal policy, a given packet is simply blocked by default. The security afforded by a positive security model–based firewall includes multiple layers of defense:

- Dramatically reduces the organization's threat envelope by allowing only those packets that meet the business needs of the organization to pass
- Provides for complete protocol validation thereby eliminating entire classes of attacks, such as buffer overflows (common in day zero attacks)
- Provides for application anomaly detection

## Positive Security Model: Gateway Considerations

While clearly a more secure alternative to the negative security model, the positive security model failed to gain popularity not due to a flaw in the model but in the authors opining because the vendors supporting it failed to keep up with the rapidly growing number of applications that it needed to support in order to work in the business environment. Simply put, if the vendor did not fully support the application, the Positive Model–based security product would in fact break the application by not allowing it's associated traffic to pass, and effectively the organization utilizing the product was not able to conduct their normal business.

If we look back to 1988, only a handful of applications were necessary to be supported in order to conduct business:

SMTP
FTP
HTTP
Finger
Telnet
Gopher

Today, the numbers of application that are used in the enterprise environment have nearly reached 1000. Failure to provide support for any one of these applications could very well prevent an enterprise from conducting its normal business.

In the early days of Firewalls, vendors that provided application proxy technologies were the first to use the positive security model in a pitch for their products. But as the number of applications began to quickly outnumber those they could provide full application proxy support for, they themselves began to include negative security model–based technologies within their products in order to simply make them useable. Quickly, the line blurred between positive and negative security models for these products as you ended up with a limited positive security model for those applications proxies that could work effectively in a given environment, and a negative security model in the form of nothing more than a packet filter with signatures (IDS) layered on top of it to provide for the identification of known bad packets to support those applications that could not be supported in a positive security model.

Obfuscation renders negative security model–based firewalls obsolete: In a negative security model, all traffic is allowed to flow freely and only that traffic that is identified as "bad" is blocked. Back in 1999 when the rate of new vulnerabilities were running at only 25 new vulnerabilities reported each month, negative security model–based firewalls could offer a reasonable level of risk mitigation as vendors could "keep up" in creating new defensive signatures. In today's threat environment with an ever-increasing number of reported application vulnerabilities combined with the use of obfuscation, we are seeing 5,500,000 unique samples of malware annually. Keeping up with the number of necessary signatures has become a trying, if not impossible, task for those responsible for creating the necessary defensive signatures.

This signature problem was clearly exacerbated with hacking tools like "VOMM" also referred to as "Evade-O-Mastic" that obfuscates Web-based exploits rendering their attack completely undetectable by negative security model firewalls and their associated signatures. Negative security model firewalls are also plagued with being unable to detect self-mutating exploits like the Straton worm, which automatically alters its program code at a faster rate, than vendors can create new signatures. In October 2006, the Straton worm was the most prevalent worm reportedly seen by security vendors on the Internet. In the month of October alone, over 300 different variants of the Straton worm were detected. Today's exploit obfuscation tools and self-modifying exploits have effectively rendered negative security model firewalls as well as other signature-based defenses such as Intrusion Prevention Systems (IPS) as obsolete.

From a firewall and positive security model perspective, Orange Book was clearly decades ahead of its time. Only now, decades later, in 2009 does a vendor seem to be "ahead of the curve" and able to support the nearly 1000 applications that may be found within the enterprise and provide for a positive security model without breaking the applications necessary for the enterprise to conduct their daily business.

## Positive Security Model: Antivirus Considerations and Application Control Considerations

Malware regularly slips through current defenses wreaking havoc within enterprise networks. Antivirus products are struggling today with their inability to keep up with both the shear number of new virus and worms (malware) that are spawned out of the dramatic increase in newly reported vulnerabilities as well as the stealth employed by current technology self-mutating malware. Antivirus products have grown to be too dependent upon signatures for detection of malware and have not placed enough emphasis on newer technologies such as advanced heuristics that can detect malware without using an associated signature. Another issue has arisen that is increasing the difficulty of antivirus products from affording a reasonable level of risk mitigation—targeted attacks. In a targeted attack, the malware is not broadly distributed across the Internet, the delivery is reduced to a finite number of targets. Antivirus vendors have grown accustomed to the luxury of the broad distribution of malware, affording them the opportunity to capture and reverse engineer the malware for signature creation early in the malware life cycle. In a targeted attack, it is highly unlikely that signature-dependent antivirus vendors will be able to capture a sample of the malware in order to create a defensive signature, hence they will be unable to offer any defensive capability. The failure of antivirus products to operate effectively without the use of signatures has perpetuated the rise in day zero attacks. This antivirus signature issue combined with the increased prevalence of targeted attacks, as compared to traditional broadly distributed malware, is quickly rendering many antivirus solutions obsolete.

Many are now beginning to recognize that the era of other negative security model–based products, such as traditional signature-based antivirus, is quickly nearing its end. A Positive Model–based alternative known as White-Listing or Application Control is quickly gaining popularity as a replacement for traditional antivirus solutions.

Table 1.1 displays the results of a recent test of AV software by Virus Bulletin. At first glance, one may conclude that a rating of 99.8% is quite effective. However, consider that the rating when applied to the 1,164,662 samples used in the test still allowed 2,329 pieces of malware through to infect a network. Consider the worst-case performance reported at 65.5% that left 401,808 pieces of malware through in the testing. Now, to fully appreciate the scope of the issue, apply the ratings from the testing to real-world numbers, such as the current reported run rate of actual unique malware samples at 5,500,000 annually. With 99.8% effectiveness in your AV solution, you are still potentially allowing 11,000 pieces of malware to slip through—more than enough to devastate and/or wreck havoc in your network.

## Negative Security Model

Also known as default allow—In contrast to a positive security model is of course the negative security model. The most popular network security products to date historically have been those that worked in a negative security model. Simply put, they rely on their ability to identify undesirable/known bad traffic and prevent it from entering. It is very much like having a list at a country's port of entry, which identifies known criminals. When people travel into the country, their passports are checked against this list, and if they are not on it, they are allowed in. This design is effective to the degree that it catches known criminals, but what about those who have not yet committed any acts of terror, or have not yet been caught for their crimes, or who should also be considered a risk because of their associations or reputation? In fact, it is not always possible to determine whether somebody, or in the case of the network, a particular packet of traffic, is undesirable based on known parameters. The most effective security policy revolves around one statement: "Trust no one." That is why the best firewalls operate on a "positive" security model, which denies all access unless it is explicitly allowed.

## Application Control

### A current generation implementation of the Positive Security Model

Application Control is quickly emerging to complement and even, perhaps, to replace traditional antivirus solutions. Rather than relying on the constant creation of new signatures to protect assets from emerging threats in a Black List or negative security model, Application Control uses a positive security model or white list approach. In the simplest of terms, controls are established to permit or deny all applications and supporting scripts and macros on all workstations across the enterprise. This approach reminds the author of the Orange Book Default Deny methodology (in limited respects)—if the application, script, or macro is not explicitly approved via the Application Control policy and confirmed via hash, it by default is not permitted to execute.

From a risk mitigation perspective, the time has clearly come for the shift from the negative security model to the positive security model. In the simplest of terms, the number of new and potentially bad things that must be blocked in a negative security model implementation now easily outweigh those that need to be permitted to facilitate the business needs of an organization. From an administrative burden perspective, the tide has turned and today it is simply more effective to manage the "known good" than to keep up with the explosive growth of the "known bad."

**Table 1.1    Results of Test of AV Software by Virus Bulletin**

| Product | Malware on Demand (%) |
| --- | --- |
| AntiVir (Avira) | 99.80 |
| Avast! (Alwil) | 99.30 |
| AVG | 95.80 |
| AVK 2008 (G Data) (1) | 99.20 |
| AVK 2009 (G Data) (2) | 99.80 |
| BitDefender 2008 | 97.70 |
| BitDefender 2009 | 97.60 |
| CA-AV (VET) | 65.50 |
| ClamAV | 88.50 |
| Dr Web | 84.90 |
| eScan | 97.80 |
| Fortinet-GW | 92.60 |
| F-Prot (Frisk) | 94.80 |
| F-Secure 2008 | 98.20 |
| F-Secure 2009 | 99.20 |
| Ikarus | 99.50 |
| K7 Computing | 92.10 |
| Kaspersky | 98.40 |
| McAfee | 93.60 |
| Microsoft | 97.70 |
| Nod32 (Eset) | 94.40 |
| Norman | 96.30 |
| Norton 2008 (Symantec) | 97.80 |
| Norton 2009 (Symantec) | 98.70 |
| Panda 2008 | 86.40 |
| Panda 2009 | 91.80 |
| Rising | 83.40 |
| Sophos | 97.50 |
| Trend Micro | 91.30 |

**Table 1.1 (continued)    Results of Test of AV Software by Virus Bulletin**

| Product | Malware on Demand (%) |
|---|---|
| TrustPort | 99.50 |
| VBA32 | 90.50 |
| VirusBuster | 89.00 |
| WebWasher-GW (3) | 99.70 |
| ZoneAlarm | 97.80 |

*Source:* Data from *Virus Bulletin*, September 2008. http://www.virusbtn.com/news/2008/09_02

The five phases of the implementation of an application control solution are

1. Discovering and monitoring the application ecosystem
2. Assigning rights
3. Pilot rollout
4. Enforcing protection
5. Fine-tuning the application ecosystem

## Discovering and Monitoring the Application Ecosystem

There are multiple approaches to establishing a baseline. One could use a third-party database of known good application hashes or simply create a custom database by scanning clean and known good machines (Figure 1.5) that had not been connected to the network or public Internet that contained the applications necessary to complete the business objectives of the organization.

## Assigning Rights

In an Application Control solution, assigning rights can be as simple as assigning all validated applications and supporting scripts to a "Everyone Group" or can be accomplished with a high level of granularity for individual users and/or groups by leveraging existing LDAP, Active Directory, or eDirectory resources (Figure 1.6). Application Control solutions often provide for integration with IT change control solutions to reduce the administrative burden of ongoing system maintenance.

## Pilot Rollout

A pilot group of users is normally selected to test the completeness and accuracy of the white list and system configuration. A good selection for a pilot group would be a set of users that does not include development and/or IT maintenance–related workstations as they typically run the most nonstandard applications. In the initial phase of a pilot program, the solution is operated in a monitor-and-report-only mode and does not implement enforcement.

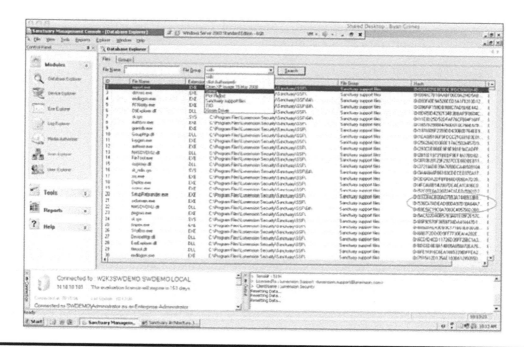

**Figure 1.5   A unique SHA-1 signature is calculated for each binary file, together with the file-name, path, size, and product version. This information is recorded on the Lumension server whitelist, defining what programs can run on all selected computers.**

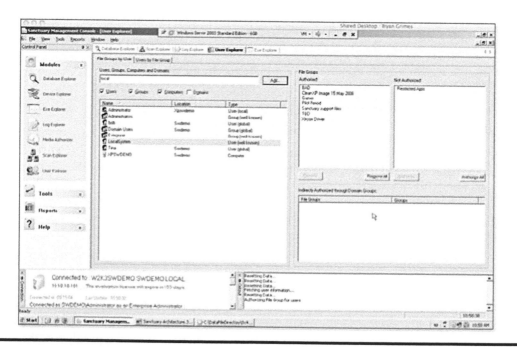

**Figure 1.6   The User Explorer module lets you use the Microsoft Active Directory to map users and groups to the whitelist.**

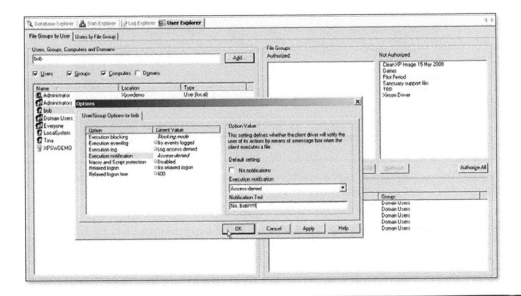

**Figure 1.7** Use warning messages to explain why applications won't run after blocking is turned on—perhaps with more information than "No, Bob!".

## Enforcement

In the pilot program, careful monitoring of exceptions will allow reconfiguration of policies to provide for operation with minimal exception alerts. As the exception list shrinks to a manageable level, the pilot can switch to an enforcement mode, whereby those applications that are not explicitly permitted for users/groups are denied, and exception reports are generated and made available to the management console, where adjustments can be made to the operating policy (Figure 1.7).

Once you are comfortable that you have developed a manageable configuration, the pilot can begin to be rolled out across the enterprise. Departments can simply be added initially in a reporting-only mode. Once confirmed to be configured properly, whereby a minimum level of exceptions are reported, the department can be switched to an enforcement mode of operation.

## Fine-Tuning the Application Ecosystem

User awareness is a big part of a successful implementation of application control. Employees must be alerted as to which applications are approved for operation on departmental workstations and which are not. If you have not prepared your employees for the change, your help desk could be overloaded. In addition, alerts can be configured to be displayed on the users' workstation to alert the users when they have attempted to run an application or script that is not permitted by policy. A carefully crafted message can go a long way in reducing help desk calls for assistance (Figure 1.8).

To facilitate an effective and manageable application control solution, the following capabilities need to be addressed by the application control vendor:

- Automated application discovery that provides flexible options to update white lists
- Spread check mechanisms that can automatically disable applications when it is discovered that too many users may have used local authorization to enable an application that potentially places the organization at risk

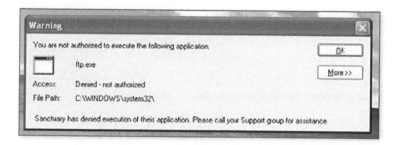

**Figure 1.8** **You can write custom warning messages for users when they attempt to launch an application that is not on the whitelist.**

- Active directory integration to facilitate automatic maintenance of users and groups used within the application control policies
- Automatic authorization of vendor software updates to eliminate the risk of automatically restricting user community's access to frequently updated applications
- Script and macro protection to extend policy enforcement beyond applications to their supporting scripts and associated macros
- Flexible file authorization to identify new files to be included in the authorization database
- Local authorization for trusted power users to offer flexibility without giving up administrative control; any locally authorized application is reported to the administrator for review
- Off-line protection to ensure that remote or disconnected users are constantly protected by keeping a local copy of respective application hashes and remissions on each machine
- Standard file definitions that include classifications of all preloaded applications across all supported operating systems

The only question remaining for moving to a positive security model in the use of application control is perhaps where it is best to implement it. Some would suggest application control is best handled at the gateway to reduce administrative burden and focus protection on a single set of protective devices. In the authors opinion, it is this kind of thinking that has brought us to the perilous point we are at today, whereby hackers that are able to pierce the perimeter defenses have an open reign within our networks. That thought along with the current increasing insider threat leads the author to conclude that application control is best accomplished in a layered approach both at the gateway and on the desktop.

An example of the benefit of positive security model–based application control:

The scenario:
Small network < 100 Windows XP Machines
Current antivirus at the gateway and on the desktop with the latest signatures
Firewall with a rule to permit internal users with Internet access over ports 80 and 443
URL filter to block access to known malicious Web sites

1. The internal user while surfing the Internet is redirected to an official-looking Web site that initiates a fake security scan of the users PC.
2. The URL was not blocked by the URL filter as the Web site had not yet been classified as a malicious Web site.
3. The page displayed on the user's PC (Figure 1.9) did not include the typical browser tool bar and the user assumed it was an official company application scanning his PC.

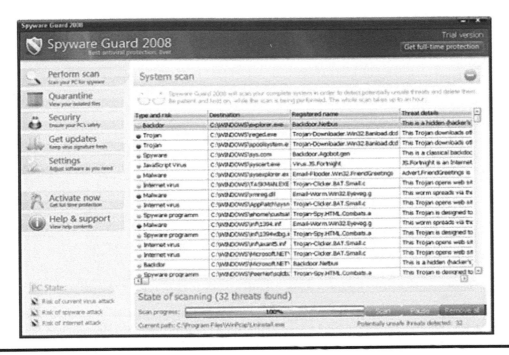

**Figure 1.9 Rogue security software is a type of misleading application that pretends to be legitimate security software; however, it provides little or no protection and may install the very malicious code it purports to protect against.**

4. When the scan was completed the user in the interest of quickly getting back to work selected to remove the malware that reportedly was found on the PC.

5. Upon selecting "Remove," the user's PC unknowingly downloaded malicious executable files to the user's PC.

6. The gateway antivirus server and the user's desktop antivirus software did not block the download as the downloaded files were using obfuscation and the antivirus signatures had not yet been updated to contain signatures for this new and seemingly one-of-a-kind obscured application.

7. Application control automatically blocked the operation of the executables by default (Figure 1.10) because they were on part of the permitted applications that the user had administrative permission to execute. Further, application control blocked the malware's attempted execution of a restricted command.

Ironically, the user's application aware firewall vendor, URL filter vendor, and antivirus vendor claims their products are proactive in that they will automatically protect the user from malware. Unfortunately the firewall did not block the malware as it did not yet have a signature for the unique malware in it's internal application filter database, the URL filter did not block the user's access to the URL that contained the malicious page as it did not yet have the proper classification for the URL that the user was redirected to, and the user's antivirus solution did not block access to the malware as it lacked a signature for the new and unique malware that was delivered. The user's so-called "Proactive Defenses" were unable to be anything that resembled "Proactive." The only real "Proactive Defense" the user experienced was their last line of defense—their positive security model–based application control.

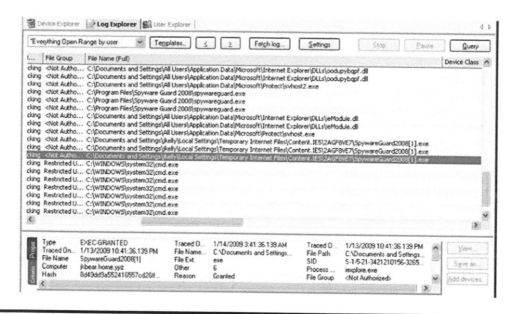

**Figure 1.10   Positive security model-based application control automatically blocked the operation of the rogue software executables by default because they were not part of the permitted applications that the user had administrative permission to execute.**

Continue with

■ Mandatory protection
■ Use of data classification labeling
■ Covert channel analysis

## *Mandatory Protection*

Mandatory protection in the form of the enforcement of the rule of least privilege was a principle component of the Orange Book. It clearly defines least privilege as a principle that "requires that each subject in a system be granted the most restrictive set of privileges needed for the performance of authorized tasks. The application of this principle limits the damage that can result from accident, error, or unauthorized use."

Perhaps one of the most recent highly visible, albeit arguably failed, implementations of mandatory protection would have to be Microsoft Windows Vista user account control (UAC). Many would argue that one of the reasons Vista has not enjoyed the popularity obtained by its predecessor Windows XP is specifically due to the implementation of UAC. In fact, reportedly, a vast majority of Vista users have disabled UAC. An example of the annoying interruptions provided by UAC is the pop-up received when a user would attempt to open the common command prompt with administrative privilege (Figure 1.11) or attempt to run any program with administrative privilege (Figure 1.12).

The problem with UAC stems from Microsoft's legacy of giving every user administrative rights by default. Simply put, UAC is perhaps Microsoft's first attempt at breaking away from the tradition of every user being an administrator by default. When a common user has standard user

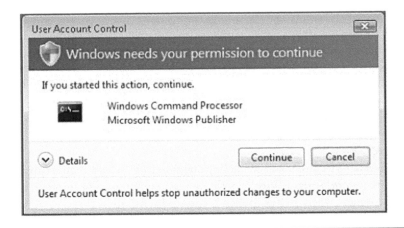

**Figure 1.11** An example of the annoying interruptions provided by UAC is the pop-up received when a user would attempt to open the common command prompt with administrative privilege.

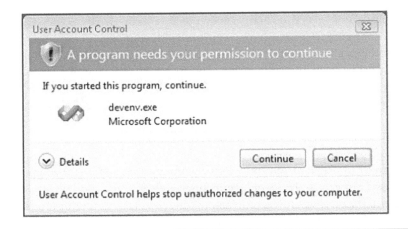

**Figure 1.12** An example of the annoying interruptions provided by UAC is the pop-up received when a user would attempt to run any program with administrative privilege.

rights in Windows Vista, UAC will pop up each and every time the user attempts to do anything where their administrative rights are necessary. Perhaps it is too much nagging interaction with the user that fueled the distain for UAC. In a Mac or Unix environment, the user by default does not have administrative rights, hence the user is only prompted when they attempt to perform a task that actually requires administrative rights and they are silently prevented from doing other things that may require administrative rights.

## Mandatory Security in the Mainstream

The U.S. government's Information Security Automation Program (ISAP) is an initiative to provide for the standardization of technical security operations. Using tools that support the Security Content Automation Protocol (SCAP) enables literally pushing standard policies out to every desktop within an organization and then monitoring those machines for compliance with the policy. While you simply will not find the words "mandatory security" within the ISAP specifications, clearly, it is a tool that can in fact be used to provide for an enterprise-wide baseline of mandatory security.

It is the policies that are used that in fact afford the baseline of the deployed security configuration—mandatory security. Further, ongoing monitoring of compliance can provide for automated compliance reporting that has become a requirement of standards such as the Federal Desktop Core Configuration (FDCC) and the Payment Card Industry (PCI-DSS) and other custom policy implementations.

A cursory review of a current FDCC policy configuration would include approximately 300 security-related requirements in a Windows XP or Vista computer. The immediate impact felt by users in an environment where FDCC policy is enforced is as follows:

- Password changes will be more frequent. Instead of every 90 days, your password will have to be changed every 60 days.
- Your login will not be saved when you log on. You will need to fill in the login and the password each time you log on to your computer.
- Administrative privileges will be taken away, which means you will not be able to download new applications. Unless you obtain a waiver to have these privileges, you will need to open a ticket with the Help Desk and have them work with your local IT support to make changes to your computer or install software.
- Some applications may not work properly because they require administrative access to the operating system, application directories, and registry keys. For example, there is a known problem with Visual Studio Suite accessing files that only an administrator can access. It has also been reported that in some cases, Remedy is unable to access the user preferences, which are stored in the user's profile, which requires administrator access.

Checklists are freely available for various FDCC configurations and are downloadable for review at http://checklists.nist.gov/chklst_detail.cfm?config_id=129.

An example of the processes involved in automating mandatory security across an entire enterprise using a SCAP-compliant product (Figure 1.13):

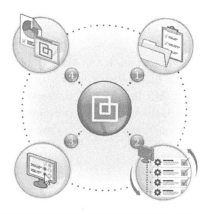

**Figure 1.13** **An example of the processes involved in automating mandatory security across an entire enterprise using a SCAP-compliant product.**

1. Manage Security Configuration Policy: Define, edit, and import/export security configuration policies and best practices by leveraging the SCAP. Automatically map these regulatory or internal security policies to your own agent policy set, enabling you to standardize and secure your endpoint configurations and easily demonstrate compliance. Thanks to open standards, security specifications can also be added or edited to create custom security configuration policies.
2. Assess Policy Compliance by Group and Device: Apply desired security specifications to your network device groups and application configurations. Automatically (or manually, where applicable) assess policy compliance with security configuration specifications for device groups as well as individual devices.
3. Report Policy Compliance Results: Demonstrate policy compliance by reporting configuration status against regulations and industry standards such as FDCC and PCI-DSS, as well as customized policies.
4. Enforce Policy Compliance: Achieve and maintain compliance with security configuration policies and best practices, leveraging automated remediation and policy enforcement.

With policies deployed across the enterprise monitoring of compliance can be an administrative burden, however, current generation SCAP implementations provide for a centralized graphical user interface (GUI) that can dramatically reduce administrative burden (Figure 1.14). Further, the centralized GUI provides for the necessary reporting capabilities that are a common component in today's regulatory environment.

Some of the very same mandatory security requirements that were perhaps principle components of the original Orange Book requirements two decades ago have clearly finally found their way in to broad use today across both government and private commercial networks. One can only wonder what impact would have occurred had mandatory security become a reality back when the Orange Book requirements were first made available. Clearly, the unquestionable benefits of

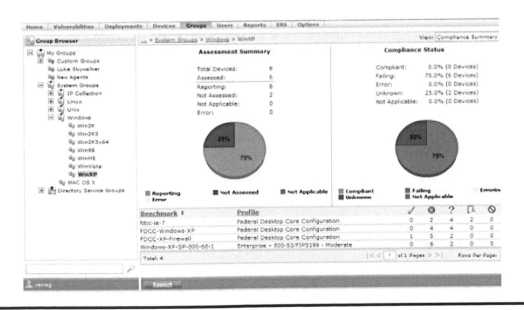

**Figure 1.14  Current generation SCAP implementations provide for a centralized graphical user interface (GUI) that can dramatically reduce administrative burden.**

mandatory security and its components such as the enforcement of the rule of least privilege would have seriously altered the threat landscape we face today.

A recent study by BeyondTrust found that 92% of critical Microsoft vulnerabilities could have been stopped or mitigated by simply eliminating the practice of giving users "administrator" rights. The study also found that eliminating administrator rights would have stopped or mitigated

94% of Microsoft Office vulnerabilities reported in 2008
89% of Internet Explorer vulnerabilities reported in 2008
53% of Microsoft Windows vulnerabilities reported in 2008.

## Use of Data Classification Labeling

The usage of a data classification and labeling scheme was a core component of Orange Book security. Used in part to enforce mandatory access control (MAC) in environments requiring high levels of security, such as government or military systems. With MAC, the inherent problems of trying to rely upon each system owner to properly control access to each access control object is eliminated by having the system participate in applying a mandatory access policy (the system owner applies the "need to know" element). This policy affords typically three object classification levels: top-secret, secret, and confidential. Each access control system subject (users and programs) is assigned clearance labels, and access control system objects are assigned sensitivity labels. The system then automatically provides the correct access rights based upon comparing the object and subject labels. Mandatory access controls allow multiple security levels of both objects and subjects to be combined in one system securely.

Today, data classification and labeling schemes are proving to be beneficial in data leakage prevention (DLP) systems as well as the automation of rediscovery and deduplication efforts.

A data classification and labeling system can go a long way in making organization's efforts to identify and secure their data more effective. The use of unique labels for files containing sensitive information can make it easier to find them, whether they are at rest or in transit.

These unique labels can be literally used like digital watermarks, and you can write IDS rules to identify them when the data is in transit. You can also use regular expressions for the tools that are used to search data at rest, using them to identify these labels and to help audit computers that should not be storing a particular classification of data.

Labeling data in eDiscovery and deduplication has been proven to be beneficial in reducing the complexity of fulfilling rediscovery efforts within large organizations. The shear volume of data contained within the enterprise has seen explosive growth (Figure 1.15). It has become common today for data labeling for data classification to become part of the normal business data life cycle, (Figure 1.16) and in at least some abstract respect has its heritage traceable back to Orange Book security initiatives.

## Covert Channels

Covert channels have long been the enabler of communications for the command and control of botnets and most recently have been adopted for the theft of data in data leakage incidents.

A "covert channel" can be described as "Any communications channel that can be exploited by a process to transfer information in a manner that violates the system's security policy." Essentially, it is a method of communication that is not part of an actual computer system's design but can

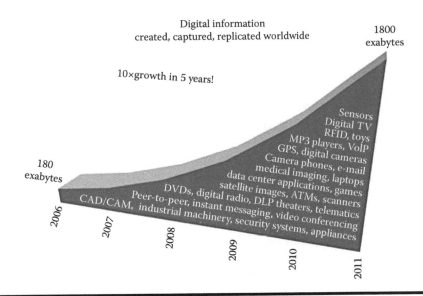

Digital information
created, captured, replicated worldwide

10×growth in 5 years!

1800
exabytes

180
exabytes

Sensors
Digital TV
RFID, toys
MP3 players, VoIP
GPS, digital cameras
Camera phones, e-mail
medical imaging, laptops
data center applications, games
satellite images, ATMs, scanners
DVDs, digital radio, DLP theaters, telematics
Peer-to-peer, instant messaging, video conferencing
CAD/CAM, industrial machinery, security systems, appliances

2006  2007  2008  2009  2010  2011

**Figure 1.15** **The shear volume of data contained within the enterprise has seen explosive growth. (Courtesy of IDC White Paper,** *The Diverse and Exploding Digital Universe,* **sponsored by EMC, Framingham, MA, March 2008.)**

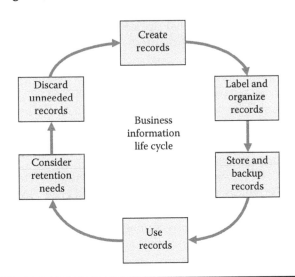

Create records

Discard unneeded records

Label and organize records

Business information life cycle

Consider retention needs

Store and backup records

Use records

**Figure 1.16** **The normal business data lifecycle.**

be used to transfer information to users or system processes that normally would not be allowed access to the information.

Covert channel exploits typically require a malicious client or server program operating on a PC outside the protected network and a malicious server or client program operating on a server inside the protected network.

The malicious PC outside the protected network would encapsulate the desired protocol within a given protocol that is allowed by the security policy of the protected network's firewall. The malicious PC on the outside of the protected network would then transmit this allowed protocol through the firewall directed to the IP address of the server running the malicious receiving program inside the protected network.

The receiving program would strip off the transport protocol, thereby leaving the original malicious data in its original protocol form. These packets would either then be used by the server running the receiving program or be automatically sent to a predetermined IP address of another server or PC within the network.

Covert channels are not a new methodology; in fact the theoretical dangers of covert channels were first addressed in the National Computer Security Center's (NCSC) Trusted Computer System Evaluation Criteria (TCSEC) as early as in 1983 and 1985.

Later in 1990, as covert channels moved from the realm of theoretical to possible, in France, Germany, the Netherlands, and the United Kingdom, a testing methodology for covert channels was developed and published: Information Technology Security Evaluation Criteria (ITSEC). In the mid-1990s, as covert channels moved from the realm of possible to probable, many papers were published outside of government that explicitly detailed covert channel exploits at the application level and, in many cases, provided working source code to build a fully functional covert channel.

One of the most recent adaptions of covert channels involved a data theft incident whereby stolen credit card data was simply added to the payload of a DNS request to move the stolen data out of the network without raising any suspicion from the network administrators.

Covert channels, in their simplest form, involve encapsulating a particular protocol that if used directly would raise suspicion over a protocol that is considered normally permitted traffic. A timely example would be IRC traffic: if an administrator saw IRC traffic flowing across the network, it would immediately raise suspicion as it has long been associated with nefarious activities. It is trivial to encapsulate the IRC traffic over the normally permitted HTTP traffic that flows across the network and escapes the detection of the network's security mechanisms.

Simply put, firewall vendors have known since the late 1980s about the risk of covert channels and yet only a select few actually did anything definitive, such as adhere to Orange Book standards for risk mitigation of Covert Channels. The problem is much broader when you consider that the vast majority of security mechanisms actually aid in facilitating Covert Channels by strictly adhering to a port-centric view of network traffic.

A good example of this failure would be the evolution of Instant Messaging (IM) and our early reliance on blocking the specific ports used by the specific IM client. IM client providers quickly realized that continued use of specific ports would allow security administrators to block their usage, so they adopted the capability to use not only the typically defined port associated with the IM client but also literally any port it could find open and available through the network's defenses. Today, you will find nearly all IM applications tunneling their traffic over the most commonly open port in a network gateway—port 80 (normally associated with HTTP).

The shortsightedness that a port-centric view brings to firewalls is still a problem today as the most popular firewalls currently in use are limited to applying their protective policies only against the specific port numbers normally associated with a specific traffic flow. Once you create a rule to allow traffic to flow through your defenses, such as opening port 80 to allow your users to have internet access with their browser, any traffic including traffic from any malicious applications that may be residing within your network have the ability to use that open port and simply encapsulate their traffic on top of the HTTP protocol and evade your ability to block it.

Historically, the author is only aware of a small number of legacy firewalls such as the Cyber Guard Firewall and Secure Computing Sidewinder Firewall (who's legacies can ironically be traced back to Orange Book) that afford the necessary application awareness to allow a specific application to use a specific protocol and to automatically deny by default any ability for a foreign protocol to be encapsulated across that permitted protocol. However, these firewalls are severely limited by the small number of protocols they can fully support, and in the current environment, some simply find them unusable as they have a tendency to break applications that they are not fully aware of.

Today, a different approach in next generation firewalls is quickly taking shape: The PaloAlto Firewall, which was noted earlier in this chapter as having the ability to control any of the nearly 1000 applications necessary to conduct business in today's enterprise environment, can be found operating literally over any port or service. Simply put, it does not classify traffic based solely on a given port or service but identifies the protocol using a combination of heuristics and learned behavior on the wire regardless of any inference to a specific port or service. This eliminates the port-centric issue of traditional firewalls and returns our ability to construct a workable deny-by-default approach to network security, whereby only those applications specifically permitted by policy are permitted to traverse the network regardless of the port or service it happens to be operating over.

Another promising approach to the covert channel issue takes a completely different approach to the problem. Rather than trying to control the ability of a malicious or undesired application from being able to move traffic across the network, Lumension Application Control eliminates the ability of the application itself from being able to operate on the workstation in the first place. The application fingerprint and centralized management approach utilized all but eliminates the administrative burden one might associate with the methodology. Using this approach brings back the ability to construct an enterprise network that is able to operate in a default deny state for any application that is not explicitly permitted by the organization's security policy. Able to support thousands of current generation and legacy applications, it can operate without the issue of legacy solutions that suffered from a severe limitation of their breadth of the applications associated with a modern enterprise.

With the ability returning to effectively enforce a default deny policy for the enterprise, we can again begin to address the covert channel issues identified decades ago in the Orange Book. For most, the remaining question is where is it best to address the issue—at the gateway or on the endpoint? In the others, opinions have been long convinced that a layered approach to network security is the only effective approach and the issue should be addressed both at the gateway and on the endpoint.

## In Closing

Long ago, those responsible for network security for those networks connected to the public Internet made a decision in a relatively immature and low-threat environment where unique threats on the wire could be measured in the hundreds annually. That ease of use and performance were more important than the ability to control a wide range of seemingly distant security threats. The security provisions of the Orange Book were relegated as being too difficult to implement, too CPU intensive to offer acceptable performance, and for the most part relegated as "old school technology" with no place in the modern enterprise.

In our current threat environment where threats are now exceeding over 5,500,000 unique malicious threats annually on the wire, current generation solutions for antivirus and firewalling have been found to be nothing short of completely overwhelmed and simply unable to scale to meet our future defensive needs and are effectively obsolete. Further, many of the risks originally addressed by the security provisions outlined in the Orange Book standards have come to fruition and unfortunately remain even today, two decades later, unsolved by the most popular solutions available in the security marketplace.

Perhaps the author is simply showing his age by taking a nostalgic look back on what could have been….. but cannot help but wonder what the threat environment we face today would be like if we had simply adopted the principles outlined in the Orange Book some two decades ago. It would most certainly not resemble the mess we currently find ourselves in today.

## About the Author

**Paul A. Henry,** MCP+I, MCSE, CCSA, CCSE, CISSP-ISSAP, CISM, CISA, CIFI, CCE, ACE, GCFA, is president of Forensics & Recovery LLC, Ocala, Florida.

# TELECOMMUNICATIONS AND NETWORK SECURITY

## Communications and Network Security

# *Chapter 2*

# Adaptive Threats and Defenses

Sean M. Price

## Contents

The survival of living organisms is often dependent on their ability to compensate for changes in their environment. The ability of an organism to compensate for changes encountered is referred to as adaptation. Predominately, the methods of adaptation involve changes in the organism's behavior, physical characteristics, or both. Some creatures are able to learn new skills or tricks that allow them to cope when changes occur. In other cases, an organism might undergo a genetic mutation that provides it with a slight advantage over its rivals allowing it to survive better given the changed conditions. Adaptation can also occur with the combination of altered behaviors and new mutations. The ability to adapt is also exhibited in the cyber realm by threats and defenses. This chapter is primarily focused on the adaptability of attacker malware and defender security tools.

Threats and defenses have evolved over the years. The emergence of the first forms of malware and hacker tools was followed by defensive tools and techniques. As new methods of attack are pursued, defensive measures arise to counter the threat. This constant struggle between attackers and defenders is sometimes referred to as an ongoing arms race (Carlsson and Jacobsson 2005). The goals of attackers and defenders are equally opposed to each other. Attackers seek to exploit a system while the defenders attempt to prevent compromises. The objectives for each of these competitors could be summarized with the following:

Threat objectives

- Discover new weaknesses
- Exploit new and old vulnerabilities
- Hide presence
- Retain a foothold in compromised systems

Defense objectives

- Counteract known threats
- Detect deviations from normal activity
- Identify abuse of the system
- Mitigate known vulnerabilities

# Evolution of Threats and Defenses

Over time the objectives of threats and defenses has not changed much. However, the methods used to achieve their objectives have substantially evolved. In the early days, threats were single purpose and could be generally categorized according to its attack vector. Initially, the taxonomy of malware was predominately marked by viruses, worms, backdoors, keystroke loggers, and Trojan horses. Human threats included hackers, crackers, and social engineers. Adaptations soon appeared with the emergence of malware such as spyware and remote-access Trojans. Similarly, the human threat evolved with the new uses of spam and phishing techniques. More recently, threats and defenses began to exhibit adaptability by use techniques from different categories (Geer 2005). The use of multiple categories is regarded as a compound threat or defense.

Attackers quickly learned that combining attack vectors enabled deeper penetration and more automation. Malware authors began to incorporate a variety of attack methods into their code. Instead of a worm simply infecting one system after another through a single exploit, it would drop packages enabling further compromise of the system. Bots, for example, are a recent evolutionary step in malware that are perhaps the most troubling. They automate much of the manual activity previously accomplished with hacker tools.

To a lesser extent compound defenses have emerged. Many security products now incorporate multiple defensive measures such as antivirus, anti-spyware, phishing filters, spam blockers, and firewalls (Greiner 2006). These efforts appear to be more about consolidation and rivalry between the products of security vendors as opposed to focused efforts to compete against malicious code. The impact of compound defenses seems much less substantial than the effect of compound attacks.

## Adapting Threats

The ability of a threat to retain its relevance is strongly tied to its capability to adapt. Automated and external human threats often exploit a weakness to gain further access within a system. As weaknesses are corrected or countermeasures put in place, the relevance of a threat is diminished. Threats must change their malware to adapt to these changes that prevent or restrict their tools from performing their devious tasks.

It is important to bear in mind that automated threats such as malware are largely dependent on the hackers that code them. Aside from polymorphism, malware adaptations are strongly linked to human intervention. Yet the source code influencing the polymorphism is a human-generated response that is driven by the need to adapt as a method of detection evasion (Christodorescu and Jha 2004). In the not too distant future, malware integrated with machine intelligence may be capable of generating original source code, discovering new vulnerabilities, and create unique methods to exploit any vulnerability. Although some might suggest that view is close to reality, there is little evidence to suggest that machine intelligence is close to achieving this level of abstract cognition. Nevertheless, it is likely that some malware will incorporate some or all of these attributes on a limited scale.

The evolutionary nature of threats is manifested from two points of view. First, changes in the behavior of the threat provide one method in which an adaptation can be achieved. In this regard, behavior reflects the actions malware takes to achieve its objectives. Relevant actions include file operations, registry manipulation, and network activity (Lakhotia et al. 2005). Process spawning is also pertinent to behavior as well. The second point of view is that of mutation. The predominate manifestations of a mutation involves changes to the code logic or structure of the binary. Changes in behavior will likely induce mutations in the underlying code. However, a mutation is also a tactical maneuver supporting adaptations that allow it to avoid detection.

## Behavioral Changes

The actions and activity of a threat is an indicator of its behavior. The longer a threat uses the same behavior the more likely it is that defenses will detect and deploy countermeasures against it. Threats, therefore, adapt by changing the methods and techniques used to attack and retain a stronghold in a victim system. Continuous adaptations in malware, such as bots, are a common occurrence (Holz 2005).

## Attack Vectors

Attackers regularly seek new methods to accomplish their objectives. An attack vector is the methods and techniques used to exploit a particular vulnerability. It is essentially the cumulative steps taken to exploit the flaw. For any given vulnerability there may exist a multitude of ways to exploit it (Ma et al. 2006). Threats can adapt their attack vector behavior by modifying the actions pursued to compromise the system.

## Vulnerability Exploitation

A threat agent may attempt to exploit one or more vulnerabilities to achieve its objective. In time, due to awareness and flaw remediation, a targeted vulnerability might disappear, become irrelevant, or prove too difficult to effectively exploit. To remain pertinent, the threat must be capable of choosing different vulnerabilities to attack. A changing list of vulnerabilities to choose from provides the threat with a means to alter its attack behavior. The affect of this behavior enables the threat to adapt to environments where some vulnerabilities are mitigated. Bots, in particular, are often coded with the capability to exploit multiple vulnerabilities (Geer 2005). Having the ability to select among vulnerability options can also make it more difficult for defensive mechanisms to target a particular threat.

## Command and Control

Much of the malware in the wild today rely on some form of command and control. This enables the threat agent to communicate with and direct the activities of the malware. With respect to botnets, command and control is recognized as an important aspect of their value (Schaffer 2006). The three main types of communication methods can be categorized as follows:

- Independent—In this category, a malware opens a communication channel and listens for commands. The listening activity could be TCP, UDP, or both types of ports. In these cases the malware threat does not know where its command will come from.
- Centralized—Some malware know how to contact their master. This could be a particular Web site or e-mail address, but the most common is an Internet Relay Chat area. In these cases the malware looks to a primary address to receive commands.
- Decentralized—One trend among attackers is to organize the malware as a collective entity. This has the advantage of ensuring the malware can survive and can make it more difficult to detect the command and control origin. This type of control is similar to peer-to-peer (P2P) networks.

A threat can adapt its behavior within each of these categories. For instance, malware using an independent method of command and control could change the port on which it is listening. It may also change the application protocol used, imitating other known services or something completely novel. Centralized threats can exhibit behavior change by contacting different or new centralized command centers to obtain instructions. Lastly, decentralized malware might try to mimic legitimate P2P, change its underlying application protocol, or use encryption. It is worth noting that a sufficiently "intelligent" malware agent might be capable of selecting among all three categories. This type of behavior could make it more difficult for network monitoring to detect its presence.

## System Interaction

In most cases, a threat exploiting a weakness results in the appearance of executable binaries on the compromised system. The binaries are usually standalone, but could be attached to other objects, in the case of a virus. These malicious software components may interact with the system in a variety of ways. Some of the most common instances follow:

- Executables—An executable file runs as an independent process. The threat might be contained entirely in the executable or it may rely on it as a way to initiate other activities such as downloading other malware.
- Extensions—A malicious library could be used to extend existent malware or have it loaded into legitimate applications allowing it run more discretely.
- Injections—Similar to extensions, a library might be injected into the execution space of another process. Some viruses create their own thread of execution within the host process. Although it is not truly an injection, the execution of a virus has many of the same implications.
- Rootkits and drivers—Malware at this level has the capability to hide its activities or that of participating malicious processes.

Threats can alter their behavior by interacting with the system through any and all of the aforementioned methods. By changing the way a threat interacts with a system it increases the likelihood that it will either avoid detection or make it more difficult to remove.

## Storage and Configuration

The code enabling the threat to execute on a system must exist somewhere in storage and also requires some configuration method to prompt its activation. Threats will alter their behavior by a variety of methods that obfuscate their storage locations. They may change their file names and/or extensions to hide their presence. Configuration entries are generally needed to assure that the threat is launched regularly.

- Obscure file and directory names—This can include names that are randomized. Some threats create random names while others select from a pre-populated list within the malware package.
- Alteration of registry entries—Some threats create their own entries or rely on the entries of legitimate software.
- Alternate data streams—Malware hiding in an alternate data stream is not easily observed with standard system tools.
- Changes to configurations files—This is similar to the methods used for registry entries.
- Masquerading as legitimate files—A threat might select a file name that is similar to legitimate software. In some cases, the threat might actually rename or replace a legitimate binary file. The malware then is loaded whenever calls are made to the replaced file. In these cases, the threat will proxy the requests to the actual library whether it is in another file or is included with the threat itself.

Malware will often change their storage locations and configuration methods to remain a step or two ahead of defensive countermeasures. This adaptive behavior of modern threats enables it to persist within a compromised system.

## Recruiting

A small number of threat agents can multiple their capabilities by duplicating their efforts. The common denominator of this behavior is to entice people to execute their malicious code. Malware are increasingly acting as the intermediary between the human threat agent and the human victim. A number of enticements are commonly used to recruit new victims.

- Trojaned freeware—An offer for a new free toy with hidden strings attaching to the victim's system.
- Pornography—The promise of a gratuitous glimpse into an act of indiscretion through a link or attachment.
- Financial—A lure to easy riches that turns out to be true for the attacker.
- Spyware—The participant is promised reduced rates or access to a particular application by using a particular software product. Often times, much more is disclosed than what was agreed to.
- Scareware—The end user is informed that their system is infected with malware and encouraged to download an antivirus tool to help clean their system. They are commonly enticed

to purchase the fake antivirus product. This is reportedly a big income generator for many attacks.

■ Phishing—Masquerading as a legitimate entity, such as an online bank, but really duping the e-mail recipient into disclosing their private information.
■ Problem solving—Unwitting participants solve reverse Turing test problems, such as CAPTCHAs, that are too difficult for malware to deduce. Often this is used with other enticements such as pornography.

### Threat Mutations

Code updates to malware has parallel attributes to evolution in living organisms. In time, a given piece of malware must adapt or it will be more readily recognized by defensive measures such as antivirus and anti-spyware tools. Mutations in this regard are essential for the malware to maintain relevance. Mutation to avoid detection is a common malware tactic (Edge et al. 2006). The following summarizes some of the reasons why threat mutations are an aspect of adaptation.

### Defeat Signatures

An unchanging or static nature of an attacker makes detection easier over time. Researchers and security product vendors constantly seek the telltale signs and behaviors of attackers. Once the attributes are learned the data is compiled into tools and techniques that can be used to detect the presence of an attacker. Threats must, therefore, change their code and alter techniques to defeat signature analysis. New versions of the malware or polymorphic techniques are common methods used to defeat signature based defenses (Hsu et al. 2006).

### Code Improvements

Some malware is just plain buggy. It is not uncommon for malware to cause poor performance or even disrupt applications (Schmidt and Arnett 2005). In recent years, the shift from hacking by rogue amateurs to those of nation-states and organized crime are accompanied by improved code reliability. Today malware is less likely to affect performance. However, it is important to consider that operating system improvements may have also contributed to more stable performance even when misbehaving applications are present. In any case, attackers will regularly attempt to upgrade their malware allowing it to better adapt to its environment.

### Detection Avoidance

Overtime malware methods have become more sophisticated. Much of the efforts for improvements are related to techniques that hide the presence of the malicious code. Malware adaptations are increasingly disguising their activities to mimic legitimate system and network activity (Borders et al. 2006). Several years ago much of the malware resided in a single executable or may have included a small number of libraries. The existences of these tools were often readily observable in the file system and could be seen as distinct processes when executing. The next evolutionary jump emerged as add-ons to existing products. Malware increased the ability to cloak their activities by taking advantage of legitimate software features that enable extensions. Examples of these include system hooks, add-ons for office productivity software, and browser helper objects. By running as a loaded module the malware avoids detection of some process monitoring techniques, but are still observable through system tools. In case of extensions the malware plays by the rules of the operating system. In contrast, other techniques such as vulnerability exploits and process injection are used to force a target application to run the attackers code of choice. These approaches to detection avoidance are more stealthy and not easily identified. The latest evolution of detection avoidance involves the use of rootkits and system drivers. These methods allow the tool itself and accomplice malicious processes to operate largely undetectable by most system and security tools. Malware with stealthy capabilities hide their behavior by intercepting and filtering application programming interface (API) calls that could be used to reveal their presence (Wang et al. 2005). The trend of malware and attackers has gone from brazen attacks defacing popular sites or sensational attacks against a well-known Internet presence to discrete compromises as chilling as any clandestine espionage activity could achieve.

## Added Capabilities

New features incorporated into malware increase its value and potentially expand the influence of an attacker. Increased capabilities represent a maturation of the malware, which is a type of adaptation for survival. For example, an update might give the attacker the capability to scan other hosts for weakness or act as a relay for other malicious activity. Increased capability enables the threat to adapt to an environment and potentially sustain or propagate its existence.

## New Objectives

An attacker may periodically change targets or attack vectors. This is a common occurrence in botnets where the bot-herder rents out the zombies to service their customer requests (Geer 2005). The ability to change objectives is a tactical adaptation that makes for a superior weapon. Older malware usually had limited objectives that were not altered. Nowadays malware can attack new targets using different vectors or exploits through the receipt of software modules embedded with the new objectives and commands (McLaughlin 2004).

## Upgrade Survival

Overtime, systems are upgraded or reinstalled. Threats must be able to adapt to new technologies for the relevance to remain. As an example, a system owner might migrate from one technology (i.e., e-mail client or Web browser) to another. An adaptable threat will be able to accommodate the change and continue unimpeded if the migration represents a vector for exploitation. Upgrades to the underlying operating system can also affect the ability of the threat to endure. Adaptable threats anticipate or respond to these changes through code changes that allow their existence to continue. Although, a threat outside of a supply chain injection may not be capable of surviving a fresh installation of the OS or applications, it can attempt to persist by incorporating itself with legitimate applications and data. A threat that carefully infuses itself with data and applications targeted by managed backups enable malware longevity due to upgrades.

## Self-Preservation

It is not uncommon for malware to disrupt, disable, or destroy security controls in a system. Some aggressive threats will alter access controls to protect themselves. Others reportedly disable host-based firewalls and antivirus software (Abu Rajab et al. 2006). This sort of activity ensures communications with the threat agent will remain intact. Yet, other malware may be so bold as to delete programs or audit data that could be used to detect or disrupt it. The techniques and methods used for self-preservation must adapt according to changes in technology and the environment of the compromised system.

## Competition

Imagine that a zombie computer is under the influence of different bot-masters. Serving multiple masters might produce erratic behavior on the machine. There appears to be an unspoken consensus in the evil realm of malware creators that a zombie should not exhibit personality disorders. This perceived consensus is most likely imaginary. In reality, some malware attack and remove other malware (Osorio and Klopman 2006). Additionally, some malware reportedly patch existing vulnerabilities (Abu Rajab et al. 2006). The reasons for this competition probably include rivalry, dominance, or economic advantage. In this regard competition among living organisms spills over into the cyber realm and is witnessed as malware on malware attacks. The escalation of malware competition is yet another dimension of the adaptable nature of threats.

## *Adaptive Defenses*

Agile defenses are necessary to counteract adaptable threats. Defensive countermeasures are continuously challenged by the rapid changes they must deal with. On one hand defenses must adapt to changes in their environment. Network expansions and new technology can easily introduce exploitable weaknesses. On the other hand, threat aggressiveness continues to escalate. The rapid evolution of malware puts continuous pressure on defenses to adapt. From the perspective of a defender, adaptation is an imperative that must meet the challenges of environmental changes while remaining competitive with adaptive threats.

Attackers continuously conduct new and inventive assaults on network defenders. New attack methods brought about by malware adaptability are met with adaptive defenses. The discoveries of new attacks are often shared in the security community. Conjectured exploits by security researchers or actual exploits discovered in the Internet are reported by numerous public and private organizations. This new information is often integrated into defensive countermeasures resulting in an adaptation to the threat.

Defenses exhibit adaptation through behavior modification and mutations. The objectives of defenses tend to be more reactionary to threat activity. In contrast, the adaptations of threats are more exploratory and proactive. In this regard, defense adaptations tend to lag those of threats.

## *Behavior Modification*

Defensive controls face more challenges than do their nemeses. Tools used to defend a system require behavior modifications to account for changes to the environment as well as proliferating and changing threats. Behavior modifications entail the methods used to accommodate the rapid changes in the organization, technology, and known threats.

## Frequency

Adaptive defenses may alter the period with which they conduct their surveillance. For instance, vulnerability scanners might ordinarily be used on a monthly basis. If the organization is experiencing substantial growth or more frequent compromises then the frequency of the control is increased. The timeframe between the moments of detection activity presents opportunity for a threat to attack a system. Increasing the frequency behavior is an adaptive approach to counteract rising malware instances.

## Breadth

Security controls are not always deployed in every possible location in a network due to resource constraints. Furthermore, a control might also peer into a narrow band of activity in its attempt to identify attacks. In some cases, the purview of a control can be expanded to cover a larger area. This could be through increased instances in a system or through expansion of the band of activity monitored. Altering the breadth of a control impacts its behavior. Essentially, an increase in the horizontal nature of the control adapts the behavior of the defensive mechanism to detect malicious activity.

## Depth

Viewing activity in a system from the perspective of the Open Systems Interconnection (OSI) model provides a vertical perspective regarding the behavior of a security control. A security control might ordinarily operate at only one layer of the model. An adaptive defensive tool might occasionally perform inspections at other layers of the model to detect attacks or actual compromises. This type of capability demonstrates a change in behavior that could be very useful in detecting adaptive threats.

## Indicators

Many defensive mechanisms rely on precompiled indicators or signatures of known attacks. Adaptable defenses have the capability to compare system activity against new and prior indicators to detect active attacks. Adaptability through indicators is one of the most predominate behavior modifications of defensive components.

## Baselines

Well-managed systems have a number of documented baselines. These include baselines for hardware, software, network connectivity, and configurations. Defensive tools with the capability to detect system components and configurations can validate baselines. Security controls with the ability to make comparisons between system changes and a documented baseline exhibit adaptable behavior.

## Learning

Perhaps the most intriguing representation of behavior modification occurs when a security control actually learns something. Machine learning techniques are commonly found in security tools designed to look for anomalous activity. Two common implementations of machine learning are used by intrusion detection and spam filtering. Intrusion detection products make use of neural networks and support vector machine algorithms (Mukkamala and Sung 2003). Spam filters typically use Bayesian techniques (Pelletier et al. 2004). In both cases, the tools learn what is normal versus what is not and raise alerts when anomalous features are encountered.

## Interactions

In the near future, technologically advanced security controls will receive data from multiple sources. This will provide the security control with the ability to form a more coherent picture of the cyber landscape. A security control with this advanced capability would be able to make predictions or advise human counterparts and other participating security controls of the current security state of the system. According to the situational awareness from the influx of data these advanced tools will exhibit behavior unlike its archaic predecessors. The interaction among these tools will form a collective that shares threat information and alters its behavior accordingly. For now, we rely on the interactions and sharing among humans to influence the most robust defensive control—the information system security professional.

## *Defense Mutations*

Most of the behavior modifications are realized through mutations of the affected defensive control. Adaptation by way of mutation is for the most part straight forward regarding security controls. It is important to note that a mutation need not necessarily be compiled. The inclusion of any sort of logic enabling adaptability qualifies as a mutation. Some of the most prominent mutations employed to achieve adaptability follow.

## Signatures

Features, behaviors, and characteristics of malware and indicators of threat activity comprise attack signatures. In many instances the files containing the signature information are compiled into a library or proprietary data file. From this perspective, the inclusion of the new signatures results in a mutation of the defensive tool.

## Rule Sets

This type of mutation is comprised of multiple "if–then" statements. Rule sets permit the logical evaluation of witnessed activity. Some rule sets are ordered to form logic trees. This allows for granular decisions based on collected information. Changes in the environment or attacker behavior may require changes in rule sets. Altering rule sets according to changes or trends enables adaptability through this type of mutation.

## Thresholds

Cumulative events can be used to activate security controls. For instance, a control monitoring access control failures might not raise an alert unless the number of failures exceeds 10 events in less than 1s. A threshold of this type is designed to detect malware behaviors given the successively repetitive failures in a period of time too fast to be driven by a human manipulating a graphical user interface. The composition and attributes of thresholds can be changed to adapt to new threats or changes in the behaviors of known malware.

## *Defensive Adaptation Weaknesses*

The traditional model used by defenders has been to shore up weaknesses or adapt to threats by deploying new or modified tools counteracting the particular threat. Often times this can be over an extended period of time after a vulnerability is disclosed and exploit code is available. Sadly, adaptive defenses are primarily reactionary. Defensive measures usually target specific types of attacks deemed imminent. Rarely, will an organization incorporate a new defensive measure that is not focused on a particular threat or attack vector that has not been experienced by the organization or industry. The main reason for this line of thinking has to do with risk. An organization may deem a particular threat, likelihood, or loss to be minimal. Due to the prevalence of risk management by way of qualitative assessments, coupled with the ever-present problem of scare resources, it is not uncommon for managers to be optimistic about their level or risk. As such, adaptive or forward thinking defenses are not commonly deployed. This has the unfortunate side effect of causing defensive countermeasures to play catch-up with the attackers. This is evident by the relentless cycle of patching and signature updating.

## Specificity

Defensive measures often rely heavily on specific signatures. The effort required to adapt to a new threat may be greater than that needed by the threat. Signature development can also require substantial time and effort to compile that can significantly lag a threat that is rapidly propagating (Edge et al. 2006). Considering the time and resources needed to detect, develop, and deploy an adaptation for a given threat it seems that attackers have the upper economic hand.

## Timeliness

The creation of a countermeasure for a given threat may be well after significant damage occurs (Cui et al. 2005). In some cases this reactive adaptation can be too little too late. It is now common for exploits for previously unknown vulnerabilities to be found in the wild (Levy 2006). In this regard defensive adaptations are entirely reactive with respect to weaknesses and exploits.

## Growth Rate

New threats are beginning to emerge at a rate faster than security defensive measures can adapt. A recent estimate claims that the volume of malicious code exceeds the production of legitimate software (Nachenberg 2008). One implication of this growth rate is that defenses may consume substantially more resources to determine if a threat is present or not. This reduction in efficiency will likely inhibit the ability of the defensive measures to adequately adapt to the ever-increasing number of threats. Furthermore, the sheer volume may also imply that a larger number of malware is circulating in the wild that are unknown to defensive product vendors. This is to suggest that false negatives (malware missed by detectors) will increase. A substantial growth rate has the effect of overwhelming our defenses by a numerically superior enemy.

## Environment

Changes in the system environment present unique challenges. Growing organizations regularly add new network equipment to accommodate a growing user base. New technologies enabling increased productivity may also include new vulnerabilities. Defenses must not only adapt to system growth but new technologies as well.

## Search Space

Adaptations that attempt to characterize what is normal in a system often fail due to complexity. Defensive techniques such as anomaly detection are commonly designed to look at everything to identify features that are not normal. This requires the defensive tool to look at the entire universe of possibilities. Tuning is often used to increase performance by reducing the search space. However, the search space is often still too large allowing false positives to persist. In some cases, items ignored by the rule set can be abused by attackers and thus avoid detection.

## Constraints

Whereas malware authors are free to attempt anything desired to achieve their objectives, defenders are much more constrained. The adaptability of defensive measures is reduced due to factors in their environment.

- ■ Financial—Adaptability often requires a monetary tradeoff. Whether the cost involves time, people, or materials the lack of sufficient financial resources can constrain defense adaptations.
- ■ Personnel—Adequately trained people must be assigned to monitor, respond, and manage defensive controls. Adaptations that are different from those existing are impacted by the abilities of those assigned responsibility. A superior adaptation is of little use if the end users are unable to implement it properly.
- ■ Performance—An adaptation must not severely degrade system performance. Whereas malware can be careless about performance issues, defensive measures with performance problems are often unacceptable even when they provide an important adaptation to a class of threats.
- ■ Usability—Defensive adaptations that are effective, but too difficult to use will not find favor with those who need them most. Complicated adaptations will be abandoned or circumvented by humans who are attempting to accomplish a particular task.
- ■ Management—A properly managed system implements change control. However, this can impede deployment of the adaptable defense. An adaptable control might be altogether avoided if it is perceived to be too difficult to manage.
- ■ Operations—Effective defenses contribute to security operations. An adaptable defense that exists in a silo inhibits the flow of security operations.
- ■ Design—Ideal security controls are built-in rather than bolt-on. Unfortunately, most adaptable defenses are bolt-on. Integration efforts may be hampered by the complexity of the tool.
- ■ Perceptions—Qualitative risk assessments might lead management to conclusions that a particular adaptable defense is unnecessary. Perceptions based on insufficient or inaccurate information inhibit the acquisition and deployment of adaptable defenses.

These constraints burden defensive adaptability. Constraints impact the ability of a defensive control to compete with the unbridled capabilities of malware encountered. The competition between adaptable threats and defenses are becoming increasingly unbalanced in the favor of malware. In this regard, attackers have a distinct advantage that is evident by the continued rise in compromises and data losses.

## Strengthening Defensive Adaptations

Security is first and foremost a people problem. Weaknesses in systems are going to occur. All security problems have their root in people. Some programmers will make mistakes when coding that is further missed by reviews and quality assurance. System integrators will occasionally put things together incorrectly. System administrators will introduce configuration errors or fail to follow procedures. Users will also make honest mistakes and fall victim to an attacker's trickery. Let us not forget that malware is an offspring of the warped efforts of bad people. All sorts of unsavory individuals such as criminals, spies, and terrorists are ultimately directing the actions of malware. Our goal as security professionals should be to not only employ adaptive defensive technology, but also to establish adaptive operations that are proactive. In this regard, the reactive nature of our current adaptable defenses can be augmented with techniques and processes that are prepared for the worst. Consider some of the following during the design, implementation, and management of security operations for information systems.

### Anticipate Compromises

Develop an attitude that the best plans will eventually be circumvented. Manage stakeholder expectations by advocating proactive measures that can be used as early warning detection of failed countermeasures. Note areas within the system that are at higher risk for compromise and conduct more frequent reviews.

### Response Plans

Contingency planning and incident response are invaluable tools that can be used to prepare for the eventual compromise in a system. Having a plan is great, but it is only as good as those who are sufficiently familiar with its guidance. The plans should be regularly practiced and updated when weaknesses are discovered. Ensure the plans address the actions required to clean the system and restore normal operations.

### Penetration Testing

Periodically attempt to break into your system. Hire reputable professionals to do the same. Use some of the same tools attackers use to compromise a system. Penetration testing should be used to exercise contingency and incident response plans.

### Operational Alternatives

Few, if any, software products have proven impervious to vulnerabilities. Unfortunately, new vulnerabilities seem to be reported weekly for some products. Critical vulnerabilities with exploitable code in the wild may subject an organization to unacceptable risk. At such times it may be prudent to deploy or have ready other products that can be used instead of the one with a critical vulnerability. Require the use of alternative applications until all instances of the vulnerable product are appropriately patched. Consider altering access controls on the affected application to prevent intentional or accidental use. The downside to operational alternatives is increased management complexity and cost. The cost of a potential exposure and cleanup should be compared with the periodic licensing and management expenses.

## Defense in Depth

Traditionally, defense in depth relies on the overlapping of policy, people, and technological countermeasures (Price 2008). Although this is a good idea it is proving too shallow. For instance, systems are often protected from malware by a policy that requires antivirus tools that are regularly updated, people to configure and use the tools, and the tools themselves deployed on workstations and servers. The problem with this approach becomes apparent when all of the mechanisms fail. Rather than use another antivirus product it would be better to implement secondary controls that could be used to detect and/or prevent virus propagation. Access controls, auditing, least privilege, network segregation, and intrusion detection are just some of the tools that can serve double duty to detect and defend against malware. But, they must be properly implemented and monitored to sufficiently detect the failure of the primary defense in depth controls.

## Monitor for Changes

Ensure system managers have complete listings of the authorized hardware devices, software components, and their configurations in the system. Frequent sweeps of these aspects of the system should be conducted. Any changes not found in the listings should be immediately investigated. Issues identified should be corrected if inappropriate or included in the system listings if authorized. Identifying unauthorized changes to hardware, software, and configuration baselines is the most effective way to determine the existence of adaptable threats.

## About the Author

**Sean M. Price**, CISA, CISSP, is an independent security researcher and consultant living in northern Virginia.

## References

Abu Rajab, M., Zarfoss, J., Monrose, F., and Terzis, A. 2006. A multifaceted approach to understanding the botnet phenomenon. *Proceedings of the 6th ACM SIGCOMM Conference on Internet Measurement*, Miami Beach, FL, pp. 41–52.
Borders, K., Zhao, X., and Prakash, A. 2006. Siren: Catching evasive malware. *Proceedings of the 2006 IEEE Symposium on Security and Privacy*, Berkeley, CA, pp. 85–91.
Carlsson, B. and Jacobsson, A. 2005. On contamination in information ecosystems. *Proceedings of the 38th Hawaii International Conference on Systems Sciences*, Bigland, HI, vol. 7, p. 185b.
Christodorescu, M. and Jha, S. 2004. Testing malware detectors. *ACM SIGSOFT Software Engineering Notes*, 29(4), 34–44.
Cui, W., Katz, R. H., and Tan, W. 2005. Design and implementation of an extrusion-based break-in detector for personal computers. *Proceedings of the 21st Annual Computer Security Applications Conference*, Tuscon, AZ, pp. 361–370.
Edge, K. S., Lamont, G. B., and Raines, R. A. 2006. A retrovirus inspired algorithm for virus detection and optimization. *Proceedings of the 8th Annual Conference on Genetic and Evolutionary Computation*, Seattle, WA, pp. 103–110.

Geer, D. 2005. Malicious bots threaten network security. *Computer*, *38*(1), 18–20.

Greiner, L. 2006. The new face of malware. *netWorker*, *10*(4), 11–13.

Holz, T. 2005. A short visit to the bot zoo. *IEEE Security and Privacy*, *3*(3), 76–79.

Hsu, F., Chen, H., Ristenpart, T., Li, J., and Su, Z. 2006. Back to the future: A framework for automatic malware removal and system repair. *Proceedings of the 22nd Annual Computer Security Applications Conference*, Miami Beach, FL, pp. 257–268.

Lakhotia, A., Kumar, E. U., and Venable, M. 2005. A method for detecting obfuscated calls in malicious binaries. *IEEE Transactions on Software Engineering*, *31*(11), 956–968.

Levy, E. 2006. Worst-case scenario. *IEEE Security and Privacy*, *4*(5), 71–73.

Ma, J., Dunagan, J., Wang, H. J., Savage, S., and Voelker, G. M. 2006. Finding diversity in remote code injection exploits. *Proceedings of the 6th ACM SIGCOMM Conference on Internet Measurement*, Rio de Janeiro, Brazil, pp. 53–64.

McLaughlin, L. 2004. Bot software spreads, causes new worries. *IEEE Distributed Systems Online*, *5*(6), 1–5.

Mukkamala, S. and Sung, A. H. 2003. A comparative study of techniques for intrusion detection. *Proceedings of the 15th IEEE International Conference on Tools with Artificial Intelligence*, San Diego, CA, pp. 570–577.

Nachenberg, C. 2008. Tomorrow's AV marks the good, the bad, and the long tail. Downloaded May 12, 2009 from http://www.infosectoday.com/Articles/Whitelisting.htm

Osorio, F. C. and Klopman, Z. 2006. An initial analysis and presentation of malware exhibiting swarm-like behavior. *Proceedings of the 2006 ACM Symposium on Applied Computing*, Dijon, France, pp. 323–329.

Pelletier, L., Almhana, J., and Choulakian, V. 2004. Adaptive filtering of SPAM. *Proceedings of the 2nd Annual Conference on Communication Networks and Services Research*, Fredericton, NB, Canada, pp. 218–224.

Price, S. M. 2008. Extending the McCumber cube to model network defense. *ISSA Journal*, September, *6*(9), 14–18.

Schaffer, G. P. 2006. Worms, and viruses and botnets, oh my! *IEEE Security and Privacy*, *4*(3), 52–58.

Schmidt, M. B. and Arnett, K. P. 2005. Spyware: A little knowledge is a wonderful thing. *Communications of the ACM*, *48*(8), 67–70.

Wang, Y., Beck, D., Vo, B., Roussev, R., and Verbowski, C. 2005. Detecting stealth software with strider ghostbuster. *Proceedings of the International Conference on Dependable Systems and Networks*, Edinburgh, U.K., pp. 368–377.

## Chapter 3

# Achieving a Global Information Systems Transformation (GIST): Foundations for Infrastructure 2.0 via Standards-Based Interoperability: IF-MAP and Beyond

David O'Berry

## Contents

# GIST: The New World Order

## *At the Edge of a Digital Abyss*

This chapter has to touch on so many topics that there is simply no way I will be able to do so to the level I want in the space allotted at the depth I need to do so. What that means is that I am going to set the table for where we are today while trying to not sound like "Chicken Little." When all hope looks lost and you think I am some kind of doomsday cultist, I am going to briefly discuss the foundation pieces that are in place as well as those rapidly evolving. The standards will be discussed conceptually as well as approached in a more actionable form where possible. It is clear we are at a tipping point for the open standards-based efforts and they are becoming not only more critical but also more practical to implement. As a whole, they are also forcing us to think differently in order to architect, collaborate, and then rapidly deploy realistic capabilities to begin to recover from where we are at present.

## *"Screw the Whales, Save the Plankton"*

The current state of the digital ecosystem is rather scary when taken in the context of just how important it is to the functioning of civilizations throughout the world. For many years, we have been in a situation where we have constantly been reacting to situations that occur versus taking a proactive stance. I have previously written on the topic of how the "threat cycle" and "product cycle" really have nothing to do with one another yet are often treated as one and the same by businesses that sell you tools to solve your problems. That has been how we have always functioned really because money most times equals resources and that equation is balanced pretty significantly to the side of the vendors. This has been acceptable to many in the past because the prime concern was pretty simply interoperability and efficiency or the lack thereof. The problem is that industry realized the real problems very late in the game and some still have not really acknowledged that things have changed. The larger vendors really do not want things to change because they have often times spent extensive resources to guarantee their stockholders some security in the various markets in which they participate. Unfortunately, fiduciary duty to shareholders and moral duty to the health of the overall world economic system run counter to one another in many instances. What the industry must realize is that the challenges have now changed significantly and cannot be looked at as anything other than a systemic cause and effect ecosystem. It is a system of dominoes driven by consumer confidence that very much resembles a frail and very tall house of cards at times. Having witnessed the financial system debacle first hand with many of you in 2008, the thing that people seem to remember most was the feeling of helplessness and how profoundly they despised being in a situation where they had little or no control over the outcome.

We quickly followed that with significant malware challenges in late 2008 and early 2009, which shook the foundations of what the world knew related to the techno-industrial revolution. The stark realization that the world was not only at the whim of a seemingly out of control technological beast but truly at the mercy of the criminal networks that wielded it, many of which had a better business model than most companies, hit home when we sat waiting to see what would happen April 1, 2009. Currently we are faced with a situation where the drivers for our world economy are the points that are least protected. Essentially, the majority of the companies that are in the security space are only in places in which they can make money. That makes sense on a microeconomic level but certainly not from a more macroeconomic point of view. Effectively we are a globally consumer-driven society and even countries that do not contribute nearly as much to the consumption side do oftentimes participate from the production perspective. What that means, in a nutshell, is that when people stop spending money we nearly immediately feel the effects and stability falters quickly. So with no real protection, the base of the food chain that drives the economies of the world is the most suspect, the most infested with malware, the most helpless, and the most at risk. That is not a recipe for success. To top that off, we are actually forced to root for the crime networks that have a profit motive to write good code because God forbid someone without a reason to keep the money flowing were to get access, through a vulnerability, to one of the larger botnets or information stores that are gathered by them. If that were to happen, then all it would take is a simple transaction involving small amounts of money and thousands of compromised bank accounts. That money could even be put back the next day but an attached message to the world would read, "We put your money back this time but can take it away at any point we choose." Imagine the potential run on the banks that could cause. It could possibly make the financial crisis of 2008 look like a very small blip on the radar. It could be a crippling blow to many economies and the house of cards would, more than likely, just come down. It looks grim but a group light on marketing but heavy on capabilities has stepped up its efforts over the last decade to fill the breach and potentially make a real difference from an open and interoperable point of view.

## *"Permeation with Representation"*

Trusted Computing Group (TCG) has been toiling in relative obscurity but has been and continues to be critical to the evolution and progression of several key standards that form a significant portion of the foundation we will discuss and they need to build on going forward to have a chance to turn the tide. Specific working groups like Trusted Network Connect (TNC) are just one arm of what the group as a whole is working on. At the same time this specific area has taken on an incredible amount of importance over the last few years as the technology curve has accelerated while the education curve has seemingly fallen off. Figure 3.1 is a chart that shows the status as of the end

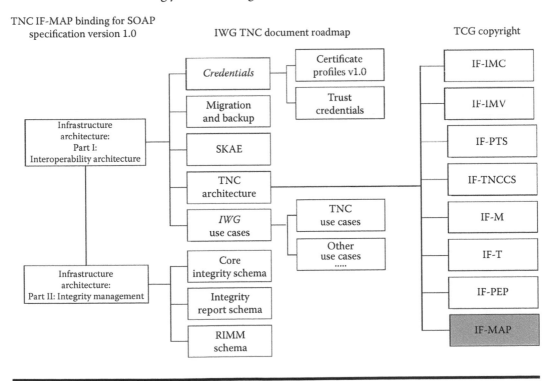

**Figure 3.1   TNC roadmap.**

of 2008 beginning of 2009 for the TNC's Document Roadmap. This was the initial document pulled directly from the TCG's Interface Metadata Access Point (IF-MAP) specification version 1.0. Establishing the initial spec was critical to progressing the initiative but at the same time uptake was not significant enough to really make an impression on the ecosystem as a whole. That changed in 2009 as specs were not only modified in some significant ways but existing specs were fine tuned and empowered with open standards-based abilities that heretofore had been mostly contained within the domain of proprietary systems. The power of that concept may at first not seem to grab you but when examined in the context of how slowly current standards develop as well as what it takes for smaller entities to contribute, the potential positive effect is amplified considerably. That being said, it makes sense to see what IF-MAP is in real-world terms, how it and corresponding specifications can be used, and why it really has a chance to make a significant difference.

## IF-MAP: In the Beginning

At the most basic of levels, IF-MAP is an open standards-based repository of information about a variety of subjects. Specifically, it provides a server mechanism that is a real-time enabler of access to network devices as well as their state and activities. The specification itself initially denoted three different capabilities, including IF-MAP Publish, IF-MAP Subscribe, IF-MAP Poll, and IF-MAP Search. These capabilities run over the wire, using Simple Object Access Protocol (SOAP), against an IF-MAP Server that in turn houses but does not validate information from all devices with the ability to publish to it. The initial metadata specifications defined for network devices include IP-to-MAC binding, Layer-2 Location, Security Events, Device Attributes, Authentication Information, and Access Request Information. They were defined and initially published in the TNC IF-MAP binding for SOAP specification 1.0 revision 25. Individually they are somewhat significant, but when you begin to put them together, they become much more compelling.

As with a TCG standard, at publication it was both open and free to use without a fee or requirement for membership in TCG or any other alliances. As previously stated, at release initial uptake existed in a plug-fest type of demonstration between a handful of vendors. The real power of IF-MAP though begins to show when you think about it and as adoption becomes broader across the entire security landscape. In the past the model involved a great deal of randomness related to vendors and their relationships to foster interworkings between various products. Essentially throughout history we have had to "hope" vendors supported a certain product or concern ourselves with a great deal of customization in order to extract, import, correlate, decipher, and then report on critical issues. While it is possible to pull this off, it is not unlike the entire problem facing our industry today, which centers around some type of assumed knowledge that simply may or may not exist. Call it the "Weenie Factor" or whatever you want, but it cripples us. Steve Hanna and I have had this conversation on and off for years and I asked him if it would be okay to share some of it. It goes something like a Letterman top ten list:

**Are you a security nerd? Here are a few telltale signs:**

- You have WPA2 enabled on your home wireless
- You use a radius server for the above because PSK is "weak"
- Your home backups are encrypted
- You have the encrypted copies stored in multiple off-site locations
- Your Web passwords are generated using an algorithm that you invented yourself
- You SSH back to servers on your home network

- You have custom rules on your personal firewall one of which had DOS'd you at some point
- You regularly run more than three different malware detection programs
- You have or had a certificate for your personal e-mail
- You installed disk encryption on your child's laptop

If you answered yes to more than one of these items, you are a security nerd. There is nothing wrong with that. I am one too and proud of it! At the same time, we must realize that most people are not like us. For most people, security does not make them feel good. Security is a necessary evil, something that they must deal with to get their job done. It is oftentimes just an evil or a block or a failure of the system as a whole. It is not unlike the "12:00 syndrome" with VCR's. Somewhere we fell off the bus and now that has worked its way up into the data centers and enterprises themselves. Instead of continuing to try and out "tech" a problem, we should seek to find efficiency through supporting interoperability without excuses. In our daily lives it should be our job to give normal people the security that they need while remaining as unobtrusive as possible. If we could do our jobs perfectly, we would design information systems that could protect themselves automatically. Users could spend less time trying to remember long passwords that change every month and complex incantations to connect back to the VPN. They could focus on their business, using smart cards and biometrics to log in. Their security duties would be focused on not falling prey to social engineering. That is plenty hard enough for most users and yet instead of moving that way by opening up the ecosystem, we have gone almost the exact opposite in many instances because we have allowed ourselves be cut off and put into silos by the same folks trying to sell us products to solve the problems they tell us we have. That seems imbalanced to me and that imbalance creates a large portion of the ecosystem issues in which we are currently mired.

The current reality we are stuck with in many cases is instead again "hoping" that the vendors stay happy with one another and praying that the next patch to whichever system needs it does not randomly break something that we have no visibility on inside a black box they created. Instead, with IF-MAP you become the pilot and not just the passenger in that deterministically you are able to use the power built within the protocol to automatically aggregate and associate information in near real time and in many cases real time from a variety of resources. It does not require vendors to be friends, it does not require them to like one another, it does not even require them to like you or even care you exist. Instead, it relies on their product to perform as it says it is going to perform and then prove that performance in a potentially heterogeneous but truly interoperable network environment. It gives the smaller vendors, through predefined data types and vendor-specific extensions, a target that cannot be moved by the behemoths in order to create lock-in and it stimulates innovation by allowing the community to potentially contribute to it's own security.

## *That Second Step Is a Dooooooozy*

While most people can agree in principle on something that seems so upfront and sensible, the real power is in not only paying lip-service to concepts but in putting rubber to the road. Broad magnanimous concepts make people feel good inside as they wax poetically about how Company C is connecting "The Human Network", while Company A to Z are "hear no evil" and "see no evil" with the third monkey seemingly missing. Luckily, Google found that monkey...at least for now! Seriously though, practical implementation of what evidently must be a radical concept to some companies, practitioners, and industry pundits maybe needs to be broken down to the simplest of examples in order for it to stick. Again, I decided to borrow from Steve Hanna simply because at it's simplest and least extensive level this is the minimum that IF-MAP brings to the security table.

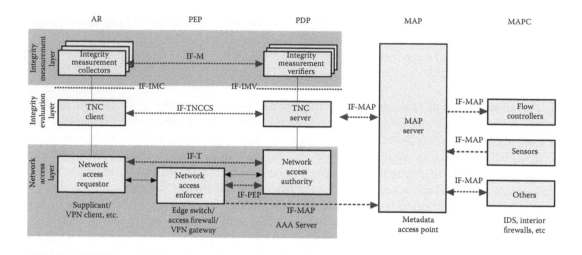

**Figure 3.2  TNC architecture with IF-MAP integrated—keeping it simple.**

Let's walk through a simple use case to see the benefits of IF-MAP. A user connects to a network through a VPN or NAC system, passing through identity checks and endpoint health checks. If the user is allowed on the network, the VPN or NAC system uses the IF-MAP protocol to store information about the user and their endpoint into the MAP. If an IDS later sees an endpoint device attacking someone or sending spam or engaging in some other undesirable behavior, the IDS can use the IF-MAP protocol to find information about that device that was previously stored in the MAP (such as the identity of the device's user). The IDS can even store an event into the MAP, reporting the bad behavior. If the VPN or NAC system has subscribed to notifications for such events, the MAP will notify the VPN or NAC system of the bad behavior using the IF-MAP protocol...[1]

So now, we see in Figure 3.2 a simple implementation that has a great deal of value in an IF-MAP based world. Capability-wise it goes up exponentially from there based on the power of the architecture to embrace products through nearly open-ended extensibility and interworking. One of the most significant aspects of the design is that from the simple diagram above, incredibly extensive maps can be developed as needs arise. This is made possible in part by the implementation of a true MAP instead of just a rehash of an extensible directory. The noticeable differences include heteroarchical versus hierarchical design, a true search capability without a separate catalog or registration server, and a much more scalable dynamic read/write capability that can be updated from nearly anywhere. Those of you familiar with X.500 and its much more popular child LDAP know the challenges associated with hierarchical directories once they reach a certain size and that issue coupled with the vast potentially chaotic looking mapping that could very well be required in each network/internetwork called for the heteroarchical approach.

## Complex Graphs May Emerge in MAP

Figure 3.3, while clearly representing just how capable the IF-MAP protocol is related to any number of decision support criteria, makes my head hurt. It serves the dual purpose of also making me thankful for those that work in our field that enjoy that sort of thing. Keep in mind that while we are concentrating on the security aspect here, the controlled chaos of IF-MAP's model

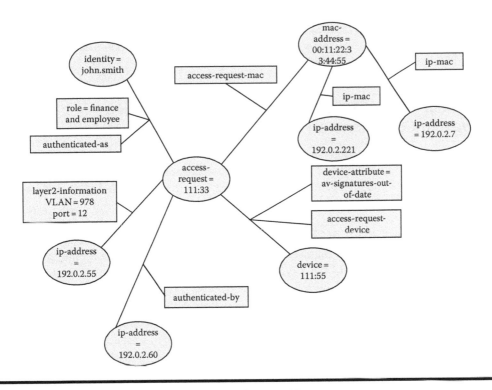

**Figure 3.3  Complex diagrams may emerge using IFMAP.**

would fit nearly any type of data required in organizations and will probably be considered for those purposes at some point in the future (Figure 3.3).

Mike Fratto wrote

> IF-MAP provides a standardized framework for network and security devices to publish device state data—such as IP address, authentication, or virtually any meaningful information—to a central repository that can be used by other applications. This repository can be used for security, asset management, discovery, or any other purpose.[2]

Stuart Bailey, the CTO and Founder of Infoblox synthesized it best:

> MAP is like a MySpace or Facebook for enterprise infrastructure security pieces that each component publishes and subscribes to.[3]

Bailey said:

> This is a community of security infrastructure devices where each device can allow its circle to know what it sees on the network, and share information.[3]

Mike's description of the "potential promise" of IF-MAP especially coupled with Bailey's analogy should hit home for practitioners because each goes to the heart of what our profession is about in many instances, context. Everything has to be considered in its own context and IF-MAP fits that way of looking at things. It has the ability to transcend a simple database to be a true open standards-based repository of all types of data that in turn will create a potential economy of scale that should lower costs and raise skill levels across the board.

## Evolution of "Threat State Databases": SETI for Security Coming to a Computer Near You

Deployment of protections coupled with correlation of the information coming back from our increasingly complicated environments is pretty much make or break going forward. In Chapter 1 "Enhanced Security through Open Standards: A path to a Stranger Global Digital Ecosystems," I mentioned and defined the flexible "Endpoints and Flowpoints" concept in a fairly generic way. This type of flex defense concept can adapt as you go to attempt to combat the increasingly intense evolution of threat and attack vectors in the next few years. The Mississippi River analogy still holds here as the sheer size and the overwhelming flood of information combine to overwhelm most if not all typical castle and moat type defenses. You cannot dam the Mississippi River but you can dam some tributaries while you watch the Mississippi and that type of thinking needs to be heavily considered for future deployments in networks. Single go/no go calls on endpoints as they come in to the network are nearly worthless in this new environment and various pieces of information need to be collected and then combined and assessed at speeds that we do not even understand yet. Again while this has existed in some form for years, the changes possible when enabled via an agile scalable framework like IF-MAP are very powerful. By sharing this information freely amongst various devices from all of the companies in your network, activity can be correlated with users to identify behavior that are anomalous eventually allowing the entity to decide the best course of action and then to enable it to take that action. Watching this diverse information stream with concepts from the past would have been nearly impossible based on both false positives as well as simply the inability of many of the practitioners in the field to fully grasp the nuances of the required skill sets for sometimes incredibly intricate manipulation of the interfaces necessary to be successful. I remember having this conversation with several of my friends and colleagues and we always came back to the question of why IF-MAP was necessary and why it mattered so much. I would bring up threats and use cases and they would detail the various things they had to approximately do the same thing. We would venture into harder core concepts and they would detail the sometimes fairly complicated data extracts and imports, the array of custom filters, the various pieces of command and control within their networks most of the time from the same company, and invariably we would broach the amount of care they had to take to make sure anything they bought fit this model. After this exercise with several friends, it became painfully clear to most of them that while they could do this it could not be and should not be an assumed skill set or even valid method of operation for our profession going forward. It simply did not scale.

Mike Fratto wrote:

> At the center of an IF-MAP-enabled system is the IF-MAP server, which stores state information. As a device changes over time, records are updated. Note that this is not a historical database—state data is only as current as the last update. Other network devices, like a NAC policy decision point, then query the IF-MAP server to determine if a host, say, successfully authenticated and completed a DHCP exchange, before allowing it to communicate on the network.[2]

IF-MAP uses a data model based on associating identifiers logically. For example, an IP address, a MAC address, and a user name are identifiers that, when linked, bind together to classify a host. Metadata is then used to describe these links. The relationship between a user name and an access request might have multiple metadata attached, including the user's role and the user name provided to authenticate.

This data is searchable by IF-MAP clients. Identifiers may be linked, facilitating searches so an IF-MAP client can discover how a particular device authenticated to the network, which user name was entered, and what IP addresses are bound to a given MAC address. This is a huge benefit—today there's no standardized way to, say, ask a Radius server which clients have authenticated, or query a DHCP server as to which leases have been given out.

As we move to drastically increase the visibility points throughout, that scalability becomes critical. As the next iterations of NBAD evolve we need to be able to truly innovate in the development of our strategies in order to enable the network to trigger responses to stimuli that begin to capture a lot more information at the first hint of trouble. The increased participation of both traditional and nontraditional endpoints in the security environment around them will allow, through IF-MAP, for the profession to potentially graduate to a "Threat State Database" as one manifestation. IF-MAP is a cornerstone of this type of concept but is only one of the tools in the box. As things like Common Uniform Driver Architecture evolve, projects like SETI can be imitated with the goal of thousands of individual clients participating in a grid working on the distributed task of a more secure ecosystem. Open source clients that serve various functions would all be IF-MAP enabled and could then possibly fill dual roles of both subscribing to information to strengthen their overall posture as well as publishing what they see around them. Effectively they each become individual sensors in their own right. This in turn allows for a weighting of input and potentially a furtherance of the vetting of information going into the repositories. This is a distributed peer review of sorts and while the input would have to be vetted to ascertain trust levels, it could be another indicator stored in the MAP that gives an additional clue as to the state of the network based more-so on what the individual clients see around and less on what they tell the network about themselves. This weighting of input could be adjusted as warranted and would potentially yield an important piece of the equation. The concept of "Federated Security" is not really new but the achievability of it has certainly been a bit of a pipe dream for some time. A truly comprehensive picture of not only your enterprise but of the portions of partner enterprises that matter to you is a potential force magnifier for defense. Real-time information flowing to an open standards-based repository allows you the ability to quickly focus efforts and resources potentially before an area becomes a concern. This on the fly tuning would simply not have been even conceivable in heterogeneous networks a few years ago and yet with the IF-MAP and TCG's newest TNC specifications, it seems like we are finally at the cusp of a true OODA or Boyd's Loop interactive decision cycle based on timely feedback to each action and decision.

## It Is Full of Stars....

Last year I wrote:

> Basically in this environment, we are watching the sampled data at different points in the system and as heuristics continue to evolve, we can decide whether or not to focus the more intensive capabilities of the forensic aspect of that network on our trouble spots. With the proliferation of headless attack vectors like printers, iPods, and iPhones there has to be a way of distributing the load of the visibility so that we have early warning indicators

before things overwhelm the core. It has been proven that core defense simply does not work because of the drastic increase in bandwidth coming from the edge, the huge liability located in the endpoint including what data it sees and what it does with that data, and new valid "malware-like" software that serves valid business purposes while fraying the nerves of the security team. As we continue to move toward the evolution of more transient and distributed network security supplicants on these clients, we need to concern ourselves with network design that allows for the inclusion of this data in real time so that when it does get here we do not have to rip and replace yet again. Buying switches that are sFlow capable should be on the agenda while paying attention to both standards adherence in the past as well as roadmap postures for the future again comes to the forefront. Paying attention to how a router supports NetFlow and whether or not the company is really participating in the standards associated with communications in general should become a main criterion for our discussions. Recognizing how we are going to put that information to use and what we need to do in order to further the evolution of the industry needs to become a prime consideration if we are every to get ahead of the curve.[4]

IF-MAP paved the way, establishing a conceptual "beachhead" and TCG wasted no time by following up this year with the release of three additional potentially powerful specifications as well as updates to three already in place. These are late additions to this chapter and cannot be explored fully right now since they are not in full production. Having said that, the potential for them when looked at as a group is staggering. First out of the gate is the IF-T Binding to TLS 1.0 (IF-TTLS). This is potentially the little engine that could as it relates to enablement of communications across the broad spectrum of IP networks. The sexiest part about this specification is that it does not require 802.1x so will function on any IP Network to enable health monitoring via intelligence embedded on a client (preinstalled or installed on the fly) that can initiate its own communication with a service menu through a new mechanism available through a modification of the IF-TNCCS specification that updated the XML-based session protocol. Feature wise, the IF-T Binding to TLS enables checking of a machine already on an IP network versus one not yet attached. It also allows very verbose assessments of endpoints due to the fact that a TLS connection generally provides larger bandwidth than tunneled EAP as well as support for many round trips as in the case when practitioners use TPM-based attestation in addition to a TNC assessment. Another benefit of using IF-T is that both the TNC-compliant client and TNC-compliant server are able to initiate an assessment when either believes an event has occurred that warrants an updated assessment.

The strength of IF-TTLS would be enough of a revision in 1 year if it stood by itself but TCG went further in attempting to help our profession do its job. First off to support IF-TTLS as well as anything else new that comes out in a distributed form, they released Federated TNC 1.0 (FTNC). Now that any IP addressable machine with a client can be assessed, they needed a standards-based way to transfer that information between security domains. TCG chose SAML assertions as the method to transfer TNC results between security domains creating three new SAML profiles. The three profiles were Roaming Assessment Profile, Web Assessment Profile, and FTNC Attribute Profile. Although only in a version 1.0, the benefits to users and practitioners comes through both improved endpoint assessment capabilities that in turn increases overall organizational security. At the same time, higher trust at host organizations could possibly result into a more substantial menu of available services. Potentially single sign-on is possible and if not that then at least simplified sign-on. You are no longer treated as an outsider to other host organizations once you have been vetted in this manner and so efficiency has strong potential to increase. Potentially overlooked in the significantly increased visibility from both the host and home site is the potential to reuse and, therefore, potentially extract further value from existing SAML and TNC-related technologies. This goes back directly to the community wanting to participate in its own safety and survival. Reuse gives you more time to innovate, which in turn gives you and others better code to reuse, continuing to cycle.

Finally, the third new specification sounds boring on the surface until you realize just how critical profiles are to mitigation of threats from headless, and in this case clientless is defined as "without a head," attack vectors throughout the network. Previously much of this was done in nonstandard ways and hence was hard to replicate and to secure from one organization to the next. Clientless Endpoint Support Profile 1.0 (CESP) attempts to standardize how all endpoints that attach to a network without clients will be treated on a class-by-class basis. At its most basic, it describes what PEPs and PDPs should do to support clientless endpoints. The benefits are substantial with clientless endpoints like printers, VoIP phones, etc., being allowed to interoperate while maintaining a much improved security posture through the use of MAC-AUTH and correlation of data. These profiles can be transported and reused and while currently there is no community creation capability, that too is a goal in order to really raise the value proposition of participation.

With the initial IF-MAP standard, TCG seemed to be staying pretty much to itself with attempts to branch out in order to push standards in certain areas. With the release of these three new specifications and the adjustments to the older ones, TCG has shown that it is here to make a real difference. The goal is evidently "TNC Everywhere" and so to that effect they no longer consider themselves limited to just WAN and LAN. They now support standards-based roaming through FTNC while stepping up as the first standards-based profile enabler for any and all devices that run on today's networks. Slowly but surely they are moving from the foundation up the stack and at each year the standards have gotten increasingly relevant to the digital ecosystem as a whole.

With everything you have read so far, this is a no brainer right? Only if consumers of the technology take an active role and push forward without shying away or giving up and letting the vendors continue to lead us. We need to get to that 50/50 partnership sooner than later.

## Standards-Based Information Sharing: Enhancing Participation and Agility

### Lead, follow, or...ok wait just lead or follow!

But follow who? Are we supposed to continue to let it occur as it has in the past number of years within the industry or are we supposed to really reclaim some type of control of our own destiny. I believe we are tired of being in silos that keep us from communicating and, therefore, cooperating with one another to the benefit of those that would like to sell us a product to solve a problem we may not have but they thought we would 18 months ago. Did you follow that? We know that coordinated security allows better automation, more room to respond, better resiliency, and better overall results in general. In the past, intentionally, the lack of communication allowed us to be separated from one another and effectively kept in silos. With those odds, it was no wonder we consistently lost our way and fell back into the old patterns. Blogs and other social media outlets are changing that aspect, breaking down the silos, and possibly enabling the next thrust forward from a capability standpoint for open standards:

In November of 2008, Chris Hoff wrote a set of blog posts over a couple of days initially based on the security state, or lack thereof, of Cloud Computing. He wrote

> I described the need for a new security model, methodology and set of technologies in the virtualized and cloud computing realms built to deal with the dynamic and distributed nature of evolving computing:

This basically means that we should distribute the sampling, detection and prevention functions across the entire networked ecosystem, not just to dedicated security appliances; each of the end nodes should communicate using a standard signaling and telemetry protocol so that common threat, vulnerability and effective disposition can be communicated up and downstream to one another and one or more management facilities.[5]

The second post came a couple days later after Hoff had been pointed to IF-MAP by a current TCG member and IF-MAP supporter. This time he writes

IF-MAP is a standardized real-time publish/subscribe/search mechanism which utilizes a client/server, XML-based SOAP protocol to provide information about network security objects and events including their state and activity:

IF-MAP extends the TNC architecture to support standardized, dynamic data interchange among a wide variety of networking and security components, enabling customers to implement multi-vendor systems that provide coordinated defense-in-depth.

Today's security systems—such as firewalls, intrusion detection and prevention systems, endpoint security systems, data leak protection systems, etc.—operate as "silos" with little or no ability to "see" what other systems are seeing or to share their understanding of network and device behavior.

This limits their ability to support coordinated defense-in-depth. In addition, current NAC solutions are focused mainly on controlling network access, and lack the ability to respond in real-time to post-admission changes in security posture or to provide visibility and access control enforcement for unmanaged endpoints. By extending TNC with IF-MAP, the TCG is providing a standard-based means to address these issues and thereby enable more powerful, flexible, open network security systems.

While the TNC was initially designed to support NAC solutions, extending the capabilities to any security product to subscribe to a common telemetry and information exchange/integration protocol is a fantastic idea.

I'm really interested in how many vendors outside of the NAC space are including IF-MAP in their roadmaps. While IF-MAP has potential in conventional non-virtualized infrastructure, I see a tremendous need for it in our move to Infrastructure 2.0

Integrating, for example, IF-MAP with VM-Introspection capabilities (in VMsafe, XenAccess, etc.) would be fantastic as you could tie the control planes of the hypervisors, management infrastructure, and provisioning/governance engines with that of security and compliance in near-time with virtualization and Cloud Computing.[5]

If he sees it then what is the deal? Chris is a smart guy and at every turn when I describe the concept to people, I at least get a positive response of some sort whether people agree that it is the right way to go or not. The positive responses with no real follow-through confounded me until I found another post by Steve Hanna that described the exact phenomenon that we see each and every time something gets traction.

Steve writes

Chris asks which vendors are supporting IF-MAP in their products. I have found that standards adoption follows the classic innovation adoption lifecycle. Innovators are the vendors and customers that have the vision and foresight to see where things must go. They are the first to create and adopt new technology. For IF-MAP, that group includes the folks who developed the IF-MAP spec and demonstrated implementations at Interop Vegas in April: ArcSight, Aruba Networks, Infoblox, Juniper Networks, Lumeta, and nSolutions. Next come Early Adopters, Early Majority, Late Majority, and Laggards. It takes at least a year for each stage: six months to turn prototypes into products and six months for the next generation of adopters to catch on. That's the timescale we've seen for the other TNC standards. So I expect to see Innovator vendors shipping products that implement IF-MAP in the next few months and Innovator customers deploying those products in the months after that. Then will come Early Adopters and so on.[1]

I thought the graph he provided potentially unintentionally highlighted the real issue that has existed for many years. The graphic he provided is the standard picture of a typical innovation adoption life cycle. The challenge is that in technology we have a skewed graphic because probably close to half of the early adopters oftentimes are de facto locked in before they make that leap to early majority (Figure 3.4).

That is what we simply cannot allow to happen at this point in time. I will not go back over the challenges we face. I will not rehash the fact that we are standing at the edge of a digital abyss or revisit the fact that we are a consumer-driven economy whose actual main drivers are the most at risk…errmm… Anyway, what I will say is that the single best way to increase the number of products that support IF-MAP is for customers to demand and then buy those products. We need to reward both the vendors who are innovators and who have used their resources to try and participate on a field they know will be level to all of those wishing to uphold the standard. We need to be supportive of the community aspect around which local centers of excellence can grow and not only

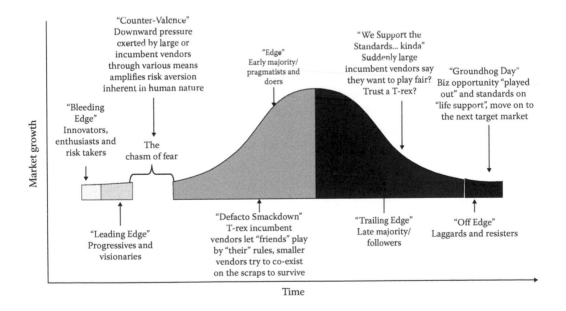

**Figure 3.4 Innovation adoption life cycle. (Adapted from Moore, G., *Crossing the Chasm*: *Marketing and Selling High-Tech products to Maintain Customers*, Harper Business, New York, 1991; and Hanna, S., The adoptive curve for IF-MAP, Got the NAC, November 11, 2008.)**

support, but actively pursue interactions across all of the lines that have been used as silo makers for us in the past. We are not Government, Health, and Education (GHE) or Small and Medium Business (SMB) or Large Enterprise, or Legal, or any of the titles vendors attach to us in order to better order their lives. What we are instead is one profession attempting to bridge a gap that we helped create. In order to even have a shot at doing that though, we need to find the things that we can make a utility and execute on them. We need to be able to rely on the community around us to assist so that each of us does not always continue to invent the wheel over and over again. We need a fulcrum in order to generate the leverage necessary to make a difference in what we do.

Mike Fratto wrote

> Whether IF-MAP achieves broad adoption depends on whether vendors actively develop integration points. IF-MAP has all the features necessary to aggregate host information in a standardized format, including enabling vendors to add their own attributes. The potential for integration is, simply, enormous. (Mike Fratto, InformationWeek)

I simply cannot say it any better than Mike does above. To that end, many of those quoted here and involved within the TCG, open group, the press, non-profits, and various government organizations have begun working toward a more active and hopefully successful role in the evolution of the standards process going forward. Currently we have to approach it from all sides. Customer advocacy, contract language, advisory councils, blogs, articles, information community based assistance, sites like opengroup.org, demandstandards.org, and truststc.org all have to be supported by our profession. It is through that coordination that we can really drive the point home and potentially snap us forward and over the early adopter's chasm. None of this is easy and with that in mind we should not make it harder than it already is by holding on to our sacred cows, old concerns, and fears that ubiquity of skill sets will make us less desirable to our organizations. The security profession has to move forward and drag some folks with us because otherwise the repercussions have the potential to be incredibly severe.

## About the Author

**David O'Berry**, CSSLP, CISSP-ISSAP, ISSMP, MCNE, CNE-I, and CSPM, is director of information technology systems and services for the South Carolina Department of Probation, Parole and Pardon Services (SCDPPPS), Columbia, South Carolina.

## References

1. Hanna, S. The Adoption Curve for IF-MAP, Got the NAC, November 11, 2008. http://forums.juniper. net/t5/user/viewprofilepage/userid/2969;jsessionid=124D8B42617DFA28E80BFC B18FF53E91.
2. Kerner, S. M. NAC 2.0 takes shape under networking giants, Internetnews.com, April 28, 2008. http://www.internetnews.com/infra/article.php/3743346.
3. O'Berry, D. Enhanced security through open standards: A path to a stronger global digital ecosystem, *Information Security Management Handbook*, 6th edn., vol. 2, H. F. Tipton and M. Krause (eds.). Auerbach, New York, 2009.
4. Fratto, M. Tech road map: IF-MAP protocol, *InformationWeek*, July 7, 2008.
5. Hoff, C. I can haz TCG IF-MAP in your security product, please…, Rational Survivability Blog, November 10, 2008. http://www.rationalsurvivability.com/blog/?p=78.

*Chapter 4*

---

# A Primer on Demystifying U.S. Government Networks*

---

## Samuel Chun

## Contents

## Introduction: 9-11 Changes Everything Including Government IT

One of the immediate impacts of the events following 9-11 for government information infrastructures was the passage of the Intelligence Reform and Terrorism Prevention Act (IRTPA) of 2004. Former President George W. Bush's signature on December 17, 2004 on the IRTPA signaled a radical change in direction for intelligence efforts by encouraging and fostering interagency cooperation. One of the most interesting aspects of IRTPA was that it clearly attempted

---

* This chapter does not contain any classified information about government networks or government network operations. All information in this chapter is freely available to the public.

to address the problems found by the 9-11 Commission in information sharing by codifying what was thought to be a solution into law.

Section 1016(a) (1) (A) of the IRTPA (Information Sharing) mandates that the President shall

(A) *Create an information sharing environment for sharing of terrorism information in a manner consistent with national security and with applicable legal standards relating to privacy and civil liberties;*

(B) *designate the organizational and management structures that will manage the ISE; and*

(C) *determine and enforce the policies, directives, and rules that will govern the content and usage of the ISE.*

Further, in Section (E), IRTPA mandates that the newly created and appointed Program Manager for the Information-Sharing environment (PM-ISE) of DNI must employ an approach that emphasizes control over access to data, in addition to networks and systems that contain it, without compromising security. Section (E) also states that the ISE must facilitate the sharing of information within and across all security levels. To summarize simply, the President is mandated to create an environment where information (including those that are classified) can be shared easily to all appropriate stakeholders without compromising security. In short, the law dictates that the U.S. government agencies changed from an "attitude of need to know" to a "responsibility to share" with enabling technologies to support this monumental change.

While it is easy to state on legislation that "everyone must share more," it is an enormous challenge to federal agencies to actually accomplish as nearly a half century of mandates and laws have created a richly complex environment that contains the most sensitive (including those that could result in grievous damage to the U.S. nation-state) in "stove-piped" enclaves with controls and cultures intended to inhibit the sharing of information. Even with the passage of the IRPTA in 2004, government networks, especially those that serve predominantly classified missions such as defense and intelligence, are riddled with the results of insular practices and inadequate information-sharing technologies of the past. For example, it is very common to have "air gapped" or "physically separated" networks that require users to have multiple PCs that are connected to entirely separate networks infrastructures (which include switches, servers, software, identities, etc.). Consequently, the PM-ISE reported in 2007 in his PM-ISE Enterprise Architecture Framework document that the current lack of capabilities in sharing and securing of information "causes proliferation of assets, ranging from multiple desktop machines for end-users to multiple server racks and associated networking equipment in back-office server rooms. This trend will continue for the foreseeable future."

## Differences and Similarities

While it is easy to assume that U.S. federal government information and communications infrastructures are identical to commercial networks in approach and technologies, the fact of the matter is that while it may use similar or even the same technologies (Microsoft, Cisco, and HP are some of the biggest federal government technology vendors) there are differences that newcomers to federal government agency IT departments struggle with when exposed to U.S. government networks. One of the primary goals of this chapter is to be a primer for those that are interested in how the U.S. federal government information infrastructures were created and some of the challenges associated in moving into a more sharing environment. This chapter is by no means the definitive treatise in how government information infrastructures operate but it is intended to give a newcomer or someone interested in joining government IT departments a topical overview.

Presented below is a general summary of the relative differences between commercial and federal government networks.

*Technologies*: The technologies deployed by federal agencies differ widely, but since the 1980s, they have gone generally toward a more COTS route in providing IT for the agency users. Ubiquitous technology vendors such as HP, Microsoft, Cisco, Dell, Oracle, and EMC make hundreds of millions in business with the federal government under Federal Acquisition Regulations (FAR) and Defense Federal Acquisition Regulations (DFAR) each year. In addition, there are numerous purpose built and proprietary systems and applications in place to support specific missions. In addition, large-scale legacy systems based on older programmatic languages such as COBOL still exist servicing millions of citizens each year. By and large, there are numerous efforts across the federal government to modernize based on customization of commercial products.

*Processes and regulations*: Federal agencies tend to be more policy and process driven than commercial organizations. This is mainly due to the myriad of regulations and directives that can apply to IT infrastructures. For example, compliance with the Federal Information Security Management Act of 2002 is a rigorous exercise that each government agency expends considerable effort in adhering to. In addition, mandates from organizations such as Office of Management and Budget (OMB) and department-specific policies generated by agencies such as DISA (Defense Information Systems Agency) exert a lot of processes and policies that need to be complied with by agency IT departments.

*People*: The practitioners and technical resources is where commercial and public sector share common ground. The technical expertise required in working in a federal government environment is not that dissimilar since the technologies tend to be ubiquitous. As a matter of fact, U.S. Department of Defense is the only federal government organization that imposes a certification requirement for security practitioners under the 8570.01 mandate. All of the 8570.01 certifications required for compliance to 8570 are commercially based (CISSP, SSCP, etc.) However, there is a level of vetting that does not exist in commercial environments since the risks involved can be extremely high. This type of vetting is usually reserved for access to the most sensitive of information—classified information.

*Nature of risk*: While the missions of the hundreds of federal agencies vary, there are a few where the risks involved far exceed that of any commercial interests. There are organizations in government whose sole mission is the defense of the state. The risks facing these organizations by inappropriate disclosure, lack of system resiliency, or data integrity can be catastrophic and can result in grievous bodily harm, loss of life, or damage to the security of the nation. It is not surprising that there are strictly controlled environments that are closed off from public and even private access without the "need to know." These environments, while small in number, do carry extraordinary risks, and the cultures of the organizations that use these environments consequently tend to be more risk averse. These classified networks, while they use classic commercially available software and hardware, are strictly controlled and closed from public scrutiny. These networks, due to the manner in which they were architected and those that are authorized to work within and with it, present some of the most challenging barriers to a more agile, sharing information environment.

## Classified versus Unclassified versus Controlled but Unclassified versus Declassified Explained

One of the first questions that will be asked when joining a government contracting company is "do you have a security clearance?" A candidate's answer will have enormous impact on the programs and projects that the practitioner will have access to when working in federal government. While most of the federal government enterprise works in an unclassified fashion (although "official use only" policies certainly do apply) using fairly well-known technologies, having a security clearance qualifies you to potentially work on projects on behalf of government programs at that person's clearance level and below.

Before getting into the particulars of the various levels of how a program (and its information) can be classified, it is important to describe how the access to sensitive, classified information is handled in the United States. It is important to first understand some basic definitions involved.

*Classified information*: Classified information refers to information that has been categorized and restricted in access to individuals or groups that has the appropriate security clearances (defined later) and requisite "need to know" to the information. There are three levels of classification in the United States: Confidential, Secret, and Top Secret. Executive Order (EO) 1329 signed by President George W. Bush in March of 2003 is the governing presidential order that regulates classified information. EO 1329 is an amendment to EO 12958, which in itself is an amendment to a long line of presidential orders dating back to President Dwight Eisenhower's order from the 1950s.

*Unclassified information*: Unclassified information refers to information that has not been classified. That does not imply that all unclassified information is releasable. See the section on Controlled Unclassified Information.

*Declassified/declassification*: Declassified information is information that has had their security classification removed. Until the introduction of the concept of "automatic declassification" by EO 12958, classified information was presumed to be of permanent value to the federal government. EO 12958 basically introduced a regular "time limit" of 25 years in which information that were legally transferred by agencies and the executive office to the National Archives would be presumed declassified unless the agency that originated them acted to exempt them in compliance with the provisions of EO 12958. This had a tremendous impact on declassifying information as 1.33 billion pages have been declassified according to the FY2006 Report to the President, Information Security Oversight Office.

*Controlled unclassified information (CUI)*: In May of 2008, the Office of the President issued a memorandum to the heads of the executive departments and agencies with the subject of "Designation and Sharing of Controlled Unclassified Information." The intent of this memorandum was to replace the Sensitive But Unclassified (SBU) designation with a framework that is intended to be more rigorous. In order for the information to be considered CUI, it must (a) not meet the standards for National Security Classification under EO 12958, as amended; (b) be pertinent to the national interests of the United States or to the important interests of entities outside the Federal Government; and (c) under law or policy require protection from unauthorized disclosure, special handling safeguards, or prescribed limits on exchange or dissemination.

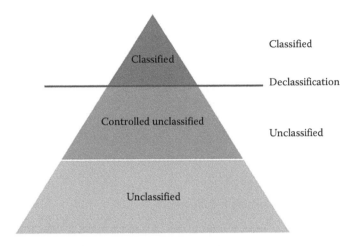

**Figure 4.1  Classification versus unclassified overview.**

Figure 4.1 pictorially represents the four terms:

## Classified Information

As mentioned earlier, classified information is generally referred to as "classified"; however, they are actually categorized further into three levels of sensitivity: *Confidential*, *Secret*, and *Top Secret*. EO 13292 dictates that "Except as otherwise provided by statute, no other terms shall be used to identify United States classified information." That means that according to EO 13292 there are no further ways to classify information than Confidential, Secret, and Top Secret.

One of the important things to note is that there are standards that are used to determine if information should be classified. Not every bit of information used by government needs to be classified in some manner. The following statements are excerpted directly from EO 13292 on the standards that are to be used to classify information. Only *if all of the following conditions are met* the information may be originally classified:

1. "An original classification authority is classifying the information."
2. "The information is owned by, produced by or for, or is under the control of the United States Government."
3. "The information falls within one or more of the categories of information listed. Information shall not be considered for classification unless it concerns:
   (a)  military plans, weapons systems, or operations;
   (b)  foreign government information;
   (c)  intelligence activities (including special activities), intelligence sources or methods, or cryptology;
   (d)  foreign relations or foreign activities of the United States, including confidential sources;
   (e)  scientific, technological, or economic matters relating to the national security, which includes defense against transnational terrorism;
   (f)  United States Government programs for safeguarding nuclear materials or facilities;

    (g)  vulnerabilities or capabilities of systems, installations, infrastructures, projects, plans, or protection services relating to the national security, which includes defense against transnational terrorism;

    (h)  weapons of mass destruction."

4.  "The original classification authority determines that the unauthorized disclosure of the information reasonably could be expected to result in damage to the national security, which includes defense against transnational terrorism, and the original classification authority is able to identify or describe the damage."

## Confidential versus Secret versus Top Secret versus Top Secret Compartmentalized Explained

Once information is deemed to meet the standards as described under the governing EO for classification, the level of sensitivity or classification is determined by the classification authority based on a set of standards. The standards are based on the potential impact to national security if an inappropriate disclosure were to occur. They are written as

**Top Secret**: "shall be applied to information, the unauthorized disclosure of which reasonably could be expected to cause exceptionally grave damage to the national security that the original classification authority is able to identify or describe."

**Secret**: "shall be applied to information, the unauthorized disclosure of which reasonably could be expected to cause serious damage to the national security that the original classification authority is able to identify or describe."

**Confidential**: "shall be applied to information, the unauthorized disclosure of which reasonably could be expected to cause damage to the national security that the original classification authority is able to identify or describe."

Top Secret level information (and programs) can be so sensitive and potentially impactful to national security that it can have additional requirements placed on the people that access it through the clearance process. For example, Sensitive Compartmented Information (SCI) requires that access be granted only to that compartment so that others that are not part of that compartment do not have access to the classified information regardless of their security clearance. Each compartment may impose additional requirements on the individuals that need access with a common one being a polygraph (full or lifestyle only). A diagram of the classification levels is presented in Figure 4.2.

## *The Clearance Process: Vetting the Individual*

While granting access to individuals to unclassified information by agencies is straightforward, granting access to classified information is actually complex. The security clearance process is the method used to determine an individual's trustworthiness and reliability before adjudicating them to be fit to receive access to classified information. While both government organizations and commercial companies that do business with government agencies can request a security clearance for an individual, only the government can grant a security clearance.

Clearances are granted (or adjudicated by an agency adjudicative authority) after a background investigation is performed by either the Office of Personnel Management (OPM) or the

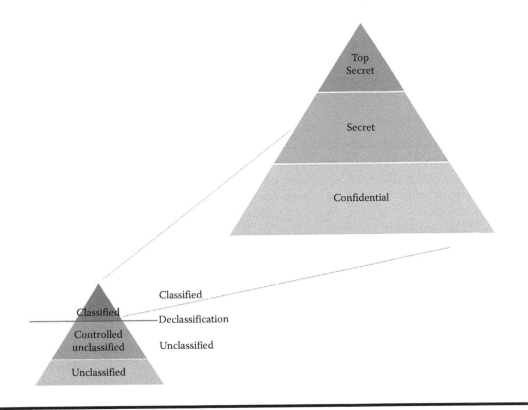

**Figure 4.2 Classified information overview.**

Defense Security Service (DSS). Depending on the clearance level requested, investigations can involve computerized checks of financial records and criminal history all the way to personal interviews of neighbors and individual polygraphs. Clearances, predictably, are mostly requested and granted at three levels: Confidential, Secret, and Top Secret.

Although security clearances "roughly" map to classification levels of Confidential, Secret, and Top Secret, individual agencies often choose to only recognize clearances adjudicated from their own agencies (which is actually technically against policy) or issue their own versions. For example, the U.S. Department of Energy grants "L" or "Q" clearances that roughly map to "Secret" and "Top Secret" levels; however, they are not generally portable to other agencies. Another notable example is that workers that work in or for the U.S. Department of Treasury or Securities and Exchange Commission can receive a clearance called "Public Trust" that does not map to any of the National Security Clearances and is not portable for access to classified information anywhere due to its less rigorous background investigations used for adjudication.

## Seems OK... What Are the Problems?

While the approach and processes for classifying information and clearing individuals seem reasonable, anyone involved in federal government information technology will readily admit that there are definite challenges with the system. One of the biggest issues in the past has been the lengthy time required for background investigations by OPM and DSS and adjudicators to grant clearances. While much progress has been made in recent years to shorten the wait time for applicants, it could still take months or even years for individuals to receive full clearances at the highest levels. OPM and DSS along with agencies are still working at the writing of this chapter in shortening the average wait times; however, the demand for cleared IT security professionals far exceeds supply and are one of the most sought after practitioners in the federal government IT support industry.

## Agency Independence

One of the most interesting aspects of U.S. federal government IT is the level of independence exercised by agencies. Whether it is due to the diverse missions of the organizations or decades of independence, agency CIO's have remarkable power to shape their IT infrastructures. Even within Cabinet level departments such as Defense, Justice, Treasury and Homeland Security there are a myriad of component agencies who operate semiautonomously. While overarching regulations such as FISMA and OMB mandates (such as OMB-13 on the federal desktop core configuration or more commonly referred to as FDCC) are complied with, other technology investments or programs are generally funded led by the individual agency themselves and generally not their cabinet level CIO's. Looking across a large cabinet level department or the entire federal enterprise is similar to looking at a jigsaw puzzle: the shapes of pieces may look different but they are intended to work together for a common mission—citizen service and safety.

Consequently, the IT infrastructure of a specific agency may look remarkably different than another even under the same Cabinet level secretary. Consequently, there are technological issues in interoperability and sharing information. As agencies have evolved their IT infrastructures independently, there have been widely varying approaches to such vendors, technologies, and services as directory/authentication, e-mail, Web services, and storage, and even security. While there have been recent efforts to have a more standardized approach to IT with initiatives such as the Federal Enterprise Architecture (FEA) and FDCC, much work remains on a coordinated effort for IT.

## Why Do I Have 5 PCs and Log In 5 Times Every AM?

Compounding the issue of a loosely coordinated IT strategy across the federal government is that agencies that are involved in maintaining national security have to have networks that are designed to protect classified information. These networks are hierarchical depending on the level of sensitivity or classification. An agency, depending on their mission, may have all levels or a subset or none. Figure 4.3 represents three hypothetical agencies and the potential networks they may contain.

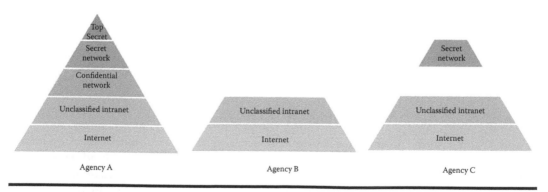

**Figure 4.3 Differences between agencies.**

In many civilian agencies, the number of networks is less of a problem. However, in environments where all levels of classified information are necessary to fulfill a mission (mainly in intelligence, homeland security, and national defense) the networking issues become complex. For example, due to the nature of the classified networks, each tend to be "air gapped" (physically separated from others) and "closed" (data flows between levels are extremely tightly controlled based on Mandatory Access Control policies). End users in these environments have multiple PCs in their work areas with separate connections to each of the networks and have multiple IDs and resources to work within the classification levels. It is not unusual for analysts at some agencies to have more than 5 PCs connected to a switch box to access multiple classified and unclassified networks. Even applications that run on these networks are not exempt from the requirement for separation. For example, even the most successful of information-sharing programs such as the Central Intelligence Agency's Intellipedia runs separately at each classification level with varying content at each level.

## Commonly Used Government Networks: The Alphabet Soup

One of the most challenging aspects of working in the federal government IT is its use of acronyms. The following presents some of the most commonly referred to federal government networks and their associated acronyms:

**NIPRNet (commonly referred to as "nipper"):** Non-Secure Internet Protocol Router Network is a network used primarily by the U.S. Department of Defense to exchange unclassified information. It is predominantly serviced by the .mil domain and is similar in use as other civilian agency internal networks.

**SIPRNet (commonly referred to as "sipper"):** Secret Internet Protocol Router Network is an IP network used predominantly by the Department of Defense and the members of the Intelligence Community to transfer classified information up to the Secret level. It is physically separated from NIPRNet due to its use to transfer classified information. SPIRNet is serviced by the .smil and .sgov domains.

**JWICS (commonly referred to as "jaywicks"):** Joint Worldwide Intelligence Communications System is a network used predominantly by the members of the Intelligence Community and the Department of Defense to transfer information up to Top Secret (and compartmented) level.

**HSDN:** Homeland Secure Data Network announced in 2004 to be a replacement for various Departmental WANs. It will operate at the Top Secret level with plans to support at TS/SCI level.

**INTELINK:** Web-based intranet information-sharing service used in the intelligence community. There are multiple versions at each classification level including an unclassified version called INTELINK-U.

**CENTRIXS (commonly referred to as "centricks"):** Combined Enterprise Regional Information Exchange System is a collection of classified networks used by the U.S. Department of Defense and Coalition allies for exchanging information in support of joint/coalition military operations. It is considered the de facto infrastructure for multinational information sharing. There are many versions of CENTRIXS with each having a widely ranging assortment of coalition allies for a common mission. For example, CENTRIXS-MCFI

(Multination Coalition Forces Iraq) is used by Global War on Terror (GWOT) allies in Iraq while the CENTRISXS-GCTF (Global Counter-Terrorism Forces) network services the U.S. military and allied partners for GWOT in a separate network. One of the long-term challenges that CENTRIXS will need to address is the creation of multiple physically separated networks that may introduce redundancy and enclaves that may not be able to communicate with each other (lack of cross domain access).

**TFIN (commonly referred to as "teefin"):** Treasury Foreign Intelligence Network is a network operating at the Top Secure/SCI level in support of the Treasury Department's Office of Terrorism and Financial Intelligence with the "twin aims of safeguarding the financial system against illicit use and combating rogue nations, terrorist facilitators, weapons of mass destruction (WMD) proliferators, money launderers, drug kingpins, and other national security threats."

## *Bell–La Padula Still Rules!*

The Bell–La Padula Model (BPM) has been the foundation of military and intelligence access control for decades. Since the early 1970s, classified networks have been built based on Bell–La Padula's approach to security—no read up and no write down. BPM forbids users at a certain classification level from reading content at a higher classification level (e.g., users in Secret networks cannot read/access in Top Secret networks) and downgrading information (e.g., users in Secret networks cannot create information in Unclassified networks). Conversely, users in lower classification levels can create or send information to higher classification levels (users in Secret networks can transfer files to Top Secret networks). The Bell–La Padula Model in effect creates a one-way information flow effect with information that is easy to send up but almost impossible to send down, as shown in Figure 4.4:

It is easy for users at lower classification networks to e-mail and transfer files to higher level networks while information transfer down to lower classification level must be done through a more rigorous (i.e., manual and slower) process. An electrical engineering analogy of a diode is

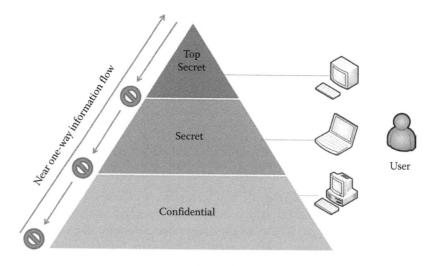

**Figure 4.4   Bell–La Padula and classified information flow.**

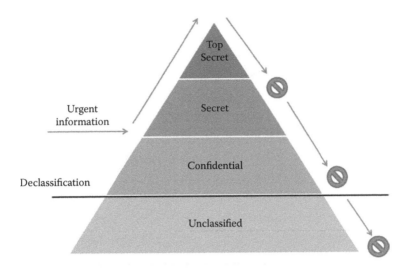

**Figure 4.5  Challenges of information sharing through classification levels.**

often used to describe the guard technologies that protect information flow between classification levels as diodes only allow an electrical charge to flow in one direction.

With the global and time-sensitive nature of homeland security and national defense, it is not difficult to imagine how this type of access control mechanism can inhibit urgent information sharing. For example, intelligence gathered by a defense organization overseas can take days to reach state and local law enforcement officials as the information must not only go through the appropriate vetting process but it must also traverse the various classification levels up and down (with delays occurring on the down side) to an unclassified state and local agency (e.g., local EMS), as shown in Figure 4.5:

While these examples and diagrams grossly oversimplify the challenges, agility in information sharing is an identified issue within and between agencies. This is one of the reasons for the PM-ISE clause in the IRTPA of 2004 and the creation of the Office of the Director of National Intelligence. Cultural and political issues aside, there are real technological problems with the ease and speed in which critical information can be shared.

## Cross Domain Solutions: Across Organizational Boundaries

There are two technologies that are extremely sought after in government to facilitate information sharing. The first is a cross domain solution (CDS). CDSs are generally intended to address the problem of being able to share information with ease (no disruptive technologies for end users) and confidence (without fear of inappropriate disclosure) across agency and even national boundaries. With unclassified, releasable information, the document can simply be e-mailed or put on a Web site for download. However, classified information is an entirely different matter since access must be restricted to specific individuals at specific periods, requiring auditing and logging of access in addition to restrictions on derivative content and in appropriate dissemination. Technologically, this is a complex issue as agencies themselves have widely differing information infrastructure, much less separate nations. In addition, classified networks tend to be closed, so rather than trying to create a secure information-sharing infrastructure, it is currently much

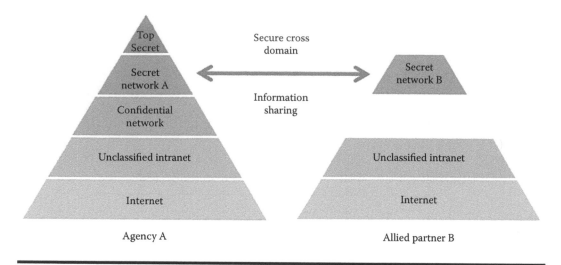

**Figure 4.6    Cross domain information sharing.**

easier, technologically, to create completely separate networks for joint mission delivery (e.g., coalition war fighting, multinational law enforcement, and public–private sector partnerships). Consequently, cross domain technologies are one of the most sought after solutions in the public sector (Figure 4.6).

## Multilevel Security: Across Classification Levels

The challenges associated with working across multiple classification levels was described earlier. Perhaps it is due to the small niche market or the complex technologies required or even the risk associated with developing a solution for this market, but industry has not been entirely successful in offering a series of robust solutions for the problem to government agencies. There have been notable successes such as the NetTop program with the NSA where a combination of VM technologies, Linux-based hosts, Microsoft Windows, and commercially manufactured PCs were integrated to perform across multiple security levels (MLS). However, successes have been rare as only a handful of providers have been able to achieve true MLS and have the solution be accredited for production implementation. While there continues to be innovation and research aimed at true MLS at different commercial companies, progress will likely continue to be slow compared to research and development aimed at producing products for a much broader market. The simplified diagram below presents hypothetical MLS solutions where users and PCs are connected either through multiple physical connections to the various classification levels from a single PC or routing/switching/VPN technologies are used to provide a single connection from a PC to multiple levels. In addition, secure information flow both up and down classification levels would also be ideal (Figure 4.7).

## The Future: Information-Sharing Environment = CDS + MLS

While it is difficult to envision any near-term solution to the MLS and CDS problems that currently exist, almost everyone uniformly agrees that a truly agile information-sharing environment, where a cleared user with the appropriate need to know on a single desktop can create, send, and

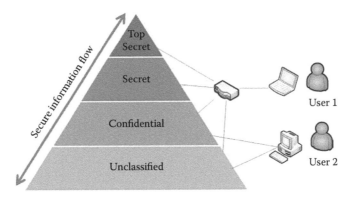

**Figure 4.7    Multilevel access.**

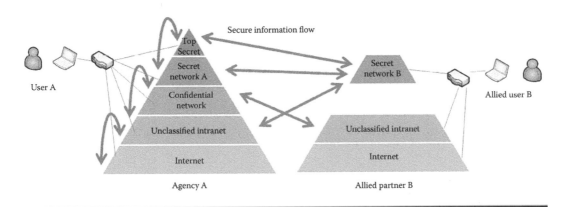

**Figure 4.8    Cross domain and multilevel combined.**

receive classified information across classification levels across domains, needs to be the future. A logical representation of such an environment where Cross Domain and Multilevel Security capabilities are combined is presented in Figure 4.8:

In this environment, information flows to the appropriate authorized users across jurisdictional boundaries (United States to allied nations) and across classified networks to ensure that the right individual has access to the information as quickly as possible. This is an antithesis to the "stove-piped" networks where information is easily enclaved due to the fear of inappropriate disclosure and lack of enabling technologies. While an environment such as this is envisioned and much effort is being expended to create it, it would be interesting to revisit the progress made by industry and government in the years to come.

## About the Author

**Samuel Chun**, CISSP, is the director of the Cyber Security Practice for HP Enterprise Services, Plano, Texas, U.S. Public Sector.

# Network Attacks and Countermeasures

*Chapter 5*

# Antispam: Bayesian Filtering

Georges J. Jahchan

## Contents

Spamming is defined as the abuse of electronic messaging to indiscriminately send unsolicited bulk messages. Its most recognized form is e-mail spam, with IM, Usenet newsgroups, Web search engines, blogs, wiki, online classified ads, mobile phone messaging, Internet forum, and junk fax transmissions being the other spam spread vectors.

Come to think of it, spam is an inexpensive method of advertising; it costs little more than the maintenance of mailing lists and that of the equipment and Internet connectivity to send spam e-mails. In other words, any individual with access to a computer that is connected to the Internet is a potential spammer. Spam has grown to alarming proportions, with the intent of spammers reaching far beyond advertising into cybercrime territory with pharming, phishing, botnets, rootkits, and other malicious uses, all of which can potentially have serious consequences for the victims (identity theft and/or financial loss).

The spam problem has grown to the point where even small businesses cannot afford to "look the other way." Businesses of all sizes consider e-mail a mission-critical application. It is relied upon for internal and external business communications. Management expects e-mail to be highly available, accessible when and where needed, and secure. To that end, measures to effectively manage spam are a business imperative.

*Information Week*, in its February 3, 2005 edition estimated the global cost of spam back in 2005 at $21.58 billion annually.* Ferris Research estimated the cost of spam in 2007 at a staggering $100 billion.[†]

Spam does not advertise itself as such, quite the contrary, spammers try to disguise the e-mails to encourage or entice recipients to read them. Early spam detection methods relied on keyword searches in the title, headers, or body of the message. Reliability was low and maintenance cost was high. Spammers quickly learned to outsmart keyword searches.

Additional controls were devised[‡]: whitelists, blacklists, and Bayesian filters. Whitelisting only delivers messages from e-mails or domains that have been preapproved by the recipient. Blacklists automatically filter e-mails based on identified individual e-mails, domains, or source server IP addresses, blocking known offenders. Bayesian filtering uses complex statistical techniques to classify e-mails based on content from past e-mails. A content-dependent score is assigned to every e-mail. E-mails exceeding a predefined score threshold are tagged as spam.

In this chapter, we analyze in detail how generic Bayesian spam filters work, probing into various methods of applying Bayes' theorem. A handful of Bayesian filtering implementations (that have been reported as particularly effective[§]) Paul Graham's, SpamProbe for MacOS, CRM114, SpamAssassin (SA), and Annoyance Filter[¶] will be examined in detail.

## Bayesian Spam Filtering Process

A Bayesian spam e-mail filter relies on the likelihood or probability of encountering certain words in spam e-mails that one is unlikely to find in legitimate e-mails. These words are not known in advance, and the Bayesian spam filter must be trained to recognize them. Initial training is performed by analyzing at least 200 known spam and 200 ham (known legitimate) e-mails. During training, the filter will adjust the probabilities that each word will appear in spam or in legitimate e-mails in its database. These word probabilities contribute to the calculation of a spam score (a numeric or a percentage value) to the e-mail, based on the weight and frequency of occurrence of certain words in the e-mail. The contribution is called posterior probability. Posterior probability is computed using Bayes' theorem.

The probability that an e-mail is spam is then computed for all words in the e-mail. If that total exceeds a preset value, the e-mail is tagged as spam (for example, \*\*\*Spam\*\*\* may be appended to the beginning of the subject line). Client-side filters look for these tags in the subject line and automatically move tagged e-mails to the junk folder without further processing.

Some implementations of Bayesian filters can optionally be configured to act earlier in the e-mail chain by "blacklisting" certain e-mails. As soon as sufficient information is received to identify an e-mail as blacklisted, the filter resets and closes the SMTP connection, thereby saving bandwidth that would otherwise be wasted in receiving spam e-mails. The disadvantage is that unlike tagging, the recipients are neither aware of such e-mails which do not reach their mailboxes, nor are they notified of their existence.

---

* http://www.informationweek.com/news/security/vulnerabilities/showArticle.jhtml?articleID=59300834
[†] http://www.ferris.com/research-library/industry-statistics/
[‡] http://articles.directorym.net/The_Fight_Against_Spam_San_Jose_CA-r906929-San_Jose_CA.html
[§] http://www.linux.com/articles/32353
[¶] http://www.fourmilab.ch/annoyance-filter/

# How Bayes' Theorem Is Utilized by Spam Filters

Bayes' Theorem is used to

1. Compute the probability that a message is spam, based on the presence of a given word in the message
2. Compute the probability that the message is spam on the basis of all of its words (or a subset thereof)
3. Identify the message as blacklisted on the basis of its header (or part thereof) and/or part of its body
4. Analyze rare words

The formula that the software uses to determine spam is derived from *Bayes' theorem* reproduced below:

$$Pr(S|W) = \frac{Pr(W|S) \cdot Pr(S)}{Pr(W|S) \cdot Pr(S) + Pr(W|H) \cdot Pr(H)}$$

where

$Pr(S|W)$ is the probability that a message is spam, knowing that the banned word is in it
$Pr(S)$ is the overall probability that any given message is spam
$Pr(W|S)$ is the probability that a keyword appears in spam messages
$Pr(H)$ is the overall probability than any given message is not spam (is "ham")
$Pr(W|H)$ is the probability that the keyword appears in ham messages

Plugging in numerical values to illustrate the theorem, assuming a spam keyword appears in 60% of spam and in 10% of ham, and that 55% of all e-mails are spam, the probability that a message with that keyword in it is spam is

$$\frac{0.6 * 0.55}{0.6 * 0.55 + 0.1 * 0.45} = 0.88 \text{ or } 88\%$$

The example above provides a use case for a single keyword. In a typical e-mail, multiple keywords can be found, each with its own set of values. The overall potential of an e-mail being spam is the combination of the individual computed keyword probabilities.

There are several methods to combine the individual keyword probabilities. The "naive" method assumes that the occurrences of the individual keywords are *independent*:

$$p = \frac{p1 \cdot p2 \ldots pN}{p1 \cdot p2 \ldots pN + (1 - p1) \cdot (1 - p2) \cdot (1 - pN)}$$

where

$p$ is the probability that the message is spam
$p1$ is the probability $p(S|W1)$ that it is a spam knowing it contains a first keyword
$p2$ is the probability $p(S|W2)$ that it is a spam knowing it contains a second keyword
$pN$ is the probability $p(S|WN)$ that it is a spam knowing it contains an $N$th keyword

The result $p$ is compared to a preset threshold; if it exceeds that threshold, the e-mail is most likely spam, and is tagged accordingly. In the English language, the "naive" assumption is, however, incorrect, as the probability of finding an adjective is affected by the probability of having a noun.

Another method used in some Bayesian spam filters is to ignore all keywords whose spamicity (see below) is close to 0.5 as they add little value to the decision. The words that are evaluated are those whose spamicity is close to zero (found mostly in ham) or close to 1.0 (found mostly in spam). A variation thereof is to only retain the words with the top/bottom $N$ spamicity values on either side of the scale.

Marcov Random Fields (MRF) [1] is yet another method of zeroing in on spam. Implemented with tweaks and hacks in CRM114, it considers all relations between neighboring words to matter, for neighborhoods with variable window size (for example, up to 3, 4, 5, 6 words). A technical discussion of MRF is beyond the scope of this document.

## Paul Graham

Paul Graham in "A Plan for Spam"* suggests an improved algorithm he later describes in Better Bayesian Filtering.† Paul starts with a relatively large set of 4000 spam and 4000 ham e-mails. He then scans the entire text including headers and embedded html and javascript, of each message. He considers alphanumeric characters, dashes, apostrophes, and dollar signs to be part of tokens, and everything else to be a token separator. He counts the number of times each token (currently ignoring case) occurs in each set. At this stage, he ends up with two large hash tables, one for each set, mapping tokens to the number of occurrences. Next, he creates a third hash table, this time mapping each token to the probability that an e-mail containing it is a spam, which he calculates as follows (in Lisp):

```
(let
        (
                (g (* 2 (or (gethash word good) 0) ) )
                (b (or (gethash word bad) 0) )
        )
        (unless
                (< (+ g b) 5)
                (max .01
                        (min .99
                                (float
                                        (/
                                                (min 1 (/ b nbad) )
                                                (+
                                                        (min 1 (/ g ngood) )
                                                        (min 1 (/ b nbad) ) )
                                                )
                                        )
                                )
                        )
                )
        )
```

---

* http://www.paulgraham.com/spam.html
† http://www.paulgraham.com/better.html

where word is the token whose probability is being calculated, good and bad are the hash tables created in the first step, and ngood & nbad are the number of non-spam and spam messages, respectively. In order to reduce false positives, the number in good is doubled. The number of e-mails in each set is used instead of their combined length in calculating spam probabilities.

When a new mail arrives, it is scanned into tokens, and the most interesting 15 tokens, where interesting is measured by how far their spam probability is from a neutral 0.5, are used to calculate the probability that the mail is spam. If probs is a list of the 15 individual probabilities, the combined probability is calculated as (in Lisp):

```
(let
        ((prod (apply #'* probs)))
        (/ prod (+ prod (apply #'* (mapcar #'(lambda (x) (- 1 x)) probs)))))
)
```

By trial and error, Paul found that words not in the hash table worked best when assigned a probability of 0.4 as it is more likely to be a clean word.

In other methods, words that the Bayesian filter is encountering for the first time (or which were not encountered in a sufficient number of e-mails during the training phase) present a special challenge. Applying the standard Bayes theorem may lead to null numerator and denominator in the case of a first encounter. In the formula below, it is assumed that the classification between ham and spam for the given keyword is a *random variable* with *beta distribution*[*]:

$$Pr'\left(S|W\right) = \frac{s \cdot Pr(S) + n \cdot Pr(S|W)}{s + n}$$

where
   $Pr'(S|W)$ is the corrected probability for the message to be spam, knowing that it contains a given keyword
   $s$ is the strength we give to background information about incoming spam
   $Pr(S)$ is the probability of any incoming message to be spam
   $n$ is the number of occurrences of this word during the learning phase
   $Pr(S|W)$ is the spamicity of this word, which is defined as

$$Pr\left(S|W\right) = \frac{Pr(W|S)}{Pr(W|S) + Pr(W|H)}$$

# SpamProbe for MacOS

Brian Burton, the author of SpamProbe for MacOS based his implementation on Paul's ideas with some tweaks and changes to improve the algorithm's effectiveness. The SpamProbe tokenizer understands HTML entity references as well as Base64 and Quoted Printable URL encoding. It allows a small set of characters to appear within terms (".", ",", " + ", "-", "_", "$") and treats all others as white space. Pure numbers are ignored but numbers linked by punctuation are retained. Tokens

---

[*] http://en.wikipedia.org/wiki/Beta_distribution

containing punctuation are further broken into sub-terms by repeatedly separating the leading portion of the term, a technique used to extract the domain name from fully qualified host names in URLs. SpamProbe uses Paul's technique of classifying some terms based on where they were found. Specifically, particular terms from the subject, to, and cc headers are specially flagged.

By default, SpamProbe scores word pairs (phrases) as terms. Longer phrases generally provide an increase in accuracy, but with diminishing returns and at a significant cost in disk space. While Paul's filter only allows each term to appear in the array once, SpamProbe allows terms to appear more than once and uses larger arrays, by default 27 terms which repeat twice.

## Annoyance Filter

Annoyance filter implements an adaptive Bayesian filter, which distinguishes junk mail from legitimate mail by scanning archives of each and calculating the probability for each word which appears a statistically significant number of times in the body of text that the word will appear in junk mail. Larger mail archives lead to more effective results (upward of 99% effectiveness has been reported). Annoyance filter is command-line driven and highly tunable, which makes it difficult to use for most users.

The excerpt below is the section of the annoyance filter manual that deals with Bayesian filter tuning/parameters:

**–biasmail** *n*

The frequency of words appearing in legitimate mail is inflated by the floating point factor *n*, which defaults to 2. This biases the classification of messages in favor of "false negatives"—junk mail deemed legitimate, while reducing the probability of "false positives" (legitimate mail erroneously classified as junk, which is *bad*). The higher the setting of *–biasmail*, the greater the bias in favor of false negatives will be.

**–binword** *n*

Binary character streams (for example, attachments of application-specific files, including the executable code of worm and virus attachments) are scanned and contiguous sequences of alphanumeric ASCII characters *n* characters or longer are added to the list of words in the message. The dollar sign ("$") is considered an alphanumeric character for these purposes, and words may have embedded hyphens and apostrophes, but may not begin or end with those characters. If *–binword* is set to zero, scanning of binary attachments is disabled entirely. The default setting is five characters.

**–newword** *n*

The probability that a word seen in mail that does not appear in the dictionary (or appeared too few times to assign it a probability with acceptable confidence) is indicative of junk is set to *n*. The default is 0.2—the odds are that novel words are more likely to appear in legitimate mail than in junk.

**–phraselimit** *n*

Limit the length of phrases assembled according to the *–phrasemin* and *–phrasemax* options to *n* characters. This permits ignoring "phrases" consisting of gibberish from mail headers and undecoded content. In most cases, these items will be discarded by a *–prune* in any case, but skipping them as they are generated keeps the dictionary from bloating in the first place. The default value is 48 characters.

**–phrasemin** *n*

Calculate probabilities of phrases consisting of a minimum of *n* words. The default of 1 calculates probabilities for single words.

**−phrasemax** *n*
Calculate probabilities of phrases consisting of a maximum of *n* words. The default of 1 calculates probabilities for single words. If you set this too large, the dictionary may grow to an absurd size.

**−prune**
After loading the dictionary from *−mail* and *−junk* folders, this option discards words which appear sufficiently infrequently that their probability cannot be reliably estimated. One usually *−prunes* the dictionary before using *−write* to save it for subsequent runs.

**−sigwords** *n*
The probability that a message is junk will be computed based on the individual probabilities of the *n* words with extremal probabilities, that is, probabilities most indicative of junk or mail. The default is 15, but there is no obvious optimal setting for this parameter; it depends in part on the average length of messages you receive.

**−sloppyheaders**
To evade filtering programs, some junk mail is sent with MIME part headers which violate the standard but which most mail clients accept anyway. This option causes such messages to be parsed as a browser would, at the cost of standards compliance. If *−sloppyheaders* is used, it should be specified both when building the dictionary and when testing messages.

**−threshjunk** *n*
Set the threshold for classifying a message as junk to the floating point probability value *n*. The default threshold is 0.9; messages scored above *−threshjunk* are deemed junk.

**−threshmail** *n*
Set the threshold for classifying a message as legitimate mail to the floating point probability value *n*. The default threshold is 0.9, with messages scored below *−threshmail* deemed legitimate. Note that you may leave a gap between the *−threshmail* and *−threshjunk* values (although it makes no sense to set *−threshmail* higher). Mail scored between the two thresholds will then be judged of uncertain status.

## SpamAssassin*

SpamAssassin (hereinafter referred to as SA) is an open source and widely used in all aspects of e-mail management. You can readily find SA in use in both e-mail clients and servers, on many different operating systems, filtering incoming as well as outgoing e-mail, and implementing a very broad range of policy actions. SA also forms the basis for numerous commercial antispam products available on the market today.

SA is a set of Perl programs that utilizes combined scores from various checks to determine if a given message is spam. SA checks are based on Perl regular expressions.

The Bayesian classifier in SA tries to identify spam by looking at what are called tokens: words or short character sequences that are commonly found in spam or ham. If I have handed 100 messages to SA, learn that they have the phrase "replica watches," and am told it that those are all spam, then when the 101st message comes in with the words "replica" and "watches," the Bayesian classifier will be pretty sure that the new message is spam and will increase the spam score of that message.

---

* http://wiki.apache.org/spamassassin/SpamAssassin

While other Bayesian filters require a large number of ham and spam messages to get started, SA can do with as little as 200 ham and 200 spam messages. In addition, custom rules can be created to address particular user needs, for example, rules targeting pill spams or foreign languages.

A sample diet pill spam set of rules by Matt Kettler* is reproduced below for reference:

```
#diet
body __ DRUGS _ DIET _ PHEN   /\bphentermine\b/i
#phentermine
body __ DRUGS _ DIET1        /(?:\b|\s)[ _ \W]{0,3}p[ _ \W]{0,3}h[ _ \W]{0,3}[e3\xE8-
\xEB][ _ \W]{0,3}n[ _ \W]{0,3}t[ _ \W]{0,3}[e3\xE8-
\xEB][ _ \W]{0,3}r[ _ \W]{0,3}m[ _ \W]{0,3}[i1!|l\xEC-\xEF][ _ \W]{0,3}n[ _ \W]{0,3}[e3\xE8-
\xEB][ _ \W]{0,3}(?:\b|\s)/i
#ionamin
body __ DRUGS _ DIET2    /(?:\b|\s) _ {0,3}[i1!|l\xEC-\xEF][ _ \W]?o[ _ \W]?n[ _ \W]?[a4\xE0-
\xE6@][ _ \W]?m[ _ \W]?[i1!|l\xEC-\xEF][ _ \W]?n _ {0,3}\b/i
#bontril
body __ DRUGS _ DIET3 /\bbontril\b/i
#phendimetrazine
body __ DRUGS _ DIET4 /\bphendimetrazine\b/i
#diethylpropion, generic of Tenuate, uncommon in spam
body __ DRUGS _ DIET5 /\bdiethylpropion\b/i
#Meridia
body __ DRUGS _ DIET6 /(?:\b|\s)[ _ \W]{0,3}M[ _ \W]{0,3}[e3\xE8-
\xEB][ _ \W]{0,3}r[ _ \W]{0,3}[i1!|l\xEC-\xEF][ _ \W]{0,3}d[ _ \W]{0,3}[i1!|l\xEC-
\xEF][ _ \W]{0,3}[a4\xE0-\xE6@][ _ \W]{0,3}(?:\b|\s)/i
#tenuate
body __ DRUGS _ DIET7 /\b _ {0,3}t[ _ \W]?[e3\xE8-
\xEB][ _ \W]?n[ _ \W]?u[ _ \W]?a[ _ \W]?t[ _ \W]?[e3\xE8-\xEB] _ {0,3}(?:\b|\s)/i
#didrex
body __ DRUGS _ DIET8 /\b _ {0,3}d[ _ \W]?[i1!|l\xEC-
\xEF][ _ \W]?d[ _ \W]?r[ _ \W][e3\xE8-\xEB[ _ \W]?xx? _ {0,3}\b/i
#adipex
body __ DRUGS _ DIET9 /\b _ {0,3}a[ _ \W]?d[ _ \W]?[i1!|l\xEC-
\xEF][ _ \W]?p[ _ \W]?[e3\xE8-\xEB][ _ \W]?x _ {0,3}\b/i
#xenical
body __ DRUGS _ DIET10  /\b _ {0,3}x?x[ _ \W]?[e3\xE8-\xEB][ _ \W]?n[ _ \W]?[i1!|l\xEC-
\xEF][ _ \W]?c[ _ \W]?[a4\xE0-\xE6@][ _ \W]?l _ {0,3}\b/i
meta DRUGS _ DIET ( __ DRUGS _ DIET1 || __ DRUGS _ DIET2 || __ DRUGS _ DIET3 ||
__ DRUGS _ DIET4 || __ DRUGS _ DIET5 || __ DRUGS _ DIET6 || __ DRUGS _ DIET7
|| __ DRUGS _ DIET8 || __ DRUGS _ DIET9 || __ DRUGS _ DIET10 )
describe DRUGS _ DIET  Refers to a diet drug
meta DRUGS _ DIET _ OBFU ( __ DRUGS _ DIET1 && ! __ DRUGS _ DIET _ PHEN)
describe DRUGS _ DIET _ OBFU  Obfuscated reference to a diet drug
```

SA processes body rules in series (one after the other), and that can take up to 65% of the total time analyzing messages. To speed things up in the latest release at the time of this writing (3.2.0), a parallel processing plug-in has been proposed "re2c" (a compiler of Perl regular expressions into

---

* http://mysite.verizon.net/mkettler_sa/antidrug.cf

C code which implements a parallel matching DFA state machine) and "re2xs" which converts basic Perl regular expressions into input for "re2c" and generates a Perl XS module.

An additional speed-up feature has been introduced in version 3.2.0: short circuit* (SC). SC enables an early spam decision if a spam score is achieved early in rule processing. The concept introduces another factor in processing: rule order. The administrator needs to specify which rules they want to allow to short-circuit the scan and the rule order can be specified in the configuration. The best practice is to run fast reliable rule first and short-circuit if hit, followed by "less cheap" reliable rules, followed by the rest. A sample is provided below for reference:

```
# local whitelists, or mails via trusted hosts
meta SC_HAM (USER_IN_WHITELIST||USER_IN_DEF_WHITELIST||ALL_TRUSTED)
priority SC_HAM               -1000
shortcircuit SC_HAM           ham
score SC_HAM                  -20
# slower, network-based whitelisting
meta SC_NET_HAM (USER_IN_DKIM_WHITELIST||USER_IN_SPF_WHITELIST)
priority SC_NET_HAM           -500
shortcircuit SC_NET_HAM       ham
score SC_NET_HAM              -20
# run Spamhaus tests early, and shortcircuit if they fire
meta SC_SPAMHAUS (RCVD_IN_XBL||RCVD_IN_SBL||RCVD_IN_PBL)
priority SC_SPAMHAUS          -400
shortcircuit SC_SPAMHAUS      spam
score SC_SPAMHAUS             20
```

## Conclusion

This chapter presented a simplified math theory of Bayes' Theorem in general, outlining representations of the theorem that are relevant to spam filtering.

It has also delved into examples of various implementations of Bayes' Theorem, each utilizing a different method to implement it. Irrespective of the details of any particular implementation, the initial effectiveness of any Bayesian spam filter is largely dependent on the corpus of spam and ham e-mails that are used to "train" it to categorize e-mails into spam or ham, based on the analysis of their content. Parameters such as the number of words utilized to categorize e-mail can also impact the filter's effectiveness and affect its performance. Such tuning is largely a matter of trial and error, each solution suggesting out-of-the-box default settings that have been proven to work in test environments.

In practice, most solutions implement one or more additional techniques of spam detection, including but not limited to DNS block lists, header and text analysis (heuristics), and collaborative filtering databases (out of the scope of this article) in an effort to improve the overall spam filtering effectiveness of the solution.

---

* http://wiki.apache.org/spamassassin/ShortcircuitingRuleset

There is no single best solution for any particular scenario. There are simply too many variables that affect the performance of spam filters (starting with proper tuning). Initial implementation tends to be labor intensive; however, once a solution has been carefully tuned (that on its own can be time consuming) and trained, spam filters continuously learn as they go, improving their own effectiveness.

## About the Author

**Georges J. Jahchan**, CISA, CISM, BS7799 lead auditor, is currently working as a senior infrastructure management consultant in the Middle East, North Africa, and Pakistan with Computer Associates (CA).

## Reference

1. Spam filtering using a Markov random field model with variable weighting schemas, in *Proceedings of the Fourth IEEE International Conference on Data Mining* (ICDM' 04), pp. 347–350, 0-7695-2142-8/04 $ 20.00, IEEE, Brighton, U.K.

# INFORMATION SECURITY AND RISK MANAGEMENT

## *Security Management Concepts and Principles*

## Chapter 6

# Measuring Information Security and Privacy Training and Awareness Effectiveness*

Rebecca Herold

## Contents

## Grades Indicate Improvement Needs as Well as Strengths

When I was growing up, there was a trend in many schools to not give grades, but instead just give a "pass" or "needs improvement" mark in an effort not to damage the "delicate self-esteem" of children. My father, who taught and was also school superintendent for a few decades, believed that was hogwash. If you do not show how well students are doing in a subject for their age and grade level, how will you be able to know where improvement is necessary? How will

---

* This is based upon an updated excerpt of the "Evaluate education effectiveness" chapter from the book *Managing an Information Security and Privacy Awareness and Training Program* by Rebecca Herold, 2005, published by Auerbach Publications.

you be able to know the specific areas in which a student needs to study more or, differently, to understand the subject better? How will you be able to know where curriculum needs improvement? How will you be able to tell if a teacher may not be living up to the standards established if you see all students are either doing very poorly, or if they are all doing exceptionally well across the board? As you can probably tell, we definitely had grades, including the minuses and pluses, within our school.

While a notable portion of the population would rather not establish any manner of measuring how well someone is doing, or how well some initiative is performing, in order to spare feelings, not measuring effectiveness is not good business. If you do not measure where your organization is as compared to where it started (your benchmark), or how close it is to meeting goals, you will not be able to clearly show how much change has occurred as a result of implementing certain business processes. This also applies to information security and privacy programs. If you do not establish some measurements, rankings, ratings, evaluations, metrics, key performance indicators (KPIs), or whatever label you want to use, you cannot demonstrate to your business leaders the value of your efforts to the business.

There has been a large amount of disagreement lately about what the correct "term" for the various types of evaluations should be called. It does not really matter whether or not a specific international evaluation term exists. What does matter is how you define the evaluations you are making within your organization that you clearly communicate those definitions and then consistently follow them.

To demonstrate the need for evaluating program effectiveness, I am going to focus on measuring the effectiveness of information security and privacy awareness and training initiatives. These same concepts can be used for other types of initiatives.

## Business Drivers for Evaluating Effectiveness

The goal of information security and privacy awareness and training should ultimately be to change personnel work habits so that they work in a more secure manner and protect the privacy of personally identifiable information (PII).

On August 22, 2007, the European Network and Information Security Agency (ENISA) released a study, "Information security awareness initiatives: Current practice and the measurement of success." It provides nice documentation validating this need to measure the effectiveness of information security education efforts to improve business. It details the awareness methods that have worked and not worked, and the various experiences of a wide range of organizations.

There are many business drivers for maintaining documented measurements to track the effectiveness of your information security and privacy program. Documented measurements

- Point out where you need to make improvements within your program
- Highlight what is working well within your program
- Show how much you have improved within specific areas of your program
- Validate to stakeholders the value of information security and privacy initiatives
- Demonstrate the need to invest in information security and privacy
- Demonstrate due care processes are in place and are actively being followed to meet compliance requirements
- Raise the awareness of information security and privacy issues
- Highlight information security and privacy risk areas
- Facilitate making better business decisions

# Components for Successfully Evaluating Effectiveness

There are many methods that can be used to evaluate the effectiveness of information security and privacy program initiatives. Do not get stuck only looking at the very specific, narrowly scoped technical measurements. While these types of metrics are useful, you also need to look at the big picture: your business enterprise.

How are information security and privacy initiatives and efforts impacting your business? You must always keep in mind that information security and privacy exists within your organization to support and protect your business and customers. Create and communicate your evaluations and measurements in terms of your business whenever possible.

When you are contemplating and planning for how you will perform your evaluations, be sure to include and document the following components:

- Evaluation topics
- Evaluation areas
- Evaluation methods
- Tangible benefits
- Intangible benefits

Do not get carried away and have too many measurements, though. After you brainstorm and document all your possible measurements, determine the ones most important for your business. You do not want to overwhelm your business leaders with too many measurements or they will not pay attention to any of them. Determine the ones that will resonate most with business.

Also determine how often to take the measurements. You will need to choose what is most appropriate for each of the topics. Some measurements will be appropriate to do once a year, and others will need to be done once a week to be meaningful.

You will also need to regularly reevaluate the measurements you have chosen and fine-tune them, replace them, or completely do away with them. As your business changes over time as a result of your training and awareness efforts, your metrics will also need to be modified.

Let us dig deeper into more of the specifics of evaluations for the rest of this chapter.

## *Evaluation Areas for Your Awareness Program*

It is important to know, and demonstrate to your business leaders, that your information security and privacy awareness efforts are valuable and are making an impact on the way your personnel do business. Before you can create measurements, grades, or effectiveness ratings, though, you need to identify the areas within which you will be looking for these metrics.

Verduin and Clark identified eight areas of evaluation for learning (*Distance Learning.* San Francisco: Jossey Bass, 1991); access, relevancy, quality, learning outcomes, impact, cost effectiveness, knowledge generation, and "general to specific." I find them useful when measuring the success of information security and privacy education efforts. Tailor them to facilitate the evaluation of your own organizational education programs by considering the questions listed with each area.

By answering the questions for each of these areas, you will be better able to identify the types of metrics you should create to answer the questions, as well as focus better on how to communicate those metrics. I will not cover how to generate the metrics in this chapter; that is a big topic and will be best discussed in a future article.

1. *Access*:
   a. What groups are you targeting for your education efforts? List the groups that handle PII, use your networks, communicate directly with your customers, and so on. Check with other areas in your organization; use your information security and/or privacy oversight group if you have one. Ask them, are there groups missing?
   b. Are all members of the target groups participating in the training offered to them? Why or why not? Are all personnel participating in awareness events? How many of the personnel have access to attend the awareness events? Are all personnel reading awareness communications? Do all personnel have access to awareness communications?
   c. Are you providing appropriate delivery methods for your target audiences? Can all your target audience access your training and awareness materials and participate in your delivery methods?

2. *Relevancy*:
   a. Is your education program relevant to your organization's business goals and expectations? Do your information security education messages have a clear link to the business goals? Do you explain how your privacy efforts support business efforts?
   b. Are your training and awareness messages and information relevant to the participants' job responsibilities? Do you clearly communicate where information security actions occur within the normal execution of business transactions? Do you relate how privacy can be impacted by misuse of PII?
   c. Does your education program have a noticeable impact on business practices? How have personnel changed the way they handle and protect PII as a result of training and awareness? Is your training content appropriate for your target participants? Does your training cover information security and privacy regulatory and policy requirements?

3. *Quality*:
   a. Does the quality of your information security and awareness materials effectively deliver the intended message? Do your communications capture the attention of your personnel throughout the training period? Does the quality of your training materials contribute to your learners' success?
   b. Do your trainers and teachers deliver quality education? Do they know how to interactively adjust to the abilities and experiences of their learners? Do they have enough background and understanding of information security and privacy to be able to answer the learners' questions?
   c. Were the conditions right for learning? Were the learners encouraged by management to participate in training? Did the learners indicate that, in their subjective opinion, they were satisfied with the quality of the training?

4. *Learning outcomes*:
   a. Is the amount of time allowed for learning appropriate for successfully understanding the message? What do your learners say about the usefulness and effectiveness of your training and awareness activities? Do you speak to the learners about the expected outcomes of your education activities?
   b. Do you tell the learners how their job activities should change as a result of taking the training? What did the learners actually learn, as evidenced through observable actions or through feedback from quizzes or follow-up surveys? Did your learners indicate they truly learned something from taking the training?

5. *Impact*:
   a. What is the impact of your education program on your entire organization? Were security and privacy activities and habits noticeably changed in a positive way following training and awareness activities?
   b. Were more information security incidents reported following training and awareness activities? Do personnel ask the information security and privacy areas more questions?
   c. What are the long-term impacts? Did the training methods promote the desired information security and privacy skills? Did job performance improve? What was the trend related to noticeable personnel work changes following each training session?
   d. Do you assist managers with determining their own workforce performance changes? Do you provide managers with communications to make them aware of the personnel changes they should notice and document following the training? Do you create related statistics to support and validate training and awareness funds?

6. *Cost effectiveness*:
   a. What time requirements are involved? Is the length of time necessary to take the training appropriate for not disrupting business work? How much time do your awareness activities take? Are education activities offered during normal work hours, during lunch, before and after work, and so on?
   b. What are the costs of the materials? Are the costs within budget? Are there ways in which cost can be reduced by partnering with other departments, or using donations from outside entities?
   c. How many people are in your targeted groups? How was training delivered? Did it allow for all personnel within the targeted groups to attend?
   d. Are you using inside or outside training and awareness resources, or both? What is the value of the method of awareness activity or training session you used compared to other awareness and training options?

7. *Knowledge generation*:
   a. Do you understand and document specifically what is important for your personnel to know about information security and privacy? Do you understand and document specifically what is important for your managers to know?
   b. Do you understand what works and what does not work within your education program? Are you actually utilizing your evaluation results?
   c. Do you account for all types of learners: visual, audio, and kinesthetic (hands-on)? Do you provide effective multimedia training methods? Do you provide awareness communications to account for all types of learners?
   d. Do you assist employees in determining their own performance success for implementing the information they received? Do you compile trend data to assist instructors in improving both information security learning and teaching?

8. *General to specific*:
   a. Do your instructors give learners enough information to allow them to evaluate their own success in implementing what they learn?
   b. Are learners told overall goals for information security and privacy, along with the specific actions necessary to achieve them? Are information security and privacy goals and actions realistic and relevant to the business?
   c. What is the necessary prerequisite general and specific information security and privacy knowledge for your personnel?

Measurements can be developed within each of these eight areas to demonstrate the value of information security and privacy activities for your business.

## Evaluation Methods

Consider using a combination of the following 18 methods for determining the effectiveness of security and privacy education within your organization.

Be sure to discuss the methods with your legal department and labor unions prior to implementation to make sure you are not violating any applicable laws, labor union requirements, or employee policies.

1. Videotape your training sessions, and review and critique to identify where you can improve delivery, content, organization, etc.
2. Give quizzes immediately following training to measure comprehension.
3. Distribute a security and privacy awareness survey to all personnel or to a representative sample. Do this prior to training to establish a baseline, then following training to help determine training effectiveness.
4. Send follow-up questionnaires to people who have attended formal training approximately 4–6 months afterward to determine how well they have retained the information presented.
5. Monitor the number of compliance infractions for each issue for which you provide training. Is this number decreasing or increasing? Why are they increasing or decreasing? Increased infractions may at first be a sign that the program has some weaknesses, but an increase in reporting infractions may instead be a result of increased awareness, which would be a success sign.
6. Measure security and privacy knowledge as part of yearly job performance appraisals.
7. Place feedback and suggestion forms on an appropriate intranet Web site.
8. Track the number and type of security and privacy incidents that occur before and after the training and awareness activities.
9. Conduct spot checks of personnel behavior. For instance, walk through work areas and note if workstations are logged in while unattended or if patient information printouts are not adequately protected.
10. Record user IDs and completion status for Web- and network-based training. Send a targeted questionnaire to those who have completed the online training.
11. Have training participants fill out evaluation forms at the end of the class.
12. Identify the percentage of your target groups that participate in training.
13. Determine if you had an adequate number of instructors with the necessary level of expertise for the corresponding training topic.
14. Determine if the training materials addressed all your goals and objectives. Identify the gaps and make a plan to fill them.
15. Review training logs to see trends in attendance.
16. Tape or film participants performing their work after training to determine if they are utilizing the skills taught.
17. Administer occasional tests to personnel. Use multiple choice, short answer, essay tests, or a combination of these. Avoid using true-or-false tests.
18. Perform interviews with past training participants as well as personnel who have not yet been trained. Use structured and unstructured interview sessions.

## Evaluating Education Effectiveness: Intangible Benefits

A successful information security and privacy awareness and training program will not only result in tangible benefits, but also intangible ones.

Intangible benefits are positive results that cannot be given monetary or numeric values, or would involve too complex calculations to create such values. However, intangible benefits have a great impact on your organization and on your bottom line. They can also be used as additional evidence of an awareness and training program's success.

The following are common intangible benefits of effective information security and privacy education programs:

- Increased compliance
- Decreased security incidents and privacy breaches
- Increased job satisfaction
- Increased organizational commitment
- Improved work climate
- Fewer employee complaints
- Fewer employee grievances
- Reduction of employee stress
- Increased employee tenure
- Reduced employee lateness
- Reduced absenteeism
- Reduced employee turnover
- Increased innovation
- Increased customer satisfaction
- Decreased customer dissatisfaction
- Enhanced community image
- Enhanced investor image
- Fewer customer complaints
- Faster customer response time
- Increased customer loyalty
- Improved teamwork
- Increased cooperation
- Conflict reduction
- Improved decisiveness
- Improved communication

A 1998 Gallup Organization study* of 2 million employees within 700 companies, based upon a survey of entirely all workers, concluded that employer-sponsored training and education is viewed by employees as a plus in recruitment and contributes significantly to retention, and that employees want more training, particularly in technology, communications, and management. Other findings within this survey include

- Eighty percent indicated training is important or very important in keeping them as employees.
- Only 50% indicated that the current training received from employers exceeded their expectations indicating that training and awareness quality can be improved.

---

* Employees speak out on job training: Findings of a new nationwide study (1998). The Gallup Organization, Survey Research Division.

## Determining Intangible Benefits of Training and Awareness

To determine the impact of information security and privacy awareness and training activities within your organization, include questions similar to those shown in Figures 6.1 and 6.2 in evaluation surveys, interviews, and focus group discussions involving your employees, training participants, managers, and trainers.

## *Evaluating the Effectiveness of Specific Awareness and Training Methods*

There are many ways to evaluate the effectiveness of the wide range of training and awareness activities. Some will work better than the others, depending upon your organization, situation, and regulatory requirements.

The following are some examples of evaluating the effectiveness of a couple of specific training and awareness methods. Modify these as necessary for your specific education and delivery methods.

## Evaluating the Effectiveness of Computer-Based Training Modules

Computer-based training (CBT) modules can be very effective for some types of training, but be inappropriate or ineffective for other types.

Whether or not you should use CBT depends on your target audience, the topic, and the amount of interaction, feedback, and inquiry necessary. In general, here are the benefits and drawbacks of CBT education in a corporate setting:

| *Employees and Training Participants* |
|---|
| 1. Are you more satisfied with your job and support for your responsibilities as a result of this training? |
| 2. Do you feel more committed to supporting the goals of the organization as a result of this training? |
| 3. Do you believe that the work climate is better as a result of information security and privacy awareness activities? |
| 4. Do you feel less work-related stress as a result of the information security and privacy training? |
| 5. Do you believe your job advancement opportunities have improved as a result of this training? |
| 6. Do the awareness and training activities motivate you to come to work each day? |
| 7. Has the training given you ideas on how to improve information security and privacy within your own team? |
| 8. Do you believe better information security and privacy practices will result in increased customer satisfaction? |
| 9. Do you believe the information security and privacy awareness and training efforts enhance the organization's community image? |
| 10. Do you believe the information security and privacy awareness and training efforts enhance the organization's investor image? |
| 11. Has the training resulted in better teamwork with your coworkers? |
| 12. Has the training provided you with the ability to make better decisions related to information security? |

**Figure 6.1  Sample training participant survey.**

| Managers, Trainers, and HR |
| --- |
| 1. Do you see increased job satisfaction in your personnel as a result of information security and privacy awareness and training efforts? |
| 2. Do you believe your personnel have increased organizational commitment as a result of information security and privacy awareness and training activities and participation? |
| 3. Has your work climate improved as a result of information security and privacy awareness and training efforts? |
| 4. Do you notice fewer employee complaints regarding information security? |
| 5. Do you receive fewer employee grievances concerning information security? |
| 6. Do you believe your personnel have reduced their stress as a result of information security and privacy awareness and training activities? |
| 7. Do you believe employees will stay with the organization longer in part because of the information security and privacy awareness and training efforts? |
| 8. Have your personnel improved their punctuality and absenteeism in part because of information security and privacy awareness and training activities? |
| 9. Have you witnessed increased innovation among your team members following information security and privacy awareness and training participation? |
| 10. Do you believe that there is increased customer satisfaction because of the changes in how your personnel communicate with them as a result of training and awareness efforts? |
| 11. Do you believe the organization has enhanced their community image as a result of providing information security and privacy awareness and training activities? |
| 12. Have you received fewer customer complaints following implementation of information security and privacy awareness and training activities? |
| 13. Are customer complaints resolved more quickly since implementing awareness and training? |
| 14. Do you believe the organization's information security and privacy efforts will result in greater customer loyalty? |
| 15. Do you notice increased personnel cooperation following training and awareness activities? |
| 16. Have your information security and privacy communications with personnel improved? |

**Figure 6.2   Sample management survey.**

- ■ *Benefits*:
    - – Can be taken by participants at a time most convenient to them.
    - – Does not require trainer interaction.
    - – Is cost effective.
    - – Participants can work at their own pace.
    - – Participants do not have someone watching over them.
    - – No associated travel expenses for trainers.
    - – More interesting for some participants than classroom training.
    - – Takes less time for the participant than classroom training.
    - – The participant can retake the portions of the CBT where more instruction is necessary.

- *Drawbacks*:
  - No human instructor interaction so may seem too impersonal.
  - Little, if any, individualization for each person's capability to understand.
  - Not as interactive.
  - Trying to find human help when necessary during the training may be hard.
  - The CBT may be poorly constructed.
  - The topic may not be best taught via CBT.
  - Errors within CBT content will be communicated and propagated to the learners.
  - Technology problems can occur with CBTs because of bandwidth, network, and similar problems.

## When Does CBT Make Sense?

A few examples indicating CBT is generally more practical than classroom- or lecture-style training includes when

- Procedural or hard-skills training is required.
- A "safe" or more comfortable learning environment is needed.
- Learners are geographically dispersed.
- Quick roll out of training is required.
- Consistency in training delivery and materials is required.
- The training topic must meet standards on an ongoing basis.
- Training is legislated, regulated, or must be based upon best practices and given to large numbers or geographically dispersed participants.
- Training can effectively be self-directed.
- A large number, such as more than 100 learners, must be trained.

## Launching CBT

Perform a needs analysis for training requirements to determine if the learners are receiving training for informational use, where a live instructor would be more beneficial, or for skills progress, where interaction with the computer would increase learning. Then proceed as follows:

1. Perform a task analysis to determine the type of information that needs to be included within the CBT.
2. Design the learning objectives for the CBT. The objectives give the learner an idea of the outcome, conditions, and how he or she will be evaluated in the CBT program. The objectives give the developer of the CBT parameters to match cognitive skills being communicated within the material.
3. Design the CBT screen designs. Create user-friendly screens with several characteristics; they should be simple as well as informative.
4. Ideally, the participant should be able to perform some sort of activity like playing a video, giving an answer to a question, or placing something on the screen by using the drag-and-drop on each screen.
5. Give the CBT participant some control over the learning experience as is appropriate. For example, for advanced or high-level topics, give the participant the option of choosing how many examples he or she wants to be given or the density of the topic context.

6. In lower level or basic participant situations, the participant may grasp the knowledge better if the program is "in charge," so that it leads the participant through the module in a very structured way, consistent from one person to another.
7. Feedback is a very important part of a CBT program. Thoughtful, informative feedback is an essential component of CBT programs and can be formative and summative feedback or evaluations. In formative evaluations, the participant's knowledge is tested on the facts that were just given, whereas a summative evaluation tests the participant about the complete CBT module. Feedback words can be standard such as "correct" or "incorrect." For correct answers, restate the idea to reinforce learning. For incorrect answers, provide an explanation and the correct answer. Then, place the reworded question again later in the module so the participant can be confident the concept is understood.
8. Other important considerations:
   a. Course organization
   b. Screen composition
   c. Colors and graphics
   d. Text placement
   e. Wording
   f. White space
   g. Text justification (left or center)
   h. Navigation toolbar
   i. Consistency
9. Perform a quality assurance review of the finished CBT to ensure that the finished product successfully meets the goals of the course. Use trainers, subject matter experts (SMEs), and a target learner or two as reviewers.
10. Obtain executive sponsorship and visible support for the training.
11. Communicate this to all your target participants. It is most effective for the communication to come from the executive sponsor.
12. Identify your primary contacts in each team and department where you are launching the training. Communicate with them your timelines for completing the training, along with directions on how the training needs to be presented, implemented, and documented within their area.
13. Obtain feedback from the primary contacts.
14. Review quiz and CBT-module results.
15. Perform business impact analysis to determine how the training affected the personnel in their daily job performance.

## Managing CBT Participation

The key to ensuring high participation in a CBT is to get the support and cooperation of your identified primary contacts throughout the organization, typically managers, who will instruct their personnel to take the CBT.

■ Have your information security and privacy champion send messages to your primary contacts asking them for their cooperation.
■ Send your primary contact a CBT implementation information package, including
   - Overview of the CBT along with learning objectives
   - Target audiences

 - Timeline for completion
 - Responsibilities for the contacts and personnel participants
 - Data collection forms
 - Sample memos for the contact to send to the participants about the training
■ Collect data forms from contacts on a date designated in the timeline.
■ Follow up with contacts who have not responded in a week of the target date. Give them one more week to have their personnel complete the training and for them to submit their data collection forms.
■ One month following completion of the CBT, send evaluation surveys to contacts to determine what impact the training had on their personnel.
■ Update the CBT content according to feedback, quiz, test results, and other identified factors from your six levels of evaluation forms.

## Effectiveness Evaluation Methods

Some possibilities include

■ Testing each participant's knowledge acquisition with an online exam following completion of the module.
■ Testing each participant's knowledge acquisition with an online quiz following each section of the module.
■ Controlling access to the exam questions and exam results.
■ Calculating the number of participants who completed the module.
■ Calculating the high, low, mean, and mode final CBT-module test results.
■ Calculating the high, low, mean, and mode results for each of the quizzes.
■ Identifying questions that had a low success rate, reviewing them, and determining if the question is bad or if the concept was not clearly communicated by the CBT curriculum.
■ Compiling reports for all the above; monitoring participation progress as well as areas of concern that may need additional training or updated content.
■ Obtaining feedback via surveys, interviews, and focus groups from the managers in the areas where the training was given.
■ Obtaining feedback via surveys, interviews, and focus groups from the CBT participants 1–3 months following completion of the CBT.

## Evaluating the Effectiveness of Awareness Newsletters

Sampling and surveys are two methods of effectiveness evaluation that lend themselves best to determining the effectiveness of many awareness activities, such as electronic awareness newsletters that are targeted at a large population.

### Sampling

Sampling is drawing information from a subset of your target group, the people you want to read the newsletter, to estimate the characteristics of the entire target population. Sampling is a good choice for newsletter effectiveness evaluation when

- You cannot collect data from the entire population to whom the newsletter is targeted.
- You do not have the time to interview the large number of targeted individuals.
- You do not have the travel budget to visit all the target population.
- Some people in the target group are difficult to reach or contact.
- You do not have enough qualified staff to conduct interviews or compile surveys from everyone.

## Sampling Procedures

Use the following steps to do sampling:

- Identify your target population
- Create a list of all members within the population
- Determine your sampling approach
- Determine your sample size
- Identify your sample participants

## Sampling Approaches

- *Probability sampling*. Ensures every member of the target population has an equal chance of being selected for the sample.
  - *Simple random sampling*. Determine what percentage of the target population to contact, and then randomly choose from the entire population. This is the most straightforward, but not frequently used, approach. It is often difficult to get a list of the entire population. Some of the employees in the list may have left the organization. The clerical effort to draw the sample may be very time consuming if the population is large. And it may not be more appropriate to select some individuals and not others.
  - *Stratified random sampling*. Divide the entire target population into groups based on such characteristics as geographic location, personnel levels, departments, etc. Then, choose an identified percentage from each of these groups (strata). This enables the evaluator to analyze the data of different subgroups and to compare and contrast the findings.
  - *Cluster sampling*. First sample a large subgroup, then sample from within the subgroup. For example, select 6 out of a total of 12 field offices, and then within each of the six chosen offices, draw a random sample of employees to contact. This is useful for reducing costs and the time required to survey people across many groups and locations.
- *Non-probability sampling*. This method does not provide information that can be generalized with confidence to the entire population. The results may be biased and could affect the usefulness of the findings. However, it is easier than the probability sampling methods.
- *Convenience sampling*. Contacting personnel who are most accessible for feedback. The evaluator does not know if these people have characteristics that bias the outcome. For example, asking for volunteers to participate may result in people who have a specific motivation to give feedback that would be completely different than if others were contacted who did not have the same motivations.
- *Purposive sampling*. Individuals are selected because of their position, experience, knowledge, or attitudes. Because the sample is not randomly selected, the findings cannot be generalized beyond those who participated.

■ *Snowball sampling.* Contact identified departments, individuals, etc., and ask them for suggestions for individuals to include in the sample. It is particularly useful when a list of names is difficult to obtain in any other way. When choosing your sampling method, take into consideration the following issues:
  – Budget, such as money is available for travel, hiring consultants, interviewers, postage, audiotapes, and other applicable materials
  – Size of sample population
  – Geographical locations of the population
  – Availability of the list of all possible people within the population
  – Data collection methods
  – How much variance exists within the population

## Determining Sample Size

You need to determine how many participants are enough. The larger the number, the more representative the results will be for the entire population. The sample size should depend on the following factors:

■ *The rarity of the event being evaluated.* If the event is rare, then a larger sample size should be used. For example, if you want feedback for an event that happens once a year, you should use a larger sample size than if you are getting feedback for an event that happens once a month.
■ *Available resources.* If you have sufficient time, resources, and personnel, draw a large sample.
■ *The degree of precision needed.* The impact of the evaluation must be considered. For example, if the evaluation involves whether the training led to reducing the amount of financial fraud resulting from access to customer data, then you will want a larger sample so you can be more accurate in determining if the benefits of the training outweigh the side effects.
■ *Whether or not the findings will be generalized.* If generalization is not a goal, then the number depends on the key evaluation questions, the number of methods being used to collect data, and what decision makers believe is sufficient to use the findings. If generalization is a goal, then you will likely need a probability sampling method.

Figure 6.3 gives you an idea of how large your sample size needs to be to have a confidence level (assurance that the results represent the total target population) of 95% with a range of 5% and 10%.

## Survey Composition

Create your survey to best obtain the feedback you need for your information security and privacy newsletters or other awareness or training activity for which you are using surveys. Solicit the opinions, beliefs, and feedback from your target group. To improve the response rate for your surveys to determine the effectiveness of newsletters, keep the following in mind.

■ Keep the survey as short and easy to answer as possible.
■ Stick with yes/no, rating (Likert), or multiple-choice answers.
■ Consider using a combination of questions.

| Population | Required Precision ±5% | Required Precision ±10% |
|---|---|---|
| Total Number of People | Sample Size | Sample Size |
| 50 | 44 | 33 |
| 75 | 63 | 42 |
| 100 | 80 | 49 |
| 150 | 108 | 59 |
| 200 | 132 | 65 |
| 300 | 168 | 73 |
| 400 | 196 | 78 |
| 500 | 217 | 81 |
| 1,000 | 277 | 88 |
| 3,000 | 340 | 93 |
| 5,000 | 356 | 94 |
| 10,000 | 369 | 95 |

**Figure 6.3   Determining responding sampling size with confidence level of 95%.**

- Use terms that the participants will understand.
- Phrase items in the same manner that participants speak them.
- Do not use "and/or" in survey items.
- Avoid using acronyms.
- Do not use double negatives. For example do NOT use a question like the following:

"Do you believe that trainees should not have to pay for their own training? Yes or No"

If the participant answers "No," it actually means, "Yes, trainees should pay for their own training."

- Avoid wording that suggests answers or biases responses in one direction. For example, do not start a question with "Isn't it true that …"
- Avoid leading or loaded questions. This is one that leads the respondent to answer differently if the question were worded in a different way.
- Avoid "double-barreled" questions that ask for more than one piece of information in the question. For example, do not ask, "Is this newsletter interesting and useful? Yes or No."
- Use plenty of white space to make the survey easy to read.
- Group items into logical sections.
- Provide clear, simple, and brief directions and instructions.
- Make it easy to return the survey, for example, via online form submission, e-mail, self-addressed, stamped envelope, etc.
- Provide advance communication, preferably from the information security and privacy sponsor, that the survey will be taking place.

- Clearly communicate the reason for the survey. For example:
  - To improve the applicability of the information to personnel job responsibilities
  - To learn the topics that are of most concern to personnel
  - To discover information security and privacy risks that were not yet known
  - To ensure that personnel are reading the newsletters
  - To improve the quality of the newsletters
- Indicate who will see the results of the survey.
- Describe how the results will be used.
- Pilot the survey before wide distribution. This will allow you to identify, remove, or revise confusing and unnecessary items.
- Notify personnel that the survey is coming within an issue or two of the newsletter and ask for their participation.
- Provide an estimate of the time needed to complete the survey.
- Allow participants to remain anonymous. You will likely want to attach some other type of stratification if you do this, such as job level, department, etc.
- Ask managers to support the survey and encourage participation.
- If applicable for sampling method, communicate to the target audience that they are part of a carefully selected sample, and that their participation is very important.
- Use one or two follow-up reminders.
- Send the survey on behalf of executive management, including the leader's signature if possible.
- Provide incentives for completing and returning the survey, for example, a coupon for a free personal pan pizza, a drawing from those participating for a free day of vacation, etc.
- Send a summary of the survey results to your participants.
- Take advantage of including survey questions within existing surveys, such as existing HR employee satisfaction surveys, whenever possible.

## Survey Questions

Think about the purpose and goals of the information security and privacy newsletter or the awareness event or training offering for which you are surveying. Construct the survey questions to determine if those goals are met. For example, consider including questions similar to the following if these are some of your newsletter goals:

- How well does the newsletter communicate recent information security and privacy incidents within the company?
- How well does the newsletter communicate incidents outside the company, which present a risk to the organization?
- How well does the newsletter communicate the organization's information security and privacy policies?
- How often do you read the information security and privacy newsletter?
- What are the reasons you do not read, or rarely read, the newsletter?
- What topics would you like to see included within the newsletter?
- What do you feel is the most helpful information currently within the newsletters?
- What do you feel is the least helpful information currently within the newsletters?
- Do you feel the newsletters should be published more often, less often, or is the current publication rate just about right?

- Which of the following types of information security and privacy newsletters do you believe are most beneficial? One that goes to all corporate personnel or those that are department-specific and tailored?
- What form of newsletter do you prefer and are most likely to read? E-mail-, paper-, or Web-based?

## Survey Administration

Here is a step-by-step high-level process for you to follow for administering surveys:

1. Identify and document the survey participants along with contact information.
2. Prepare the surveys for distribution.
3. For mailed surveys, prepare return envelopes.
4. Compose a cover letter to accompany each survey. It is ideal to have the executive sponsor sign the letter. The cover letter should state the purpose, give instructions, and other items as applicable from the list of 30 items provided earlier.
5. For mailed surveys, prepare envelopes for mailing.
6. Create a survey tracking form to record each participant's name, the date the survey was sent, and when it was received.
7. Record the receipt of surveys as they are returned. Even if they are anonymous, you can count the forms to determine how many participants have responded. You will need this to determine the response rate.
8. Follow up with those who do not return the survey to help increase your response rate.

## *Education Effectiveness Evaluation Checklist*

Create a checklist to help you keep on track with establishing baseline measurements, delivery measurements, and impact measurements that you collect within the education effectiveness evaluation framework. For a complete set of evaluation forms and charts, see my book *Managing an Information Security and Privacy Awareness and Training Program.*

Use any of the forms in conjunction with this checklist to help you plan and implement your own, customized information security and privacy education evaluation framework.

1. Establish the information security and privacy training and awareness schedule.
2. Identify your goals for each training and awareness activity.
3. Obtain executive support for the awareness and training program.
4. Create an inventory detailing your training and awareness activities and associated information. Use this inventory to track progress with your education program.
5. Identify your awareness and training contacts for each location.
6. Send your contacts the training and awareness schedule, along with a memo from your executive education sponsor.
7. Create an effectiveness evaluation framework for each training and awareness event/activity and fill in the information you have so far.
8. Three weeks before each education activity, send your contacts a baseline pre-evaluation form.
9. Two weeks before the activity, follow up with contacts who have not yet returned their completed baseline pre-evaluation form.

10. Send the appropriate contacts the information privacy and security education effectiveness evaluation at the time the activity is scheduled to occur.
11. One week following the activity, follow up with contacts who have not yet returned their completed information security education effectiveness evaluation.

## Consistently Measured Evaluations

Some believe that unless you can assign an exact number to your measurements, your measurements are not meaningful. Poppycock! There are many ways in which you can measure your effectiveness; through metrics, percentages, ratings, rankings, KPIs, grades, and any other type of label you want to use. The most important consideration to make them truly useful is that they need to be consistently measured and applied.

Some argue that meaningful evaluations should not be subjective. Yes, there are many methods of evaluating effectiveness that can and should be objective. Specific measurements, such as the cost in dollars, the number of hours used, the numbers of questions correctly answered, and so on, are valuable. However, there are also some very valuable measures that are necessarily subjective. Consistent and useful measurements can be obtained if your subjective measurements are clearly defined, and examples provided.

For example, it is important to know that the management in each of the departments are supporting awareness and training efforts. However, trying to measure this with an objective numerical value is hard, if even possible, to do. Management support is not a mathematically accurate concept. But you can determine a measurement for management support based upon clearly observable management characteristics and actions. Some possible measurements for information security and privacy education management support include the following:

1. *Unacceptable.* Management did not make awareness communications available to staff. Management did not send staff to available and applicable information security and privacy training sessions. If you want a value assigned instead of the "Unacceptable" label, use the value "1."
2. *Needs improvement.* Management sends some, but not all, staff to information security and privacy training sessions. Management occasionally, but inconsistently, provides awareness communications to the staff. If you want a value, use "2."
3. *Satisfactory.* Management consistently sends most staff to information security and privacy training offerings. Management consistently gives staff access to awareness communications. Use the value "3" if you want.
4. *Better than expected.* Management sends all staff to training regularly and always to usually returns training evaluation forms. Management actively and visibly encourages all staff to participate in awareness events. The value "4" would correlate with this label.
5. *Role model.* Management has incorporated information security and privacy training into staff job requirements and performance appraisals. Management urges staff to create information security and privacy awareness communications tailored to their own areas, along with participating in corporate awareness activities.

Subjective evaluations can tell a lot about awareness efforts in addition to other metrics if they are consistently applied.

## Your Measurements Are Unique to Your Organization

Effective use of information security and privacy measurements can have a profound impact on your business. As you gain a better understanding of your business and move closer to achieving important goals, your day-to-day work will become easier and your staff will be more accountable for the measurements that matter. You will make sound information security and privacy decisions based upon consistently generated measurements that are created in the context of business.

I see too many organizations try to use a cookie-cutter approach to establishing information security and privacy measurements. I see too many vendors pushing their cookie-cutter metrics onto organizations, only to subsequently have the organizations realize they are trying to measure something that is not applicable to them.

The axiom generally attributed to Peter Drucker holds true for information security and privacy efforts, "You can't manage it if you can't measure it." You also cannot be successful in your efforts if you do not maintain measurements. Organizations must establish metrics based upon their own unique organizational characteristics. They can use ideas obtained from others, but their ultimate metrics must be customized to fit their organization.

# About the Author

**Rebecca Herold**, CISM, CISA, CISSP, FLMI, is an information privacy, security, and compliance consultant, author, and instructor.

# Chapter 7

# Managing Mobile Device Security

E. Eugene Schultz and Gal Shpantzer

## Contents

# Introduction

Of all the recent trends in technology, few have been as pervasive as the growth of mobile computing technology. Whereas not too many years ago smart phones, personal data assistants (PDAs), and wireless networks were somewhat of a rarity, the opposite is very much true today.

Many types of mobile computing devices now exist. Laptops, not exactly newcomers to the mobile computing arena, continue to be prevalent, but the number of smart phones now owned and used both in the business and personal arena is growing disproportionately. PDAs continue to be popular, as are multifunction devices such as BlackBerry devices. Detachable media such as universal serial bus (USB) devices ("flash drives") are also very much part of the mobile device mix.

Mobile computing exists in many contexts. As many organizations have moved increasingly to "officeless" environments, mobile computing has bridged the gap resulting from not always having wired technology available. The same applies to telecommuting; telecommuters are increasingly connecting to organizations' networks from wireless networks. "Road warriors" such as sales personnel may connect to numerous wireless networks using one or more mobile devices during a typical workday. In larger organizations, employees are working in distributed environments, using wireless to connect to a central network while they are in a meeting in one building and then connecting via wireless when they change physical locations. The use of detachable media such as USB flash drives to transfer files and executables from one computing system to another constitutes yet another common use of mobile computing technology.

# Advantages of Mobile Computing

Mobile computing is becoming increasingly essential in a wide variety of usage contexts because of the many advantages that this technology offers. In a nutshell, the advantages boil down to increased productivity and efficiency. Users with mobile computing devices can quickly and conveniently connect to a network, enabling them to engage in a plethora of tasks, including quickly accessing files, executables, applications, and databases all of which can be used for a myriad of purposes. Data portability is often a particularly critical consideration. Mobile users can bring data stored on mobile computing devices with them to use in a wide variety of situations such as sales calls and corporate briefings; they can also analyze such data at their convenience. The fact that today's mobile devices now typically offer many hundreds of gigabytes of storage makes data access via mobile devices even more advantageous. Additionally, wireless technology allows users to quickly and conveniently connect to organizations' networks to check e-mail and participate in instant messaging to keep abreast of the latest developments.

Without mobile computing, the physical location of network connection spots becomes a huge obstacle to users. Users would otherwise have to wait until they are able to connect via conventional methods, usually via wired networks, but in some cases via Internet cafes (with all of the associated security risks). Most individuals need constant Internet connectivity, and in the business world, having this level of connectivity is critical to profitability.

Cost savings are another significant advantage of mobile computing. The cost associated with wired networks is considerably higher than for wireless networks. Wireless networking precludes the need to install and maintain network cabling within buildings. Additionally, smart phones and PDAs are often sufficient for mobile users' needs; the cost of these devices is well below conventional computing systems. Furthermore, the ease and speed with which users of mobile computing devices can connect to networks typically results in sizable productivity gains.

Finally, mobile computing devices can also deliver functions that "normal" computers cannot. For example, some mobile computing devices support open communication with wireless switches configured to serve as load request proxies between mobile computing devices and one or more mobile services server(s) on wireless networks. A mobile services server furnishes provisioning data to each wireless switch, which can then transport these data to each mobile computing device. The provisioning data are used to set security parameters on each mobile computing device and to configure software applications, thereby maximizing their security. Additionally, phone services are supported on many mobile computing devices, and many also have a built-in camera.

# Mobile Computing Risks

With all the advantages of mobile computing and mobile computing devices also come a wide variety of security-related risks. These risks are described in this section.

## Susceptibility to the Same Attacks as Conventional Systems

Previously, applications and technologies for mobile users were different from traditional ones. Before they became PDAs with powerful computing capabilities and storage capacity, cell phones were in reality just mobile phones with specialized operating systems and very limited functionality. Security risks were primarily tied to three issues: (1) the privacy of data that flowed in the "air" on its way to and from the organization's network; (2) the need for organizations to open ports in their firewalls to let the data in; and (3) the risk that thieves might steal the unprotected mobile computing devices themselves, thereby gaining access to the data on them. Serious risk from earlier mobile devices was limited because their functionality and storage capacity were very limited. Risks previously in large part applied to Wireless Application Protocol (WAP)-enabled cell phones, PDAs and wireless data entry systems, and attackers required a different skill set from the one needed to attack other types of computers. The opposite is now true. As mobile devices have become more powerful, they are now subject to same type of attacks as conventional computers, since they now have more complete operating systems and popular, widely deployed applications, making them vulnerable to the same malware and interactive attacks that have plagued Windows and other systems for years.

## "Always-on" Connections

Today, being connected 24/7 is a critical productivity issue. At the same time, however, an "always-on" connection is an almost ideal target for an attacker, who has virtually unlimited time to launch attacks. In contrast, conventional workstations are often if not usually turned off after normal work hours.

## Reduced Ability to Control Devices

Mobile devices are often out of the immediate control of an organization's security staff, creating a plethora of complications and risks, including the following.

### Reduced Ability to Monitor User Actions

Overseeing mobile employees' behavior and ensuring that they adhere to their employer's security policies and procedures is normally much more difficult.

### Operation Independently of an Organization's Network and Network Security Features

Most of the monitoring and filtering tools that organizations use to enforce policies and to protect systems and devices within networks are geared toward the central office, not the mobile computing environment. These tools are built into the organization's network(s), and are thus very difficult for users to circumvent when users directly access the network(s). The opposite is, however, true of other networks to which mobile users connect. Additionally, mobile devices are used outside of the office, where they are not as protected as at the corporate office, resulting in a higher likelihood of malware infections and other security breaches. At some point in time, they are connected to the corporate network, where they may introduce malware that would otherwise have been blocked by network security mechanisms such as firewalls and virus walls.

### Increased Risk to an Organization's Conventional Network(s)

New entry points into an organization's network(s) are created by mobile device access to the network. These entry points, most of which are not likely to be nearly as security as conventional entry points, comprise new potential avenues of attack.

## Increased Difficulty of Installing Software and Patches, as Well as of Troubleshooting

Given that mobile devices are so often out of the reach of system administrators, performing normal maintenance and software (including software with security functionality) or patch installation is usually considerably more difficult. Troubleshooting installations that do not go well is also generally much more complex for the same reason. Additionally, the sheer variety of mobile devices, from laptops to PDAs, creates complexity challenges for organizations. Management must consider the following when selecting mobile devices for standardization, or for exceptions to standards.

## Increased Difficulty of Configuration Management

Configuration management of mobile computing devices is more difficult for the same reason that installing and troubleshooting software and patches on these devices is.

## Increased Difficulty of Performing Backups and Restores

Many mobile devices are not backed up as frequently as desktops and servers at corporate headquarters. This is due to several limiting factors: One is the now frequently mentioned problem of mobile computing devices not being accessible to system and network administrators. Another is ignorance and neglect on the part of mobile computing users, who may not know how to make a backup, or if they do, may overlook the importance of doing so. Bandwidth and processing power are other factors, in that they create a large backup window for networked backup systems. This forces mobile users who know how to make backups and who are motivated to do so to use cumbersome local backup methods such as USB drives or even smaller devices. The same limitations also apply to performing system restores.

## Elevated Risk of Virus/Worm/Trojan Horse Infections

Mobile devices sometimes lack full-function malware protection available on their conventional workstation counterparts. If the packages are available, they are not necessarily centrally managed by the corporation. In the case of certain mobile devices, there are still no malware protection products available. Furthermore, even if antivirus software is installed, mobile device users often delay downloading the latest updates because downloading updates is slow in bandwidth-poor wireless networks.

## Elevated Risk of Shoulder Surfing

Shoulder surfing (e.g., at airports and in airplanes) is a particularly dangerous threat with mobile computing devices.

## Elevated Risk of Use of Unauthorized Software

Many mobile devices, even if owned by an organization, are self-administered by end users. This gives end users complete control over the configuration of installed operating systems and applications, as well as the ability to install further applications, often from untested third parties that may not be fully compatible with the operating system, built-in applications, and third-party management and security applications installed on the device. Legitimate applications installed by the end user are often not as rigorously tested for interoperability and security defects before they are sold to the public. They are also not updated as often for security patches as the applications from the larger software publishers, who have formalized security development processes that take into account prerelease architecture and post-release security patches. Additionally, users may unknowingly download software that appears useful, but that is in reality malicious. Furthermore, mobile user actions often cannot be monitored by system and network administrators; so users may be able to download peer-to-peer software without being detected.

### Elevated Risk of Unauthorized Integrity Changes to Sensitive/Proprietary Data

Even in organization with strong controls in the mobile computing arena, a certain amount of sensitive or proprietary data is likely to be downloaded to mobile devices. Because these devices cannot normally be protected as well as conventional computing systems, the likelihood of unauthorized integrity changes due to malware infections, unauthorized access to mobile devices' hard drives, user error, or attacks that result in data modification is higher.

### Elevated Risk of Mobile Computing Devices Being Used without Owner's Knowledge

Mobile devices are inherently more subject to unauthorized use than their desktop counterparts at an organization's office(s). In a normal office, physical security is more stringent than in the home office or on the road. A given desktop machine at a typical office is not accessible to a multitude of people who are not employees and who are thus not in an organization's building itself. An executive with a corporate laptop often leaves the laptop around the house; children and friends often engage in Web surfing and other activity on this computer, thereby exposing the computer to additional threats such as malware at malicious Web sites.

### Increased Risk of Unauthorized Interception of Communications

Mobile devices are designed to use wireless networks at an organization's office(s) or in a wireless hotspot in a foreign country. Communicating back to the corporate network via a Virtual Private Network (VPN) is not always possible with every mobile device, however. Some PDAs are, for example, initially released as "hot" consumer items. It may take a generation or two for basic enterprise-level security features to be built into these devices. Additionally, even if a wireless network is encrypted, the encryption that is used may be so weak that cryptanalysis of the message content may require only seconds. The risk of unauthorized interception of network communications from mobile computing devices is especially high when the mobile user is in foreign countries where business travelers are targeted by local governments and businesses for intellectual property theft and competitive intelligence.

### Increased Risk of Denial of Service

Denial of service is a special worry in mobile computing environments. One of the major reasons is that wireless networks are subject to a variety of very difficult-to-prevent attacks, such as traffic flooding and frequency jamming.* Also, as mentioned earlier, firewalls, intrusion prevention systems, and other barriers at the entrance to many organizations' networks generally filter the overwhelming majority of the malicious incoming traffic (such as multitudes of malformed packets designed to produce denial-of-service conditions).

## Ease of Downloading Illegal Music or Movies

Bandwidth shaping and URL filtering at the corporate office is a standard way to conserve bandwidth resources, monitor employee productivity, and prevent objectionable, copyrighted, and illegal material from settling into the corporate network. Mobile devices are less controllable than the desktop workstations at a typical organization's office(s), since the mobile device's traffic is not usually forced through the corporate proxy server and/or URL filters when a mobile device is not directly connected to the organization's network(s). Therefore, mobile users are generally able to more readily connect to file-sharing sites in which illegal music or movies can be downloaded.

## Risks Due to Built-in Cameras and Microphones

Many mobile devices have built-in cameras and microphones. Cameras pose elevated security risk because pictures of documents and computer screens are one way to purloin information onto personally owned devices. Cameras may also be remotely controlled via malware and take pictures or video clips without the legitimate end user's awareness. Microphones built into mobile devices can also turn mobile devices into a tool for eavesdropping on sensitive conversations.

## Increased Difficulty of e-Discovery and Archiving

Records management within organizations is a growing concern for those in charge of IT and legal departments. IT and legal counsel must work together to formulate and implement defensible and repeatable policies and procedures that are properly responsive to legal requests for discovery in litigation. e-Discovery is becoming an increasingly important component of records management. Knowing exactly what files exist and where (i.e., in which particular server or workstation) each is stored is difficult in conventional computing environments; in mobile computing environments, this endeavor is even more difficult.

## Increased Difficulty of Forensics and Investigation Efforts

Incident response and internal investigations in the digital realm are now a fairly routine part of normal operations in many organizations. Nonstandard devices such as many types of mobile computing devices become technical and legal challenges if the proper forensics hardware, software, and standard procedures to successfully and defensibly extract data from the device are not available.

---

* Frequency jamming is flooding a particular frequency channel with noise, thus overwhelming normal communications that occur on that channel.

---

**Case Study in Complexity and Unwelcome Surprises: The iPhone**

Security managers sometimes have to make exceptions to policies that ban unsupported devices. The iPhone is a wildly popular mobile device that is rapidly taking over market share from traditional PDA players, despite a lack of availability of some security features and third-party tools, especially as compared to the Blackberry, Palm, and Pocket PC platforms that have had more time to mature in the security realm. The iPhone has become more enterprise friendly with features added to the product after its initial release. However, there is an interesting twist to the iPhone story. The iPhone requires installation of iTunes, an Apple application, on a laptop or desktop, to activate the phone and to install software updates. Apple's iTunes also comes with Quicktime, a media player program. So, having an iPhone requires installation and management of a separate Web-enabled desktop application and a media player on a desktop or laptop system. These two additional applications have numerous vulnerabilities. To further complicate things, in early 2008, Apple bundled its Safari Internet browser along with the iTunes application, so installing iTunes also installs Safari onto the desktop/laptop system that runs iTunes. The iPhone example demonstrates that the mobile device itself is not the only security-related problem for the enterprise: There are other security-related issues such as whether or not e-mail sync capabilities to exchange servers exist, whether network encryption is available, and whether antivirus functionality is present; these must be carefully evaluated and addressed. Furthermore, ISMs must also adequately understand and deal with the way devices such as the iPhone are deployed and managed as well as the particular types of preinstalled software on these devices. ISMs need to work with owners of these devices to make informed decisions concerning costs versus benefits that will ultimately drive mobile device security standards such as standards for iPhones.

---

# Management Strategies

Given the number and magnitude of security-related risks inherent in mobile computing, mitigating these risks should be a very high priority for the organizations that use it. Unfortunately, too often due to failure to genuinely understand the seriousness and pervasiveness of mobile computer–related risks, this is not the case. In other instances, ISMs may genuinely understand these risks, but for one reason or another they have deployed piecemeal approaches and/or purely technical solutions, both of which will almost invariably result in unacceptably large amounts of residual risk.

The better alternative is to use a systematic and comprehensive top-down approach. This approach should include the following steps and/or components.

## *Creating a Strategy or Plan for Dealing with the Mobile Computing Security*

This first step in mitigating mobile computing risk is achieving a high-level understanding of mobile computing and its potential advantages and disadvantages with respect to business and/or mission drivers within an organization. After achieving and documenting this level of understanding and communicating it to senior-level management and obtaining feedback, the ISM should create a high-level strategy or plan for securing mobile computing environments. This strategy should describe the basic objectives in dealing with mobile computing risks as well as the types of policy or policies and standards that will be necessary in combating these risks. It should also state the types of resources (monetary, personnel, and technological) that are likely to be necessary to achieve the long-range goal and why, the types of obstacles that are likely to be encountered and what to do if each one manifests itself, and how progress toward achieving the long-range goal (mitigating mobile computing security risk to an acceptable level) will be monitored. The ISM should brief senior management concerning the major elements in this plan and should once again obtain their feedback and modify the strategy or plan accordingly.

The strategy or plan for dealing with mobile computing security must be aligned with the strategy or plan for the information security practice as a whole. Just as the overall information security strategy or plan must be aligned with critical business and/or operational drivers, so should the strategy or plan for achieving mobile computing security. If the overall information security strategy calls for tolerating risks that other organizations might not be willing to accept because a business is aggressively pursuing profitability with all the associated business risks, the strategy for security mobile computing environments must reflect a similar posture. In this case, a mobile computing strategy might allow use of mobile devices that are not all that conducive to security because the devices might uniquely support a new, aggressive sales initiative. The same principle applies to an organization that is risk adverse regarding business risks—in this case, only mobile devices that are conducive to achieving high levels of security are likely to be suitable.

## *Performing a Risk Analysis for the Mobile Computing Environment*

One of the next critical steps is performing a comprehensive risk analysis that covers mobile computing devices, networks, and operations. This step is critical in that if performed correctly, it enables the ISM and others to genuinely recognize and understand the types of risks that mobile computing poses and the magnitude of each risk. For example, an organization that routinely assigns laptop computing systems to employees who develop marketing strategies must evaluate associated risks such as the cost of current and new strategies falling into the hands of competitors due to loss or theft of the laptops and using vulnerable mail servers other than those owned and operated by the organization to send and receive mail while employees are away from the office.

The risk analysis process should include vulnerability and threat analyses* in an organization's mobile computing environment. Additionally, risk analysis (including a vulnerability and threat analysis) for this environment should not be a one-time activity, but should (as in the case of an overall risk analysis) rather be repeatedly performed at appropriately spaced intervals (e.g., once a year). Ideally, a risk analysis on an organization's mobile computing environment will as soon as possible be integrated into the overall risk analysis process.

Finally, the scope of a risk analysis for the mobile computing environment must be appropriate if the risk analysis is to produce valid and meaningful results. Many types of mobile computing technology currently exist. Given the many vulnerabilities and threats that exist for each type of mobile computing technology, it is tempting to conduct a risk analysis for mobile technologies that are not currently used, but that are likely to be used sometime in the future. Yielding to this temptation is extremely unwise, however, in that risks associated with technologies that are yet to be implemented cannot be genuinely assessed and understood. Newly implemented technologies

---

* To the surprise of many information security professionals and others, a number of vulnerabilities in each particular type and make of mobile computing device usually exists. These vulnerabilities can allow unauthorized access to file systems, cause denial of service, allow for unauthorized capture and or decryption of encryption keys, and much more. Obtaining vulnerability information may, however, be considerably more difficult than with conventional operating systems and applications. Some mobile device vendors have over the years been very unresponsive to security-related vulnerabilities found in their products; others have gone out of the way to communicate these vulnerabilities to their customers and to patch them.

must instead be assessed for risk at their time of their implementation as part of the overall change management process. At the same time, however, proactively collecting and evaluating information about the possible security implications of new and developing mobile technologies is essential.

## Creating a Breakout Policy for Mobile Computing Security

Another critical step in suitably mitigating mobile computer risks is creating a policy—a "breakout" policy for using mobile devices. There should be one high-level information security policy for each organization and other more-specific ("breakout") policies that provide details about provisions within the high-level policy and also provide direction concerning specific areas such as what constitutes acceptable use of computing systems are usually also necessary. Given the level of risk involved, mobile computing now warrants creating a breakout policy for mobile computing security. This policy should address many important issues, which include the following.

### Ownership

A provision that states that every mobile computing device is the exclusive property of the organization that has bought and/or issued it should be included in this policy. Individuals to whom these devices are issued should also be advised that each device is subject to immediate repossession by the owning organization for any reason.

### Usage Authorization

Who may use mobile devices and for what reasons? Must mobile computing device usage be approved in advance by a cognizant manager, and if so, must devices that are used for official company business be issued by the organization, or may personally owned devices be used?

### Use of Approved Software

Must all software installed on each mobile device be on an organization's approved product list, or may other software also be installed and used?

### Required Data Protection Measures

Who is the owner of the data that reside in each mobile computing device and what responsibilities does this person have in protecting the data? For example, any restrictions concerning the types of files that can and cannot be stored on and transferred to/from mobile computing devices need to be stated. Additionally, is disk encryption required, and if so, what type and strength of encryption is required? The same applies to encryption of data transmitted over networks. What measures are required to safeguard as well as escrow encryption keys?

### Required Physical Security Measures

This part of a mobile computing breakout policy should cover many physical security issues. At a minimum, it should prohibit leaving mobile devices in any location in which the likelihood of theft is higher than normal (e.g., in a locked or unlocked car). In the case of laptops that store sensitive and/or proprietary information, more extreme measures such as installation of GPS devices that allow for stolen laptops to be tracked are appropriate.

## Usage Location Restrictions

Where can and cannot mobile devices be taken and used? For example, may devices such as smart phone be taken on international travel? May devices that have built-in cameras be used in areas of buildings where sensitive and/or proprietary information is discussed and/or printed out?

## Responsibility and Accountability of/for Devices

A mobile computing policy should also state that each person who owns any mobile computing device is accountable for that device and that that person should use all reasonable measures to prevent the theft or damage of that device. Each person must upon discovery of a potentially missing device immediately report this to a designated entity or group such as physical security.

## Training and Awareness: Requirements and Content

As will be discussed in more depth shortly, training and awareness requirements for mobile computing device users and IT administrators need to be included in the mobile computing security breakout policy. At a minimum, these individuals should be required to take some kind of training concerning risks associated with mobile computing, required logical and physical security measures (including any procedures that must be followed), prohibited types of usage, and what to do if a device is lost or stolen before they actually start using any mobile computing device. Requiring IT administrators to receive special training concerning how to install and maintain antivirus and anti-spyware software in these devices, how to patch vulnerabilities, how to make backups, and how to detect and respond to security breaches in these devices is also highly advisable.

## Acceptable Use Policy

Acceptable use provisions for traditional and mobile computing overlap considerably, yet a separate acceptable use policy may be necessary because of differences between the two computing environments. For example, in the mobile computing environment, "piggybacking," i.e., obtaining a wireless network connection by connecting to a nearby wireless network that has weak or no security, is a real temptation to mobile computing users. The closest thing to "piggybacking" in a conventional network environment is finding a unsecured terminal and then using it to access a network to which a negligent user has already been authenticated. In most cases, however, the need to "piggyback" is much greater with mobile users who are away from their normal computing environment. Defining and explicitly forbidding "piggybacking" is thus appropriate in a mobile computing security breakout policy. Similarly, because of the typical ease of using mobile devices to download movies and music without authorization,* specific admonitions against doing so need to also be included in such a policy.

---

* Firewalls that block peer-to-peer access to file sharing sites are often used in conventional networking environment, thereby greatly reducing users' ability to illegally download movies and music. However, once mobile users are away from the office, they can usually connect to such sites without the intervention of the organization's firewalls.

## Consequences of Policy Violations

The consequences (anything from warnings to reprimands to termination of employment) for violating this policy must also be delineated.

## *Selecting and Implementing Controls*

What types of controls are suitable for risk mitigation in which types of mobile computing environments and devices and what criteria should be used? This section answers these questions.

### *Types of Controls*

The types of controls selected depend on the particular environment or device in question. For example, if an organization cannot control mobile device access to a wireless network (such as in the case of home users gaining access to an organization's network via wireless networks in their own homes or if users access local networks at airports to access their organization's mail and calendar servers), the following kinds of controls are appropriate:

- Antivirus and anti-spyware software
- Secure network protocols (SSH, SFTP, and so on)
- Secure e-mail
- VPNs for all remote connections
- Policy-enforcing software (e.g., software that drops connections in which peer-to-peer protocols are used)
- Personal firewalls
- Hard drive encryption
- Host-based intrusion detection and intrusion prevention

If, however, an organization controls mobile device access to wireless networks, the following kinds of controls are appropriate:

- Network isolation—either segregating wireless networks from conventional networks or making wireless networks part of virtual LANs* (VLANs)
- Scaling back power on wireless transmitters to reduce the likelihood of "war driving," discovering unprotected access points by driving or walking around a physical area with a device or computer that can pick up wireless transmissions
- Having strong authentication at all access points
- Deploying secure gateways
- Secure network protocols
- Secure e-mail
- Encrypting all network traffic (e.g., using WPA† and ultimately to the IEEE 802.11i standard‡

---

* Virtual LANs or VLANs are local area networks in which computers are not within the same physical LAN, but yet the switch that sends network traffic to and from them acts as if they are.
† WPA is wireless protected access, a specification for interoperable security enhancements in wireless networks.
‡ An IEEE (Institute of Electrical and Electronics Engineers) standard for a security protocol for wireless networks that was developed to replace older, less secure encryption protocols.

- Hard drive encryption
- Media access control (MAC) address filtering, such that only pre-known, approved MAC addresses are allowed to connect to the wireless network
- Making all names of access points and disabling service set identifiers* (SSIDs) difficult to guess
- Disabling SSID broadcasts
- VPNs for all connections
- Network access control (NAC) to reduce the likelihood that virus-infected and vulnerability-laden devices can connect to the network
- Deploying servers that provide security at intermediate connection points, especially when wireless devices also support Voice over IP (VoIP)
- Host-based intrusion detection and intrusion prevention
- Network-based intrusion detection and intrusion prevention tools

Potential controls for Bluetooth devices include the following:

- Antivirus and anti-spyware software
- Keep any Bluetooth network(s) separate from other networks
- Application-level security controls—these are especially important in mobile computing security because applications that run on mobile devices are often developed without much concern for security
- Vendor products that associate user identities to the keys used in Bluetooth link encryption
- Servers that enforce security-related procedures and mechanisms (e.g., biometric authentication, end-to-end encryption, and so forth)
- NAC
- Hard drive encryption
- Backup software in which backups are regularly initiated by clients within devices

Note that in the previous examples, obtaining an acceptable level of security would not necessitate implementing all or possibly even most of the listed controls. If nothing else, the lack of financial resources that information security practices usually face would prevent purchasing most or all of these controls. At the same time, however, implementing only one or two of these controls would not be a wise strategy given the need for defense-in-depth or layered defenses. Multiple layers of controls need to be in place in case one or more security controls are bypassed or defeated.

## Controls Selection Criteria

Potential controls need to be evaluated on the basis of numerous criteria, including the following.

### Effectiveness

Some types of technical controls for mobile computing devices are simply more effective in mitigating certain kinds of risks than others and are thus, all things considered, better

---

* An ID that is used to distinguish one wireless local area network (LAN) from another.

candidates for selection and deployment. For example, personal firewalls for these devices provide better protection by preventing intrusions into these devices than do passwords used in the authentication of these devices.

## Strength of Authentication

Surprisingly, some controls for mobile computing devices offer relatively weak (if any) authentication. Strength of authentication should be a major consideration during the selection of controls for these devices.

## Defense in Depth

Whenever practicable, controls should be selected and deployed in accordance with the defense-in-depth principle. Multiple layers of defense can thwart attacks in which one or more controls have been defeated or bypassed.

## Compatibility with Other Software and Features on Each Mobile Computing Device

Technical controls for each mobile computing device need to run compatibly with other software running on the same device as well as features built into that device. Some kinds of antivirus software may, for example, falsely detect anti-spyware software as malware and may thus isolate it in the same manner that it isolates viruses it detects.

## Performance Considerations

Although most mobile computing devices' processor speed and random access memory (RAM) have increased substantially in recent years, most of these devices do not have as good performance as standard desktop machines, let alone servers. Installing additional software and/or enabling features that hurt performance can cause mobile devices to become intolerable. Selecting technical controls that do not interfere significantly with performance is thus essential.

## Ease of Installation and Maintenance

Given that mobile devices are frequently used in places where they are not accessible to system administrators, ease of installation and maintenance is a particularly important consideration.

## Usability

Using many types of mobile computing devices is not particularly easy from a usability point of view. Technical controls that are implemented on these devices should thus not compound usability problems.

## Cost

The financial cost of technical controls should be reasonable. This is an especially important consideration given the sheer number of mobile devices that organizations are currently using. This number will also certainly only grow in the future. The ISM should also consider that up front costs are only the first of a number of costs over the life cycle of a security product; maintenance and upgrade costs must also be considered.

## Vendor Considerations

Vendor reputation, support, and reliability should also have a major bearing on the decision whether or not to buy a particular technical control for mobile computing device security.

All things considered, however, the major driver for selecting controls should be costs versus benefits. Ideally, a control should yield many times more benefits in terms of amount of risk mitigation than the cost in terms money, disruption, and so on.

## *Creating Security Standards and Procedures for Mobile Computing Security Technology*

Once controls have been selected and implemented, standards and procedures for the technology used to counter mobile computing risks should follow soon.

## *What Standards Need to Cover*

Standards must specify acceptable parameters for mobile computing security technology, such as the number of days between updates of antivirus software. At the same time, however, standards are likely to vary greatly, depending on the policy provisions for mobile computing security, the particular context(s) in which mobile computing is used, and the particular types of mobile computing technology that are being used within an organization.

## *What Procedures Need to Cover*

Procedures must as much as possible be focused on the system and network administrators who administer mobile devices, because these individuals will in most cases be the ones who have sufficient technical skills to be able to perform that many tasks (e.g., installing software and performing maintenance tasks) that need to be completed for the sake of security. Given the propensity for user error combined with users' general lack of technical knowledge, procedures for mobile computing security must also be designed to keep users out of the loop as much as possible.

Procedures need to at a minimum address all of the following issues.

## Inventorying All Mobile Computing Devices

Several studies indicate that a substantial (up to 40%) percentage of mobile computing devices are lost or stolen within 2 years of their purchase. Additional studies show that a disproportionate percentage (up to 75%) of all mobile device thefts is committed by insiders (employees, contractors, and so forth). Regularly (e.g., once a month) inventorying all mobile computing devices is thus an extremely critical theft and loss mitigation measure. Procedures need to establish ways that those charged with keeping inventories can locate each mobile computing device at specified time intervals and to report missing devices. Procedures should include escalation methods to be used when business-critical devices are missing.

## Enabling Security-Related Features

Mobile computing devices tend to be small in physical size. Functions (including security-related functions) thus tend to be represented by small icons or may be buried in menu structures that may be as deep as five or six levels. Consequently, enabling security-related features tends to be difficult. Procedures must specify the features to be enabled, how to enable them, and how to set any associated parameters in accordance with standards.

## Installing Security Software

Only a few years ago, security software such as antivirus software and anti-spyware software was not widely available for mobile computing devices, but now it is. However, as in the case of enabling security-related features, installing security software on mobile computing devices tends to not be very intuitive. Procedures must thus delineate the steps involved in security software installation as well as how to set parameters that determine how the software works.

## Penetration Testing

One of the major failings in security mobile computing devices and wireless networks is neglecting to conduct penetration testing, yet penetration testing is one of the best ways to find vulnerabilities in mobile computing devices. The ISM must ensure that thorough procedures for penetration testing these devices as well as procedures for eliminating any vulnerabilities that are found are developed.

## The Patch Management Process

Patching mobile computing devices is one of the most difficult tasks in the IT arena. The reason is that mobile computing devices are so often out of the direct control of the IT staff within an organization. In contrast, conventional computing devices are normally put in one fixed location within a building and connected to a particular network and subnet, things that are very conducive to remotely pushing patches into these devices using a patch server. Procedures must specify how and how often patches for mobile computing devices are to be installed. The number of vendor products that simplifies patch management for mobile computing devices has slowly grown over time. Some of these products check for the presence of each device on an organization's network. If the device is found, a patch server checks the device to determine whether each patch has been installed. If not, the patch server automatically installs each missing patch.

## How and How Often to Review Audit Log Data

Many types of mobile computing devices now have their own audit logs. Capturing audit data does not do any good, however, unless someone or something (e.g., a security information and event management tool) analyzes the data. Procedures must thus state how and how frequently audit/log data need to be reviewed as well as archived.

## Performing Backups and Restores

Mobile computing devices are "strange beasts" in that although more of them have complete operating systems than ever before, some of their functions are less straightforward than for conventional operating systems. Backups and restores are two of these functions. Whereas attaching tape drives to conventional systems for the purpose of backing up or restoring them is generally trivial, the same is by no means true for most mobile computing devices. Special procedures and solutions for backups and restores therefore need to be created for many types of these devices.

### Responding to Incidents Such as When Mobile Computing Devices Become Lost or Compromised

Finally, given the above average probability that mobile computing devices will be lost or stolen or will have a data security breach, procedures for responding to such incidents need to be created. Although these procedures are likely to be very similar to incident response procedures for conventional computing devices, the threat profiles and eccentricities associated with mobile computing devices dictate the need for special steps. For example, eradicating a virus in a mobile computing device for which no antivirus software currently exists is different from eradicating a virus in a Windows PC.

## Training and Awareness

Ensuring that mobile computing device users and system and network administrators who install and maintain these devices have sufficient training is a critical part of achieving adequate control over mobile computing risks. Users must at a minimum be taught the provisions of the breakout policy for mobile computer security so that they are more likely to do what is required of them and to avoid doing what is prohibited. Users must also be told not to download files that are sent to their mobile devices unless they are expecting the files to be sent, and also to avoid surfing unknown Web sites with these devices. System and network administrators need training concerning initial configurations of mobile devices, how to properly install additional software (such as security tools), how to install patches, how to back these devices up, and much more. The fact that mobile devices are so often completely out of the reach of system and network administrators coupled with the eccentricities and mysteries that go with many of these devices makes training for these individuals a much more important than average requirement.

## Intrusion Detection

Mainstream network-based intrusion detection systems (IDSs) such as Snort are capable of identifying some attacks against mobile computing devices. These tools generally have no trouble detecting denial-of-service attacks, attempts by viruses and worms to scan other systems and devices, and many other kinds of malicious activity. However, many attacks against mobile computing devices are against *specific* types of mobile devices, each of which has its own particular vulnerability profile. In this case, mainstream IDSs do not fare very well—the missed detection rate tends to be very high. The best solution is to purchase and install host-based IDSs designed specifically for each type of mobile computing device that is being used. This solution is, however, usually limited in that when a host-based IDS detects an attack against a mobile device, the fact that the mobile device is often not connected to an organization's network frequently results in the alert that is sent to a central IDS within the organization's network being dropped or blocked by some intermediate barrier such as a firewall at the entrance to the network being used by the mobile user or a spam wall. Additionally, although host-based IDSs for mobile devices are available for a number of these devices, they are not available for many others. The bottom line is that at this point in time it is not likely that an intrusion detection effort in connection with mobile computing is likely to be very successful. Still, getting started is better than doing nothing at all, and planning for the future, when host-based IDSs for a larger proportion of mobile devices are likely to be available, is necessary.

## Incident Response

Incident response for attacked and/or compromised mobile computing devices is another extremely challenging endeavor. As discussed earlier, the basic problem is that mobile devices are so frequently out of the direct control of an organization's system and network administrators, often rendering basic incident response measures such as immediately isolating compromised systems impossible. Additionally, the previously discussed problem of computer forensics for mobile computing devices being more difficult than normal, in large part due to a dearth of forensics products designed for many of these devices, presents even more challenges to mobile computing incident response efforts. Nevertheless, the ISM should ensure that incident response procedures for mobile computing devices are written on a best effort basis, frequently tested, and appropriately distributed.

## Business Continuity Planning

The ISM must also consider mobile devices in business continuity planning. One of the most overlooked facts in the IT arena is the importance of many mobile computing devices to an organization's business interests. Consider, for example, the importance of a CEO's PDA on which notes related to strategic planning are stored. The loss of this PDA could possibly have extremely adverse consequences for the organization, not merely because the PDA might fall into the hands of competitors, but also because of the potential value of the intellectual property that the CEO may or may not be able to recreate at a later point in time. Although mobile computing devices do not fit into classic business continuity and disaster recovery models very well, at a minimum these devices can and should be regularly backed up. As mentioned previously, special procedures for backing up mobile computing devices need to be created and updated as necessary.

## e-Discovery

The ISM must select and implement solutions for challenges (as imperfect as they may be) that mobile computing creates for e-Discovery. Having a mobile computing device policy that limits the types of files that can be stored on these devices is the right place to start. This policy should in most cases state that files containing personal and/or financial data cannot be stored on mobile computing devices. The disposition of documents, e-mail messages, instant messenger (IM) conversations, and other communications to and from the mobile device should all follow the corporate records management policies for retention. This can be a daunting technical task, because many mobile devices are self-administered and lack centrally managed software that works with archiving backend systems. Lamentably, the end user will thus have to properly synchronize the device to a corporate server, desktop, or laptop that will then be incorporated into the archiving and discovery process. Similarly, destruction and disposal of information stored on mobile computing devices should be considered. Alternatively, the ISM can use data de-duplication technology to ensure that one and only one copy of each file is stored and that it is stored in a known location, and having periodic audits of files stored on mobile computing devices. Additionally, a few vendor tools can help with the e-Discovery challenge in mobile computing environments by indexing and cataloging files stored on mobile devices and then reporting the file names and paths to a central e-Discovery server. This technology is in its relative infancy; nevertheless, it may be suitable for the current needs of some organizations, and it promises to become considerably better in the future.

## Compliance Monitoring

Creating policies, standards, and procedures related to mobile computing security does little good if there is no enforcement that accompanies it. The ISM is the first line of enforcement, so the ISM must (in conjunction with the IT organization and other stakeholders) systematically check whether the requirements in the policies, standards, and procedures for mobile computing security are being met. The ISM must also use good judgment in determining whether or not requested variances should be approved, and must be reasonable in creating action plans for dealing with out-of-compliance situations in which it is not practical for business or other reasons to comply by an established date.

## Conclusion

Mobile computing is an extremely dynamic arena, as is virtually every aspect associated with it, security very much included. As such, the ISM must at a minimum devote a great deal of effort to understanding the boundaries within the organization's network in which and out of which mobile computing exists and how these boundaries change over time. The ISM must constantly track mobile computing usage and learn of new mobile computing technologies that seem to inevitably surface within an organization so that new security-related risks can be identified, evaluated, and mitigated. The types and values of information that are remotely stored on mobile computing devices and transmitted in mobile computing environments as well as the applications that run in mobile computing environments will inevitably change over time; these, too, need to be tracked and the resulting risk needs to be considered and, if justified by a cost-benefit analysis, mitigated. Ensuring that new, appropriate provisions are added as needed to an organization's mobile computing security policy is also imperative.

Reducing security risk associated with mobile devices and mobile computing environments to an acceptable level is a very difficult task, one in which so far very few organizations have been truly successful. As the use of both wireless networking and handheld mobile devices in organizations continues to grow, the struggle to achieve this goal in the face of significant budget constraints is likely to become even more challenging. The ISM must thus now more than ever before assume a much more active role in ensuring that a process for planning and phasing in proper controls for mobile computing is in place.

## About the Authors

**E. Eugene Schultz**, PhD, CISM, CISSP, is the chief technology officer at Emagined Security, an information security consultancy based in San Carlos, California.

**Gal Shpantzer** is a trusted advisor to chief security officers of Fortune 500 corporations, Silicon Valley start-ups, large universities, and national nonprofits organizations.

*Chapter 8*

# Establishing an Information Security Program for Local Government

Robert K. Pittman, Jr.

## Contents

## Introduction

Many of us are survivors based on experiences and challenges that all of us face throughout life. These challenges include the careers and jobs that we work and spend an enormous amount of time on a daily basis for many decades that eventually lead to a gratifying retirement. At least, this is the hope and goal. Employees that seem to be flourishing with satisfying retirement packages are employed at various levels of government (e.g., federal, state, and local). Government or public-sector jobs differ from corporations or private-sector jobs in numerous facets. Some of these differing facets are providing an enormous amount of services to citizens and constituents throughout our nation.

The consumers of government businesses are essentially supported by the public. The public is comprised of its citizens, constituents, and businesses such as nonprofits, corporations, including government agencies at all levels. There is a relationship among everyone that involves citizens in terms of governments and associated organizations interrelating their programs and services on behalf of the public. At least, this is one of the goals of government, since they are providing services that a corporate business would not even consider. The plethora of services being provided to the public and its citizens are social services, general government, health care, and public safety.

Some of the countless government social services programs are addressing and supporting low-income families, foster care, emancipated youths, and general relief payments for food and housing for the disadvantaged. Other services consist of property value assessment, property tax payment, requests for a birth certificate, marriage license, or a death certificate, as well as simply registering to vote, in part, constitutes general government services. Our citizens, from the time they are brought into this world and throughout their lives will require health-care services. Medical and mental-health care including public health issues will always be of the highest concern to all levels of government that involve all ages. It may seem obvious that public safety services are at the top of the list with heath care as well. The security of our homeland, borders and ports protection, law enforcement, and protecting our loved ones is an area where government visibly plays a significant role.

All of the aforementioned government services are provisioned externally to the citizens. The perspective on services provided internally would be contrary to corporate, in terms of the existence and loyalty of a significant amount of employee's labor unions (i.e., civil service rules), attractive sustained retirement packages, consistent health and dental benefits, career and job advancements within the same government level where opportunities exist at different departments, branches, and agencies, and are knowingly supporting a cause or the greater good.

Regardless of what lens we use to view government and corporate, the lens illustrates that obvious differences do exist. Many of the services to the public are intangible where government employees have a fond appreciation.

By viewing government at the 80,000 ft level and viewing through the looking glass, differences exist from an employee and organization perspective. Local government (i.e., county and city) organizations have differences in contrast to corporations. Obviously, corporate stock shares and job security are some of those differences. However, establishing an information security program has significant differences within local governments contrary to corporations.

To establish an information security program in local government involves an array of focal points that must be addressed within the initial 18 months by the chief information security officer (CISO), chief security officer (CSO), or information security manager (ISM). In some recent information security forums and industry writings, the term chief risk officer (CRO) may have a significant role as well. It is imperative that these focal points are addressed in terms of having them established and adopted by the organization:

- Enterprise information security policies
- Information security steering committee (ISCC)
- Enterprise information security program
- Enterprise information security strategy
- Identify the organization health level based on an information security risk assessment
- Enterprise and departmental (or agencies) computer emergency response teams (DCERTs)
- Enterprise security engineering teams (SETs)

Each of the above focal points can be categorized as your "Lucky 7." Throughout this chapter these points will be referred as Lucky 7. For that information security professional that addresses these points will be "lucky," and the others will not be as "lucky" in terms of continued employment with that particular organization since the primary responsibility exists in the information security unit. This may sound harsh. However, at the end of the day, the organization's business and services being provided to the citizens and constituents have the expectation that their confidential, sensitive, and personally identifiable information (PII) is secured and protected. It is the job of the information security professional to accept the challenge and responsibility to ensure that the organization stays away from any press or media release announcing a data breach, or perhaps, a breach of trust. As information security practitioners are aware, there has been a plethora of announcements in the press and media on organizations (public and private sectors) that experienced computer security breaches. These are in corporate America, colleges and universities, health-care organizations, as well as the 26 million veterans' records with PII that was the responsibility of the federal government Veteran's Administration (public sector) and T. J. Maxx's record setting 45.7 million credit and debit card owners (private sector).

## Organizational Governance

It seems more apparent that the public sector leverages a security-related event to promote an information security program, or at the minimum, obtain a funding source to support a project or initiative. Despite the consequences of failure or compromise, security governance is still a muddle. It is poorly understood and ill-defined, and, therefore, means different things to different people. Essentially, security governance is a subset of enterprise or corporate governance. Moreover, one could identify governance as security responsibilities and practices, strategies and objectives for security, risk assessment and management, resource management for security, and compliance with legislation, regulations, security policies, and rules.

Information security governance is "the establishment and maintenance of the control environment to manage the risks relating to the confidentiality, integrity, and availability of information and its supporting processes and systems."

From a local government perspective, in terms of county government that is governed by a five-member board of supervisors and the chief executive officer (CEO). The CISO, departmental information security officers (DISOs), and the ISSC or a security council comprises the information security governance.

A federated organizational structure is the norm for the majority of local government organizations. If the discussion is county or city government, there are numerous business units or departments that serve unique and differing business purposes. Because of these unique business units, comprehensible governance is vital to the success of any information security program. This governance involves a strategic organization framework (Figure 8.4) that provides a clear illustration of the involved players. The "Security Triangle" or Figure 8.3 is a framework that is doable for the CISOs organization regardless if their information technology is decentralized, centralized, or a managed-security service. Additionally, a local government organization can be deemed as an organization with 30 or more corporations, in terms of having 30+ county departments with distinct businesses as they serve their respective constituents' (Figure 8.1).

The Security Triangle must be supported by the organization's senior management; however, articulation of this support should be achieved by the development of board-adopted policies. These policies are similar to the corporate world where the board of directors and CEO can adopt policies. However, information standards and procedures can be approved by an information security council.

| Public Sector | Private Sector | Public Corporation |
|---|---|---|
| Director | Owner | Board of directors |
| Deputy director/branch manager | Vice-president | Executive management |
| Division chief | Manager | Middle management |
| Section manager | Manager | Supervisory management |
| Associate | Employees | Employees |

**Figure 8.1  Public sector versus private sector and corporate organizations.**

# Organizational Culture and Behavior

Bruce Schneier is an internationally renowned security technologist and author, as well as the go-to security expert for business leaders and policy makers. Currently, he is the chief security technology officer for BT Managed Security Solutions. He states, in his book *Beyond Fear, Thinking Sensibly about Security in an Uncertain World*, that security is all about people: not only the people who attack systems, but the people who defend those systems. If we are to have any hope of making security work, we need to understand these people and their motivations. We have already discussed attackers; now we have to discuss defenders.

Schneier also states that good security has people in charge. People are resilient. People can improvise. People can be creative. People can develop on-the-spot solutions. People are the strongest point in a security process. When a security system succeeds in the face of a new or coordinated or devastating attack, it is usually due to the efforts of people.

If it was not obvious prior to reading this chapter, it should be obvious now that people play a significant role as part of any information security program. And it is the culmination of people that defines organizational behavior and its culture. Organizational culture is the culture that exists in an organization, something akin to a societal culture. It is composed of many intangible phenomena, such as values, beliefs, assumptions, perceptions, behavioral norms, artifacts, and patterns of behavior. It is the unseen and unobserved force that is always behind the organizational activities that can be seen and observed. Organizational culture is a social energy that moves people to act. "Culture is to the organization what personality is to the individual—a hidden, yet unifying theme that provides meaning, direction, and mobilization."

Organizations are assumed to be rational–utilitarian institutions whose primary purpose is the accomplishment of established goals (i.e., information security strategy and initiatives). People in positions of formal authority set goals. The personal preferences of organization employees are restrained by systems of formal rules (e.g., policies, standards, and procedures), authority, and norms of rational behavior.

These patterns of assumptions continue to exist and influence behaviors in an organization because they repeatedly have led people to make decisions that "worked in the past." With repeated use, the assumptions slowly drop out of people's consciousness but continue to influence organizational decisions and behaviors even when the environment changes and different decisions are needed. They become the underlying, unquestioned, but largely forgotten, reasons for "the way we do things here"—even when the ways may no longer be appropriate. They are so basic, so ingrained, and so completely accepted that no one thinks about or remembers them.

In the public sector, it seems that almost every employee has worked at least 20 years or more. In retrospect, they may have only worked many years less. Reality sits in when many employees consistently echo the aforementioned phase, "the way we do things here." Being the CISO attempting to implement one of your many information security initiatives, this echo seems to sound loudly increasing exponentially with the employees that will be affected by implementing a change to their environment. This type of behavior illustrates the presence of a strong organizational culture.

A strong organizational culture can control organizational behavior. For example, an organizational culture can block an organization from making changes that are needed to adapt to new information technologies. From the organizational culture perspective, systems of formal rules, authority, and norms of rational behavior do not restrain the personal references of organization employees. Instead, they are controlled by cultural norms, values, beliefs, and assumptions. In order to understand or predict how an organization will behave under varying circumstances, one must know and understand the organization's patterns of basic assumptions—its organizational culture.

Organizational cultures differ for several reasons. Some organizational cultures are more distinctive than others. Some organizations have strong, unified, pervasive cultures, whereas others have weaker or less pervasive ones; some cultures are quite pervasive, whereas others may have many subcultures existing in different functional or geographical areas.

In contrast, there are some "prescriptive aphorisms" or "specific considerations in changing organizational cultures"; when this occurs, your information security program (i.e., Lucky 7) along with its processes and practices will flourish with positive outcomes:

- Capitalize on propitious moments
- Combine caution with optimism
- Understand resistance to culture change
- Change many elements, but maintain some continuity and synergy
- Recognize the importance of a planned implementation
- Select, modify, and create appropriate cultural forms
- Modify socialization tactics
- Locate and cultivate innovative leadership

Altered organizational culture is merely the first—but essential—step in reshaping organizations to become more flexible, responsive, and customer driven. Changing an organizational culture is not a task to be undertaken lightly, but can be achieved over time.

| Organizational Target Group | Desired Behavior |
|---|---|
| Board of supervisors/city council | Endorsement |
| Executive management | Priority |
| Middle management | Resources |
| Supervisory mangement | Support |
| Employees | Diligence |
| Constituents/consumers | Trust |
| Security program | Execution |

**Figure 8.2 Stakeholders' desired behavior.**

Organizational cultures are just one of the major tenets that constraints the establishment and building of an information security program. As a CISO, or an information security practitioner within your organization, you should have had at least some interaction with the various target groups (i.e., stakeholders) to grasp an awareness of their behavior. Figure 8.2 illustrates the expected behavior of the target groups and the desired behavior to assist in driving your program. This chart will provide benefits when you rate each stakeholder from your perspective.

## The Information Security Executive in the Organization

The University of California at Los Angeles (UCLA) legendary men's head basketball coach John Wooden, wrote "there is a choice you have to make in everything you do, so keep in mind that in the end, the choice you make makes you." Nowhere is this more evident than the relationships that are established throughout your organization as well as external to the organization. Surround yourself with people who add value to you and encourage you. At the minimum, having photographs or prints hanging from your office walls of individuals that have achieved greatness, regardless of what industry will provide an added psychological benefit when tough decisions must be made. Having established strong relationships is an excellent indicator of a strong CISO; however, staying visible in the organization is equally important.

People can trace the successes and failures in their lives to their most significant relationships. Establishing relationships are part of our livelihood in terms of family, personal, professionally, and business. Moreover, as the CISO, when establishing an information security program and chairing an ISCC meeting with your security peers or colleagues in your organization, those relationships are imperative to your success. Effective CISOs have learned how to gain the trust and confidence of the executive team. The CISO must remember that security is easy to sell if the focus is on the benefits to the company.

The CISO is the information security executive (i.e., executive management); regardless if we are referencing public or private (i.e., Corporate American) sector organizations. An organization's CISO must address the big picture and must rely on timely and actionable risk information that enhances their ability to make decisions that will drive local government efficiencies and operational effectiveness.

In local government, many CISOs are using a matrix reporting structure and either report to the chief information officer (CIO) or the CEO, and ultimately the city manager, board of supervisors (Board), or city council (Council). Actually, this matrix model can only function in this fashion as long as no operations responsibilities are incorporated. In other words, the daily operational activities and tasks would collide, at the minimum, with the strategic and tactical mindset of the information security practitioner. This model has brought this author numerous successful implementations of information security projects and initiatives.

However, there are many other ways to organize the security function and they all have advantages and disadvantages. Better CISOs understand it is not important how security is organized, or the hierarchical structure. The key to success is the support structure the CISO is able to build among the executive team. However, the manner in which security is organized will change the methods and processes a CISO will use to be successful. Effective CISOs will adapt their approach to the most advantageous organizational structure. The two primary organization structures most common are (1) matrix structure, in which the CISO is an enterprise-level (or corporate level for private sector) organization and the security staff report in the business lines, or (2) the CISO has direct responsibility for the implementation and operations of security.

Smart CISOs understand that they do not need to have all the security staff in their direct reporting line. Be ready for decentralization. Being a powerful CISO is not about how many staff you manage; it is about how many staff you can influence. Drive the difference of security any way you can—through direct staff, matrix staff, and supporting staff to reach the security program goals and initiatives. Large organizations have already implemented a matrix organization or are seriously reviewing how to manage the business lines more effectively. Be prepared to manage in a matrix organization.

Regardless of the reporting structure, decisions must be made to eliminate press clippings in tomorrow's local newspaper, or perhaps the national news. The CISO cannot be risk-averse. All information security practitioners should think quantitatively. This does not necessarily mean doing calculations. Rather, it means thinking about things in terms of the balance of arguments, the force of each of which depends on some magnitude.

Some local government organizations are forward-thinking companies that have recognized that business and information technology (IT) executives (e.g., CIO, CISO, or Chief Technology Officer) need to establish standardized, repeatable ways to identify, prioritize, measure, and reduce business and technology risks, both collaboratively and effectively. Moreover, security executives who were accustomed to working in their own silo must now consider all business-related risk areas to align initiatives (e.g., business and applications system migration projects and customer-based applications to enhance e-government/e-services) properly with exposures.

Collaboration and communication is sunshine on its brightest day. Team relationships and/or team meetings are training gold nuggets. If the opportunity exists, inviting individuals to attend selected meetings within your security program can go a long way to helping them understand the scope and breadth of security. Make them an honorary member of the team. This has been done on several occasions to break through the myopia barrier. In addition, if other groups will let you attend a team meeting or two, go for it. This seems very simple, and is, but can be unbelievably powerful.

It is very true that there is success in numbers from an empirical perspective, where teams can drive your information security program. There are two types of teams that should be implemented to support an information security program: proactive and reactive.

We call the proactive measures teams SETs. All of these teams develop and review policies, standards, procedures, and guidelines. These teams are usually experienced and knowledgeable in terms of the technical, culture, and organizational perspectives. These teams address host strengthening and isolation, policy and operating procedures, malware defense, and application security, to name a few. However, there will be opportunities where a proactive team will be formed to address a point-in-time project. For example, our implementation of an Internet content filter was a win–win because of the formulation of a SET from development of the technical specifications to enterprise deployment. Once deployed throughout the organization, the team was no longer required.

A reactive team addresses an enterprise-wide CERT. This team reacts to situations that potentially impact or have impacted the enterprise network, servers, applications, workstations, etc. This is reactive in nature. However, the use of a structured methodology while responding, resolving, and reporting the incident is vital. The use of well-maintained and clearly written documentation (e.g., narratives, matrixes, and diagrams) for responding to incidents, and using a standardized incident reporting form are crucial. It may be obvious that by defining the various types of information security incidents to report will provide one of the numerous performance metrics that can be established to measure a portion of the operational aspects of your program.

# Information Security Policies, Standards, Procedures, and Guidelines

One of the major components of an information security program is the formulation, collaboration, and adoption of information security policies. These written policies cannot survive without associated supporting standards, procedures (some private-sector organizations uses standard operating procedures or SOP), and guidelines. Personally, having clear, distinct, and physically separated policies, standards, and procedures would provide benefits to your overall information security program.

Charles Cresson Wood, well known in the information security industry as a leader for information security policy development, has emphasized to segregate information that has different purposes. Specifically, one should formulate different documents for policy, standards, procedures, and guidelines. This structure provides numerous benefits to the responsible owner of these documents in terms of ease of modification to maintain currency and relevance, reviews and approvals are more efficient, and requests for any single type of document can be distributed on a need-to-know basis that protects the security and privacy of the written information, where applicable.

Policy is defined as the rules and regulations set by the organization. Policies are laid down by the management in compliance with applicable law, industry regulations, and the decisions of enterprise leaders and stakeholders. Policies, standards, and procedures are mandatory; guidelines are optional. However, policies can be used to clearly define roles and responsibilities of the information security program, including the CISOs, steering committee, etc. Moreover, policies are written in definite language and require compliance. Failure to conform to policy can result in disciplinary action, termination of employment, and even legal action.

Information security policy governs how an organization's information is to be protected against breaches of security. Familiar examples of policy include requirements for establishing an information security program, ensuring that all laptops are deployed with automatic hard disk encryption software, employees' Internet usage, security awareness and training, malware (e.g., anti-virus, anti-spam, and anti-spyware) defense, and computer incident reporting for employees, to name a few.

Information security standards can be an accepted specification for software, hardware, or human actions. These standards can be de facto, as well, when they are so widely used that new applications routinely respect their conventions. However, the written format is preferred and recommended from the perspective of an information security professional and information technology professionals including auditors.

A software standard can address a specific vendor's solution for anti-virus software protection. In fact, from a defense-in-depth perspective an organization may be standardized on two vendor's solutions. If particular organizations have implemented all Cisco Systems, Incorporated (Cisco) network devices, they could conclude that their hardware standard for network infrastructure is Cisco. There are many standards to address human actions or even their behavior. For example, to address a potential computer security breach, a standard will address actions to be performed by specific employees' roles, responsibilities, and timelines for an appropriate response.

Procedures prescribe how people are to behave in implementing policies. For example, a policy might stipulate that all confidential and private data network communications from employees working or traveling and desire to connect externally to the enterprise network must be encrypted. This would constitute previously identified software and hardware (perhaps an adopted standard for communicating externally) required to be implemented based on policy. The corresponding procedure (the "how-to") would explain in detail each step required to initiate a secure connection using a particular virtual private network (VPN) or some other technology.

Policies, standards, and procedures as previously stated are mandatory. However, guidelines are not mandatory. Guidelines could be used as a documented standard or procedure where invariably in the future could be transformed and adopted into a standard or procedure. Establishing guidelines assists in identifying the usefulness, and the trial of specific security controls for future adoption. For example, if an organization prefers the usage of Windows Mobile operating system for all mobile devices and there is a small community within the organization that prefers the proprietary Blackberry device, a guideline would be feasible to address appropriate security controls for the Blackberry device, where a standard would address appropriate security controls for all Windows Mobile devices. Eventually, the Blackberry security controls guideline would be transformed into a standard after a greater acceptance within the organization was achieved. This eliminates the use of a de facto standard in this example.

All documents should use suitable policy resources including the aforementioned Charles Cresson Wood's Information Security Policy Made Easy, government (e.g., National Institute of Standards and Technology (NIST), National Security Agency (NSA) Security Guidelines, and RFC 2196), industry bodies (e.g., International Standards Organization (ISO) 17799/27002 and CoBIT), and commercial (e.g., Microsoft) organizations in preparing to formulate policies and standards.

The writing style should state what employees can do and what they cannot do, use of short sentences, written at a tenth grade level similar to the model newspapers use, review and improve (i.e., Sunset date), or adapt policies regularly, circulate drafts showing changes in policies to stakeholders and interested participants prior to adoption, and articulate major changes to senior management (e.g., Department Heads, Counsel, CIOs, and Privacy Officers) within the enterprise.

## The Information Security Organization

The organizational culture and behavior, the CISO as the information security executive, and the organization structure are the dependent variables in establishing an information security program. The framework that has been proved at numerous local governments west of the Mississippi River, regardless of workforce size is the "Security Triangle" (Figure 8.3). This framework has paid dividends in having clearly defined roles and responsibilities, while addressing defense and offense strategies. In other words, these strategies are the previously stated reactive and proactive teams that allow for continual collaboration with stakeholders vertically and horizontally throughout the public-sector organization.

The following Information Security Strategic Organization diagram (i.e., Security Triangle) depicts an example from a local government (i.e., county government). It illustrates the CISO at the top of the organization that may report to a CIO or CEO, as previously stated. The ISSC is composed of the DISOs. This will provide a forum for all information security-related collaboration and decision-making. This deliberative body will weigh the balance between heightened security and departments performing their individual business. The ISSC responsibilities will be to

- Develop, review, and recommend information security policies
- Develop, review, and approve best practices, standards, guidelines, and procedures
- Coordinate interdepartmental communication and collaboration
- Coordinate countywide education and awareness
- Coordinate countywide purchasing and licensing
- Adopt security standards

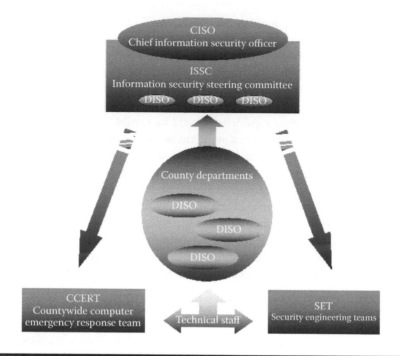

**Figure 8.3    Information security strategic organization "Security Triangle."**

The DISOs are responsible for departmental security initiatives and efforts to comply with countywide information security policies and activities. They also represent their departments on the ISSC. To perform these duties, the DISO must be established at a level that provides management visibility, management support, and objective independence. DISO responsibilities include

- Representing their department on the ISSC
- Developing departmental information security systems
- Developing departmental information security policies, procedures, and standards
- Advising the department head on security-related issues
- Department security awareness programs
- Conducting system security audits

The countywide CCERT will respond to information security events that affect several departments within the county that must be coordinated and planned. The CCERT is comprised of membership from the various departments, and are often members of the DCERT. The CCERT team meets biweekly to review the latest threats and vulnerabilities, and ensure that membership data is kept current. The CISO participates in their activities as well as leads the response to cyber-related events. Efforts include improved notification and communication process, and ensure that weekend and after-hours response is viable. Additionally, training will be conducted to provide forensic capabilities to the CCERT team members, but specific to incident response in terms of maintaining chain of custody of electronic evidence.

The information security strategic framework (Figure 8.4) developed to support a local government is designed to address organization, people, processes and technology, as they relate to information security. The strategy is based on the principle that security is not a one-time event; but, must be

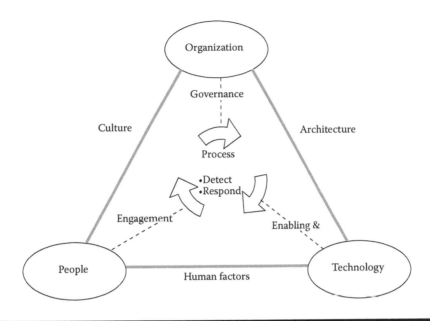

**Figure 8.4 Information security strategic framework.**

a continuously improving process, an emergent process that addresses changes in business requirements, technology changes, new threats and vulnerabilities, and a need to maintain currency with regard to software release levels at all levels within the security network, server, and client arena. It also is based on the realization that perfect security is an impossible goal and that efforts to secure systems must be based on cost of protective measures versus risk of loss.

As the CISO or ISM, many of these protective measures are identified in an information security strategy, as a necessity. A documented strategy that is annually reviewed is imperative to ensure currency of the projects and initiatives for that particular fiscal year. It is prudent that as the information security practitioner you align your security projects, initiatives, and activities with the annual budget process of the organization. This will provide a means and awareness to senior management that funding is mandatory to sustain a true information security program that will reduce risk. This strategy must clearly articulate the mission and vision of the program. Additionally, information security program goals and objectives are articulated in the strategy, in terms of short- and near-term timelines. For example, your high-level goals can be derived from the 12 information security domains that are articulated in the ISO 27002 standard. The objectives will support the stated goal that should apply to your organization's required level of security protections. The strategy will assist in the CISO's ability to achieve the stated goals and objectives over a defined period of time.

## Conclusion

Today's information security professional practitioner is increasingly being challenged in numerous facets that are warranted based on the numerous threats and vulnerabilities that exists in the world. Government organizations are among us and throughout the world, as well. Rather, we are discussing local government or private-sector organization challenges, some specific areas are unique to government, such as the diversity of businesses and services under a single organization (i.e., county or city government), the type of businesses that warrants differing security and privacy protections, multiple legislations and regulations that sanctions departments within a local government organization, and perhaps most of all the culture issue because of the civil service rules that provides difficulty when employee termination is being considered.

The CISO responsibilities range from establishing and sustaining relationships with executive management, learning about the organization's culture and behavior, constantly being visible and communicating the security message throughout the organization, having formulated clearly defined policies, standards, and procedures, and establishing a governance structure that comprises and establishes a successful information security program.

In today's global society, a career path definitely exists for information security practitioners that would ultimately lead to holding a position as a CISO or CSO. This chapter including and this book will hopefully provide dividends throughout your career as a practitioner. However, having a business acumen, IT experience, and enormous leadership skills are a few of the major tenets in striving to be an outstanding and successful CISO. On the other hand, IT training curriculum does not usually include managerial skills such as leadership, team building, collaboration, risk assessment, communication skills including negotiations, as well as psychology, philosophy courses, are not usually provided.

## About the Author

**Robert K. Pittman, Jr.**, MPA, is a public sector employee and a doctoral degree candidate at the University of Southern California, Los Angeles, California.

# *Policies, Standards, Procedures, and Guidelines*

## Chapter 9

# A Business Case for ISO 27001 Certification

Tom Carlson and Robert Forbes

## Contents

## Introduction

While your organization's marketing and sales teams attempt to leverage security as a market differentiator, information security leadership faces the daunting challenge of "doing more with less." This chapter sets out the benefits and provides a business case for an information security management system (ISMS) that conforms to the ISO 27001 standard.

## Background

ISO 27001, the internationally accepted and recognized standard for ISMSs, was developed and supported by the member nations of the International Organization of Standardization (ISO), an organization chartered by the United Nations. The ISO 27000 series of standards evolved from the British Standard BS 7799. Originally published in 1995, Part One of BS 7799, the Code of Practice (aka the implementation guide), is now the basis for ISO 27002 (formerly known as ISO 17799). Part Two of BS 7799, first published in 1998 is the auditable ISMS set of specifications, now embodied in ISO 27001. There are other standards in the series, both published and in progress, covering ISMS implementation guidance (27003), information security metrics (27004), risk management (27005), and a guide to Information Security Management auditing (27008).

# Intended Use

ISO 27001 is intended to provide guidance on how to manage information security for an organization. To expand on this, the ISO standard is focused on an organization as a whole, including all information types, systems, people, policies, processes, and technologies.*

An ISMS built and certified to ISO 27001, in addition to its internal benefits to the organization, can also provide defensible due diligence for potential clients, users, and/or other parties. The latter sections of this chapter will demonstrate a number of benefits resulting from implementation of the standard.

First, let us look in detail at the ISMS and how it can be used by an organization to "package for success."

We can all agree that although we have been *practicing* information security for a long time, the *management* of information security has been inconsistent at best. The concept of a quality-based ISMS, codified in the ISO 27001 standard, is a classic example of interdiscipline synergy, porting proven quality management techniques into the security discipline.

What is a management system?

Management: direction or control

System: a collection of practices bundled to provide some form of service

Management System: that collection of practices to direct or control the provision of a service

Note that from the definitions above, the service provided could be any service from any program. For the purposes of this chapter, the services will be information security services.

Once an organization makes the decision to proactively direct or control its information security activities (i.e., managing rather than practicing), an ISMS can be crafted. This is where we can borrow valuable lessons from, believe it or not, the discipline of packaging.

What are some typical functions of packaging?

- It presents the product to the end user in an appealing manner
- It protects the product during transport and storage
- It provides instructions on how to set up and use the product
- It informs the end user on where to turn for help

With these functions in mind, let us look at some common scenarios with "bad" packaging. Any parent who has been severely challenged as they attempted to assemble a child's new toy, will understand the impact of "bad" packaging.

|  | *Bad Packaging Example* | *Problem* |
|---|---|---|
| Appearance | Dingy box with no pictures or motivating text | No appeal to procure the product |
| Communication | Incoherent documentation | Message not getting across |
| Direction | Assembly instructions with no illustrations or insufficient detail | Inconsistency in assembly |
| Structure | Poorly labeled piece parts | Not clear what part is what |
| Packing | Damaged cartons | Missing or unusable piece parts |
| Feedback | Unresponsive/inadequate Customer support | No recourse |

* Note that organizations may choose to certify all or a reduced section of their environment.

Packaging has vastly improved over the years, although bad examples certainly still exist. In contrast, let us look at an organization that is well known for their packaging—the Swedish modular furniture merchandiser, IKEA.

| | IKEA Packaging | Result |
|---|---|---|
| Appearance | Pictures of the product in action and features list | Creation of desire and motivation |
| Communication | Documentation tailored to the audience in both proper language and content | Clear and unambiguous knowledge transfer |
| Direction | Clear instructions with sufficient detail to ensure success | Consistency in assembly |
| Structure | Each part clearly labeled, usually with a spare part or two just in case | No confusion regarding what goes where |
| Packing | Engineered cartons | Safe arrival of all piece parts |
| Feedback | Help desk | When all else fails, the ability to reach out for help |

Note how IKEA (and certainly others) have overcome traditional packaging problems and derived a marketing benefit, as well as usable products. Through the use of focus groups and customer feedback, their products are attractively packaged, with a high probability of customer satisfaction.

By now, you are probably saying to yourself, "What does this have to do with information security?" As a tactical initiative to manage a strategic information security program, an ISMS must

- Be supported by those that use or are bound by it
- Be easy to use and maintain for those that are affected
- Have a mechanism for stakeholder satisfaction

Returning to our packaging analogy, here are some typical "bad" packaging issues common in the security arena:

| | Management Example | Problem |
|---|---|---|
| Appearance | No benefit identified for stakeholders | No appeal to participate |
| Communication | Documentation written with inconsistent or inappropriate use of terminology | Message not getting across |
| Direction | No defined processes | Inconsistency in execution |
| Structure | Undefined taxonomy | Not clear what controls goes where and at what level of detail |
| Packing | Best practice ("best guess") based selection of controls | Inadequate or missing controls |
| Feedback | Unknown/undefined responsibilities | No accountability |

Here are some typical solutions enacting by nothing more than proper packaging of existing practices already being done by most information security organizations:

| | *ISMS Packaging* | *Result* |
|---|---|---|
| Appearance | The Service Delivery model provides for clear definition of benefits and can be integrated into the ITIL[a] service catalog | Services can be "marketed" within the organization with clearly defined benefits. In addition, service satisfaction can be measured |
| Communication | A glossary of terms assists in linguistic consistency | Clear communication |
| Direction | Defined and documented enterprise standards and processes | Clear direction at all levels as to what to do and how to do it |
| Structure | Well-defined documentation taxonomy | Identification of audiences and audience needs |
| Packing | Risk-based selection of controls | Defensible and measurable controls |
| Feedback | Clearly defined roles and responsibilities | Accountability |

[a] ITIL: Information Technology Infrastructure Library: Concepts and policies for managing information technology infrastructure, development, and operations.

Note how effective ISMS packaging has overcome traditional management problems and creates both stakeholder appeal, as well as tangible management benefits. Through the inclusion of stakeholders in a facilitated process, as well as attention to stakeholder feedback, the ISMS is both comprehensive and comprehensible, with a high probability of stakeholder satisfaction.

Standards such as the ISO 27001 and ISO 9001 intentionally specify only the requirements of a management system, and are implementation-neutral. ISMS implementations may therefore vary both in look and feel. Proper packaging, however, makes a huge contribution to success.

Once the decision is made to do more than practice information security, the next logical conclusion is to create an ISMS based upon the proven quality concepts embedded in ISO 27001. But not all management systems are created equal. Although an ISMS may meet the requirements of ISO 27001, proper packaging can make the difference between a "lip service" management system and a true management system that brings actual added value to the organization.

Then, and only then, will an organization yield the benefits as detailed below:

1. *Market differentiation*

   The ISO 27001 certification is accepted globally, and its adoption rate in the United States while still not comparable to some other nations, is on the rise.* Organizations, large and small, have felt increasing pressure from current customers, potential customers, and regulators, to adopt a defensible, risk-based ISMS, as opposed to abiding by the customary and

---

* See www.isocertificates.com for a complete listing of organizations who have attained the ISO 27001 certification.

vague reliance on "best practices" or other standards that are not specific to the discipline of information security, e.g., SAS 70 Type II. The effort involved in raising the maturity of the security program to a certifiable level is proof to clients and potential clients that your organization is actively maintaining its information security posture.

*Benefit*: The ability to stand apart from your competition. Attaining ISO 27001 certification means joining an exclusive group of companies and is a highly effective market differentiator for your company. Your competitors are most likely already looking at or moving toward ISO 27001 certification. You can get there first.

*Bottom line impact*:

a. Increased selling opportunities by offering a mature and capable ISMS, certified to an international standard.

b. A greater potential to land business where touting your company's security is a critical element, including opportunities to work with clients seeking to do business with a company that has a certified security program already in place.

2. *Proactive versus reactive security management*

ISO 27001 provides a set of criteria in the form of management system requirements and control objectives that are based on intelligent and risk-based practice from various industries and countries. Organizations can then use these criteria as the basis to determine what they should be doing to manage information security, and the flexibility to decide how. This allows the information security function to be proactive in developing, deploying, managing, and maintaining an information security program. Information security is no longer forced into a constant "fire-fighting" mode and the usual lack of efficiencies is avoided.

In turn, a proactive, defensible approach to information security yields a reduction in response effort to the rising volume of information security questionnaires that an organization receives from clients and potential clients. Given the increasingly cumbersome regulatory environment, detailed inquiries are often defended as "doing due diligence," even though such inquiries impose a significant time and workload burden on the receiving organization. However, with proactive security management, the organization has a ready answer to any and all security questions, and has no need to "reinvent the wheel" every time a new inquiry is received. Often, customers are willing to accept the ISO 27001 certification in lieu of answering lengthy and proprietary questionnaires. Further, security-conscious organizations are hesitant to provide detailed information regarding implemented controls; thus, a comprehensive response such as "We are ISO 27001 certified" is preferred.

*Benefit*: Holding an ISO 27001 certification is widely accepted proof of a reliable, defensible, standards-based information security posture. It confirms to both management and clients that your organization is proactively managing its security control responsibilities.

*Bottom line impact*: Reduced effort and time to respond to inquiries; shortening the sales cycle, and reducing the number of audit or review cycles, thereby increasing efficiencies.

3. *Information risk management*

ISO 27001, with its process-based and risk-driven approach, provides a mechanism to integrate information security into your company's overall risk management strategy. Using the common language of risk management, business executives can now be presented with information security in its proper context of asset protection and risk mitigation, without a need to explain the intricacies or jargon of the discipline.

*Benefit*: By making information security decisions on the defensible basis of risk management, the information security practitioner and business manager can employ a common terminology.

In addition, the information security function becomes more integrated with the organization as a whole.

*Bottom line impact*: Increased understanding and acceptance of the role of information security in the organization's overall risk management strategy.

4. *Time-based assurance*

   Adoption of the ISO standard requires implementation of an ongoing management component or "continuous process improvement." Organizations are required to not only identify what is in place now, but monitor, review, and change controls if the environment dictates such change. ISO 27001, like other ISO management standards, is based on the W. Edwards Deming model of *Plan, Do, Check, Act* (PDCA) to achieve continuous improvement.

   If your organization must respond to customer security inquiries, there is nearly always a requirement for annual renewal or periodic review. Once certified under ISO, the ISMS will be subject to annual surveillance audits and recertification every 3 years. These independent audits performed by the certifying authority offer proof to your management and your clients that the ISMS is operating in a satisfactory manner with continuous improvement.

   *Benefit*: ISO 27001 certification is a dynamic process, requiring at least annual audits and periodic renewal of the certification. This offers independent proof of ISMS adequacy and the ongoing benefit of continuous process improvement. It offers clients and management proof that the ISMS continues to meet due diligence.

   *Bottom line impact*:

   a. Proves to management that the program is operating effectively and has a positive return on investment.

   b. Reduces the effort to provide ongoing compliance assurance to customers and regulators.

5. *Process definition and metrics*

   Another benefit of ISO 27001 is its requirement to define information security services and the supporting processes. For some organizations, it will be the first time they have thoroughly addressed and defined the structure of their information security group. In other cases, the implementation of the standard yields defined process flows and assigned responsibilities for services delivered both to "customers" within the organization and for services delivered to information security by other parts of the organization, such as Information Technology, Human Resources, Audit and Legal Counsel. By defining processes, inputs, outputs, and responsibilities, the role of information security is emphasized and awareness is increased across the organization.

   Process definition also yields an unambiguous basis for security metrics. These metrics are essential to measure both the effectiveness of the program and its progress through the PDCA or continuous improvement cycle.

   *Benefit*: Management gains a clear window into the results of its security investment, and better insight info which security processes are working well and which need improvement. This increased visibility helps to make the case for the information security group and often can serve as a model for other parts of the organization.

   *Bottom line impact*: Concrete results and metrics help to justify security budgets. Better management understanding of the challenges and opportunities faced by the information security function leads potentially to both a larger role in the organization and the ability to at least sustain and possibly increase management funding. Moreover, metrics can be used to demonstrate opportunities to streamline processes and make more efficient use of available resources.

6. *Consistent third-party governance, risk, and compliance (GRC) management*

Consistency between internal and external parties is another challenge organizations face today, and the problem is only getting worse. How can you make sure that your requirements are being implemented, measured, managed, and communicated? Contract or service agreement language often does not address specific requirements for the preservation of information confidentiality, integrity, and availability. A supplier risk assessment or audit can check to see if security expectations are adequately met, but by itself, this activity does not communicate the actual requirements or criteria.

With an ISO 27001-based ISMS, third-party requirements, specifications, empowerment, and communication are an integral part of the system. These elements can then be provided to the third parties or service providers. What does this mean? It means that you can raise your level of assurance by knowing that the third parties are "on the same page" as your company. Suppliers are able to deliver services at desired levels and with processes and security measures which are defined, visible, and accountable to you.

*Benefit*: Clear communication of security requirements to third parties and scheduled periodic reviews of compliance with such requirements.

*Bottom line impact*: Third parties with a full understanding of requirements can provide more accurate pricing for services and are not "surprised" near the end of the contract process with unanticipated demands. Periodic compliance assessments become a scheduled part of third-party governance with specific, stated objectives and increased focus on defined remediation tasks where necessary.

7. *Legal and regulatory compliance*

The legal and regulatory environment is increasingly more rigorous, and unfortunately, increasingly more burdensome. Recently introduced law and regulation often requires a risk-based approach and informed-choice decision making to achieve compliance. Both of these qualities are inherent in an ISO 27001 ISMS, along with a defined responsibility for the Legal department to advise security of pending legislation. A risk-based, structured approach to security management, policies and standards, means accommodating shifts in the regulatory environment can often be accomplished as part of the normal review and update cycle rather than an ad hoc, reactive mode. When changes are required, they can be accomplished incrementally rather than as a major overhaul.

*Benefit*: The risk-based decision making inherent in an ISO 27001 ISMS means the system shares a common basis with many new legal requirements. Changes to the ISMS can be made in an orderly, incremental fashion.

*Bottom line impact*: Legal and regulatory compliance is accomplished through an ongoing change process, often using maintenance cycles rather than unplanned efforts or forced reaction. Disruption to the business is lessened, and compliance is achieved through simple alignment rather than repetitive and unplanned reengineering of security policies, standards, and practices.

8. *Defensibility*

ISO 27001 begins by requiring organizations to define a risk methodology, then to perform an assessment of their security practices based on this methodology. With the risk assessment in hand, information security and management together make informed choices regarding which controls must be applied, and justify these choices. The list of controls in Annex A of the standard are not simply "best practices" but rather a set of independent, reasoned choices formulated and signed off on by more than 170 countries. Within the context of the ISMS, each choice can be defended on the basis of evaluated risks and defined controls. There is no "gray area" and no reliance on individual interpretation of security practices, no matter how well intended.

*Benefit*: Referencing decision making to an independent standard and valid risk assessment means the organization can easily defend and justify its choices to management, customers, and regulators.

*Bottom line impact*: Using a defined and defensible set of information security controls means reduced effort and confusion in explaining security choices. This can shorten audit cycles and provide important reassurance to both management and clients that information security is based on informed-choice decisions, not just common practices.

## Conclusion

The future of assurance for information security and security risk management lies with the utilization of proactive frameworks, based upon internationally recognized standards. By providing defensible, risk-driven, and process-based information security practices in a manner that is packaged for success, the organization can achieve the following goals:

1. Increased ability to earn and maintain business from its customers
2. The ability to differentiate its services from those of its competitors
3. Speed to compliance in the legal and regulatory environment
4. Better alignment with management requirements and allotted resources
5. More comprehensive and ongoing governance over third-party services
6. Concrete metrics to justify security budgets

## About the Author

**Tom Carlson**, CISSP, is a principal consultant and ISMS practice lead for Information Security Management Systems (ISMS) and ISO 27001 certification.

# Chapter 10

# Achieving PCI DSS Compliance: A Compliance Review

Bonnie Goins Pilewski and Christopher A. Pilewski

## Contents

Government, corporate, and industry compliance has become a mainstay of business life for the world's population. This is due to the recognized need for secured operations, facilitated through the implementation of appropriate controls and governance mechanisms. This also includes security standards for corporations, such as the Payment Card Industry Data Security Standard (PCI DSS), sponsored by Visa. Details on the organization's Web site state that "beginning January 1, 2008, Visa will implement a series of mandates to eliminate the use of non-secure payment applications from the Visa payment system. These mandates require acquirers to ensure their merchants and agents do not use payment applications known to retain prohibited data elements and require the use of payment applications that adhere to Visa's Payment Application Best Practices (PABP). PABP-compliant applications help merchants and agents mitigate compromises, prevent storage of prohibited data and support overall compliance with the Payment Card Industry Data Security Standard (PCI DSS) and the *Visa U.S.A. Inc. Operating Regulations.*"

The purpose of this chapter is to educate the security practitioner in the field regarding PCI DSS compliance requirements (Standards). Information based on the international standards (i.e., ISO 17799/27002 and ISO 20000), best practices, and control frameworks (i.e., CobiT, NIST) is also provided in the discussion of the implementation of controls within the standard.

Security practitioners and organizations alike should take note that, while this chapter is targeted toward compliance with the PCI DSS, the recommendations for implementation detailed within could be expanded and used by the organization in building or enhancing its enterprise security program.

# Payment Card Industry Data Security Standard

*Requirement 1: Install and maintain a firewall configuration to protect cardholder data*
As stated in the PCI DSS version 1.2, "all systems must be protected from unauthorized access from untrusted networks, whether entering the system via the Internet as e-commerce, employees' Internet access through desktop browsers, employees' e-mail access, dedicated connection such as business to business connections, via wireless networks, or via other sources. Often, seemingly insignificant paths to and from untrusted networks can provide unprotected pathways into key systems. Firewalls are a key protection mechanism for any computer network."

The following components contribute to this requirement, as stated in Version 1.2 of the Standard:

Establish firewall and configuration standards (1.1): Components include the following: a formal change control process that ensures approval is obtained and testing occurs for all changes to the firewall configurations, including rulesets, and for network connections; a current network diagram, including wireless networks, is in place that represents the location of connections to cardholder data; firewalls present at the boundary between the zoned architecture, that is, firewalls in place at all Internet ingress/egress points and between perimeters of the DMZ, particularly at the boundary between the DMZ and cardholder systems and data; detailed information about the individuals and groups responsible for administration of cardholders systems and data; a full formal and documented business justification for open ports and services; and the requirement for formal and documented review of all firewall configurations and rulesets every 6 months.

Build a firewall configuration that restricts connections between untrusted networks, i.e., external and any system components in the cardholder data environment (1.2): Components include the following: the restriction of both inbound and outbound traffic to only that which is necessary for the environment; ensure that router configuration files are properly secured and synchronized; and implement perimeter firewalls between any wireless networks and allow only the traffic required for the cardholder environment, denying all other traffic.

Prohibit direct public access between the Internet and any system component in the cardholder data environment (1.3): Components include the following: implement a DMZ to restrict protocols traveling from the public zone (i.e., the Internet) to the secured zone (i.e., cardholder data is present); restrict public traffic to the DMZ only (i.e., public access to the secured zone is prohibited); prohibit any direct routes between the public zone and the secured zone; prohibit the passing of internal addresses from the public zone to the DMZ; outbound traffic from the secured zone must pass through IP addresses in the DMZ only (i.e., no direct outbound traffic from the secured zone to the public zone is allowed); implement stateful inspection (i.e., dynamic packet filtering); locate any databases containing cardholder data in the secured area; implement IP masquerading (i.e., NAT, PAT) to prevent internal IP addresses from being exposed to the public zone.

Install personal firewall software on any mobile and/or employee-owned computers with direct connectivity to the Internet (for example, laptops used by employees), which are used to access the organization's network (1.4): This component ensures that mobile and computing devices, particularly those not within control of the organization, maintain at minimum the same level of protection as organizational assets.

## Change Control and Configuration Management

The foundation for the implementation of robust change control and configuration management processes must start with formal, documented, and approved policies, standards, and procedures detailing the processes. The practitioner may wish to use ISO 20000 or IT Infrastructure Library (ITIL) practices to build an internal change control and configuration management capability. It is important to note that provisions for emergency changes must also be formally documented and approved by senior management.

Implementation guidance for this effort can be found in Section 9 (Control processes) of the Code of Practice for Information Technology Service Management (ISO 20000-2).

*Requirement 2: Do not use vendor-supplied defaults for system passwords and other security parameters*
As stated in version 1.2 of the PCI DSS, "Malicious individuals (external and internal to a company) often use vendor default passwords and other vendor default settings to compromise systems.

These passwords and settings are well known by hacker communities and are easily determined via public information."

The following components contribute to this requirement, as stated in Version 1.2 of the Standard:

Default passwords provided by hardware and software vendors must always be changed by the organization (2.1): Components include the following: all default settings in wireless networks must be changed and strong encryption for authentication and transmission must be implemented.

Standards configurations must be developed for all cardholder system components (2.2): Components include the following: all cardholder systems must be dedicated, with the data segregated; disable all unnecessary ports, services, and functions on cardholder systems; ensure security functions are enabled on cardholder systems to prevent unauthorized use.

Encrypt all access to cardholder systems that is not performed directly at the console (2.3). This ensures that data streams cannot be read by unauthorized persons or systems.

If cardholder systems are collocated with a shared hosting provider, the organization must meet requirements as dictated by Visa. In particular, cardholder systems and data must be segregated from other systems at the collocation (2.4). This ensures that the confidentiality and integrity of cardholder data are not breached by unauthorized persons or systems.

*Requirement 3: Protect stored cardholder data*

As stated in version 1.2 of the PCI DSS, "Protection methods such as encryption, truncation, masking, and hashing are critical components of cardholder data protection. If an intruder circumvents other network security controls and gains access to encrypted data, without the proper cryptographic keys, the data is unreadable and unusable to that person. Other effective methods of protecting stored data should be considered as potential risk mitigation opportunities. For example, methods for minimizing risk include not storing cardholder data unless absolutely necessary."

The following components contribute to this requirement, as stated in Version 1.2 of the Standard:

Keep cardholder data storage to a minimum. Develop a data retention and disposal policy. Limit storage amount and retention time to that which is required for business, legal, and/or regulatory purposes, as documented in the data retention policy (3.1). This will ensure that cardholder data can be properly maintained and protected by the organization.

Authentication data must not be stored after authorization, regardless of the protection mechanisms used (3.2). Components include the following: storing the full contents of any of the magnetic strip data from the card is strictly prohibited; the card verification code (CVC) or value (CVV) may not be stored in any media post-authentication; storage of the personal identification number (PIN) or encrypted PIN block is strictly prohibited.

Account numbers (PAN) must be masked when displayed (3.3). This ensures that the account number will not be accidentally divulged to unauthorized persons through shoulder surfing.

The PAN must not be readable when stored (3.4). Components include the following: in the event disk encryption is used to protect the PAN, the decryption keys cannot be tied to a user or system account.

Cryptographic keys must be protected against disclosure and/or misuse (3.5). Components include the following: keys must be restricted to as few custodians as possible; keys must be securely stored while in use and in escrow.

Ensure that all policies, standards, procedures, and processes for key generation, key distribution, key management, implementation, storage, revocation and escrow are formally documented and implemented (3.6), to include acknowledgement of responsibility for these functions.

*Requirement 4: Encrypt transmission of cardholder data across open, public networks*
As stated in version 1.2 of the PCI DSS, "Sensitive information must be encrypted during transmission over networks that are easily accessed by malicious individuals. Misconfigured wireless networks and vulnerabilities in legacy encryption and authentication protocols can be continued targets of malicious individuals who exploit these vulnerabilities to gain privileged access to cardholder data environments."

The following components contribute to this requirement, as stated in Version 1.2 of the Standard:

During transmission of cardholder data over an open and/or public network, strong encryption and security protocols must be used (4.1). This includes transmission from wireless networks.

Account numbers must never be sent unencrypted over any medium (4.2).

*Requirement 5: Use and regularly update antivirus software or programs*
As stated in version 1.2 of the PCI DSS, "Malicious software, commonly referred to as "malware"—including viruses, worms, and Trojans—enters the network during many business approved activities including employees' e-mail and use of the Internet, mobile computers, and storage devices, resulting in the exploitation of system vulnerabilities. Anti-virus software must be used on all systems commonly affected by malware to protect systems from current and evolving malicious software threats."

The following components contribute to this requirement, as stated in Version 1.2 of the Standard:

Implement antivirus software on all systems that house cardholder data (5.1): ensure that these programs can detect, recover, and protect against all malware.

Ensure that all installed antivirus software is activated, running effectively and is generating audit logs (5.2).

*Requirement 6: Develop and maintain secure systems and applications*
As stated in version 1.2 of the PCI DSS, "Unscrupulous individuals use security vulnerabilities to gain privileged access to systems. Many of these vulnerabilities are fixed by vendor-provided security patches, which must be installed by the entities that manage the systems. All critical systems must have the most recently released, appropriate software patches to protect against exploitation and compromise of cardholder data by malicious individuals and malicious software."

The following components contribute to this requirement, as stated in Version 1.2 of the Standard:

Ensure that all systems holding cardholder data are patched as required, with critical patches installed no later than 30 days after issuance (6.1). This will assist in ensuring that exposures are corrected within operating systems and applications.

Build a vulnerability assessment process (6.2). This will help the organization to continue to identify exposure (vulnerabilities) as they exist in the organization's network, infrastructure, applications, and physical facilities.

Develop software in accordance with the Software Development Lifecycle (SDLC), industry best practices and the PCI DSS (6.3). Components include the following: testing of all security patches, to include validation of input, error handling, secure cryptographic mechanisms, secure communications and role-based access control implementation; separation of test and development environments, as well as administration and use of these environments; the use of test data only (no live account numbers) for testing in the development/test environment; segregation of administration of these environments; and the removal of any test data prior to going live with the systems or updates; removal of any custom items introduced into the code prior to production; review of the source code for any vulnerabilities.

Implement change control procedures to any system components (6.4), including documentation of impact, senior management approval, testing, and a formal back-out plan.

Develop all code based on secure coding standards, such as those present in the OWASP standards (6.5), including, cross-site scripting (XSS), injections, malicious code execution, information data leakage, unsecure direct object references, cross site request forgery, broken authentication management, unsecure cryptographic access and communications, and failure to restrict URL access.

Establish vulnerability assessment methods for applications (6.6); this will assist the organization in performing a comprehensive vulnerability management review.

*Requirement 7: Restrict access to cardholder data by business need to know*

As stated in version 1.2 of the PCI DSS, "To ensure critical data can only be accessed by authorized personnel, systems and processes must be in place to limit access based on need to know and according to job responsibilities. "Need to know" is defined as the case when access rights are granted to only the least amount of data and privileges needed to perform a job."

The following components contribute to this requirement, as stated in Version 1.2 of the Standard:

Limit access to cardholder systems and data to those with "need-to-know" (7.1). Limits to access include limited access to privileged accounts (i.e., administrator accounts), assignment of permissions based on role, authorization for receiving permission to access an organization's resources and the implementation of software to assist with provisioning access control.

Establish control of systems that have multiple users based on users' need to know (7.2) and include coverage of system components, assignment of access based on role, and setting a "deny-all" default setting.

*Requirement 8: Assign a unique id to each person with computer access*

As stated in version 1.2 of the PCI DSS, "Assigning a unique identification (ID) to each person with access ensures that each individual is uniquely accountable for his or her actions. When such accountability is in place; actions taken on critical data and systems are performed by, and can be traced to, known and authorized users."

The following components contribute to this requirement, as stated in Version 1.2 of the Standard:

All users must have a unique user ID to log into cardholder data and systems (8.1).

Along with this ID, a user must also have either a password or two-factor authentication mechanisms to assist with login (8.2).

Incorporate two-factor authentication for remote access (network-level access originating from outside the network) to the network by employees, administrators, and third parties (8.3).

Render all passwords unreadable in storage and transmission through the use of strong encryption (8.4).

Ensure proper user authentication and password management is implemented for non-consumer users and administrators on all system components (8.5)

*Requirement 9: Restrict physical access to cardholder data*

As stated in version 1.2 of the PCI DSS, "Any physical access to data or systems that house cardholder data provides the opportunity for individuals to access devices or data and to remove systems or hardcopies, and should be appropriately restricted."

The following components contribute to this requirement, as stated in Version 1.2 of the Standard:

Facility entry controls should be used as a means to restrict and monitor traffic into and out of facilities containing cardholder systems and data (9.1). Components include the following: use of properly placed video cameras to record traffic; restriction on the use of publicly available network jacks; restriction of the use of handheld devices and wireless networks.

Create, implement, maintain, monitor and enforce policies, standards and procedures for visitors (9.2). This allows the organization to promote a process for tracking visitors to facilities, particularly those which contain cardholder systems or data.

Ensure that visits are properly processed (9.3). Components include the following: ensure visitors are authorized; ensure visitors are given a badge to wear during the entire time on the site; ensure that visitors are asked to return the badge prior to leaving the facility.

Implement a manual or automated visitor log to "check in" visitors to the facility (9.4). Information captured should include name, company/title, escort, time in, and time out. Logs should be retained for at least 3 months.

Backups of media should be securely stored, preferably at an offsite location such as the organization's collocation site for business continuity (9.5).

Any media, be it electronic or paper, must be securely stored if it contains cardholder data (9.6).

Maintain control over all media distribution (i.e., both internal and external) (9.7). This includes media classification so it can be properly handled and transporting the media by trusted courier.

Management must approve any move of cardholder data from its secured location (9.8).

Storage of and access to cardholder data must be strictly controlled (9.9). The maintenance of data inventory logs facilitates this process.

Cardholder data and media must be destroyed when no longer required for business purposes. Hardcopy materials should be appropriately shredded, burned, or made into pulp to render the data unreadable. Electronic data must likewise be rendered unreadable through permanent wiping or full media destruction, as appropriate.

*Requirement 10: Track and monitor all access to network resources and cardholder data*

As stated in version 1.2 of the PCI DSS, "Logging mechanisms and the ability to track user activities are critical in preventing, detecting, or minimizing the impact of a data compromise. The presence of logs in all environments allows thorough tracking, alerting, and analysis when something does go wrong. Determining the cause of a compromise is very difficult without system activity logs."

The following components contribute to this requirement, as stated in Version 1.2 of the Standard:

Implement a process that links an individual user to administrative permissions (10.1) so that these individuals can be tracked and held accountable for any access violations correctly attributed to them.

Implement automated audit trails (10.2) that track: individual access to cardholder systems and data; monitor all audit trails from administrative-level users; track all audit log access; the use of authentication and identification mechanisms; initialization of audit logs; and creation and deletion of system-level objects.

Record audit trail entries for all system components for each event (10.3). Include user identification, date and time, type of event, success or failure indication, the origin of event, and the identity (or name) of the affected resource.

Synchronize all critical system clocks and times (10.4).

Secure audit trails against tampering (10.5).

Review all logs for system component issues at least once per day (10.6).

Retain the audit trail for at least 1 year, with 3 months present for review and analysis (10.7).

*Requirement 11: Regularly test security systems and processes*
As stated in version 1.2 of the PCI DSS, "Vulnerabilities are being discovered continually by malicious individuals and researchers, and being introduced by new software. System components, processes, and custom software should be tested frequently to ensure security controls continue to reflect a changing environment."

The following components contribute to this requirement, as stated in Version 1.2 of the Standard:

Perform wireless network vulnerability assessments at least quarterly (11.1) to determine exposures present in the environment; if this is not possible, implement a wireless IDS/IPS and follow the monitoring processes mentioned prior in this Standard.

Run internal and external network vulnerability scans at least quarterly or whenever there is a change in the network status (11.2) to determine exposures present in the environment.

Perform internal and external network and application penetration testing at least quarterly or whenever a significant change is introduced into the network to determine exposures present in the environment (11.3).

Monitor all network traffic with intrusion detection or intrusion prevention systems to alert authorized persons of any issues with traffic or intrusion (11.4).

Deploy file integrity software that alerts authorized parties of tampering with cardholder files and data (11.5). Ensure that file comparisons are performed at least weekly.

*Requirement 12: Maintain a policy that addresses information security for employees and contractors*
As stated in version 1.2 of the PCI DSS, "A strong security policy sets the security tone for the whole company and informs employees what is expected of them. All employees should be aware of the sensitivity of data and their responsibilities for protecting it. For the purposes of this requirement, "employees" refers to full-time and part-time employees, temporary employees and personnel, and contractors and consultants who are "resident" on the company's site."

The following components contribute to this requirement, as stated in Version 1.2 of the Standard:

Create, implement, maintain, monitor and enforce a formal and documented security policy which addresses PCI DSS concerns, requires a threat, risk and vulnerability assessment and includes a review at least once per year or when the environment changes (12.1).

Create, implement, maintain, monitor and enforce formal and documented standards and procedures which operationalize the security policy (12.2). Ensure there is a provision for review and update of the deliverables at least annually or when there is a change to the environment.

Create, implement, maintain, monitor and enforce formal and documented appropriate use policies for the technologies used with cardholder systems and data (12.3). This includes formal and documented management approval, authentication for technology use, a list of all devices and authorized users, labeling of devices with the owner, his or her contact information and the purpose of the device, acceptable use and network location, a list of approved products, automatic disconnection from remote access after a prescribed period of discontinued use, activation of vendor products for remote maintenance only when needed to perform the job function.

Prohibit the download of cardholder data to local machines or mobile devices (12.4) when connecting remotely.

Assign security responsibilities to an owner (12.5), to include creation, implementation, maintenance, monitoring and enforcement of a formal and documented security policy; the monitoring and subsequent analysis of security alerts, as well as distribution to the proper resource(s); creation, implementation, maintenance, monitoring and enforcement of a formal and documented incident management and reporting plan; administration of user accounts; monitoring and controlling of all access to cardholder data.

Create, implement and maintain a security awareness training program (12.6) that is presented to resources at last annually and is formally acknowledged by all staff and contractors.

Perform employee background checks on all staff working with cardholder data and systems (12.7).

If cardholder data is shared with a service provider (12.8), prepare a list of all service providers, maintain a formal and documented service-level agreement for cardholder systems and data, ensure vendors are screened to determine if they are appropriate to task and develop a formal and documented program to monitor service from the vendor.

Create, implement, maintain, monitor and enforce a formal and documented incident response plan (12.9), in order to be prepared for internal or external attacks.

# Implementing Controls for PCI DSS Compliance

## Approvals (Control Process)

Approvals can be completed and documented through the use of either an automated workflow process or a manual review cycle. Proper documentation includes authorized signature on the configuration itself or on a cover sheet that is attached to the requirement or change control deliverables. An archived and/or electronic copy of the approval should be securely maintained for future use. This recommendation can be used for all areas of the PCI DSS which require such approvals.

## Leadership (Section 6, ISO 27002)

Assignment of accountable senior management for completion of PCI compliance is critical to the organization's success. While it is not mandatory that the same resource be dedicated throughout the life of the compliance initiative, dedication provides continuity and stability to this important initiative. Formal documentation of the assignment, along with signatures from senior management, should be completed as part of this compliance objective.

## Exceptions (Section 5, ISO 27002)

While it is advisable to construct policies, standards, procedures, plans and programs such that they may govern the organization's PCI compliance function without the need for exceptions, it is clear that an exception over time may be required. The organization should implement a formal and documented exception process that is followed for every exception requested. Information documenting the exception should, at minimum, include

Requestor
Department
Date of request
Affected policy deliverable
Scope of the exception
Reason for the exception request
Documentation to support the need for the exception
Signature of departmental manager indicating the exception has been reviewed and is authorized by departmental management

Approval from senior management prior to authorizing the exception and noting it in the policy deliverable

The exception process should itself be reviewed annually, approved by senior management and updated as required.

## Cyber Security Policy (Section 5, 27002)

Paramount to communicating expectations to staff, business partners and third parties is the creation of a comprehensive security policy, relative to people, process, data, technology, and facilities. The policy should encompass all identified areas of the Code of Practice for Information Security Management (ISO 17799/27002).

Sample policies are available in abundance on the Web, covering a variety of topics. Policies are communication of management expectations and should not, therefore, detail how to perform a function; this is left to procedural documentation. A policy should contain, at minimum

Introduction or background
Purpose
Scope
Definitions
Policy statement
References, including corresponding policies, standards, and procedures
Information on the version and effective dates
Approval by senior management

It is important to note that processes for implementation, maintenance (including annual review and update), monitoring for effectiveness and enforcement must also be considered and, if implemented, reviewed, and updated at least annually.

## Asset Management (Section 7, 27002)

In its truest sense, asset management surrounds the data (information) classification effort within the organization, as it applies to cardholder information assets. Once classification is completed, proper controls must be applied to protect the information. The implementation guidance from ISO 27002, Section 7 (Asset Management) can assist the organization in building an appropriate classification scheme and performing the assessment of information assets. Policies for proper labeling and handling, based on the classification, should be included either in the security policy or implemented as a stand-alone policy requirement. Formal and documented standards and procedures should also be created, approved by senior management and implemented. Note that all this documentation will also require maintenance, monitoring, and enforcement.

In terms of applying controls to the assets for the purposes of protection, there are a number of frameworks, in addition to the ISO standards, that can be used to determine a desired control set for PCI compliance. Controls detailed in the CobiT framework, as well as controls described in NIST Special Publication 800:53A, will give the organization a control set from which to select its protections. Once controls are selected, they should be formally documented, planned, approved by senior management and applied to the assets.

## *Awareness (Section 8, ISO 27002)*

Periodic security awareness training within an organization can be accomplished through a variety of means, including formalized in-class and computer-based training. Regardless of the method selected, a formalized and documented approach should be implemented. A good reference for the building of this program is available through NIST Special Publication 800:50. It is important to note that, in this case, awareness training must be provided for all staff with PCI responsibilities and/or access to PCI data.

## *Training (Section 8, ISO 27002)*

The same methodology as mentioned above can be used for the completion of a PCI training program for affected staff. Content will vary, as the purpose of this training program is to socialize staff with the requirements for PCI compliance and to establish their roles in the compliance objective.

## *Personnel Risk Assessment (Sections 4 and 8, ISO 27002)*

All staff with access to PCI data and/or systems must be assessed for risk prior to the granting of access to these systems. There are a variety of methods for performance of this objective; it is advisable for the resource or team performing this function to enlist the help of the Human Resources and Facilities departments to complete this requirement.

Access control considerations for this part of the PCI standard have been discussed earlier in this chapter.

## *Physical Access Controls (Section 9, ISO 27002)*

Organizations are required to document, implement, and operate controls for the provision of physical access to cardholder systems and data. Acceptable controls for physical access include

Proximity cards
Security personnel, such as a guard contingent, centralized operations center and so on
Specialty locks (magnetic remote access control locks, mantraps, and restricted access locks)
Devices that promote two-factor authentication, such as biometric devices, tokens, and so on

Implementation guidelines for this work can be reviewed in Section 9 (Physical and Environmental Security) of the Code of Practice for Information Security Management (ISO 17799 (27002)), NIST Special Publications 800:53A, 800:39, DS5: Ensure Systems Security, DS12: Manage the Physical Environment (CobiT).

## *Monitoring Physical Access (Section 9, ISO 27002)*

Physical access to cardholder systems and data must be continuously monitored ($24 \times 7 \times 365$). Monitoring should include both automated controls, such as alarm systems, and human controls, such as review of physical access points by PCI cleared personnel. Monitoring should be formal and documented.

Implementation guidelines for this work can be reviewed in Section 9 (Physical and Environmental Security) and Section 10 (Communications and Operations Management) of the Code of Practice for Information Security Management (ISO 17799 (27002)), NIST Special Publications 800:53A, 800:39, DS5: Ensure Systems Security, DS12: Manage the Physical Environment (CobiT).

## Logging Physical Access (Section 9, ISO 27002)

Physical access to PCI secured areas must be logged. Acceptable methods for logging include

Automated logging, such as those produced by use of proximity cards
Camera/DVR recording of entrance to and exit from the PCI physical access points
Manual review of visitor logs, recordings, and log files generated by automated means
Logging must identify the individual gaining access and the time of access. Logging must be performed 24 × 7 × 365.

Implementation guidelines for this work can be reviewed in Section 9 (Physical and Environmental Security) and Section 10 (Communications and Operations Management) of the Code of Practice for Information Security Management (ISO 17799 (27002)), NIST Special Publications 800:53A, 800:39, DS5: Ensure Systems Security, DS12: Manage the Physical Environment (CobiT).

## Disposal or Redeployment (Section 9, 27002)

Requirements in this area of the PCI standards mandate that cardholder systems set for either disposal or redeployment undergo the permanent removal of PCI information from the system. The processes must be formally documented. In addition, records of removal must be maintained for these systems.

Implementation guidelines for this work can be reviewed in Section 9.2.6 (Secure disposal or reuse of equipment) of the Code of Practice for Information Security Management (ISO 17799 (27002)), NIST Special Publications 800:53A, 800:39 and DS12: Manage the physical environment (CobiT).

## Maintenance and Testing (Section 9, ISO 27002)

In order to determine that PCI physical access controls are implemented properly and are operating effectively, they must be tested and maintained. This testing and maintenance cycle cannot exceed 1 year. Any records related to outages must be retained for a minimum of 1 year from the outage.

Implementation guidelines for this work can be reviewed in Section 9 (Physical and Environmental Security) of the Code of Practice for Information Security Management (ISO 17799 (27002)), NIST Special Publications 800:53A, 800:39, DS5: Ensure Systems Security, DS12: Manage the Physical Environment (CobiT).

## Electronic Security Perimeter (Section 10, ISO 27002)

In any secure architecture, creation of zones is essential to ensure that assets requiring heightened protection are segmented off from more public-facing areas of the network. In addition, the secured zone will often receive expanded control implementation. Paramount to this activity for PCI DSS is the segmentation of cardholder systems and data from non-cardholder systems and data.

When the architecture has been implemented, a detailed network diagram should be completed to accurately reflect the zones, including assets and access points to those zones.

Implementation guidelines for access control can be obtained from Section 10 (Communications and Operations Security and Section 11 (Access Control) of the Code of Practice for Information Security Management (ISO 17799 (27002)), NIST Special Publications 800:53A, 800:39 and DS-5: Ensure Systems Security (CobiT).

## Monitoring Electronic Access (Sections 10, 11, and 12, ISO 27002)

For the purposes of this section, monitoring refers to the tracking of unauthorized access into the electronic security perimeter, through access points to the network and to dialups using non-routable protocols. Implementation of monitoring tools that provide automated alerts is highly desirable; however, it is equally important that logs generated by the monitoring are periodically and formally reviewed by skilled staff. This function can also be outsourced, should the organization desire. At minimum, network-based monitoring must be undertaken; however, the organization may also opt to conduct host-based monitoring as a part of this effort.

Implementation guidelines for this work can be reviewed in Section 10.10 (Monitoring) of the Code of Practice for Information Security Management (ISO 17799 (27002)), NIST Special Publications 800:53A, 800:39, DS5: Ensure Systems Security, ME1: Monitor and Evaluate IT Performance and ME2: Monitor and Evaluate Internal Control (CobiT).

## Cyber Vulnerability Assessment (Sections 10 and 12, ISO 27002)

In order to determine whether PCI assets are appropriately protected, a technical vulnerability assessment must be performed at least annually on these assets. It is also highly recommended that the organization perform both internal and external technical security assessments for this effort. A baseline PCI assessment could include

Network discovery, using tools such as IPSonar, Nmap, others
Discovery of all access points to the secure (PCI) zone, using tools such as Internet Scanner
Port and services scanning, using tools such as ISS and Microsoft Baseline Analyzer
Scanning for default accounts and passwords, using tools such as Dumpsec
Password cracking, using tools such as John the Ripper, Cain, and Abel
Scanning SNMP community strings, using tools such as Internet Scanner
Configuration reviews (manual process) of network devices, servers and workstations, as included in the PCI assets for the organization (automated or manual)
Any additional assessments services desired by the organization (such as social engineering, penetration testing using tools such as Metasploit, application security testing using tools such as AppScan, and so on)

Post-assessment, the results of the assessment, along with a description of the method for conducting the assessment, must be formally documented and presented to the organization for review and comment, as appropriate. The National Security Agency Information Assurance Method (NSA IAM) and NSA Information Evaluation Method (NSA IEM) are good examples of a unified assessment system; information on this method is publicly available at the NSA Web site.

Guidelines for this work can be reviewed in Section 12.6 (Technical Vulnerability Management) of the Code of Practice for Information Security Management (ISO 17799 (27002)), NIST

Special Publications 800:53A, 800:39, DS5: Ensure Systems Security, PO9: Assess and Manage IT Risks (CobiT) and Section 6.6.3 (Security Risk Assessment Practices) in the Code of Practice for Information Technology Service Management (ISO 20000-2).

### Test Procedures (Section 10, ISO 27002)

It is imperative that any changes to systems containing cardholder data are tested to ensure that they do not adversely impact operations or any other system. These include configuration changes, such as the implementation of security patches, service packs, operating system upgrades, and so on. Formalized and documented test procedures are required for compliance in this area. All testing performed must reflect the production environment for the PCI.

Implementation guidelines for this work can be reviewed in Section 10 (Communications and Operations Management) of the Code of Practice for Information Security Management (ISO 17799 (27002)), NIST Special Publications 800:53A, 800:39, DS4: Ensure Continuous Service, DS5: Ensure Systems Security, DS9: Manage the Configuration (CobiT).

### Ports and Services (Section 10, ISO 27002)

In order to secure systems appropriately, the "hardening" of hosts must be completed. This entails the disabling of ports and services that are unnecessary for normal or emergency operations. If it is not possible to disable a port or service due to technical infeasibility or for business reasons, it is necessary to implement compensating controls to provide the same level of protection as would be achieved through disabling of the port or service.

Implementation guidelines for this work can be reviewed in Section 10 (Communications and Operations Management) of the Code of Practice for Information Security Management (ISO 17799 (27002)), NIST Special Publications 800:53A, 800:39, DS4: Ensure Continuous Service, DS5: Ensure Systems Security, DS9: Manage the Configuration (CobiT) and Section 9 (Control processes) of the Code of Practice for Information Technology Service Management (ISO 20000-2).

### Security Patch Management (Section 10, ISO 27002)

This objective requires the organization to evaluate relevant security patches for applicability and implement them as appropriate. In the event that an organization decides not to implement a relevant patch, it must formally document the justification for doing so and indicate the compensating controls put in place to protect the PCI assets.

Implementation guidelines for this work can be reviewed in Section 10 (Communications and Operations Management) of the Code of Practice for Information Security Management (ISO 17799 (27002)), NIST Special Publications 800:53A, 800:39, DS4: Ensure Continuous Service, DS5: Ensure Systems Security, DS9: Manage the Configuration (CobiT) and Section 9 (Control processes) of the Code of Practice for Information Technology Service Management (ISO 20000-2).

### Malicious Software Prevention (Section 10, ISO 27002)

PCI assets must be protected from viruses and malicious code. Antivirus and malicious software tools must be implemented as a result. If for any reason the tools cannot be implemented, the organization must document compensating controls that provide the required protection for the assets.

Implementation guidelines for this work can be reviewed in Section 10 (Communications and Operations Management) of the Code of Practice for Information Security Management (ISO 17799 (27002)), NIST Special Publications 800:53A, 800:39 and DS5: Ensure Systems Security.

## Security Status Monitoring (Section 10, ISO 27002)

Monitoring in this area of the PCI standards is related to the monitoring of systems versus the network. This is referred to as security event monitoring. This monitoring is typically performed in the server and workstation environments. Event logs can be sent to an aggregated log server for easier review and maintenance. Dependent upon the operating system, this can be done with or without an additional software package for log forwarding. This work can be performed in-house or outsourced. The organization must document the approach, implement automated alerting where possible (manual where not) and ensure that logs generated are securely stored for 90 days, with the exception of logs documenting reportable incidents, which must be securely stored based on the organization's retention policy for incidents.

Implementation guidelines for this work can be reviewed in Section 10.10 (Monitoring) of the Code of Practice for Information Security Management (ISO 17799 (27002)), NIST Special Publications 800:53A, 800:39 and DS5: Ensure Systems Security (CobiT).

## Access Control (Section 11, ISO 27002)

Access control for PCI should include considerations not only for electronic access control, but for physical access control as well. As a foundation, formal and documented policies, standards and procedures for performance of this work should be completed and approved by senior management. The policies may be incorporated into the security policy or may appear as stand-alone policies, as desired. In addition, processes performed must be formally detailed and approved as well. At a minimum, the following processes should be included:

The process for determination and assignment of permissions to staff with need-to-know for PCI compliance

The process for creation, implementation, maintenance (including periodic review), and monitoring of access control lists for both electronic access and physical access to PCI assets

The process for periodic of review and update of electronic and physical access lists

The processes for provisioning of electronic and physical access, preferably based upon role (RBAC), including management authorization

The processes for deprovisioning of electronic and physical access, including management authorization

The processes for creation and assignment of access control mechanisms (such as proximity cards, tokens or fobs, and so on)

The processes for third-party electronic and physical access

Inputs to these processes would likely come from Human Resources (relative to role assignment, which is typically based upon job function or description), Facilities and Corporate Security (physical access).

This requirement also reflects the need for proper control of access, through implementation of protections and configuration management. In particular, the organization should ensure that network devices, such as firewalls, are configured with rules that implicitly deny and explicit allow; ports and services that are not necessary for job function are disabled; appropriate use banners are implemented on PCI assets; and that protections implemented are formally documented.

Implementation guidelines for access control can be obtained from Section 11 (Access Control) of the Code of Practice for Information Security Management (ISO 17799(27002)), NIST Special Publications 800:53A, 800:39 and DS-5: Ensure Systems Security (CobiT).

### Account Management (Section 11, ISO 27002)

While this objective shares commonality with the Access Control requirements mentioned prior in the chapter, there are additional requirements to be met for Account Management. The previous Access control section delineated the need for a formal and documented provisioning process to be carried out by authorized personnel. The same is true for meeting this compliance objective. In addition, there is a stated need to perform a review of access, at least annually, in a formal and documented fashion. Formal procedures should be documented to detail mechanisms for performing this review.

The requirements for handling of shared, generic, and vendor default passwords are also noted here. Where possible, these passwords must be changed to a unique, strong password. If there is a business justification or technical infeasibility, it must be demonstrated that there are compensating controls to address this issue and to protect PCI assets. Note that a policy for password maintenance is required for PCI compliance.

Implementation guidelines for this work can be reviewed in Section 11 (Access Control) of the Code of Practice for Information Security Management (ISO 17799 (27002)), NIST Special Publications 800:53A, 800:39 and DS5: Ensure Systems Security.

### Cyber Security Incident Response Plan (Section 13, ISO 27002)

The Incident Response Plan must minimally include

Procedures to help to differentiate among PCI events, incidents, and reportable security incidents

Identification of the PCI Incident Response Team, along with documentation of the members' responsibilities

Formal documentation of PCI incident handling procedures, and communication plans.

A formal and documented process for reporting all security incidents.

Formal and documented process for updating the Incident Response Plan.

Formal and documented process for an (at least) annual review of the Incident Response Plan

Formal and documented process for (at least) annual testing of the Incident Response Plan is required, to include at least a desktop drill, a full simulation exercise, and, if possible, the response to an actual security incident.

Implementation guidelines for this work can be reviewed in Section 13 (Information Security Incident Management) of the Code of Practice for Information Security Management (ISO 17799 (27002)), Section 8 (Resolution processes) of the Code of Practice for Information Technology Service Management (ISO 20000-2), NIST Special Publications 800:53A, 800:39, DS5: Ensure Systems Security, DS8: Manage the Service Desk and Incidents and DS10: Manage Problems (CobiT).

## Recovery Plans (Section 14, ISO 27002)

A recovery plan (i.e., Business Continuity Plan) is required for all PCI assets. This Plan must be reviewed at least annually. This Plan must include specific actions for disasters, based on both severity and duration of the disaster, as well as responsibilities for those personnel affected by the Plan.

Implementation guidelines for this work can be reviewed in Section 14 (Business Continuity Practices) of the Code of Practice for Information Security Management (ISO 17799 (27002)), The Code of Practice for Business Continuity Management (BS 25999-1), NIST Special Publications 800:53A, 800:39, DS4: Ensure Continuous Service, DS10: Manage Problems and DS11: Manage Data (CobiT).

## Exercises (Section 14, ISO 27002)

A formal and documented process for (at least) annual testing of the Recovery Plan is required, to include at least a desktop drill, a full simulation exercise, and, if possible, the documented response to an actual disaster.

Implementation guidelines for this work can be reviewed in Section 14 (Business Continuity Management) of the Code of Practice for Information Security Management (ISO 17799 (27002)), The Code of Practice for Business Continuity Management (BS 25999-1), NIST Special Publications 800:53A, 800:39, DS4: Ensure Continuous Service, DS10: Manage Problems and DS11: Manage Data (CobiT).

## Plan Maintenance (Section 14, ISO 27002)

Any lessons learned as a result of a recovery should be incorporated into the Recovery Plan. This information should be added to the Recovery Plan in such a way that information which is still viable is preserved. Changes must be communicated to staff, either through formal training or by computer-based means.

Implementation guidelines for this work can be reviewed in Section 14 (Business Continuity Practices) of the Code of Practice for Information Security Management (ISO 17799 (27002)), The Code of Practice for Business Continuity Management (BS 25999-1), NIST Special Publications 800:53A, 800:39, DS4: Ensure Continuous Service, DS10: Manage Problems and DS11: Manage Data (CobiT).

## Backup and Restore (Section 14, ISO 27002)

Processes and procedures for backups and restores must be formally documented. It is also advisable to test these procedures to ensure they correctly capture these critical functions. Any documentation contributing to this work could also be included in this requirement.

Implementation guidelines for this work can be reviewed in Section 14 (Business Continuity Practices) of the Code of Practice for Information Security Management (ISO 17799 (27002)), The Code of Practice for Business Continuity Management (BS 25999-1), NIST Special Publications 800:53A, 800:39, DS4: Ensure Continuous Service, DS10: Manage Problems and DS11: Manage Data (CobiT).

### *Testing Backup Media (Section 14, ISO 27002)*

Testing of backup media is essential to ensure that the media is viable and restores can be appropriately completed in a timely fashion. Backup media must be tested at least annually.

Implementation guidelines for this work can be reviewed in Section 14 (Business Continuity Practices) of the Code of Practice for Information Security Management (ISO 17799 (27002)), The Code of Practice for Business Continuity Management (BS 25999-1), NIST Special Publications 800:53A, 800:39, DS4: Ensure Continuous Service, DS10: Manage Problems and DS11: Manage Data (CobiT).

# Conclusion

The security, infrastructure, and compliance requirements set forth in the PCI DSS standards can present challenges for the organization required to comply. Fortunately for the practitioner, there are many resources, vetted by the international community, to assist with implementation. A considered selection of controls can also make the job much easier for both the practitioner and the organization. Regardless of the control implementation chosen, the organization should allow sufficient time, resources, and dollars for a robust compliance effort.

# About the Authors

**Bonnie Goins Pilewski,** MSIS, CISSP, NSA IAM, ISS, is a senior security strategist at Isthmus Group, Inc., Madison, Wisconsin, where she is the co-practice leader for IGI's security practice.

**Christopher A. Pilewski,** CCSA, CPA/E, FSWCE, FSLCE, MCP, is a senior security strategist at Isthmus Group, Inc., Madison, Wisconsin.

# References

BS 25999, Part 1: Code of Practice for Business Continuity Management, 2006.
ISO/IEC 17799, International Standard: Code of Practice for Information Security, 2005.
ISO/IEC 27002, International Standard: Code of Practice for Information Security, 2007.
ISO/IEC 20000, Part 2: Code of Practice for Information Technology, 2005.
Payment Card Industry Data Security Standard version 1.2, Visa.com, 2008.

# Risk Management

## Chapter 11

# Leveraging IT Control Frameworks for Compliance

Todd Fitzgerald

## Contents

A variety of laws and regulations have surfaced over the past decade in an attempt to strengthen the security of information stored within the companies to which the information assets are entrusted. As a result of the laws that have been enacted, various security control "standards" and "frameworks" have evolved and become popular means to meet the requirements of the laws. Since laws and regulations are intentionally developed at a higher, "what needs to happen" level vs. the "how to secure the information" level, the standards and control frameworks become valuable tools to ensure that security is planned, organized, implemented, tested, and monitored.

    Governance, risk, and compliance (GRC) is a term that has been embraced primarily by the vendor community in recent years in recognition of the fact that companies are struggling with the plethora of controls that must be implemented to meet the extensive requirements of the laws and regulations. Governance is simply the structure, policies, and practices that are put in place by the organization to ensure that the controls are adequately communicated, carried out, and enforced by engaging direction and support at the appropriate organizational level. Risk is the act of making informed decisions about the losses that the company is willing to accept given a breach of security and building the appropriate mitigating risk strategies to reduce the risk to acceptable levels defined by the business. Compliance is ensuring that the controls are being adhered to on an ongoing basis, thereby increasing the likelihood of a reduction of risk and increased adherence to the governance intended by the organization.

The three components of GRC are necessary for adequate security controls; however, implementing them does not ensure that a security program is adequate. Compliance is a necessary control which has been recognized by governments for centuries. Criminal acts, by their very nature, are forms of noncompliance with the laws that are in place. Take driving a car for example. As a teenager obtains his or her driver's license, the diligent parent warns about the downside of not following the laws, reckless driving, speeding, and paying attention to parking and vehicle regulations. The teenager says, "Sure dad, no problem" and forgets 5 min later as they morph into their busy teenage social network of friends and peer pressure, away from the constant mom/dad reminders. They do not realize at the time the consequences of their actions. Or, maybe they do subconsciously, but it is not the most important thought in their daily "work life." Time goes on, piling up speeding tickets, tickets for excessive window tinting, unpaid parking tickets... until one day, they have the opportunity to pay their own car insurance! The parent at that point transfers the risk to the child, and then the learning of true cost of noncompliance begins. The risk is ultimately acknowledged and accepted, and new mitigating strategies are put in place, such as better driving. Organizations are made up of many busy "teenagers," each of which are influenced by their peer work groups and need to be educated as to the future costs of noncompliance to the security controls. Adopting a control framework is a good start; however compliance must be addressed as an ongoing, deliberate strategy.

## So, What Are the Control Frameworks?

Control frameworks and security standards are often interchangeable terms depending upon the creator. Just to confuse things further, ISO27001 posits an Information Security Management "system" (ISMS) and the controls are contained within the ISO27002 "Code of Practice." The National Institute of Standards and Technology (NIST) Special Publication 800-53, entitled Recommended Security Control for Federal Information Systems, breaks the controls into 17 control "families" and three "classes" (Managerial, Operational, Technical) of controls. COBIT defines a framework the same as a Control Framework, which is defined as a tool for business process owners that facilitates the discharge of their responsibilities through the provision of a supporting control model. Alternatively, COBIT defines a standard as a business practice or technology product that is an accepted practice endorsed by the enterprise or IT management team.

For the purposes of this discussion, control frameworks, controls, and standards are interchangeable, as the "intent" of each of them is to provide some definition to a practice or set of practices which if performed, will protect the organization's information assets. These consist of documented, executed, tested, implemented, and monitored controls which reduce the risk of threats succeeding against the company vulnerabilities.

The following are some examples of the control frameworks/standards which address information security requirements:

*Health Insurance Portability and Accountability Act (HIPAA):* The final rule for adopting security standards was published in February 20, 2003, which required a series of administrative, technical, and physical security procedures for entities to use to assure the confidentiality of Protected

Health Information (PHI). The standard was intentionally non-technology specific and intended to provide scalability to small providers and large providers alike.

*Federal Information Security Management Act of 2002 (FISMA)*: The primary purpose is to provide a comprehensive framework for ensuring the effectiveness of security controls over information resources that support federal operations and assets. The law also provided funding for NIST to develop the minimum necessary controls required to provide adequate security. The government publishes an annual report card based upon their assessment of compliance with the framework.

*National Institute of Standards and Technology (NIST) Recommended Security Controls for Federal Information Systems (800-53)*: The standards and guidelines reference the minimum set of controls that must be implemented to protect the federal system based upon the risk level determined. Implementation of the 17 families of security controls establishes a level of "security due diligence" for the federal agencies and the contractors which perform work for the government. These standards are very comprehensive, freely available, and an excellent resource to supplement the other control frameworks.

*Federal Information System Controls Audit Manual (FISCAM)*: Issued by the General Accounting Office, this provides guidance for Information Systems auditors to evaluate the IT controls used in support of financial statement audits. This is not an audit standard, but is included here because auditors are typically testing the control environment in government audits using this standard. There has been increased emphasis on the use of NIST 800-53 controls and the NIST 800-53A Assessments, however FISCAM is still utilized by government auditors and, therefore, it is worthwhile to understand the contents.

*ISO/IEC 27001:2005 Information Security Management Systems Requirements*: Provides a model for establishing, implementing, operating, monitoring, reviewing, maintaining, and improving an ISMS. This was an evolution from British Standard BS7799-2 and ISO17799.

*ISO/IEC 27002:2005 Information Technology Security Techniques—Code of Practice for Information Security Management*: Provides 11 security control clauses (Security Policy, Organizing Information Security, Asset Management, Human Resources Security, Physical and Environmental Security, Communications and Operations Management, Access Control, Information Systems Acquisition, Development and Maintenance, Incident Management, Business Continuity Management, and Compliance). The code of practice specifies the controls necessary and the implementation guidance by specifying the controls that may be chosen to build the ISMS specified through application of ISO/IEC 27001:2005.

*Control Objectives for Information and Related Technology (COBIT)*: A framework and supporting toolset that allow managers to bridge the gap with respect to control requirements, technical issues and business risks, and communicate that level of control to stockholders. COBIT can be used to integrate other standards as an umbrella framework. COBIT gained increasing popularity through implementation to demonstrate compliance with Sarbanes–Oxley regulations, which were enacted in 2002 to require management and the external auditor to report on internal controls over financial reporting.

*Payment Card Industry Data Security Standard (PCI DSS)*: A set of comprehensive requirements for enhancing payment account security, formed by several major credit card issuers, to facilitate the broad adoption of a comprehensive security standard.

*Information Technology Infrastructure Library (ITIL)*: ITIL is a set of books published by the British government's Stationary Office between 1989 and 1992 to improve IT service management. The framework contains a set of best practices for IT core operational processes such as change, release and configuration management, incident and problem management, capacity and availability management, and IT financial management. ITIL's primary contribution is showing how the controls can be implemented for the service management IT processes.

*Security Technical Implementation Guides (STIGS) and National Security Agency (NSA) Guides:* Configuration standards for Department of Defense Information Assurance, however freely available and used as the basis for technical standards for many private organizations. These standards, if implemented, support many of the high-level requirements specified within requirements such as FISMA, HIPAA, PCI, NIST, GLBA, COBIT, ISO27001, etc.

## The World Operates on Standards

The obvious fact about standards is that they are useful and the world is made up of many of them, from the minimum weight in the passenger seat that must be met before the airbag protection will become active, to the specification of the size of a #8 screw, to the standard formats for electronic data interchange of electronic transactions between healthcare providers, payers, and clearing-houses. Standards ensure that products are built to specifications and allow us to "simplify" the complexity of the world by creating a common deliverable and common language. Imagine if every time a manufacturer wanted a product built they had to design a screw that could be potentially different from any other screw a manufacturer created! Not only would this process be very expensive, it would also be very time consuming for the customer and the supplier, and would be very error-prone. Non-standardized processes also slow down the delivery of the product or service. Henry Ford recognized many years ago that there were efficiencies and increases in quality by creating vehicles which looked the same and were painted the same color (black). While they were actually available in other colors, the primary color produced was black for efficiency. Imagine if stoplights were each made with different colors to represent stop–slowdown–go. Imagine roadways that used different types of striping to indicate passing vs. non-passing lanes based upon the state that you lived in! The world would be very chaotic with each individual interpreting the colors and passing lanes as they drove, many times potentially making the wrong decision.

Sometimes we like the standards, sometimes we do not. Sometimes, they just do not make intuitive sense to us, nor do they seem effective. For example, the Transportation Security Administration (TSA) originally did not allow nail clippers on the airplane, and reversed the decision in 2005 after negative public opinion. Lighters were also subsequently allowed in July, 2007 by the Federal Aviation Administration. Laws, regulations, and the standards which support them are sometimes developed without the extensive analysis of their necessity, or in reaction to a major event and the need to "do something," only to be rescinded later for their lack of effectiveness. This is understood, as government and private industry must react to make demands and situations, making decisions on the data available at the time. In defense of the TSA, decisions to limit what was brought on an airplane had to be made quickly on the heels of September 11, 2001, and their focus was on objects which had the potential to harm. Thus, the standard of "no nail clippers" was enacted. Liquid restrictions were placed on travelers due to an incident where the chemicals could be used to create explosives. By the time of this publication, due to new technology scanning, the "no liquid" standard may also disappear.

## Standards Are Dynamic

Over time, the standards evolve, and they change to meet the societal and technological needs. While the intent of many security standards appears to stay the same over time, the underlying technologies that must be supported are constantly changing. Just as in the "no liquids" on airplanes were first introduced, and then evolved into "as long as the liquids are 3oz or less and fit in a 1qt baggie," and then may morph into "no requirements at all" due to investments in more advanced scanning technology, information security standards also need to change.

Most control frameworks are written at a higher, broader level, which provides flexibility to implement controls to satisfy the specific technological request. For example, the ISO27002:2005 Information Technology Security Techniques (Code of Practice) control 10.5.1d indicates that "the back-ups should be stored in a remote location, at a sufficient distance to escape any damage from a disaster at the main site." This leaves much interpretation up to the implementer of the standard—how far away is far enough? Before Hurricane Katrina inflicted extensive damage on New Orleans, Louisiana, and other surrounding areas in 2005, many individuals felt that storage a few miles away was sufficient. Today, when companies are assessing their business continuity plans, they typically point to Katrina, and quickly decide that 50–100+ miles away would greatly reduce the risk. Others have invested in new replication technologies and the availability of inexpensive storage to ensure availability of the information.

Changing environments necessitate the ability to change the implementation strategies to meet the lower cost of technology, increased effectiveness of controls, and conformance to emerging regulations.

## The "How" Is Typically Left up to Us

As the aforementioned example illustrates, the good news is that the standards may be written to be flexible over time. The bad news is that they are written to be flexible over time. In other words, standards often lack the specificity of the "how" that would be useful to implementing the standard. Obviously, this is by design; however, it leaves the implementer of the standard to "figure out" based upon the available alternatives what the best method of implementation should be for their particular environment and cost constraints.

The "best practices" terminology has received criticism over the past several years, as the beauty is in the eye of the beholder. A practice that works for one organization may not fit for another. One organization may implement a policy banning USB drives due to their small size, while another may allow them as long as the contents are automatically encrypted with the company-approved software. Still another may prohibit their use by policy to most users, but allow adoption by those which establish a business need (as specified in ISO27002:2005 10.7.1f), as well as taking the additional step of controlling access through active directory authorization and a vendor product. Which is the "best practice"? It depends on the organizational culture, appetite for risk, cost constraints, etc. It may also be the case that the individuals within the organization do not have access to sensitive information, thus limiting the exposure.

Therefore, the "best practice" for an organization must take in many factors not defined within the individual standard. Typically, an organization would be prudent to follow the trends within their particular vertical industry, and pay attention to what the "herd" is doing. If 70% of the sheep are heading for the hills, it may be worth heading in that direction. It is also important to understand why, as the 10% going another direction (assuming 20% are standing still), may be headed to a better best practice. In the tape backup example, maybe the 10% that are utilizing online, high-speed compressed disk-to-disk backup strategies are the "best practice" that is right for the organization.

Whatever these practices are named for our individual organizations, each must recognize that the practices must satisfy the standard and where they do not, sufficient business justification and risk acceptance must be documented. In this manner, the standards become the reference point for making informed business decisions.

## Key Question: Why Does the Standard Exist?

Before deciding the "how" to implement the standard, it is a useful exercise to examine the selected control within the standard and analyze why does this control exist in the first place? What threat is it addressing? What would the risk be to my organization if I decided to ignore addressing the control? In other words, how is implementing the control increasing the security, protection, or information assurance of the information assets within the organization? Understanding the "what if I don't" can quickly lead to a deeper understanding of the "intent" of the control, vs. trying to ensure compliance with every detail of the control.

For example, if there is a control within the standard which says that logs of activity to the system must be retained for 1 year, access must be restricted to only those with a need to know, understanding why this standard exists will contribute to "how" it should be implemented. If the intent of the control is to be able to go back and analyze incidents, then the individuals who need read access are the systems security operations team, or those responding to the incidents. The files may also need to be online if there is a frequent occurrence of investigation. Alternatively, the logs may not be able to be reviewed due to resource (human) constraints, and may necessitate the investment in a security incident management tool which aggregates and correlates the information.

Understanding the intent of the control also assists in interpreting the terminology used within the control. The standards are promulgated by many different organizations, committees, and geographic representations. The NIST uses terminology in the 800-53 standard (Recommended Security Controls for Federal Information Systems) with roots in the Government Sector that would be familiar to many accustomed to working for or contracting with government agencies. Contrast that with the IT Governance Institute's COBIT framework that is reviewed by an internationally represented committee.

## Compliance Is Not Security... But It Is a Good Start

Checking off each of the controls specified within a standard is analogous to completing the weekend honey-do list at home... it may be "done" at the end of the weekend, but wait for the household auditor to see if it was done "well." When the Health Insurance Portability and Accountability Act (HIPAA), Gramm–Leach–Bliley Act (GLBA), Federal Information Security Management Act (FISMA), Payment Card Industry Data Security Standards (PCI), and other regulations arrived on the scene, some organizations reviewed the "Compliancy with the standard" as the primary goal, and subsequently created a checklist approach to satisfying the controls with the minimum that would be needed for "compliancy," without the benefit of a real risk assessment. The danger in this is that the security controls implemented may prove to be ineffective to addressing the vulnerabilities of the organization and the threats that they face.

However, even though compliance with standards may not be sufficient to mitigate the risk level to an acceptable level for the organization, the fact that the organization is adopting a control framework provides the opportunity to create a baseline and enhance the security level over time. Without such a framework in place, there is less chance that the environment will be secure, as items can be missed too easily.

## Integration of Standards and Control Frameworks

Each of the standards and control frameworks contributes in their own way and the astute security professional will become familiar with each of them. COBIT provides an excellent overall framework which ties business goals, governance drivers, business outcomes and IT resources, processes, and goals together. ISO27001 provides a nice framework for establishing the ISMS, ensuring that risks are assessed, controls are implemented, management is actively involved, and the documentation is up to date. NIST 800-53 provides the detailed controls with tailored enhancements with the specifications for assessing the controls (800-53A document). HIPAA Final Federal Security Rule provides the framework for implementing protection for the Healthcare vertical industry. The Federal Information Security Management Act (FISMA) relies on the controls specified by NIST to comply with the regulation instead of creating a new set of controls. The ITIL provides the control areas for providing effective and efficient service delivery, and overlaps the security areas specified in the other control areas.

Several organizations, such as NIST and the IT Governance Institute have recognized the commonality of these standards as evidenced by their work in mapping controls between HIPAA, NIST 800-53, COBIT, FISMA, ITIL, and others. While the wording, level of the control, and measures for assessment may have different criteria, there is much commonality amongst the controls. For example, controls regarding configuration management and the need to develop baselines may not be specifically called out in HIPAA and FISMA as they are in ISO27001 and NIST, however, the need for securing the computing devices are represented within the controls for technical controls and the implementation of systems security plans.

## *Value of Audits*

Once a control framework or set of standards has been chosen and implemented, it is imperative that the framework be audited on a regular basis internally and externally. Gaps in process are typically uncovered during these audits, and if these gaps are mitigated quickly, over time, the security program becomes more complete. Care must be taken to address reasonable risk, as it is rare that an organization will execute every control every time. What is important is that there are mitigating or compensating controls that catch the anomalies before they become major issues, and prompt follow-up and correction actions are taken. Audit testing of the control frameworks will take many forms including interviewing, determining, and testing samples; performing vulnerability assessments; reviewing policies and procedures; and conducting external penetration tests.

Each audit should be viewed as an opportunity to determine the effectiveness of the control framework and potentially modify the existing controls.

## *Final Thoughts: Control Framework Convergence*

Why cannot we have just one standard? On the surface, this appears to be a simple, logical question. As Eckhart Tolle promotes in his book, *A New Earth*, individuals create stress in their lives by not accepting "what is." The reality is that laws and regulations will continue to emerge from different organizations and as security professionals, adapting to the emerging laws and regulations and applying the appropriate standards and control frameworks will be key. This is not to say that efficiencies cannot be gained, as controls can be implemented which would support multiple control frameworks. Sometimes, a control only needs to be tweaked to satisfy multiple controls/standards.

Over time, the practices that are common do emerge and become generally accepted. Even as recent as a few years ago, laptops were not universally encrypted by companies, with IT departments citing the expense, complexity, lack of necessity, files stored on the network by company policy, etc. So what was the tipping point that changed the practice to companies encrypting the laptops? It was when the veteran's administration lost a laptop containing information on 26.5 million veterans in 2006 which caused public outrage at the situation. Today, few companies would want to admit that they are not encrypting their laptops due to the shift in the herd mentality to encryption. The sheep have headed for the hills, and the slow sheep are vulnerable to being left behind. Upon reviewing the standards and control frameworks, it is clear that the requirements for protecting "mobile devices and media" were specified prior to 2006. It could be argued that proactive attention to these frameworks would save much in the long run. The Veterans Administration suffered in terms of public reputation and financially ($20 million lawsuit to settle claims), all which could have been avoided. What happened to this government agency could happen to any of our organizations if the controls are not in place. Adherence to the control frameworks and standards increases the likelihood that breaches will not have a devastating effect on the confidentiality, integrity, or availability of the information assets.

Control frameworks and standards provide the roadmap to build a successful information security program. Once in place, continuous review of the policies, standard operating procedures, and implementation of the controls will enhance the effectiveness of the program. Monitoring through audits accompanied by corrective actions and tracking enables refinement of the control framework and standards to reduce the risk of a security event impacting the business in a significant way. Think of the various security control frameworks as each contributing in some way to the infrastructure of a super 6-lane freeway. Rather than managing our security programs by ourselves, on an old gravel road at 20 miles per hour, it is time to get on the superhighway supported by the strong plethora of control frameworks and standards and enjoy the ride!

## About the Author

**Todd Fitzgerald**, CISSP, CISA, CISM, is the director of systems security and systems security officer for United Government Services, LLC, Milwaukee, Wisconsin.

## Suggested Reading

Cobit 4.1, IT Governance Institute, http://www.itgi.org

Defense Information Systems Agency (DISA), Security Technical Implementation Guides (STIGS), http://iase.disa.mil/stigs/stig

Federal Information Security Management Act of 2002 (FISMA), November 27, 2002, http://csrc.nist.gov/drivers/documents/FISMA-final.pdf

Federal Information System Controls Audit Manual (FISCAM), GAO/AIMD-12.19.6, January 1999, http://www.gao.gov/special.pubs/12_19_6.pdf

GAO/AIMB-12.19.6, Federal Information Systems Controls Audit Manual (FISCAM), January 1999, http://gao.gov/special.pubs/ai12.19.6.pdf

Guide for Assessing Controls In Federal Information Systems, http://csrc.nist.gov/publications/nistpubs/800-53A/SP800-53A-final-sz.pdf

Health Insurance Portability and Accountability Act (HIPAA), August 21, 1996, http://aspe.os.dhhs.gov/admnsimp/nprm/sec13.htm

Information Technology Infrastructure Library, http://www.itil-officialsite.com/home/home.asp

ISO/IEC 27001:2005 Information Security Management Systems Requirements, http://www.iso.org/iso/iso_catalogue/catalogue_tc/catalogue_detail.htm?csnumber=42103

ISO/IEC 27002:2005 Information Technology Security Techniques—Code of Practice for Information Security Management, International Organization for Standardization (ISO), http://www.iso.org/iso/iso_catalogue/catalogue_tc/catalogue_detail.htm?csnumber=50297

National Institute of Standards and Technology, Special Publications, http://csrc.nist.gov/publications/PubsSPs.html

National Security Agency, Security Configuration Guides, http://www.nsa.gov/snac

Recommended Security Controls for Federal Information Systems, Special Publication 800-53, http://csrc.nist.gov/publications/PubsSPs.html

Seventh Report Card on Computer Security, http://republicans.oversight.house.gov/FISMA

Tolle, E., *A New Earth: Awakening to Your Life's Purpose*, Penguin, New York, 2005.

## Chapter 12

# Rats in the Cellar and Bats in the Attic, "Not Enough Depth to My Security"

Ken M. Shaurette

## Contents

## Introduction

What comes to mind when you think of security? I guess that would depend on what one is trying to secure.

For an organization, technology has come a long way over the past decade, which has helped to detect network intrusions or breaches of security to keep critical organizational data confidential.

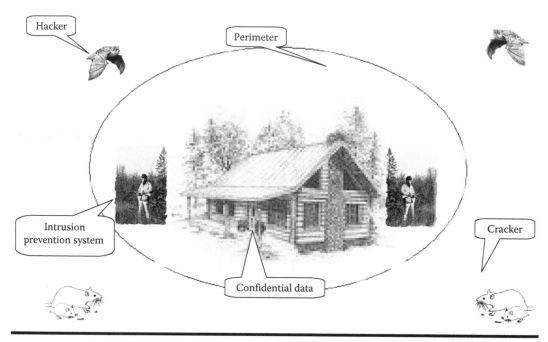

**Figure 12.1   Real-world risk management.**

With technology we now have ways to look at literally a mountain of data to determine if an incident is occurring or has occurred.

For an individual protecting their home, there have been advances as well. However, there are still the same variables that continue to cause the organization or home to be at risk. Those variables are people, time, and exposure to new and changing threats.

I would like to share a couple of stories, draw some analogies to how we secure our organizations, add some perspective to common security processes that every organization evaluates when performing network penetration testing and maybe, just maybe, you will find some advice based on real-world experience related to managing risk with vulnerability assessments and penetration testing (Figure 12.1).

## You Bat'ch You

It was early summer in northern Wisconsin and I planned a trip to the cabin. This is the time of year to travel north to the cabin and get things ready for the summer. Cabins need summer preparations just like at the end of the season when they need preparations before winter. There are a number of chores and preparations that must be completed so the family can enjoy another summer at the cabin. There is always a checklist of items, which include chopping wood for camp-fires and clearing paths for nature walks or to provide open paths for riding the all terrain vehicle (ATV), but once all the chores are completed it is well worth the effort. The cabin becomes a refuge for rest and relaxation from the stress of hectic work schedules and the strains of day-to-day risk management—helping organizations protect their critical assets.

Similar efforts are necessary when comparing winter and summer preparations to the activities that an organization undertakes to protect their network. The difference in the corporation is that the preparations must be proactive, constant, and there is no time to relax. An organization must perform processes such as updating antivirus and undergo continuous efforts to patch applications, databases, and operating systems against new and changing vulnerabilities' (just like keeping the cabin ready to survive winter or ready to handle a busy summer). Performing vulnerability assessment (VA) and penetration tests are like walking around the cabin, checking the trails, and making sure that basic cabin facilities are functioning properly to protect the cabin and its contents from criminal activity (thieves and kids who might like to just cause property damage) and even mother nature's creatures (bats and mice) and conditions (storms and snow). These preparations in an organization not only provide the organization their competitive ability to grow but also protect the confidentiality, integrity, and availability of information assets to comply with customer expectations or regulated and legislated requirements.

After a very busy day working around the cabin, I was just about ready to settle in for the evening, relax by the fire, and kick up my feet. I was relaxing in the living room by the fire with the lights off just enjoying its warm glow. Suddenly, I saw something out of the corner of my eye fly past my head. It took me a couple of seconds to be able to process what I just saw. I jumped to my feet quickly and turned on the lights.

Hmmm, there it was, just as I thought, a bat. For me personally, bats are not one of my most favorite creatures; in fact, even though I consider myself a hunter and active outdoors person, I am very squeamish when it comes to bats. I had to ask myself, first, how am I going to get this thing out of the cabin and second, and more important; how did it get in the cabin in the first place? Without figuring out number two I was going to continue having problems even if I took care of this incident.

> Sound familiar to your risk management efforts at your organization? Deciding how to handle an incident and reevaluating your current protections?

I quickly assembled my anti-bat tools in preparation of doing battle. Anti-bat tools, well I grabbed a pair of leather gloves, two of the kids butterfly nets, and my trusty work boot, just in case I had to do a little fast footwork with this critter. Remember I really don't like bats?

> Sound familiar to assembling your incident response team, equipping them with the tools they need for incident management and to protect the organization from the event?

Just so you can get a clear picture of how I looked. I was now wearing a pair of blue jeans, a long sleeve flannel shirt, boots, leather gloves, a hat and I had a butterfly net in each hand. I know it's a myth about bats flying in your hair, but my earlier experience with it flying by my head had me thinking it's better to be safe then sorry.

I contained the bat to the living room by closing all doors to every room, so I was now ready to go on the offensive. If you have had an experience with a bat before, you probably already have guessed that I much underestimated the speed and agility of my foe.

> What? Butterfly nets used as my combat tools against a bat. It is important when handling an incident to be prepared to have the proper tools in order to properly handle the incident and protect the organization combating an intruder.

I found it hanging on the wall in the corner of the living room. Just as I was getting close it took off and began flying around the cabin again. Those butterfly nets came in handy as I found myself swinging with both nets simultaneously only to come up empty handed. I chased the intruder (bat) around the cabin living room area for about an hour until it suddenly flew into a very small hole near the fireplace where the rock wall firewall connects to the wood interior siding. It had apparently made its escape.

> Monitoring systems and event management help identify and track an incident, possibly even giving evidence of an intruder's actions.

I was very tired from the day's chores and with the incident with the bat intruder, so I called it a day and went off to get some sleep. However, I did make sure to put some basic protections in place for the bedroom. I made sure the door was closed and added one more thing to the list of chores for tomorrow, which was to figure out how the bat intruder got into the cabin.

> Regular vulnerability and penetration assessments can help to identify potential areas of concern where an attacker in the corporate environment might exploit to access information assets.

Okay, it is clear my home incident response process needs a little more planning, but it is hard to plan for all possible scenarios. For your organization, the important thing is to have an incident response plan defined. Once a process is in place and steps are defined, your focus is clearer and you are less likely to miss something, especially if you are gathering evidence that might need to support litigation at some point in the future. This way you are not relying solely on the skill of the staff to react and make proper decisions quickly under a probably stressful situation to resolve the incident.

The next morning I needed to do an external perimeter assessment of the house, as well as investigating possibly holes inside, especially by the fireplace. I could identify a small hole where the screened-in porch connects to the house. It is on the same wall where the chimney for the fireplace is located. I proceeded to climb up onto the porch roof and inspect the external perimeter where the porch was an add-on after original construction. I found that bats had chewed a small hole in the area where the porch integrated to the cabin and this was where they were able to gain access to the interior of the cabin. There were also some gaps along the eaves of the house which were probably caused over time by lack of regular maintenance and the effects of ice and cold winters. *This evidence shows, like in our corporate computing environments, that maintenance is not something we can just do a couple times a year, it must be ongoing.*

After I climbed down from the roof, I headed to the local hardware store to get the tools I did not have to begin patching things, close the holes.

I returned ready to complete the necessary maintenance to eliminate the vulnerabilities that had made it possible for an intruder to invade the cabin. I climbed back up on the roof of the porch and began patching. My first priority was to patch the hole where the roof connected to the cabin. This would minimize the potential for future intruders. Suddenly I heard a scratching sound and little squeaking noises coming from the eaves of the main roof. I subsequently pounded on the eave with my fist and several bats came pouring out of the gaps. (Did I mention that I didn't particularly like bats?) Needless to say I was a little startled by this. I started waving my arms rapidly to protect myself, like they were attacking me. It is scary how little room there is on a 12 ft by 12 ft porch roof to make a quick get away unless I was willing to risk a 10 ft drop, so my movement was limited.

Sometimes in our corporate environments budget and other resources limit our ability to protect our systems to best practices. We have to make do to the best of our ability within the limitations that are posed to us. Management, regulations and legislation will still expect that adequate protections are in place.

Once everything finally settled down and there appeared to be no bats around the roof or in the eaves, I steadied my chalk gun and plugged every gap, crease, and hole. I eliminated all of the vulnerability that I could find. After the maintenance project on the porch roof was complete, I called it a day, figuring I deserved a little time to rest and relax. Now, I can look back, since this incident occurred a few years ago and I, fortunately, have not had a reoccurrence since.

Just as all of us face day-to-day challenges of protecting our homes from intrusion, organizations face constant battles to protect their critical and confidential information. Nothing sends a chill down a CEO's spine like hearing about a security breach. Yep, the one where your first reaction is to take a deep relaxing breath, in through the nose out through the mouth just like you were getting ready to deal with a bat.

Organizations need to be on constant vigilance, keeping watch on potential intruders, monitoring and analyzing the perimeter and the interior for vulnerabilities. Thankfully, organizations have the technology available that can make the tremendous burden of keeping a constant vigil over vulnerabilities easier.

However, organizations cannot let their guard down, just like the story about the bat intruder, vulnerabilities were minimized, but one day my wife opened the door and let a mouse into our house. This action reminds us that people need to be aware and careful in their actions to avoid opening any holes unintentionally making our environments vulnerable even if only for a few moments.

The remainder of this chapter will continue to discuss the vigilance and some of the measures that organizations take to minimize vulnerability and manage risk to the confidentiality, integrity, and availability of their data.

# Vulnerability Assessments and Penetration Testing

Planning and preparation are keys for any risk assessment. Vulnerability assessment in conjunction with penetration testing help when doing complete diligence to test both technical and process-oriented controls protecting an organization's data.

## *Penetration Testing versus Vulnerability Assessment*

For years there has remained a certain amount of confusion about the difference between a network penetration test (PenTest) and a network VA. Too often, they are classified as the same thing or one is confused for the other when in fact they are different. One common misrepresentation is the PenTest is from the outside and a VA is of the inside. While penetration testing does sound a lot more exciting, experience has told us that most organizations need to start with a comprehensive VA and not the more intrusive PenTest.

While they are similar projects and can cover many of the same areas; a critical difference is that a PenTest is typically more aggressive and more intrusive. The PenTest involves trying to break into components of the computing environment to prove they are vulnerable. Essentially, the PenTest in that sense is providing evidence that the VA and associated processes to perform maintenance, patch and mitigate identified vulnerabilities are effective.

A concern with a PenTest is that it can be more risky, since the tester may exploit flaws in hardware, database, Web, or software components of the production environment, which could cause instability and potential outages.

## The Penetration Test

A *penetration test* is a method of evaluating the security of a computer system or network by simulating an attack by a malicious hacker. PenTest should be a goal-oriented test. Sometimes, a PenTest will identify a trophy, the target that signifies success of a penetration. The process involves active analysis for weaknesses, technical flaws, or vulnerabilities. The idea is to attack a predetermined target. It is like trying to break into the vault, fill a bag with money, and walk out of the bank without being stopped. It does not matter how many ways it could be done, the question is whether it can be done. Analysis is carried out from the position of a potential attacker, and could involve active exploitation of vulnerabilities. The extent to which penetration was successful along with vulnerabilities found is reported with an assessment of their impact and recommendations for mitigation. Pen testing can help to find the mistakes that other approaches might miss, such as a problem with configuration or architecture that could get overlooked in other reviews. The PenTest usually goes deeper than most audits. Be prepared for the different impact that a PenTest will have on the time resources of target environment personnel.

In reality, the PenTest cannot find all vulnerabilities in a target environment. Limitations will be based on the resources and constraints of a test. These limitations may include

- Scope of testing (e.g., internal, external, applications, human firewall)
- Time, this includes both elapsed time and how many hours are contracted for an ethical attacker to attempt to penetrate.
- Access by the PenTest, this is important to the objective of the testing and to some level dictated by scope of testing.
- Methods and expertise of the tester.
- Testing that will not result in a denial of service. This can limit diversionary attacks and other activities that might make an attack more likely to be successful.

## The Vulnerability Assessment

A VA is more like a review or an audit. VA is the step an attacker performs to identify vulnerabilities, internal or external including network, system, database, and application or Web site components. A key distinction is the VA identifies vulnerabilities versus exploiting the worst of them. It is like walking around the bank looking for unlocked doors or open windows. It does not matter if a particular goal is completed; the challenge is to identify as many likely areas of exposure that could lead to a variety of compromised assets. Vulnerabilities that are found can be categorized, prioritized for risk, and reported with their potential impact, likelihood, and recommendations for mitigation.

Some potential purposes for your VA include

- Demonstrate due care
  - Infrastructure patching
  - Intrusion prevention
  - Software development

- Security awareness
- Discovery
- To justify funding

## *Comparing and Contrasting*

Which one delivers an organization the most value? Answering that depends on the maturity of your risk management. Unless vulnerability assessments have been performed for a while and vulnerabilities actively corrected, organizations will be much better served by conducting the vulnerability assessment. The reason being is that a PenTest is typically more time consuming and more expensive. A VA answers the question: "What are our weaknesses and how do we fix them?" A PenTest typically answers the question: "Can someone exploit our vulnerabilities and to what extent can they access information?" A VA works to improve security posture and develop a more mature, integrated security program, whereas a PenTest's most common use might be to prove to doubting management that vulnerabilities can be exploited, by showing evidence of the break-in (the Trophy). Depending on the tools used during a high-quality VA, the need to do PenTesting can be minimized. The VA tool may perform some basic PenTesting, such as testing default passwords.

Most organizations should start with vulnerability assessments, act on the results; and when confident with mitigation, consider the penetration test. The PenTest should be performed by a different third party than the VA. As components of an overall risk management program, both vulnerability assessments and penetration tests can have their purpose and should be performed regularly (the VA at least annually, more often in an environment such as PCI/DSS) to ensure continuous risk management.

# A Hacker's Process

Let us take a look at the process a hacker could take in breaching an organization's network. Plan, discover, attempt penetration, more discovery, more penetration attempts and the process is repeated until they are either successful, they give up, or get caught. Then they move onto the next target (trophy) identified in the planning stage.

This is very similar or is actually the same process that is involved with the penetration test as described above.

The one thing a hacker typically has on their side is time and if they can be patient. It is often only a matter of time before they will be successful. The same is often true with the PenTest, scoping how many hours will be used and the elapsed time are important to a test's effectiveness. Given enough time to test during a penetration test will typically result in finding a vulnerability to penetrate and with sufficient elapse time the testing can be done in such a way that it is very unlikely that it will ever be detectable.

Let us take a brief look at how different types of penetration tests are performed, and what tools are involved from the planning stages to execution. There are four functional areas to consider: external perimeter, internal network, wireless environment, and social engineering.

## *Social Engineering*

Social Engineering, more positively identified as security awareness testing, is a method that can be used to educate the organization's employees to have good judgment when encountering anomalous activity. Just like testing the perimeter firewall, it is important to test the "human firewall," the employee. This kind of activity targets the vulnerability I alluded to earlier when I mentioned my wife letting the mouse in the house. Providing my wife greater awareness of how to be more careful so she can prevent an incident like the mouse coming in the door of the house. While testing my wife to be more careful might be a little difficult and not real practical, testing employees to ensure they follow good data handling is a valuable step to improve protection of data.

## Physical Security

One area of social engineering testing involves physical visits that look for vulnerabilities in an organization's nonpublic presence to view information that might be left in plain sight. A social engineer might start by reviewing and evaluating various physical access points to the facility. The test might use some of the following types of attack scenarios, including costumes to dress accordingly for the role:

- Help desk employee
- Executive attending a management meeting
- Delivery person
- High-profile IT vendor representative
- Fire extinguisher service personnel
- Maintenance or janitorial staff

This test can identify the internal availability of "live" network ports that could be used for technology based penetration activities after an attacker might gain physical access. A social engineer could place a rogue wireless access point (WAP) or a specifically configured laptop on the network and attempt to obtain a network connection and penetrate the network from that device. Physical access may even be authorized, such as a vendor or auditor connecting a WAP for ease of printing, or maybe just having their laptop's wireless active and insecure.

## Password and E-Mail/Web Site Spoofing

Another social engineering attack might test a sample of personnel using the following types of tests:

- Telephone-based social engineering—Sometimes also called pre-texting, this type of an attack's goal could be to elicit login credentials, or directly get personal data on a customer.
- E-mail and fake Web sites—A social engineering test might find e-mail addresses that employees have posted on the Internet using their company e-mail address. This may be in technical support chat (i.e., Listserv) rooms and on social networks (e.g., Facebook, MySpace, Twitter, and LinkedIn). Many e-mail addresses that could be valuable targets are often available on corporate Web sites. The goal of this type of testing would be to determine how an employee would deal with unsolicited actions from unknown sources.

Once these activities are complete, an organization may have a good idea how their existing security awareness plan is working. Experience shows that most organizations that have undergone this type of service were surprised. A talented social engineer has the ability to take advantage of the trust that many people inherently have to help, especially in organizations that are service oriented. Kevin Mitnick, renowned as a hacker, in reality was not at all technical, but was very good at exploiting people's trust and also at masquerading in positions to gain trust to get information.

For a hacker, social engineering activities are just one step in the process. Obtaining key pieces of information, such as types of applications or systems or a user's credentials to use in order to gain access, increases a penetration's potential for success. This information is almost always used for future penetration.

This reminds me of another story about the cabin. One of the other joys of owning a cabin in northern Wisconsin is that each fall and spring there is the unglamorous task of eliminating mice. Mostly they are discovered in the cellar but on occasion I will see one in the house. A mouse is somewhat an unpleasant creature and I can tolerate them better than bats; however, they can cause a great deal of damage and if not taken care of, costs could mount.

I find myself continually checking the perimeter of the cabin looking for possible entry points (vulnerabilities) and closing them one at a time. But still each year as the cabin ages new vulnerabilities are discovered, an ever so small crease, hole, or crack that provides an opening for mice to get in. These types of things are expected, so plan for it, dealing with the vulnerability by adding insulation (applying network, operating system, application, or database patches), replacing a door or filling in the gaps with some caulk (upgrades to newer vendor releases or replacing an out-of-date firewall).

As mentioned earlier, my wife went to feed our Old English sheepdog one morning, not thinking (a lapse in awareness), she had left the bag of open dog food on the deck the night before. When she stepped outside with the food dish she left the door open and in her first scoop of food out pops a mouse, jumps down onto the deck, and scurries right into the house. You could almost hear the mouse say, "Thank You!" Of course the alarm is sounded, my wife and daughter immediately begin to start screaming, the dog starts barking and running around the perimeter of the kitchen alerting me that an intruder has entered. We all recognized these as the more frustrating situations when we just hold the door open for those pesky mice, the intruders to come right it (employees open malicious attachments, visit unauthorized Web sites, or choose poor passwords).

As you would expect, my incident response team was immediately put into motion, I dropped everything and began to hunt the little critter down. Fortunately, with the Old English sheepdog circling the kitchen barking, the mouse froze under the table and I was able to capture it with my trusty butterfly net and I place it back outside. It is almost like the dog herded the mouse to confine where it would go to under the table. Imagine this as one of the secondary layers in the organization's defense in depth. I should not really be that surprised an Old English sheepdog is bred to herd sheep. I think if we would have still had our Yellow Lab, she would have just ran it down stepped on it and ate it. Labs will eat just about anything, both food and not food items. Trust me on that, I have many stories to tell. Each different type of dog can have different approaches but either would have been just as effective. Just like different security technologies handle intrusions or specific potential vulnerabilities differently.

## Wireless Environment

Wireless is an extension of an organization's internal network. It can extend an organization's internal network outside the perimeter. At this point, almost everyone is aware that wireless is inherently insecure, but with proper security can be made more secure. Wireless technology is easy to set up but can be a bit more difficult to adequately secure. However, there are secure wireless configurations that make penetrating the wireless networks harder and makes it take more time and effort for the attacker. Some of them are basic changes in default configuration settings.

As is with any type of penetration testing, the first part of performing a Wireless PenTest focuses on external WLAN (wireless LAN) Discovery. The goal is to look for active APs (access points), workstations, and laptops associated with the target organization and attempt to identify the configuration of those devices. The Discovery includes determining if any open WAPs are available, if configuration errors exist and the security level and encryption type that may be configured on the APs. There are many tools available for use during the discovery. One such tool from the Back Track 3 suite is called Airodump-ng. This free tool collects much of the information needed to perform additional attacks and identifies potential attack vectors. Other noncommercial tools that can be used for discovery include Kismet, Netstumbler, Ministumbler, Commview, Wifi Hopper, Wirelessmon, Airopeek, and Wellenreiter.

The process for attacking a wireless environment is essentially the same whether it is being performed internally or externally from the parking lot or street. Once the discovery step is complete, a variety of next steps could be taken. Those include asking several "ifs":

1. If there is an unencrypted wireless network, then sniff and port scan IP range and continue to gather information of workstation or laptops connected to that network. Look for bridged systems that are both connected to the wired network and wireless network.
2. If the Wireless environment is using WEP encryption, then attempt a WEP attack. The biggest challenge for cracking WEP is collecting enough initialization vectors. Three tools (Airodump, Aireplay, and Aircrack) running in conjunction with each other can be very effective in cracking any WEP key. One only needs time to collect the initialization vector required to initiate the cracking process. That is what Aireplay is used for. Once an active access point and associated workstation or laptop is identified, Aireplay can be used to send authentication and de-authentication requests to assist in generating traffic quickly. Both penetration testers and/or hackers do not like waiting around too long if they do not have to.
3. If the Wireless environment is using WPA/WPA2 encryption, then capture EAPOL handshake and attempt a WPA/WPA 2 dictionary attack. The same challenges apply to cracking WPA as WEP. The tool that would be used would be Aircrack.
4. If LEAP is being used for the wireless network, then attempt to break LEAP by using Airodump to capture the traffic and use Asleap to collect any authentication requests and crack the password.
5. If the discovery identifies a client configuration where wireless clients are "listening" in peer-to-peer mode, known as AD-HOC, then…. To clarify this issue, when a user reviews a list of wireless access points by which to connect, occasionally an AD-HOC "base station" or access point (typically it is just another wireless client in AD-HOC mode) will appear in the list. If the user either manually attempts to connect to this AD-HOC base station (or configures the client to connect to ANY base station, infrastructure *or* AD-HOC), the user's wireless client will store that attempted association. Then, when the user moves the wireless client to a new location and there are no access points that the current configuration selects in priority, the client will attempt to search for whatever it was connected to last. If the previous connection attempt was to an AD-HOC base station, the client will, in effect, become an AD-HOC base station in its attempt to search for its missing partner. Because this behavior occurs automatically and sometimes when the computer that hosts the wireless client is also connected to a wired network through the Ethernet interface, an attacker could connect to the wireless AD-HOC base station and compromise the computer and its wired Ethernet interface.

6. If you were able to observe wireless clients that were "roaming" for a wireless access point to which to connect, then in most cases, these wireless clients are *also* connected to the secure, internal, wired network via an Ethernet adapter. Then one could create a mobile, promiscuous access point that rapidly rotates the broadcast SSID of observed client beacons in order for "free roaming" clients to connect. The mobile access point could also host a DHCP server so that clients were automatically given an IP address, to which the "attacker" could scan each unsuspecting client and exploit vulnerabilities.

As you can see, if there is a will there is a way when it comes to successfully penetrating a wireless network. It is simply a function of time.

## External Perimeter

Attacking or attempting to penetrate the external perimeter starts similarly to that of a wireless or internal penetration attack that is beginning with reconnaissance and discovery. External PenTest activities typically include Google searches for e-mail addresses, reviewing technical forums, and blog posts. The goal is to identify e-mail addresses that might be used to populate user lists for authenticator enumeration. Other activities include

- Running WHOIS searches to identify IP address ranges and getting confirmation of ownership.
- Performing an initial assessment of Web-based applications accessible by BROWSER only. This involves rendering publicly accessible browser pages to identify "low-hanging fruit" and establish a prioritized testing framework.
- Looking at DNS resolution to identify resolution and reverse resolution of IP addresses and corresponding "fully qualified domain names" (FQDN) to also look for discrepancies or anomalies.
- Doing port mapping using redundant NMAP scans and performing port scans against identified targets.

One of the next steps in the external penetration attack would be to perform specialized scans against Web servers. Tools that can be used are commercial scanners such as WebInspect, Nikto, Paros proxy, WebScarab, Wisker/libwisker, Burpsuite, Wikto, Acunetix WVX, Appscan, WFUZZ, N-Stealth, and potentially others, depending on the Web server or application server discovered. These scans are intended to identify information about the supporting architecture, such as internal IP addresses, application servers, and databases running on the inner application tiers. The tools can identify various vulnerabilities including poor coding practices in Web application programming, and dangerous files/CGIs.

These types of scans can be "noisy/loud" in terms of network attack activities. If an organization has an intrusion detection system (IDS), the activities might be noticeable and the organization could quickly respond appropriately to prevent penetration. That is unless secure socket layer (SSL) ports are leveraged to do the scans.

Most attackers will identify which servers offer SSL and will launch specialized scans on these systems first to maintain a "stealth" level of activity to avoid being detected. If the attacker is unable to identify if an organization has an IDS, then the servers that do not offer SSL will usually be attacked last, if at all, to continue to work undetected.

The penetration tester or attacker would also perform an assessment of non-Web exposed services. This would involve review of exposed banners, leveraging acquired username lists in an attempt to authenticate, attempting to bypass authentication, and an attempt to compromise exposed services. The goal of using the service(s) will be to access internal resources. Tool selection and strategy will depend upon the exposed services that are discovered.

### Internal Network

An internal penetration test or attack follows a similar format as an external. An internal attacker typically has an advantage. Their advantage is that they often understand the systems and the placement of the valuable assets that they wish to attack because they are often an employee with credentials to access resources associated with their role within the company. So there is time on their side to gain access to confidential information they are not supposed to access.

If the attacker is not an employee, they might start by locating an open "active" network jack in a location that would not be too conspicuous. The tester or attacker would then start information gathering and vulnerability analysis on devices that are visible on the internal network. Typical devices that are discovered by the penetration tester include servers, workstations, databases, printers, firewalls, routers, Web servers, e-mail servers, and ftp servers.

The tools used would be a port scanner such as NMAP and a vulnerability scanner like Nessus.

Based on an attacker's results and the targets that are identified, the exploit activities could be performed. The specific attack vectors are dependent upon exposed services and vulnerabilities associated with the exposed hosts and services. Subsequent penetration attack strategy and tool selection depends on the discovery.

# Conclusion

Vulnerability testing (i.e., assessment—VA) and penetration testing (i.e., assessment—PenTest) are not the same thing! They have much in common, are both a form of assessment, and when done correctly will help an organization manage their risk. They both have their place and should be part of a robust risk management program. The simplest difference in a "pure" sense is that the VA is less intrusive than the Pentest. Maturity of vulnerability management is very important before stepping into a Pentest. Pentesting will typically include the processes of scanning for vulnerabilities (i.e., discovery), which is the main process of the VA.

What are some of the motivators for VAs and Pentests?

- Compliance/fear
- Means to justify other initiatives
- New management eager to learn
- "True believers"

Anticipated benefits to a vulnerability assessment/PenTest can include

- Learning something new
- Validating and quantifying concerns
- Standardizing communication of vulnerabilities
- Establishing common language and tools
- Satisfying the auditors and regulators

The vendor selection process is an important step. Before selection, an organization must exercise due diligence when choosing a vendor to ensure the ethics and morals of not only the organization, but the individuals performing the assessment. This should include background and reference checks. Be sure to select a vendor who not only has employees with the skill to compromise the latest exploits but who can be trusted. These authors are not for hiring the "reformed" hacker, but we will leave that discussion for another day and time. If penetration testing is successful, you will want to have confidence that if any data is breached it will be handled in a secure and professional manner. You want to know that the exploits will not be published or talked about except in the management report to your organization.

Information security technology can be a life saver when identifying vulnerabilities and to stop many security incidents, but the processes of incident response plans are also crucial to minimizing potential impact. This means not just the technology of intrusion detection, but what to do if an attempt is detected. Every organization's security awareness and training programs must include reminders and proactive measures to keep not just the technology firewall, but the human firewall well prepared for the potential attack.

Oh. Did I ever tell you about the problem I had with bees...

## About the Author

**Ken M. Shaurette**, CISSP, CISA, CISM, IAM, is an engagement manager in Technology Risk Manager Services at Jefferson Wells, Inc. in Madison, Wisconsin.

# Chapter 13

# The Outsourcing of IT: Seeing the Big Picture

Foster Henderson

## Contents

Outsourcing information technology (IT) jobs has benefits if properly managed and conducted in a manner that doesn't jeopardize the loss of strategic or corporate assets. Unfortunately, the common practice is to solely focus on reducing costs and not applying the same amount of attention or diligence in addressing security issues. This problem encompasses ethical issues, losses in revenue in the long run, and a clear and present danger to our national interests. If we as a nation continue sending high-technology jobs overseas, should we trust the electronics or software when it appears in military applications, hardware, or other critical infrastructures that support a nation so dependent on technology?

## Background

The Central Intelligence Agency (CIA) stated within its *World Factbook* of 2008 the following:

> The US has the largest and most technologically powerful economy in the world, with a per capita [gross domestic product] GDP of $48,000. In this market-oriented economy, private individuals and business firms make most of the decisions, and the federal and state governments buy needed goods and services predominantly in the private marketplace. (CIA, 2008).

The GDP is defined as the final goods or services a country produces within a given year (CIA, 2008). An example of the United States's technological power is evident throughout twentieth-century history.

The United States as a nation is responsible for a majority of the greatest twentieth-century inventions that propelled its technologically powerful economy. Below is a sampling of those inventions:

- Computers
- Integrated circuits
- Lasers
- Fiber optics
- Telephone (traditional and cellular)
- Air conditioning and refrigeration
- Television
- Airplanes
- Internet (National Academy of Engineering, 2009)

The CIA estimates the world's GDP at $70.65 trillion; the United States's GDP is the second largest in the world, surpassed by the European Union by $380 billion, and is estimated to be nearly $14.58 trillion or 21% of the world's estimated GDP (CIA, 2008). The next closest country is China at $7.8 trillion or 53% of the United States's GDP (CIA, 2008).

Melton (2004) wrote at the end of the Cold War that the former Soviet Union was not able to adapt to the new global economy and lacked the telecommunications infrastructure to compete as a modern superpower; yet, it maintained a nuclear arsenal to destroy the world. The Cold War era has been replaced with the digital byte in today's economic and digital warfare. Future superpowers will be those nations that successfully compete in today's economic environment.

From a monetary viewpoint, how can lesser developed nations or businesses from those nations seek to compete in today's environment? How can they narrow the gap between their country and the United States, for example? One strategy is to simply obtain the technology they cannot afford to develop themselves. Think about it from a business point of view. It makes sense. Call it what you like: borrow, steal, copy, or acquire a technology. Let someone else expend valuable resources to perform the research and development of a product and simply pick up on the tail end with the production. This leads to my next point.

# Today's Business Environment (Globalization)

Business is war. Clausewitz (1832) stated in his chapter "Art or Science of War," the following:

> It is a conflict of great interests which is settled by bloodshed and only in that it is different from others. It would be better, instead of comparing it with any Art, to liken it to business competition, which is also a conflict of human interests and activities; and it is still more like State policy [politics], which again on its part, may be looked upon as a kind of business competition on a great scale (pp. 202–203).

I used the quote from a classic book to illustrate today's global business environment with all its underlying motivations and risks, which must be considered. For example, in a *Federal Computer Week* article titled the "Outsourcing Hole," French wrote the following:

> A terrorist cell looking for an advantage against the powerful U.S. military trains a group to be software programmers, who then infiltrate companies that have sent their software development work overseas. Working for those companies, the programmers surreptitiously put vulnerabilities in software (French, 2004a).

In too many instances, chief executive officers (CEOs), chief information officers (CIOs), or other decision makers do not account for the strategic impact that their decision to outsource IT will have on their own company or country. These decisions are being made solely on the basis of the expected cost savings without taking into account other potential problems or issues associated with outsourcing IT. Specifically, these decision makers tend to overlook critical information about the topics listed below:

- Turnover of personnel
- Insider threats
- Data security/protection
- Espionage cases
- Business cases
- Cost reduction expectations
- Business impact
- Ethics
- Project risks
- Cultural barriers
- Infrastructure risks
- National interests (includes geopolitical)

If one doesn't buy French's analysis as a possibility, here's another example of the risk.

In February 2002, nearly 6 months after September 11, 2001, Paul Wolfowitz, Deputy Secretary of Defense, signed Department of Defense (DoD) Directive (DoDD) 8000.01, Management of DoD Information Resources and Information Technology, [policy] that mandated the Services and individual organizations, which comprise the DoD, to perform the following actions summarized below:

- Before applying IT resources, determine whether or not if private industry or another government organization could provide the same product or services at a lower cost.
- Maximize the use of commercial-off-the-shelf (COTS) products for military acquisitions related to DoD IT and national security systems (NSS).
  - NSS is defined as U.S. government telecommunications or information related to intelligence, cryptological activities, command and control of military forces, equipment or control of a weapon or weapon system, or fruition of military or intelligence missions.
- Outsource non-core or inherently non-government business functions to another government organization or private sector when it made good business case or decision.
- Custom designed products shall be avoided or isolated to minimize severe impacts to project schedules or budgets.

On February 10, 2009, the above policy was canceled, updated, and renamed DoDD 8000.01, Management of the Department of Defense Information Enterprise (ASD NII/DoD CIO, 2009). This policy is consistent with DoD's existing acquisition policies and now states:

- Acquisitions shall allocate risk between the U.S. Government and contractors
- Tie contract payments to performance
- When applicable, take maximum advantage of COTS technology
- Information solutions are to be structured, brief, with a delivered and measurable net benefit
- Outsource noncore or nongovernmental functions to another U.S. Government entity or the private sector when it makes appropriate business case (ASD NII/DoD CIO, 2009)

The benefits of COTS can be illustrated throughout IT history. Xerox developed the first personal computer, but it was too expensive to market because everything was developed from scratch. IBM's personal computer (PC) was released in August 12, 1981, and was IBM's first computer built from off-the-shelf parts distributed by outside vendors. It used an existing Intel 8086 chip that IBM had licensing rights from Intel to manufacture (Bellis, 1999a). The development of IBM's PC is an early example of outsourcing, where Microsoft developed a 16-bit operating system (OS) that it called MS-DOS. A more modern example is Boeing outsourcing to Chinese vendors, which has had a major consequence, as discussed later in this chapter.

## Outsourcing Types

Bierce and Kenerson (2007) define outsourcing as "the transfer or delegation to an external service provider the operation and day-to-day management of a business process. The customer receives a service that performs a distinct business function that fits into the customer's overall business operations." They state there are two principal types of outsourcing: traditional and greenfield. They define those respective terms as follows:

> …employees of an enterprise cease to perform the same jobs to the enterprise. Rather, tasks are identified that need to be performed, and the employees are normally hired by the service provider. In "greenfield" outsourcing, the enterprise changes its business processes without any hiring of personnel by the service provider. For example, the enterprise might hire a startup company to provide a new service, such as wireless remote computing, that was not previously managed internally (Bierce and Kenerson, P.C., 2007).

Now, from that definition we can see the more commonly known types of outsourced services, technology services and business process outsourcing (BPO). For further clarification, outsourcing practice terms "nearshore" and "offshoring" will be used. These words refer to geographical locations according to whether the outsourced work is sent outside the country. The term "offshoring" primarily used within the United States refers to those jobs or services sent overseas as a result of outsourcing (Pfannenstein and Tsai, 2004). A key benefit is that the labor pool is cheaper overseas when compared to wages within the United States to perform the same task. Nearshore outsourcing refers to those locations where outsourced work occurs within the same four major times zones as the United States (Rao, 2004). Another term that won't be used in this chapter but is a used business practice is "insourcing." Rao (2004) described insourcing as "attempts to reap the dual advantages of low-cost offshore environments" (p. 20). Specifically, some U.S. companies will hire foreign technology workers as employees at established offshore IT centers who receive the same training, tools, support, and follow the same developing outlines as their U.S. counterparts (Rao, 2004). The one exception is that these workers come from poorer countries and are paid less than their U.S. counterparts. The reason for this practice is to eliminate some of the risks associated with outsourcing IT, specifically software development, to third-party vendors (Rao, 2004).

## Risk Management

"As soon as you have anything of value, you are at risk of losing it—it is just that simple" (Tiller, 2004, p. 1064). As added value along the same thought process: what are you protecting, and why is it important to protect? If an individual, corporation, or country does not know what is worth protecting, then the security plan is flawed from the start. Risk management involves first identifying the risk, knowing the probability for it occurring, and then being able to respond to that threat or vulnerability. There are four things an individual, company, or nation can do with risk. You can ignore it, accept it, transfer it (insurance policy), or mitigate it. Mitigation involves reducing risk to an acceptable level where the consequences of that event are recoverable. For example, outsourcing touches upon the one key item or one common thread this nation and its underlying businesses was built upon that propels our economy: intellectual property (IP).

## Intellectual Property

*Merriam-Webster's Dictionary of Law* (1996) defines IP as "property that derives from the work of the mind or intellect; specifically: an idea, invention, trade secret, process, program, data, formula, patent, copyright, or trademark or application, right, or registration relating thereto" (Dictionary.com, 2009). As previously mentioned, there were nine bulletized items briefly mentioned at the beginning of this chapter (i.e., within Today's Business Environment subheading). The first four bullets will be discussed in detail because they are integrally connected to the one item most corporations are attempting to protect: IP. As a reminder, the four items were

■ Turnover of personnel
■ Insider threats
■ Data security/protection
■ Espionage cases

History is a teacher that provides a useful method for understanding the value of IP and why it should be protected. For example, Bill Gates, cofounder of Microsoft, and Steve Jobs, cofounder of Apple, both took tours of Xerox's Palo Alto Research Center. Jobs first visited the site and was inspired by the work Xerox was performing with the Graphic User Interface (GUI) involving pull-down menus and point and click features (Bellis, 1999b). Bill Gates was hired to work on software for the Macintosh, which was released in 1984, and Gates released Windows 1.0 in 1985. Mesa (1998) states

> ....Bill Gates feared Apple would sue him due to the fact that his OS was looking a lot like the Mac OS. So on November 22, 1983, John Sculley, then CEO of Apple, signed an agreement to allow Microsoft to use Mac OS technology in exchange for further development of Microsoft software for the Mac. This single event would be one of the biggest mistakes in the history of the micro-computing industry.

When Steve Jobs complained that Gates had stolen designs from the Mac, Gates' reply appearing in *MacWeek* was "Hey, Steve, just because you broke into Xerox's house before I did and took the TV doesn't mean I can't go in later and take the stereo" (Mesa, 1998). Later, Bill Gates worked on the next OS for IBM PC, which was OS/2 to replace the MS-DOS OS. The deal went bad and as a result Gates took that information from working for IBM and turned it into what is now known as Windows NT. IBM later sued and lost due to contractual language within the licensing agreements.

Fortunately, the aftermath from the lawsuits still benefited the U.S. economy (i.e., among Apple and Microsoft, and Microsoft and IBM) and jobs were created within this country as a result of a disputed IP owner(s); however, it can be assumed Apple and IBM wouldn't see it that way. What if this 1980s timeline were moved up 20 years and occurred in a foreign country where a U.S. company was offshoring? Are companies conducting background investigations on offshoring employees and who would be the IP owner if this occurred today?

## Data Security/Protection

IP is something a majority of companies have difficulty grappling with or even understanding. Michael Croy (2004) stated "Most business managers say their data must be highly available, but few identify which data needs to be highly accessible and which data can be stored in less accessible locations" (p. 20). This point is important because with offshoring, most companies use data centers. These data centers are usually located in remote regions where the infrastructure isn't in the company's control, but a vendor's control located in another country. Also consider the fact that in 2003, it was estimated that 1 out of every 500 data centers experienced a computer disaster (Margeson, 2003), and application failure was the number one reason in most outages (Roden, 2004). "The loss of critical knowledge is seen as the greatest source of work-force related risk around outsourcing" (Pfannenstein and Tsai, 2004, p. 75). While this statement was specifically focusing on the intellectual assets that will be discussed shortly, it also refers to loss of digital information.

For example, the importance of data security and protection should become evident by discussing Boeing's outsourcing with China. It was previously mentioned that airplanes made the National Academy of Engineering's twentieth century's greatest engineering achievements list. According to Owen Herrnstadt (2008), Boeing has worked with China for three decades in various business dealings to include manufacturing training, raw materials, and parts. As a condition for Boeing to sell its 747 to Air China, parts of the plane had to be assembled in China (Herrnstadt, 2008). During his Congressional testimony (U.S. Congress, 2008), Herrnstadt stated that there has been technology transfers "offsets" (as described previously within Pfannenstein and Tsai's (2004) article). China Daily (2007) stated, "China is now Boeing company's largest foreign supplier of parts, with US $2.5 billion of live contracts for aircraft products, a senior Boeing official said here on Thursday" (para 1). More troubling is that earlier *USA Today* (2004) reported, "China studies building its own large aircraft." In addition, on March 27, 2007, Cameron et al., (2007) wrote an article in the *Financial Times* titled "China to challenge Boeing and Airbus." The *Financial Times* article stated that China was going to pursue building its own airplanes rather than buy from Airbus or Boeing.

Strictly focusing on raw data (i.e., the electronic form in bytes), what guarantees are in place to ensure that data in transit (transmission) or storage is being properly protected from prying eyes? There are specific regulations that have privacy requirements for U.S.-based companies. Below are a few regulatory requirements:

- The Privacy Act of 1974
- Health Insurance Portability and Accountability Act of 1996 (HIPAA)
- Sarbanes–Oxley Act of 2002 (Sox) (public company accounting reform)
- European Data Protection Directive (Rao, 2004)
- California SB 1386 (Blum, 2004)
- Gramm–Leach Bliley Act (Blum, 2004)

Failure to comply with the above regulatory requirements can result in steep financial or disclosure penalties (Blum, 2004).

## Turnover of Personnel

Bangalore, India, has experienced rapid growth as a result of being one of the larger IT outsourcing hot spots, which has created a dynamic labor market. Turnover rates for that region are reported to be from 15% to 20% and there are associated indirect IT costs as a result of training new employees and loss of knowledge associated with turnover (Davison, 2004). Also any knowledge or experience gained working in a particular project (i.e., what does work and doesn't work), the best business practices to use, etc., is lost when an employee leaves. Overby (2003) stated the cost for turnover of vendors is as high as 35% in India. A Deutsche Bank research conducted by Schaaf (2005) stated that India's employee turnover in call centers is 50%, and among IT providers the range of turnover is from 15% to 30%. There is also the question what's to stop an individual from working with another competitor on a similar project and using what they learned from the previous job in their new position with a new employer?

## Insider Threats

By law, companies have to provide employees 60 days notification prior to outsourcing their jobs. Most of those employees who would be notified in this instance are probably aware that the main reason they are losing their jobs is to reduce the company's payroll. Insider threats pose more security consequences than an outside hacker because an insider is an employee who has more access rights or privileges to company assets than a stranger not associated with the company. It is safe to assume that insider threats would increase due to the backlash associated with employees losing their jobs because of outsourcing. For example, a credit union employee with system administrator access was terminated and had his account disabled. Unfortunately, the credit union forgot to remove the individual's remote network access or change the password that led to the credit union's network being sabotaged and unavailable for three days. The 2004 Computer Security Institute (CSI)/FBI Computer Crime and Security Survey was based upon 481 participants and 59% of those respondents reported insider abuse of their network totaled $10,601,055 (CSI/FB1, 2004). CSI's 2008 Computer Crime and Security Survey stated that insider abuse was the second-most frequently occurring problem reported by 44% of its 420 respondents; down from 2007s 59% of previous respondents reporting insider abuse (CSI, 2008).

## Espionage Cases

Sun Tzu's *Art of War* is a timeless classic written around 500 BC. The last chapter in his book is titled, Employment of Secret Agents. Sun Tzu's fourth principle states, "…foreknowledge cannot be elicited from spirits, nor from gods, nor by analogy with past events, nor from calculations. It must be obtained from men who know the enemy situation" (Tzu, 500 BC, p. 145). Michaelson (2001) further elaborated with a modern Sun Tzu interpretation stating, "While you get their secrets, protect your own" (p. 132).

As a result of economic espionage, one company in particular no longer exists: Ellery Systems, Inc. (Texas A & M, n.d.). Ellery was working on distributed computing technology software. An employee from Ellery Systems went to China and returned, resigned, and proceeded to download the source code and sent it to a friend in China. The employee later admitted to meeting with Chinese officials. The cost to develop the source code was $950,000with an estimated market value in the billions (Texas A & M, n.d.). In November 2001, two men were arrested in San Francisco's airport en route to China caught with suitcases packed with microchip designs, equipment, and other trade secrets (Konrad, 2003). Court documents stated that the Chinese government wrote in documents discovered in the homes of the suspects indicating their work is "extremely useful to the development of China's integrated circuit industry" (Konrad, 2003).

Weiss (n.d.) discusses several interesting espionage facts within an article that are summarized and highlighted below:

■ The Soviets performed "successful clandestine effort to obtain technical and scientific knowledge from the West" (Weiss, G, n.d.).
   − The operation process was code named "Line X"
■ A Soviet citizen visiting Boeing's facility had glue on his shoes to obtain metallurgic samples.
■ A Soviet delegation applied for a visa to visit a light-emitting diode watch manufacturer; however, three days before their arrival they expanded the trip to include computer and semiconductor firms.
   − The intentional last-minute change prevented the DoD the necessary time to object and this maneuver was within legal constraints; thus nothing could be done
■ In the early 1970s, the Soviets proposed purchasing 50 planes from financially strapped Lockheed with the stipulation Lockheed build and equip those planes in their country.

- Line X obtained thousands of documents, samples, and technology in radar, computers, and semiconductors.
- In the mid-1990s, the Soviet science advisor wrote the Soviets trailed the West 15 years in military and civil technology and a Soviet-made supercomputer was the most glaring absence illustrating this fact (Weiss, n.d.).

The United States caught onto the Soviets' Line X operation and deliberately slipped faulty programmed computer chips, a rejected NASA space shuttle design, stealth technology, and more into what the Soviets were covertly acquiring from U.S. companies and the U.S. government (Weiss, n.d). The various stolen technologies eventually made their way into military equipment and turbines used within the Soviet's gas pipeline (Safire, 2004). *The New York Times* printed an article based upon Thomas Reed's 2004 book and Gus Weiss' historical account. The effects of sending the Soviets bogus technology led to an estimated three-kiloton blast in the Siberian wilderness in 1982. This occurred because the computer chips and software was designed to pass Soviet quality control tests, yet when put into operation, exceeded the gas pipeline's tolerance (Safire, 2004).

Some of this may appear like something from a Tom Clancy novel or as in the case with the Soviets, it is ancient history and someone may say that the Cold War is over and that this does not apply in today's climate. During the Cold War, the United States sent naval submarines to tap into Soviet cables lying on the ocean floors (Drew et al., 1999). The point is why bother using outdated and expensive Cold War tactics when there is offshoring or the Internet in which nearly everything is connected? Michaelson (2001) wrote in the *Art of War for Managers*, "The vision of what the organization wants must be planned with an awareness of reality" (p. 3). Furthermore, on the same page, he further states

> A common mistake is to consider planning as only a mental process, an idea in our head that simply looks at the past and adjust for the future. If your plan is not in writing, you do not have a plan at all. Instead, you only have a dream, a vision, or perhaps even a nightmare (Michaelson, 2001, p. 3).

Michaelson (2001) went on to state the following:

> There is evidence that Asian nations readily apply Sun Tzu's lessons on "secret agents." A survey of 1300 companies conducted by the American Society of Industrial Security revealed China and Japan head the list of foreign countries possessing the greatest economic espionage threat. However next in line were France, Great Britain, and Canada (p. 132).

A more recent assessment within the Annual Report to Congress on Foreign Economic Collection and Industrial Espionage, FY [U.S. fiscal year] 07 (2008) stated, "Many European countries appear to face industrial espionage threats from China, Russia, and others that are similar to threats facing the United States, according to the media" (p. 2).

The semiconductor industry has changed its strategy from building new plants in Taiwan and instead has chosen to locate them in China (*Manufacturing & Technology News*, 2003a). China has changed its value-added tax to a 14-point advantage in their favor, which is attracting the semiconductor industry to that country. A *Manufacturing & Technology News* (2003b) article indicated, "The U.S. government should require that China provide full protection for intellectual property and increase enforcement of IP because lack of enforcement enables the piracy of semiconductor designs." *Manufacturing & Technology News* published an article describing a debate over defense offsets within Congress. An offset is when foreign countries require transfer of technology or manufacturing capacity in order to receive a contract (i.e., from American companies). The term "economic bribery" was used to describe this practice by one senator (*Manufacturing & Technology News*, 2004a,b).

## The Business Case and Expected Cost Savings

Most of the information recently discussed is overlooked in comparison with saving a U.S. dollar. Verton (2003) indicated a 2003 Gardner study, which concluded that in 2004 "80 percent of U.S. companies will consider outsourcing critical IT services, including software development, to countries such as India, Pakistan, Russia and China". *CIO* magazine conducted a survey with its readers in January 2004, and 49% of the survey's 340 respondents indicated outsourcing was the main reason to lower costs (Ware, 2004).

Earlier it was stated there are four ways to treat risk: ignore it, accept it, transfer it, or mitigate it. The CSI/FBI 2004 Computer Crime Survey indicated 72% of the respondents do not have an external insurance policy to transfer cyber security risks (CSI/FBI, 2004). The 2008 CSI Computer Crime Survey indicated a mild increase from 29% (2007's results) to 34% of the respondents stating they have insurance policies (CSI, 2008). And some of the risk management issues discussed earlier, in regard to complying with regulatory compliance statues, may actually contradict the initial expected cost savings. Blum (2004) briefly discussed within his article the fact that companies may find that the expected cost savings may evaporate when proper risk management practices, such as conducting audits on software code and background checks on offshore employees, are carried out. Kliem (2004) wrote this regarding outsourcing .... "these risks are potentially more numerous and disabling, with the possibility of offsetting the potential gains from outsourcing in the long run" (p. 23). Specifically, the initial expected or cost savings from outsourcing will be reduced when you take into account the severance pay, monitoring the contract performance, providing oversight, legal consultation expenses for the awarding the contract, relocations cost, and dual payrolls (i.e., before a corporation transfers U.S. jobs overseas).

## Business Impact

"Organizations simply lack the means and experiential research to assign value to the knowledge they are transferring and receiving" (Feeney et al., 2004, p. 7). If organizations or individuals don't understand the value assigned to knowledge, more commonly known or referred to as "IP assets," the business impact of outsourcing is unknown and won't be known until it may be too late. Businesses are either simply unaware, ignoring, or simply accepting the risks. Security is overhead to most companies and it affects the total net profit. Without knowing all the risks and benefits associated with a decision to outsource and properly manage risks, the same outcome or sequence of events discussed earlier (e.g., from Ellery Systems, Inc.; Xerox; Apple Computer; IBM; and possibly Boeing in the distant future now having to compete against China) will be repeated again.

To use the Boeing example again, it was stated that Boeing's latest project the 787 is two years behind schedule due to the various problems with its outsourced partners and is making plans to bring the work back in-house amid pressure customers may cancel orders (Weber, 2009). If an individual is under the assumption that this is an isolated case or that Boeing is being singled out, far from the contrary. Overby (2006) wrote,

> In the past year alone, 47 percent of companies have prematurely ended an outsourcing arrangement, according to research by Diamond Management and Technology Consultants. Forty-three percent of them brought the work back in-house, indicating it may not have been a good decision to farm out the function in the first place (para 4).

## Ethics

"We have one of the few societies, the only one I can think of right offhand, where your health care is tied to your job, so that when an American company has to hire, they have to think about health care" (Congressman Frank, 2004, p. H2054). People are losing their jobs as a result of globalization and old jobs are being lost or destroyed while new ones are being created. The problem is that while new jobs are being gained or created, it is often at a reduced pay scale and loss of benefits (Congressman Frank, 2004). In the past, education was one method of ensuring job stability or security within this country. "The jobs being outsourced are the jobs we used to retrain people for" (Congressman Frank, 2004, p. H2057). President Obama (CBS News, 2009) stated. .... "that over the last decade, the average worker, the average family have seen their wages and incomes flat. Even at times where supposedly we were in the middle of an economic boom, as a practical matter, their incomes didn't go up" (p. 7).

The Economic Policy Institutes' briefing paper (Herrnstadt, 2008), which was referenced within Herrnstadt's Congressional testimony (U.S. Congress, 2008), briefly stated the following:

- Within the United States, over 3 million jobs lost due to offsets the past few years
- Sited a U.S. government report that over 16,000 jobs lost each year between 2002 and 2005 due to defense industry offsets
- Sited a 1996 GAO study where McDonnell Douglas machine tools were shipped to China's business (i.e., another offset) that was transferred to a Chinese producer of military equipment
- Sited an Aerospace Industry Commission report stating aerospace account for 15% of the United States's GDP
  - Nearly 500,000 aerospace jobs lost since 1990 due to offsets (Herrnstadt, 2008)

The intent of the H-1B and L-1 visa was to allow U.S. companies to recruit foreign employees as a result of the shortage of technical people during the ".com" boom. However, the H-1B and L-1 visa program is now being abused because companies are employing foreign workers at reduced salaries rather than available unemployed high-tech U.S. workers (e.g., Silicon Valley area). For example, Humphries was a 1996 Stanford graduate who lost her quality assurance engineering job at Palm (i.e., maker of the popular handheld PDA and Palm One software). Humphries described how she had to train her Indian replacement and before a Congressional hearing was quoted in the article saying "....we have companies more concerned about the bottom line than they are in preserving U.S. jobs" (*Manufacturing & Technology News*, 2003a,b). Interestingly, a finding from a *CIO* magazine survey indicated only 12% of its respondents stated their reason to use outsourcing resulted from a lack of qualified workers or scarce skills (Ware, 2004). Ironically, McCormack (2005) within his article detailed that the Defense Science Board stated DoD was the most logically to lead and encourage a national solution to save the U.S. semiconductor industry rather than them making a recommendation to Congress or the commerce department as it's a private sector issue that started the problem. Private corporations such as Dell, Apple, HP, etc., manufacture laptops either in Taiwan or China, and Intel corp. has manufacturing plants across the globe.

Sectors such as law enforcement, the intelligence community, or the DoD routinely require processing confidential to highly sensitive data (i.e., classified). Yet, it is common knowledge that this group uses COTS software for their OS and databases. The ethical question to pose is this: if a specific vendor is a key provider or source for software used in this particular business process climate is that vendor informing its clients that the software is being outsourced? This issue was partially addressed within a DoD *Interim Defense Acquisition Guidebook*. Unfortunately, the procedures listed are not mandatory and are at the discretion of acquisition program managers (French, 2004a,b). Within the IT security profession, program managers are notorious for their focus on cost-cutting principles and not using that same diligence as in cutting costs to address security issues because that increases the costs for their project. French (2004a,b) wrote an article titled "Setting Boundaries" describing a summary of the security rules for foreign affiliates involved with software development based upon the previously mentioned policy. It is located below:

■ Vendors must indicate whether foreign affiliates participated in software development
■ Foreign affiliates employed as contractors to DoD to develop or modify code must have security clearances (i.e., extensive background investigations performed) equivalent to the level the software's intended use
■ DoD software coded by foreign affiliates must be reviewed by software quality assurance employees for malicious content (French, 2004a,b)

## National Interest (United States and Others)

As previously mentioned, it is common knowledge that the DoD and U.S. government heavily use Microsoft's operating system (OS) software and COTS computers. It was announced in February 2003 that Microsoft would provide its OS source code to China and other countries. Apparently, Congress had no issue in allowing Microsoft to release the source code, and in a partial defense, Microsoft was responding to the open source OS threat that was eating into its market share. As it may not be perfectly clear, the security concern is this: since Microsoft released its source code the question is whether or not the intelligence community, DoD, or law enforcement agencies or other federal departments have experienced increased attempts by someone writing virus or malicious code attempting to penetrate those IT systems based upon weaknesses in the Microsoft source code? What does this have to do with outsourcing?

IT professionals at a security conference in South Carolina questioned the reliance on offshore software developers, which is ultimately putting companies and the U.S. economy at risk (Verton, 2003). Attendees at the security conference raised common concerns about work being sent to China. Verton (2003) wrote "....China has a significant economic espionage program that targets U.S. technology." Furthermore, another voiced concern was that some software was being developed in "....countries in Southeast Asia, particularly Malaysia and Indonesia where terrorist networks are known to exist" (Verton, 2003). During the same technology meeting it was acknowledged that Oracle outsources some of its software developmental work to companies based in India and China; however they are only granted read access (Verton, 2003). Just a thought, but wasn't Abraham Lincoln reportedly self-taught from reading? A Government Accountability Office (GAO) report stated "DoD officials' control over software, particularly which goes into weapons platforms is lacking" (French, 2004a,b). In addition, the Office of the National Counterintelligence Executive (2008) key finding to Congress stated:

> The United States remains the prime target for foreign economic collection and industrial espionage by virtue of its global technological leadership and innovation. Collectors from across the globe—private businessmen, scientists, engineers, students, and foreign military and intelligence officers—engaged in economic collection activities against the United States in Fiscal Year 2007 (FY 2007), according to information amassed by the Counterintelligence (CI) Community. While collectors came from a large number of countries, those from fewer than 10 nations, including both allies and adversaries, accounted for the bulk of targeting activity (p. ii).

Hopefully, it is clearly evident that outsourcing not only in values U.S. interests, which corporate leaders should consider, but also those of other nations or companies who have their own agendas.

## Mitigations of Risks (Outsourcing)

### Trusted Foundry

The National Security Agency and DoD have voiced similar security issues and concerns over the shift of semiconductor manufacturing capacity offshore (*Manufacturing & Technology News*, 2004a,b). As previously mentioned, the Defense Science Board, recommended that DoD take the lead to save the U.S. semiconductor industry (McCormack, 2005). The NSA and DoD are funding a "Trusted Foundry" initiative owned by IBM. The deal with IBM will allow NSA and DoD to move away from their heavy reliance on COTS technology and to obtain designs of various technologies with strict guidelines and procedures to ensure reliability of that technology (*Manufacturing & Technology News*, 2004a,b). As a follow-up to his previous article, and in response to the Defense Science Board's earlier recommendation, McCormack wrote the DoD has stepped up the program to include microelectronics in its supply chain and that 10 companies were accredited as "trusted" suppliers (2008).

### Trusted Software

The federal government has provided a number of valuable resources to IT professionals through the National Information Assurance Partnership (NIAP). NIAP involves the initiative to increase information technology security by collaborating with industry in security testing, research, and the development of information assurance methodologies. From NIAP came the Common Criteria Evaluation and Validations Scheme (CCEVS), which is jointly managed by the National Security Agency and National Institute of Standards and Technology (NIST). The CCEVS established a national program for the evaluation of information technology products. This program is known as Common Criteria (CC) and it is identified as International Organization for Standardization (ISO) 15408. Under CC there are seven protection profiles. A firm understanding of the CC's protection profiles, which also include seven evaluation assurance levels (EAL), is important for various reasons (Henderson and Craig-Henderson, 2004). "The CC will permit comparability between the results of independent security evaluations" (ISO, 1999). In laymen's terms there are strict guidelines that must be followed and documented and these must be verified by an independent lab.

*Investigation*

Nothing takes the place of truly informed decision. Thoughtful and strategic planning has to occur first before diving in and claiming money can be saved. A review of the Boeing case, discussed several times, is a perfect example. Specifically, if an organizational management performs the following:

■ Carefully inventories and catalogs its IP and assigns values
■ Performs the necessary background checks of outsourced personnel
■ Checks the political climate, safety, of the outsourced host's infrastructure
■ Prepares a project risk management plan
■ Performs a return on investment with clearly defined metrics to measure success

That organization won't be within the 47% of companies to prematurely end an outsourced deal. Instead, it will be within the 53% of successful companies (Overby, 2006).

## Conclusion

Outsourcing IT jobs has benefits, if properly managed and conducted in a manner that doesn't jeopardize the loss of strategic or corporate assets. Having a clear inventory or understanding of what an organization's intellectual property is and properly managing and having a plan for protecting those "assets" is when an informed decision to outsource IT jobs can be rationally made. Otherwise, in the somewhat near future, those companies outsourcing today without the proper planning are not only creating their competition but are also continuing to create harm to their own nation in the long run.

## About the Author

**Foster Henderson**, CISM, CISSP senior recovery planner, NSA IAM, is an information assurance (IA) consultant for the United States Department of Defense. He is currently an information assurance manager covering a wide range of IA matters.

## References

ASD (NII)/DoD CIO (2009). Department of Defense Directive Number 8000.1, Management of the Department of Defense Information Enterprise. Retrieved March 22, 2009, from http://www.dtic.mil/whs/directives/corres/pdf/800001p.pdf

Bellis, M. (1999a). Inventors of the modern computer: The history of the IBM PC. Retrieved December 4, 2004, from http://inventors.about.com/library/weekly/aa031599.htm

Bellis, M. (1999b). Inventors of the modern computer: The history of the graphical user interface or GUI—The Apple Lisa. Retrieved December 4, 2004, from http://inventors.about.com/library/weekly/aa043099.htm

Bierce and Kenerson, P.C. (2007). Outsourcing law. Retrieved March 26, 2009, from http://www.outsourcing-law.com/what_is_outsourcing.htm

Blum, D. (2004). Weigh risks of offshore outsourcing. *Network World*. Retrieved November 2, 2004, from http://www.networkworld.com/columnists/2004/0308blum.html?fsrc=rss-outsourcing

Cameron, D., Done, K., and McGregor R. (2007). China to challenge Boeing and Airbus. *Financial Times*. Retrieved March 29, 2009, from http://www.ft.com/cms/s/0/62138fe6-d575-11db-a5c6-000b5df10621.html?nclick_check=1

CBS News. (2009). Transcript: Obama press conference March 24, 2009: The President Takes questions from the White House Press Corps. *CBS News*. Retrieved March from http://www.cbsnews.com/stories/2009/03/25/politics/100days/main4891818.shtml

China Daily. (2007). China becomes largest foreign supplier of Boeing parts. *China Daily*. Retrieved March 27, 2009, from http://www.chinadaily.com.cn/china/2007- 09/07/content_6088635.htm

Clausewitz, C.V. (1832). Vom kreige: Translation published by Routledge & Kegan Paul Ltd 1908. Art or Science of War (pp. 202–203). London, U.K.: Penguin Classics.

Common Criteria: Common Criteria for information technology security evaluation Part 1: Introduction and general model. (2004). National Institute of Standard and Technology.

Croy, M. (2004). The business value of data. *Disaster Recovery Journal*, Summer 2004, 17(3), 20.

CSI/FBI Computer Crime and Security Survey. (2004). Federal Bureau of Investigation. Retrieved September 15, 2004, from www.go.csi.com

CSI Computer Crime and Security Survey. (2008). CSI. Retrieved March 25, 2006, from http://www.gocsi.com/forms/csi_survey.jhtml

Davison, D. (2004). Top 10 risks of offshore outsourcing. *CIO* magazine. Retrieved November 2, 2004, from http://searchcio.techtarget.com/news/article/0,289142,sid182_gci950602,00.html

Department of Defense Directive Number 8000.1, Management of DoD Resources and Information Technology. (2002). Assistant Secretary of Defense (Command, Control, Communications, and Intelligence {ASD (C3I)}).

Dictionary.com. (n.d.). Intellectual property. Retrieved March 21, 2009, from http://dictionary.reference.com/browse/property?db = legal&q = property

Drew, A., Drew, C., and Sontag, S. (1999). *Blind Man's Bluff: The Untold Story of the American Submarine Espionage*. New York: Perennial.

Feeney, D., Hindle, J., Lacity, M., and Willcocks, L. (2004). IT and business process outsourcing: The knowledge potential. Information Security Management. Retrieved November 15, 2004, from www.ism-journal.com

Frank, B. (2004). Employment problems in America. U.S. Congressional Record–House, pp. H2054–H2059.

French, M. (2004a). The outsourcing hole. *Federal Computer Weekly*. Retrieved October 25, 2004, from http://www.fcw.com/fcw/articles/2004/0719/pol-outsource-07-19-04.asp

French, M. (2004b). Setting boundaries. *Federal Computer Weekly*. Retrieved November 2, 2004, from http://www.fcw.com/fcw/articles/2004/0719/pol-outsource2-07-19-04.asp

Henderson, F. and Craig-Henderson, K. (2004). Security architecture and models. In Krause, M. and Tipton, H. (eds.), *Information Security Management Handbook*, 5th edn. (pp. 1531–1554), Boca Raton, FL: Auerbach Publications.

Herrnstadt, O. (2008). Offsets and the lack of a comprehensive U.S. policy. Economic Policy Institute. Retrieved March 29, 2009, from http://www.sharedprosperity.org/bp201/bp201.pdf

Insider Threat Study: Illicit cyber activity in the banking and finance sector. (2004). United States Secret Service/CERT Coordination Center/SEI.

International Organization for Standardization, ISO/IEC 15408-1:1999. Information technology—Security techniques—Evaluation criteria for IT security—Part 1: Introduction and general model, 1999.

Kliem, R. (2004). Managing the risks of offshore IT development projects. Information Security Management. Retrieved November 15, 2004, from www.ism-journal.com.

Konrad, R. (2003). Judge to hear motions in Silicon Valley economic espionage case. *The Detroit News Technology*. Retrieved March 23, 2009, from http://www.highbeam.com/doc/1P1-85920329.html

Manufacturing & Technology News. (2003a). Engineers fear offshore outsourcing is contributing to high jobless rates. Retrieved November 6, 2004, from http://www.manufacturingnews.com/news/03/1104/art1.html

Manufacturing & Technology News. (2003b). How China is quickly capturing the world's semiconductor industry. Retrieved November 6, 2004, from http://www.manufacturingnews.com/news/03/0804/art1.html

Manufacturing & Technology News. (2004a). $600 million over 10 years for IBM's 'Trusted Foundry' chip industry's shift overseas elicits National Security Agency, Defense Department response. Retrieved October 19, 2004, from http://www.manufacturingnews.com/news/04/0203/art1.html

Manufacturing & Technology News. (2004b). 'Buy American' raises its head once again; This time in a battle over defense 'offsets.' Retrieved October 19, 2004, from http://www.manufacturingnews.com/news/04/0707/art1.html

McCormack, R. (2005). Defense Science Board tells military to develop a grand strategy to save the U.S. semiconductor industry. *Manufacturing & Technology News*. Retrieved March 25, 2009, from http://www.manufacturingnews.com/news/05/0422/art1.html

Margeson, B. (2003). The human side of data loss. *Disaster Recovery Journal*, Spring 2003, 16(2), 48. Retrieved from http://www.drj.com/articles/spr03/1602-08.html

Melton, H.K. (2004). Spies in the digital age. *Cable News Network (CNN)*. Retrieved November 29, 2004, from http://www.cnn.com/SPECIALS/cold.war/experience/spies/melton.essay/

Mesa, A. (1998). Apple and the GUI. Retrieved December 4, 2004, from http://applemuseum.bott.org/sections/gui.html

Michaelson, G.A. (2001). *Sun Tzu: The Art of War for Managers*, Avon, MA: Adams Media Corp.

National Academy of Engineering. (2009). Greatest engineering achievements of the 20th century. Retrieved March 27, 2009, from http://www.greatachievements.org/

Office of the National Counterintelligence Executive. (2008) Annual report to congress on foreign economic collection and industrial espionage, FY07. Retrieved March 27, 2009, from http://www.ncix.gov/publications/reports/fecie_all/fecie_2007/FECIE_2007.pdf

Overby, S. (2003). The hidden cost of offshore outsourcing: Moving jobs overseas can be a much more expensive proposition than you may think. *CIO* magazine. Retrieved October 25, 2004, from http://www.cio.com/article/29654/The_Hidden_Costs_of_Offshore_Outsourcing.

Overby, S. (2006). How to say no to outsourcing. *CIO* magazine. Retrieved March 28, 2009, from http://www.cio.com/article/25356/How_to_Say_No_to_Outsourcing?page=1

Pfannenstein, L.L. and Tsai, R. (2004). Offshore outsourcing: Current and future effects on American IT industry. Retrieved November 15, 2004, from www.ism-journal.com

Rao, M. (2004). Key issues for global IT sourcing: Country and individual factors. Retrieved November 15, 2004, from www.ism-journal.com

Roden, K. (2004). Building a business case for disaster recovery planning. *Disaster Recovery Journal*, Summer 2004, 17(3), 76–77.

Safire, W. (2004). The Farwell dossier. *The New York Times*. Retrieved October 19, 2004, from http://courses.dce.harvard.edu/~cscie160/FarewellDosier.html

Schaaf, J. (2005). Outsourcing to India: Crouching tiger set to pounce. *Deutsche Bank Research*. Retrieved March 25, 2009, from http://www.dbresearch.com/PROD/DBR_INTERNET_EN-PROD/PROD0000000000192125.pdf

Tiller, J. (2004). Outsourcing security. In Krause, M. and Tipton, H. (eds.), *Information Security Management Handbook*, 5th edn. (p. 1064), Boca Raton, FL: Auerbach Publications.

Texas A & M Research Foundation. (n.d.). Espionage killed the company. Retrieved December 11, 2004, from http://rf-web.tamu.edu/security/Security%20Guide/Spystory/Ellery.htm

Tzu, S. (500 BC). *The Art of War: Translated and with an Introduction by Samuel. B. Griffith*, Oxford, U.K.: Oxford University Press.

United States Congressional Congress. (2008). Testimony of Owen E. Herrnstadt. USCC. Retrieved March 28, 2009, from http://www.uscc.gov/hearings/2008hearings/transcripts/08_07_16_trans/herrnstadt.pdf

USA Today. (2004). China studies building its own large aircraft. *USA Today*. Retrieved March 29, 2009, from http://www.usatoday.com/travel/news/2004-03-15-china-jets_x.htm

Verton, D. (2003). Offshore coding work raises security concerns. *Computer World*. Retrieved March 16, 2010, from http://www.computerworld.com/s/article/80935/Offshore coding work raises security concerns

Weber, J. (2009). Boeing to Rein in Dreamliner outsourcing. *Business Week*. Retrieved March 29, 2009, from http://www.businessweek.com/bwdaily/dnflash/content/jan2009/db20090116_971202.htm

Weiss, G.W. (n.d.). Doping the Soviets: The farewell dossier. Retrieved October 19, 2004, from https://www.cia.gov/library/center-for-the-study-of-intelligence/csi-publications/csi-studies/studies/96unclass/farewell.htm

*The World Factbook*. (2008). Central Intelligence Agency. Retrieved March 25, 2009, from https://www.cia.gov/library/publications/the-world-factbook/index.html

# Chapter 14

# Understanding Information Risk Management

Tom Carlson and Nick Halvorson

## Contents

## What Is Information Risk Management?

The discipline of information security may be considered as a subset of an organization's overall risk management strategy. Information security is a focused initiative to manage risk to information in any form. Risk management concepts, when applied to information risk are readily managed within the context of an information security management system, or ISMS. An ISMS is a process-based program management approach and furnishes a framework from which to administer risk management processes.

## Why Information Risk Management?

Robust risk management processes identify and quantify areas of information risk, and allow for the development of a comprehensive and focused risk treatment plan.

- A clearly defined risk assessment methodology is a mandatory component in legal/regulatory compliance.
- The corresponding risk treatment plan documents informed choice, decision making, and organizational due diligence.

## Background

Business is all about risk and the management of any enterprise is in some manner enterprise risk management. Traditionally, the term risk management has been focused on financial and fiduciary business risk. The increased importance of information confidentiality, integrity, and availability in managing an enterprise has caused the recognition that information risk is equally concerning the health and well-being of an enterprise and should be managed accordingly.

## How Is Information Risk Management Implemented?

### The Nature of Risk

Risk may be strategic, tactical, or operational.

### Strategic Risk

Strategic risk is risk to the existence or profit of the organization and may or may not have information security significance. Such risk includes regulatory compliance and fiduciary responsibility, as well as risk to the revenue and reputation to the organization.

### Tactical Risk

Tactical risk is risk to the information security program's ability to mitigate relevant strategic risk to information. Such program risk includes the ability to identify relevant regulations, identify and justify control objectives, and justify information security initiatives.

### Operational Risk

Operational risk is concerned with the ability to implement the tactical risk–based control objectives. Such risk includes budget, timelines, and technologies.

### The Process of Risk Management

In its most basic form, the Risk management process is a closed loop, or iterative, providing a feedback mechanism for continuous process improvement (Figure 14.1).

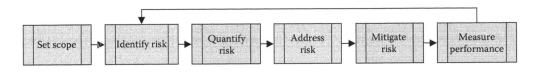

**Figure 14.1    Risk management process.**

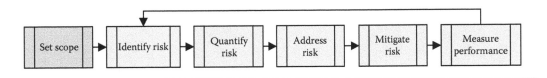

**Figure 14.2    Set scope.**

The current ISO 27005 standard addresses the application of this process as an information security technique. A process-based ISMS provides the framework within which to implement this technique.

## Step 1: Set Scope (Figure 14.2)

### Information Security Program

A comprehensive information security program should address strategic, tactical, and operational risk. An information security program is a strategic risk initiative, managed by a tactical risk–based ISMS. This structure allows ready identification and mitigation of operational risk. For example:

- The scope of strategic risk is enterprise wide and focused on the risk-mitigating services required by the enterprise.
- The scope of tactical risk is program wide and focused on the risk-mitigating processes required by the strategic services.
- The scope of operational risk is based upon a discrete domain that stores, transmits, or processes information in any form. This domain-specific risk is focused on the people, procedure, and products that integrate into risk-mitigating processes.

An ISMS-based information security program is conducive to scoping and managing multiple risk domains while simultaneously identifying and maintaining both vertical alignment and horizontal dependencies (Figure 14.3).

## Step 2: Identify Risk (Figure 14.4)

### Threat Forecasting

Threats are *negative events* that occur when a vulnerability or weakness is exploited. Threat forecasting is a proactive process to predict future risk based on identified or perceived vulnerability.
   Threats span the organization at all levels.

- Threats may be strategic, or enterprise wide such as regulatory noncompliance.
- Threats may be tactical based upon organizational vulnerabilities such as ineffective programs.
- Threats may be operational based upon technical vulnerabilities.

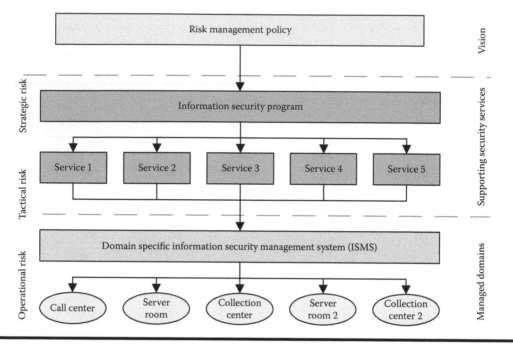

**Figure 14.3  ISMS-based information security program.**

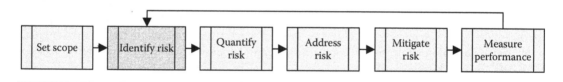

**Figure 14.4  Identify risk.**

Threat forecasting examines multiple information sources, or sensors. Threat sensors may include

■ Legal/regulatory analysts
■ Program reviews
■ Technical bulletins from vendors or analysts

The potential rate of change to the threat environment must be considered, and may drive the frequency of triggering the threat forecasting processes. For example, a strategic threat such as noncompliance with emerging regulations typically has a longer tolerable reaction time than an operational threat such as emerging technical vulnerabilities.

## Incident Evaluation

Incidents are threats that have occurred, or in other words, a vulnerability has been exploited to cause an event resulting in an incident. Incident evaluation, although triggered reactively, is proactive because of the "lessons learned" that can be utilized to both identify the underlying vulnerabilities and predict future probability of reoccurrence. Forensic, or "root cause" analysis

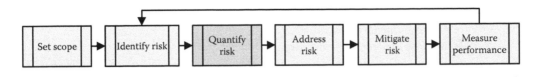

**Figure 14.5   Quantify risk.**

will illuminate technical and procedural weaknesses, and performance analysis will illuminate efficiency and effectiveness weakness.

## Step 3: Quantify Risk (Figure 14.5)

### Risk Assessment

The processes of threat forecasting and incident evaluation identify relevant threats and vulnerabilities; however, relevant threats and vulnerabilities are not necessarily risks. Identified threats and vulnerabilities must be quantified to determine the existence and magnitude of risk within the applicable environment. Quantified risk allows for defensible prioritization of remediation efforts as well as informed choice (defensible) decision making.

### Assessment Scope

*Strategic assessment*
Strategic risk assessments look at enterprise business processes that span multiple domains. Not all assessed business processes have information risk.

*Tactical assessment*
Tactical risk assessments look at the ability of the information security program to identify and mitigate relevant strategic risk to information.

*Operational assessment*
Operational risk assessments look at a domain's ability to meet tactical control objectives in protecting specific information assets. Technical vulnerability assessments are an example of a specifically focused type of operational risk assessment.

**Assessment Framework** — A risk assessment framework assists in maintaining structure during the risk assessment process since it may be difficult to make sense of the diverse collection of threats and vulnerabilities that flow from "worst-case" scenario brainstorming. A risk assessment framework allows both organization of thought and recognition of relationships between this diverse collection of threats and vulnerabilities. Starting with the premise that information risk is based upon breaches of *confidentiality*, *integrity*, and *availability*, a risk assessment framework can be further subdivided into, for example, intentional and accidental components. Further subdivisions result in creation of a "threat tree" that allows organized "cataloging" of risk, and enhances the ability to ask and analyze appropriate risk questions. For example:

*Threat*: Breach of confidentiality

■ Intentional disclosure
  – *Vulnerability*: Poorly vetted employees

■ Unintentional disclosure
- *Vulnerability*: Unencrypted information
- *Vulnerability*: Ineffective media disposal

Note the structured thought process resulting in discrete vulnerabilities being mapped to a common threat.

**Risk Quantum** — Risk quantification is based upon identification of relevant variables that are then incorporated into a risk rating algorithm. A quantitative assessment requires much more effort than a qualitative assessment, but may be necessary when, for example, using the resultant risk rating to make financial (quantitative) decisions. Typical qualitative risk quantification utilizes two independent variables, probability (likelihood), and harm (impact). Risk-rating algorithms vary in sophistication depending on the level of detail and accuracy required to be furnished by the assessment.

*Probability* — Probability may be seen as having three attributes. Total probability must take into consideration all aspects:

■ *Frequency*: how often the scenario can be expected to occur
■ *Simplicity*: the level of effort required to create the scenario
■ *Motive*: the determination of the attacker

Frequency and simplicity are relevant for each vulnerability, whereas motive is relevant to the organization. For example, an externally facing firewall has a high probability of penetration attempts (frequency) but a low probability of success (simplicity). A defense contractor or financial institution may generate more focused attention than a home PC user (motive).

*Harm* — Harm is the impact successful execution of the event would cause the organization. Since harm is many times aligned to a particular tangible asset, another view sometimes used in risk assessment is value where value is perceived in terms of availability, and harm perceived as absence. This view is more common in enterprise business process risk assessment.

**Raw Risk** — The identified vulnerabilities quantified through an algorithm (of your choice) utilizing the independent variables of probability and harm constitute raw risk, or risk before the application of controls. Raw risk serves as a baseline of your threat exposure or risk environment. Raw risk also acts as the basis of "before and after" views, modified as controls are factored in to calculate residual (post-control) risk. An unacceptable level of raw risk serves as the justification for implementing mitigating controls.

## Step 4: Address Risk (Figure 14.6)

### Risk Tolerance

Having identified and evaluated the risks attached to specific vulnerabilities, the risks must be addressed. Decisions on risk are based upon the organization's risk tolerance thresholds and include the following options:

**Avoid Risk** — Risk may possibly be avoided, for example, by relocating a data center.

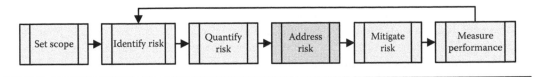

**Figure 14.6   Address risk.**

Transfer Risk — Risk may be transferred to someone with a higher risk tolerance, for example, an insurance company.

Accept Risk — Risk may be accepted although diligence requires care regarding

- Who is authorized to accept what level of risk
- How is risk acceptance based upon "informed choice decision making"
- Whether the aggregation of accepted risk remains tolerable

Mitigate Risk — Risk may be mitigated to an acceptable level through the application of compensating controls.

## Step 5: Mitigate Risk (Figure 14.7)

It is not practical to completely eliminate risk, only to reduce risk to an acceptable level.

## Control Objectives

Control objectives serve as the glue to bind specific vulnerabilities to specific controls. Defining control objectives is the first step in deriving the corresponding control requirements to mitigate the risk associated with the vulnerability. Control objectives give a risk-based justification to allocation of resources.

## Selection of Controls

Once control requirements have been derived from control objectives, tangible controls may be selected.

Discretionary Controls — Discretionary controls are controls that can weigh cost versus benefits. In general, the cost of mitigating a risk needs to be balanced with the benefits obtained. This is

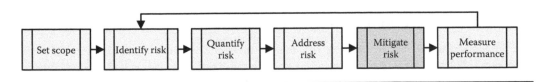

**Figure 14.7   Mitigate risk.**

essentially a cost-benefit analysis on "at what cost" the risk is acceptable. It is important to consider all direct and indirect costs and benefits whether tangible or intangible and measured in financial or other terms. More than one option can be considered and adopted either separately or in combination. For example, mitigating controls such as support contracts may reduce risk to a certain degree, with residual risk transferred via appropriate insurance or risk financing.

**Mandatory Controls** — Mandatory controls differ from discretionary controls in that cost has no bearing on the selection of mandatory controls. These are controls that *must* be implemented in order to mitigate specific risks. There may be no risk acceptance option due, for example, to legal and regulatory requirements.

## Risk Treatment

**Development of Action Plan** — The organization requires a treatment plan in order to describe how the chosen controls will be implemented. The treatment plan should be comprehensive and should document all necessary information about

- Proposed actions, priorities, or time plans
- Resource requirements
- Roles and responsibilities of all parties involved in the proposed actions
- Performance measures
- Reporting and monitoring requirements

Action plans may have strategic, tactical, and operational components, and should be in line with the culture, values, and perceptions of all stakeholders.

**Approval of Action Plan** — As with all management plans, initial approval is not sufficient to ensure the effective implementation of the action plan. Senior management support is critical throughout the entire life cycle of the plan. By its nature, an ISMS is an empowerment vehicle for risk treatment, with clear trickle down authority documenting management support and authorization to the highest levels.

**Implementation of Action Plan** — An important responsibility of the action plan owner is to identify requirements and procure necessary resources to implement the plan. This may include such tangibles as people, process, and products, the component parts selected to meet the required control objectives. In the event that available resources such as budgets are not sufficient, the risk of not implementing the action plan must ultimately be accepted by someone. The risk management model allows transference of risk to a willing risk acceptor, and the ISMS framework provides the means of transference.

## Step 6: Measure Performance (Figure 14.8)

A critical success factor (CSF) for the risk management process is to strategically reduce risk to an acceptable level. A key performance indicator is the tactical ability to reach this steady state, or equilibrium, through the judicious selection and deployment of efficient and effective controls. Operational metrics can be used to evaluate control efficiency and effectiveness.

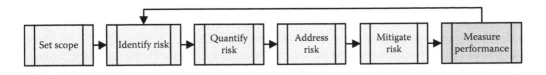

**Figure 14.8 Measure performance.**

## Risk Metrics

There are various types of risk metrics that may benefit the information security program.

Process Metrics — A process by definition has a CSF defining the successful execution of the process. The CSF is evaluated via process key performance indicators. Key performance indicators are evaluated via process metrics. Whereas process design deals with process effectiveness, process execution deals with process efficiency. For example, a risk-mitigating operational "incident response" process (a reactive control) has been designed to be tactically effective, but the performance indicators look at operational efficiency factors such as "time to respond."

Program Metrics — Program metrics typically measure process effectiveness. These tactical process effectiveness metrics require a "history" against which to measure, with value being enhanced by history length. This type of evaluation is synergistic with maturity modeling since maturity modeling is by nature history based.

Environmental Metrics — Environmental metrics are of value when trying to evaluate an organization's risk profile and resultant risk strategy. For example, a response process (reactive control) may be triggered frequently, giving insight into the external environment. This metric says nothing about the efficiency or effectiveness of the information security program, but may add justification to its existence or tactics.

## Control Attributes

Controls in this context may be seen to have two independent attributes

Maturity — As risk treatment progresses, controls remain in varying degrees of maturity. Factoring in the maturity level of the various types of controls on a standardized scale allows the ability to quantify effectiveness in progress toward meeting control objectives and the resultant reduction of risk.

Weight — Controls may be considered:

- Directive
- Preventive
- Detective
- Reactive

In some environments, there is merit in weighting the value of a specific category of control. For example, in a risk-intolerant environment such as the nuclear industry, a preventive control may be far more valued than detective and reactive controls and should be weighted accordingly.

## Residual Risk

Residual risk is the risk that remains after risk treatment. Residual risk is derived from raw risk, with an algorithm typically utilizing risk-mitigating control attributes to modify the raw risk environment. Untreated residual risk is essentially de facto accepted risk. Since the objective of the iterative risk management process is to reduce residual risk to an acceptable level, the risk management process may therefore require multiple passes to reach this goal. For example, a vulnerability management process that tracks the system patching life cycle may require multiple iterations before an acceptable residual risk of 5% unpatched (95% patched) is achieved.

# Conclusion

Information security is a focused application of risk management, managing risk to information in any form based upon the risk criteria of confidentiality, integrity, and availability. An information security program is hence a subset of an organization's risk management program, and is readily managed within the context of a process-based ISMS. ISMS and risk assessment frameworks add structure to the information security program, clearly delineating risk roles and responsibilities. A process-based approach is repeatable, defensible, and extensible, offering metrics to optimize efficiency and effectiveness while reducing risk to an acceptable level.

# About the Authors

**Tom Carlson**, CISSP, is a principal consultant and ISMS practice lead for Information Security Management Systems (ISMS) and ISO 27001 certification.

**Nick Halvorson**, CISSP, is the information security manager for Merrill Corporation headquartered in St. Paul, Minnesota.

# Chapter 15

# The Sarbanes–Oxley Revolution: Hero or Hindrance?

Seth Kinnett

## Contents

A headache. A frustration. A nightmare. Each of these terms comments on the seemingly universal sentiment over Sarbanes–Oxley (SOX). A review of available journal literature surrounding SOX reveals the frustrations facing companies affected by SOX. Supporters of heavy regulation might dismiss these responses as typical or expected reactions by the business world. Certainly regulatory requirements are not always embraced by the corporate community, but SOX appears to have rattled them even more than ever. But the purpose of this essay is not to debate the worth of the regulations, nor to justify them. Rather, we will begin our discussion by examining the impacts that SOX compliance has wrought upon various institutions. Having established the vast environment affected by the SOX legislation, we will then turn to particulars of implementation such as pain points, costs, and frustrations, including those by actual people within the organizations affected. Finally, we will synthesize this information to determine the high-level impact and potential benefits of SOX on organizations and how it will affect their ability—better or worse—to thrive in the evolving business environment.

To begin, it is important to understand that SOX is not a narrow initiative. In fact, "according to the Public Company Accounting Oversight Board, 15,000 U.S. companies, 1,200 non-U.S. based companies and 1,423 accounting firms spread across 76 countries are affected by SOX" (Braganza and Franken 2007). This example is eye-raising to many who falsely assume SOX applies only to financial institutions. In fact, SOX applies to financial reporting, which is something that every company—to some degree or other—conducts as part of its business. While financial institutions may have additional requirements or challenges, SOX is a far-reaching initiative affecting many organizations. "In particular, Section 404, which deals with management's assessment of internal controls, affects CIOs and information technology departments" (Brganza and Franken 2007). We will examine financial institutions in some level of detail, however, as an emblematic institution that finds itself complying with the SOX mandates, but we will also draw examples from other industries. There are a number of considerations surrounding SOX that apply to multiple business verticals. By way of providing background, we should note that SOX is a piece of regulatory legislation passed by the U. S. Congress in 2002. The impetus for the legislation came most publicly from scandals, but also "business structures and reporting processes have become increasingly complex, leading to redundancies and inefficiencies" (Giniat and Saporito 2007). Put another way, the enactment of SOX reflected a "need to enhance the independence of SEC financial statement audits by shifting responsibility from audit oversight and auditor selection to an audit committee composed of three independent directors, and prohibiting auditors from providing certain consultation services to clients" (Drexler 2006). The regulation has a number of components and nuances that are of import to companies, but at a high level, "the main effect of Sarbanes–Oxley is to move the ultimate responsibility for the accuracy of financial reports from the outside auditor to the company's management" (Needleman 2008). The SOX environment as 2008 draws to a close is an evolved one as more and more organizations gain their footing in implementing controls and developing an appropriate compliance strategy. Most companies had knee-jerk, reactive responses to SOX. They began hammering their IT departments to implement the required controls. Indeed, "much of SOX addresses IT functions, as IT is an integral component of financial transaction processing in any enterprise" (Needleman 2008). This response, while perhaps effective in the short term, is dangerous. As time continues to pass and it becomes increasingly clear that SOX is not going away, "controls must not be viewed as a single event, but as a changing process that must be monitored and reviewed on a regular basis" (Kumar 2006). While the "Band-aid" approach may have worked in 2003 and 2004 and even 2005, most companies now already have addressed the basics. "Now that companies have completed the initial implementation of SOX controls, it is time to create a framework for ongoing, sustainable SOX compliance" (Kumar 2006). The issue of control specificity within SOX is one that has been the subject of some debate.

> While Sarbanes–Oxley may have initially been viewed as a panacea for better reporting, some of its critics argue that the initial implementation of the law has focused too much on the detailed process-level controls instead of on the company-level monitoring controls. In effect, the critics contend, there has been too much focus on a coverage-based approach instead of a risk-based approach (Giniat and Saporito 2007).

Throughout this discussion we will examine a combination of specific, IT control considerations as well as broader initiatives such as company culture and how it may affect an environment of compliance.

To the former, one spillover benefit of regulation has been the economic benefit to software companies that have responded to SOX by deploying new tools to provide the controls so many technology departments desperately need. Applications such as the Axentis Financial GRC Suite "[provide] base services, including organization management, knowledge management and communication management, as well as reporting and analytics, and audit trail tracking. To these base services, the application adds risk and control management, which directly addresses Section 404 concerns" (Needleman 2006). While it is never a good idea to view a software application as a complete business solution, these applications can contribute toward positive discussions about how to shape an organization toward a culture of compliance and accountability. Those two words underscore the very purpose of SOX and bring us back to a remembrance of the unfortunate issues that brought about the legislation in the first place.

It is important to place this sort of discussion within a practical industry context so as to frame it in as real an environment as possible. The financial industry will serve well in this regard. We will examine high-level fraud and compliance in this field as well as the specific impacts, costs, and benefits that compliance has placed on this vertical. First, it is critical to note that this is an industry that certainly contributed to the advent of SOX. As an example, "in the *2006 ACFE Report to the Nation on Occupational Fraud & Abuse*, 14 percent of the 1134 fraud cases reported by the Certified Fraud Examiners who investigated them were from the banking/financial services industry" (Magliozzi 2007–2008). Since then, they—like all verticals—have had time to change their ways and respond to the effects of regulation. As we noted above, this is the time for companies to transition away from their control-based responses and look toward a sustainable strategy. This will be a challenge, but one which may prove very beneficial. "Many financial institutions, including asset management companies, hedge funds and companies undergoing their initial registration process, operate with manually intense processes. Automating these processes can yield improvement in the quality of the control environment, while reducing significantly the cost of SOX compliance" (Magliozzi 2007–2008). Still, the challenge of moving IT resources away from the day-to-day grind of support and reactivity toward long-term process-improvement initiatives is a large one. Particularly in this environment in which financial institutions are struggling simply to survive, the short-term costs of strategic initiatives are perceived as far greater than the long-term benefits. To make matters worse "for financial institutions, the cost of SOX compliance is exacerbated by the costs associated with the myriad other laws and regulations with which they must comply" (Magliozzi 2007–2008). There is a need—if for no other reason than sanity—to view SOX in a more positive light than reflexes dictate. Smart companies will use the SOX regulations to help them update their systems, processes, and security. "A financial institution should aim to make the SOX effort efficient while improving overall quality over time…. Positive change can occur as companies move from a manual, detective and ad hoc state to a more evolved systems-based, preventive and managed state" (Magliozzi 2007–2008). But unfortunately many financial institutions have not adopted this model. In an article written in late 2007 for *Bank Accounting & Finance* Magazine, author Rick Magliozzi made it clear that progress still needs to be made, writing that "reducing the cost of SOX compliance and improving the quality of the key business processes are needed if the financial institution is to remain competitive in today's marketplace" (Magliozzi 2007–2008). One bit of relief may be in store for banks and financial institutions, however, in the form of greater flexibility on the part of the SEC as they have "endorsed the recommendations of the agency's professional staff to eliminate 'waste and duplication' in companies' compliance with the Sarbanes–Oxley Act" (SEC…. 22). Of course, it may be some time before all the efficiencies are put into place, and organizations rarely have the time, energy, or resources to take steps back to strategically analyze these kinds of issues. We will now take a closer look inside the inner workings of an organization and examine some of the issues facing executives as they strive to comply with SOX. Considering the political and power-play issues inherent in this kind of situation, companies may find that the specific technical requirements of SOX are, in fact, the least of their worries.

In a truly fascinating article, authors Ashley Braganza and Arnoud Franken studied the relationships between C-level executives as they interact within the context of implementing and executing on SOX compliance. The study is very revealing into the sorts of political and power games that take place within the corporate environment, and the SOX challenge is certainly not immune from these games. This examination provides a very distinct insight into our discussion, as it allows us to deviate from simply analyzing a particular business environment and the technical and operational business considerations surrounding SOX compliance and allows a brief examination of the human function within this process. It is important for everyone involved in the compliance process to understand the human element, for it is the most difficult to mediate or to predict its impact. In their study, the authors examined CEOs, CFOs, CIOs, and auditors.

Early in their article they reveal that they "use power relationships as the basis for [their] analysis because previous empirical research shows that CIOs have relatively little power in organizations" (Braganza and Franken 2007). In one example cited in their study, the authors described the power relationships taking place between the CIO and the CFO in the context of the 404 SOX requirements. "The CFO's influence is directed at pushing 404 requirements on to the IT department; whereas the CIO seeks to create the environment for the finance department to understand IT" (Braganza and Franken 2007). In this same example, the CIO of the company in question is part of an organization in which he does not have direct access to the CEO, "which can be of concern especially where the CIO has a significant role to play in the implementation of 404. Moreover, it implies the CIO has access to the CEO via the CFO, which gives the CFO a political edge over the CIO" (Braganza and Franken 2007). An organization with this type of structure is in trouble. Sarbanes–Oxley is clearly a complicated process that requires an efficient and intelligent use of company resources. The amount of people involved and the challenges implicit simply in achieving compliance are numbered and great, and there is absolutely no room for political posturing among C-level executives. By marginalizing the CIO, the CEO of this organization has actually hurt his company overall by failing to acknowledge the critical role that technology plays in not just SOX compliance, but in making the organization run smoothly each and every day. Other examples in this study, while exhibiting some level of variance, basically underscore the larger point that the CIO is—as the authors suggested at the beginning of the study—at the bottom of the proverbial totem pole when it comes to executives. It is difficult to draw conclusions about how or why this hierarchy evolved or how it has persisted. Auditors, armed with this information, should be encouraged to form strong relationships with the CIO and to be understanding of his position in the firm. The CIO is an important player and, when treated as more than just an implementer of controls, may have valuable insights to lend to the SOX compliance process. The authors of the study suggest that "CIOs widen their base of relationships and develop new internal power and influence relationships when implementing 404 compliance" (Braganza and Franken 2007).

We have now examined what SOX is: a number of control-specific issues that companies must understand in order to comply with the regulation, and external challenges such as politics and power games that executives might find themselves in during this process. Ultimately, however, the government has a responsibility to impose regulations to support the best interests of the people. Clearly, in a capitalist system, it is imperative that companies are reporting accurate and honest financial data and it is in the best interest of the public for them to do so. We must also consider, however, the impact of these regulations on companies and ensure that the benefits realized by regulation do not outweigh the costs—both direct and indirect—on companies.

In an article for *Strategic Finance* magazine, Paul Sharman likens the SOX process to a long car trip. In this analogy, "the final destination Congress defined was 'more reliable auditor certified financial disclosures.' The travel planner is the Securities and Exchange Commission (SEC) and its new subsidiary, the Public Accounting Oversight Board (PCAOB)" (Sharman 2007). In Sharman's estimation, the trip is not going very well, with costs outweighing those predicted by lawmakers. "As a result, the U.S. has been slowly losing ground to other countries whose markets aren't as cumbersome and restrictive" (Sharman 2007). During difficult economic times it can be tempting to rollback regulations in favor of corporate growth and profitability. What many neglect to realize is that it may be the previous lack of regulation that caused circumstances to turn so dire in the first place. Realizing, however, that it is difficult to deny the challenges that SOX has placed upon American businesses, it is more reasonable to suggest targeted reforms to streamline compliance requirements without sacrificing quality and accountability. We now turn to outlining some specific shortcomings that others have analyzed and which would appear to be positive targets for reform.

Areas for improvement exist throughout the SOX compliance process, from documentation requirements to external auditor accountability and standards. To the latter, "IMA and FEI (Financial Executives International) research indicates there is massive variability between various audit pass/fail graders. Even graders from the same CPA firm vary in their views on how much and what kind of controls are enough to pass. The grading criteria that auditors are using are far from clear and haven't been empirically validated as appropriate" (Sharman 2007). This is not such a surprising finding. It is challenging to strike a balance between mandating specifics and trusting professionals to use their expertise to make decisions. Depending on the research, however, it may be useful to define a more targeted list of requirements for auditors. There appears to be a large degree of dissatisfaction with the SEC across multiple areas of the SOX process. Some research suggests that the SEC was too reliant on existing systems and processes and did not provide targeted means to address specific new challenges brought about by SOX. According to Sharman, "the SEC in effect abdicated responsibility for providing adequate guidance for management to assess and report on internal control by assigning the PCAOB the responsibility to develop external auditor guidance in the form of Auditing Standard No. 2 (AS2). The problem is that the PCAOB's mission and guidance are intended to support the external auditors—using decades-old thinking and very traditional audit standards" (Sharman 2007). Couple this anti-executive orientation with the political implications we already discussed facing executives, and it is not too difficult to see how SOX can become a significant challenge for businesses. Reforms to this portion of the regulation should focus on developing a new innovative guidance for executives, clearly outlining high-level points that they can follow. These do not necessarily have to replace lower-level auditor specifications, but executives are used to big-picture views throughout their jobs, and SOX regulators should strive to capitalize on this where possible. The SEC has already begun to respond to "suggestions" for improvement. After the SEC eased some compliance requirements, the response was generally favorable.

> "To a great extent, the new SEC rule and the new auditing standard by the Public Company Accounting Oversight Board deliver what we've hoped," says George Yungmann, senior vice president of financial standards at the National Association of Real Estate Investment Trusts based in Washington, D.C. The new rules allow companies to conduct a top-down, risk-based analysis of their internal controls, says Yungmann, rather than getting into a hyper-detailed review. "It brings us up out of the weeds," he says, "and the new rules are intended to be scalable for companies." (Filisko, 2007)

These are the kinds of adjustments that are understandable and necessary for a young mandate such as SOX. Businesses could assist in this improvement by providing targeted feedback and analysis as opposed to brute force lobbying or complaining, which has largely been the status quo.

Despite the frustrations we have examined so far, SOX is not entirely a negative initiative. Consider that organizations may even be better off for having been forced to comply with SOX. One article notes that "while SOX compliance can seem like an added burden, the upside is that creating a SOX-compliant credit function pays off handsomely in terms of achieving repeatable and transparent processes and procedures, increased efficiencies, and more accurate reporting" (10 Credit Pros... 2). It is important to understand how SOX's best intentions can actually make businesses better. The beginning of making this a reality comes from the organizational culture, and "organizations should not regard voluntary compliance with the Sarbanes–Oxley Act as an end in itself; it should be part of a larger enterprise risk management initiative" (Giniat and Saporito 2007). Authors Edward Giniat and Joseph Saporito examine the not-for-profit healthcare industry as one that could benefit from a voluntary SOX compliance initiative. They argue that "many of the unfortunate surprises that have hurt healthcare organizations' reputations recently could have been avoided—or at least anticipated—by more effective risk management and more transparent reporting" (Giniat and Saporito 2007). SOX certainly can provide the catalyst toward a greater organizational awareness into information security and security controls. For some industries, they may not have explored security to a very deep degree at all. SOX can be an important first step toward a more secure organization, and public demand has begun to support the push for tighter accountability. As noted in a magazine catering to accountants, one author writes that

> Non-SEC-registered entities, including governments and not-for-profit organizations, face pressures similar to those present in for-profit corporations to mismanage accounting, mislead their auditors, or influence auditor judgment with lucrative consulting projects. Third parties for nonregistrants, such as banks, venture capitalists, hedge funds, and regulators, are just as vulnerable to financial reporting abuses as are investors in publicly traded companies (Drexler 2006).

This public trend is the kind of nudge that companies often need to begin a process as challenging as SOX compliance. One elusive benefit of SOX is the attention to fraud and audit concerns that have plagued many smaller businesses in the past but which never received sufficient national attention. At one end of the extreme, "discoveries of fraud in Nassau County's school system led New York State Comptroller Alan Hevesi to reinstitute the state's school audit department and hire 89 auditors" (Drexler 2006). We must caution, however, that SOX is not the end of the process, but rather the beginning and "SOX compliance by itself is not sufficient to account for risk where the root causes are in operations, compliance, and strategic activities" (Giniat and Saporito 2007). Rather than operate reactively and scrambling to implement specific SOX controls—as many companies have that we have explored thus far—organizations would be well benefited "to incorporate SOX compliance into a larger, integrated enterprise risk management (ERM) approach that tailors their SOX compliance to their specific needs while ensuring that other types of risk also receive critical attention. In this way, they can apply a coordinated approach to addressing many of the root causes of risk facing their organizations" (Giniat and Saporito 2007). This larger enterprise initiative can be the strategic driver or umbrella under which SOX tactical measures may operate. ERM may have been viewed as a "nice to have" in the past, but one benefit of SOX is that security best practices are much more widely known and implemented than they may have been in the past. In addition to the benefits of the controls themselves, "ERM engages leadership... by ensuring that they use a common language and methodology to identify, measure, prioritize and manage risk. It also creates a framework and process to improve the focus and efficiency of governance and to link the risks the organization faces to its strategy and decision-making process" (Giniat and Saporito 2007). This strategic approach is also more cost-effective to companies as it exposes them to fundamental principles of information security such as confidentiality, integrity, and information availability. As Giniat writes, "ERM helps the organization's executive leadership understand diverse risks and place those risks on a common platform that takes into account each risk's likelihood of occurring and its potential magnitude of impact should it occur" (Giniat and Saporito 2007).

We have seen that SOX can conceivably bring a number of benefits to an organization, despite the perceived hassles. While many organizational leaders might admit that in the long run they agree SOX can help their organization, they resent the short-term costs and challenges. These are reasonable concerns, particularly for small businesses. A study conducted about the banking industry can help to provide a representative example of the impacts of SOX compliance on the company bottom line. The banking industry is a particularly interesting example since it is quite familiar with regulations and compliance issues. "The Federal Deposit Insurance Corporation Improvement Act (FDICIA) of 1991 required significant auditing, corporate reporting and governance reforms for all banking institutions with more than $500 million in assets" (Borgia and Siegel 2008). FDICIA was perhaps the weightiest regulation for banks prior to SOX. Even though "SOX was modeled after FDICIA…, the provisions of SOX go far beyond those of the model and require an audit of the internal controls of an SEC registrant throughout the year" (Borgia and Siegel 2008). We have already examined the circumstances surrounding SOX's development, but the profitability figures found in this bank study are important to be noted and they do drive forward the case for intelligent reform. The study compared public and private banks. The latter, being excluded from the SOX requirement, were hypothesized to be more profitable than public banks that had to expend capital on SOX controls and compliance.

> The results of the study are fairly telling about how SOX affects profitability of public bank holding companies. ROA increased only 4% for public companies from 2001 to 2003, but it increased twice as much (8%) for private companies. ROE showed even greater differences for public and private entities. For public companies, ROE increased 3%, whereas private companies experienced an 8% increase. Clearly, SOX had a negative initial impact on the profitability of public bank holding companies (Borgia and Siegel 2008).

While we do not have access to studies for every industry vertical, it is clear that SOX compliance weighs on the company budget. "The total average cost of Sarbanes–Oxley Section 404 compliance reached $1.7 million last year [2007], according to a newly released survey by Financial Executives international. The poll of 183 companies found that total audit fees for U.S. accelerated filers averaged $3.6 million, a slight increase of 1.8 percent from the previous year" (Costs… 7). It is important to note that corporate expenses are not necessarily cause for public concern. Considering the reputations most corporations in America have today, many people would be inclined to shrug with disinterest when presented with these types of figures. The danger comes when, in the aggregate, companies and particularly small businesses begin to find their budgets weighed down with these types of recurrent fees that prevent them from adequately taking care of their employees or participating and contributing to civic initiatives. Americans have a vested interest in the success of their economy, so streamlining an initiative like SOX has the potential to help both businesses and consumers.

Overall, SOX—like any piece of regulatory legislation—is not perfect. It is also in its infancy, so we should not be terribly surprised that it still has flaws that need to be corrected in order to provide a reasonable and appropriate regulatory environment that will achieve its primary goal of mandating accurate and reliable financial reporting. A balance must always exist between regulators and the regulated, and there are bound to be pain points throughout the process. Changes, while slow, have begun to trickle down from the SEC as business pains and shortcomings of the existing SOX rules become clearer and more widely known. Yet businesses continue to paint a relatively grim picture of SOX. Even the most vigorous supporters of regulation* must admit SOX has not been the most effective or intelligent mandate to come out of Washington. Corporations must strike a balance and foster a culture that embraces risk management initiatives rather than treating them as a chore that must be completed, as many companies still do. Where items need to be reformed, they ought to be and they should be reformed rapidly so as to ease the potential burden to companies who, like the American people, are struggling. To some, SOX reform cannot come quickly enough and it is viewed as an imperative to the prosperity of the United States enterprise. "If America's global competitiveness and position as the world's preeminent capital market is to be maintained, the time to make sweeping changes to the current SOX regime is now. If U.S.-listed companies want change, the time to lobby for real change is now" (Sharman 2007). With the dawn of a new era of politics and American civics, we may just find that capitalizing on the benefits of SOX and making it into a positive economic driver for businesses is truly within our reach.

## References

Borgia, C. and Siegel, P. H. How the Sarbanes–Oxley Act is affecting profitability in the banking industry. *The CPA Journal*, pp. 13–14, August 2008.

Braganza, A. and Franken, A. SOX, compliance, and power relationships. *Communications of the ACM*, 50, 97–102, September 2007.

Costs analysis of 404. *Practical Accountant*, p. 7, June 2008.

Drexler, P. M. Could Sarbanes–Oxley benefit non-SEC-registrant audits? *The CPA Journal*, pp. 6–9, June 2006.

Filisko, G. M. SOX auditing rules eased. *National Real Estate Investor*, p. 118, July 2007.

Giniat, E. and Saporito, J. Sarbanes–Oxley: Impetus for enterprise risk management. *Healthcare Financial Management*, pp. 65–70, August 2007.

How 10 credit pros meet the challenge of SOX compliance. *Managing Credit, Receivables & Collections* newsletter, p. 2, December 2007.

Kumar, S. Finding a framework for sustainable SOX compliance. *Pulp & Paper*, September 2006.

Magliozzi, R. The dawn of Sarbanes–Oxley efficiency and effectiveness: A financial institution perspective. *Bank Accounting & Finance*, pp. 43–46, December 2007–January 2008.

Needleman, T. SOX compliance software—Lots to choose from. *Accounting Today*, September 2006.

Needleman, T. SOX compliance: More than a single approach. *Accounting Today*, pp. 22–27, September 8–21, 2008

SEC supports streamlined SOX compliance. *Practical Accountant*, www.webCPA.com.

Sharman, P. A. The winding road of SOX compliance. *Strategic Finance*, pp. 8–10, January 2007.

---

* Such as this essay's author.

# APPLICATION SECURITY

## *System Development Controls*

## Chapter 16

# Data Loss Prevention Program

## Powell Hamilton

## Contents

One of the major challenges for today's IT security professional is having a strong awareness of the type of data and value of the data they are protecting. No matter how robust the technology, or how vigorous the monitoring systems, intellectual property (IP) can find a way to leak onto less secure systems and devices for which they are not intended.

Traditional information technology (IT) strategies have focused on the external threats that emphasize broader protection methods and often overlook internal threats and vulnerabilities. These strategies assume a malicious person is willing and motivated to break through the network barriers and penetrate critical systems. This "Barbarians at the Gate" mentality loses the focus that the main asset to protect is data.

Protecting the data, rather than protecting the system, is the risk-based approach that guides security practitioners to focus on security controls on systems processing, transferring, and storing high-value or sensitive data. The problem is most IT professionals have little knowledge of what type of data their systems are processing and what value is placed on the data. Therefore, the IT professional focuses on protecting computer systems, rather than data protection.

To compound the problem, business owners (i.e., data owners or data custodians) often do not have a strong understanding of the value of their own data. Therefore, little emphasis is placed on security controls and safeguards.

The old phrase used in criminal cases, "Follow the Money," can be slightly altered in the business environment to "Follow the Data." If an organization follows the data, they can focus their security controls on these systems.

## What Is Data Leakage?

What is meant by data leakage is easy to understand. Data leakage is the separation of IP from its intended place of storage. Most of the time, the IP is stored in a location with less security controls, than where it was intended. Data leakage can occur in many ways. The most common method is for an employee to violate corporate policy and copy the IP to a less secure system or their personal computer or removable device. Other methods include human error, technology mishaps, system misconfiguration, sabotage from a disgruntled employee, or possibly, a system breach from a hacker.

## Common Sources of Data Leakage

Some leakage may be intentional and others may be from human error or a system misconfiguration. The following outlines some common examples of data leakage:

- An employee needs to create a report. The employee extracts the data from a secure system and conducts the analysis on a less secure system, such as desktop or their notebook device. After the analysis has been complete, the employee does not properly dispose the information.
- A new or upgraded application is being implemented on a test system. Personal identifiable information (PII) is used to ensure the system is working properly. After the tests are completed, the PII is not removed or disposed of.
- Processes for conducting secure backups are not established. The backup tapes are stored in a nonsecure environment and a curious intruder removes the tape to examine the content.
- Outdated hardware is donated to a charitable organization. Before the system is delivered, the hard drive is not properly cleaned and sensitive information is not removed.
- A home-grown application is developed to interface to the public. The application developer lacks secure coding experience and writes the program with leakage errors. These types of applications can provide a malicious hacker with unauthorized access to sensitive data.
- In some cases, the improper configuration settings or inadequate security controls for shared drives have been implemented. The permissions of the file and directory structure allow anyone to access the information. The organization has a loosely guarded policy toward its propriety information, whereby data becomes easily accessible to everyone.
- A disgruntled employee with privileged access to sensitive data may act maliciously and steal information. The information is copied to a nonsecure system or device (such as a memory stick).

Although it is common for data leakage incidents to occur internally, it is also common for data to leak due to hackers, social engineering, phishing attacks, and even dumpster diving. These attacks can spread sensitive information from system to system.

To cope with data leakage, many organizations have implemented several security solutions. Solutions can range from establishing policies and procedures, increasing education and awareness, to building a full Data Loss Prevention (DLP) program.

## What Is Data Loss Prevention?

DLP, also known as Data Loss Protection, is the process and methodology to detect and prevent the unauthorized transmission or disclosure of sensitive information. DLP depends on a combination of people, processes, and technology as its strategic control foundation. These control elements work together to help ensure data is utilized in its intended manner.

DLP is one of the least understood technologies. Before businesses think to implement a sound DLP program, they must have a solid discovery tool to drive the effort. Although a discovery tool is important, there are several components needed to build a successful DLP program.

## Components of a Data Loss Prevention Program

The potential legal liability and damage to brand reputation from exposure of sensitive data has encouraged security leaders to implement a DLP program. A DLP program can be constructed in many ways. The following diagram illustrates a unique model.

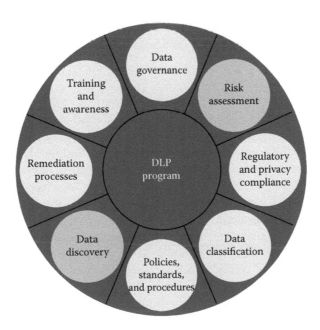

Most DLP solutions rely on technology. Although technology is an important aspect, it takes manpower resources (or personnel resources) and processes to build a holistic DLP program.

## DLP Governance

A first step in a DLP program is to establish Governance. DLP Governance encompasses the overall management of the DLP program. From a security standpoint, DLP governance is the act of protecting data and monitoring the flow of where the data travels. Although this sounds easy to accomplish, this can be a challenging task within a large organization.

A governance program includes a governing body or a committee to define policies and procedures and a plan to implement those procedures. In a large organization, this group needs to consist of individuals who have a strong understanding of the organization's industry, business objectives, internal processes, and the corporate culture.

This group is not responsible for managing data directly, but is responsible for creating the rules (policies) and the methods (procedures) for storing, accessing, and handling data. Along with creating policies and procedures, the group needs to define the responsibilities of the owners and/or custodians of the data and outline the accountability for the data, specifically how the data is processed, stored, archived, and transmitted internally and externally.

The makeup of this group should include multiple departments (i.e., HR, Legal, Compliance, Information Systems, and IT Security). The relationship, roles, and responsibilities of the group are discussed within the "Emergence of departments" section of this chapter. This group will need to establish a working structure to help resolve complex issues. The mishandling of data can cause apprehension and panic, even if it was conducted inadvertently.

The structure of a DLP governance initiative will vary not only with the size of the organization, but with the desired objectives it hopes to accomplish. For example, an organization may want to only identify and track the movement of sensitive data. Once an alert has been delivered, the offender's management will be notified to address the issues. In a stricter environment, the sensitive data may be blocked and quarantined and the offender may be disciplined with stringent punishment.

Overall, the governance of a DLP program is an important first step for establishing a DLP program. Similar to many unsuccessful intrusion detection system (IDS) implementations, a DLP system without a structure and governance will more than likely fail.

## Risk Assessment

Conducting a risk assessment is a good second step in any DLP program. The main purpose for a risk assessment is to identify all types of data within your network and to identify threat and vulnerabilities related to this data. Non-Public Data (financial, business, HR, legal, and regulatory data), PII (social security numbers, credit card information, personal health data), and IP (patents, trademarks, design plans) are examples of data that need to be identified. Once this information has been identified, a flow analysis needs to be conducted to identify all systems and devices the data either resides on or flows through.

For example, the HR department may utilize employee information. This information is stored on a centralized server utilizing a second server with a proprietary database. To access this information, the HR employee connects their intranet Web browser to the server (i.e., three-tier architecture). In this simple scenario, the devices transferring and storing data are the employee's desktop workstation, network components connecting to the server, the server itself, and a separate server maintaining the proprietary database. Each of these systems needs to be evaluated to determine threats and vulnerabilities that may put the data at risk.

This exercise needs to be conducted for all types of data being utilized within the organization. A comprehensive DLP solution ultimately has to protect all potential risk points in your organization.

There are several approaches and methods available for conducting an accurate risk assessment. The following Internet sites provide excellent information to accomplish this goal:

*Control Objectives for Information Technology (COBIT)*: Developed by IT auditors and made available through the Information Systems Audit and Control Association (ISACA). COBIT provides a framework for assessing a security program, developing a performance baseline, and measuring performance over time. Additional information can be obtained on the Internet at www.isaca.org/cobit.htm.

*NIST Documents on Risk Assessment*: The U.S. National Institute of Standards and Technology has published several documents that outline frameworks for conducting technology risk assessment and evaluating information security. Additional information can be obtained on the Internet at csrc.nist.gov.

*Operationally Critical Threat, Asset, and Vulnerability Evaluation (OCTAVE)*: Developed by the Computer Emergency Response Team at Carnegie Mellon University. OCTAVE provides measures based on accepted best practices for evaluating security programs. Additional information can be obtained on the Internet at www.cert.org/octave.

*Common Criteria (International Organization for Standardization (ISO) 27001)*: The common criteria represent an international standard for testing the effectiveness (functionality and assurance) of most security products/systems. Additional information can be obtained (purchased) on the Internet at www.iso.org.

*SysTrust*: Developed by the American Institute of Certified Public Accountants and the Canadian Institute of Chartered Public Accountants. SysTrust provides a framework for evaluating controls for information systems assurance. Additional information can be obtained on the Internet at www.aicpa.org/assurance/systrust/index.htm.

## Regulatory and Privacy Requirements

Identifying regulatory and privacy requirements is essential for an organization to ensure that the organization is compliant and privacy goals and confidentiality policies are supported by its practices, thereby protecting confidential information from abuse and the organization from liability and public relations problems.

In the past, regulatory requirements were usually issued by the federal or state government. Today, regulatory requirements are not only mandated by public bodies, but now private organizations are driving forced mandates as well (i.e., payment card industry—PCI). Just about every industry sector has some type of regulatory and/or privacy requirements. A few of the more common requirements are as follows:

- 21 CFR Part 11 (FDA)
- Australian Privacy Legislation
- BBB Online (privacy standards)
- California AB 1950
- California SB 1386

- Canadian Privacy Act
- Children's Online Privacy Protection Act (COPPA)
- Data Protection Act 1998 (UK)

- FCRA (Fair Credit Reporting Act)
- Federal Energy Regulatory Commission (FERC)
- Federal Law for Data Protection (BDSG)
- FERPA (Family Educational Rights and Privacy Act)
- FIPPA (Freedom of Information and Protection of Privacy Act)
- Gramm–Leach–Bliley Act (GLBA)
- Health Insurance Portability and Accountability Act (HIPAA)
- Other State and Local Privacy Regulations

- Electronic Communications Privacy Act of 1986 (ECPA)
- European Union (EU) Data Privacy Directive
- FACT Act (Fair and Accurate Credit Transactions)

- Payment Card Industry Data Security Standards (PCI DSS)
- Sarbanes–Oxley Act

Having a strong understanding of what regulatory requirements apply to your organization and what types of security controls are required, need to be identified. Most organizations do not have a strong understanding of their requirements, or their interpretations of those requirements are different from the regulators. Thus, most organizations are operating in a noncompliance mode.

A successful DLP program needs to take initial steps to identify and understand their regulatory requirements. The following table is an example chart for collection and tracking regulatory requirements and privacy issues.

| Regulatory and Privacy Requirements | HIPAA | SB1386/AB700 | PCI | EU Data Privacy Directive | Sarbanes–Oxley Act | GLBA |
|---|---|---|---|---|---|---|
| Departments | | | | | | |
| Human resource | × | × | | × | × | × |
| Legal | × | × | × | × | × | × |
| Compliance | × | × | × | × | × | × |
| Marketing and sales | | | × | × | | |
| Information systems | × | × | × | × | × | × |
| Manufacturing | | | × | | | |
| Information systems | × | × | × | × | × | × |

Once all the regulatory and privacy requirements of a company have been identified, the organization now has a stronger understanding of the type and the amount of information it must protect.

## Data Classification

Data classification is the process of classifying information data according to its value and sensitivity to the organization. Data classification provides the proper prioritization of an organization's assets and resources, which will result in the appropriate level of controls to be applied to each system, accordingly.

Data should be categorized in terms of sensitivity within an organization's environment (i.e., public, confidential, secret, and private, etc.). Business requirements should drive the classification process and should be directly related to data classes.

Once data requirements have been established and IP has been identified, classification categories can be assigned. A typical data classification program should conduct the following:

- Develop a standard or policy for data classification.
- Identify data type by departments.
- Identify administrator/custodian/users for each data type.
- Identify systems maintaining, processing, or storing each data type.
- Specify the criteria of how the data will be classified and labeled.
- Create an enterprise awareness program.

The data classification program will add additional controls to limit the access and movement of sensitive data, reducing the amount of data that is leaked within the organization.

## Risk Rating Factors

The following risk rating factors can be used to measure the level of risks for data:

| Data element | Data elements are the information an organization desires to protect. They can be financial records, marketing information, human resource records, etc. |
|---|---|
| Data value | This risk factor is based on the value of the data. It considers the financial impact if the data that was exposed is altered or lost. |
| Threat agents | Threat agents consider the human-caused or technology-based events such as the accidental deletion of records or denial of service attacks by cybercriminals. |
| Confidentiality risk | The confidentiality risk element is the risk of exposure. This risk rating considers the harm to the organization if the information were to be disclosed. Categories of "Internal Use Only," "Confidential," and "Most Confidential" have been assigned to each data item. These categories match the existing data classification descriptions in place and are based solely upon input from the business areas. This is the sensitivity element. |
| Integrity risk | The integrity risk element rates the risk of unauthorized modification or deletion of information. |
| Availability risk | The availability risk element considers the loss of productivity due to systems or data not being available. This is the criticality element. |
| Data classification | The Data Classification element is an overall rating of the potential exposure. This rating summarizes the other elements so a comparison and prioritization can be performed. |

## Risk Rating Scale

The following rating chart describes the criteria used to rate the value of data and the risk rating within the environment.

| Rating | Definition |
|---|---|
| Low | *Low*: The likelihood that the identified risk will have a significant impact on the business is remote |
| L / M | *Low/medium*: The likelihood that the identified risk will have a significant impact on the business is a low possibility |
| Medium | *Medium*: The likelihood that the identified risk will have a significant impact on the business is possible |
| M / H | *Medium/high*: The likelihood that the identified risk will have a significant impact on the business is probable |
| High | *High*: The likelihood that the identified risk will have a significant impact on the business is a high possibility |

## Data Classification Level

The following is an example of Data Classification schema:

*Private*: Information that is highly sensitive and is an internal document. For example, pending mergers or acquisitions, investment strategies, or research information that could seriously damage the organization if such information were lost or made public. Information classified as Private has very restricted distribution and must be protected at all times. Security at this level is the highest possible.

*Confidential*: Information that, if made public or even shared around the organization, could seriously impede the organization's operations and is considered critical to its ongoing operations. Examples would include accounting information, business plans, sensitive customer information, medical studies, and similar highly sensitive data. Such information should not be copied or removed from the organization's operational control without specific authority. Security at this level should be very high.

*Internal*: Information not approved for general circulation outside the organization where its loss would inconvenience the organization or management but where disclosure is unlikely to result in financial loss or serious damage to credibility. Examples would include internal memos, minutes of meetings, and internal project reports. Security at this level is controlled but normal.

*Public*: Information in the public domain; annual reports, press statements, etc., which has been approved for public use. Security at this level is minimal.

## Business Segment Detail Data Analysis

The following is an example of a chart listing detailed data analysis of the type of data and relevant risk ratings.

| Data Element | Depart. | Owner | Application | Storage Type | Server | Data Value | Number of Threat Agent | Confid. Risk | Integrity Risk | Availability Risk | Data Class. |
|---|---|---|---|---|---|---|---|---|---|---|---|
| HR data | HR | Fred Thomas | People soft | DB | Server1 | High | L / M | High | M / H | Medium | Private |
| Network share | All users | Mark Swanson | Network share (Prod) | Network share | Server2 | Medium | M / H | L / M | L / M | L / M | Confidential |
| Legal transcripts | Legal | Brad Wong | Network share (legal) | Network share | Legal server3 | High | M / H | High | Low | Medium | Private |

## Policies, Standards, Procedures

Sound policies, standards, and procedures are fundamentals for an effective DLP strategy. They ensure that the organization's data is protected at a level appropriate to its value. It is critical not only to create sound policies, standards, and procedures, but also to ensure that they are updated on a regular basis.

Within the realm of DLP, *policies* are the starting point before a company can establish standards and procedures, which allow an organization's DLP solution to operate more securely and efficiently. *Standards* are mandatory activities, actions, rules, and regulations designed to provide the DLP policies with the support, structure, and specific direction required to be meaningful and effective. *Procedures* spell out the specifics of how the DLP policies and the supportive standards will actually be implemented in an operating environment.

Your DLP policies should be based on your compliance and privacy needs. Some examples would include

- Acceptable Use Policy
- Computer, Telephone and Network Usage Policy
- Contractors and Third Parties Policy
- Exceptions to Policy
- Change and Problem Management Policy
- External Network Connections Policy

- Glossary of Terms
- Hard Copy Information Policy
- Incident Reporting Policy
- Information Contingency Policy

- Information Security Roles and Responsibilities
- Logon and Authentication Policy

- Personnel Security Policy
- Physical Security Policy
- Remote Access Policy

- Risk Management and Information Classification Policy
- Security Awareness Policy
- Software Compliance Policy
- System Security Audit and Review Policy

Once your policies have been created, policies search rule sets will be created to support the data discovery phase.

Policy creation is not a one-time operation. DLP policies should include technological requirements, as well as business requirements. For a discovery tool to be effective, IT and business units must collaborate on developing policies that protect the company's assets, but are also flexible enough to allow employees to be successful with their job requirements.

Once policies are created and rule sets are established, the IT team should expect to engage the business units to help update the policies on a regular basis, using feedback from the user community. One method to obtain user feedback is to collect explanations of why a policy-breaking action should be allowed to occur. This feedback will help strengthen policies and will provide an overall view of the business functions needed within the environment.

## Data Discovery

Data discovery (also known as e-discovery) refers to any process in which electronic data is assessed. In the process of data discovery, data of all types can be searched. This can include electronic mail (e-mail), text, images files, databases, spreadsheets, Web sites, and computer programs. Digital data can be electronically searched with ease, whereas paper documents must be scrutinized manually. To help support a data discovery effort, most technicians utilize a data discovery product.

Data discovery products are tools that help organizations identify sensitive information by matching predefined patterns or algorithms to flag matches to those definitions. There are many different types of products architectures. Some are software-only, some are appliance based, some require user credentials, and some require agents to be installed on target systems. Regardless of their form, most of these products are based on either scanning "data-in-motion" on the network or scanning "data-at-rest" (i.e., data files or databases) on servers, workstations, desktop, and even laptop systems.

Once data discovery has identified a policy violation, the system can be configured to handle the event in a variety of ways. In the case of "data-in-motion," the administrator can be alerted and the data can be blocked or quarantined for further investigation. In the case of "data-at-rest," the administrator can be alerted and a copy of the data can be obtained. In either case, sensitive data can be captured and addressed according to the organization's internal procedures.

Regardless of the amount of security controls implemented, the chance of IP leaking out is highly likely. This is why a data discovery assessment should be conducted on a periodic basis. Data discovery is one of the key elements of a DLP program. Access to a strong discovery tool and knowledgeable staff can assist most organizations in implementing a solid DLP program.

## Remediation Processes

There are several process steps within the remediation phase. These steps are visually displayed below.

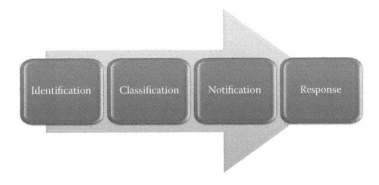

## Identification

Before a policy violation can be remediated, it first needs to be identified. A major challenge with DLP is determining which data is real-leaked data and which data is a false-positive detection. In today's business environment, the amount of data traveling through the network and stored on disk drives is almost overwhelming. Nevertheless, the challenge needs to be managed and processes need to be in place beforehand. Should a violation be discovered, proper methodology can be implemented and the cause of the breach accurately determined.

Should a violation be discovered, enough information needs to be collected to determine the next steps.

## Classification

Once the data has been identified, it needs to be classified as far as the type of data and its severity level. The type of data will support notification steps (i.e., who needs to be notified) and the severity will help determine the urgency for addressing the issue. The classification schema should leverage the data classification model discussed earlier in this chapter. An example classification chart would be as follows:

| Departments | Urgency | | | |
| --- | --- | --- | --- | --- |
| | *Private* | *Confidential* | *Internal* | *Public* |
| Human resource | × | | | |
| Legal | × | | | |
| Compliance | | × | | |
| Marketing and sales | | × | | |
| Information systems | | | | |
| Manufacturing | | | × | |
| Information systems | | × | | |

where

| Severity | Action |
| --- | --- |
| Private | Immediate contact needs to occur. Data should be blocked or quarantined. |
| Confidential | Contact needs to occur within a timely manner. Data should be blocked, quarantined, or at least a copy of the data taken. |
| Internal | Urgency is low; the contacts should receive a voice mail or e-mail notification. A copy of the data should be taken for future reference. |
| Public | Public data is not an issue. No action required. |

## Notification

Based on the type of data and its severity, determined in the previous step, the notification step will identify the proper owner of data and the urgency to take action. This information should be predetermined and escalation procedures should be developed to hand off the issue to the data's owners. Notification procedures should, at a minimum, contain the following:

■ Department
■ Contact
■ DLP role
■ Office/cell number

## Response

Once a violation has been identified, classified, and the correct people have been notified, the violation must be responded based on the classification and severity level. Part of the response would include an assessment and an investigation.

Assessment begins as soon as a violation is identified. The relevant DLP team members need to collect all relevant data and work with business owners to determine the business impact on the organization. The DLP team members and the data owners need to coordinate a plan to efficiently contain the distribution of the sensitive data and address the offenders to ensure the violation does not occur again.

At a minimum, the DLP team and data owners should

- Identify all types of data the offender has access to
- Start logging and recording the offender's activity
- Suspend access to additional sensitive data

Investigation is undertaken to determine the method and extent of the incident. The method is the technical vehicle allowing data to be transferred. The extent includes the boundary and the magnitude of the circulation of the data.

During the investigation process, ensure the following information is captured:

- The data and time of the violation
- The source of the data
- The destination of the data
- Data violation

Regulatory Compliance—One of the outcomes of the assessment and investigation phases is to determine if any steps need to be taken to meet regulatory requirements. (i.e., "California SB1386—Protection of Personal Data").

The DLP Leaders will work with Compliance and Legal Counsel to determine if compliance violations have occurred. If violations have occurred, the DLP Leaders should call an incident meeting with the DLP team, Compliance, Legal Counsel, and Executive Management. This meeting should determine the following:

- Determine what data was affected
- Determine if outside help is required
- Determine if law enforcement should be notified
- Determine the best notification method to use

## Training and Awareness

It is important for an effective DLP solution to interact with the organization's employees so that they have a strong understanding of why certain activities are inappropriate and could be harmful for the organization. Not all violations are conducted with a harmful intent. An employee may want to work at home and e-mail sensitive data to their personal, less secure public account. Although the intent is good, the action is not. Ongoing education will help reinforce correct behavior and provide the employee with guidance on how to correctly handle sensitive data.

When organizations educate and highlight the dangers of data loss, violations are reduced dramatically. Over time, as the employees become more familiar with corporate policy, the overall security awareness practices increase throughout the organization.

## Emergence of Departments

With the technology advancements of DLP tools, the emergence of multiple departments becomes necessary to ensure data is handled in an appropriate manner. Functional relationships need to be defined so sensitive information is not exposed to the wrong person. The following model displays an example of a DLP department relationship structure.

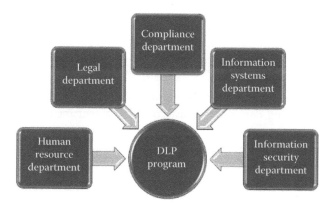

Although it depends on the organization's structure, the above model displays a common relationship (i.e., interest) structure, with each department responsible for a particular role and responsibility.

*Legal Department*: The Legal department must be involved in any DLP program. The legal department will have the role and responsibility for creating and/or approving policies and procedures. The first set of policies the legal department must create and/or approve is who has access to certain types of discovered information. For example, the legal department needs to create a policy ensuring that IT personal are not reviewing HR data. The legal department will also need to create a policy and a process for policy violations. With today's technology, it is easy to identify policy violations. The difficult part is acting on the policy and determining the level of damage to the organization. Overall, the legal department needs to provide legal oversight to ensure the DLP program is not being misused.

*Human Resources Department*: The Human Resource (HR) department's involvement would be that of a reviewer of data and enforcement. As a reviewer, HR policies violations need to be flagged and assessed by an HR representative. Sensitive information such as salaries, social security data, and other PII needs to be restricted and protected. As an enforcer, the HR department would be required to handle any personnel issues, which may lead to a reprimand or possible termination of employment.

*Compliance Department*: The Compliance department will have the role and responsibility to ensure the handling of data does not violate any compliance requirements. For example, the transfer of HIPAA or PCI data from its secure location to a less secure, unauthorized location could violate a compliance requirement. An employee may not be aware that their actions violate compliance; therefore, an intervention may help protect the company and educate the employee.

*Information Systems Department*: The Information Systems (IS) department's role and responsibility is to install and maintain tools that are used to identify violations of DLP policies. In the case of a network solution, the IS department would provide logical access to the network and would provide physical accommodations for the DLP hardware.

*Security Department*: The Security department is the owner of the DLP program. As the owner, it would also be the functional custodian of the tools used to monitor and/or discover policy violations. Although it would be the application owner, this does not mean it would receive and take action for all the alerts. As stated earlier, each designated group (i.e., Legal, HR, Compliance, etc.) would receive and manage their own issues.

# Legal Challenges

Employee monitoring of their staff's activities has always occurred within the workplace environment. Early monitoring was as simple as walking the floor to ensure the employee was at their desk working away. Today, due to technological advancements, the workplace environment has widened its boundaries. Virtual environments have allowed employees to work in remote locations and, in some cases, work at their home. Although technology has provided the employee with the freedom to work remotely, technology has also provided the employer with tools to monitor their activities, without the employee's knowledge.

The practice of monitoring employee's activities without their knowledge has become a controversial issue. Although most organizations have their employees sign an acceptable use policy, privacy expectations can be out-of-alignment between the employee and the employer.

## Federal and State Laws

There are several federal and state laws governing workplace privacy. The most popular federal law is the Electronic Communication Privacy Act of 1986 (ECPA). ECPA was enacted to extend federal wiretap laws to new forms of communication. The prior law, the Omnibus Crime Control and Safe Streets Act of 1968, protected only those communications that could be overheard by an individual. The statue did not address communication technologies such as e-mail, instant messaging, file transmittals, faxes, pagers, and cellular or cordless telephones.

This later legislation disallows employers to monitor their employee's communications. Although it is disallowed, the ECPA has several exceptions for monitoring electronic communications. The three most relevant to the workplace are (1) where one party (i.e., the employee) consents, (2) where the provider of the communication service can monitor the communications, and (3) where the monitoring is conducted in the ordinary course of business.

On October 26, 2001 new legislation was enacted, called the Uniting and Strengthening America by Providing Appropriate Tools Required to Intercept and Obstruct Terrorism (USA PATRIOT) Act. This new law amended a number of laws, including the ECPA. The changes made by the PATRIOT Act to ECPA addresses two situations, (1) the manner in which government authorities can compel disclosure, and (2) whether or not an organization can make a voluntary disclosure to government authorities.

The USA PATRIOT Act also amends ECPA by adding a new voluntary disclosure exception for emergency situations. Under this exception, if a service provider reasonably believes that an emergency exists involving immediate danger (i.e., death or serious physical injury), assistance from and disclosure of information to a law enforcement agency is justified.

Every state has some type of privacy law as well. These laws, also known as tort laws, are often viewed as the primary sources of protection for privacy of electronic communications. The most common tort that would apply is the tort of invasion of privacy.

The biggest controversy with workplace privacy laws is the reasonable expectation of privacy. Most employees have a different expectation of privacy than their employers. An organization must take significant steps to ensure the expectation of privacy is understood.

The Legal department should be heavily involved in every DLP program. Their lack of involvement could easily lead to an unsuccessful program if the structure, processes, and procedures were ill-defined and an employee's expectations of privacy are not properly communicated. Even if an organization constructs a solid program on the front-end, back-end issues with handling a policy violation can be challenging, especially from a legal standpoint.

Disciplinary action taken against an employee violating policy can always be a challenge. The organization needs to ensure all policies are in order and that the employee is well informed about the policy and its consequences.

## DLP Resource Challenges

Today, implementing a DLP program can be cost-prohibitive for most organizations. The cost of procuring a product and deploying dedicated security resources to manage and investigate alerts has been limited to large enterprises. Mid-tier organizations traditionally resort to improving their policies and procedures, increasing employee awareness, and in some cases, implementing some type of e-mail or file encryption. The simple fact is, most mid-tier organizations have not been able to afford the emerging technology and do not have the IT resources to manage a program.

With advancements in technology, an increasing number of DLP vendors, and increased awareness of the value of a DLP program, costs are reducing and next-generation solutions are becoming economically feasible.

## Benefits of a Data Loss Prevention Program

The following illustrates some of the benefits for creating a DLP program:

- *Prevent data leakage*
  Prevent accidental or malicious loss of data by insiders or hackers, even when data is disguised.
- *Reduce cost of investigation and reputation*
  Reducing costs in investigating data loss can also reduce the cost of rebuilding damage to an organization's reputation.
- *Facilitate early risk detection and mitigation*
  Implementing a DLP program will help identify data leakage and will help ensure information is in its proper place.
- *Increased comfort level with senior management*
  Implementing DLP controls will help assure senior management that proper security safeguards have been implemented, allowing them to concentrate on other critical business issues.

## Conclusion

A DLP program reduces the risk of exposure of sensitive information. Although some of the DLP processes and procedures may appear to be redundant to existing security safeguards, creating a separate program would strengthen existing security controls and would initiate new methods for detecting data leakage. Implementation of a program will also provide management with greater control and understanding of what type of data is being transferred through the network. Organizations faced with compliance requirements need to be proactive and initiate a program to address compliance obligations.

## Chapter 17

# Data Reliability: Trusted Time Stamps

Jeff Stapleton

## Contents

The technology shift from pen and ink documents to electronic bits has dramatically increased data flows and information quantity during the past 70 years, but at the same time has adversely affected its quality. The information age initially required data entry operators to translate pen and ink information into data bits, but today information sources are the data bits and conversely the paper is now printed afterward, relying on the data bits interpreted by software programs. This software abstraction layer introduces a data reliance problem that ultimately can only be addressed using cryptography to implement trusted time stamp technology.

## Pen and Ink Reliability

More than 5000 thousand years ago, the Sumerians are thought to have invented the written language using styli and clay tablets. The Egyptians and Mayans often captured their hieroglyphics in stone, while the Chinese used turtle shells and ox bones. Regardless of the language, such physical media have a certain permanence about it. Even today, thousands of years later, we can still read these carvings. The Egyptians are also accredited with using papyrus and ink as early as 5000 years ago, which the ancient Romans adopted over 2500 years ago. Papyrus writing, clay tablets, wooden tablets, and waxed tablets may not have the same permanence as stone carvings; but nonetheless their physical characteristics provide a sense of authenticity and integrity, which has transferred to the modern-day paper and ink. Indeed, important documents requiring integrity were captured on paper using pen and ink, such as accounting ledgers and contracts, with handwritten signatures and personal seals (e.g., signet rings and hand stamp devices in wax or ink) providing authenticity.

Pen and ink documents have inherent characteristics; they are tangible and have tactile feedback. An individual can feel the paper, smell the ink, and read the document with an unaided eye. Paper documents are static and stable such that appropriate procedures can preserve their custody (e.g., chain of evidence). A document can be filed away and locked up in a filing cabinet. Paper records are to some extent indelible and durable, such that alteration or unintentional destruction can be easily detected. The paper, the ink, and the manufacturing processes can be enhanced to such an extent that governments use it to print currency.

The originality of a pen and ink document is perceived to have worth, merit and reliance. Ancient scribes painstakingly used to copy documents by hand, sentence by sentence, word for word, letter by letter. Today, paper documents can be copied using modern imaging systems, they can then be mailed or faxed to multiple parities, and stored in filing cabinets for later reference. The authenticity of an original document is often determined by handwritten signatures that are distinguishable from copies.

## Evolution to Electronic Data

Prior to computer availability, information was captured and processed by humans using pen and ink documents. The availability of electronic computing in the 1940s and the commercialization of mainframe computers in the 1950s ushered in the need to transform pen and ink information into electronic data. Data entry operators read handwritten or typed documents as the data source and keyed information for computer processing. The 1960s introduced the minicomputer, which led to the transition of data capture from documents to data capture directly into computer systems. The microcomputer in the 1970s completed the data-capture transition, and inevitably transformed the paper document source from humans using pen and ink to printing documents from electronic bits. The data flow has literally reversed the direction "paper then computer" to "computer then paper," and subtly transformed the reliance from paper to electronic data. It is this transformation that lost the inherent characteristics of pen and ink and introduced the unreliable nature of electronic data, adversely affecting paper documents.

Data bits can exist in volatile memory such that an unexpected loss of power will allow the data to fade away over a relatively short period of time. For longer periods data bits are stored on magnetic or physical media depending on the retention or the usage requirements. Magnetic media include computer hard drives, tapes, flash memory on smart cards, and even magnetic stripe on credit cards. Physical media include CD-ROM, DVD, and other optic-based tokens.

Regardless of the medium, such data bits cannot be read directly; rather, humans rely on electronics and software to read, interpret, and display the information. Further, data bits can be perfectly duplicated (each bit is either a "0" or a "1") an infinite number of times without the ability to discriminate between the original and a copy.

The article *Spoliation of Digital Evidence* [1] discusses the evolution of more accurate forensics tools to *determine the provenance of evidence, as well as likelihood of spoliation.* Court cases are now addressing digital evidence issues, such as computer equipment ownership, preserving unaltered electronic data, controls over digital data to prevent spoliation, and even meta-data, which is information about data such as modification dates and file sizes. As the courts become more familiar with digital evidence and forensics experts continue to testify as expert witnesses, organizations' need for proactive integrity controls (versus reactive processes) will continue to increase and eventually will become a core element of the enterprise security policy and practices.

# Electronic Data Unreliability

Application software is designed to read, interpret, display, and even edit data files. Data files have a specific format and syntax such that sufficient modifications may corrupt the data to the extent that the designated application can no longer read the file. However, adversarial modifications may change the semantics of the file without affecting the format or syntax. Examples abound ranging from e-mails to contracts in which a dollar amount may be changed, a decision might be reversed, or a date could be manipulated. In many cases the modification would go undetected, while with others the change triggered an unexpected event and scrutiny.

The Sarbanes–Oxley Act of 2002 (Public Law No. 107-204) commonly called "SOX" was passed in response to a number of major corporate and accounting irregularities. Essentially SOX requires that publicly traded companies evaluate and disclose the effectiveness of their internal controls as they relate to financial reporting, and that appropriate controls over financial data be implemented where such controls are found to be lacking. There are several reported instances of time manipulation and data modification, where financial statements, audit reports, letters of credit were falsified and backdated to provide the appearance of compliance. See the Information Assurance Consortium's *Wall of Shame* [2] for details.

The article "Life after Sarbanes–Oxley" [3] discusses the "data-generation event" (DGE) separate from data "views" and the unreliability of paper printouts. The authors take the following positions:

- *First, it may be argued that the provision by the enterprise of views for audit, and the corresponding audit of views by auditors, constitute* prima facie *violations of Sarbanes-Oxley Section 302. This is because certifications are not being made on reliable business documents but on unreliable views.*
- *Second, the government and the courts traditionally have recognized that internal control requirements apply to electronic information-security infrastructures. If material weaknesses (for example, the ready ability of an insider to reset a system clock and undetectably alter, delete, or substitute digital accounting records) could lead to a material misstatement (as it has in the cases previously cited), a Sarbanes–Oxley violation might ensue.*

Backdating stock options is the granting of restricted employee stock options by a company at an exercise price equal to the value on the date that the grant is apparently made; however, the date chosen for the grant date is cherry-picked to select a date when the price of the stock was advantageously lower after the fact. These events incorporate time manipulation where the stock option letter is backdated such that the statement appears to be issued on the older grant date rather than the current date. This practice gained the attention of the *Wall Street Journal* (WSJ) and the Securities Exchange Commission (SEC). For more information refer to "The options backdating fiasco" [4] presentation at the RSA 2007 Conference. Not an illegal practice *per se*, although the legal profession is still debating this point, the impact to the company and stock-holders of having to reissue earning statements to the SEC and the Internal Revenue Service (IRS) has been in the multimillions. See the Information Assurance Consortium's *Wall of Shame* [2] for details.

Mutual funds' late trading incorporates data modification where trades that have been held past the final bell are submitted in a batch to the stock exchange. The practice of late trading is currently an acceptable SEC process but the consequences of altering the trades after the fact are well recognized by the securities industry. See the Information Assurance Consortium's *Wall of Shame* [2] for details.

These days software developers are notorious for bugs and vendors are well known for issuing endless patches. Information technology (IT) professionals are constantly on guard for current security patches, they rely on quality assurance (QA) practices to ensure that software is well behaved, and use antivirus software to prevent unauthorized software modification. However IT operates under the presumption that the executable software has not been intentionally manipulated during the software development life cycle (SDLC). See the Information Assurance Consortium's *Wall of Shame* [2] for details.

Sensitive data such as health-care information is susceptible to manipulation as demonstrated in the example x-rays shown in Figure 17.1. The newly created file might further be backdated and substituted for the original. Such time manipulation and data modification could be used to grant insurance coverage on an otherwise declined policy, provide justification for unwarranted medical treatment, or any number of other health-care-based fraud instances.

Further, electronic data can easily be copied and duplicated an infinite number of times with no distinction between the original and a copy. Clearly when the data is software related this can be a manufacturing benefit; however, replication might allow unauthorized distribution. Such

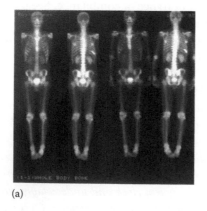 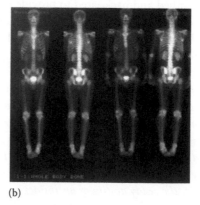

(a)                                              (b)

**Figure 17.1    Manipulating zeros and ones. The digitized full-body bone scan on the left (a) shows cancerous lesions on two ribs in the second and fourth images. The altered image on the right (b) shows the patient miraculously cured thanks to the advanced treatment called Adobe Photoshop®. (From B. Rothke, et al., LAW-403, RSA Conference, San Francisco, CA, 2007.)**

may be the case of downloadable or physically distributed software. Further, when the data is business information or unauthorized duplication of software, replication might allow the loss of intellectual property. It is often desirable to identify the compromised point and authorized party for purpose of reparation. However, when data can be modified or backdated by the first party providing information or second party receiving or replicating information, no parties can rely on the data unless a third party can verify the information.

Ironically, additional controls are necessary in order for electronic data to reclaim reliance that has become lost with outmoded pen and ink documents. Data in storage can be protected by physical barriers and access-control measures in a controlled environment. However, access controls can fail, and whenever the data is removed from its controlled environment (e.g., whenever it is viewed) the stored information requires cryptographic integrity solutions. In all circumstances, data in transit can only be protected using cryptographic solutions.

## Cryptography Schemes

There are several well-known and established uses of cryptography with its advantages and disadvantages. Each cryptography scheme is presented and its characteristics are described.

### Data Encryption

Data encryption is the best understood use of cryptography. A modern encryption algorithm such as Triple DES or AES uses a symmetric key to encrypt cleartext and produce ciphertext, and the same key is used to decrypt ciphertext and recover the cleartext. Encryption provides data confidentiality, which can be defined as the protection of information from unauthorized disclosure. Two-party transmission as shown in Figure 17.2—symmetric encryption is where the sender (A) and receiver (B) have previously and securely exchanged a symmetric encryption key. The sender encrypts the cleartext, transmits the ciphertext to the receiver, and the receiver decrypts the ciphertext to recover the cleartext. Any third-party eavesdropping on the transmission can only access the ciphertext. However, note that encryption by itself cannot provide integrity as the eavesdropper can modify the transmission and the receiver might not detect the modification depending on the format and syntax of the cleartext.

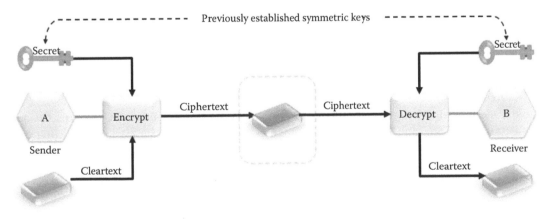

**Figure 17.2   Symmetric encryption.**

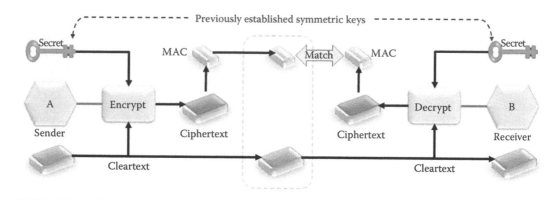

**Figure 17.3　Message authentication code.**

## Message Authentication Code

A message authentication code (MAC) is a symmetric scheme that uses encryption to provide rudimentary data integrity and limited authentication. Two-party transmission as shown in Figure 17.3—message authentication code is where the sender (A) and receiver (B) have securely exchanged a symmetric MAC key. The sender encrypts the cleartext, derives a MAC from the ciphertext, and transmits both the cleartext and the MAC to the receiver. The receiver encrypts the cleartext, derives a MAC from the ciphertext, and compares the MAC received with the newly generated MAC. If the two match, then neither the MAC nor the cleartext message has been modified and the receiver has validated the data integrity to itself. Further, the receiver has authenticated the sender to itself since only the two key holders could have generated the MAC. However, note that the MAC does not provide authentication to a third party in the case of a dispute since either the sender or the receiver could have generated the MAC and consequently the cleartext.

## Encrypted Hash

An encrypted hash is a combination of using a hash function with data encryption to achieve both data confidentiality and data integrity. A good hash function is a compression algorithm that demonstrates several important properties including the following:

■ High compression rate, which means that the length of the output must be significantly shorter than the length of the input. This is necessary so that very large inputs are reduced to outputs that are small enough to use with other cryptographic schemes.
■ One-way function, which simply means that the input cannot be determined from the output. This also implies that an inverse function does not exist or is infeasible to calculate.
■ Low collision rate, which basically means that the number of possible outputs from an infinite number of inputs have equal probability. For example, a bad hash function is one that maps every input to the same output value. Conversely a good hash function has the characteristic that the output is mathematically representative of the input.

Two-party transmission as shown in Figure 17.4—encrypted hash is where the sender (A) and receiver (B) have previously and securely exchanged a symmetric encryption key. The sender first

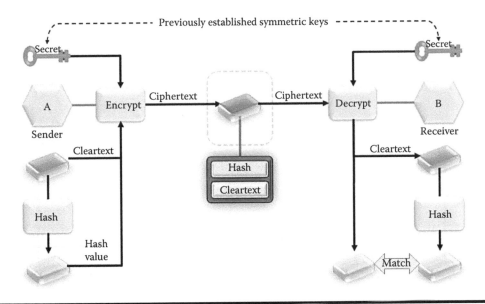

**Figure 17.4  Encrypted hash.**

generates a hash value of the cleartext, encrypts the hash value and the cleartext, and transmits the ciphertext to the receiver. The receiver decrypts the ciphertext to recover the hash value and the cleartext, generates a hash from the cleartext, and compares the hash value received with the newly generated hash value. If the two match, then the ciphertext has not been modified and the receiver has validated the data integrity to itself. Further, the receiver has authenticated the sender to itself since only the two key holders could have generated the ciphertext. However, the encrypted hash has the same issue as the MAC, as the ciphertext does not provide authentication to a third party in the case of a dispute since either the sender or the receiver could have generated the ciphertext and consequently the cleartext and the hash value.

## *Keyed Hash*

The keyed hash is similar to an encrypted hash except instead of encrypting the cleartext and hash value together, the cleartext is combined (not encrypted) with the symmetric key and then the hash function is used to generate a hash value. The combination algorithm uses several "exclusive or" functions (XOR) to create the input to the hash function so that the output is a "keyed hash" value. Two-party transmission as shown in Figure 17.5—keyed hash is where the sender (A) and receiver (B) have previously and securely exchanged a symmetric encryption key. The sender generates the "keyed hash" from the cleartext, and transmits both the cleartext and the "keyed hash" to the receiver. The receiver generates a "keyed hash" from the cleartext, and compares the "keyed hash" received with the newly generated "keyed hash." If the two match, then neither the "keyed hash" nor the cleartext has been modified and the receiver has validated the data integrity to itself. Further, the receiver has authenticated the sender to itself since only the two key holders could have generated the "keyed hash." However, the "keyed hash" has the same issue as the MAC, as the "keyed hash" does not provide authentication to a third party in the case of a dispute since either the sender or the receiver could have generated the "keyed hash" and consequently the cleartext.

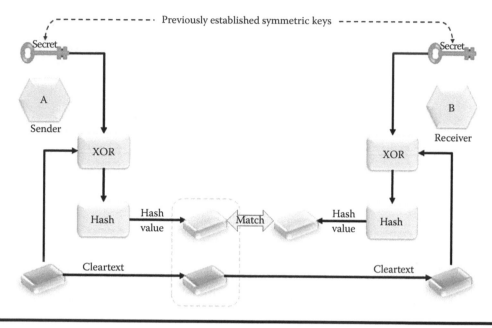

**Figure 17.5    Keyed hash.**

## Digital Signature

A digital signature is an asymmetric scheme that uses a hash function and a digital signature algorithm to provide enhanced integrity and authentication. Two-party transmission as shown in Figure 17.6—digital signature the sender (A) has an asymmetric key pair, designated as the public key and the private key, and the sender has established its public key with the receiver (B). The sender creates

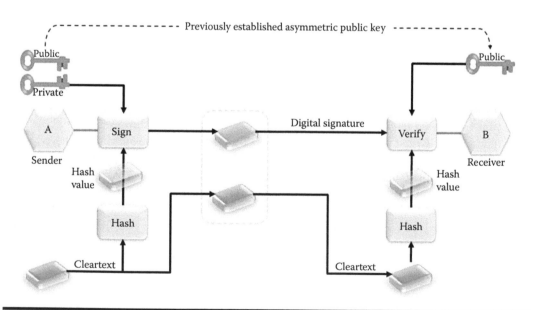

**Figure 17.6    Digital signature.**

a hash value from the cleartext using a hash function; generates a digital signature using the hash value, the private key, and the sign function; and transmits the cleartext and the digital signature. The receiver creates a hash value from the cleartext using the same hash function, and verifies the digital signature using a verify function. Note that the digital signature can only be generated using the private key that is under the control of the sender, but the digital signature can be verified by anyone using the sender's public key. Since only the sender can generate the digital signature, the cleartext has authenticity provable to any third party. However, the integrity is impermanent since the sender could modify and backdate the cleartext with a new valid digital signature. Different relying parties might receive dissimilar information, or the same relying parties might receive discontinuous information, whose valid digital signatures convey a false sense of reliability [5].

From an information-security perspective, data reliability must be based on a cryptographic technology whose integrity scheme can be validated by any independent third party to a verifiable time source [6]. Trusted time stamps are in fact such an integrity scheme that can provide not only data reliability, but also have the capacity for enhancing digital signatures.

## Trusted Time Stamps

Trusted time stamps can use one of several cryptographic methods but for this explanation the method described will be using digital signatures. An independent Time Stamp Authority (TSA) provides time stamp tokens (TST) to requestors, which relying parties can depend upon. Two-party transmission as shown in Figure 17.7—TST provided by the TSA has an asymmetric key pair, designated as the public key and the private key, and the TSA has established its public

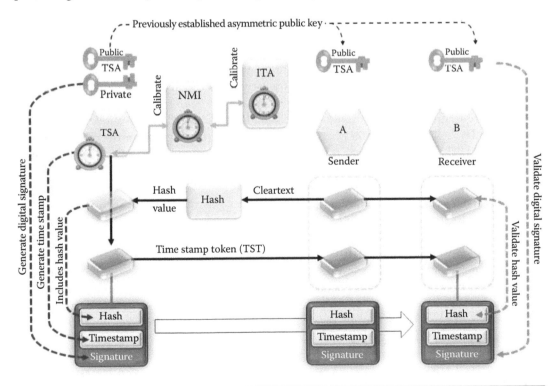

**Figure 17.7  Time stamp token.**

key with both the sender (A) and the receiver (B). The sender (who is the requestor for this scenario) generates a hash of the cleartext and submits a request with the hash to the TSA. The TSA generates a TST by incorporating the sender's hash value, generating a time stamp from its clock, and generating a digital signature using its asymmetric private key. The TSA returns the TST to the sender. Note that the TSA never has access to the original cleartext. The sender can then transmit the TST and the cleartext to the receiver (who is the relying party for this scenario). The receiver first verifies that the TST corresponds to the cleartext by validating the hash value, and then validates the TST by validating the TSA's digital signature using the TSA public key which verifies the binding between the hash value and the time stamp. The receiver can then rely on the time and integrity of the cleartext.

The time stamp is reliable as it is derived from the TSA clock. The TSA clock is calibrated to a National Measurement Institute (NMI), which similarly calibrates its clock to the International Timing Authority (ITA). The ITA is the Bureau International des Poids et Mesures (BIPM) near Paris, France [7]. The United States actually has two NMI, the National Institute of Standards and Technology (NIST) Time and Frequency Division [8] and the United States Naval Observatory (USNO) [9]. Note that the Global Positioning System (GPS) clocks are calibrated to the NIST and USNO atomic clocks and, therefore, GPS can be used by a TSA to calibrate its clock and generate a time calibration report.

Unlike digital signatures the sender cannot modify and backdate the cleartext. The TST ensures the reliance of the data integrity, the authenticity of the TSA, and the trustworthiness of the time stamp. Similar to digital signatures the TST is verifiable by any third party using the TSA's public key. The receiver can now truly rely on the data, hence the term "data reliance" versus "data integrity." Further, trusted time stamp technology can also be used to extend the reliability of public key infrastructures (PKI) by enhancing the sender's digital signature.

It is important to recognize that trusted time stamping technology is not a panacea. The TST must be applied to the workflow at the proper sequence of events, otherwise the data reliance is no more useful as locking the proverbial barn door after the horses have already left. For example, a requestor could generate several different messages prior to an event and obtain a TST for each message. The optimal message could then be chosen and used after the event. A classic case might be late trading. In this scenario an unscrupulous trader generates two messages, a "buy" message and a "sell" message, and obtains a TST for both. Depending on the outcome of the targeted stock, the optimal message is submitted after the closing bell, but the TST indicates a pre-closing time. The TST provides reliance that the message was generated before the closing bell, but in this case it does not provide anything useful regarding the actual submission of the order. The TST obtained by the trader before the order was submitted is an improper implementation. Rather the TST should be obtained by the stock broker at the time of submission to thwart the unscrupulous trader. Of course an unscrupulous stockbroker could practice the same deception, so the problem has not been solved; it has only been shifted in the workflow. A proper solution for this scenario might include a TST at every message-exchange point in the workflow between participating entities. Note that this scenario discussion has ignored the fact that the TSA is required to log all TST generation events [10] such that the extra messages would easily be discoverable in an investigation should collusion between multiple parties result in fraud.

Two-party transmission as shown in Figure 17.8—signature TST is where the TSA has an asymmetric key pair and the sender likewise has an asymmetric key pair. TSA has established its public key with both the sender (A) and the receiver (B), and the sender has established its public

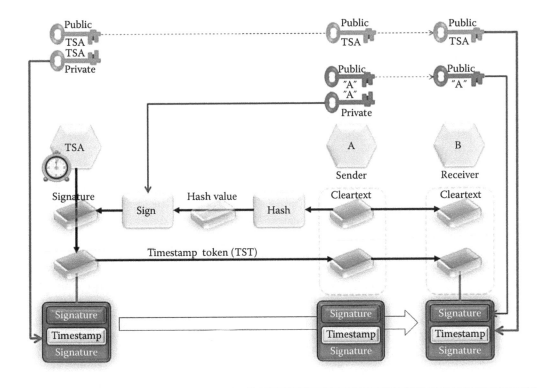

**Figure 17.8   Signature TST.**

key with the receiver. The sender generates a digital signature from the cleartext using its asymmetric private key and submits the digital signature (instead of just hash) to the TSA. The TSA generates a TST using its normal process, the difference being that the TST contains the sender's signature, and returns the TST to the sender as usual. The sender can then transmit the TST and the cleartext to the receiver. The receiver first verifies that the TST corresponds to the cleartext by validating the sender's digital signature using the sender's public key and then validates the TST by validating the TSA's digital signature using the TSA public key. The receiver can not only rely on the integrity of the cleartext as it pertains to the time stamp, but also knows with certainty when the sender signed the cleartext. Since the TST is verifiable by any third party using both the TSA's and the sender's public keys, the receiver now has strong authentication and data integrity demonstrable to a verifiable time source.

The concept of a cryptographically secure digital timestamp (CSDT) was described in "Preserving public key hierarchy" [11]. The CSDT is essentially a proprietary implementation of a TST customized for a specific application environment, namely the issuance of a public key certificate by a Certification Authority (CA). Both schemes have a requestor (for the CSDT it is the CA), the equivalence of a TSA (for the CSDT it is called a Timing Authority), and a relying party (for the CSDT it is the certificate users). The CSDT provides the additional assertion as to when the CA signed the public key certificate such that in the unlikely event of a CA root asymmetric key pair being compromised, the relying party might still trust the existing certificate. This of course presumes that the point in time at which the compromise occurred is known such that any certificate issued prior to the compromise might still be trusted.

## Standardization

TSA technology, policy, practices, and processes are codified in the National American Standard X9.95 *Trusted Time Stamp Management and Security* [10]. This standard is an enhancement of two other standards, the Internet Engineering Task Force (IETF) Request for Comment (RFC) 3161 Internet X.509 PKI Time Stamp Protocol (TSP) [12] and the international standard ISO/IEC 18014 Information Technology—Security Techniques—Time-Stamping Services [13]. There are significant differences between the documents as detailed in the *Trusted Time Stamp Standards* [14] and summarized here.

- X9.95 includes digital signatures, message authentication codes (MAC), linked tokens, and the transient key method. ISO/IEC 18014 does not include the transient key method and RFC 3161 only supports digital signatures.
- X9.95 includes roles and responsibilities for four entities, the Time Source Entity (TSE) such as the NMI and the ITA, the Time Stamp Authority (TSA), the TST requestor and the TST verifier. ISO/IEC 18014 does not include the TSE and RFC 3161 only address the TSA.
- X9.95 contains over 150 specific and detailed requirements, whereas ISO/IEC 18014 has 22 and RFC 3161 has 9 requirement statements.
- X9.95 provides both Abstract Syntax Notation One (ASN.1) and Extended Markup Language (XML) definition for various objects including the Time Calibration Report, the Time Stamp Request, the Time Stamp Response, the Time Stamp Token, the Verification Request and the Verification Response. ISO/IEC 18014 and RFC 3161 provide ANS.1 definitions for a subset of the same objects, however the objects are interoperable.
- X9.95 has complete message flows and error handling for Time Calibration, Time Stamp Acquisition, and Time Stamp Verification. ISO/IEC 18014 and RFC 3161 do not provide any message flows or error handling, but error codes are defined.
- X9.95 provides example policy and practice statements, whereas ISO/IEC 18014 and RFC 3161 do not address the topics.
- X9.95 provides 22 control objectives and 237 evaluation criterion for use by a qualified professional to assess (or audit) a TSA or other trusted time stamp implementation entity. ISO/IEC 18014 and RFC 3161 do not provide any assessment or evaluation material.

Note that ISO, IEC, and X9 standards undergo 5-year reviews and revisions so it is likely that the differentials listed above will change in the near future. Further note that there are other proprietary content integrity and time-and-date stamp services that likewise rely on various cryptographic solutions. As of this writing, there are no regulatory or industry requirements for using trusted time stamps or for existing TSAs undergoing formal assessments based on any industry standards beyond the usual accounting practices such as the Statement on Auditing Standards No. 70 (SAS 70) for third-party service organizations.

## Conclusion

Regulatory and legal precedents are occurring today that are harbingers for proactive data integrity controls. Cryptography is a key element in achieving data confidentiality, data integrity, and authenticity for electronic data; however, not all cryptographic schemes are equivalent. Symmetric cryptography can provide limited data integrity and authenticity between participating parties but cannot provide such assurance to a third party. Asymmetric cryptography can provide authenticity provable to a third party but with impermanent data integrity. However, data integrity must include a trustworthy time element, and, therefore, to distinguish between "data integrity" methods in use today and the advanced trusted time stamps, the term "data reliance" has been introduced. Trusted time stamps are the next-generation technology that can provide data reliance services that are demonstrable to independent third parties.

## About the Author

**Jeff Stapleton** is the CTO with Cryptographic Assurance Services with over 25 years experience in the cryptography, security, financial, and healthcare industries.

## References

1. S. W. Teppler, Spoliation of digital evidence: A changing approach to challenges and sanctions, *The Scitech Lawyer*, 6(2), FALL 2007, Section of Science & Technology Law American Bar Association.
2. Information Assurance Consortium, *Wall of Shame*, www.infoassurance.org
3. S. W. Teppler Esq., B. Nearon, J. Stanley Esq., and J. Burton Esq., Life after Sarbanes-Oxley: The merger of information security and accountability, *Jurimetrics J*. 45 379–412 2005.
4. B. Rothke, B. Nearon, S. Teppler Esq., and J. Stapleton, The options backdating fiasco: Time-based data control issues leads to compliance problems, shareholder lawsuits and criminal indictments, LAW-403, RSA Conference, San Francisco, CA, 2007.
5. J. Stapleton, P. Doyle, and S. Teppler Esq., Digital signature paradox, 6th IEEE Information Assurance Workshop, West Point, NY, April 2005.
6. J. Stapleton, Digital signatures are not enough, *ISSA J*. 4 1 January 2006.
7. Bureau International des Poids et Mesures, http://www.bipm.org/
8. Time and Frequency Division, National Institute of Standards and Technology, http://tf.nist.gov/
9. United States Naval Observatory, http://www.usno.navy.mil/
10. American National Standard X9.95 *Trusted Time Stamp Management and Security*, 2005 www.x9.org
11. G. C. Grabow, Preserving public key hierarchy, in H. F. Tipton and M. Krause (eds), *Information Security Handbook*, 6th edn., New York: Auerbach Publications, 2007.
12. RFC 3161 *Internet X.509 PKI Time Stamp Protocol* (TSP), August 2001 www.ietf.org
13. ISO/IEC 18014 *Information Technology—Security Techniques—Time-Stamping Services*, www.iso.org; www.infoassurance.org
14. J. Stapleton, Trusted time stamp standards: A comparison and guideline of the American national standard X9.95 trusted time stamp management and security, Information Assurance Consortium, 2007.

*Chapter 18*

*Chapter 18*

# Security in the .NET Framework

James D. Murray

## Contents

Since its formal introduction in 2002, the Microsoft.NET Framework has become the standard development platform for mobile and desktop applications, Web sites and Internet services, and enterprise-class software solutions running on Microsoft Windows. The .NET Framework itself is a managed environment used to provide a structured development platform for creating and managing many types of software solutions.

Microsoft created the .NET Framework in response to the need of a standardized platform for

■ Designing general-purpose, network-distributed, and Web-based applications
■ Providing platform-independent services for those applications to use
■ Managing (monitoring and controlling) applications running in a Windows environment

The ultimate purpose of the .NET Framework is to free developers from making decisions such as writing codes based on system dependencies, creating nonstandard services, and implementing low-level security, and instead focus on development based on the business goals of the needed solution. As stated on the Microsoft Developer Network (MSDN) Web site, the .NET Framework is designed to fulfill the following objectives:

■ To provide a consistent object-oriented programming environment whether object code is stored and executed locally, executed locally but Internet distributed, or executed remotely.

- To provide a code-execution environment that minimizes software deployment and versioning conflicts.
- To provide a code-execution environment that promotes safe execution of code, including a code created by an unknown or semi-trusted third party.
- To provide a code-execution environment that eliminates the performance problems of scripted or interpreted environments.
- To make the developer experience consistent across widely varying types of applications, such as Windows-based and Web-based applications.
- To build all communication on industry standards to ensure that codes based on the .NET Framework can integrate with any other code.

It is interesting to note that all of these objectives have security implications, either directly or indirectly. Security in a computing system is often expressed as a trust in the precision, reliability, and confidentiality of the system. This fact is realized by Microsoft and is expressed in Microsoft's Trustworthy Computing initiative.

## Trustworthy Computing

In 2002, Microsoft launched its Trustworthy Computing initiative in an effort to ensure the delivery of secure, private, reliable, and helpful computing experiences for all users. The four key goals of this initiative are

- Security to ensure the confidentiality, integrity, and availability of a system and its data, and to provide resilience to attack.
- Privacy to provide reliable control over how the information stored by a system is accessed and protected.
- Reliability to guarantee that a computing system is dependable, is available when needed, and performs at the level expected.
- Business practices that help discover effective and responsible solutions to business customer's problems with product, services, or interactions.

The .NET Framework supports Trustworthy Computing by allowing developers to write .NET applications that make use of Windows libraries and services, which provide technical support for these four goals. Developers using the .NET Framework may create applications that support host and user authentication, information privacy, and ensure reliable operation and resiliency against errors and attacks.

## Releases of the .NET Framework and Windows

Since the first beta release of .NET in 2000, there have been subsequence releases of .NET (1.1, 2.0, 3.0, and 3.5) that have extended the capabilities of the .NET Framework, including the security framework. Therefore, not all security features detailed in this article are available in all versions of the .NET Framework.

It is also useful to know that not every release of the .NET Framework runs on every version of Microsoft Windows, or even comes preinstalled on most versions of Windows:

- .NET Framework 1.0 was released in January 2002, and ran only on Windows 98, Windows NT 4.0, Windows 2000, and Windows XP. .NET 1.x also runs on later releases of Windows, but is never preinstalled on any Windows distribution.
- .NET Framework 1.1 was released in April 2003, and came preinstalled on Windows Server 2003. Release 1.1 added support for security features such as Code Access Security and levels of trust.
- .NET Framework Version 2.0 was released in November 2005, and featured many additions and updates, especially to the .NET security engine. This is the last version of .NET to support Windows 2000, Windows 98, and Windows Me. No distribution of Windows includes .NET 2.0 preinstalled.
- .NET Framework 3.0 was released in November 2006, and came preinstalled on Windows Vista and Windows Server 2008, and can only be installed on Windows Server 2003 with Service Pack 1 (and later) and Windows XP with Service Pack 2 (and later). Release 3.0 contains new major features, but no major architectural changes.
- .NET Framework 3.5 was released in November 2007, and comes preinstalled only on Windows Vista with Service Pack 1 (and later). This release includes mostly fixes and improvements, but nothing security related.
- .NET Framework 4.0 is due to be released in 2009.

Improvements in security are present in each release of .NET from 1.0 through 2.0. .NET 3.x uses the same Common Language Runtime as .NET 2.0 and has no significant changes in security that requires updating applications from .NET 2.0. To make full use of .NET security features, it is recommended that .NET applications and all Windows systems use (at least) .NET 2.0.

## Java and .NET

The .NET Framework is conceptually identical in many respects to the Java platform. The Java Virtual Machine, Java byte codes, and Java class libraries have equivalents in .NET as the .NET Common Language Runtime, Common Intermediate Language, and the Framework Class Library. Both Java and .NET can run applications that are either compiled before execution or Just-In-Time compiled as they are executed. In addition, both support applications developed to run from a command line shell, a GUI shell (the desktop), in a Web browser, or a mobile device.

Some notable differences between Java and .NET are

- Java has been widely ported to many operating platforms (e.g., Windows, UNIX, Linux, OS X), while Microsoft's implementation of .NET is only available for Microsoft Windows.
- Microsoft supports the implementation of hundreds of programming languages that use the .NET Framework, while Sun Microsystems only supports the use of the Java language for the Java platform.
- Portions of the .NET Framework are formalized by the ISO/IEC and ECMA as international standards, while Sun Microsystems exclusively controls the Java standard.
- Most of the Java software platform is licensed as free and open source under the GNU General Public License, while the .NET Framework remains largely closed source and proprietary to Microsoft.

■ Java is a third-party software for Microsoft Windows, while Microsoft itself develops the .NET Framework. Therefore, the .NET Framework may be perceived as having better integration and accessibility to the Microsoft Windows environment than does Java.

All the similarities and differences aside, both Java and .NET have many of the same goals, including developing better, useful, and more secure applications more quickly by writing less code, and distributing all applications more easily and securely.

## .NET Framework Security

The .NET Framework provides a variety of security-related features and services that developers may choose to include in the design of their .NET applications. Services such as authentication, private network communications, secure data storage, and data encryption are available to all .NET applications as needed.

.NET also provides security features that run transparently in all .NET-based applications, requiring little or no configuration by the developer or system administrator. The continual monitoring of a running .NET application for invalid input, illegal access, and security policy violations are performed continually at the application level.

.NET also provides a security model in which all .NET applications must run. The model determines what permissions are granted to the code running in a .NET application and defines and enforces the security boundaries of each .NET application. This security model runs independently of the Windows user context-based model.

### .NET Security by Domain

To better understand the security features of the .NET Framework, it is useful to categorize them using the (ISC)2 CISSP Common Body of Knowledge (CBK). Exhibit 18.1 lists the major .NET security features and their corresponding CISSP CBK domains.

## Security Inside the .NET Framework

How .NET security works must be understood through the features and mechanisms that form the components of the .NET Framework itself. Some components, like assemblies and the Common Language Runtime, are indispensable parts of .NET security. Security features, such as user authentication and string encryption, are only used if needed by an application. Still other mechanisms, such as garbage collection, are not specifically security features, but are very important for the secure operation of a .NET application.

### Common Language Runtime

The .NET Common Language Runtime (CLR) is the virtual runtime environment that controls the execution of .NET code on the Windows platform. The CLR provides all the services essential for running a .NET application including memory management, thread management, type checking, exception handling, garbage collection, and security. The CLR itself is

**Exhibit 18.1   .NET Security Features in Relation to the CISSP CBK Domains**

| Security Domain | Supporting Features | Benefits |
|---|---|---|
| Access control | Role-based security | Authentication |
| | Host-based access control | Authorization |
| | Logging and event reporting | Accountability |
| Application security | Code access security | Resiliency to error, misuse, and attacks |
| | Applications domains | |
| | Input validation | |
| | Isolated storage | |
| | Secure strings | |
| Cryptography | Secret key cryptography | Privacy and confidentiality of data |
| | Public key cryptography | Authentication and non-repudiation of data ownership |
| | Cryptographic hashing | Use of common and formalized standards of cryptography and cryptosystems |
| | Digital signatures | |
| | Random number generation | |
| | Security API interfaces | |
| Security architecture and design | Host-based security integration | Integration and conformance to Windows platform security |
| | COM/DCOM integration | |
| | ASP.NET security | |
| Network security | Secure network protocols | Use of common and accepted standards of secure network communications |
| | Security provider interfaces | |
| | PKI interface | |

Microsoft's implementation of the Common Language Infrastructure (CLI) standard defined in ISO/IEC 23271:2006.

The CLR acts as the security watchdog of the .NET environment. It constantly checks for illegal instructions that would affect the integrity of the application or violate the security policy of the hosting environment. If the code in a .NET application attempts to commit an illegal operation, either accidentally or on purpose, it is prevented from doing so by the CLR. The security operation of the CLR is a compliment to the security policies of the Windows-operating system and does not override host-based or domain-based security mechanisms.

## Managed Code

Managed code is any application code whose execution is controlled directly by the CLR. Applications written using a .NET language are not compiled to native machine code, and, therefore, are not directly executed by the CPU. Instead, .NET applications are compiled to Common Intermediate Language (CIL, formerly known as Microsoft Intermediate Language, or MSIL) and Just-In-Time (JIT) compiled to native machine code at run-time. The JIT stage is when checks for security and consistency are performed.

Managed code also does not support the use of unmanaged pointer types in application code. Memory pointers are a constant source of problems involving uninitialized memory references (wild pointers), code stepping beyond memory object boundaries (overflow or overruns), and pointing to data objects that no longer exist in memory (dangling pointers). Such problems cause memory faults in a program's execution. They are also a possible source of security vulnerabilities from arbitrary code execution attacks that change the memory location stored by the pointer. None of these problems exists in managed .NET applications.

## Unmanaged Code

Unmanaged code is any application code executed outside of the control of the CLR. This includes all programs compiled to a binary image, all Windows-operating system APIs, and all COM/DCOM components. When unmanaged code is called by a managed .NET application, the operation of the unmanaged code is not controlled by the CLR; therefore there can be no assurance of secure and correct operation of the unmanaged code by the CLR. For reasons of both reliability and security, it is often a development constraint that .NET applications are designed to only use managed code by only calling classes and methods implemented in the .NET Framework.

## Assemblies

In .NET, an assembly is a library that stores the managed code used by a .NET application. An assembly contains the pre-complied CIL code, class libraries, and localized resources used by the application. An assembly will also contain *metadata* used to identify the object types, attributes, and security permissions in the managed code, and versioning, locality, and deployment information about the .NET application. An assembly itself is a set of files JIT compiled and executed by the CLR to run a .NET application.

## Strong-Named Assemblies

Code signing is used to enhance the security of .NET assembles. When an assembly is signed with a digital signature, it is said to have a *strong name*. A strong name is created from the assembly's text name, version number, locale information, a public key, and a digital signature. A strong name provides a unique identity for an assembly, allowing integrity checking to be performed before the assembly is loaded into memory. If the integrity check fails, a security exception is generated and the assembly is not loaded.

Assembly authentication is provided using an Authenticode signature. Authenticode enables signing an assembly using an X.509 certificate stored in a Public Key Infrastructure (PKI) repository. The assembly's publisher signs the assembly using a private key, and the authentication is checked using the corresponding public key stored in a trusted certificate authority. If the publisher's identify cannot be verified, the .NET application user is asked (via a pop-up dialog box) if the publisher is trusted or not. Both strong names and Authenticode are especially important for identification of assemblies deployed in mobile and Web-based environments.

Strong names also help prevent a long-standing problem with Windows involving multiple versions of the same library installed on the same computer. This "DLL Hell" causes applications to load the wrong version of a shared library file, which can cause security problems and often the source of program failures. Strong names allow a specific .NET application to use only the version of an assembly it is built for, and for multiple version of the same assembly to be installed on a single computer and not to cause problems.

## Type Safety

Type safety is the ability to prevent operations on an object that is not appropriate for its data size or type, such as writing a string value to an integer object. Such operations can cause memory violations that may result in the unstable operation of the application or cause the application to crash. In rare circumstance, such errors are also exploitable as security vulnerabilities.

Type safety verification is provided both at compile-time by the .NET language used to write the application and at run-time by the CLR. Coding errors that could cause a type safety problem are flagged as warnings or errors by the .NET compiler. Type safety also provides *memory safety* by preventing the referencing of arbitrary memory locations by a .NET application. This includes the execution of code on the program stack or heap commonly used in buffer overflow attacks.

## Bounds Checking

Bounds checking is the ability of an object to autonomously control the allocation of memory it uses to store data. String and StringBuilder are examples of .NET Framework classes that perform their own bounds checking. If a string is assigned to an object instantiated from either of these classes, the object will check if its internal buffer is large enough to store the sting data. If it is not, either the size of the buffer will be increased or an exception will be thrown indicating sufficient storage space does not exist. In either result, a buffer overflow condition will not occur.

## Security Exception Management

Security exceptions are events generated when the CLR detects a security error in a .NET application. Security exceptions can result from authentication failures, insufficient permission to perform an operation, invalid strong name detection, and from arithmetic overflows and underflows. Developers are responsible for writing code in their applications that handle all security exceptions generated by the .NET Framework.

## Garbage Collection

Garbage collection is the mechanism that allocates and releases memory managed by the CLR. Although not considered a security feature, garbage collection does prevent some common security vulnerabilities, such as memory leaks and premature deallocation, found in programming environments where developers are required to control memory deallocation explicitly in their code. Garbage collection does not securely overwrite memory before it is deallocated, nor has it control over unmanaged memory or resources, pointer types, and static variables. The application developer must, therefore, implement extra security measures if the secure destruction of data objects is required.

## Code Access Security

Code Access Security (CAS) is a security model in .NET that enforces the access limitations an assembly has to specific protected resources and restricted operations. Different assemblies in a .NET application may have different levels of trust depending on their publisher and origin of their code. CAS uses the integral security features of the CLR to perform higher-level administrative operations on running code, such as authenticating assemblies before they are loaded and checking permissions when code attempts to access resources. CAS is, therefore, an abstraction of both the CLR and the features of .NET used to prevent managed code from performing operations for which it is not trusted.

### Evidence-Based Security

Windows uses a user-based security model in which all operations are granted or denied based on the security context of the user performing the operation. The CAS uses an evidence-based security model based on identifying information provided by assemblies and trusted application domain hosts. The evidence-based security model is independent of the security context of the user, and is applied on top of Windows' user-based security and does not replace it.

### Evidence

Evidence is information obtained from an application domain host or .NET assembly and compared to system or user security policies to determine what permissions the host or assembly has. Assembly evidence is created when the assembly is coded and built by the developers, but before it is signed. Evidence that may be present in an assembly includes

- The strong name (digital signature) validated by the CLR when the assembly is loaded.
- A cryptographic hash value of the assembly.
- The Authenticode X.509v3 signature of the software publisher.
- The physical folder and path where the assembly's files are located.
- The URL of the Web site from which an assembly originates.
- The URL where an assembly is located.
- The Internet Explorer security zone of an assembly.
- Custom information added to an assembly by the application developers. This can include simple data, such as date the assembly was approved for release, or stronger data, such as additional public keys to be used for authentication.

A trusted application domain (e.g., Web browser, Web server, operating system shell) hosting the .NET application passes both its own evidence and the assembly's evidence to the CLR when the assembly is loaded. The evidence is evaluated against the current enterprise, machine, application, and user security policies to determine the permission the assembly will have. If the host is not trusted to control evidence, the CLR uses the same security permission it uses for the host itself.

Not all evidence is regarded with equal trust. Assembly evidence is not considered as trustworthy as evidence provided by a trusted host. Strong names and Authenticode signatures are also considered stronger evidence because they are difficult to modify and forge.

### Security Policies

CAS enables system administrators to configure security policies allowing the CLR to determine what operations an assembly is permitted to perform. The policies are a mapping of assembly evidence to a set of operations that the assembly's code has authorization to perform. For example, an assembly originating from a trusted and authenticated source may have the ability to write to the Windows event logs, while an unauthorized assembly originating from the Internet may not.

Managed code can make permissions requests, allowing an assembly to request only the level of permission it needs to perform its operations. Code that cannot be granted its minimum permission request is not loaded, and the application generates a security exception when it is first started and not at a later time when the application is running.

Like the Windows security model, .NET policies can be configured for different scopes, including enterprise, machine, user, and application domains. Policies are set by the system administrator and are evaluated by the CLR when the application is run. The CLR determines the trust of the assembly from the permission and assigns a level of trust from a predefined set of permissions defined for a .NET application.

## Application Domains

Operating systems provide isolation by running each application in a separate process. This isolation provides a security boundary that does not allow a process to inadvertently access the memory or private resources of other processes. The CLR can provide further security boundaries by creating application domains within a single process. Each application domain isolates objects within an application from each other, much the same way processes are isolated by the operating system.

Application domains are a primary mechanism used by CAS for enforcing security boundaries and checking run-time security. When an assembly is loaded by the CLR, it is placed in its own application domain and cannot access objects in any other application domains unless it is trusted to do so. Each application domain, therefore, has its own security permissions and level of trust. An assembly in an application domain can be unloaded without affecting all other application domains. This ability allows applications domains to perform sandboxing of potentially unsafe code, but also increase application performance and control application memory utilization as well.

## Application Security

.NET applications, components, and services are built on top of a standard library called the Framework Class Library (FCL). The FCL contains thousands of classes and methods that extend functionality to all applications that use it. Many implicit security operations are implemented directly in the code in the FCL, including parameter value checking and access permission restriction. All .NET applications, therefore, contain security-minded code, although a .NET application developer may never write a single line of code with security in mind.

## .NET Framework Security Namespaces

The FCL orders related classes into groups called *namespaces*. All .NET classes are referenced within the context of a namespace to isolate them into functional groups, and to prevent any ambiguity between classes that have the same name. Namespaces are very similar in concept to folders in a file system, with files being the classes. The FCL itself can be regarded as the Application Programming Interface (API) for .NET itself.

The base namespace for most security functions is *System.Security*. Several other namespaces also contain security-related classes. The following is a listing of all of the security-related namespaces in the FCL:

- *System.IO.IsolatedStorage* provides access to secure storage locations for isolating data by the context of the current user, domain, and assembly creating the store.
- *System.Net.Security* provides authentication and encryption for secure network communication between hosts using SSL.
- *System.Runtime* provides control over services used by the .NET security engine, including garbage collection.
- *System.Security* is the base class for all CLR security functions.
  - *System.Security.AccessControl* provides auditing and rule-based access control over securable objects.
  - *System.Security.Authentication* defines the type of authentication to be used with an SSL connection.
  - *System.Security.Cryptography* provides the base cryptographic services of .NET, including encryption and decryption, cryptographic hashing, message authentication, and random number generation.
    - *System.Security.Cryptography.Pkcs* enables applications to use the Public Key Cryptography Standards (PKCS) supported by .NET, including message signing, key exchange, requesting certificates, and PKI.
    - *System.Security.Cryptography.X509Certificates* enables applications to use X.509 v.3 certificates for reading and distributing public keys.
    - *System.Security.Cryptography.Xml* enables applications to create and validate XML digital signatures to provide integrity or message authentication for data.
  - *System.Security.Permissions* provides controlled access to operations and resources based on security permissions and Windows security policy.
  - *System.Security.Policy* allows the CLR to determine operation based on security policy using code groups, membership conditions, and evidence.
  - *System.Security.Principle* defines a principal (Windows group or user) that represents the security context under which manage code is run.
  - *System.Security.RightsManagement* provides an application access to the Microsoft Windows Active Directory Rights Management Services (AD RMS) for controlling application-created content.
  - *System.Security.SecurityException* provides notification when a security error is detected by the CLR.
- *System.Web.Security* provides security features specifically for ASP.NET managed code in Web server applications. Security features includes Windows, Forms, and Microsoft Passport authentication, URL and file authorization, and access to Active Directory.

## Isolated Storage

The .NET Framework supports the concept of isolated storage for the creation of safe, private, virtual file systems for each .NET application. Isolated storage can be used when a computer's file system does not provide sufficient isolation or protection for a user's data from untrusted code, or an application is not sufficiently trusted to allow it access to the Windows file system and registry. A typical use of isolated storage is to store application settings and user preferences, so they are hidden from access by untrusted code. The use of isolated storage also removes the need for the developer to write code for creating file names, checking file paths, and verifying that the application has read and write file permissions.

Every assembly run under the user's context is given its own private area in the user profile folder on the local system disk in which to store data. Access to this folder is based on either application identity or user identity, and conditional access is based on assembly evidence and application domain. Roaming profiles are used with isolated storage to allow an application's isolated stores to travel with the user's roaming profile. System administrators can control isolated storage by configuring the size (quota) of the allocated space, clearing the space, and setting the security policies. Administrators also have unrestricted access to all of the current user's isolated stores.

## Secure Strings

A common security problem with running applications is that they often store sensitive information as readable clear-text in memory and do not properly dispose of the information after it is no longer needed. This type of data leakage is sometimes observed in programs that accept a password for authentication and then fail to overwrite the password before removing it from memory. In .NET, string data is stored in memory as clear-text that is not automatically overwritten before it is removed from memory, leaving the string data to remain in memory even after the string object has been destroyed and garbage collection has occurred.

To remedy the possibility of string data exposure, the .NET Framework provides a SecureString class that is used to store string data in memory in an encrypted data format. To a .NET application, SecureString objects behave as normal strings, with the string data itself being encrypted when it is initialized and modified. A SecureString object can store data as either read–write or read-only, and can be forced to clear its data and immediately remove it from memory without waiting for garbage collection to occur. The data in a SecureString object is also not visible or accessible via COM.

# Security Architecture and Design

The .NET Framework provides both a security model and architecture of its own and integration with the security architecture of the Windows operating system. The .NET concept of application security is built on the top of the security model for the entire Windows platform. .NET is not inherently capable of bypassing or overriding Windows system or network security settings.

## Windows Host Security

The Windows security policy supports the concept of security zones. These predefined zones are used to segregate the location of code based on its physical location and levels of trust of its region.

The zones are My Computer, Intranet, Trusted, Internet, Untrusted, and NoZone, and are configured using the Internet Options applet in Control Panel, or the Security tab on the Microsoft Internet Explorer options panel.

Zones allow the CLR to determine how to trust code based on its identity. This is especially important for ASP.NET applications, whose code originates partially from the local machine and partially in an environment accessed via a Web browser. The CLR can run the local code with full trust, while allowing only partial trust for the mobile code running in the browser, effectively sandboxing the mobile application from the local environment.

## COM and DCOM

The Component Object Model (COM) is the Microsoft protocol and interface standard for inter-process communications between software components residing in different processes on the same machine. ActiveX is an interface model based on COM that allows Windows programs to run hosted in Web browsers, and is identical in concept to Java applets.

Although the .NET Remoting feature is a functional replacement for COM, .NET is fully capable of communicating securely and reliably with unmanaged COM components. .NET WinForm and WebForm controls offer a much more secure replacement for ActiveX components. The versioning and signing of .NET assemblies removes the "DLL Hell" created by COM components. And .NET assemblies can expose COM interfaces of their own.

The Distributed Component Object Model (DCOM) is the Microsoft protocol and interface standard for communications between software components residing on separate, network-connected machines. DCOM supports an RPC encryption protocol that provides encryption of all packets in an RPC channel. The Remoting and XML Web Services features of the .NET Framework are the functional replacement of DCOM (and COM+) in .NET applications.

## ASP .NET

ASP.NET (Active Server Pages for .NET) is an application framework used by developers for the creation of Web applications, Web sites, and Web services. ASP.NET is built on top of the .NET Framework, and uses .NET the same way that other .NET applications do.

Security features typically employed by ASP.NET applications include authenticating, registering, and managing users; authorizing access to Web site features; and provisioning application, provider, and database configurations. Many of these high-level features are implemented directly in ASP.NET and not in .NET itself. However, ASP.NET does benefit greatly from the security features inherent in the .NET Framework.

The security concerns specific in ASP.NET are those of any Web site, including SQL Injection and Cross Site Scripting (XSS) attacks. ASP.NET contains features used to prevent these types of attacks, such as automatic validation of all HTTP GET and POST Request variables, disallowing the illegal modification of pre-populated data controls, and preventing directory traversal that would read–write outside of the document root. Input validation applied by ASP.NET on WebForm field data defeats malformed URL and SQL Injection attacks.

Web Services provide cross-platform communication between heterogeneous systems, and are used quite extensively in Service-Oriented Architecture (SOA) and Software as a Service (SaaS) designs. The security of Web Services is greatly increased by using the authentication and data encryptions features available in the *System.Web.Security* namespace of the .NET Framework.

## Levels of Trust

In .NET 1.0, all ASP.NET Web applications ran with full trust, making them unable to apply the rules of Code Access Security. Starting with .NET 1.1, the system administrator is allowed to configure the trust level of an ASP.NET application, ranging from full unrestricted access to no access execute-only permission. Allowing different parts of a .NET application to operate at differing levels of trust blocks the more vulnerable parts of an application, such as a WebForm, from accessing the more privileges features of the .NET Framework while not impairing the access by more trusted code in the same ASP.NET application.

# Access Control

Access control uses the operations of authentication, authorization, and accounting to identify a subject; determine what objects the subject can and cannot access; and record an audit trail of the subject's actions. The .NET Framework provides features allowing applications to perform these access control operations as needed.

## Authentication

The .NET Framework supports three methods of user authorization and authentication: host based, role based, and custom. Host-based authentication uses Windows authentication to determine the identity and permission of a user based on a Windows local or domain user account. Role-based authentication allows users to be authenticated based on a role, which can be application defined or based on Windows groups. Custom authentication allows the developer to implement an application-specific authentication scheme.

ASP.NET is fully integrated with the authentication mechanism used for a Windows domain or network using NT LAN Manager authentication, or Kerberos for single sign-on capability. Other authentication schemes available to ASP.NET applications include digest authentication with MD5, using digital certificates to mutually authenticate both the client and server, and custom authentication schemes created by developers.

## Role-Based Security

.NET contains a generic, role-based security mechanism that allows the CLR to make authentication and authorization decisions based on the identity and roles of a principle running the application. A *principle* is typically a Windows user account, with the groups to which the user belongs acting as the roles. Using Windows user accounts to determine access permissions for an application allows an administrator to change the permissions without also requiring an update and redistribution of the application. Principles can also be subjects in other systems, such as Active Directory or SQL Server, or a customized identity unrelated to user accounts.

Role-based security verifies that a principle has a role that allowed it to perform a requested operation, such as creating a file or loading an assembly. Role-based security is commonly used in ASP.NET applications; however, any type of .NET application may use role-based security as needed.

## *Authorization*

Authorization is the process of determining what access permission an authenticated principle has concerning a specific object. In Windows, applications are authorized to access specific objects based on the context of the user, group, or computer successfully authorized by the application. Access to objects is granted based on the authenticated user's NTFS permission. These permissions are ACL based and can use either an "allow all, except…" or a "deny all, except…" permissions scheme.

ASP.NET applications may also use NTFS permissions to access objects as if they were users logged on locally to Windows or on to the Windows domain. Authorization rules can also be specified in Web services, and access granted or denied to a specific object based on user name or role specified in a URL.

## *Accounting*

Accounting refers to the ability of an application to create an audit trail of its activities in the form of a log file or log records in a database. The .NET Framework provides access to the Windows event-logging service for reporting application information to the Windows administrator. Developers may design .NET applications to report suspicious user activity, including attempted unauthorized access, the use of privileged features, and changes in the user's security context. The .NET Framework also supports the services needed for implementing event-reporting protocols, such as syslog and SNMP.

# Network Security

The .NET Framework provides applications access to network security services available on the Windows platform. Standardized network encryption and authentication services are available for low-level TCP/IP sockets and higher-level network and Internet communications. .NET applications may create encrypted communication channels, access secure Web sites and Web services, use Public Key Infrastructure services for authenticating and decrypting data, and securely exchange information with non-Windows-based network hosts. All secure networking protocols supported by .NET are found in Windows 2000/XP/Vista and later releases of Windows.

## *Secure Network Communications Protocols*

The Hypertext Transfer Protocol Secure (HTTPS) is the use of the Hypertext Transfer Protocol (HTTP) over an encrypted network security protocol, such as SSL or TLS. The use of HTTPS is to ensure confidentiality of HTTP transactions and to prevent eavesdropping and man-in-the-middle attacks. SSL and TLS are used with certificate-based authentication systems and provide packet traffic encryption. Although commonly used by ASP.NET applications, any .NET application may utilize network protocols associated with the Internet and the World Wide Web.

SSL, TLS, and HTTPS provide a secure, point-to-point communications channel between host applications. For creating a secure, host-to-host communications channel, .NET provides interfaces to protocols such as IP Security (IPSec) and Layer 2 Tunneling Protocol (L2TP). IPSec is an open standards communications framework that supports network-level peer and origin authentication, data integrity and confidentiality, and packet replay protection. L2TP is used to create Virtual Private Network (VPN) connectivity between two hosts and IPSec is used to create a secure (authenticated and encrypted) communications channel.

### Security Support Provider Interface

The Security Support Provider Interface (SSPI) is an interface to the Windows security system enabling Windows applications to create secure communications channels. Protocols available include NTLM, Kerberos v5, digest authentication (using MD5), and SSL. A .NET application can also use SSPI for encryption and authentication for TCP channels that it creates between hosts over a network or between processes on the same machine. SSPI is the Microsoft implementation of the Generic Security Service API (GSSAPI) standard documented in RFCs 1508 and 1509.

# Cryptography

Cryptography is an essential technology for supporting the confidentiality and integrity of data, authorization and non-repudiation of subjects, and access control of objects. The .NET Framework enables applications to use many of the standardized cryptographic algorithms commonly used for secure data storage and network communications. Also supported is the ability to extend the .NET Framework with custom third-party and developer-created cryptographic features.

### Microsoft Cryptographic Application Programming Interface

Most cryptographic services are not implemented within the .NET Framework itself, but instead reside within the Windows operating system. The Microsoft *Cryptographic Application Programming Interface* (CAPI, formerly known as the Microsoft CryptoAPI) is a Windows API use for providing cryptographic services to the Windows operating system and applications. The .NET Framework provides a managed interface to CAPI services for use by .NET applications.

CAPI includes symmetric and asymmetric encryption algorithms, cryptographic key generation, message digests, digital signing, and random number generation. Also provided is support for network protocols that used cryptography, including SSL, TLS, and IPSec. Cryptographic devices, such as Smart Card interfaces used to provide single sign-on capability to a Windows workstation or application, are also supported.

### Cryptographic Service Providers

The .NET Framework provides applications access to CAPI cryptographic services through the use of *Cryptographic Service Providers* (CSP). CSPs are the implementation of the cryptographic services installed and used on Windows, and are what FIPS publications refer to as *cryptographic modules*. The .NET Framework provides an interface to CSPs and enables .NET applications to access CAPI services using managed code.

### Changes in CAPI

The features in CAPI itself are improved both in new releases of Windows and through periodic updates. The actual cryptographic services available to a .NET application will depend on the release of the .NET Framework the application uses and the release and patch level of the

Windows system the application is running on. For example, Windows Vista includes compliance with FIPS 140-1 Level 1 for cryptographic module support, but compliance with the same standard was not available in Windows XP until the release of Service Pack 3.

Windows Vista also introduced an update to CAPI know as *Cryptography API: Next Generation* (CNG). CNG provides improvements for legacy CAPI cryptographic algorithms and supports a number of new algorithms from NSA Suite B, including Elliptic curve cryptography (ECC), Elliptic Curve Digital Signature Algorithm (ECDSA), and Elliptic Curve Diffie–Hellman (ECDH). Service packs and other updates to Windows also provide bug fixes and security features to CAPI.

## Encryption and Decryption

Through CAPI, the .NET Framework supports the use of several standard algorithms capable of encrypting and decrypting data in a file stream, memory stream, or network stream. Symmetric algorithms supported include RC2, RC4, DES, Triple DES, AES, and Rijndael. Asymmetric algorithms supported include RSA, DSA, and Diffie–Hellman (key agreement). The actual algorithms available to any .NET application on any Windows system depends upon the release of the .NET Framework and the CSPs installed.

## Cryptographic Hashing

Cryptographic hashing is an integrity-checking mechanism that allows a unique, fixed-sized value (the message digest) to be generated from a corresponding collection of digital data, such as an e-mail message or image file. The .NET Framework supports the use of many standardized cryptographic hashing algorithms, including MD2, MD4, MD5, SHA-1, SHA-256, SHA-384, SHA-512, and RIPEMD-160.

Cryptographic hashing algorithms that also use a secret key in combination with the digital data input are known as Hash-based Message Authentication Codes (HMAC), or simply as *keyed hashes*. Using a secret key, HMAC algorithms can verify both the integrity and the authenticity of digital data. HMAC algorithms supported by the .NET Framework include HMAC-MD5, HMAC-SHA-1, HMAC-SHA-256, HMAC-SHA-384, HMAC-SHA-512, and HMAC-RIPEMD-160.

All cryptographic hashing algorithms supported by the .NET Framework are available to all .NET applications, and are used by many other security protocols supported by .NET, including SSL, TLS, and IPSec. The .NET Framework also supports the ability of developers to create their own cryptographic hashing and keyed hash algorithms.

## Digital Signing

Digital signing is a primary method for verifying the integrity and authenticating the sender of digital information. A digital signature is a combination of cryptographic hashing (message digest) and public key (asymmetric) cryptography. The .NET Framework supports digital signing using the Digital Signature Algorithm (DSA) as described by FIPS 186-2 Digital Signature Standard (DSS), and Elliptic Curve DSA (ECDSA) described in ANSI X9.62-2005.

## Public-Key Cryptography Standards

Public-Key Cryptography Standards (PKCS) is a collection of cryptography standards created by RSA security for promoting and expediting the implementation of systems that use public key cryptography. The .NET Framework supports several PKCS key types, including those used for creating public/private key pairs and the Digital Signature Algorithm (PKCS #1), Diffie–Hellman key exchange algorithm (PKCS #3), signing and encrypting messages for PKI (PKCS #7), cryptographic tokens for Smart Cards and single sign-on (PKCS #11), and using the Personal Information Exchange Syntax Standard (PKCS #12).

## Random Number Generation

A *Random Number Generator* (RNG) is an implementation of an algorithm used for creating sequences of random, non-repeating values. An RNG is considered strong if there is an extremely small chance that a duplicate set of values will be produced by multiple calls to the RNG. Cryptographic algorithms are used to ensure the strength (or *quality*) of random numbers produced by a RNG.

CAPI implements an RNG that provides a cryptographically secure pseudo-random number generator (CSPRNG). (The term *pseudo* is used to indicate that the sequence of values generated is not truly random, and is instead only an approximation of random values.) CSPRNG is suitable for creating cryptographic key streams and initialization vectors for stream and block ciphers, and for generating passwords, salts, nonces, and one-time pads. CSPRNG is based on the RNG specified in the FIPS 186-2 standard for Windows 2000, XP, and Vista, or on NIST SP 800-90 for Windows Vista with Service Pack 1 and Windows Server 2008.

## Data Protection API

The .NET Framework also provides managed access to other security APIs not associated with CAPI. The Data Protection API (DPAPI) is an operating system service and a legacy API, available since Windows 2000, and used to protect data such as passwords, encryption keys, and database connection strings using encryption. The main advantage of using DPAPI is that it enables Windows applications to use data encryption without the need of managing secret encryption keys.

# .NET Framework Security Issues

The .NET Framework itself is software, and, therefore, .NET and all the applications built using it are subject to the same possible vulnerabilities and exploits as any other software installed on the Windows platform. Misconfiguration, excessive security permissions, design and coding errors, and flaws in legacy Windows components can all possibly cause security-related vulnerabilities. Even certain aspects of the design of the .NET Framework itself leaves it open to possible attacks.

A search through the vulnerability advisories at Secunia.com shows past releases of .NET to have a variety of security-related problems, including boundary errors aiding the execution of arbitrary code, buffer overflows resulting in denial of service, and invalid data allowing the bypassing of security restrictions. These types of vulnerabilities do not only exist in .NET, but are also found in many unmanaged Windows components (DCOM, GDI+, WMI, etc.) called by the .NET Framework.

Vulnerabilities also result from misconfiguration of security-related features when software is written, built, installed, or run. Developers may make mistakes in designing and implementing code that results in security vulnerability that the .NET Framework cannot possible compensate for. Not understanding the need for encryption, authentication, restricted code access, or requiring an application to be run with unnecessarily elevated privileges are all security design issues.

.NET applications themselves can aide in their own attack. If .NET assemblies are distributed as unobfuscated CIL code, or with debugging information included, they will be much easier to reverse-engineer and possibly alter for malicious purposes. Application diagnostic messages can contain information that can be very useful to attackers, such as physical path names and component version numbers. Applications that are designed or configured or provide verbose diagnostics logging—perhaps written to the Windows event log or a log file—may be leaking information aiding in their own misuse.

The possibility of yet undiscovered security-related problems in the .NET Framework stresses the need to update Windows machines with the latest services packs, hotfixes, and monthly Microsoft updates as they become available. Both system administrators and application developers are responsible for testing applications for proper and secure behavior before any new system or application updates are distributed into a production environment.

## Conclusion

The .NET Framework is a vast and feature-packed platform for the creation of the smallest programs to the largest software solutions. .NET provides transparent security to make the default operation of .NET applications secure, and provides services making the deliberate implementation of security-related features quick and easy.

However, using .NET for developing applications is not a panacea for all Windows platform security issues. Although the .NET Framework assists developers in writing secure application, it can do very little to ensure that developers always follow best practices for write secure code, including the appropriate security mechanisms in the application's design, and that security is considered and implemented at every stage of the development process.

Many aspects of application security are outside of the scope of the .NET Framework, including risk mitigation, threat modeling, following best practices, and writing secure code. Design decisions, such as not to use data encryption or user authentication, are not the concern of .NET. There is also very little .NET can do about an administrator's choice to allow the use of excessive permissions, weak passwords, or revoked certificates. The .NET Framework is software platform used for helping developers create secure Windows applications, and not an iron hand of security that prevents developers from creating and running insecure applications.

## About the Author

**James D. Murray**, GSEC, CISSP-ISSMP, CISA, CISM, is the information security official for the Office of MMIS Services in the NC Department of Health and Human Services (DHHS), and information security lead within the NC Medicaid Management Information System development project.

# CRYPTOGRAPHY

*Crypto Concepts, Methodologies, and Practices*

*Chapter 19*

# Cryptography: A Unifying Principle in Compliance Programs

Ralph Spencer Poore

## Contents

## Cryptography: A Unifying Principle in Compliance Programs

Compliance programs generally require one or more of the following attributes: confidentiality, integrity, and assurance of the identities of entities involved. Cryptographic measures are uniquely qualified to implement these attributes. This chapter describes how the tools of cryptography can act as a unifying principle in compliance programs.

### Compliance Regimes

Compliance with regulatory, quasi-regulatory, and contract requirements and industry standards first requires an understanding of what applies to your enterprise. In an ideal world, your legal department would know this and advise the enterprise accordingly. In practice, however, this is almost never the case. The vastness of legal jurisdictions, specialties, and industry standards overwhelms most corporate legal departments. They, in turn, depend on compliance officers, department management, corporate management, internal audit, and specialty areas (e.g., information security, HR, and IT) to provide them with specific compliance program information that they can research.

Although the spectrum of compliance programs is vast, the chapter focuses on two areas: protection of privacy and of identity. Privacy is clearly important in many industries including health care and financial services—two heavily regulated industries with mandatory compliance regimes. The ability to identify authoritatively is essential to both commercial and governmental transactions. Identity theft is a major and escalating problem.

Table 19.1 lists examples of cryptography-related compliance requirements, i.e., sources of rules that either require cryptography explicitly or have an implicit and practical requirement for cryptography. Note that several states (e.g., California, Massachusetts, and Nevada) have laws that provide their citizens protection regardless of where the data actually resides.

Once an enterprise understands the compliance programs it must put in place, the enterprise should take a unified approach to policy, standards, procedures, and technology. This can save time and money. The old 80/20 rule applies: 80% is common to almost all compliance programs and 20% is unique. This also applies to cryptographic security measures.

## Privacy

In support of privacy requirements, encryption can limit constructive access to information. This is an essential tool in protecting information in transit. It is also a useful tool in protecting stored information on removable media (including laptop computers). Many compliance regimes have privacy as one required element. Health Insurance Portability and Accountability Act (HIPAA), for example, has an entire body of regulations on privacy. The European Union and its member countries also have extensive privacy rules.

## Integrity

Cryptography can provide message or transaction integrity. In business transactions, the integrity of the transaction is often more important than its secrecy. The use of digital signatures, message authentication codes (MAC), and similar cryptography-based error-detection mechanisms can reduce fraud by preventing undetected changes to messages. The integrity of underlying accounting transactions, for example, is an important element of Sarbanes–Oxley (SOX).

## Authentication

Authenticating the source, the destination, or the authority of a transaction is important in many compliance regimes. Cryptography can play an important role in accomplishing this. The binding of information to an identity may provide a relying party with a level of trust on which to base a business relationship. Access control depends on authentication of an identity. Password, security token, or biometric identity systems often use cryptography as an essential element.

## Cryptographic Key Management

Cryptographic security measures depend on several factors including selecting the appropriate algorithms for the intended purpose, securely implementing the cryptography, and properly managing the cryptographic key life cycle.

**Table 19.1 Cryptographic-Related Compliance Requirements**

| Law, Regulation, Standard | Requirement | Cryptography |
|---|---|---|
| Gramm–Leach–Bliley Act (15 U.S.C. §§ 6801 et seq.) | Requires administrative, technical, and physical safeguards to maintain the security, confidentiality, and integrity of the information | Implicit |
| Health Insurance Portability and Accountability Act (Pub. Law No. 104-191 §§262,264: 45 C.F.R. §§160-164) | Regulations issued on both privacy and security | Implicit in privacy rules; explicit in security rules |
| Privacy Act (5 U.S.C. §552a) | Requires the establishment of appropriate administrative, technical, and physical safeguards to ensure the security and confidentiality of records. | Implicit |
| Fair and Accurate Credit Transactions Act of 2003 (FACT Act) (Public Law 108-159) | Protection of account numbers and expiration dates on receipts | Explicit (but alternatives may be possible) |
| Sarbanes–Oxley Act of 2002 (SOX) (Public Law 107-204) | Sec. 802 addresses altering documents by amending 18 USC §1519 | Implicit |
| OMB Memorandum 06-16 *Protection of Sensitive Agency Information* (06-23-2006) | Provides a security checklist for use by federal agencies to protect personally identifiable information (PII) during transmission, storage, and remote access. The checklist contains five mandatory and four conditional action items depending on whether PII is transported, stored, or accessed remotely | Explicit |
| OMB Memorandum 07-16 *Breach of Personally Identifiable Information* (May 22, 2007) | Required agencies to develop and implement a breach notification policy and identified three "simple and cost-effective steps" to reduce PII breach risks which included using encryption. | Explicit |

*(continued)*

**Table 19.1 (continued)   Cryptographic-Related Compliance Requirements**

| Law, Regulation, Standard | Requirement | Cryptography |
|---|---|---|
| California: *Security Breach Notice*—Civil Code sections 1798.29, 1798.82, and 1798.84. [SB 1386 (2003) & AB 1950 (2004)] | SB 1386 states that any breach of the security of the data must be reported in the most expedient time possible following the discovery of the breach to any resident of California whose unencrypted personal information was, or is reasonably believed to have been, acquired by an unauthorized person. Theft of encrypted data is specifically exempted in SB 1386 and AB 1950 | Explicit |
| Massachusetts: *Standards for the Protection of Personal Information of Residents of the Commonwealth* (201 CMR 17.00) | This law requires all portable personal data about any Massachusetts resident to be encrypted. The law applies to data transmitted over public networks and to data stored on a laptop or on any type of removable memory device | Explicit |
| Nevada: *Restrictions on transfer of personal information through electronic transmission* (NRS 597.970 (January 10, 2008)) | "A business in this State shall not transfer any personal information of a customer through an electronic transmission other than a facsimile to a person outside of the secure system of the business unless the business uses encryption to ensure the security of electronic transmission." | Explicit |
| Payment Card Industry (PCI) Data Security Standards (DSS), Version 1.2 (October 2008) | Cryptography is specifically cited as a means of protecting sensitive information | Explicit (but alternatives may be possible) |
| PIN Security Compliance ("TG-3") | Required by interchange networks, e.g., NYCE® Payments Network, PULSE® Network, and STAR® Debit & ATM Network. This is all about encryption | Explicit |

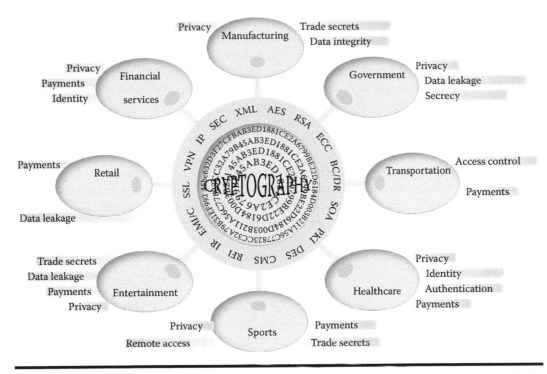

**Figure 19.1  Business uses of cryptography depicts the many forms and uses of cryptography in various industries. (Courtesy of Cryptographic Assurance Services LLC, Arlington, TX, 2009.)**

As shown in Figure 19.1, organizations use cryptography often without intention. That is, off-the-shelf products on which organizations rely use cryptography, and the defaults are rarely what management would choose if developing a cryptographic security policy. Having a documented policy on the application of cryptography to an organization's compliance program is one step in unifying the otherwise disparate elements of compliance regimes.

## Unifying Cryptographic Compliance

The process for developing a unified cryptographic compliance program begins with collecting and creating documentation. Here are recommended steps:

1. Document an inventory of crypto-using products in your organization. Include information on the cryptographic functions supported, the business purpose for the product, and the following technical data:
   a. Cryptographic algorithm or algorithms supported by the product
   b. Key lengths used/supported by the product
   c. Cryptographic testing criteria (if any) met by the product (e.g., FIPS 140, ISO/IEC 15408, and X9.24)
2. Produce a network diagram that includes all paths that support some cryptographic security measure. Indicate protocol, form of cryptography used (e.g., symmetric key or asymmetric ("public") key), and algorithm used (e.g., two-key triple-DES, AES, or RC4). Give the keys names that you can reference in your documentation.* This diagram is especially important

for compliance regimes that allow network segmentation as a scope-narrowing principle (e.g., PCI DSS). Some compliance regimes require a network diagram as part of their compliance reporting (e.g., PIN Security Compliance—commonly referred to as a TG-3 Assessment).

3. Identify cryptography that is done in cryptographic hardware (e.g., host security module [HSM], tamper-resistant security module [TRSM], or physically secure device [PSD]). For some compliance regimes such devices are required.
4. Identify cryptography that is done in software. Determine how the cryptographic keys are generated, stored, and managed. This step will often identify weaknesses that may require remediation.
5. Collect copies of all documented procedures associated with cryptography in your organization. This may include vendor manuals, local processes, computerized scripts, logs, and control forms.
6. Determine which business processes fall under which compliance regimes. For those that require (or benefit from) cryptography determine if the cryptography in place addresses the requirement.
7. Ensure that compliance documentation reflects the applicable contribution made by cryptography.

Operational processes associated with the cryptographic key life cycle are also unifying principles. In accordance with ISO standards (ISO 11568-1 and ISO 11568-4) a cryptographic key life cycle consists of the stages shown in Figure 19.2. Those stages are briefly described here.

*Generation*: Key generation involves the creation of a new key for subsequent use.
*Storage*: Key storage involves the holding of a key in one of the permissible forms.
*Backup*: Key backup occurs when a protected copy of a key is kept in storage during its operational use for potential recovery.
*Distribution and loading*: Key distribution and loading is the process by which a key is manually or electronically transferred into a secure cryptographic device.

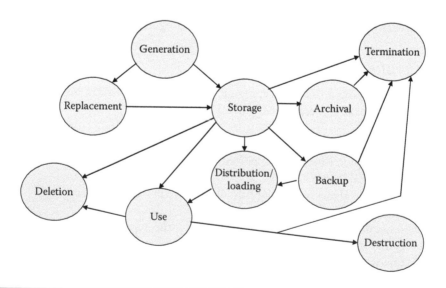

**Figure 19.2 Cryptographic key management life cycle. (Courtesy of Cryptographic Assurance Services LLC, Arlington, TX, 2009.)**

*Use*: Key use occurs when a key is employed for the cryptographic purpose for which it was intended.

*Replacement*: Key replacement occurs when one key is substituted for another when the original key is known or suspected to be compromised or the end of its operational life is reached.

*Destruction*: Key destruction ensures that an instance of a key in one of the permissible key forms no longer exists at a specific location. Information may still exist at the location from which the key may be feasibly reconstructed for subsequent use.

*Deletion*: Key deletion is the process by which an unwanted key, and information from which the key may be reconstructed, is destroyed at its operational storage/use location. A key may be deleted from one location and continue to exist at another, e.g., for archival purposes.

*Archive*: Key archive is the process by which a key that is no longer in operational use at any location is stored. Archival of keys is usually for evidential purposes, i.e., when the business has reason to believe that a future legal action may require the ability to reconstruct an historic transaction or prove its authenticity. Archived keys should have clear retention periods.

*Termination*: Key termination occurs when a key is no longer required for any purpose, and all copies of the key and information required to regenerate or reconstruct the key have been deleted (irrecoverably) from all locations wherever they existed.

By having a uniform set of policies and procedures for cryptographic key management, the organization saves time and money in development, training, and compliance assessment, and often through standardization that permits fewer products and associated maintenance.

## Summary

Cryptography is pervasive. The use of cryptographic security measures underlies many compliance regimes. Intentional, documented use of cryptography can provide the foundation for unification of compliance programs. Unified compliance programs save time and money, reduce complexity and increase reliability.

## About the Author

**Ralph Spencer Poore**, CFE, CISA, CISSP, CHS-III, CTGA, QSA, is the chief cryptologist for Cryptographic Assurance Services LLC, Arlington, Texas.

## Further Resources

ANSI & ISO Standards, webstore.ansi.org
Compliance White Papers, it.toolbox.com/vendors/white-papers/view-results/?term=compliance
Cryptographic White Papers, www.cryptographicassuranceservices.com; www.cryptography.com/resources/whitepapers/index.html
NIST Cryptographic Materials, csrc.nist.gov
Privacy White Papers, epic.org/

# SECURITY ARCHITECTURE AND DESIGN

## *Principles of Computer and Network Organizations, Architectures, and Designs*

# Chapter 20

# Best Practices in Virtualization Security

Shanit Gupta

## Contents

*If you want to be on the cutting edge then be ready to bleed.* Virtualization in many ways is on the cutting edge of technology. More importantly, it continues to transform our IT infrastructure that was not possible using the physical environment. While the technology of virtualization is widely respected, the ability to secure a virtualization infrastructure is passionately debated.

I am of the opinion that virtualization by itself does not make the system more or less secure. The risks that we see on a physical environment manifest themselves a little differently in a virtualized environment. However, it is important to note that virtualization introduces new layers. Each layer increases the attack surface that can result in attack and compromise. The enterprise-wide adoption of the technology is fairly recent, which increases the fear of the unknown. In this chapter, we go through some of the tactical and strategic steps that can be taken to better secure the virtualization infrastructure.

## Main Components

- VirtualCenter
- Virtual machine
- ESX Host
- Data storage
- Policy and compliance thoughts
- Virtualization security products
- Strategic thoughts

### ESX Host

The core of the ESX Host is the virtualization layer. This is a lightweight kernel that is capable of virtualizing the hardware and running multiple operating systems simultaneously on the same physical system. This virtualization layer is popularly known as the hypervisor. The hypervisor along with the other support modules make up the ESX Host. It is easy to see why the hypervisor or in fact the ESX Host would be a valuable target. Once the Host is compromised, all virtual machines running on the Host can be compromised.

While it seems that the ESX Host would be a most likely target of attack and penetration, there are multiple design decisions that help bolster the security of the hypervisor. The most important consideration is to maintain the guest isolation. VMware embedded several design and implementation controls to ensure that one guest cannot compromise another guest of the Host in ways that would otherwise be not possible in a physical environment. Additionally, a small footprint and the highly optimized kernel that is designed specifically for virtualization limits the attack surface of the ESX Host. However, besides the hypervisor, we have several other components in the ESX Host that have a network interface attached to them and if compromised can jeopardize the integrity and confidentiality of all virtual machines on the ESX Host.

ESX Host's service console is developed from the base image of Red Hat Enterprise Linux 3 Server, Update 6. While the service console feels like a Linux system, it is heavily customized and lightweight. It, therefore, should not be treated like a regular Linux console. Many Red-Hat Package Manager (RPM) packages that would otherwise be available on a Linux system will not be available on the ESX service console. Even if they are available on ESX Host the administrator cannot assume them to function like regular RPM packages because they may be customized to meet the hypervisor requirements. Considering the factors mentioned above, the administrator should pay special attention while deploying any tools that have not specifically been developed for ESX Host.

## Patches

Do not apply patches released by Red Hat on ESX Host. While this may seem like a contradiction to security best practices, Red Hat patches may not be compatible with your ESX Host and should, therefore, not be applied on the same. An administrator should subscribe to security notifications issues by VMware. These notifications can be signed up at http://www.vmware.com/security under "Sign-up for Security Notifications."

## Server Management

The `redhat-config-*` commands that are used to manage a Red Hat system will not be available on the ESX Host. Similarly, there is no graphical interface like the X server present. Most configuration and server management will need to be performed using vmfstools and `esxcfg-*` commands present on the ESX Host. If the user prefers a user interface, consider the use of VI Client or the VirtualCenter for configuring the ESX Host. While many configurations can be performed using these tools, the administrator will need to use the service console for some advanced configurations and hardening.

## Security Tools

Many vulnerability scanners and security analyzers are not designed to work with the ESX Host and the hypervisor. In most cases, these analyzers will detect the ESX Host to be a Linux server and identify vulnerabilities that are not applicable for ESX Host. They may also offer steps and procedures to remediate the vulnerability. It is not recommended to follow these steps as they may not apply for ESX. Unless the scanners are designed for ESX Host, it is not recommended to use them to analyze the ESX Host.

If the administrator follows the security best practices detailed in the hardening guide and/or in sections below, it will not be necessary to deploy host-based security tools like antivirus, IDS, or IPS. Unless they are designed specifically to work with the ESX Host, it is recommended they are not deployed on the ESX system.

# Hardening Steps for ESX Host

This section details some of the configuration best practices that we can follow to better protect the ESX Host and thereby the virtual machines running on it. We will assume the use of VirtualCenter for managing the ESX Host. Most configurations mentioned below can be performed using VirtualCenter. Some may need the administrator to have Console access or SSH access to the ESX Host.

## *Controlled Root Access*

Limiting *root* user access is the first and most important step toward securing ESX Host. The *root* user controls the ESX Host, which in turn controls every other VM. It is, therefore, easy to understand the significance of this account.

By default, remote access to root account using SSH is disabled. If for any reason remote access for root is enabled, disable the root login by modifying the /etc/ssh/sshd _ config file and change the line from PermitRootLogin yes to PermitRootLogin no.

*Note*: Before performing this step, ensure that you integrated the ESX Host with active directory or have created a lower privilege user account on the system that can remote login the system. If remote access for *root* is disabled and no other accounts are configured, then you will not be able to remote access the server.

We also need to configure the sudo and/or su privileges for the regular user to be able to perform some privileged operations. The use of sudo provides better accountability of user actions as all sudo operations are logged. In contrast, if su is used, then only the fact that the user elevated the privileges will be logged.

## *Strong Password Policy*

The basic principle of strong password policy is important even with ESX. The two biggest factors of a strong password policy are

1. Password aging
2. Password complexity and lockout

## *Password Aging*

The steps to change the default password aging restrictions on ESX are
  Step 1: Log on to the service console and gain privileged access (root or equivalent) on the Host
  Step 2: Make the change using the following commands

- To change the maximum number of days a user can keep a password:
  - esxcfg-auth --passmaxdays = <number _ of _ days>
  - where <number _ of _ days> is the maximum number of days before password expiration.
- To change the minimum number of days between password changes:
  - esxcfg-auth --passmindays = <number _ of _ days>
  - where <number _ of _ days> is the minimum number of days between password changes.

- To change the warning time before a password change:
  - esxcfg-auth --passwarnage = <number _ of _ days>
  - where <number _ of _ days> is the number of days of advanced warning a user receives before a password change is due.

## Password Complexity and Lock Out

The ESX server uses the pam _ cracklib.so plug-in to set the rules that users must observe when creating passwords and to check password strength during the creation process. The default rules provided by pam _ cracklib.so plug-in may not be enough for some high-risk environments. In such cases, the administrator can configure the environment and set custom rules.

To change the password complexity requirement, the privileged user can enter

esxcfg-auth --usecrack=<retries> <minimum _ length> <lc _ credit> <uc _ credit> <d _ credit> <oc _ credit>

where

<retries> is the number of retries the user is allowed before ESX Server locks them out of password change mode.

minimum _ length is the minimum number of characters a user must enter to make the password acceptable. This number is the total length before any length credits are applied.

One length credit is always applied so, in effect, the password length is one character less than the minimum _ length parameter you specify. Because the pam _ cracklib.so plug-in does not accept passwords of fewer than six characters, calculate the minimum _ length parameter so that users cannot drop the password length below six as a result of subtracting the length credits.

lc _ credit is the number by which the minimum _ length parameter is reduced if the user includes at least one lowercase character in the password.

uc _ credit is the number by which the minimum _ length parameter is reduced if the user includes at least one uppercase character.

d _ credit is the number by which the minimum _ length parameter is reduced if the user includes at least one digit.

oc _ credit is the number by which the minimum _ length parameter is reduced if the user includes at least one special character, such as an underscore or dash.

For further protection, you can enforce account lockout after too many unsuccessful login attempts. To configure the ESX service console to disable the account after three unsuccessful login attempts, add the following lines to /etc/pam.d/system-auth:

```
auth required /lib/security/pam _ tally.so no _ magic _ root
account required /lib/security/pam _ tally.so deny=3
no _ magic _ root
```

To create the file for logging failed login attempts, execute the following commands:

```
touch /var/log/faillog
chown root:root /var/log/faillog
chmod 600 /var/log/faillog
```

If the pam _ cracklib.so plug-in does not provide sufficient password strength enforcer for your environment, then you can consider the use of pam _ passwdqc.so plug-in. All available options for the plug-in can be viewed by *man* pam_passwdqc.

## Authorization Controls for Privileged Operations

### Substitute User Privileges

The ability to become the super user is a powerful feature and should, therefore, be closely guarded. Once a user elevates his privileges to super user privileges, then the commands executed by the user may not be logged and, therefore, go unidentified. Only the members of the wheel group should be allowed to become *root* after having successfully authenticated to the system. This can be achieved by editing the /etc/pam.d/su file. Uncomment the line that reads

```
auth required /lib/security/$ISA/pam_wheel.so use_uid
```

This configuration setting will only allow members of wheel group to change their effective user identifier to root. Only allow very limited users to be part of the wheel group.

### Perform Actions as Super User

The use of sudo is a safer way to grant administrators access to privileges commands without having to give them root access or even making them part of the trusted group. The permissions for users of different groups and the commands they can execute can be controlled by editing the /etc/sudoers file. The list of commands and groups depend on the environment and the user groups created. Security best practices to consider while configuring the sudo users are

- Create a special group and only allow members of that group to use sudo.
- Do NOT permit users to execute su using sudo.
- Use aliases to configure user roles and apply necessary authorization control. It is easier to add users to aliases than to add and remove them from every sudo command specification.
- Use the global authentication scheme that is configured using the esxcfg-auth command. This is set by using service=system-auth as the authentication means in /etc/pam.d/ sudo file.
- Require user to enter their password while performing sudo operations.
- Enable extended logging for all sudo operations performed by the user.

## Active Directory Integration

Many organizations tend to use the Active Directory for central user management and administration. ESX Host includes services that can integrate with the existing directory services.

There are several advantages of integrating ESX Host with the directory services. Most significant of them include the following:

1. Large enterprises tend to have an established environment with many users and creating trust with an existing authentication authority is easier than recreating all required users in ESX Host.
2. Reducing the number of authentication systems reduces the number of user names and passwords each user must remember. Users are more likely to follow recommended practices for creating strong passwords when they have fewer passwords to remember. Reusing any password, even a strong one, for multiple accounts effectively weakens the security of an authentication system. This can be avoided by using a centralized user management system.

The esxcfg-auth tool makes authentication with Active Directory possible by configuring a plug-gable authentication module (PAM) and modifying the ESX Server system's configuration.

To accomplish directory services integration, execute the following commands:

Step 1:

```
# esxcfg-auth --enablead --addomain=DOMAINAME.com --addc=DC1.
DOMAINAME.com
```

This configures the global authentication scheme to use active directory–based authentication for the domain DOMAINAME.com with the domain controller DC1.DOMAINAME.com.

Step 2:

```
# useradd UserName1
```

This will create a user with user name UserName1 with permission to use the service console.

## Disable Unnecessary Services on the Host

Services increase the footprint of any software especially the services with network access. Every open port in the system increases the attack surface thereby increasing the potential for misconfiguration and compromise. By default, ESX Host limits the number of services and does not start any clear text-based communication channels. The default firewall setting only allows a list of known services to use the associated incoming and outgoing ports.

The list of services started by default on the ESX server are listed in the screen shot below.

All other incoming and outgoing ports are explicitly blocked by the firewall on the ESX system. If any ports need to be opened on the ESX system, they can be opened using the command esxcfg-firewall –o <port,tcp|udp,in|out,name>

The table below lists the services and the ports that can be blocked provided the condition specified is fulfilled.

| Service Name | Identification in esxcfg-firewall Command | Port Number | Traffic Type | Disable Condition |
|---|---|---|---|---|
| CIM service location protocol | CIMSLP | 427 | Incoming and outgoing UDP and TCP | If not using CIM-based software for monitoring or management |
| NFS client | nfsClient | 111, 2049 | Outgoing TCP and UDP | If not mounting NFS-based storage in the service console |
| VMware consolidate backup | VCB | 443, 902 | Outgoing TCP | If not using VCB for backup |
| CIM over HTTP | CIMHTttpServer | 5988 | Incoming TCP | If not using CIM-based software for monitoring or management |
| CIM over HTTPS | CIMHttpServer | 5989 | Incoming TCP | If not using CIM-based software for monitoring or management |
| Licensing | LicenseClient | 2700, 27010 | Outgoing TCP | If using only host-based licensing |
| SSH server | sshServer | 22 | Incoming TCP | If all management is done via VirtualCenter, VI Client, or through third party agents |
| VirtualCenter agent | vpxHeartBeats | 902 | Outgoing UDP | If not managed by VirtualCenter |

## Secure SNMP Configuration

SNMP agent on ESX Host can allow remote management tools to monitor status information on many critical operations. Further, it is possible to obtain configuration information about the virtual machines and the state of hardware components like CPU, Network, Disk, and other failures. While ESX supports SNMP version 1, 2c, and 3, it is recommended to only use SNMP version 3, which provides authentication and privacy of messages between the agent and the management console. In the least, administrators should consider configuring a non-default community string and restricting the hosts that are allowed to query.

The link http://net-snmp.sourceforge.net/tutorial/tutorial-5/demon/snmpd.html provides detailed steps to configure SNMP using the snmpconf script. The administrator can choose community names, specify the restricted host list, and also configure SNMP v3 using the script. The script is available on ESX 3.5.

## Configure Proper Logging

System logs are a key resource in identifying technical and security issues. They help reconstruct a chronological order of the actions performed on the system. Monitoring tools rely on logs collected on the system to identify any unusual or unsafe activity. It is, therefore, vital that the logging on ESX be set according to recommended best practices.

### Log File Size

Log files should be restricted in size but at the same time configured to collect an adequate amount of information. If the log files are not restricted in size, then they may keep growing and eventually exhaust all available disk space thereby missing important log information and causing a denial-of-service attack. If the log file size is too small, then important logs may get overwritten.

The key is, therefore, to choose a log file size that will not exhaust disk space and cannot be filled up easily thereby resulting in loss of information.

The settings for log files vmkernel, vmksummary, and vmkwarning can be configured in the directory /etc/logrotate.d/. It is recommended that the vmk* file size be raised from 200 k to 4096 k. Further enable compression on the log files. The duration to keep the logs may be governed by the corporate policy.

Similar setting can be made for /etc/logrotate.conf master log configuration file. It also dictates the defaults for log file rotation, log file compression, and the duration for which older log files should be stored and maintained.

### Remote Logging

The syslog daemon performs logging on the ESX system. By default, the log files are stored under /var/log directory. Syslog can be configured to send the logs to a remote logging server. The use of a dedicated logging server is recommended in a production environment. This reduces the likelihood of log compromise in the event that the ESX server is compromised or corrupted. Central management of the logs also makes it easier for a monitoring tool to gain a holistic view of the activities and identify malicious activities on the system and network.

Syslog behavior is controlled by the configuration file /etc/syslog.conf. The logs can be sent to a remote log server by adding the name of the host where the log files should be sent, for example, to send the storage monitor-related messages to the server logserver.companyname.com add @<logserver.companyname.com> at the end of the line local4.*. This will look like local4.* @<logserver.companyname.com>

Similarly, the other entries in the syslog can be configured to send logs to the log server. An important point to keep in mind is that the log files are transmitted in clear to the log server and so the log server and the ESX server should be hosted on an isolated and restricted network to prevent the compromise of log information.

After the `syslog.conf` file configuration is complete, the syslog daemon needs to be sent the HUP signal to reread the config file. The command to do the same is

```
#kill -SIGHUP '/bin/cat /var/run/syslogd.pid'
```

## Time Synchronization

To ensure that all events are recorded in the right order, it is important to keep time synchronization between all devices. It is, therefore, best to use the same relative time source, and the source should be configured to an agreed upon time standard such as UTC. This configuration makes it easier to correlate the user actions between different log files. The time synchronization can be configured using an NTP system by following the instructions listed below:

1. Logon to the console and gain super user privileges
2. Make a copy of /etc/ntp.conf for backup
3. Add the following lines to the /etc/ntp.conf file to select NTP servers from a pool
   restrict 127.0.0.1
   restrict default kod nomodify notrap
   server 0.pool.ntp.org
   server 1.pool.ntp.org
   server 2.pool.ntp.org
4. Edit file /etc/ntp/step-tickers and add the following lines
   server 0.pool.ntp.org
   server 1.pool.ntp.org
   server 2.pool.ntp.org
5. Enable NTP access through the firewall
   esxcfg-firewall –enableService ntpClient
6. Restart the NTP service
   service ntpd restart
7. Configure the service to auto start
   chkconfig –level 345 ntpd on
8. Synchronize hardware clock to NTP synchronized local clock
   hwclock –systohc

Refer the VMware knowledge-based article for more details on NTP configuration. http://kb.vmware.com/selfservice/microsites/search.do?language=en_US&cmd=displayKC&externalId=1339.

An automated script to set up the NTP can be obtained at http://www.vmcolonel.net/?p=13

## Maintain File System Integrity

There are several important configurations and binary files on the ESX Host that are not intended to be changed very often. It may, therefore, be useful to have a file integrity verifier to ensure that the files were not edited out of the change control cycle. The file checksum can be calculated at the end of configuration changes. The results can be stored securely offline. Periodically, the checksum can be verified to ensure that the files have not been tampered with because of unauthorized access or changes. Many different factors can be considered to calculate the checksum including the file contents, size, location, and file permissions. Commercial products available for ESX can help implement this security measure.

Some key files and folders to consider for integrity checks are

- /etc/fstab
- /etc/group
- /etc/grub.conf
- /etc/host.conf
- /etc/hosts
- /etc/hosts.allow
- /etc/hosts.deny
- /etc/krb.conf
- /etc/krb5.conf
- /etc/krb.realms
- /etc/logrotate.conf
- /etc/logrotate.d/
- /etc/login.defs
- /etc/modules.conf
- /etc/motd
- /etc/nscd.conf
- /etc/ntp
- /etc/nsswitch.conf
- /etc/ntp.conf
- /etc/openldap/ldap.conf
- /etc/pam.d/system-auth
- /etc/passwd
- /etc/profile
- /etc/resolv.conf
- /etc/securetty
- /etc/ssh/sshd _ config
- /etc/snmp
- /etc/sudoers
- /etc/shadow
- /etc/vmware—Multiple configuration and kernel files

Besides monitoring these files for integrity, it is also advisable to periodically backup these files. In the event that a compromise is detected, it will be easier to restore the system if system backup is available.

## Disable Auto Mount on for USB Devices

ESX Host automatically mounts the USB devices that may be connected to the server. The drivers are preloaded to detect and mount a USB device attached to ESX Host. This may allow a user with physical access to the ESX Host to connect a USB device and execute malicious code on the server. It is advisable to disable auto mount on USB devices. A privileged user will still be able to manually mount the USB device if it is connected to the server. This will prevent an attacker from attaching devices with malicious code.

To disable to the auto mount on USB devices, edit the `/etc/modules.conf` file and place a # symbol before the line usb-controller.

# Configuring ESX Host

## *Network Isolation*

Systems attached to a network are at considerable higher risk of attack and compromise. The risk is increased if the systems are accessible to untrusted and potentially malicious users. The attacks do not always originate from external users. In many instances, internal users or even privileged administrators in the organization may pose a risk. It is, therefore, best to reduce the attack surface of the virtualized infrastructure.

Network isolation is perhaps one of the most important and effective ways to increase the security of virtualization infrastructure. While it seems like a straightforward and intuitive solution, it is one of the most common misconfigurations in the virtualized world. Much of it can be attributed to insufficient planning and incorrect design of the virtual networks. In the next section, we look at some of the security best practices and procedures to isolate the virtual networks.

During the configuration of ESX, an administrator has the option of creating a default virtual machine port. If this option is chosen, a *virtual machine port* group is created on the same network interface as the service console. It is easy to see how this can allow a malicious virtual machine to sniff sensitive and often unencrypted (logs, VMotion) information belonging to the service console. It can also allow a virtual machine to launch man-in-the-middle attacks against the console and disrupt network operations. Considering these threats, it is recommended to isolate the network operations for the virtual infrastructure.

To begin with, we will start identifying the different networks segments. Broadly, we can divide the networks into two segments.

## *Management*

This network will be used to troubleshoot and configure the virtual infrastructure. The systems that need to be on the management segment are

1. ESX Hosts
2. VirtualCenter
3. Client tools like VI Client, custom, or third-party tools using VI SDK
4. Syslog server
5. Database server
6. Backup servers
7. Host monitoring systems
8. Any third-party management systems
9. Storage systems

## *Operational Networks*

The operational network is used by the virtual machines running on the ESX Host(s) to perform their business goals. The systems on the operational networks will be

1. Virtual machines
2. Security devices (IDS/IPS/DLP, etc.)
3. Other systems (physical or virtual)

It is important to note that not all management systems will need to be on the same network segment. Similarly, the trust relationship within systems on the operational network will also have multiple levels and different categories. They will, therefore, need to be grouped and configured in more granular segments based on the organization network.

The more important need is to isolate systems based on their roles and the trust relationship with other systems on the network. For instance, the traffic communicated between the ESX Host and the Syslog server is unencrypted and unauthenticated, which may allow a malicious system on the same network to compromise the integrity of the logs. Similarly, the virtual machine state that is transmitted from one ESX Host to the other during a VMotion process is unencrypted, which may allow man-in-the-middle attacks. These systems, therefore, cannot be hosted on a network that is accessible by other untrusted and potentially malicious systems.

All systems that are not exclusively operated by the privileged administrators can be considered untrusted and should not share the network with managed hosts.

Network isolation can be achieved using one of the two different ways:

1. VLAN (virtual local network) tagging for different isolated networks
2. Physical segregation of networks using different virtual switches and physical uplinks

It may be useful to note that not all experts trust the VLAN tagging to be secure and effective. While VLAN tagging by itself does not offer security, it is a good first step to isolate the networks. With correct network configuration, it is possible to isolate systems on different trust levels on different VLANs.

The other option of physical isolation provides a much more conceptually straightforward way to isolate networks. However, this comes at a much higher price of additional routers. Further, it requires multiple physical network interfaces as there is a one-to-one mapping between VLAN port and physical port.

## ESX Virtual Switch Tagging (VST Mode)

In virtual switch tagging, multiple port groups are created on each virtual switch. Each port group created in a virtual switch can be assigned a unique VLAN ID. All systems connected to a particular port group with uniquely assigned VLAN IDs are isolated from systems on other port groups on the same or different virtual switch. If two port groups in the same virtual switch are assigned the same VLAN ID, then the traffic between the 2 port groups is shared.

Virtual network adapters associated with virtual machines may then be configured to connect to these user-defined port groups. The virtual adapters connected using a user-defined port group inherit and abide by the policies defined within the port group.

A VLAN ID between the ranges of 1–4095 can be specified. It is recommended to not use VLAN IDs of 1, 1001–1024, and 4095. These VLAN IDs are reserved for default VLAN, Cisco VLANS, and virtual guest tagging mode. The use of VLAN ID 1 can cause a denial of service as ESX drops traffic with this VLAN ID. VLAN ID 4095 causes the port group to use trunk mode. This is useful in the event that the operating systems are installed with VLAN drivers to manage their own VLAN tags. While this is rare, there are some conceivable reasons for doing so. Most organizations do not use this feature and, therefore, the VLAN ID 4095 should not be used.

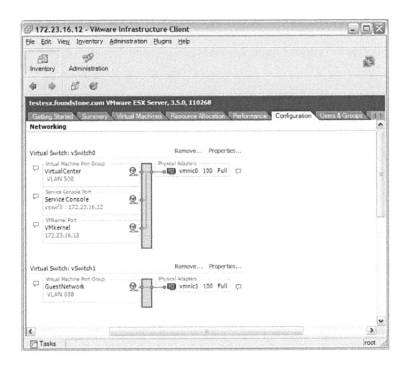

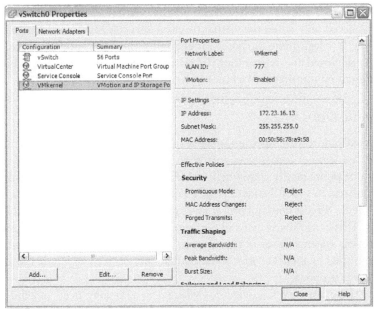

It is important to clearly label all port groups to avoid any misunderstanding and misconfiguration of systems. This will decrease the likelihood of virtual machines being attached to unauthorized networks. It is also important to note that if VMotion is currently in use between different Hosts, then the Hosts should have the same port group label. If the port group labels do not match, VMotion will fail.

## Layer 2 Security Settings

ESX provides 3 options to enforce Layer 2 (OSI Stack) security measures on the virtual machines. They are

1. MAC address changes
2. Forged transmissions
3. Promiscuous mode

### MAC Address Changes

When a virtual machine is instantiated, it can have one or more network interfaces. Each network interface is assigned a MAC address at the time of creation. These MAC addresses can be assigned statically or dynamically by the administrator.

The operating system and the administrator typically have the ability to change the MAC address for any network interface on any operating system. When a new MAC is assigned, network packets are stamped with the MAC address that is assigned to that network interface. This can allow a malicious virtual machine to masquerade as another system on the network and receive their network traffic.

By default, the ESX Host does not prevent a virtual machine to change its MAC address. ESX Host provides an option to reject these MAC address changes. If this option is set to "Reject," ESX will not allow the operating system to change the initial MAC address. If the virtual machine tries to change the MAC address, ESX will disable that virtual port on the virtual machine. The port will be re-enabled only when the virtual machine sets the MAC to the initial value.

There are very few legitimate purposes for changing the MAC address once the system has been successfully deployed and is operational. It is, therefore, recommended to change the setting to "Reject" to not allow the virtual machine to change its MAC Address.

### Forged Transmissions

It is similar to MAC address changes in the sense that the virtual machine will send packets using a MAC address that was not initially assigned to it. As opposed to MAC address changes, the virtual machine is not permanently changing its MAC. It is only sending out network packets with a forged MAC address to spoof the identity of a victim.

By default, the ESX Host does not prevent a virtual machine from sending packets with forged MAC addresses. This can allow systems to perform ARP spoofing and enable man-in-the-middle attacks against other systems. If the option is set to "Reject," the ESX network stack compares the MAC address stamped on a packet with a virtual machine's actual MAC. If the addresses do not match, the packet is dropped.

Once again, there are very few scenarios where a system may need to send packets with a forged MAC address. They should be treated as exceptions and by default all virtual switches (including the port groups) should be configured to reject forged transmissions.

### Promiscuous Mode

Many network cards can be placed in the promiscuous mode. In a regular mode, the network card only accepts the packets destined to it and ignores all other packets. However, if the card is placed in a promiscuous mode, the network card accepts all network packets passing through the system.

This will allow the system to sniff traffic belonging to other systems. Some of this traffic may be sensitive and unencrypted. This will, therefore, allow the "sniffer" to gain access to sensitive information that he should otherwise not have access to.

By default, ESX Host is configured to reject a virtual adapter's request to operate in promiscuous mode. This will prevent a virtual machine's network adapter from gaining access to traffic that is not destined to it. While this setting can be changed, it is recommended to not change this setting.

There are some legitimate uses for enabling promiscuous mode for monitoring systems, for example, the IDS system, tracking and troubleshooting system, or for debugging purposes. However, they are more of an exception. These systems could be placed in a separate port group and the promiscuous mode can be enabled only for that port group while it is set to reject for all other switches and groups.

## Boot Time Passwords

### GRUB Password

Physical access to systems by an attacker can be damaging. Most organizations, therefore, take adequate measures to physically secure systems from intruders. However, not all attack scenarios can be prevented, especially when the data center access is shared with many other administrators or if a hosting service is in use. An attacker with physical access to the system can boot the system into single user mode and gain root access. It is, therefore, advisable to use a GRUB password to prevent an unauthorized user from booting into single user mode. The user will be prompted for this password if they try to boot the system into a single user mode. To set a GRUB password, follow the steps below:

- Type grub at the command line. Ensure that you have root privileges.
  #grub
- Type md5crypt to generate an MD5 hash of the password. This prevents clear text access to the password. When prompted for the Password, enter the password you want to use.
  grub> md5crypt
  Password: **********
  Encrypted: $1$Pdmiq$W7rfsJjSEfzuOzKzbsPx21
- Encrypted: provides the MD5 hash of the password entered.
- Add the line password -md5 <Hashed Password> to the file /boot/grub/grub.conf. Make sure that you copy the hash provided by md5crypt correctly.

Now if any user tries to edit the GRUB options, the user will be prompted for a password.

### BIOS Password

Another way to compromise a system with physical access is to boot the system using a removable device. An attacker can reboot the ESX system, change the BIOS settings, and make the first boot device the removable media. He can then attach the removable media which has a Linux distribution with Rescue mode. Once the attacker boots in Rescue mode, he can mount the ESX file system and change the root user's password. This will allow him to gain complete control of the ESX Host. It is, therefore, important to set up a BIOS password that makes it difficult for an attacker to change the boot priority and gain super user access on the ESX Host.

It is common knowledge that BIOS passwords can be circumvented by an attacker with physical access. They act more as a deterrent that make it harder for an attacker to gain access to the system. To prevent against a dedicated attacker with physical access, full disk encryption may offer the best protection.

## Require Certificate Validation

All components in a virtualization infrastructure rely heavily on SSL to ensure the confidentiality and integrity of information. All communication from the client tools (VI Client, VI API, VirtualCenter, Web Access) rely on the administrators to deploy certificates signed by a trusted third party. Without trusted certificates, all communication is vulnerable to man-in-the-middle attacks. Further, it is very hard for users to differentiate between a self-signed certificate used by a component from a certificate warning issued because of a man-the-middle attack launched by an attacker.

During the installation of the virtualization components, self-signed certificates are deployed to get the system up and running. Extended use of self-signed certificates can raise the risk of attack and compromise through a man-in-the-middle attack. It is, therefore, recommended to deploy certificates that are signed by a trusted third party. Once certificates signed by trusted third party are deployed, the system should be configured to reject any self-signed or invalid certificates.

### Replace Certificate on ESX

To replace the certificate on the ESX host, follow the steps mentioned below:

1. Log in the ESX as root
2. Change directory to `/etc/vmware/ssl/`
3. Backup the files `rui.crt` to `rui.crt.bak` and `rui.key` to `rui.key.bak` (`rui.key` is the private key and `rui.crt` is the certificate)
4. Upload the new certificate and the private key and place them in `/etc/vmware/ssl/` with the name `rui.crt` and `rui.key`, respectively
5. Ensure that the owner of the both the files is user and group root
6. Ensure that the permission on the certificate file remain 644 (read/write for root, read for group, read for others)
7. Ensure that the permission on the private key file remain 400 (read for root, no permissions for anyone else)
8. Restart the web server by executing `/etc/init.d/mgmt-vmware restart`

### Replace Certificate on VirtualCenter

To replace the certificate on the VirtualCenter

1. Log on the system that has VirtualCenter. You should have administrative privilege on the system
2. Go to C:\Documents and Settings\All Users\Application Data\VMware\VMware\VirtualCenter\SSL\
3. Backup the files `rui.crt` to `rui.crt.bak` and `rui.key` to `rui.key.bak` (`rui.key` is the private key and `rui.crt` is the certificate)
4. Besides the certificate and the private key, you will also need a PFX (Personal Information Exchange) format file for the Windows system

5. Create the PFX file using openssl

   *openssl pkcs12 -export -in rui.crt -inkey rui.key -name FQDNforVirtualCenter -out rui.pfx*
6. Upload the new certificate, private key and the PFX file in C:\Documents and Settings\All Users\Application Data\VMware\VMware\VirtualCenter\SSL\
7. Restart the VirtualCenter management service to load the new certificates

## Enable Certificate Checking on the VirtualCenter

To enable certificate checking

1. Log in to a VirtualCenter server using the VI Client.
2. Click Administration > VirtualCenter Management Server Configuration.
3. Click SSL Settings in the left pane and enable the Check host certificates checkbox.
4. Click OK.

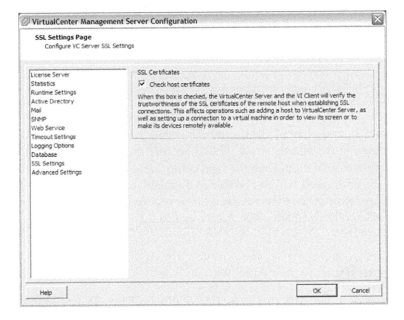

## Re-Encrypt the Database Password

Once the default certificates are replaced with custom certificates signed by a trusted third party, the VirtualCenter will not start the next time. This is because the password used to connect to the database is encrypted using the old certificates. For this purpose, it is important to re-encrypt the password using the new certificate.

To do this, follow the steps mentioned below:

1. Stop the VirtualCenter service
2. Open command prompt and change directory to C:\Program Files\VMware\Infrastructure\ VirtualCenter Server\
3. Run vpxd.exe -p
4. Enter the database password when prompted
5. Start the VirtualCenter service again

### Configure Virtual Infrastructure Clients to Verify Certificates

Once the valid certificates are deployed on the Hosts and the VirtualCenter, an administrator can enable certificate validation for the VI Client. This is only relevant if the user had chosen "Do not display any security warnings for ..." was initially checked. Now that the valid certificates are installed, it is important to no longer ignore the security warnings.

The security warning preferences are set in [HKEY_CURRENT_USER\Software\VMWare\ Virtual Infrastructure Client\Preferences\UI\SSLIgnore\] of the system running VI Client. Under this key is the name of all hosts for which the security warning will no longer be displayed.

Remove the VirtualCenter and Hosts that are now configured with a valid SSL certificate. The SSL warning should no longer appear for these systems as the certificates used by these systems are signed by a trusted third party.

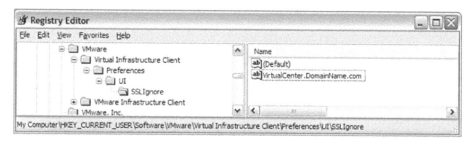

It is important to note that all client communication initiated from a Linux system will be vulnerable to a man-in-the-middle attack. This is because the client tools on a Linux system do not perform certificate validation. Even if a valid certificate is deployed on the ESX Host and the VirtualCenter, the client tools will not be able to differentiate a valid certificate from an invalid one. It is, therefore, recommended to not use a Linux system to operate the client tools including VI Client, VI Perl Toolkit, VI SDK, Web Access, and RCLI.

## Storage Security

ESX Host can store a Virtual Machine on local SCSI disks, a Fiber Channel storage area network, iSCSI storage area network (SAN), or via Network File System (NFS). In the most common use cases, virtual machines are stored as .vmdk (Virtual Machine Disk format) files within an ESX server's VMFS (Virtual Machine File System) datastore.

While the security considerations for storage files on local SCCI disks and NFS are fairly common best practices, security considerations concerning storage area network are more involved. Two common methods of increasing the security for a SAN are by logical partitioning of information in different segments through the use of zoning and masking.

### Zoning

A zone divides and partitions the available resources into multiple logical groups. A group of servers with similar business need to typically access the same zone. Zone switches access control HBAs (host bus adapters). They control which HBA can connect to which service processor. A server cannot access devices in outside zones. SAN switches also restrict SAN traffic within each zone. An example use of the zones is to create different zones for trusted and untrusted environments.

The ESX systems in a test environment can be configured to use a different zone from the ESX systems in a production environment. This will reduce the risk of attack and compromise.

## Logical Units Masking

Logical units (LUN) masking is used to implement access control on the files that the users are aware of and have access to. It restricts users from accessing files that are present on the same storage unit. LUN masking is enabled at the storage array level by admitting only specific fabric WWNs (World Wide Name) to access the LUN within the array. By default, the Host that has access to a given fiber port can potentially access all LUNs accessible by that port. To restrict access, access control is enforced on the HBA using a masking utility that is part of the HBA. This masking utility allows editing the WWNs visible to a host down to the set authorized for that host.

## Raw Device Mapping

ESX supports mapping of a raw storage device to a virtual machine using a proxy file present on the VMFS volume. This proxy file contains all metadata used to redirect disk access to the raw storage device. It allows a virtual machine to access the details of the underlying LUN. A virtual machine can pass raw SCSI commands to the LUN. The ability to pass raw SCSI commands to a LUN is very powerful and should be restricted to only privileged and highly trusted systems.

## Secure iSCSI Deployment

An ESX Host can be configured to use the iSCSI-based storage area network instead of the fiber channel. An iSCSI is a specialized high-speed network-based protocol that connects the server to a storage system using Ethernet. The availability of storage devices over the Ethernet increases their attack surface considerably. Incorrectly configured iSCSI devices can potentially allow an unauthorized user to connect and mount a LUN which he should otherwise not have access to. This poses a significantly higher risk when compared to a fiber channel–based SAN. If fiber channel is used, a virtual machine has no means to access the SAN directly. The virtual machine is not provided the virtual fiber channel HBAs. They can only access the disks that have been assigned to a virtual machine using virtual SCSI adapters. Considering the security profile, a fiber channel may be considered as a safer storage system.

There are well-established hardening best practices that can be employed to make iSCSI devices secure from attack and compromise.

## Network Isolation of iSCSI

The most important step to securing the iSCSI device is to isolate it from an untrusted network. An iSCSI device should only be accessible on an isolated or private LAN where limited trusted systems are hosted. The use of a separate VLAN may serve well to isolate the storage network.

If the iSCSI device is accessible to virtual machines or other untrusted systems, then they are open to attack and compromise. All iSCSI communication except Challenge Handshake Authentication Protocol (CHAP) is clear text and can be compromised using a man-in-the-middle attack. It is, therefore, recommended to create a separate isolated network for ESX and iSCSI communication.

The management console of the device should also be protected from unauthorized access. Administrators should only be able to access the management console from a management VLAN or restricted systems.

### *Require Challenge Handshake Authentication Protocol to Connect to iSCSI*

ESX only supports the use of CHAP authentication to connect to iSCSI devices. It does not support other authentication protocols like Kerberos, Secure Remote Protocol, or public key encryption. Further, bidirectional authentication is not supported. Only the initiator can authenticate to iSCSI devices and each initiator can only support one set of credentials for all targets.

It is recommended to configure the iSCSI SAN to require authentication from the initiators. This will ensure that any attacker with access to the iSCSI device will not be able to connect to and mount the LUNs that he should not have access to.

## Security Banner

US Department of Defense recommends the use of warning banners. The banner should indicate the name of the organization that owns the system and the fact that the system may be monitored. The banner should also indicate that by proceeding to use the system the user is consenting to the monitoring terms stated.

The organization's legal team should review and approve the content of the warning banner. For the most part, warning banners should be consistent across the organization expect for any location or system-specific messages. A sample message can be found at http://www.usdoj.gov/criminal/cybercrime/s&sappendix2002.htm

### *ESX Host*

Web Access

To configure the warning banner on the ESX Host Web interface, embed the banner in the file /usr/lib/vmware/hostd/docroot/index.html

Similarly, the file /usr/lib/vmware/webAccess/tomcat/apache-tomcat-5.5.26/webapps/ui/WEB-INF/jsp/scriptedInstall/login.jsp will need to be modified to embed the security banner in the login page.

### *Console and SSH Access*

To enable the security banner for console and the SSH access, embed the banner in the following files:

```
/etc/issue
/etc/issue.net
/etc/banner
/etc/motd
/etc/issue.emergency,
```

Further edit the file /etc/ssh/sshd_config and replace line

```
#Banner /some/path
```

with

```
Banner /etc/banner
Restart SSH
service sshd restart
```

# VirtualCenter

VirtualCenter is the central management station that allows administration of all ESX Hosts and the VirtualMachines. It mediates several advanced features available on the Virtual Infrastructure like High Availability, Distributed Resource Scheduler, and VMotion.

When an ESX server is added to a VirtualCenter, the VirtualCenter creates a powerful vpxuser account on the ESX Host. This account is used by VirtualCenter to perform all the operations on ESX Hosts. ESX server, therefore, has a trust relationship with the VirtualCenter. If the VirtualCenter is compromised, then all ESX Hosts and the virtual machines on each ESX Host may be at risk. The security of VirtualCenter, therefore, warrants very stringent security standards.

## VirtualCenter Host Controls

VirtualCenter needs to run on a Windows Server 2000 or newer and all security controls that would otherwise be applicable to a Windows Server should be implemented for a VirtualCenter. This includes and is not limited to antivirus, antispyware, intrusion detection systems, and a firewall.

An administrator can also consider running the VirtualCenter as a virtual machine. The key benefit of running the VirtualCenter as a virtual machine is to provide high availability (HA) and take snapshots. The HA feature ensures that the VirtualCenter is migrated to a different ESX Host in the event of a server failure. Similarly, system snapshots can help the administrator restore the VirtualCenter if a system patch or an application makes the system unstable.

## Implement Network Isolation

VirtualCenter only needs to communicate with the Virtual Infrastructure components like the ESX Host, Licensing Server, Update Manager, and other virtualization add-ons. VirtualCenter should, therefore, be hosted on an isolated management network that is separate from an operational network. Regular users should not be able to connect to VirtualCenter. Further, during normal operation, VirtualCenter does need to access the Internet. A combination of isolated network with no Internet connectivity will significantly decrease the attack surface for VirtualCenter.

## Firewall

VirtualCenter can receive network communication from many different interfaces. These include the VI Client, the Web Interface, the Remote CLI, the Scripting Toolkit and the third party Addons that use the SDK. Not all of these network interfaces may currently be in use. Further, there may be other ports like NETBIOS that may not be used.

The use of firewalls can be considered to disable or even restrict access to these ports. The firewall can be configured to only allow a restricted set of systems to access the management interface. The list of services and the ports used by VirtualCenter are mentioned below.

| Port Number | TCP or UDP | Incoming or Outgoing | Service Description |
| --- | --- | --- | --- |
| 80 | TCP | Incoming | HTTP access for non-encrypted traffic. By default redirects the user to port 443. |
| 443 | TCP | Incoming | HTTP access using SSL. All VirtualServer clients use this port including the VI Client, Web interface, and SDK. This is the only required port for VI Client and VirtualCenter communication. |
| 902 | TCP and UDP | Incoming TCP, outgoing UDP | ESX Access and Heartbeat |
| 27000–27010 | TCP | Incoming and outgoing | Licensing transactions. Applicable if Licensing Server is installed on the same host. |

## Disable Unnecessary Services

VirtualCenter should be hosted on a separate system with very few other shared services. Ideally, only the VirtualCenter and the Licensing Server should be hosted on this system. All other services that are not necessary to support the VirtualCenter and the Licensing Server should be disabled. This can include services like IIS Web server, printer services, e-mail server, and dhcp server. Unnecessary services and applications increase the number of input points that can be used by an attacker to compromise the system. Therefore, the number of input points in a system should be kept to the lowest possible.

## Authentication and Access Control

Authentication to VirtualCenter may be supported through local Windows-based authentication or through integration with ActiveDirectory. If the VirtualCenter host is not part of an Active Directory domain, then local system administrators will have access to the VirtualCenter. If the host is a member of Active Directory or a domain controller, then administrators on the domain have administrative access on VirtualCenter.

There are several advantages of using VirtualCenter as a member of Active Directory Domain. Some of the key ones are

1. Centralized management of users and roles. Users could be made part of a group or a role. This limits the number of user accounts that need to be tracked and changed in the event of a change in user role.
2. Password policy enforcement: It is easier to establish and enforce one good password policy throughout the domain than to configure several individual policies for every environment.

3. Ease of use: The user is likely to choose one good password with adequate complexity than choose several different ones with varying requirements. If a user has many accounts, then he may end up writing his credentials down which may be easily accessible to others.
4. It is possible to enable pass-through authentication for a VI Client using a short to "C:\ Program Files\VMware\Infrastructure\Virtual Infrastructure Client\Launcher\VpxClient. exe" -passthroughAuth -s virtualcenter.domainname.com

If the VirtualCenter is not part of the domain controller, then the users can still be configured on VirtualCenter using local Windows accounts. It is desirable to create a separate Windows account with regular user privileges and make that user an administrator for VirtualCenter. This will eliminate the need to provide Windows administrative account to the VirtualCenter administrator. Where possible, it is recommended to integrate VirtualCenter with the Active Directory domain for all the advantages mentioned above.

## Roles and Permissions

VirtualCenter supports a very matured and sophisticated system of roles and privileges. These roles and privileges determine a user authorization on the objects. An administrator can configure the roles and privileges to control user permissions at a very granular level. Roles and permissions can be configured to set authorizations for various operational and administrative tasks on the available object. The objects may be a data center, clusters, hosts, virtual machines, or any resource group.

By default, VirtualCenter supports two groups of roles: One is system roles and the other is sample roles. The system roles are *no access, read-only, and administrator.* System roles cannot be edited or deleted. Users and groups can be added or deleted from system role.

The sample roles are provided as suggestions. The permission for the sample roles can be modified to meet an organization's needs. Further, administrators can create custom roles to meet the requirements of the environment. It is important to create roles that only support the intended tasks and do not provide the users with elevated privileges.

The task of assigning roles and privileges to a large base of users can be a fairly involved. A user can gain privileges from the permissions that were applied hierarchically downward to an object. Permissions can also be overridden by setting different permissions on the lower object. Finally, a user may be a member of two or more roles and groups. In such cases, a union of the permissions may take effect. A combination of these different rules can easily cause confusion resulting in unintentional consequences. It is, therefore, recommended to plan user roles and permissions well before making actual configurations in VirtualCenter.

## Database Security

The databases supported by VirtualCenter include Microsoft MSDE, SQL 2000/2005 SP1, and Oracle. The use of MSDE is not recommended for a production environment. Some of the security considerations while using the database are

1. Install the database on a separate server with adequate network controls like VLANs and firewalls.
2. Harden the database by removing unnecessary procedure calls, unnecessary databases and users, and installing all the applicable security patches.

3. Shared database use with other applications is not recommended. Other applications may have user accounts with privileges not restricted to their own database. Malicious application owners or an SQL injection vulnerability in other applications can result in complete compromise of Virtual Infrastructure.
4. Configure VirtualCenter to use an account with restricted privileges. This user should only be able to
   a. Select, update, insert, and delete queries
   b. Execute stored procedures

## Logging and Monitoring

VirtualCenter governs the important configuration settings for the virtualization infrastructure. It is, therefore, important to log and monitor the actions performed on the VirtualCenter. While most of the actual configuration is stored on the database, some important configuration and logs reside on the VirtualCenter's file system. An organization's logging policy might require periodical backup and monitoring of these files.

The logs files are located at the following locations:

| VirtualCenter Log Files | C:\Documents and Settings\All Users\Application Data\VMware\VMwareVirtualCenter\Logs\* |
|---|---|
| VirtualCenter Web Server Log Files | C:\Program Files\VMware\Infrastructure\ VirtualCenter Server\tomcat\logs\* |
| License Manager | C:\WINDOWS\Temp\lmgrd.log |

A menu option in VirtualCenter management console allows the administrator to back up all VirtualCenter and ESX Host logs using the VI Client.

Select File > Export > Export Diagnostic Data

- If connected to an ESX Host, the logs for ESX Host will be collected.
- If connected to a VirtualCenter Server, the user can choose the ESX Host(s) to gather the logs from.

Another convenient option is to run the Generate VirtualCenter Server log bundle command from the VMware program file menu. This will capture all troubleshooting and debugging information including the relevant Windows registry entries, configuration files, and all log files for VirtualCenter.

This task can be easily automated by the administrator to periodically obtain the information and compare the state to the previous configuration.

# Virtual Machine

The virtual machines running in a virtualized environment should not be treated any different from the virtual machines running in a physical environment. There may be a few exceptions for cases like clustering services and virtual machines using Guest Tagging for VLANs but for the most part, all security considerations applied for physical systems should also be applied for virtual machines.

## *Virtual versus Physical World*

Systems are not inherently more or less secure because they are virtualized. The security of a virtual system largely depends on the configuration and security measures applied on the system. Virtualization adds a few new attack vectors and also provides a few measures to bolster the security of a virtual machine but these measures are independent of the need to secure the virtual machine itself. It is, therefore, important to apply all security controls of the physical world to a virtualized system. These controls may include and are not restricted to the following:

1. Harden the guest operating system. Default operating system installations are deployed with unnecessary services, default accounts, and in some cases weak file permissions. It is, therefore, important to follow a system hardening guide to lockdown the system.
2. Deploy security solutions like antivirus, antispyware, firewall, intrusion detection systems, and monitoring agents. It may also be important to connect them to a central management console that monitors and updates these tools on a periodic basis.
3. Patch all systems regularly. In the current environment, by the time a vendor releases a security patch, the vulnerability is often being exploited in the wild. It is, therefore, important to patch systems as soon as possible. This does not eliminate the need to test the patches well to ensure that they do not cause any conflicts with critical applications. The use of virtualization can make it easier to take snapshots and revert back in case any unexpected event occurred.

## *Use Templates*

Templates provide a fast and efficient way to create new virtual machines. A template image is a base image of a virtual image that can be used to create and deploy live virtual machines. There are several advantages of using templates. Some of the key ones are

1. Templates can be configured to be a hardened base operating system with all necessary security controls, latest patches and service packs, and all security policies pre-configured. This ensures that the systems are better secured when initially deployed.
2. Reduced deployment time. The time needed to deploy a new virtual machine is reduced with the use of templates. The templates will probably have the necessary tools, applications, and drivers installed thereby reducing the likelihood of configuration errors and the deployment time needed for new systems.
3. It is easier to update templates along with the applications and the security tools to the latest available service packs, patches, and updates. The server update process that would otherwise take several different individual tasks is now part of the template.

There are some security considerations that need to be considered with the use of templates. Some of the key things to consider with the use of templates are as follows:

1. *License violations*: Templates are mobile, activated guest images that can contain commercial licensed software. It is easy to make several copies of the template without purchasing the necessary number of licenses. This can result in unintentional license violation. While this does not directly result in compromise of a system, it can have financial and public relations impact on an organization.

2. *Hidden secrets in templates*: Live virtual machines generated from templates may have embedded hidden secrets that can be exploited by a malicious user to gain access to other systems on the network. The most common technique employed by an internal penetration tester to gain access to privileged systems on the internal network is password reuse. Templates could potentially contain services running as privileged accounts. If a malicious user has administrative control on the virtual machine, then by dumping the LSA secrets the administrator on the virtual machine can gain access to clear text passwords of the service accounts. These credentials could then be replayed on other systems to gain privileged access to them. Similarly, if the password to administrator (or root) account is the same on all systems, then a user with administrator-level access on the system can crack the password hashes. In some scenarios, the user may not even need to crack the hash. They can directly *pass the hash* to gain privileged access to other systems.

## Loss of Virtual Machines

At a fundamental level, virtual machines are comprised of a bunch of files. If an attacker can gain access to the vmdk files, then he can easily upload the complete virtual image on a remote private server. Similarly, an attacker can mount the vmdk(s) using the VMDK Disk Mount utility and directly write to the underlying file system. This can allow an attacker with access to virtual machine files to inject code and replace system files with backdoors. It is, therefore, important to secure the storage system and ensure that the users do not gain access to VMDK files. Organizations can also consider the use of full disk encryption techniques to ensure that an unauthorized user cannot manipulate the virtual machines even if he has access to the VMDK files.

## Resource Overcommitment

Using the virtual infrastructure, it is possible for the administrators to overcommit on the resources between virtual machines. This means that the ESX administrator can allocate virtual machines memory and CPU power such that the sum of individual assignments can exceed the total available resources. While this configuration allows optimal utilization of resources, the successful operation of the system hinges on the assumption that virtual machines will play nice and only consume resources when they need them. Further, by default, all virtual machines have the same priority on the resources. However, not all virtual systems may be equally critical. If any virtual machine acts malicious, then it can easily consume all available resources thereby causing a denial-of-service attack on more critical systems. It is, therefore, important to set minimum limits on the resources that should be available for the key critical systems. This will ensure that these systems will at least have the minimum resources required to be stable. It is also important to monitor the resource consumption by virtual machines to ensure that no machine is trying to consume all resources. Further, an administrator can set tasks to take necessary action like suspend, shutdown, or reboot a virtual machine in the event that a virtual machine is causing performance degradation to other systems. Similarly, an administrator can set up alerts to notify them if unusual resource consumption is detected.

## Isolation Based on Trust Levels

VMware has incorporated several architectural designs to enforce virtual machine isolation. The Hypervisor is designed to ensure that one virtual machine cannot access resources belonging to other virtual machine in a manner that is not possible in the physical environment. While that works well most of the time, security researchers periodically identify vulnerabilities that can potentially allow an attacker on a virtual machine to break the isolation and gain privileged access on another virtual machine. These vulnerabilities eventually get patched but there is always a window of exposure between the time that the vulnerability is discovered and the vulnerability is patched.

Organizations that require a very high level of security can consider a defense-in-depth strategy. The defense-in-depth strategy recommends only hosting virtual machines on the same trust level on an ESX Host. While this approach provides better protection against less trustable systems, it does come at the additional hardware and operational costs.

While the isolation provided by VMware can be considered strong and the ESX administrators can only deploy systems on the same trust level on the same ESX Hosts, all systems are still interconnected through the network. The most effective isolation technique will be to isolate systems based on network segments.

All virtual machines on the same network segment are open to attack and compromise from other virtual systems present on the same network. A malicious user on one virtual machine can perform attacks like sniffing traffic, ARP spoofing, IP spoofing, and MAC spoofing. These attacks can alter the traffic flow, provide clear text access to sensitive information, or help an attacker launch a man-in-the-middle attack.

Considering the different risk level of systems on the same network, it is important to segment the network based on the business roles, trust levels, and criticality of systems. Virtual machines can be separated by different physical network connections or through the use of VLANs.

## Virtual Machine Isolation Settings

There are several isolation settings that can be made for a virtual machine or a group of virtual machines that can provide defense-in-depth measures. It may be advisable to perform these hardening steps on all virtual machines unless there is a legitimate business purpose for not doing so.

## Disable Copy and Paste

By default, the Copy and Paste feature is enabled for all virtual machines. This allows a user with remote access to a virtual machine console to copy and paste information between the virtual machine and the system where remote access is running (host). While this is a convenient feature, it allows the processes and users on the virtual machine to access the clipboard of the host system. If a user on the host system copies any sensitive information to the clipboard and moves focus to the remote virtual machine, the virtual machine process can gain access to the information on the clipboard. Users on the host system will not even be aware that the processes in the virtual system are able to access the information on the clipboard. It is, therefore, recommended to disable the Copy and Paste feature between the host and the virtual machine.

To disable Copy and Paste feature, make the following configuration changes

| Name | Value |
|------|-------|
| `isolation.tools.copy.disable` | True |
| `isolation.tools.paste.disable` | True |
| `isolation.tools.setGUIOptions.enable` | False |

## Limit Log File Size

The logs created during virtual machine operation are written to the `vmware.log` file. This file is present on the same VMFS volume as other files for the virtual machines. All troubleshooting and debugging information from the virtual machine is written to this file. A malicious virtual system can potentially exploit this feature of logging information to consume all available disk space and cause a denial-of-service attack. To effectively mitigate the disk exhaustion attack, the administrator can set a limit on the total size and the number of log files that will be created. The key is to choose a file size and number of files that collect adequate information but do not tax the storage space. VMware recommends 10 different log files with maximum size of 100 kB each. This configuration will collect most of the important information needed for logging and debugging purposes and will not consume too much system resources.

The system will automatically enforce the log file checks and will delete the old log files in the event that the maximum file size and file number is reached for all files.

| Name | Value |
|---|---|
| `log.rotateSize` | 100,000 |
| `log.keepOld` | 10 |

## Limit VMX File Size

Virtual Machines can provide system-specific information to ESX Host that is written to VMX file. These are name–value pairs that have no predefined format and can be of any length. If no upper limit size is specified on the name–value pairs, then the VMX file can grow out-of-bounds and it can result in a denial-of-service attack. In ESX 3.5, the size for this GuestInfo is limited to 1 MB by default.

An administrator can change this setting using the tools.setInfo.sizeLimit setting in the VMX configuration file. The absence of this setting places a default size limit of 1 MB.

A more stringent setting disallows the guest system from writing any name–value pairs to the VMX file. This may be a recommended setting for some production systems that are not expected to change during the course of operation. It can be set using the setting
isolation.tools.setinfo.disable true

## Disable Unnecessary Devices

The administrators can decide which devices are needed for the virtual machine and only allow connection to those devices. Other devices like serial and parallel port and CD/DVD drive may not be needed on the virtual system.

Some of these removable devices may have residual information. If the virtual machine is allowed access to these devices, then the users on the virtual machine can potentially gain access to this information.

| Device Name | Configuration Parameter <X> Signifies a Device Identifier | Value (True or False) |
|---|---|---|
| Floppy drive | Floppy<X>.present | False |
| Serial port | Serial<X>.present | False |
| Parallel port | Parallel<X>.present | False |

All unnecessary devices that are not needed should not be enabled for the virtual machine. To disable the use of a device, the device presence can be set to false.

## *Other Configuration Settings*

Users within the virtual machine should not be able to connect or disconnect the available devices. Only the administrators should be able to configure the virtual machine with devices. To prevent a user within a virtual machine from connecting or disconnecting a device, the administrator can set the configuration

```
isolation.device.connectable.disable = "TRUE"
isolation.device.edit.disable = "TRUE"
```

Lower privileged users within the virtual machine can invoke the disk-shrinking utility to reclaim unused space and decrease the size of a virtual disk. Repeated use of disk shrinking can cause the virtual disk to defragment and shrink thereby becoming unavailable and causing a denial-of-service attack on all users. To prevent users from invoking the disk-shrinking utility, configure the following settings

```
isolation.tools.diskWiper.disable = "TRUE"
isolation.tools.diskShrink.disable = "TRUE"
```

# Tools for Virtualization

## *Virtualization Malware*

A lot is being debated about virtualization security and will continue to be the case. Over the last 4 years, several proof-of-concept malware and virtualization detection tools have been released. One of the virtualization-specific infection techniques is known as Hyperjacking. In this attack, a malware converts an operating system into a virtual machine and operates as Hypervisor. It is transparent to the applications and operating system itself. Some of the prominent virtualization-based malware discussed in the community are Blue Pill, Vitriol, and SubVirt.

Blue Pill is a virtualization-based malware originally targeting the Windows Vista operating system. Since then, the project has evolved and now works on different architectures and platforms. In simplistic terms, the Blue Pill concept SubVirts the base operating system or the Hypervisor and moves it to a virtual machine. Once infected, the malware itself will run like a Hypervisor between the host operating system (could be a hypervisor) and the hardware. The authors of this proof of concept malware claim it to be 100% undetectable. One of the main reasons that the malware is claimed to be undetectable is because it uses no system hooks, therefore, the traditional methods of rootkit detection no longer apply.

These claims have been heavily challenged in the community. Many claim that the techniques that would be used to inject the malware into the Hypervisor or the base operating system can be detected and stopped. Some others claim to have the technology to detect virtualization-based malware like Blue Pill.

There are other Hyperjacking tools like SubVirt and Vitriol. Vitriol developed by Dino Dai Zovi uses Intel's virtualization technology (VT-x) to infect the Mac OS X. SubVirt was a similar proof of concept virtualization malware developed by researchers at the University of Michigan targeting the Virtual PC and VMware Workstation on x86 platform.

The main idea for all these rootkits remains the same. Some of them are more weaponized than others.

SubVirt: http://www.eecs.umich.edu/virtual/papers/king06.pdf

## Detecting Virtualization

Most commercial virtualization solutions make no attempt to hide the fact that the guest operating system is running as a virtual machine. There are many different ways to detect virtualization. These include looking for artifacts inside the virtualized environment. Some of the easily identifiable signs include

- Process, files, and registry keys present inside the guest operating system.
- Inside memory. Several operating system structures are located on different address ranges in virtual machine when compared to a virtual machine. In particular, the location of interrupt descriptor table register (IDTR) provides a good indication of the kind of virtualization environment used. The other operating system structures like global descriptor table and local descriptor table can also be referenced to determine the virtualized environment.
- Virtualization-specific hardware. This includes motherboard make and model, MAC addresses, USB controller, audio controller, and SCSI devices.
- Invoke nonstandard instructions and observe the behavior. Some nonstandard x86 instructions are supported by VMware, Virtual PC, and Xen.
- The timing discrepancy between two operations performed in physical and virtual mode can also be used to detect the presence of virtualization.

A non-privileged user can use any combination of the methods listed above or more to detect operations in a virtual machine. However, the significance of such detection is getting smaller. In the past, some malware detected operation in a virtual machine and terminated itself. This was done to avoid being monitored. The assumption was that the virtual machines with their unique ability to take snapshots and revert to snapshots will be used to study malware.

Virtualization is now increasingly being adopted in a production environment and its use is only expected to grow. In the future, instead of terminating themselves, malware and attackers can use the virtualization detection techniques to launch attacks targeting the specific virtualized operating environment.

Some of the popular virtualization detection tools are

1. RedPill
2. Nopill
3. ScoopyNG (Scoopy Doo and Jerry combined)
4. VMDetect

## Future of Virtualization Security

In February 2008, VMware announced the release of VMsafe security technology. VMware partnered with several security vendors that can leverage the powerful features of VMsafe APIs to provide security solutions that were not available in the physical world.

The VMsafe technology opens the operations on ESX Host to provide security vendors much more fine-grained access to Hypervisor and the operations on the virtual machine. VMsafe-based security solutions will be able to provide several unique features.

## CPU and Memory Scanning

Using the VMsafe APIs, the authorized security product will be able to monitor CPU state and virtual machine memory pages for all the virtual systems on an ESX system.

## Network Monitoring

All network communications through any virtual switch can be monitored using VMsafe. This will include traffic for all virtual machines and the ESX Host.

## Process Monitoring and Execution

VMsafe APIs will allow process execution control within a virtual machine. This will allow the security tools to monitor the modules loaded, executables launched, and the operations performed by all binaries.

## Storage Scanning

All virtual machines' storage files can be mounted, scanned, and edited using the VMsafe APIs. Security tools will be able to scan for malicious content within the file system. Further, all file system operations can also be governed.

There are several benefits of VMsafe APIs that make the technology promising.

## Agent-Free Security

The key benefit of using VMsafe-based products will be the agent-less security. Administrators will no longer need to deploy a security tool on every operating system. One of the major challenges with the physical world is that once a system is compromised, it is difficult to trust any operation on that system. In most cases, malware and security tools operate at the same permission level. This allows the malware to disable the security software and render it useless. With the use of VMsafe technology, agents will no longer be needed to be deployed on the virtual machines. They will operate outside the influence of the malware, which can allow more effective control and higher standards of security.

Further, agents will not need to be deployed, updated, and maintained on every system. Any virtual system present on the ESX Host could automatically be part of the protection profile.

## Comprehensive and Integrated Network Security

All network traffic from all virtual machines across different ESX Hosts can be integrated and monitored using the VMsafe technology. Security products can enforce more granular network policies for virtual machines. Malicious content can be blocked or filtered before it actually reaches the virtual machines. Further, the need to deploy complex and expensive hardware devices can be reduced.

## Security Bottlenecks Can Be Reduced

Most security tools tend to be resource intensive. They tend to have a large footprint and consume valuable resources. In some cases, this causes a contention of resources on a system that delays critical business operations. With the use of VMsafe technology, most security operations are performed without consuming the resources of the virtual machine. The scanning and monitoring of the content and operations are performed outside the scope of a virtual machine.

This is especially important for critical business systems that support high-priority operations. Even if the security tool fails or crashes, this will not directly affect the operation of the virtual system.

### Concerns about VMsafe

The powerful features of VMsafe if abused by malicious systems can result in significant damage to the infrastructure. Some of the most obvious concerns are

1. VMsafe APIs will allow the security vendors to perform some very powerful operations on the ESX and the virtual machines. What prevents a malicious virtual machine from masquerading itself as a security tool and invoking the same function?
2. To perform some of the security features that were mentioned, the security tools will have direct access to the core functioning of the Hypervisor. While measures can be taken to run the operations outside the context of the Hypervisor, the ability to influence CPU, memory, network, and storage will raise concerns about Hypervisor integrity.

Given the importance of security, we can be sure that there will be considerable thought given to these and several other security concerns arising with the use of VMsafe. We can also be sure that there will be design flaws, bugs, and vulnerabilities. While we trust the vendors to design the products securely, it will be our responsibility in the security community to verify and test these claims.

## About the Author

**Shanit Gupta** is a principal consultant at Foundstone, Mission Viejo, California.

## References

http://www.vmware.com/pdf/esx3_esxcfg_auth_tn.pdf
http://www.vmware.com/support/esx21/doc/esx21admin_snmpagents.html
http://www.inlab.de/balanceng/vi3_35_25_3_server_config.pdf
http://kb.vmware.com/selfservice/microsites/search.do?language=en_US&cmd=displayKC&externalId=1003070
http://kb.vmware.com/selfservice/microsites/search.do?language=en_US&cmd=displayKC&externalId=1517
http://www.vmware.com/pdf/vi_vcserver_certificates.pdf
http://pubs.vmware.com/vi35/server_config/wwhelp/wwhimpl/js/html/wwhelp.htm?href=sc_cover.1.1.html
http://www.cisecurity.org/tools2/vm/CIS_VMware_ESX_Server_Benchmark_v1.0.pdf
http://www.accessmylibrary.com/coms2/summary_0286-9909942_ITM
http://www.vmware.com/pdf/esx25_rawdevicemapping.pdf
http://www.vmware.com/pdf/esx_lun_security.pdf
http://iase.disa.mil/stigs/stig/esx_server_stig_v1r1_final.pdf
http://www.vmware.com/pdf/vi3_vc_roles.pdf
http://www.eecs.umich.edu/virtual/papers/king06.pdf
https://www.blackhat.com/presentations/bh-usa-06/BH-US-06-Zovi.pdf
http://viops.vmware.com/home/docs/DOC-1079
http://www.iseclab.org/papers/detection.pdf
http://handlers.sans.org/tliston/ThwartingVMDetection_Liston_Skoudis.pdf
http://www.offensivecomputing.net/files/active/0/vm.pdf
http://www.vmware.com/technology/security/vmsafe/usecases.html

## Chapter 21

# Everything New Is Old Again

Robert M. Slade

## Contents

Once upon a time, it was fun going to computer trade shows. All the vendors were doing new things. Novel ideas sprouted like weeds. It was exciting.

But that was once upon a time, very long ago.

Somewhat more recently I was doing a course on "Emerging Technology" for a local college. As the course went on, the students kept asking why we weren't studying this or that technology. Basically, it was because those technologies weren't actually new or emerging: they were old technologies under new names. I introduced the class to Slade's Law of Computer History: those who do not learn the lessons of computer history are doomed to buy it all again—repackaged.

Don't believe me? You think Twitter is the latest new thing? We used to have a system that allowed you to publish your current activities and plans, and made it possible for anyone (who was interested) to access them. It was called finger.

Into blogging are you? You like the fact that people with similar interests can find each other, post their thoughts and opinions, and comment on those of others? We used to do that on something called Usenet News.

So, you're a 13th-level sorcerous battle maid on *World of Warcraft*, having built up a stock of magical pruning saws? Other than the graphics, what's the difference between that and rogue?

Allow me to present a few more examples.

# Virtualization

Virtually everyone has heard the "new" term "virtualization." That's because virtually every vendor has jumped on the virtualization bandwagon. Virtually anything can be virtualized, it seems.

Also, virtually nobody can agree on what virtualization really means. Virtualization seems to be a conflation of two old ideas: virtual machines (what do you think VM and VMS stood for?), and distributed computing (which is now being sold as "cloud computing," an amazingly cloudy concept that'll be dealt with in a moment).

We used virtual machines a lot in the old days, and they were great for security. We used them as goat or bait machines for viruses. Very secure way to protect yourself when dealing with dangerous software.

Of course nowadays they use virtualization in some virtually explosive ways. Like putting your Kerberos KDC on the same physical box as your Web server.

## Cloud Computing

At one time, everybody stored their programs and information in some mysterious, far off, ill-defined entity. It was called a "mainframe," or sometimes just "the computer." Nobody stored anything locally: you really couldn't, on a terminal.

So then we got microcomputers, or personal computers, or desktop machines. And people stored everything locally. And then found out that there were problems with not making backups, getting viruses, and stuff like that.

In the mid-1990s, the Internet was getting big, thanks to this new technology called "the World Wide Web." And people started to write programs that ran in the application you used to access the Web, called a browser. And all of a sudden people had this wonderful idea that you wouldn't need to store your programs locally anymore, they could be stored, in bits and pieces, all over the Internet. And so could your data!

And everyone who has ever looked at a network diagram knows what the Internet is. It's a cloud.

Well, when people started to actually try and store programs and data on the net (in the cloud), they got into a big fight over whether they would use a freely available and open technology, or one from The Vendor Who Controlled Everything—Trust Us. And then they decided that maybe it really wasn't that great an idea.

Until it came back with a new name...

## CloudAV

And, even within the idea of cloud computing there are specialties.

A few media sources seem to be picking up a press release from the University of Michigan [1]. This reports on "CloudAV," a project and a series of papers about having antivirus detection run "in the cloud" rather than on the PC [2].

As usual, there seems to be some misunderstanding about what is going on here. CloudAV is not really a new approach, it is simply the use of multiple scanners, which the AV research community has advocated for years. It's like having a bunch of scanners installed on your desktop, or a system like Virustotal [3], with the exception that the scanners run on different computers so you get a bit of performance advantage (absent the bandwidth lag/drain for submitting files to multiple systems).

# ROSI

Return on Investment. (In security.)

Return on Security Investment.

It doesn't exist. But it keeps on coming back from the grave, no matter how many times we try to kill it.

OK, we can say that spending money on security keeps you from losing more money somewhere down the road. But "investing" in security isn't going to bring in revenue. (Well, unless you want to try and estimate the extra business you got from being a "safe" company to do business with.)

We can also try to do quantitative risk assessment or analysis, and, therefore, be able to do something of a cost/benefit analysis of individual controls. (Of course, a lot of people have done a "quick and dirty" qualitative cost/benefit analysis, and figured out that the cost of doing a quantitative risk analysis outweighs any possible benefit in terms of the greater accuracy of your cost/benefit analysis.)

Undeterred, now that we are in an economic quagmire, the media has started to spin ROSI as the way to ensure that you get the most out of your security investment.

Columnists love fairy tales…

# Intelligent Automation

Wait a minute, I thought automation, by definition, was supposed to involve some measure of intelligence?

Oh, but it's a specialized form of automation.

First we have to go way, way back. Back to the days of random security technologies, when you had all kinds of different security technologies. And they all had to be managed. Separately.

And then, oh joy, someone (either Marcus Ranum or Steve Bellovin, take your pick) invented firewalls! And we wouldn't have to manage security anymore! And there was rejoicing!

Until we figured out that we were going to have to manage the firewalls.

And then someone invented Intrusion Detection Systems! And there was rejoicing!

Until we figured out that we were going to have to manage the IDS.

And then some marketing department invented IPS. And by this time, becoming jaded, we were asking questions. Like, what's the difference between IDS and IPS. (Oh, really? An IPS prevents a packet getting through, rather than just detecting it? Then what's the difference between an IPS and a firewall? Oh, really? An IPS is more intelligent? How so? Well, depends on which marketing department you ask. That's what you get for using terms invented by marketing departments.)

But that "intelligent" business seems to have had a bit of magic in it. We've always had network monitoring, of one sort or another. For a long time we've had tools to help us sort through our logs (after all, even IDS is only a form of real-time log analysis). And people have been trying to sell us all "management" systems, to help with the work of, well, managing all the security bits and pieces. So why not get a log analysis package, bolt on a few other items (maybe virus scanning or something), and call the whole thing "intelligent!"

Hey, presto! A new marketing term!

## Native Client

Google has garnered a lot of interest with its radically new idea, released under the name Native Client. You can read the announcement [4] and download the research paper (in PDF [5]).

That idea sounded so familiar I just knew it had to have been done before.

It has. It's just a dressed up version of an activity monitor. The oldest form of antivirus technology actually implemented. In fact, it dates back to the days just slightly before the first PC viruses, when people were trying to prevent damage by some of the early PC trojans that were being shared on BBSs.

Or, if they take it far enough, and if you like, you can call it a form of virtual machine. And we are back to where we started this article.

## Convergence

Or, converged communications, if you prefer.

I mean, c'mon. We've had VoIP for a while. (Before that we had H.323. Even before that we had Internet telephony, although it didn't work all that terribly well.)

Of course, from our perspective in security, convergence is a great thing for job security. Just think, we can take all the problems we have in networking, and all the problems we have in telephony, and roll them up into one big insecurity.

(Surprise, surprise: bad guys are breaking into home and small office VoIP PBXs and using them to make telemarketing calls [6].) (Most recently with Skype.) (Although don't get me wrong: I've nothing against Asterisk per se, and I'm sure it's a great system if well managed.)

## Baked in Security

Now, believe me, I have only the greatest of sympathy with the intent of this phrase. Yes, I agree that we've been hamstrung and hampered by insecurities due to sloppy programming, and we desperately need to have more secure software development practices.

It's just nothing new, that's all.

I mean, we've been preaching this for years. Decades, really. Ask any old programmer what he, she, or it was taught way back in the old days.

Structured programming. Top-down programming. The waterfall method.

And documentation. I especially like internal documentation. If you don't like documentation, you can have a moment of pity for my (occasional) programming students. When they hand in a project it has to have internal documentation in the source code, and it has to be clear and make sense. (They lose marks if they don't and it doesn't.) As far as I'm concerned, if you can't say what you are doing, you don't know what you are doing.

And if you know what you are doing, you do it right.

## Web 2.0

Or, social networking, if you prefer.

Let's face it, the net is social. The money that went into creating computer networks, and the Internet itself, may have been intended for specific purposes, but as soon as it was there, people, being people, were being social.

As soon as the Internet was out of the test bed (and probably before that), and even before it was known as the Internet, people were using e-mail. A lot. For social things. What are the longest running Usenet "news" groups and mailing lists of any types? Lists of jokes and discussions of science fiction. Social stuff. (Yeah, the SF geeks are pretty antisocial, by "normal" standards, but for them this stuff is the ultimate in sociability.)

So, what's new? Oh, "social" networks have the users generate content? What do you think mailing lists are? OK, blogs make it a bit easier to search archives. But archives of mailing lists have been around for a while too. (And this "easier" stuff is highly subjective. Some blogs can be pretty difficult to plow through in order to find content of interest.)

And what about the Internet itself? It's the last word in user-created content. The protocols and programs that run the net were primarily created by individual users, seeing something they wanted to do, and writing something that would do it. As Dave Clark famously put it, "We believe in: rough consensus and running code."

Works pretty good, doesn't it?

## VDI

Argh! YASMA! (Yet Another Stupid Marketing Acronym.) VDI pops up in my e-mail. And when I search for it (using two kettles worth of carbon emissions), what do I find? "Virtual desktop infrastructure." In other words, thin client, or cloud computing, or just plain virtualization.

It is to weep.

## How to Spot the Next Big Thing that Spots Next Big Things

A new company is telling everyone which new companies are worth investing in [7]. Is this something we should get into?

"The software measures the 'buzz' surrounding a company via blogs and media reports along with a variety of factors including website traffic."

We should all blog and Twitter about this.

Then we should all blog about how blogging is so last year.

## Vulnerability Management

Yes, we have to know, assess, analyze, and manage vulnerabilities. Yes, it is a complicated task. So now this is the next big thing, is it?

Well, when you look at it, it is the same task we have always had to do under the name "risk management." Except that it is in a smaller compass and more limited extent and application. Nothing particularly wrong with concentrating on one aspect at a time—as long as you realize that is what you are doing. Not thinking that you are somehow seeing something new.

## Compliance

"Comply" used to be a verb. It used to mean that you would follow instructions.

Not any more. Now "compliance" is the important thing. You have to "have compliance." (Preferably at least five yards' worth.)

And what kind of compliance are we to have? Well, as Tanenbaum has said, the great thing about computer standards is that there are so many of them. And, if you don't like those, there will be more next year. We have the ISO 27000 family (which basically says you have to do information security). There is PCI DSS (which basically says you have to do information security). There is COBIT (with the middle three letters in small caps, which basically says you have somebody demonstrate that you are doing information security).

One of the definite biggies, recently, is the Sarbanes–Oxley Act of 2002 [8]. This act basically says that, if you have a company that is traded on the stock market, you have to tell people how much money you are making. (This allows people to bet on whether you will continue to make money. That's what the stock market is all about: betting.) And it even says that you have to have internal controls on whether you are being accurate about how much money you are making. Section 404 (say, isn't that the code for "file not found?") says that you have to have controls on your systems.

(A moment of thought for this "internal controls" business. If someone is going to lie about how much money they are making, what makes you think they won't lie about whether or not they are telling the truth?)

What a radically new idea! Have controls on our information systems! (Hmmmm, no, wait, I've heard the word "controls" used before. It had something to do with doing information security...) Anyway, it's a new idea to have it legislated, right? Well, not really. Way back in 1977, the Americans had this thing called the Foreign Corrupt Practices Act [9], which talked about the internal controls you had to have on your accounting books and systems. As a matter of fact, at about the same time the Committee of Sponsoring Organizations of the Treadway Commission created something called COSO (which stood for Committee of Sponsoring Organizations) that has been suggested as guidance for internal controls for doing information security. The banking industry even got into the game with the Basel II guidelines (which is kind of ironic in view of that Foreign Corrupt Practices business).

## Etc.

Is crimeware new? Of course not. Even phishing is just using the same kind of login trojan as has been around for as long as we've had login screens. The ever-so-modern cross-site-request-forgery (CSRF) is just a form of the man-in-the-middle attack that we've known about forever. Recently,

I saw someone use the term "time to protection," which is just another way of saying plain old "window of opportunity." Even endpoint security (or Network Access Control [NAC] or Data Leakage Protection [DLP]) isn't new: 20 years ago Sophos had something called D-Fence that implemented the concept (although in a simpler, and therefore more robust, way).

## Conclusion

Sorry, marketing guys. There are new ideas out there. But you have to go and find them. Not just dress up the same old ideas (that didn't work before) and give them a new name.

## About the Author

**Robert M. Slade**, CISSP, is a data communications and security specialist from North Vancouver, British Columbia, Canada.

## References

1. http://www.ns.umich.edu/htdocs/releases/story.php?id=6666
2. http://www.eecs.umich.edu/fjgroup/cloudav/
3. http://www.virustotal.com/
4. http://google-code-updates.blogspot.com/2008/12/native-client-technology-for-running.html
5. http://nativeclient.googlecode.com/svn/trunk/nacl/googleclient//native_client/documentation/nacl_paper.pdf
6. http://www.networkworld.com/news/2008/120608-fbi-criminals-auto-dialing-with-hacked.html
7. http://news.bbc.co.uk/go/em/-/2/hi/technology/7900463.stm
8. www.sec.gov/about/laws/soa2002.pdf
9. http://www.usdoj.gov/criminal/fraud/docs/statute.html

# OPERATIONS SECURITY

## Operations Controls

## Chapter 22

# A Brief Summary of Warfare and Commercial Entities

Rob Shein

## Contents

Throughout past history, civilian commercial entities have not been the primary targets of warfare and have even been avoided as targets. In the earliest days when such groups existed, they did not make feasible targets in and of themselves. Such organizations existed within the physical boundaries of nation-states, such that attacks upon them could only be conducted within the scope of much larger, comprehensive attacks upon the nation-states themselves, or the castles/cities in which they were located. The concept of weakening an enemy by focusing on causing economic impact exclusive of significant loss of life simply did not exist, and even if one were to focus military efforts on disruption of commercial activity, it inevitably involved a focus on killing civilians. In those days, the only means of warfare was kinetic warfare, using spears, swords, ballistic weapons, explosives, and so on. Non-kinetic warfare, also known as cyber warfare, was not an option as there simply was no digital infrastructure through or against which to leverage attacks.

Trade, both between and within nation-states and cities, was conducted using material goods, which in and of themselves were transported by people. As a result, the notion of warfare even for the specific purpose of halting or impeding such trade necessarily involved direct attacks on civilians. This fact remained in effect from the feudal era on until the late twentieth century, and as a result, by the time warfare (especially aerial warfare in general and bombing in particular) allowed for the capability to target commercial entities specifically, the Fourth Geneva Convention, provided some degree of protection. There have been exceptions to the degree with which nations have followed the Geneva Conventions, but these exceptions have tended to stand out as just that: exceptional events, accidents (such as a bomber crew targeting the wrong building through genuine human error), or the misbehavior of nation-states that were judged to be barbaric for their actions. Despite these outlying events, the general fact has been that nations have sought to target counterforce (military) targets and avoid damage to countervalue (civilian) targets. As kinetic warfare has evolved, this differentiation has only grown; the advent of precision-guided munitions has reduced the civilian death toll from bombing raids to numbers so low as to have been unimaginable during earlier conflict. Where once entire neighborhoods would be bombed in the course of attacks on a single building of military value, it is now considered a tragedy if a single civilian building is destroyed as a result of human error or incorrect information. In a sense, the protection of civilian industry was a beneficial side effect of the Geneva Conventions, given the fact that one could not deliberately attack a commercial enterprise without physically harming or killing its employees. Such organizations also experienced reduced risk from their geographic distance from theaters of warfare, and their attack surface was relatively small compared to that of the military itself. A shop owner need not fear the destruction of his business by a war that was fought thousands of miles away.

In the late twentieth century, this began to change. Now, as the methods, processes, and doctrine around cyber warfare have evolved, the above-described world has nearly reversed itself. Attacks using non-kinetic means are nonlethal in nature, and do not even incur physical harm; as such, the Fourth Geneva Conventions do not apply. Furthermore, while the IT infrastructure of the military is often sequestered (with varying success, admittedly) into enclaves, private industry is heavily interconnected with a great deal of exposure to the digital world and all of its inhabitants.

## Non-Kinetic Warfare and Civilian Exposure

There exists a larger problem with the evolution of non-kinetic warfare as a form of low-intensity conflict during peacetime. While non-kinetic warfare offers the potential for impact without loss of life, it also broadens the battlefield in a fashion that has not been seen since the advent of the airplane. Even worse, it has extended the theater of combat to organizations that have never before been responsible for defending themselves against nation-state aggressors. Most conflict on the globe is considered "low intensity," meaning that it takes the form of guerrilla warfare, insurgency, special operations, and other such means. Even current wars between the United States and its enemies in Iraq and Afghanistan may be considered this, from the perspective of its enemies, since they themselves do not engage in large military maneuvers on defined fronts. The days of two large armies amassing their forces to face off on a battlefield with clear battle lines are no more, except between two smaller powers in a regional conflict of only local interest.

What this means in broader terms is that the world's major powers have an incentive and model through which to conduct non-kinetic warfare against potential adversaries, even in peacetime. Between themselves, this category of nation-states typically participate in low-intensity conflict through clandestine operations and special warfare to avoid becoming enmeshed into full-fledged conflict, and the additional deniability that inevitably comes from information warfare makes cyber warfare an attractive means of conflict. Furthermore, the overwhelming military superiority of the United States—in terms of kinetic warfare—provides an equally overwhelming incentive for smaller nations to adopt cyber warfare for other reasons. Simply put, cyber warfare provides an economically cheap means of asymmetric warfare that is unlikely to incur a conventional military response from a much larger power.

## Differentiation between Nation-State and Cybercriminal Actors

There are several things about cyber warfare that differentiate it from hacking related to other motivations. Originally, hackers (or "vintage hackers," as they shall be described here) were people with extraordinary expertise and talent, but typically benevolent motivations. It was not uncommon for a hacker to notify the sysadmin of a compromised system as soon as a hack was successful, both informing them of the way they gained access and of how to prevent it in the future. The key motivation was a quest for knowledge and greater expertise, combined with a lack of a legitimate outlet for their skills. While their actions were unquestionably illegal, there nonetheless existed a consistent morality to these individuals, and they rarely caused the havoc they were capable of. Later came the time of the "script kiddie," once Internet access became commonplace, hacking tools became more widespread, and a far lesser degree of skill was needed to break into vulnerable systems. These individuals lacked the expertise or moral fiber found in their predecessors, typically defacing Web sites with profane messages just to gain bragging rights. Dealing with this group has been little more than a matter of implementing best practices for security, as the threat posed by them has proven to be particularly sophisticated. Most recently, criminal organizations have adopted hacking as a means toward generating revenue through extortion, embezzlement, or identity theft. This threat has been gaining in sophistication and scope, and still poses an evolving challenge to both individual people and private organizations.

A nation-state leveraging offensive cyber warfare with hostile intent, however, embodies the worst aspects of all three groups. The sophistication and expertise of the vintage hacker, the indiscriminate scope of the script kiddie, and the targeted hostile intent to maximize damage of the cybercriminal combine. In addition, cyber warfare units of military and intelligence organizations are furnished with unprecedented resources. The vintage hackers and script kiddies both did their work on a shoestring budget; while criminal organizations are better funded, they still have limited resources plus a significant need to avoid capture and prosecution. A nation-state's offensive cyber warfare assets, however, have plentiful resources and training, and no fear of criminal prosecution for their acts. They operate within save enclaves from which they have little fear of facing retribution for whatever they may do. The morality of their acts is typically limited to that of the government they serve; as two of the more sophisticated cyber warfare actors are North Korea and China, this is a chilling thought indeed.

## Addressing the Threat: Private Organizations on the Front Line

So, the question becomes this: what can be done about managing the risk imposed by these developments? Even the largest multinational private companies have never had more than a limited capability to address the challenges of warfare, even when operating in conflict regions. Smaller organizations are still grappling with the threat imposed by cybercrime and nuisance hacking, neither of which typically represents the same degree of threat posed by a motivated nation-state actor. In contrast to information about typical hacking elements, where information is plentiful and openly available, information about the true capability and intent of cyber warfare elements is typically classified and not available for public consumption. So, while financial organizations and entities that process large number of credit card transactions have been properly forewarned that they are being targeted by criminal organizations, for example, other industries may not be aware of the fact that they are being targeted by the operators of other countries for reasons not directly related to their core business.

Fortunately, while the motives and degree of sophistication possessed by attackers may vary, the nature of vulnerability does not. Technical vulnerability to one form of attack is the same regardless of whomever may seek to exploit it. The challenge is that a more sophisticated and determined actor will leverage vulnerabilities in combination to greater effect while more capably evading detection. Additionally, while major private organizations (like members of the Fortune 100) will likely themselves be targeted directly and subjected to the full brunt of an attack, smaller organizations need only be more secure than the norm to avoid significant attacks.

The governments of many nations are aware of this new form of risk that their citizenry now faces, and steps are being taken in an effort to manage the risk. The current Obama administration in the United States is making bold moves toward a national policy to improve the cybersecurity in the private sector, for example. How effective such measures will be has yet to be seen, as the organizations and individuals tasked with such things have historically been given few tools with which to affect any true measure of change. Even within civilian government, positions typically tasked with responsibility for cybersecurity on a broad scale have lacked any kind of budgetary control, therefore rendering them incapable of imposing or facilitating change.

## The Other Side of the Coin: Cyber Partisans

Despite the fact that many nation-states have invested significant resources into developing their offensive cyber warfare capabilities, to date most activities seem to have been carried out by sympathetic civilians, apparently with little more than tacit and indirect support from the nation on whose behalf they act. Examples of this include the coordinated attacks by Russian citizens (some not even located in Russia) on Estonia and Georgia in 2008. Chinese military doctrine allows for and welcomes this manner of leveraging civilian actors, and the People's Liberation Army has even carried out military cyber warfare exercises involving use of these units. This has tended to keep the impact of attacks limited, either in terms of duration or in terms of strategic impact, and denies the attackers the benefits of state-funded vulnerability research related to exotic technologies like Smart Grid/advanced metering infrastructure (AMI), embedded devices, or SCADA environments. An appropriate description of the potential role of such civilian hackers acting in support of a nation-state is of partisans. In the case of cyber warfare, they are able to act in the nation of their enemy, unlike partisans of the more traditional form in kinetic warfare who act as an insurgent resistance. Otherwise, the metaphor holds, as these "cyber partisans" strike at targets of opportunity from the digital woods to foment disorganization and chaos among those they consider to be the enemy.

This concept is not so new, in a manner. In 2001, after a Chinese fighter collided with a U.S. electronic surveillance plane off the coast of the Hainan Peninsula, a "hacker war" erupted between Chinese and United States–friendly hackers. In that day and age, the distributed denial-of-service attack was relatively new and infrequently employed; instead the method of choice was Web site defacement. Vulnerabilities still abounded among public Web servers, cybercrime had not come to fruition, and there was still great social value placed within the underground hacking community on bragging rights gained by defacing random Web sites. Ironically, in hindsight, it is considered likely that this conflict did not develop organically, but rather as the result of the questionable journalism of Michelle Delio, who authored a story in *Wired* magazine claiming that Chinese hackers were preparing to unleash attacks upon the United States in retaliation for American hegemony. Acting in response to the article, Western hackers attacked Chinese sites, and thus the "war" began. Later, Delio stated that the war was over... and as simply as that, the exchanges seemed to cease. (It is worth noting that Delio was later exposed as having manufactured information for a number of her articles, and is no longer used by *Wired* magazine as a contributor.) "Jericho" of the organization Attrition.org titled the whole affair with the phrase, "Wag the Delio," at a presentation given at the Black Hat Briefings. Other examples of mass Web site defacements in support of one national cause or another relate to Pakistani interests, the Palestinian–Israeli conflict, and curiously enough a mass dispute in South America over which country produces the best "pisco," which is a liquor distilled from grapes in both Peru and Chile. The same ease with which nation-states attack each other with cyber warfare also translates to irate private citizens with the desire to overreact on a global scale. It may well be that unlike traditional terrorists, such people have not endured more than annoyance by the general populace because there has yet to be any significant loss of life, or other reason to see them as more than a nuisance. As would be expected given the trivial basis for some of these exchanges, the true motivation is to inflict damage on information technology assets, with the nationalist motivation merely providing a thin veneer of legitimacy in the eyes of the attacker. Unfortunately, as cyber warfare increasingly becomes a tool of formal nation-states, the problems posed by such people will become more apparent.

One of the great challenges posed by the acts of such individuals is the difficulty they add to the task of attributing attacks to nation-state entities. When one cannot be sure that an attack is committed by a nation, or simply on behalf of that nation by sympathetic elements, it becomes difficult to wield the tools of international accountability. Even more troubling is that such people could conceivably trigger larger conflicts or adversely affect ongoing diplomatic negotiations between nations, since they cannot be assumed to recognize the true and full impact of their acts. Just as peace negotiations have often been disrupted or even halted by a single act of aggression using kinetic violence, so might similar discussions be threatened by an act of cyber warfare, particularly since the aggressors would be unlikely to claim responsibility for their acts. It is not difficult to imagine a regime that is trying to appease two different constituencies going to the negotiating table, but also fomenting such attacks so as to avoid alienating too many of its supporters; the mere possibility of such a thing in (for example) Pakistan would be enough to jeopardize talks with other nations should an independent group carry out such an attack on their own, even without even tacit approval from their own country.

Two recent examples highlight how tenuous the connection can be between the individual hackers and the countries on whose behalf they act. In the recent attack on Georgia by pro-Russian activists, one of the two coordinating Web sites behind the attacks (www.stopgeorgia.ru) was actually hosted by a small Russian company that, in turn, had leased its server from a London shell company which operated out of a mail drop; that company is owned by a Russian national living in the Netherlands which leased a server block from a major hosting and services firm in Texas. The participants of the forum themselves were from multiple nations, apparently joined by little more than Russian patriotism and the ability to wreak havoc with Georgian networks through the use of distributed denial-of-service attacks and vulnerability research. Finally, within these forums, there was a "journeyman-apprentice" approach, whereby the more experienced and capable hackers took on a leadership role, and subordinate tasks were meted out to less seasoned actors. In a situation like this, assigning responsibility, blame, or criminal liability is an obvious nightmare.

Another way in which such behavior clouds matters is where the actors for cybercrime and cyber warfare overlap. It follows that a populace that is highly represented with regard to criminal operations like the establishment and operation of botnets, illicit online activities, and cyber-based fraud will also serve just as well for cyber warfare. The problem that arises is in the motivation that some governments have in protecting such enterprises to some degree, so as to maintain a capability for later use should the need arise.

## Regulatory Efforts to Defend Critical Infrastructure

There is one way in which government agencies and industry coalitions can affect change to cybersecurity in the private sector. Regulatory standards related to security can be developed and implemented as a driver toward greater security. In many cases, the standards act mostly to create a driver for funding and support of cybersecurity within organizations; in other cases, they provide guidance as to best practices and requirements to get to a more secure state. There have been few regulatory standards yet that have much direct relevance to the threat posed by cyber warfare, but one such set of standards is put forth by the North American Electricity Reliability Corporation (NERC). A particular subset of the NERC standards, known as NERC Critical Infrastructure Protection (or "NERC CIP," as the standards are known), focus on information security for critical assets related to the generation, management, and transmission of electricity in North America.

NERC CIP is comprised of nine standards, CIP-001 through CIP-009. CIP-001 is rarely discussed, as it merely describes the need for a process whereby sabotage is reported to the appropriate entity within the Department of Energy. But CIP-002 through CIP-009 cover the gamut of information security practices, from user security awareness training and personnel security to backup procedures. Currently in its first iteration, NERC CIP is currently succinct and lacking in specific details or guidance on many topics. A new iteration is currently in development, which is expected to reflect a radical shift in methodology toward a framework based around NIST standard 800–53. In addition, the scope of NERC's requirements is expanding to include additional forms of power generation and transmission assets.

## Information Warfare Doctrine: The View of Data as Both Sword and Castle

The concept of attacking cyber infrastructure using logical attacks is not difficult to grasp, but simply performing such attacks for their own sake fails to elevate one's effect (or relevance) above that of the chaos-inducing cyber partisans discussed earlier. The true benefit of any form of warfare lies in its integration with other forms. This is an already established doctrine in terms of kinetic warfare doctrine, whereby troops on the ground move after aerial attacks have severely damaged enemy emplacements, which in turn were first observed using various reconnaissance and intelligence-gathering methods. While attacking, the troops have the ability to call upon artillery strikes, close air support, or armor to support their mission. This is known as "combined warfare," and is the norm on today's battlefield. But what happens when the concept of information... both as a weapon and as an objective to be attacked or captured...comes into play? The Chinese People's Liberation Army (PLA) has been a pioneer in thought around this question, and while their doctrine is still evolving they are remarkably open in their thinking, at least to those who can read Mandarin.

There exist two primary objectives that compete for primacy in the context of information warfare. One is the control of information, either in the sense of gaining access to it or denying access to it. The other is influence over that information. The two concepts may sound vague and unrelated to warfare until one considers the way in which they can be applied. For example, denying access to information could take on the form of using logical attacks to cause an air defense system's radar to lie; if the enemy cannot perceive the intrusion into its airspace of an invading force, that becomes a remarkable tactical advantage to the invader as it would provide obscurity about the scale and composition of the attack while maintaining total surprise until the last possible minute. If the same effect were to be sought using kinetic warfare (i.e., bombing the radar installations) then the element of surprise would be lost, and the only benefit would be denial of information about how the attack was progressing at the early stages. To apply the alternate objective (influence over information) would be to cause the radar systems to false positive at times, showing things that are not there. Eventually, the information produced by the radar systems would be considered so unreliable as to be nearly worthless, thus degrading the quality of decisions made based upon that data. This seems like the lesser of the two approaches until one recognizes that it is far easier to make fake objects show up on a screen than it is to selectively hide the ones that you wish to keep hidden.

Most notable is that even formal Chinese information warfare doctrine does not distinguish between countervalue and counterforce targets in terms of escalation. It is not considered a more aggressive act to attack a bank or other civilian target (countervalue) than it would be to restrict the scope of an attack to military targets (counterforce), for example. In fact, the result of this aspect of doctrine tends to favor attacks against private organizations for the numerous reasons listed earlier. Furthermore, this reality has been acknowledged by leading members of the Chinese cyber warfare community on many occasions.

# The Evolution of Technology and Impact on Vulnerability to Cyber Warfare

As a result of recent spikes in the price of petroleum products, attention focused on energy conservation. Fortunately, a number of technologies have recently come into maturity to address such a need, and as a result new phrases have started appearing in the vocabulary of the news: "Smart Grid," "AMI," "Smart Metering," "Demand Response," and so on. These refer to a set of enabling technologies, which provide the ability to do things that were never before possible with the power grid:

> AMI: Uses "smart meters" that monitor electrical usage at individual homes in 15 min increments (instead of the 3 month increments that are the current norm) and throttle power consumption by noncritical devices like air conditioners and dishwashers in response to spikes in demand (or unforeseen drops in power generation). These communicate back to the central power utility company via wireless protocols of various forms, and communicate with devices inside the home using protocols like ZigBee.

These meters have a feature called "remote disconnect," which permits a utility to toggle power delivery to a home or office with a command sent to the meter, saving cost and time needed to handle disconnects and reconnects. This feature also facilitates services like payment in advance for power, much like a prepaid cell phone; when the balance runs low, the household is alerted so that they may top off their balance with more funds.

Smart Grid: Refers to a set of technologies that provide additional control capability to the power grid using devices like "reclosers" (which can remotely force tripped power connections to be reestablished) and capacitors. By leveraging the information gleaned from AMI, Smart Grid allows routing of power around downed lines and better management of the power generated by uncertain sources of generation (like windmills), among other things.

There are obvious security ramifications to replacing current power meters (which are mechanical in design) with computerized systems that have the ability to turn appliances off while they report back wirelessly to a power company. These implications have also been covered by the media, including one story where a vulnerability in key management for a specific brand of AMI meter was discovered. Unfortunately, there is more hype than truth to the discussion of these vulnerabilities at the moment. Even more unfortunate is that sooner or later, significant vulnerabilities will likely be uncovered. Either way, this expansion of information technology into a realm of infrastructure provides new opportunities for attackers to wreak havoc from afar. By gaining access to the "head end" system of an AMI infrastructure, which accepts data from and sends commands to the meters, it would be possible to trigger a mass disconnect of tens or even hundreds of thousands of meters simultaneously. Such an event is called a "mass load-shedding event," and would cause an outage similar in both nature and scale to the power outage suffered in the Northeastern United States in 2003.

The good news is that the potential for abuse of these technologies has not gone unnoticed. A number of organizations have sprung up to address security with Smart Grid and AMI solutions, and the offerings put forth by some vendors are also quite promising. Standards around communications and data security, a taxonomy for defining security domains within AMI infrastructure, and a vibrant working group dedicated to the discussion of security requirements all exist and are proving to be viable in addressing the risk. The power grid will remain a target of interest to hostile actors, and successful breaches have occurred outside the United States, but the picture is not nearly as gloomy as it could be, and it is getting better as time passes.

# Addressing the Threat

While single private organizations have few options against a determined cyber warfare attacker (above and beyond proper information security practices), as stated earlier it will be uncommon for a foreign actor to be focused specifically on any single company in particular. Instead it ends up being more like the joke about two men running from a bear, where the punch line states "I only need to outrun you." There is a great deal of protection afforded the fact that nation-states rarely take such bold action unless there is a specific and deliberate reason, and globalization greatly narrows the potential number of reasons to attack a corporation or civilian organization of any significant size (while smaller ones are quite unlikely to pose much interest to foreign nations at all). And while the behavior of cyber partisans is not so measured and restrained, they are largely not of great impact unless they band together and work in concert.

Which brings the threat to three different forms. One, an organization that is smaller, relatively immature in information security measures, and thus useful as a stepping stone in attacks on other organizations. The second is of organizations that, for some reason, have gained the attentions of groups with nationalist, environmental, or other motivators. The third contains organizations which themselves are tightly linked to national drivers and infrastructure. Examples of this third group include defense contractors, financial institutions, and public utilities.

## Cyber Warfare as a Threat to Small/Medium Civilian Organizations and Individuals

Within the first group, as stated above, the primary goal of an attacker would be merely to gain a foothold in their infrastructure for the facilitation of attacks on other organizations. This tactic is nothing new, and a more granular form of it takes place even within well-secured larger organizations. Incident response teams have noticed that many attackers choose to take control of relatively unimportant IT assets, and remain dormant until the time comes to exploit the control they already have. This takes place only when there is sufficient cause for them to reveal the penetration and tip their hand. The same can and does happen on a national scale, where smaller, less-defended environments are used for the staging of attacks against more vigilant targets; this allows for some degree of obfuscation regarding the source of the attack, and adds flexibility should the intended final target notice an attack and start blocking the networks from which it originates. Thus, in a time of open, no-holds-barred cyber warfare between any two factions, this segment of the population would be more heavily hit than normal, both in terms of the number of attacks and the effect of already-compromised machines being more heavily leveraged to perform attacks.

## Cyber Warfare as a Targeted Threat for Non-State Causes

The second group involves a greater risk of facing a determined attacker, but still lacks the risk inherent in a coherent, well-coordinated attack by a large or well-supported group. Still, an attacker who is bound and determined to bring harm to or gain entry to a target is far more dangerous than one who is merely looking for a target of opportunity. These organizations will tend to be larger, and thus better protected, but not themselves useful targets for cyber warfare. In the event of greater conflict between nations, however, the equation changes for organizations within this group. The largest of multinational corporations are themselves tightly bound to foreign nations with significant cyber warfare capabilities for outsourcing and manufacturing; this almost provides a kind of hostage situation whereby an attack upon them would inevitably (and quickly) incur harm upon the attacking nation. Companies from Accenture to General Electric to General Motors all rely heavily upon their operations in other nations. This, combined with the ways in which our economies interact, would not only serve to cause any harm to be shared by both the attacker and the target, but in some cases would actually cause far greater harm to the attacker's economy. In the recent worldwide downturn, it has become apparent just how slim a margin the economic powers of Asia have been maintaining in their fight to compete globally; once things slipped backward even a small amount, that margin was eliminated and disaster ensued on a regional scale. The same event would be triggered by a successful and devastating attack on a large multinational corporation by China, for example, except in this case only China would suffer the impact, and the other countries in the region (particularly Taiwan) would actually benefit, as they would pick up the slack. The phrase, "Globalization stops wars," is at least as true with cyber warfare as it is with kinetic warfare. For those few nations who possess a significant cyber warfare capacity but lack significant economic ties to the rest of the world (the best example of this is North Korea), their lack of economic ties is accompanied by both a lack of large-scale connectivity to the rest of the world and a lack of large groups of motivated actors in other countries. As a result, an attack by such a nation would be easily stopped merely by severing the links between that nation and the rest of the Internet.

## Cyber Warfare as a Threat to Organizations of Interest to Nation-State Actors

This final group has the most to fear from cyber warfare, given that they comprise organizations that would be specifically targeted by the disciplined, well-resourced actors of nation-state entities. Fortunately, these are also typically organizations that have had to face a significant and sophisticated threat model to begin with for other reasons (e.g., the same financial organizations that would be attacked by another nation for countervalue economic impact tend to have a lot of money, and have always been targeted for purposes of theft and fraud) and, therefore, have highly evolved defensive capabilities. In addition, this segment of the population holds the fewest members, has the highest level of collaboration with officials in the intelligence and defense sectors, and is likely to get the quickest and most effective response from government agencies in the event of an attack. In some situations (particularly organizations that have some degree of overlap with the defense industry) attacks on this segment of the population would fall under the definition of counterforce attacks. In even rarer cases, these organizations are already adept at defensive cyber warfare operations, since they already provide services to the military and government in that capacity. So, while the potential threat to this group is the greatest, they are also far better prepared than any other component of private industry.

# Fear vs. Reality: Cyber Warfare in the Press and in Reality

On a final closing note, it is wise to discuss the differential between what is likely to occur and what some reports in the popular media envision in terms of cyber warfare and how it would be conducted. Some of the visions come from books or film, and, therefore, cannot be seriously faulted; after all, these are venues of entertainment, not education. But news media tends to follow similar plotlines in their conceptualization of cyber warfare, to the detriment of popular perception and, eventually, efforts to prepare for the future. So this chapter will close with a bit of debunking.

The first basic rule of cyber warfare is this: cyber warfare rarely causes new things to occur. What instead is more probable is that an attack, at most, could cause something minor that happens occasionally to happen a great deal at once, either in terms of scale or in terms of frequency. The challenge there is that since these are things that can happen for other reasons, there are usually already ways to prevent them or mitigate their impact. The classic example of this concept is the "green lights in all directions" idea. This has both shown up in popular film and in the dire warnings of "experts" on the topic of cyber warfare. The idea is that as more cities integrate networks over their municipal operations, including stoplights and traffic management systems, a hacker could take control of the network and cause traffic lights to show a green signal in all directions at once, causing car crashes. The truth of the matter is that many things have been proven to cause a traffic signal to attempt to do this, like corrosion, rodent infestation, human error in installation, electrical failure, and so on. As a result, the circuitry of these traffic light controllers is designed with an inherent failsafe. Should the controller attempt to display a pattern that would be considered dangerous (like all green lights in all directions), it fails into a failsafe mode, with blinking yellow or red lights in all directions. Anyone with significant driving experience has seen this phenomenon. Getting control of the signal controller via the Internet will not override this circuitry; it is inherent to the wiring of the signal itself, to make it as reliable a failsafe as possible.

Another fallacy pertains to the production of food. One example was the warning that hackers could take control of the machines involved in the production of children's cereal and increase the amount of iron being put into the food until it would be toxic. This also fails as a threat when one considers the real-world situation, and how such an event would actually play out. For one thing, the additive in food used to provide supplemental iron (iron sulfate) is used in trace amounts normally; to poison someone with it, the amount would have to be increased by multiple orders of magnitude. Consider also the fact that iron sulfate is dark green in color. The cereal would have a rather peculiar appearance, which I doubt would go unnoticed by people working at the production facility, much less the child presented with a bowl full of the stuff. Even more interesting is the odor and flavor of iron sulfate, which is not in the least bit appetizing. Getting a child to eat a bowl full of cereal laced with enough of it to harm him would only be possible in a household so draconian that the child would probably be tough enough to eat barbed wire and still survive the experience in the first place. And finally, it would not go without notice that the mixing machines would be going through iron sulfate at an unprecedented rate, requiring refills thousands of times more often than normal. So again, when one considers the operational world in which this attack would need to be successful, one can see that it would have very limited chances of success on any level, for a wide number of reasons.

Another fabled attack that is coming to the forefront in the news is the notion that attackers could take the entire Internet off-line. Oddly enough, this one has more truth to it than fiction, in that such a thing is conceivable. Testifying before the United States Senate in 1999, "Mudge" of the group L0pht stated that he could take the Internet down within approximately 30 min. This was later borne out to be entirely plausible, as 4 years later a series of vulnerabilities in a protocol called BGP (Border Gateway Protocol) were revealed. There were earlier indications of these flaws, going back to that same year when a person known as "Batz" (who was a friend of Mudge) gave a talk on "Security Issues Affecting Internet Transit Points and Backbone Providers," during which he detailed how attacks using BGP could result in the rerouting or even denial of traffic routing between major components of the Internet. An analogy would be the global destruction of all points of travel across bodies of water, mountains, desert, or other impassable terrain.

The problem with this scenario was detailed by Mudge in the sentence that followed the proclamation that hackers could demolish the Internet so quickly. He posed the simple question of asking why they would do such a thing, and sever the links to rich sources of information instead of exploiting them. And this point still holds true today. While most of the issues surrounding BGP have been addressed, there are probably other issues waiting to be found. But for a cyber warrior to "take down" the Internet makes little sense; it would be like an invading army blowing up a bridge that still lay before them.

In some cases, for brute force reasons (such as the attacks on Estonia and Georgia by hackers sympathetic to Russian causes), a limited version of this may be performed against a single nation, but for larger countries with significant connectivity to other parts of the world, such a thing is not feasible without causing numerous effects to friendly networks. The amount of traffic needed to perform a denial-of-service attack against the entire United States, for example, would cause backscatter traffic that would more than overwhelm the rest of the Internet, including the networks of the attacking country. Furthermore, the earlier-described economic interdependence of nations provides a strong disincentive to perform this kind of attack at all. And above all else, the cyber warfare doctrines of all companies with sufficiently advanced capabilities to perform such an attack would instead dictate that they exploit access to resources, rather than cut off the ability to continue to do so.

## About the Author

**Rob Shein** is a cyber security architect for HP's Security and Privacy Professional Services division, where he provides security consulting to a wide range of clients in the private and public sector.

# Chapter 23

# Information Destruction Requirements and Techniques

Ben Rothke

## Contents

The inability to discard worthless items even though they appear to have no value is known as compulsive hoarding syndrome. If the eccentric Collyer brothers had a better understanding of destruction practices, they likely would not have been killed by the very documents and newspapers they obsessively collected.

While most organizations do not hoard junk and newspapers like Homer and Langley Collyer did, they do need to keep information such as employee personnel records, financial statements, contracts and leases, and more. Given the vast amount of paper and digital media that amasses over time, effective information destruction policies and practices are now a necessary part of doing business and will likely save organizations time, effort and heartache, legal costs, as well as embarrassment and more.

In December 2007, the Federal Trade Commission (FTC) announced a $50,000 settlement with American Mortgage Company of Northbrook, Illinois, over charges the company violated the FTC's disposal, safeguards, and privacy rules by failing to properly dispose of documents containing consumers' credit and personally identifiable information. In announcing the settlement, the FTC put all companies on notice that it is taking such failures seriously.

A $50,000 settlement might seem low when measured against the potential for financial harm to individuals as a result of the company's negligence, but in addition to the negative PR for

American Mortgage, the settlement includes an obligation to obtain an audit, every 2 years for the next 10 years, from a qualified, independent, third-party professional to ensure that its security program meets the standards of the order. Any similar failures by this company during the next decade will be met with more severe punishment. That, indeed, is a very costly lesson.

In today's litigious environment, there are a plethora of aggressive lawyers that would love to devour your organization for failure to take due care around document and media destruction.

This chapter looks at the key areas to ensure that your organization does not fall prey to such lawyers when it comes to the physical destruction of documents and records.

## Every Organization Has Data That Needs to Be Destroyed

Besides taxes, what unites every business is that they possess highly sensitive information that should not be seen by unauthorized persons. While some documents can be destroyed minutes after printing, regulations may require others to be archived from a few years to permanently.* But between these two ends of the scale, your organization can potentially have a large volume of hard copy data occupying space as a liability, both from a legal and information security perspective.

Depending on how long you have been in business, the number of physical sites and the number of people you employ, it is possible to have hundreds of thousands, if not millions, of pages of hard copy stored throughout your company—much of which is confidential data that can be destroyed.

The National Association of Corporate Directors provides some excellent guidelines in their Record Retention and Document Destruction Policy. From trademark registrations, safety records, to retirement and pension records and much more, there is a lot that needs to be retained. But once that retention period is over, much of those documents can be destroyed. Below is a partial list[†] of the types of information that absolutely should be shredded when no longer needed:

| Account Records | Activity Sheets | Advertising | Applications |
|---|---|---|---|
| Appraisals | Bank statements | Bids and quotes | Budgets |
| Business plans | Canceled checks | Client lists | Contact lists |
| Corporate tax records | Correspondence | Customer records | Disciplinary reports |
| Educational reports | Expense reports | Financial statements | Forecasts |
| Formulas, product plans, and tests | General service information | Health and safety reports | Internal reports |
| Legal documents | Lottery tickets | Magnetic media | Maps and blueprints |
| Marketing plans | Medical records | Microfilm/microfiche | New product information |
| Payroll documents | Performance appraisals | Personnel files | Plastic credit and ID cards |

---

* Some basic records retention schedules can be found at http://www.shredquick.com/pdfs/Records_Retention_Schedule.pdf
† From http://www.shredquick.com/whatshred.asp

**(continued)**

| Account Records | Activity Sheets | Advertising | Applications |
|---|---|---|---|
| R&D reports | Sales forecasts | Specification drawings | Strategic reports |
| Strategies | Supplier PO's | Supplier reports | Supplier specifications |
| Test scores/class rosters | Training information | Treatment programs | Encryption key management information |

Besides the regulatory and ethical issues around keeping those hard copies secure, the reality is that many of your competitors would love to get their hands on the documents that you are throwing out. And even if your competitors are not combing through your dumpsters, others may do so and attempt to sell your secrets to your competitors.

For those who think that dumpster diving is a security threat of the past, check out Steve Hunt's fascinating video Scoring big in corporate dumpster diving. He recently did a dumpster dive in Chicago and found confidential wire transfer information, a laptop, and others treasures in the dumpster. His adventure took all of 3 min and he astutely advises companies to do their own dumpster diving tests.

In addition, the current recession means that organizations may have to deal with disgruntled and angry employees as well as those who think their job or company will soon be eliminated. With that, the risk of misuse of sensitive information is even greater.

Simply put, effective document destruction practices prevent information from falling into the wrong hands. Perhaps the most pervasive example of this is credit card charge receipts, which are retrieved from trash bins by dumpster divers often with the intent of using the information for online or telephone orders. Many businesses discard such payment information without effective destruction controls. If such controls are not used, the information unearthed from the post-fraud investigation could be extremely embarrassing to explain to customers, and it could also turn into a PR nightmare or an expensive legal problem.

## Just Trash It All: The Enron Approach

Once made aware of the need, many organizations take a knee jerk reaction by gathering all stored hard copies and simply disposing of them. But that does not solve the problem for a number of reasons.

First, there are legal and regulatory requirements that mandate that paper documents be retained for specific periods of time. Additionally, throwing things directly into the dumpster exposes companies to dumpster divers. As detailed above, dumpsters can be a great source of information.

There is another reason why the trashing of daily records without appropriate destruction is dangerous. If you simply throw out trash and it gets into your competitors' hands, they can easily correlate and learn about your business activities.

By way of example, SIM software can take seemingly disparate log items and correlate them into an active attack; so too with your trash. Your daily activities are similarly manifest in your trash. From daily activities, phone records, travel plans, RFP submissions, memos, and much more, your business can be exposed if this information is not properly destroyed.

If Enron is the poster child for inappropriate document destruction, those organizations seeking to do document destruction precisely should consider obtaining the Media Disposal Toolkit from Network Frontiers. The toolkit contains everything an organization needs to know about data disposal. It includes a spreadsheet of unified common controls, work breakdown structure with processes and procedures, and a data deletion management documentation on the policies and standards that organizations must adhere to in order to be in compliance with global regulatory mandates.

## Regulatory Issues

Various regulations must be taken into consideration also. For example, Sarbanes–Oxley (SOX) addresses the destruction of business records and documents and turns intentional document destruction into a process that must be carefully monitored. If the process is not followed, executives can find themselves under indictment. Having formally documented data retention, policies are a requirement.

SOX raises the legal stakes for destruction of corporate documents and includes numerous provisions that create and enhance criminal penalties for corporate fraud and obstruction of justice. SOX section 1102 makes it a crime, punishable by fine and imprisonment for up to 20 years, to corruptly alter, destroy, mutilate or conceal a record, document, or other object with the intent to impair the object's integrity or availability or use in an official proceeding or to obstruct or impede an official proceeding. SOX section 802 states that "whoever knowingly alters, destroys, mutilates, conceals, covers up, falsifies, or makes a false entry in any record, document, or tangible object with intent to impede, obstruct, or influence the investigation or proper administration of any matter within the jurisdiction of any department or agency of the United States... or in relation to or contemplation of any such matter or case, shall be fined under this title, imprisoned not more than 20 years, or both."

Another relevant regulation around disposal is the Fair and Accurate Credit Transactions Act of 2003 (FACTA). Enacted in June 2005 requires businesses and individuals to take appropriate measures to dispose of sensitive information derived from consumer reports. Any business or individual who uses a consumer report for a business purpose is subject to the requirements of the Disposal Rule, a part of FACTA that calls for the proper disposal of information in consumer reports and records to protect against *unauthorized access to or use of the information.*

The rule applies to people and both large and small organizations that use consumer reports, including consumer reporting companies, lenders, insurers; employers; landlords; government agencies; mortgage brokers, car dealers; attorneys; private investigators; debt collectors; individuals who pull consumer reports on prospective home employees, such as nannies or contractors; and entities that maintain information in consumer reports as part of their role as a service provider to other organizations covered by the rule.

A benefit of having a formal document destruction process and using product such as the Media Disposal Toolkit is that since you are doing document destruction properly, your organization does not have to worry about every new regulation, as such practices are likely compliant with whatever new regulation comes out.

## *Hard Copies Should Be Destroyed on a Formal and Regular Basis*

Imagine you are the manager of a large medical practice, which is being sued after 10,000 pages of medical records found their way into the hands of an investigative reporter or thief. When asked by the plaintiff's lawyer how you get rid of hard copies, an answer such as "Lenny the computer guy does it whenever he can" is akin to pleading guilty. In contrast, "We have an outside bonded, National Association of Information Destruction (NAID) certified company empty our security containers and shred the contents on a weekly basis" will likely shield you from significant liability.

The issue also is not necessarily how often the data is destroyed; rather, whether it is done on a formal basis, based on risk factors specific to the organization. As part of effective oversight, a formal system of information destruction must be created and implemented. If data destruction is indeed performed in a formal, documented manner, and your destruction schedule is done on a scheduled basis, the plaintiff's lawyers will have much less to use, which could likely be judged positively by a jury.

Two good examples of formalized procedures are the confidential document handling procedures from Purdue University and the Iowa State University document destruction operating plan. A Google search will give you many more, which you can use as a base for your program.

One of the most important aspects of a formal plan for information destruction is *consistency*. If an organization is inconsistent in what it destroys, this shows a lack of due diligence, in addition to the appearance of attempting to hide something.

As part of this formal process, realize also that there are many elements to data destruction that must be built into the process. One of them is the concept of a *data destruction moratorium*. The reason for this is that there are times when an organization must *stop* its data destruction activities. If a legal discovery request is received, policies must be in place to ensure that all organized and periodic data destruction activities must immediately be placed on hold until the Legal Department determines whether these destruction activities jeopardize sought-after data.

As to a formal process, there was a company that used a goat as their document shredder. While perhaps effective from a shredding perspective, it is clearly not a best practice approach, nor is it likely their lawyers signed off on that method. A goat eating away at paper is fine for the farside, but has no place in a formal document disposal process.

## *Security Containers*

As the need for information destruction has caught on, the ubiquitous security containers from companies such as Shred-it are found in many organizations. It is a good idea to have such containers readily available so staff can easily dispose of information that is no longer needed.

Containers generally come in three sizes:

- *Executive consoles*: Generally used in high-profile environments. They have front loading which frees up the top space for office equipment and the doors swing open for easy removal and can be keyed alike. Approximate measurements are 40″ × 19″ × 19″.
- *Large containers*: Ninety six gallon security containers are used for heavy document production centers, purging sites, warehouses and high-traffic offices are especially popular for overflow conditions. Approximate measurements are 43″ × 24″ × 37″. They have the capacity to hold up to 15 boxes of paper.

■ *Bulk containers*: Used for larger production centers, areas that generate large quantities of confidential data and some e-scrap material. Approximate measurements are 38″ × 43″ × 29″ and can accommodate up to 650 + lbs of material.

As part of a security awareness program, make sure that employees are trained in the proper disposal and destruction of sensitive materials. You want to make sure that employees place papers in these designated locked destruction containers and *not* in trash bins, recycle bins, or other publicly accessible locations. Also, make sure that they do not place materials that do not need to be shredded in these bins. Since many destruction companies charge by the bin or pound, placing documents in these bins that do not need to be shredded is a waste of money.

Some organizations use these secure information containers only for sensitive, but not highly confidential or secret information. Some organizations have polices that require highly confidential or secret information, because it is so sensitive, to be immediately destroyed. This lessens the risk that someone could break into a locked destruction container, or even steal the whole container and then break into it at another location.

## In-House or Outsource

Document destruction, like other services, can be done in-house or outsourced. Which is the best way to go? Like every decision, the correct answer is the proverbial—*it depends*.

There are two predominant types of shredding services available: plant-based (off-site) and mobile (on-site).

■ *Mobile-based shredding*: Mobile shredders have the actual shredders on the truck itself. Mobile shredding companies provide bins or consoles for their customers and on scheduled days, the truck arrives at the place of business and the customer service representative (CSR) collects the bins, or console bags, takes them to the truck, and shreds the material on the customer's premises. After completion, the CSR will typically leave a certificate of destruction. Since the shredding operation is done on the customer's property, it is assumed to be more secure since nothing leaves unshredded. Often the customer will board the truck to ensure their sensitive material is indeed being destroyed.

■ *Plant-based shredding*: This is a typical off-site service where the plant has large industrial shredders. On the scheduled day, the CSR collects the bins or console bags, places them in his secure truck, and transports them back to the remote plant where the bins are unloaded into a secured area. The collected bins are later staged for shredding, which can occur days later. Some view this as an insecure method since the documents may be left unattended. One other major caveat is that plant-based shredders may sort the material to maximize its recycling value which can put your organization at risk. Some of these off-site shredding companies are simply glorified recycling companies that get top dollar for recycling paper, *your paper*. Since their staff will sort the documents, they have the opportunity to take them. So before you choose a plant-based service, make sure you investigate them accordingly.

When dealing with an outsourcer, ensure that they are NAID certified. NAID is an independent organization that certifies destruction companies. Its certification program checks a shredding company's compliance in 22 critical areas, including everything from shred size to employee background checks. When it comes to something as critical as information destruction—caveat emptor.

Unscrupulous shredding companies will claim to be NAID certified just to get your business. Make sure to ask for a copy of their NAID Certified certificate as proof of their standing.

So what *it depends* gives you the right solution? There are potential security issues with both solutions. Mobile shredding is done with the CSR alone there and since the CSR is alone on the truck, they may have access to your confidential material.

With a plant-based approach, various plant employees have access to the material during the sort process. A paper sorter could conceal a sensitive document on his person and leave the property with it.

The bottom line is that either solution requires an amount of trust, but the final decision must be customer-based on what they feel the most secure solution is. This decision, like most, is a trade-off between the level of security and cost.

A third solution is to do it yourself. While this may seem cheaper in the short term, it can often be more expensive. And if you do it internally, there must be policies and procedures to ensure that destruction of sensitive information must be performed only with approved destruction methods including shredders or other equipment approved by the information security department.

Irrespective if you use a mobile-based shredding or a plant-based shredding service, ensure that the service provider is NAID certified and that all documents are secured until they are destroyed. A good service level agreement (SLA) is to make sure documents are completely destroyed within 24 h and a certificate of destruction is provided upon completion of this process.

## Conclusions

It is clear that document destruction in today's world must be part of a good system of business processes.

But the bottom line is that if your organization is not careful about what they do not dispose of, it could become your competitors' good fortune and your worst corporate nightmare.

## About the Author

**Ben Rothke**, CISSP, CISM, PCI QSA, is a New York City–based senior security consultant with BT INS, Santa Clara, California.

# BUSINESS CONTINUITY PLANNING AND DISASTER RECOVERY PLANNING

## *Business Continuity Planning*

# Chapter 24

# Integrated Business Continuity Planning

James C. Murphy

## Contents

This chapter is written for information security professionals charged with creating or improving the existing business continuity plan (BCP) within his or her organization. This chapter assumes that such professionals have a general working knowledge of the information security common body of knowledge, and yet may need a supplementary document detailing the general concepts. The emphasis within the chapter is less on what are the components of the BCP and the specific organizational task forces or committees, but on how to accomplish the necessary preparations and tasks.

Business continuity management (BCM) planning is a body of knowledge that does not lack for resources. Table 24.1 is only a sampling of available documentation and plans that are available (albeit obtaining many of the standards documents require a fee). The list in this table is intended only as a short beginning; dozens of other sources and sets of documentation are available. Though there are many organizations contributing to the professionalism of BCM planning, two have great history and presence, the Disaster Recovery Institute International (DRII) and the British Continuity Institution (BCI). Both have robust certification programs and have contributed sets

**Table 24.1    Selected Business Continuity Management Resources**

| |
|---|
| **Organizations** |
| Business Continuity Institute, http://www.thebci.org/ |
| Disaster Recovery Institute International, https://www.drii.org/ |
| **Government plans** |
| National Incident Management System, 2008, http://www.fema.gov/pdf/emergency/nims/NIMS_core.pdf |
| National Response Framework, 2008, http://www.fema.gov/pdf/emergency/nrf/nrf-core.pdf |
| The National Strategy for Pandemic Influenza Implementation Plan, 2006, http://pandemicflu.gov/plan/federal/pandemic-influenza-implementation.pdf |
| National Infrastructure Protection Plan, 2009, http://www.dhs.gov/xlibrary/assets/NIPP_Plan.pdf |
| Treasury Board of Canada Secretariat, Operational Security Standard, Business Continuity Planning (BCP) Program, http://www.tbs-sct.gc.ca/pol/doc-eng.aspx?id=12324 |
| Public Safety Canada, Emergency management, http://www.publicsafety.gc.ca/prg/em/index-eng.aspx |
| **International standards** |
| DRII—Professional Practices for Business Continuity Planners, https://www.drii.org/professionalprac/index.php |
| BCI—General Practice Guidelines, http://www.thebci.org/gpg.htm |
| NIST SP 800-100, *Information Security Handbook: A Guide for Managers*, 2006, NIST SP 800-34, Contingency Planning Guide for Information Technology Systems, 2002, http://csrc.nist.gov/publications/PubsSPs.html |
| ASIS International—Organizational Resilience: Preparedness and Continuity Management Best Practices Standard, http://www.abdi-secure-ecommerce.com/asis/ps-907-37-1842.aspx |
| National Fire Protection Association 1600: Standard on Disaster/Emergency Management and Business Continuity Programs, 2007, http://www.nfpa.org/aboutthecodes/AboutTheCodes.asp?DocNum=1600 |
| BS 25999-1:2006: Business continuity management, Part 1: Code of practice, BS 25999-2:2007: Business continuity management, Part 2: Specification, http://www.pas56.com/index.htm |
| Standards Australia—*HB 221:2004*, Business Continuity Management, *HB 292-2006*, A practitioners guide to business continuity management, http://www.saiglobal.com/shop/script/PortalBusiness.asp |
| Canada Standards Association Z1600, Emergency management and business continuity programs, http://www.shopcsa.ca/onlinestore/GetCatalogDrillDown.asp?Parent=4773 |
| Singapore: Technical Reference 19: 2005: Business Continuity Management, http://psbcorp.com/BCM2007.aspx |

of practices and guidelines that have become de facto industry standards. The U.S. government, through the Department of Homeland Security (DHS) has established a set of national plans and a framework that has great potential for offering a controlled regional response to crises of all kinds. The Canadian government also has a similar set of plans and structures. Several standards are available for use, and more are underway.

In July of 2008, the U.S. DHS made an agreement with ANSI-ASQ National Accreditation Board (ANAB) to implement certification requirements for the private sector. This was based on Title IX of Public Law 110-53 *Implementing the Recommendations of the 9/11 Commission Act of 2007* (http://www.fema.gov/news/newsrelease.fema?id=45280). The ultimate result will be an accreditation and certification program for U.S. private sector organizations. Based on that, ASIS International and the British Standards Institution announced plans for developing an American BCM Standard. The first meeting for drafting the plan was held in January, 2009, in Alexandria, VA (http://www. asisonline.org/guidelines/guidelines.htm), and the draft is under development and review.*

Standards are foundational for a security professional to develop a framework for the BCM framework. Appropriate compliance will offer assurance to the organizational stakeholders (and stockholders) that the framework will meet industry-wide expectations for safety, security, and prompt attention to organizational process restoration. In attempts to address an extensive range of issues and conditions, standards offer an idealized approach to BCM planning, and often business professionals will assume that a selected standard document actually depicts a single, comprehensive plan that can be introduced, established, and implemented as a single organizational effort. Unfortunately, those engaged in this process may assume the need to start from scratch with the selected standard, building a set of plans and structures according to the standard. Such an effort may inadvertently disregard existing organizational documentation and processes that are vital to the ultimate BCP, and which may result in duplications of effort or redundant plan components.

Therefore, in addressing compliance, security professionals need first to be aware of any existing plans and work efforts that will affect or be affected by the larger BCP. They also need to adapt the components of the standards to meet the specific organizational characteristics and requirements in order to make the BCP usable within the organization. Standards may be comprehensive and detailed, but often the standards documentation does not provide the depth of detail and pragmatic approaches necessary to tailor the plan to the organization. This usability is the basis for the design of this chapter. A reasonably trained, organizationally experienced security professional can hopefully adapt the concepts within this chapter to craft an appropriately targeted plan.

A large organization—characterized by a campus of several buildings and possibly several locations across a community or the country, and with a workforce size of several hundred to several thousand—will have opportunity for more distribution of the responsibilities of a BCP into separate plans and committees. Smaller organizations—characterized by a single or very few locations in one (or perhaps less than one) building, and with a workforce size of a few dozen to a few hundred—will have fewer committees and plans but no less responsibility for the sake of the future of the organization and its relationships. Small organizations which lease or rent part (or all) of a building will have to coordinate some of the response plans and sequences with the building owner/manager, but the responsibilities and expectations of the lease contract pertaining to crisis response should be clarified and documented as part of the planning.

Every business initiative deserves to be under scrutiny for cost benefits and savings, and BCM planning must be included. An efficient BCM planning process can not only enable recovery and

---

* *Full disclosure*—at the time of writing this chapter, this author is a reviewer of the U.S. BCM Standard development process as administered by ASIS and BCM.

restoration after major and minor crises, but it can also drive a top-to-bottom review of practices, processes, underlying information dependencies, and the supporting technical infrastructure. An existing business process that is not easily recoverable for any number of reasons may be a target for reduction or elimination. While not a major decision factor, *process recoverability* may prove to be a new consideration for existing and new business initiatives. Another suggested new consideration may be *data retention efficiency*. In part because storage technology has become much more affordable, organizational data and information has begun to accumulate beyond the terabyte into the petabyte range. Such capacity is proving to be more and more difficult to back up routinely. With additional pressures from e-discovery requirements, eliminating unnecessary stored data will undoubtedly enhance data recoverability.

The plan process itself must also be efficiently conceived and administered, especially as it becomes a repeatable, cyclical program, finding its place among other major organizational initiatives. Let it not be unsaid that a well-crafted BCM plan will more than prove its worth to an organization during and after a major crisis, and the absence of such a plan will almost certainly mean the demise of the organization. Let it also not be unsaid that a BCM plan is a vital component of any organization that seeks to protect its information assets through time and in anticipation of interruptions, large and small. A BCM plan is not simply a control for residual risk.

## Challenges in Responsibility Scope and Terminology

Most information security professionals have understood by experience and training that the recovery of technology and restoration of systems and data (the classic disaster recovery planning) was primarily the responsibility of the technical or security organizational units. Within the past decade, as the executive level has been confronted with requirements for more visible involvement with data protection, other organizational units have become involved. Information auditors are being trained to administer business continuity processes, sometimes including the information protection and recovery. Because of recent major regional crises, safety and emergency response professionals are being trained to address *disaster recovery* from a hazards management perspective. In fact, all three professional groups—auditors, information security professionals, and emergency response professionals—are being trained to assume responsibility for establishing and managing a command and control center at the onset of a major crisis. Without integrated planning, coordination, and communication, the tragic scene of each of the three groups claiming the center stage in a crisis could be more real than imagined. This vitally important collaboration is the primary driver behind the details of this chapter.

Even the use of the term *security professional* can lead to confusion, as this author discovered recently. At a recent conference of health and safety professionals, I presented a seminar encouraging cooperation between "safety and security professionals" in which I intended to introduce concepts of information security and offer points of potential collaboration. To my surprise at the apparent frustration of some of the attendees, I was informed that some of the audience expected the presentation to address safety and police or guard professionals! I strongly suggest as we professionals involved in protecting data interact with diverse audiences that we identify ourselves as information security professionals!

The term disaster recovery has long been associated with the recovery of and restored access to the computer, network, information components, and business data systems of an organization. As the awareness of the need increased for a recovery plan for the larger organization, BCM planning became the inclusive term, with disaster recovery as one of the subordinate plans. However, many organizations with a strong physical security or safety component have long associated the terms *disaster, crisis,* and *emergency* as near synonyms in making plans for response and recovery, which has often led to problems in planning and coordinating disaster recovery programs. I suggest that the term disaster recovery should be given back to the safety/emergency response organizations and business units, and that the historic single process be divided to emphasize the appropriate ownership and responsibilities. I suggest *process continuity*, to describe the restoration of business processes that rely on information components. This is within the scope of responsibility of organizational unit data owners. *Information continuity* describes the restoration of access to systems, servers, and networks that support those business processes as more appropriate and descriptive of the actual efforts.

There is also a potential problem in the use of the term *incident*. For several years within the information security domain, and the context of information security and BCM planning, the term *incident* is associated with an *event* (which can be any interaction with the information technology (IT) and resources) that produces a negative impact. Such an impact can be a compromised password, a stolen laptop, a successful Internet attack, the presence of an unrecognized person, and many others. That definition is relatively small in scope, and is intended to encourage the prevention and detection of activities before they precipitate larger crises. The problem is that certain national and international business continuity initiatives have begun to use the term *incident* to be nearly synonymous with *crisis* or *emergency*. The U.S. DHS has created the massive and well-crafted National Incident Management System (NIMS) and the system's inclusive components, e.g., incident action plan, incident command post, incident command system, and incident management team—all using the definition of *incident* to mean *crisis* or *emergency* (see Table 24.1). Also, the National Fire Protection Association (NFPA) 1600 Standard on disaster/emergency management and business continuity programs (see Table 24.1) uses the term *incident* in the same context as the NIMS. Other BCM standards and planning organizations use the same context for the term *incident* (e.g., BS 25999-1, Code of Practice]. And, safety professionals are adopting the same terminology of the NIMS (e.g., American Society of Safety Engineers publication *Emergency Incident Management Systems*, http://www.asse.org/cartpage.php?link=emergency).

Even though information security professionals have defined and used the term *incident* for an arguably longer time than the business continuity and risk management professionals, the overwhelming usage of term definitions by the business continuity professional domain, may prove that the momentum is moving away from the original information security concept, and reconciliation of the definition will be difficult. CERT (Web site link) uses the term *computer security incident response*, which may be the appropriate alternative. I suggest another alternative, since computer security incidents are not the only incidents that require attention: *internal incident* (e.g., internal incident management), in order to distinguish the concept from the usage by the business continuity domain, retain the familiar information security referential usage with little modification and include the broader scope of internal problems that could lead to larger problems.

## Chapter Preview

> Overriding Perspectives
> Organizational Responsibilities
> Organizational Assessment
> Integrated BCM Plans/Processes
> Crisis Onset and Response

This chapter has five major sections, beyond the Introduction, each with several subsections. The first section, "Overriding Perspectives," gives an indication of some of the concepts or emphases—human safety, information access restoration, and process restoration. Also increasingly, major disasters are no longer local to individual organizations, but require interaction among local and regional organizations and control centers. In the second section "Organizational Responsibilities", I describe the importance of executive participation—not simply approval and funding. And, the integrated participation throughout all units of the organization is vital. For large organizations, no single organizational unit can perform all the responsibilities of the BCM plan alone, although the BCP needs to have a single point of origin and contact.

In the third section "Organizational Assessment," I emphasize capturing the core organizational characteristics and the existing documentation and organizational structures as an efficient means of beginning the BCM planning. This will also include documenting the breadth of external relationships including local community neighbors and regional crisis recovery groups, as well as business relationships. In some organizational units, plans may already exist that address specific continuity processes. Within the fourth section, "Integrated BCM Plans/Processes," I present the details of the individual plans and how they can be integrated. I describe the plans and responsible business units as conceptual. Not all organizations will be the same size or have the same structure, and some may combine processes and planning efforts under a single business unit. Security professionals need to be more concerned about addressing the concepts than whether named committees and plans match those documented here.

Because most efforts described here are plans, I suggest that all plans include a strategic (long range, 5–10 or more years) and a tactical (within one business year or season) aspect, and suggest some simple measures of maturity for the plans. Within each of the plans, I indicate the responsible organizational unit, and any teams or special units created by the plans. In response to the growing concerns internationally for pandemic events, including naturally spreading diseases and bioterrorism, I integrate components to address these needs within the appropriate plans.

Finally, in the section "Crisis Onset and Response", I suggest a sequence of cascading events for an actual crisis response. This sequence will also identify the points of integration among the plans and components.

# Overriding Perspectives

*Business Continuity Management Planning has context!*

Overriding Perspectives
  Human Safety Is Most Important
  Process/Service Continuity Is the Emphasis
  Information Is the Focus
  *Disasters Are No Longer Local!*

## *Human Safety Is Most Important*

The human component is arguably the most important resource of any size organization. Without doubt, therefore, the most important perspective in developing the organizational BCP is human safety and protection. This includes not only the workforce of the organization, but the extended families of the workforce individuals, and the people in the near vicinity of the organization who may be affected by emergency circumstances originating within the organization. This is certainly apparent to manufacturing or large healthcare organizations, where the understanding for compliance to regulatory mandates for workforce or care recipients permeates throughout the life of the organization. This should also be apparent to organizations of all sizes and industry sectors. Most large organizational safety units will already have plans and processes for emergency recognition, response, and evacuation. Many organizations may not have considered planning for work activities in the absence of a facility. Some large organizations may be in a position to provide vital temporary shelter for their own workforce and for nearby individuals as well.

After intense, destructive disasters, many of the organizational workforce may be lost in the disaster, and many others may relocate from the area of the disaster. Plans must account for the loss of workforce after large disasters.

Pandemic diseases and bioterrorism activity may result in mandatory quarantine episodes where workforce members may be compelled to stay away from the organizational buildings or campus, or some may be trapped by circumstances within the buildings.

## Process/Service Continuity Is the Emphasis

Proactive organizations have developed change management strategies for relocation, expansion (or reduction), mergers, and acquisitions. Each of these activities include process continuation plans during the changes. Within a crisis situation, the process continuity planning is similar, but response and implementation must be at a much more rapid pace. These plans developed under the larger umbrella BCM plan must emphasize definitive and comprehensible steps for restoring how the organization will reorganize and restart vital business processes. Although most of the processes will have an information component, some may not actually involve data or information, but the steps still need to be defined. The steps must be clear for workforce members who may be new to the organization, and they also must define working in temporary locations and include manual capabilities, if necessary.

Process continuity planning may offer opportunities for identifying efforts that may need reengineering for better recoverability. If a defined process is tied to outmoded technology or represents duplication or redundancy or is considered no longer critical, process consolidation or elimination may be the answer. It will be important to address any organizational processes and services which may be part of a chain of efforts or vital service on which other organizations and communities depend.

## Information Is the Focus

In developing the larger BCP, the focus on planning must be on the organizational data and information. Without the workforce, the organization will have a prolonged recovery; without the data and information, the organization will not recover! Regulatory requirements for health and safety of the workforce, such as OSHA or HIPAA, warn that the inability to produce health and safety information on demand can result in fines, even if the organization has suffered loss from a major disaster.

Data and information define the organization, regardless of the primary products or services provided as income sources. Protecting the organizational information is of highest importance, and that protection should be part of every business cycle, not just as a part of long-term planning. Minimally, organizations must enable data backups to remote locations, a practice that has been standard in all IT management units for decades. Successful BCM planning also includes contingencies for replacement of organizational technology—servers, workstations, and networks. However in the aftermath of recent large regional disasters in many parts of the world, it has been seen that the restoration of technology may take much longer that anticipated, because the competitive demand across the region will be extremely high. At that time, recovery contracts with technology vendors may be useless! Such a bottleneck in the supply of technology will undoubtedly skew previously documented planned time objectives for recovery and restoration of business processes. Even more consequential was the loss of workforce, not necessarily from injury or death, but from permanent departure.

Therefore, *it cannot be understated* that it is of highest importance that business data and information must be the primary target of a successful BCP. Even if restoration of technology hardware is much slower than anticipated and even if the workforce is much reduced and takes longer to restore, as long as the historic and current (at least to the date of the last backup) information is still available and protected in a remote location, then the organization will have a much better opportunity to return to viability.

### Disasters Are No Longer Local!

Most historic BCM planning have concentrated on the organizational building or campus, but it is clear from recent crises that other organizations as well as local and regional communities are affected by the disaster or crisis at an organizational location. A crisis on a single floor of a building can block access to other untouched tenants in the same building. A fire in a single building can certainly spread to other buildings in an urban setting. Organizations that manufacture or store hazardous chemicals or other products constitute a threat to local communities if the crisis is a fire or a flood that can disseminate dangerous products.

In the United States, the recent crises over the past several years has resulted in National Infrastructure Planning, and FEMA has established extensive training for individuals and professionals in how to respond to regional crises. State and local governments have also established homeland security programs that mandate appropriate planning among government agencies. Several local nongovernment organizations have brought the concepts of emergency planning to schools and private family homes. Private organizations are also being encouraged to develop planning relationships with these public and community groups. Organizational BCM planning must include the contact information for the government and community efforts and make allowances for including some of the contacts in regional planning.

# Organizational Responsibilities

*No single organizational unit can do it all.*

```
Organizational Responsibilities
    Executive-Level Coordination
    Mandatory Internal Collaboration
    Strategic Planning
    Operational/Tactical Planning
    Plan Maturity Measurement
```

## Executive-Level Coordination

Many large organizations have entered into the BCM planning by setting aside an internal committee to pull all the pieces and documentation together in a grand effort that often takes many months. Sometimes the committee is led by a consultant, either an individual or a team. Depending on the size of the organization and the existing status of some of the supporting planning and documentation, this type of effort may be necessary. However, in most medium to large organizations, it should not be assumed that the responsibilities for planning, implementing, and participating in the creation, evaluation, and testing of the BCP can be accomplished by a single committee or at least in a reasonably acceptable time frame.

All BCP standards (no exception) will assert that successful planning and preparation require commitment and participation from the executive level of the organization. Where appropriate, a commitment of support from the board of directors would be most appreciated and beneficial, since the directors often are the ultimate source for funding. Ultimately, a committee formed with executives as the primary participants will be in the best position to act as the overriding steering committee of all other committees and plans. The executives would reduce the effectiveness of the ongoing management of the BCP if their participation was only as a token appearance at the beginning of the effort. It is not enough for the executives only to give permission, or simply to open the purse strings. Executives must play a part in the overall planning and the ongoing administration of a successful BCP, even if some of the tasks are delegated to a subset of the executives or their direct reports. For organizations of all sizes, the persistent participation of executives will set the proper tone for the participation of all levels.

## Mandatory Internal Collaboration

Organizations of all sizes have complexities that reflect differences in responsibilities and therefore division of skills and labor. Each organizational business unit will also have different information foundations and different information relationships among each other and among external partners. The BCP must include participation from all organizational units whose product or service and foundational information are critically important to the organization's integrity. Since one of the outcomes of a complete BCP is the safety of the organizational workforce, the complete workforce should be aware of the plan as it is crafted and refined.

The BCM plan and the subordinate, integrated plans must be initiated before major disasters occur. This is most obvious to practicing business continuity professionals, but regretfully, some organizational executives tend to postpone plans until the cost is prohibitive and the organization is limited in its ability to withstand or recover from a crisis. The most effective planning is made a part of the organizational business life cycle along with other accepted support activities. In fact, BCM planning within a given organizational unit should not be seen as expanding the unit's work responsibilities, but as a process for documenting the work responsibilities with an emphasis on recoverability. As referenced above, the planning must account for the overriding principles— human safety, process continuity, information focus, and community responsibility.

## Strategic Planning

All of the subordinate plans need to be integrated as other traditional organizational plans. Since most major organizational subunits have strategic as well as tactical or operational planning, so should the efforts involved in creating the BCP. Strategic plans for some business processes may project 5, 10, or even 50 years in the future; therefore, by nature some of the strategic planning may outlive members of the planning committees. Strategic plans may document repeatable or cyclical processes, which may span months or years, and which include long-term organizational changes and maintenance requiring capital expense commitments. These processes are often primarily administrative, including organizational hierarchy changes, responses to workforce growth (or shrinkage), and evolving regulatory response. Across a wide variety of industries, research activities also necessitate a strategic view since outcomes of research are unpredictable.

Organizations craft tragic plans for long-term external relationships, such as business partners, competitors, suppliers, customers, and regulatory agencies. Information and business continuity will require the same strategic relationship planning as well. Suppliers of hardware and software technology will evolve along with their products, and suppliers of technical services will change as the technology and information requirements of the organization change. The evolving technology environment will be paralleled by the evolving threats to information from the Internet in general and from individuals who directly target organizational information for monetary gain. Strategic plans involving information protection and continuity will need to be more attuned to the stages within organizational information life cycles, as the information migrates from inputs to outputs, archives, and even elimination.

## Operational/Tactical Planning

All network-based organizations are actively involved in tactical or operational planning for technology and information management as part of periodic (annual, if not more frequent) business cycle changes. Organizational growth and decline will result in increase or decrease in technical service requirements and increasing emphases on information retention will affect the local and remote storage requirements for data protection. This type of planning is usually tied strongly to the annual operational budget, with flexibility for short-term operational planning to replenish supplies and replace outmoded or worn equipment.

Operational planning also prepares for short-duration interruptions to information access or availability due to power problems or human accidents. This planning includes adequate staffing for answering internal calls for assistance, to keep systems, servers, and other network components up to date with the latest upgrades and patches, and to monitor the networks for component failure or intrusion attempts. Organizational safety professionals also create and maintain tactical plans for hazards management and human protection from industrial accidents. Many of these incidents may be addressed by service contracts with vendors supporting various technology components, which also require monitoring for service compliance.

## Plan Maturity Measurement

Organizations are facing the need to become more responsible in maintaining and improving plans, whether strategic or tactical. Critical plans affecting core business functionality can no longer be static and thus require measurements to track improvement and maturity through time. This is increasingly important to ensure that the plans outlive committee memberships and to track more effectively the changes in the organizational information and technology requirements.

There are certainly several standards-based maturity tracking disciplines that address various aspects of organizational processes, including software design and development, and overall organizational information management. Many of the standard efforts require investment in external consulting to implement and coordinate over time. I suggest here a simple view consisting of four levels of maturity that summarizes the expectations of most of the standards and allows for various-sized organizations to ensure the consistency of the individual plans involved in the overall BCM planning.

## Initial Plan Creation

Poorly documented, loosely coupled processes and ad hoc conceptual plans do not constitute a plan sufficient to address targeted needs and responsibilities. The rule of thumb for many conceptual plans and policies has been that if it is not written down and authorized, it does not exist. For the BCM planning, there will be several interrelated plans, each of which will have separate but complementary domains within the larger BCP. The first stage for all of them has to be that the plans are documented and appropriately authorized by the executive level. This also applies to the integration plan that ties all the individual plans into an operable master BCM plan.

## Plan Testability/Changeability

Once a plan has been created and documented, it remains in a conceptual mode that will need to be tested and managed within its own organizational domain or unit. Only by examining the plan in context, if only a tabletop discussion, can the effectiveness and efficiencies be validated. These tests must be within a consistent periodicity that is appropriate to the organization's size and distribution. Some smaller organizations may be able to test once each year or business cycle. Larger organizations may require several individual tests of business units throughout the year. Tests will be most effective if the problems identified will result in appropriate modifications, which must be made within a controlled, auditable process. Modifications also include updates based on organizational and personnel changes through the periodic testing cycles.

## Plan Integration

As individual plans are created and tested, the actual integration across the larger organization will not occur without the participation of the senior management executive levels. As will be explained in more detail below, the integration of the individual plans require attention and oversight only found at the decision-making, expense distribution levels of the organization. This oversight can begin as a separate plan from the organizational domain plans and can form the foundation for the creation, documentation, and testing of all the other plans. The testing of the integration plan itself will certainly change as the more localized plans are established and tested. Smaller organizations cannot ignore the need to integrate the individual plans, even if the organizational size means that most of the plans may be created, documented, and tested by a single organizational unit.

## Integrated Plans as Part of Organizational Identity

Ideally, an organization will establish a mature BCM planning mode and methodology when the BCP is considered integral to the organizational culture. When BCM planning changes and test results are made part of annual organization reports and presentations to the public as well as to the board of directors, and the contributions of individual executives to the integrated planning and management of the BCP are appropriately recognized, then all the rest of the workforce will accept the importance of BCM to the future of the organization.

# Organizational Assessment

*Business Continuity Planning is rarely* de novo

> Organizational Assessment
>     Business Characterization
>     Existing Documented Internal BCM
>         Plans/Policies/Procedures
>     Existing Internal BCM Structure
>     Existing External Relationships

## *Business Characterization*

As mentioned earlier, common characteristics of many existing BCM standards include the idealized breadth and scope of the components of the plan, which is justified by the need to address BCM planning in a large variety of organizational sizes, structures, and industry sectors. Because of such a characterization, each organization must be attentive to document its unique characteristics, especially as they will affect how the organization is reestablished and restored after a major crisis. Documenting these characteristics will be critical to the recovery process, especially if much of the recovery is handled and administered by individuals who are not part of the organization. Undoubtedly, much of this documentation will already exist but perhaps in inconsistent forms and formats.

The organizational documentation begins with core business values—unique points of sensitivity that may be part of the organizational philosophy, industry sector, and/or products or services produced. Many of the points of sensitivity are because of the organizational regulatory environment constraining the industry sector, e.g., health care, manufacturing, waste management, construction, etc., all which have specific requirements for products or services produced, protection of records, and responsibilities for surrounding communities. Each organization will have goals and objectives surrounding the products or services produced, in areas such as quality, capacity, growth in size, and breadth of products. Based on those goals and constrained by the regulations, organizations may have business development plans such as expansions, mergers, and acquisitions, some of which may be actively underway when a major crisis strikes. All of these documents will be necessary to restore the organization, especially if commitments and contracts have been established.

For each of the products and services, and for the business goals and plans, there will be a set of supporting data and information foundations, including external data sources, internal data stores and archives, and specific information processing and protecting requirements. These data/information foundations are often taken for granted until a crisis demonstrates their vital importance. Establishing a BCM planning process may offer an important opportunity to document the ties between business processes and goals and the data/information foundational requirements. Integral to the information foundation is the technology—hardware, networks, and software—required to render the information useful. Vital to the information and technology are the people—the IT professionals that implement and maintain the information environments. Documenting all of this can be part of the periodic organizational impact assessment, described further in Section 24.4. Such an exercise can be useful in heightening the awareness through all levels of the organization to the importance of the information and support environments and for identifying potentially unnecessary or obsolete practices and technology that can be de-emphasized or eliminated.

Finally, organizational characteristics include the actual physical location or locations of all buildings, owned or leased, and all important topographic or geographic features, which may affect crisis management. These include points of transportation ingress and egress, nearby bodies of water, nearby potentially hazardous terrain, e.g., dry forests, rocky slopes, geologic faults, larger, taller buildings, etc. Again, much of this may exist in various formats, but documenting these characteristics will help in anticipating potential crises, and/or consequences of crises.

## Existing Documented Internal Business Continuity Plans/Policies/Procedures

In attempting to implement the components within a given standard as specific requirements to be explicitly fulfilled, individual organizations may overlook or ignore existing sets of plans, however well documented and organized, that actually address important components of the BCM planning. The organization may already have BCPs and disaster recovery plans in various organizational units. These can be vitally important jump starts for developing a larger integrated BCM plan. Larger organizations may already have risk management planning documentation, and associated plans for annual audits and assessments. Some organizations may have formal privacy/quality/regulatory responses, based on industry sector or product/service characteristics. Manufacturing organizations undoubtedly will have safety and emergency response plans based on regulatory requirements, as well as a robust workforce awareness and training program. Hopefully, most organizations, large and small, will have existing enterprise information security policies and plans that may include security incident response management and information protection and continuity planning.

## Existing Internal Business Continuity Responsibility Structure

If such plans and documentation exist, then undoubtedly some measure of organizational structure exists as well. There may be individuals already identified with some of the plans and processes described above. The existing structures need not have the same titles and role descriptions outlined in some of the Standards documents, but they do need to be related to the functions expected by the Standards documents. Even if some structure exists, for a successful BCM plan, the structure must be tied to the organizational hierarchy in a way that elevates the importance of the roles and ties it to the decision makers and spenders.

Organizations that have less structure will need to identify (beyond the decision makers and spenders) the responsibilities for privacy/regulatory response, compliance assessment and audit, safety and physical security, information security, and data protection (which may be distinct from IT support). The common factor in most of these roles is that though there may be individuals with delegated responsibility to implement them, the foundational responsibility for each is within the executive level of the organization. This again highlights the importance of tying the overall BCM planning to the executive level.

## Existing External Relationships

As highlighted in Section 24.1, *disasters are no longer local!* Even when the crisis is within a single building, organizations still do not respond in isolation. This cannot be underemphasized based on the recent regional disasters. As part of the responsible gathering of organizational character-istics, the collection must include external relationships. Most organizations will already have documentation about supply chain or business partners. It will be vital to understand and clarify the responsibilities (on both sides of the contract) during a major crisis. This is also vital for restor-ing the organizational roles and relationships after the crisis, whether in a temporary recovery location or in a permanently restored setting. Critical vendors who provide vital raw materials and services must also be documented, including technology vendors and support organizations. The documentation must certainly include contact information but also license and service numbers and contract responsibilities.

Beyond the business requirements, external relationships include the local community surrounding the organizational buildings or campus. Building and keeping "good neighbor" relationships will become critically important during and after major crises. If the crisis or emer-gency is localized to an organizational building, it may be necessary to disrupt the local com-munity to bring crisis response, such as fire fighting equipment, through local communities. For larger organizations, and especially health care organizations, the surrounding community may seek shelter or other types of services that may be lost in the surrounding community. Larger organizations may consider stocking levels of canned goods, dry goods, and bottled water for such opportunities. Organizational workforce members undoubtedly will include parents of school-age children, thus it will be of major benefit to identify school locations and be ready to assist work-force parents with their family concerns.

Finally, organizations must become aware of federal, state, and local emergency response efforts, and especially local organizations that seek to bridge the response planning of govern-ments, the community, and the private business/industry. If a crisis is regional, such a bridge will be vital to ensuring a coordinated response across all sectors. Large and small organizations must take the time to become acquainted with such efforts, and to become involved in community-wide crisis response planning.

## Integrated Business Continuity Management Plans/Processes

*Out of many, one!*

> Integrated BCM Plans/Processes
> Coordination Plan
> Communications Plan
> Risk Management Plan
> Internal Incident Management Plan
> Safety and Emergency Response Plan
> Process Continuity Plan
> Information Continuity Plan

All organizations, regardless of size, will require an anchor plan for BCM, and the accompa-nying anchor of control and administration. From that, a number of organizational unit-specific plans will be coordinated. In this section, I suggest six organizational plans, which address com-ponents and processes required for successful recovery after major crises. Each organization may name these plans or concepts differently, or divide or combine them in different ways, all based on the organizational size and complexity.

For each plan, I suggest the organizational unit responsible for creating and/or administrating the plan, and describe the accompanying committee, if appropriate. I also recommend strategic considerations, which will carry the plan through subsequent years or business cycles, which will include pandemic issues that each plan must address. It should become immediately evident that all the plans and concomitant committees interact—one committee will gather information that feeds the plans for another committee, and much of the responsibility of the executive coordination committee (ECC) involves assimilating and maintaining reports and other output from the other plans. Finally, I recommend tactical components for each plan to be addressed within each business cycle, or as a part of regular operational processes. The tactical components will change much more frequently than the strategic components.

The actual *plan* will be the summary documentation describing appropriately the committee makeup and the associated strategic and tactical components. Therefore, the complete BCM plan will be the compiled documentation from all the plans. The documentation of the combined plan must be dynamically maintained and protected, allowing for authorized periodic updates and modifications, and accessible for timely review, testing, and prompt implementation as needed. A variety of business continuity systems and tools are available for use and adaptation; but the BCM plan must determine the software and tools, and not the other way around! The driving determinations for tools and storage of the plan are usability and accessibility.

## Coordination Plan

The coordination plan is the anchor for all other plans and processes for the BCM plan. Organizational *senior executives* must initiate and implement this plan and be responsible for leading this effort through an ongoing BCM ECC, which will include representatives from the other plans and from various organizational units as needed.

### Strategic Components

The ECC establishes the command and control team (CCT), which is the group that administers the BCM plan during and after a crisis onset from a predetermined command center. The ECC is the ongoing presence of the CCT; it may consist of rotating members, some of whom may be on the CCT as well. The CCT will not be a standing team, but will take form at the onset of a major crisis, and it will be responsible for all organizational decision-making during and after the crisis. Its composition must be defined and representative roles must be identified. The most important responsibility of this ECC, and ultimately the CCT, is to keep abreast of the legal responsibilities that the organization will face during a major disruptive crisis, such as regulatory requirements for personnel safety, product or service quality, and protected information accessibility.

The CCT will establish the emergency responsibility hierarchy, initiate the communications plan, and determine the allocation of funds and the availability of any insurance claims in anticipation of an emergency. The ECC will be responsible for selecting the command and control center location and the temporary relocation site for the organizational recovery, if necessary, based on recommendations from other organizational units. The ECC will determine the staff augmentation requirements during the recovery stages, with input from organizational units. Based on the funds and insurance, the ECC will determine the spending plan during and after the crisis onset.

For pandemic considerations, the ECC must understand the legal liability if data cannot be recovered in a timely manner from a quarantined location, and must document the data protection requirements for the organization during a reduced workforce due to quarantine or social distancing mandates.

The ECC will also formally establish the other BCM plans, if they are not already in force, and will initiate the communication strategies among the other committees and with external contacts.

### Tactical Components

The ECC must collect, organize, and maintain the local and regional contacts for community, state, and federal crisis management groups, and identify representatives for periodic meetings of the groups. The committee will also track the maintenance of all the other plans, insuring that documentation is updated, and plans are tested appropriately. The most important tactical consideration for the ECC is to define the requirements for declaring a formal disaster or emergency, and to declare the initiation of the crisis response plans. This must be a single decision, made with participation from other organizational committees.

## Communications Plan

This plan establishes the eyes, ears, and mouth for the CCT, and is also implemented by the organizational *senior executives*, with appropriate unit representatives. This plan establishes the communications team (COMT) who will define and document organizational communications at all levels prior to and especially during a major crisis.

### Strategic Components

The COMT will also implement and administer the organizational training unit to address a broad range of training including personnel safety, information security, incident response, and emergency recognition and response. Many manufacturing and construction organizations may already have a strong safety training and awareness program that can be expanded to include the other subject matter. For BCM planning, the more the workforce is aware of emergency response, the more efficient that response will be.

This plan will also document organizational relationships on all levels—workforce, customers, vendors, partners, and supply chains—and supply the contacts and procedures for emergency circumstances. The CCT will be the point of origination for official communications to the media from the organization during a crisis response.

### Tactical Components

The COMT will insure that all contacts are documented and that the lists are maintained. The team will also research technologies and procedures for keeping in contact with workforce members and their families, including hotlines, call trees, and various messaging services. The training unit will insure that the workforce is made aware of the conditions that could lead to a major crisis, and the appropriate ways to respond, including recognizing security incidents, following the proper chain of notification, and following emergency evacuation planning based on periodic training and review programs.

## Risk Management Plan

The risk management plan will be administered by the organizational units that address internal audit, privacy, or quality control. Of course, organizational size and complexity will determine the specific unit responsible for risk management. This plan will also be addressed in more detail within another chapter of this book. Characteristically, the plan assigns a compliance/internal audit (CIA) unit to address regulatory responsibilities. For the BCM planning purposes, the risks involved with managing the information component of the processes are the primary scope. Also for the BCM plan, assessing positive outcomes of risks is a potential distraction, since the most effective use of BCM planning resources is to control, if not prevent negative outcomes. Evaluation for positive outcomes belongs much higher or earlier in the organizational decision process.

## Strategic Components

Much of the strategic work of the risk management plan is to measure, for each organizational business process, the components of risk, and from those components, to analyze the risk for each of the processes.

### Assessment of Criticality

This component determines the relative importance, or value, of each business process asset to the mission and goals of the organization. First, the specific process must be described sufficiently for replacement or temporary staff to activate the process. Then, the data/information foundation for the process must be documented. This includes the types and capacity of data and information, the server and network technology, as well as the support staff. In terms of the BCM plan, the criticality of the process is the overall cost of the loss of the process, which is evaluated from three perspectives:

- *Actual Value of the Process.* The importance of the process to the organizational bottom line; and the effect of the loss of the process to the continuation of the organization.
- *Replacement Cost.* This includes not only the organizational staff and activities engaged in implementing the process, but the technology and staff supporting the data management involved with the process.
- *Regulatory or Legal Liability.* The impact of the interruption of the process or service to the neighborhood or community, the effect on partner/customer contracts, and the regulatory penalties for delaying or failing to restore the process and its associated information.

From this assessment, the business processes and their supporting information and technology can be ranked by value and/or cost of replacement.

For each system(s) supporting the process, certain targets can also be determined during this assessment. The *recovery time objective* (RTO) is the time required to restore a system or process to functionality, and the *recovery point objective* (RPO) is the desired state or point in (recent past) time at which the system is to be restored. Another target often included is the minimum time to recover (MTR), which takes into account the logistics involved in recovering the technology, data, and systems. In the event of a pandemic crisis, this assessment must account for the effects of a reduced workforce on this process.

## Assessment of Threat Ecology (Sources, Activities, Probability)

The complete threat assessment must document the sources, the activities involved with this threats, and the probability of each threat occurring within the organizational setting. The threat *sources* for most of the processes at the same location will be the same, with minor exceptions. Generally, threats are summarized under three main categories:

- *Human*: Directly personal activities, including internal and external sources involving social engineering, unauthorized access or behavior (e.g., apparent hallway strangers, "dumpster diving"), errors, theft, vandalism, and terrorism.
- *Environmental*: Weather-related threats, other natural disasters such as fire, earthquakes, and pandemic diseases.
- *Technology-* or *Information-Based*: Malicious software of all kinds, whether from external Internet-based sources and/or internal accidental or deliberate activities. These also include malicious use of wireless technology, unauthorized network sniffing, email phishing, and spamming.

Of course, most technology-based threats are perpetrated by humans, but the exploitation of technological skills and the application of technological controls differentiates these from the directly personal human activities. Most of the threat sources are easily identified using commonly available sources. Documenting the threat *activities*, whether human or network-related, will help determine the controls or countermeasures for the threats. Threat *probability* is frequently assessed in a subjective measurement (e.g., high, medium, low), but can be measured with more precision. This assessment must include those threats that affect human safety as well as threats to the data and information.

## Assessment of Vulnerabilities

Organizational vulnerabilities are the openings, faults, or absences, accidental or deliberate, which allow threats to affect negatively the information resource and interfere with the process or service. Vulnerabilities can be categorized in three ways:

- *Physical* or *Structural*: Building or room problems that allow some of the personal and/ or environmental threats to act. These can include broken or absent entry controls, doors, or window locks lighting (for visibility); building construction problems, new incomplete construction or older deteriorating structures; and location proximity to potential natural threats, such as steep slopes with loose rock or lacking vegetation, lakes or rivers prone to flood, or regions with recent history of wind storms.
- *Technology-* or *Information-Based*: Network, hardware, or software problems that allow threats to penetrate the systems and servers. Specific examples are out of date or poorly designed operating systems, applications or systems or devices, poor system software change management, poor access management, and poor network and server protection management.
- The absence of *Operational Structures/Processes/Practices*: The absence of process barriers may inadvertently permit human- or technology-based threats to act or penetrate. These can include incomplete (e.g., unsigned) or missing policies and procedures, poorly defined or undocumented processes, all of which can permit or fail to detect successful threats.

Based on the assessment, it may be possible to *aggregate vulnerabilities* in ways to enable efficient implementation of controls, e.g., many network vulnerabilities can be controlled with intrusion detection/prevention devices, or uniform access control processes can control unauthorized access to different systems; many physical vulnerabilities can be controlled by consistent door locks and lighting.

## Assessment of Controls Sufficiency

There are several controls categorization schemes available to document and correlate the controls for the vulnerabilities and threats. The selection of a scheme will depend on the organization's industry sector or regulatory requirements. By definition, the control of a threat is essentially the control of a vulnerability through which the threat is actualized; therefore, in the context of providing protection and controlling access to the data and information, the most appropriate targets of the controls and countermeasures are the vulnerabilities as indicated above. Controls or countermeasures for asset loss cost of restoration can include reducing the technology costs of the restored process, e.g., moving to less expensive platforms or systems requiring fewer person-hours of support.

After the recommended controls are identified, and an initial gap analysis is performed, the controls efficiency assessment is intended to follow up on the gap analysis by determining if an active controls assessment is actually in place, and if there are any required controls that are absent.

## Analysis of Risk from Assessments

To be precise, in an information management context, risks themselves are neither identified nor are they directly managed. Threats, threat probabilities, vulnerabilities, and the value (or loss impact) of the information component of the business process can be directly measured and managed. Risks associated with specific processes can be determined, or calculated by the combinations of the components. The classic equation defines the assessment process succinctly:

$$\text{Risk} = \text{Threat (Probability)} \times \text{Vulnerability} \times \text{Asset Value (loss)}$$

Risk is then identified as the probability of a monetary loss. The complete analysis means that risk is calculated for all organizational business processes. From this analysis, the value/cost ranking of the business processes can be augmented by the probability of the threats and cost of vulnerability controls. This analysis can indicate the high-value, high-risk processes, which can lead to a priority of process recovery for the BCM plan. The same analysis can indicate the data or information supporting the processes that can be classified by protection importance, which could indicate the most confidential data or information deserving the highest protection from integrity loss or unauthorized access, and requiring the highest availability.

## *Tactical Components*

For risk management, the tactical processes include planning and implementing annual internal assessments, as well as assessments for changes in the organization that affect the protection of critical assets and the associated data/information. Internal and external audits will be administered or coordinated from the CIA unit or other appropriate organizational units. Each of the assessments and audits will undoubtedly result in changes and updates to the overall risk management plan or subsets of the larger plan.

## Safety and Emergency Response Plan

Undoubtedly, most manufacturing or construction organizations will have robust plans for protecting people during and after a major crisis. Other organizations, depending upon size and complexity, will have physical security and/or safety plans. This planning effort is administered by the organizational safety/physical security (SPS) unit. Characteristically, in most organizations, the safety plan is implemented and maintained by a single or a set of safety/emergency response teams (SERT).

### Strategic Components

The most important strategic component is that people come first! People are gradually being acknowledged as the most important and valuable organizational resource, therefore providing for the safety and protection of people during and after crises offers a strategic advantage to the restoration of the organization. SPS units administer physical site control, assessing, and controlling potential threats to human safety. Organizations that deal in potentially harmful materials or substances, either as raw materials or products, will conduct hazards assessments to protect people from the substances or materials. The SPS unit also will determine criteria for recognizing emergencies, whether they are internal or external. This group also develops evacuation plans from within structures and possibly egress plans away from dangerous locations. Also, the SPS unit will develop the temporary relocation plan to account for restoration of processes and services immediately after the crisis.

For pandemic issues, the SPS unit will need to define and plan quarantine evacuation plans. These differ from rapid, emergency evacuations because they may allow for slow egress from buildings or campuses. This type of slow evacuation will allow for gathering personal material, laptops, and documents that will be important in continuity of processes. Also, this type of evacuation will allow for a phased lock-down of buildings and information resource locations and allow for appropriate restrictions to be implemented. In the case that individuals will be left inside for technical support efforts, the SPS unit must also prepare stores of food and water.

### Tactical Components

As part of ongoing organizational support, the SPS unit will work with the IT unit to administer the organization's requirements for power and internal climate conditioning to protect the technology resources. Appropriate internal engineering management will help reduce energy-based threats and vulnerabilities, potentially reducing the impact of a major crisis. The SPS unit must be prepared to tailor the emergency response, drawing from the overall strategic plan and based on the nature of the crisis and its onset. The SERT will be responsible for implementing the temporary relocation plan at the onset of a crisis. During the crisis, the SERT will have the primary responsibility for building and site safety.

After a crisis onset and the move to the temporary location, the SPS unit and teams will be responsible for administering the cleanup, decontamination, and/or disposal of damaged structures and materials. Finally, this unit will plan and manage the return from the temporary location and conditions to a restored or new organizational location.

## Internal Incident Management Plan

The growing danger to organizational integrity posed by the increasingly intense threats from malicious software and the human perpetrators of this software have increased the importance of the organization internal incident response team (IIRT) and plan. This plan is primarily initiated from within the IT unit with close involvement and cooperation of the SPS unit and because of anticipated legal complications, the senior executives. This collaboration is responsible for developing the internal incident response plan and the closely aligned forensics assessment plan. The activities of the IIRT are predominantly tactical and operational as they respond to notices from all quarters about lesser and greater incidents.

## Strategic Components

The strategic activities of the team entail developing and maintaining plans that will address crucial circumstances, such as human threat activities, internal and external network attacks, and legal consequences of the responses to these activities. These carefully prepared plans and procedures will need to be reviewed and vetted by the executives and by legal representatives, certainly internal but perhaps external as well. Ideally, this team is a separate group from SPS and IT units, which may not be the case in smaller organizations. Working with the IT group, the IIRT will develop an escrow protection plan for sensitive system passwords, encryption keys, and lists of authorized administrators and delegates who will be able to acquire the lists and use them in the response and recovery phases of a major crisis. Working with IT, the IIRT will develop a structured and authorized process for acquiring the escrowed information and a process for allowing the authorized individuals to enter the building to assess and document the status of the infrastructure. The IIRT will develop plans and procedures to coordinate the collection of internal incidents from various sources. Any observable interruption of information-based services must be documented and correlated with other events or internal incidents to determine patterns or sequences that may help control a problem and prevent it from escalating and/or repeating in the future.

Process steps for a response plan can be found from a number of resources, but all have similar sequences:

■ *Prepare*: The development of the plan represents the preparation. All IIRT members will need to become skilled at following the details of the plan.
■ *Strengthen*: Based on the preparations and in cooperation with IT and SPS units, the internal infrastructure can be strengthened with appropriate countermeasures and controls that will eliminate or reduce the impact of incidents. Also, working with the organizational training unit, a set of awareness and training programs can be developed from the plan that will bring the workforce members into appropriate participation with the overall response.
■ *Detect*: Discovering, identifying, analyzing, and reporting the types of incidents will be an integral part of the training for the workforce; anyone should be able to notice, assess the significance, and report on occurrences as soon as possible. The IIRT must be the single point of contact, even if the team will not necessarily address or correct every internal incident. The uniform collection process will be vital for correlating events that may at first notice seem unrelated.

- *Contain/eliminate*: Working with other organizational units, the IIRT will direct the appropriate response to the incident or sets of incidents, including how to capture the most amount of data and evidence about the incident, when to block the source of the incidents, and how to remove the effects of the incident from the infrastructure. The IIRT will determine how to control the evidence, whether physical or digital so that the evidence can be useful if a legal or criminal investigation ensues.
- *Restore*: For information-based incident activities, the IIRT will work with the IT unit to determine the recovery from the activities, assuring that the sequence of events is documented, potential witnesses are identified, and evidence is appropriately collected and protected. After such efforts are underway or under control, then the internal and external networks can be restored and if backups are necessary, affected servers and workstations can be recovered.
- *Report*: No internal incident response is complete until all the activities are documented and reported to the organizational executives and if appropriate, the external legal or criminal authorities. This will also include appropriately handing over any documentation or evidence for the activities.
- *Review*: Every response activity offers a chance to review the internal incident response plan and make corrections or additions, and to enhance the training to the workforce.

## Tactical Components

The most significant burden of the IIRT will be in the ongoing tracking of the reported network and systems intrusions, evaluating server and system halts and interrupts, responding to personal observations by workforce members, and correlating all the activities. The team will also review system, network, and other activity logs collected by various audit logging systems to evaluate activities and patterns. The IIRT will also constantly review Internet threat assessments and software vulnerabilities as reported by various Internet-based security organizations.

## Process Continuity Plan

The organizational business unit managers are identified as the data owners for the information resource supporting the business processes. After a major crisis, the data owners will actually direct the restoration of the systems based on the backups preserved for this purpose. The IT group will certainly provide the technical capability for the restoration. Each unit data owner will create a restoration plan for validating the incorporation of the backup data into the restored system and determining the availability of the system. Depending on the size of the organization, there may be many process continuity plans!

## Strategic Components

The primary strategic component for each unit data owner in developing the restoration plan is the criticality assessment of risk management plan. The unit data owners will participate in the criticality assessment, which will not only determine the priority of the restoration among other processes, but also the RTO, RPO, MTR, and any other restoration objective appropriate to the specific process. Additionally, the unit data owners will work with the IT unit and the system vendors to arrange for systems and usage licenses and keys for restoration on new technology.

## Tactical Components

At the declaration of the recovery plan by the CCT, each organizational business unit will first implement the unit emergency organizational hierarchy for structural continuity. This will also enable the continuity of regulatory response and restore the policies and procedures specific to the unit. As the recovery proceeds, the unit data owners will coordinate with IT for the activation and configuration of the temporary network and infrastructure. According to priority sequence, the backed up data and information, and new copies of the application software will be restored to the temporary infrastructure. The unit data owners will be responsible for testing the restored systems and authorizing the restoring of the process to the appropriate user community.

The unit data owners will work with existing staff or temporary workers to carry out the processes in coordination with the organizational staffing plans. As the permanent organization location is restored, the unit data owners will initiate a similar set of restoration plans to move back to the permanent location.

## Information Continuity Plan

This plan is clearly within the scope of the IT unit, though the activities are dependent on input from the CIA unit (including auditors and legal staff), the SPS unit, and the organizational business unit data owners. In fact the information continuity plan cannot exist in isolation—it is by definition and make up an integrated plan. In many larger organizations, the information security management (ISM) unit, which addresses the planning for overall data protection, may be separated hierarchically from the IT unit, which administers the networks and server infrastructure, implements the security practices, and acts as stewards of the organizational data, as directed by the units referenced above.

The IT unit will have the expertise to keep abreast of advances in the various technical arenas and will add value by proactively recommending changes while supporting the existing infrastructure. It will also perform the backups and archives of data as required, and in direct relation to the internal incident management team and the SERT, the IT staff will act as eyes and ears to respond immediately and report problems as they occur. The IT unit ideally will identify an IT Recovery Team (ITRT) to be at the forefront of crisis recovery implementation to restore data to the temporary infrastructure. This team will develop and maintain the information continuity plan for responding to a crisis. Historically, the information continuity plan has been a complex activity, coordinating technology, vendors, backup media, and workforce demand, but it is important to recognize that the primary goal of this plan is *to restore access to data and information*. Keeping this goal in mind can help simplify decisions about how data is protected in general, and choices about the replacement architecture and infrastructure.

The preparation and documentation of the information continuity plan can require an investment in time if little has been documented historically and based on organizational size. Several external service agencies offer consulting services to initiate and document the plan. Many of these will also be able to participate at varying levels of effort at the onset of the crisis and the activation of the plan.

## Strategic Components

Most of the strategic components of this plan reflect the actual strategic responsibilities of the IT unit. As the IT staff track advances in technology, evaluation and adoption is a function of such things as business direction, capital cost, and effects of infrastructure change. From a continuity perspective, other considerations for new technology must be resistance to interruptions (short duration, less than one workday) and recoverability (from short or long interruptions), which may be less a function of new devices and more a reorienting of existing processes and perhaps creativity in architecture and infrastructure planning. Targets for reorientation and creativity include the following areas.

## Decoupling

This refers to the separation of server and networking components that classically were contained within a single cabinet. This is reflected in tiered architectural designs where the processing function is separated from input/output and storage, e.g., a single console connecting to redundant servers which are also connected (along with other redundant pairs of servers) to a storage area network (SAN). These multiply connected sets of redundancies constitute a tiered architecture such as service oriented architecture (SOA). With other design considerations, this can potentially enable replacement or addition of component parts without noticeable interruptions to services and data.

## Redundancy

Storage redundancy has been available for years, and is continually being refined with more storage capacity and more intelligence within the units to detect problems. As server technology shrinks in size and cost (rack mounts and blades), capabilities for clustering, either in pairs or more, and automatic failover after failure are becoming more affordable. Many larger organizations are building redundancy in network architecture, including redundant network hubs (at a distance) and redundant pathways. Higher network speeds and protocols are allowing for remote mirrored servers offering a complete duplication of the server environment. Virtual technology is not itself physical redundancy, but again, with the reduction in size, it is conceivable to construct redundant virtual servers.

The challenge for process recovery is to document all configurations and where remote mirroring is implemented, documenting the latency and daily differences in active data. As redundancy and virtual capabilities increase, the cost of software and system licenses will change and vendor service contracts must account for appropriate licenses and keys for duplicate servers and server images.

## Resilience/Disaster Tolerance

Innovations in server and operating system technology bring the potential for near immediate recognition of power loss and data preservation, including automatic shutdown and recovery after power restoration. With redundancies throughout the architecture, it is possible to conceive of no network downtime or zero-time recovery, which would be important for threats leading to short-duration interrupts, but less so for major crises. New technologies are also bring better fire and water protection to server and array cabinets, cabling, and server rooms and buildings.

## Remote Storage

With the higher network speeds and protocols, remote storage and backups are more affordable both in time and money. As described above, organizations can more efficiently implement remote data mirroring or file shadowing. With the reduced cost for storage, organizations may consider retaining idle arrays at distant locations for rapid recovery needs. Based on experiences in recent environmental crises, most large, and many small or medium organizations are establishing remote centers for backup and archive, either with separate organizational locations or perhaps through reciprocal agreements with business partners. Smaller organizations also have access to remote storage service agencies, whose services may include simple data backups, data archives, and data recovery hot- or warm-sites.

Serendipitously, storing mirrored or daily backed up data may offer a sea change in information recovery. As long as the remote location is sufficiently distant, and the stored systems are duplicates of the primary location, and the data is no older than one workday prior to the crisis onset, this practice may simplify the recovery process. Once a recovery work site is established, including work space, workstations, and network connectivity, then the time consuming and cumbersome processes—acquiring new servers, recovering backup media from a remote location, initiating all operating systems and applications, and finally reloading the data itself—may be obviated by simply pointing the recovery site network to the remote server location.

## Desktop Simplification

Many organizations have suffered data loss of various scopes because of organizationally sensitive data being stored on desktop workstations. As a response, many have attempted a variety of data backup schemes from implementing mounted server directories to actual remote backup of many or all workstations. The situation has grown much more complex with portable storage devices and mobile computing becoming part of the organizational practices. Some organizations are turning to networked terminals, a technology that harkens back to pre-desktop workstation times. In the strictest architecture, the desktop device will have no internal storage, and no external storage connections. All desktop software and data will be mounted remotely at start-up and all data will be kept in protected storage arrays within the organizational data center. One of the technologies supporting that is the *blade PC*, which is conceptually similar to blade servers. This has the potential for greatly simplifying the management of large numbers of desktop workstations, since the blade PCs will be much more easily updated, protected, and serviced. Additionally, virtualization offers the potential for PC images to exist on data center servers. Virtualization on desktop PCs may offer flexibility in application processing, but may not help with the protection, updates, and potential data loss since the workstations themselves remain on workforce desktops.

## Outsource All Server and Storage Management

Large and medium organizations may have an historic investment in technology to such a degree that duplicate storage and server capability is too expensive. These organizations will continue to rely on contract recovery service vendors who will provide fee-based, on-demand server facilities (cold-, warm-, or hot-sites) or other vendor-supplied recovery services. As infrastructures evolve toward smaller server sizes, some of the large organizations are beginning to create recovery services among remotely located data centers, each serving the recovery needs of the other location.

Smaller organizations, especially those who are recent start-ups with little historic technology, may opt for the complete outsourcing of all technology devices and support. Service agencies are expanding to provide complete computing and data management services to small and medium organizations, even supplying and supporting desktop workstations. All backups, data recoveries, and technical support could be handled by the service agency, and potentially, the customer organization may need no salaried technical workforce. Another innovative alternative to outsourcing is the concept of cloud computing, where all processing capability and data resides within a remote vendor's domain, allowing a customer organization to connect through secure Web interfaces to the vendor's systems services.

Such arrangements with remote vendors have great promise and may reduce technology management costs. However, they must not be adopted hastily; they will require carefully created contracts specifying service scope, service response timeframes, change management, data protection requirements, assurance of data protection, and regulatory and legal liabilities for failure to full the contract.

For pandemic issues, there are two main considerations for the IT support group:

## Reduced Workforce

In an active pandemic, several workforce staff may be absent, whether from suffering from actual symptoms or from the practice of social distancing, which reduces the active workforce on site to reduce the opportunity for infective agent spread. Strategic plans will need to include how to support critical systems (from the risk management plan assessment of criticality) with a reduced staff. This may be addressed by appropriate cross training of staff to be able to fill in at different roles and timeframes. The process and procedure steps must be documented so that temporary staff who may not be familiar can at least follow instructions. It will be important to identify the minimum systems necessary to keep the organization's service processes in action, some systems and servers may be able to be shut down temporarily. A reserve of supplies—paper, tapes, print cartridges, etc.—should be kept separately from the standard set of supplies in the case that external service agencies may be unavailable. In the case of a quarantine declaration, food and water supplies should also be kept strictly for that purpose. Finally, IT will need a shutdown triage plan, allowing for a careful, controlled backup and shutdown of the servers if the staff is reduced, or if the organization is completely shut down. This correlates with the quarantine evacuation, described within the safety and emergency response plan, during which no structural damage occurs.

## Remote Workforce

In the event that the organization is shut down, but the servers and networks are still functioning, it may be necessary to implement a remote workforce plan where staff connect to the network through the Internet. This will require capacity planning for the network hub, since many more workforce staff will be making remote connections. New policies and procedures will be needed to ensure secure connections and access control procedures are in force. Potentially, new workstation or laptop technology will be needed to ensure high-speed connectivity, either wired or wireless. It may be necessary to increase the voice connectivity as well.

One consequence of a high volume of remote users will be the capacity of the public Internet access services. Many vendors may not be able to handle such a peak load increase, especially if the effects of the pandemic are widespread. Organizations may consider contracts for multiple ISP alternatives or working together with the local community to arrange for ad hoc rapid bandwidth increases during pandemic events.

## *Tactical Components*

The primary tactical/operational goal of the IT unit is to prevent (or reduce the potential for) service interruption to data and information flow within the organization. This involves addressing the organizational business process technology and information requirements, and responding to the regulatory requirements for restricted access to private data. For the IT workforce, this means the active implementation of the strategic plans for managing the architecture, infrastructure, and processes. The day-to-day activities feed back to the strategic planning with new requests and recommendations based on growing organizational needs. From the information continuity perspective, these activities target reducing vulnerabilities to interruptions, small and large, and enhance the overall recoverability of the technology components.

One of the primary means of controlling service interruptions is often overlooked before it is too late. Inadequate staffing is indeed a vulnerability, if the workforce is overloaded and is not able to address service requests in a timely manner. If increased staffing is difficult, then service contracts with external agencies is a viable alternative. Historically, the IT workforce were considered prime targets for reduction and/or outsourcing, based on relative ignorance of the decision makers. Where there is a heavy investment of technology infrastructure, internal staff who develop familiarity over time with the technology and the organizational requirements prove to be much more efficient in responding to problems than outsourced, temporary staff.

The technology itself requires constant attention and periodic maintenance (another function of adequate staffing) to allow proactive anticipation of problems instead of retroactive cleanup. As the infrastructure within a single data center increases, the power and environmental conditioning requirements will also increase, which highlights the importance of strategic views on technology changes. Loss of power or failure to maintain the appropriate temperature can result in the loss of the complete technical infrastructure.

Whether or not staffing problems can be resolved, other service interruption controls can reduce interruptions. Implementing the strategic perspectives on redundancy in the technology components and devices will reduce single points of failure in the infrastructure; if one of a paired set of servers fails, the failover capability can provide near seamless continuity of service. With redundancy, the service maintenance and upgrades can be performed separately while the other member of the pair is kept active. Redundancy can also be implemented in connectivity—each of the paired servers can have paired connections to the storage switches, which also can have paired connections to the storage array. The decoupling of the infrastructure components allows for replacing or adding processing technology or storage capacity without bringing down the infrastructure. Server virtualization potentially reduces the number of independent server units, and therefore the complexity of the infrastructure. It can also reduce the staffing requirements needed to maintain separate servers.

Backup of data and information can be a labor-intensive effort, especially if tapes and other small media are incorporated. Server-to-server backups, whether adjacent or remote, can reduce the live system impact of backups, and allow the data on the backup server to be separately copied to external media, if necessary. Automated, remote server backups can provide strong data protection in anticipation of a major crisis, but may require additional staffing for support.

As part of the maintenance of the organizational infrastructure, recoverability can be enhanced by periodically reducing the infrastructure variability, simplifying the support effort, and eliminating out-of-date software and hardware technologies. Vendors characteristically will curtail or eliminate support on products that are too far out of date. Older applications that have little use are targets for assumption into new technologies and systems.

## Summary of Planning

Apart from the coordination plan, all the other plans represent ongoing active processes within the various organizational business units. The coordination plan is specifically for activation at the onset of a major crisis, but it still needs to be developed and documented by the executives.

The ECC should periodically tap into the planning schemes, including testing results and status of documentation, of all the other units and the subordinate plans. That itself is one of the most important disciplines within the BCM planning program, and one of the reasons that the overall coordination must be at the executive level, if not at the board level. If planning control and accountability is not mandated, the subordinate planning programs will slip in priority within the organizational units.

The biggest challenge for all the plans will be to find ways to test appropriately—if the plans are not tested, then they are not viable. For large organizations, it may be necessary to establish a formal testing program that operates year-round and sequentially tests the major plans and the organizational unit process recovery plans. For most of the major plans described above, the most efficient testing may be to have detailed tabletop walk-through tests, which include all major participants (even from other business units) and which allows a testing leader to take the plan through various crisis scenarios and validate the documentation for process flow and completeness. One of the scenarios may be to scale back from a complete recovery implementation if in fact the crisis is more regional than organizational. The organizational representatives may participate in regional crisis response activities even if the physical structure and information resources of the organization are still intact. Live testing for many of the plans, such as safety evacuations and hazard containment may be required by regulations. Testing data backup media is extremely important, even if it is not a formal system recovery test. It may also be important to test selected system recovery processes for the highest critical systems.

As stated in this chapter, and in many more documents and venues, people are the most important target for crisis recovery, and they are the most important resource for implementing the recovery. It will be increasingly necessary for organizations to develop a culture of security—personal safety, data privacy, hazard containment, and recognition of potential problems. Organizations that seek longevity cannot afford an ignorant workforce, and the elimination of ignorance rests in the hands of the executives and board of the organization.

# Crisis Onset and Response

*Today is too late!*

> Crisis Onset and Response
> Crisis Recognition
> Organizational Impact
> Scope Impact
> Declaration
> Emergency Response
> Incident Management
> Information Continuity
> Process Continuity
> Recovery Termination

This section suggests several sequence steps after the onset of a major crisis (see Table 24.2). These are idealized, and meant to represent a wide range of decisions and responsibilities that all

**Table 24.2 Integrated Business Continuity Plan Outlines**

| | Coordination Plan | Communications Plan | Risk Management Plan | Safety and Emergency Response Plan |
|---|---|---|---|---|
| Responsibility | Senior executives | Senior executives | Privacy/quality/audit unit(s) | Safety/physical security unit(s) |
| Participation | Unit representatives | Unit representatives | IT, safety units | Training unit |
| Team/committee | Executive coordination committee<br>Command/control team | Communications team<br>Training unit | Compliance/internal assessment/audit units | Safety/emergency response team(s) |
| Strategic components | Establishment of other plans | Workforce awareness training | *For each defined business process:* | People first! |
| | Legal responsibilities | Relationship communication | Criticality assessment | Safety/evacuation training |
| | Emergency responsibility hierarchy | Media communication | Threat ecology assessment | Site control |
| | Spending plans | Regulatory communication | Vulnerability assessment | Hazards assessment |
| | Staff augmentation plans | | Controls sufficiency assessment | Emergency recognition |
| | Temporary relocation site | | Analysis of risk from assessments | Evacuation plans coordination |
| | Communications plan | | | |

| | | | Consequences of reduced workforce (each defined business process) | Quarantine evacuation |
|---|---|---|---|---|
| Pandemic issues | Legal liability for unrecoverable data | | | Phased lock-down |
| | Requirements for data protection | | | Controlled facility access |
| | | | | Emergency food/water stores |
| Tactical components | Identification of local/regional contacts | Community coordination | Periodic Review | Tailored emergency response |
| | Definition of disaster/emergency | Internal messaging | Annual internal assessments | Temporary relocation |
| | Declaration of disaster/emergency | Workforce family communication | Annual external audits | Building/site safety |
| | Assessment/maintenance of other plans | Communications technology | Timely updates to plans | Cleanup, disposal, and decontamination |
| | | | | Termination of recovery activities |
| | | | | Return from temporary location |

*(continued)*

**Table 24.2 (continued)  Integrated Business Continuity Plan Outlines**

| | Incident Management Plan | Process Continuity Plan | Information Continuity Plan |
|---|---|---|---|
| Responsibility | IT, safety units; senior executives | IT, unit representatives | IT unit |
| Participation | Unit representatives | Organizational unit process and data owners | Safety unit representatives |
| Team/committee | Internal incident response team | Process continuity team(s) | IT recovery team |
| Strategic components | Structured, authorized response | Criticality assessment of risk management plan | *Creative architecture/infrastructure* |
| | Coordination of incident collection | Organizational development strategic plans | Technology redundancy |
| | Escrow/protect passwords, keys, critical lists | Regulatory compliance plans | Technology resilience/disaster tolerance |
| | Forensics preparation | | Remote data storage |
| | | | Outsource server and storage management |
| Pandemic issues | | | Plans for reduced workforce/social distancing |
| | | | Plans for remote workforce; increased network/Web access |

| | Incident Management Plan | Process Continuity Plan | | Information Continuity Plan |
|---|---|---|---|---|
| Tactical components | Network/systems intrusions | Initiate emergency organizational hierarchy | | *Crisis/service interruption prevention* |
| | Personal observations | Provide procedure continuity | | Control technology/service interruption |
| | System halts/interrupts | Coordinate with IT for temporary technology restoration | | Reduce islands of technology |
| | Threat assessment | Restore services/processes in temporary configuration | | Reduce technology variability/ obsolescence |
| | | | Initiate temporary staffing plan | |
| | | | Timing of temporary structure breakdown | |
| | | | Return from temporary state or location | |

organizations will need to determine prior to the actual crisis. Depending on the size, organizations may combine some of the responsibilities under a more appropriate set of organizational units, and rearrange the sequence of events to suit the organizational structure.

## Crisis Recognition

It is clearly understood that the most prevalent crises that trigger response and recovery plans are weather related (e.g., see the FEMA map links: http://www.fema.gov/hazard/index.shtm). Fires are perhaps the next major category of crises that trigger a formal response. Although the prevalence of Internet malware and network attacks are increasing, it is neither clear how many of those attacks trigger formal crisis response and recovery plans, nor is it clear if such attacks reach the same breadth and scope as environmental, weather, or expansive fire-related crises. Nonetheless, each organization will have to be diligent in tracking and responding to low-level incidents and Internet attack attempts lest they result in a loss of processing capability within the organizational network.

A crisis may be recognized by anyone in the organization, but if the processes are in place the report will make its way through either the IIRT or the SERT to the ECC, and if appropriate to the CCT. Of course, for regional crises, news from the public media may reach all committees and the workforce at nearly the same time. From any source, the crisis recognition needs to be brought as soon as possible to the ECC who will call the CCT to action, which will officially initiate and administer the response (Table 24.3).

## Organizational Impact

The first consideration is the impact of the crisis, internal to the organization and external to the surrounding community and region. The CCT will simultaneously solicit organizational impact reports from the ITRT and the SERT for the state of structural and safety problems and the condition of the network and infrastructure. The severity of these reports (or lack thereof) may signal the quick end of the crisis and the CCT activities. If the severity is sufficient (which most certainly is a subjective determination), then the CCT will initiate the response plan. The first effort will be to instruct the Legal and CIA Units to evaluate the organizational responsibilities during and immediately after the crisis response. At this point, the CCT will determine from the reports whether or not the crisis involves a pandemic circumstance. If so, the team will implement the pandemic plan and initiate the appropriate evacuation or quarantine response.

## Scope Impact

At the same time as the organizational impact review is initiated, the CCT will instruct the COMT to contact external crisis teams for the impact beyond the organization. The COMT will be the official voice of contact for the organization under the direction of the CCT. The COMT will also instruct the predetermined organizational representatives to report to regional command centers for participating in the regional response and to keep the COMT abreast of the community and regional activities. The COMT will also contact all subordinate plan teams for preparation of activity.

**Table 24.3   Crisis Onset Response Sequence**

|  | *Responsible Unit(s)* | *Activity/Role/Function* |
|---|---|---|
| Crisis recognition | Internal incident response team | Observe/report internal incidents |
|  |  | Implement internal incident response plan |
|  | Safety/emergency team | Observe/report external or internal crises |
| Organizational impact | Coordination team | Receive/collate internal and external crisis alerts |
|  |  | Contact safety and IT units for effects on people, structures, information |
|  |  | Contact legal, compliance units for regulatory effects and responsibilities |
|  |  | Determine pandemic effects—evacuation, quarantine, remote/reduced workforce |
|  |  | Alert all responsible teams/units |
|  | Internal incident response team | Track/report correlated incidents |
| Scope impact | Communications team | Contact local/regional centers for breadth and intensity of crisis |
|  |  | Delegate participants to regional local crisis control center |
| Declaration | Command and control team | Declare official response implementation |
|  |  | Establish command and control center; activate relocation hierarchy |
|  |  | Based on predetermined thresholds, initiate response and recovery plans |
|  |  | Initiate emergency spending plan—accounting, payroll, expenses |
|  |  | Initiate remote location readiness plan |
|  |  | Acquire/establish networks, workstations, communications, furniture, etc. |
|  | Communications team | Contact workforce, establish family communication capability |
|  |  | Contact partners, customers, health care providers, media |
|  |  | Contact vendors and initiate technology replacement and license adjustment |
|  |  | Distribute/coordinate temporary communications technology |

*(continued)*

**Table 24.3 (continued)   Crisis Onset Response Sequence**

|  | *Responsible Unit(s)* | *Activity/Role/Function* |
|---|---|---|
| Emergency response | Safety/emergency team | Hazard assessment—ascertain human effects of exposure to hazards |
|  |  | Structural assessment—evaluate damage effects on people and processes |
|  |  | Set organizational perimeter protection |
|  |  | Establish ingress (rescue, firefighters) and egress (evacuation) pathways |
|  |  | Coordinate immediate personal aid—health, food, shelter |
|  |  | *Environmental/Pandemic assessments:* |
|  |  | Initiate evacuation/quarantine plans (time of day, intensity of Pandemic) |
|  |  | Coordinate food, shelter needs of internally quarantined groups |
| Incident management | Internal incident response team | Assess potential for information leakage, theft at organizational site |
|  |  | Acquire escrowed lists for timely and appropriate use |
|  |  | Monitor temporary network infrastructure for intrusions |
|  | IT recovery team | Collaborate with Internal Incident Response Team for technical support |
| Information continuity | IT recovery team | Activate recovery location technology—servers, workstations, network connectivity, vendor licenses |
|  |  | Initiate system builds—OS, licensed software, etc. |
|  |  | Acquire/reload backup data |
| Process continuity | Unit data owners | Test and activate systems (predetermined RTO/MTR sequence) |
|  |  | Initiate production processes in recovery location |
|  | IT recovery team | Coordinate testing and production loads with unit data owners |
| Recovery termination | Command and control team | Determine restoration completion of permanent site |
|  |  | *After other team activities (below):* |
|  |  | Declare return to permanent site |

**Table 24.3 (continued)   Crisis Onset Response Sequence**

| | *Responsible Unit(s)* | *Activity/Role/Function* |
|---|---|---|
| | Safety/emergency team | Determine/report safety of restored permanent site |
| | IT recovery team | Initiate planning for restoration from temporary location |
| | | Restore networks, workstations, servers, licenses from temporary location |
| | Unit data owners | Initiate planning for restoration of production processes from temporary location |
| | | Initiate production processes in restored permanent location |

## Declaration

The CCT will be the sole source for the formal declaration of the crisis in order to activate the organizational recovery plan. Depending on the size of the organization, the decision may be made by one person or the whole team, but a single source timing and of the decision is imperative. The declaration by prior understanding sets in motion a series of cascading events, triggers the initiation of all the subordinate plans; no separate command is to be expected by the subordinate plan administrators. However, if the crisis conditions have not interrupted all services and structures, some of the subordinate plan administrators may be advised to scale back pending further developments.

The CCT will activate the recovery hierarchy and establish the command and control center, which must be away from the crisis location. Then the team will initiate the emergency spending and accountability plans and set in motion the necessary insurance claims. Then, the temporary relocation site can be prepared, and all previously defined replacement technology, network infrastructure, furniture, and communications capability can be acquired, installed, and configured. If the temporary relocation site is provided by a service agency, then the relocation contract and plans will be implemented. If a temporary workforce supplement is necessary, then the CCT will initiate contact with temporary staffing agencies.

The declaration will also trigger the COMT to contact the workforce with the prearranged process, and seek to provide communication and coordinate assistance to families. The COMT will alert all organizational partners, customers, debtors, etc., to the status of the ongoing response and recovery. As the temporary relocation site is being prepared, the COMT will also contact vendors for replacement technology and license adjustment, based on previously collected instructions from the IT Tech Support Staff. If appropriate, the COMT will acquire and distribute the temporary communications technology, again based on previously arranged plans.

## Emergency Response

The SERT will be the primary on-site contacts for ascertaining the potential hazards within the organizational location, including toxic hazards and structural damage. Within the location, the team will set an organizational perimeter to prevent anyone from entering, whether part of the workforce or not. The team will also coordinate with local and regional authorities for establishing pathways for ingress of emergency vehicles and the egress of the workforce, especially any who may be injured. Where needed, the team will implement or coordinate the personal aid for injuries and temporary shelter and food.

If there are pandemic conditions, the SERT will initiate the appropriate quarantine and evacuation plans, based on advice or mandates from local and/or regional authorities. The team will also release and distribute food and other needs for workforce who may be remaining within the buildings for predetermined reasons.

## Incident Management

The IIRT will continue vigilance for any other threats that may exploit the structural and technical vulnerabilities associated with the crisis onset. This team may be involved with forensics assessments and gathering evidence especially if the crisis appears to be of internal origin, such as a fire or an explosion. The team will also initiate the monitoring of the temporary location network prior to restoring the replacement systems and data.

If there is damage to the network infrastructure, the team will work with the ITRT to estimate the damages and to identify recoverable systems and data storage. If the organizational network is still intact, the team will work with the IT Technical Support to heighten the intrusion detection and prevention capabilities of the monitoring devices. Representatives of both the internal incident management team and the ITRT will follow the procedures to recover any escrowed lists of passwords or encryption keys for use during the recovery period.

## Information Continuity

The efforts of the ITRT reflect the classic disaster recovery planning involved with restoring access to data and information. Once the recovery site is set up with replacement servers, workstations, and network connectivity, and the vendor licenses and keys are acquired, the ITRT will prepare the architecture for organizational use. The team will load the appropriate operating systems and tools, and build the applications systems required. Following that, the team will acquire the backup data media and restore the data to the temporary infrastructure.

## Process Continuity

In close coordination with the ITRT and the information continuity plan, the organizational business unit data owners will assist in the reconfiguration of the application systems and test the systems with the restored backup data. The prearranged RTO and MTR sequences will determine the order of the processes. Only the unit data owners can release the production systems for user activities.

## Recovery Termination

The CCT will necessarily keep abreast of both the temporary relocation efforts and the reestablishment or reconstruction of the original location. When the original location is close to completion, the CCT will initiate the plans to terminate the temporary recovery activity and return to the restored location. The process will be quite similar to the temporary location recovery activities, with hopefully much less need for safety and hazards protection. The team will instruct the SERT and ITRT to assess the safety of the restored site and to initiate the preparation of the restored site networks and infrastructure. Once configured, the unit data owners will again test and authorize the restored systems for production status. The relocation back to the restored location will also follow a predetermined sequence, based on the size and complexity of the organization.

## About the Author

**James C. Murphy**, GSEC, CISSP-ISSMP, CISA, and CISM, is the information security official for the Office of MMIS Services in the NC Department of Health and Human Services (DHHS), and information security lead within the NC Medicaid Management Information System development project.

# Chapter 25

# CERT/BERT: Community and Business Emergency Response

Carl Jackson

## Contents

# Foreword

The Department of Homeland Security defines a *first-responder*[1] as those individuals who in the early stages of an incident are responsible for the protection and preservation of life, property, evidence, and the environment, including emergency response providers.

Today, there is no accurate estimate of the number of trained and certified first-responders in the United States. The U.S. Department of Defense has warned of the piecemeal manner in which the federal government's assistance program for first-responders was initially created and expanded across agencies and departments. This largely uncoordinated effort has resulted in a number of problems and shortcomings in the effort to improve the nation's overall preparedness. According to Richard Falkenrath, former senior director of policy and plans at the Office of Homeland Security and currently the deputy commissioner of counterterrorism of the New York City Police Department, "The specifics of the program have been determined not by any guiding strategic concept but by discrete, uncoordinated legislative and appropriations and administrative initiatives."[2]

Also, according to Bruce Baughman, director of FEMA's Office of National Preparedness (ONP), "Even the best prepared states and localities do not possess adequate resources to respond to the full range of terrorist threats."[3] In fact, over the past 5 years, numerous reports have identified problems with the federal effort to train first-responders and have called for a reform of the numerous federal assistance programs created to support these professionals.

For some time, many private sector *executive managers, event crisis coordinators*, and *continuity planning professionals* have become increasingly aware of the gap that exists between the ratio of employees in their organizations versus the number of immediately available civil first-responders.

At this writing, the U.S. First Responders Association (http://www.usfra.org/), a nonprofit network of *firefighters, EMS, rescue, police officers, military*, and *civilian support teams*, estimates that there is far in excess of 17,000 open positions in these professions. These positions are for all categories of position titles and agency openings relating to support and execution of first-responder responsibilities.

# Background

Subsequent to the September 11, 2001 attacks on the United States, the newly formed Department of Homeland Security[4] (DHS), established the National Incident Management System (NIMS). In DHS's words, "NIMS provides a systematic, proactive approach to guide departments and agencies at all levels of government, nongovernmental organizations, and the private sector to work seamlessly to prevent, protect against, respond to, recover from, and mitigate the effects of incidents, regardless of cause, size, location, or complexity, in order to reduce the loss of life and property and harm to the environment."

The NIMS command and management component is comprised of the following elements:

- Incident command system (ICS)
- Multiagency coordination systems (MACS)
- Public information

Taken together, all three of these elements of top-down and unified command and control infrastructure are the most visible aspects of the DHS incident management infrastructure and are normally executed with a sense of urgency during times of crisis.

## Incident Command System

The ICS component of NIMS is designed as a standardized, on-scene, all-hazards incident management approach that

- Allows for the integration of facilities, equipment, personnel, procedures, and communications operating within a common organizational structure
- Enables a coordinated response among various jurisdictions and functional agencies, both public and private
- Establishes common processes for planning and managing resources

The command and control organization and communications structure of the ICS is utilized by all levels of the government including *federal, state, tribal,* and *local.* As well ICS has been voluntarily adopted by many nongovernmental and private sector organizations (*i.e., businesses, educational organizations, etc.*). ICS is applicable across disciplines providing a structured command and control environment comprising five major functional areas: *command, operations, planning, logistics, and finance/administration.* All of these functional areas may or may not be used based on the needs of the response personnel reacting to a particular incident.

## Multiagency Coordination Systems

The MACS component of NIMS allows all levels of government and all disciplines to work together and coordinate activities much more efficiently and effectively. Multiagency coordination occurs across the different disciplines of the ICS structure involved in incident management, across jurisdictional lines, or across levels of government. This multiagency coordination has been utilized on a regular basis whenever personnel from different agencies interact in such activities as preparedness, prevention, response, recovery, and mitigation (Figure 25.1).

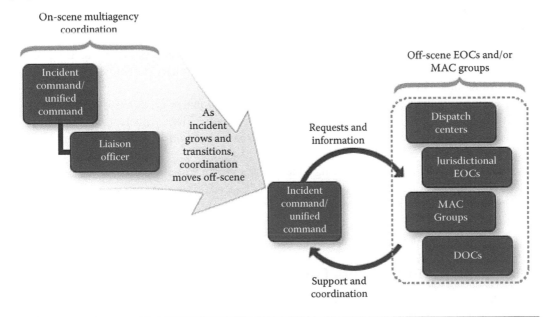

**Figure 25.1 Multiagency coordination systems overview. (From Federal Emergency Management Agency, http://www.fema.gov/emergency/nims/MultiagencyCoordinationSystems.shtm)**

## Public Information

The public information component of NIMS consists of the processes, procedures, and systems to communicate timely, accurate, and accessible information on the incident's cause, size, and current situation to the public, responders, and additional stakeholders (both directly affected and indirectly affected). Public information must be coordinated and integrated across jurisdictions, agencies, and organizations; among federal, state, tribal, and local governments; and the private sector.

The government provides a *Glossary of NIMS related terms* at the following URL for anyone interested in further understanding (http://training.fema.gov/EMIWeb/IS/ICSResource/Glossary.htm).

# Private Sector Integration

*So, what is the relevance of NIMS to the private sector organizations like businesses and educational organizations?*

NIMS provides an effective and efficient emergency response command and control structure that can be rather easily adopted by private sector organizations in planning for and documenting crisis management plans.

## Integration into Crisis Management Plans

Private sector organization crisis management planning is an integral part of the continuity planning process of the enterprise. Its most important objectives are to provide managers with a quickly activated and streamlined mechanism to assist them in managing the enterprise during the crisis/disaster situation. They do this by providing resource support and more importantly in facilitating communications with both internal crisis and recovery teams as well as with critical external parties (*the press, key stakeholders, civil authorities, important customers, clients and suppliers, etc.*).

Should a crisis arise, organization's crisis management team(s) must be activated to manage the crisis until conclusion. Typically, this support would be in the form of facilitated communications, resource allocation and access, and any other help required by the business and/or information technology recovery teams to facilitate rapid recovery and continuation of time-critical business process functionality.

Adopting and integrating the ICS concept into the company's crisis management structure gives the management a leg up on carrying out these vital objectives. Adherence to the ICS command and control model provides company crisis management with significant benefits and will enhance all aspects of response and recovery.

Utilization of the ICS model during times of crisis by businesses promotes the coordinated exchange of information that is so critical to rapid crisis response and mitigation. This provides business management, crisis management, and continuity planning teams with a valuable and structured synchronized means to exchange vital information, both internally and externally.

# Community and Business Emergency Response Teams

Given the NIMS and ICS background discussion above, it should be apparent at this point there are many advantages of adopting the ICS process in the private sector. As a way of providing private sector organizations with a model of how to most effectively achieve this, company managers should merely look to what many communities have done along these lines.

Referred to as the community emergency response team (CERT[5]) program, dozens of public entities have established CERT programs that serve as an outstanding example of how best to systematize community crisis response processes for a widespread or regional crisis. CERT is a key supporting component of the overall NIMS infrastructure with its ability to help communities organize management structure and communication paths. A properly implemented CERT program provides communities with the tools necessary to help them react to emergencies in a rapid and synchronized way utilizing ICS. CERT has enjoyed a widespread implementation among state, county, city, and other governmental agencies within the United States.

## The Role of Community Emergency Response Teams

The CERT program is designed to teach people about crisis and disaster preparedness and accompanying hazards that could seriously impact their communities and it provides training in essential disaster response skills, like

- Fire safety
- Light search and rescue
- CERT team organization
- Disaster medical operations

Through the CERT training that potential team members receive, they will be prepared to assist other folks in their neighborhood or workplace should disaster arise until professional first-responders are available, which in some cases could be hours or even days.

As volunteers go through the CERT training, they gain a much better understanding of the possible threats to their communities so that they may take the most appropriate steps to reduce the impact. Should a crisis occur that overwhelms local community first-responders, CERT members are then in a position to provide aid and comfort until help arrives. And even when assistance is available, CERT members can provide helpful information to first-responders accordingly.

Through participation in CERT, community leaders and volunteers are acknowledging that without outside assistance, they must be prepared to help themselves until significant aid can be brought in from the outside. This also acknowledges the fact that following a major disaster, first-responders who normally respond rapidly to supply fire and medical services simply will not be able to meet the overwhelming demand for life-safety services. A simple fact of life under these circumstances is that the numbers of casualties, potential communication interruptions or even complete failures, possible street blockages, etc., will all combine to severely hamper first-responders from providing aid.

CERT organization resources are available on the Web. For instance, an organization called *Citizen Core*[6] (http://www.citizencorps.gov/cert/index.shtm) recommends a number of steps to start a CERT within their Web site:

- Identify the program goals that CERT will meet and the resources available to conduct the program in your area.
- Gain approval from appointed and elected officials to use CERT as a means to prepare citizens to care for themselves during a disaster when services may not be adequate.
- Identify and recruit potential participants. Naturals for CERT are community groups, business and industry workers, and local government workers.
- Train CERT instructor cadre.

- Conduct CERT sessions.
- Conduct refresher training and exercises with CERTs.

On the Web site referenced above *Citizen Core* also provides guidance on

- Starting a CERT program
- Registering a CERT
- Obtaining CERT specific training
- Finding CERT resources
- Locating other CERT organizations

The well respected *Citizen Core* CERT National Newsletter can also be found at that URL.

# Business Emergency Response Teams Program
## The Role of BERT

As with community CERT teams, likewise, businesses must also acknowledge that without outside assistance, they must prepare themselves to help themselves until significant assistance can be brought in from the outside. An outgrowth of the CERT concept, the American Red Cross and other organizations have been advocating the formation of Business Emergency Response Teams (BERTs) within the private sector. Business, educational organizations, and others are being asked to consider the implementation of a BERT organization. BERT is very closely related to and structured in a similar manner for businesses as the CERT program is for government entities.

## Why BERT?

Sometimes, unfortunately, organizational management may not be aware of the need for a BERT program internally. There are several tools the practitioner can use to begin educating management on the need for BERT. For instance, Figure 25.2 presents a convincing argument by addressing the wide disparity of community first-responders on duty at any given time versus the numbers of citizen casualties who would need assistance. Such a wide divergence of numbers demonstrate that in a significant regional or area wide disaster, civil first-responders would be badly stretched to the point of breaking, and citizens would be forced into taking care of themselves as well as their neighbors.

## Benefits of BERT to the Enterprise

There are several benefits that can accrue to an organization that implements and maintains a successful BERT program. These benefits include, but are certainly not limited to, the following:

- Enhanced State OSHA compliance
- Lowered insurance related costs
- BERT recognition by local fire and police agencies (potentially)

Why a company BERT?

Situation: The *American Red Cross* and the *State of California OES* tell us that in the event of a major Southern California earthquake, we should all expect to and be prepared to be on our own for at least 72 h.

| • Facts: | Company locations | | |
|---|---|---|---|
| | #1 | #2 | #3 |
| Population: | ~84,000 | ~48,000 | ~428,000 |
| Visitors/company employees: | ~10,000 | | |
| Total population: | ~94,000 | ~48,000 | ~428,000 |
| On duty police officers: | 12 | 20 | 35 |
| On duty fire fighters: | 39 | 10 | 29 |
| Total first responders: | 51 | 30 | 64 |
| Ratio: | 1800:1 | 1600:1 | 6700:1 |

- • We need to answer these questions:
  - • What do we do if there is a major disaster event at one of our locations?
  - • What happens if we are on our own?
  - • What do we do it there are multiple casualties?
  - • What happens if 911 is down?
  - • Do we have enough trained internal first responders?
  - • Do we have enough supplies?

- • Assist in answering management's question: "Are we ready?"

**Figure 25.2  Why a company BERT?**

- ■ Fulfilling responsibility to company employees
- ■ Having the company location named as a *Disaster Triage Drop-Off**location
  - – Paramedic/ambulance colocation
  - – Medical personnel marshalling area
- ■ Workers compensation credit (potentially)
- ■ State emergency services credit (potentially)
- ■ Corporate citizenship (to the local community)

# Establishing a BERT Program

At the outset, it is wise to establish a *BERT Management Team* with the organization to oversee the development and implementation of the program. Components of BERT program formation might include

- ■ Obtaining executive sponsor support and leadership
- ■ Identification of company locations in need of BERT

---

* Potentially making the company eligible to be recognized and used by local fire and medical agencies as a medical marshalling area during times of emergency. The reasoning is that if medical agencies understand that BERT training and triage is utilized at this location, they may be more likely to designate the location as a marshalling area as they would understand that the company's personnel are trained in triage and have performed adequate screening of critically injured people. This is as opposed to a company where no prescreening has occurred, thereby requiring medical authorities to perform triage themselves, stretching scarce resources, and thereby slowing response.

- Preparing a written program description including definition of a BERT charter, outlining the BERT organization structure, participant and volunteer roles and responsibilities, funding, training plans, internal awareness communications plans, etc.
- Identification of volunteer business emergency responders who work in the business and are familiar with the area
- Preparation of draft management communications regarding BERT
- Analysis of existing business emergency response plans and groups within the enterprise that support those plans (*i.e., company security, facilities management, IT emergency response and business continuity planners, etc.*)
- Organizing and oversight of BERT training
- Development of BERT maintenance plans
- Continued long-term administration of the BERT program

## BERT Costs

One of the very first questions that will be asked will be on the topic of cost. An organization that has not attempted to form a BERT in the past will naturally be concerned about the expenses involved for start-up. Figure 25.3 estimates expenses for a company with three locations with roughly 3000 employees spread across those locations.

As can be seen in this very simple example, the estimated costs are allocated to two categories: the first being the cost of initial start-up, while the second is an estimate of annual maintenance expenses. Of course, there are important cost elements that have been left off this simple example: the cost of employee time in training and participating in BERT-related events, etc.

| Company BERT program | Estimated first year BERT start-up costs | | | Notes |
|---|---|---|---|---|
| | Location 1 | Location 2 | Location 3 | |
| Costs | | | | |
| BERT materials | $ 15,000 | $ 15,000 | $ 15,000 | Extinguishers, radios, backpacks, etc. |
| Misc BERT consulting | $ 10,000 | $ 10,000 | $ 10,000 | CPR training, Haz-Mat abatement, etc. |
| Primary BERT training | $ 15,000 | $ 15,000 | $ 15,000 | Outside consulting |
| Contingency | $ 5000 | $ 5000 | $ 5000 | Unknowns |
| | $ 45,000 | $ 45,000 | $ 45,000 | $ 135,000 |

| Company BERT program | Estimated annual BERT maintenance costs | | | Notes |
|---|---|---|---|---|
| | Location 1 | Location 2 | Location 3 | |
| Costs | | | | |
| Refresher training | $ 2000 | $ 2000 | $ 2000 | Certification fees—Red Cross |
| Materials | $ 2000 | $ 2000 | $ 2000 | New and replacement |
| Training | $ 6000 | $ 6000 | $ 6000 | New BERT members |
| Consulting | $ 5000 | $ 5000 | $ 5000 | Annual drill assistance |
| Contingency | $ 3000 | $ 3000 | $ 3000 | Unknowns |
| | $ 18,000 | $ 18,000 | $ 18,000 | $ 54,000 |

**Figure 25.3  BERT start-up and maintenance cost estimates.**

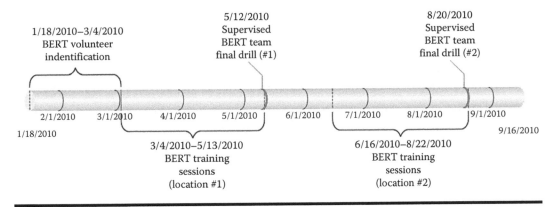

**Figure 25.4  BERT training schedule.**

## BERT Training[7]

The typical American Red Cross BERT course is generally 28 h long for each volunteer that trains them in first-responder disciplines. The course prepares business first-responder teams to respond during emergency and disaster situations. It consists of seven 4 h modules:

- Introduction to emergency preparedness
- Emergency response
- Medical module 1
- Medical module 2
- Search and rescue
- Team organization and management
- Course review and disaster simulation

## Timing of BERT Training

The following sample BERT training schedule timeline (Figure 25.4) is a MS Visio representation of how an organization with two different geographical locations may want to address training at both with scarce training resources:

## Equipping the BERT Teams[8]

To learn more and find out how you can help your community, please contact citizencorps.gov. The following CERT checklist, which is also very applicable to a checklist that BERT team members might use, is recommended *by Citizen Corps* (www.citizencorps.gov/cert/downloads/training/PM-CERT-AD-Unit1Rev2.doc):

---

### COMMUNITY EMERGENCY RESPONSE TEAM MEMBER EQUIPMENT/SUPP/FIRST AID CHECKLIST

The following equipment and supplies are recommended as a minimum supply cache for all CERT teams. The equipment and supplies should be maintained at or near the team staging area.

#### EQUIPMENT/SUPPLY

- Nylon/canvas bag with shoulder strap
- Water (two canteens/bottles per search and rescue team)
- Dehydrated foods
- Water purification tablets
- Work gloves (leather)
- Goggles
- Dust masks
- Flashlight or miner's lamp
- Batteries and extra bulbs
- Secondary flashlight or light sticks
- Utility knife
- Note pads
- Markers:
  - Thin point
  - Thick point
- Pens
- Duct tape
- Masking tape (2 in.)
- Crescent wrench

#### First aid pouch containing:

- 4 × 4 gauze dressings (6)
- Abdominal pads (4)
- Triangular bandages (4)
- Band-Aids
- Roller bandage
- Scissors

---

## Executive Management Communications

Once executive and mid-level managers are on board, the BERT management team can take over to provide initial organization, preparation of budgets, selection of volunteers, training, and the like.

Box 25.1 is an example of the wording of an executive management communication intended for all managers within the enterprise.

---

**BOX 25.1   SAMPLE EXECUTIVE MANAGEMENT
BERT PROGRAM ANNOUNCEMENT**

Date:

Good Morning (Afternoon);

Given threat of serious regional disaster scenarios in our area, *Executive Management* is pleased to announce the initiation of a *Business Emergency Response Team* (BERT) program at Company.

The primary purpose of the BERT program is to put us in the position to help us help ourselves should severe regional emergencies, like earthquakes, result in significant delays by local city, county, or state first-responders to come to our aid.

Under the BERT program, we will provide training to individuals who have volunteered to help respond to emergency situations at company locations.

When emergencies happen, *Company Business Emergency Response Team* members will have been trained to provide critical support to first-responders, provide immediate assistance to victims, and organize spontaneous volunteers for our primary business locations.

Members of the *Company BERT Management Team* will be asking for volunteers within the next few weeks. We are anticipating that each of the company locations will require approximately (number here) BERT members.

The *Business Emergency Response Team* training is free, will be conducted during business hours, and is comprised of seven 4 h modules:

Session 1: Introduction/course overview/basic emergency preparedness
Session 2: Fire suppression/evacuation basics
Session 3: Search and rescue
Session 4: Triage/stabilization and extrication/medical operations/disaster first aid
Session 5: Medical operations/disaster first aid II
Session 6: Team roles and operational organization/NIMS—SIMS system orientation
Session 7: Final drill exercise

Following completion of initial training, BERT members will meet periodically to ensure they stay current on training and to participate in periodic drills as needed.

On behalf of the executive management, please note that as we move through the initial stages of forming the company BERT program, we are asking the cooperation of all managers in assisting in the identification of volunteers, and then for allowing selected BERT volunteers to participate fully in BERT training and other activities. It is not anticipated that the time needed by BERT volunteers will in any way be onerous.

Our *BERT Management Team* will be utilizing the company intranet site and other communication mediums to reach out to company BERT volunteers and their managers very soon.

Should you have any questions, please feel free to contact _____.

Best Regards,

/CEO signature/

## Summary

The 9/11 attacks as well as the many natural and man-made disasters of late have all combined to raise awareness and recognition that our civil first-responders may well be hard pressed to provide enough aid in a timely manner. We know that even under optimum circumstances, there is often a very serious deficit of civil first-responders as compared to the numbers of people that would require life-safety and/or medical attention immediately following either an area wide or regional disaster or a major terrorist attack.

One solution discussed has been the adoption and adherence to an ICS command and control model. A properly implemented ICS together with CERT/BERT team formation will provide enterprise crisis management with significant benefits and will enhance all aspects of response and recovery. Utilization of the ICS model during times of crisis by businesses promotes the coordinated exchange of information that is so critical to rapid crisis response and mitigation and, thereby, provides business management, crisis management, and continuity planning teams with a valuable and structured and synchronized means to exchange vital information, both internally and externally.

BERT and CERT are about readiness, people helping people, rescuer safety, and doing the greatest good for the greatest number. BERT/CERT is a positive and realistic approach to emergency and disaster situations where citizens will be initially on their own and their actions can make a life-and-death difference to us, our loved ones, coworkers, and/or neighbors. Through training, citizens can manage utilities and put out small fires; treat the three killers by opening airways, controlling bleeding, and treating for shock; provide basic medical aid; search for and rescue victims safely; and organize themselves and spontaneous volunteers to be effective.

FEMA defines an emergency as "any unplanned event that can cause deaths or significant injuries to employees, customers, or the public; or that can shut down your business, disrupt operations, cause physical or environmental damage, or threaten the facility's financial standing or public image."

To help prepare ourselves to withstand such a serious unplanned event, this chapter has attempted to provide potential solutions *to prepare ourselves to help ourselves*. And, at the end of the day, this preparedness may be all we have that stands between us and tragedy.

## About the Author

**Carl Jackson**, CISSP, CBCP, is the former director of the Business Continuity Program at Pacific Life Insurance Company in Newport Beach, California.

## References

1. Section 2 of the Homeland Security Act of 2002 (6 U.S.C. 101).
2. R. A. Falkenrath, The problems of preparedness: Challenges facing the U.S. Domestic Preparedness Program. BCSIA Discussion Paper 2000-28, ESDP Discussion Paper ESDP-2000-05, John F. Kennedy School of Government, Harvard University, December 2000, p. 4.
3. B. Baughman, Testimony before the Subcommittee on Military Procurement, Committee on Armed Services, U.S. Senate, March 5, 2002.

4. Department of Homeland Security, http://www.dhs.gov/xprepresp/
5. CERT, http://www.citizencorps.gov/cert/
6. Citizen Core, http://www.citizencorps.gov/cert/index.shtm
7. Business Emergency Response Team Training [BERTT],Orange County, California, http://oc-redcross.org/Education/course.aspx?c=3744
8. CERTT and BERTT Kits & Equipment for Community Emergency Response Teams, http://www.cpr-savers.com/emergency/cert-kits-equipment.html (CPR Savers & First Aid Supply LLC)

# LAW, REGULATIONS, COMPLIANCE, AND INVESTIGATION

## *Major Categories of Computer Crime*

# Chapter 26

# Cyberstalking

Micki Krause Nozaki

## Contents

## Introduction

In 1998, J. Reid Meloy wrote: "Stalking is an old behavior, but a new crime." [1]

A decade later, we can state: Cyberstalking is a new behavior and an even newer crime. This chapter will address the what, who, why, where, and how of cyberstalking, including the many definitions of the word and the behaviors demonstrated by cyberstalkers; where and how cyberstalking is done; who propagates this potentially criminal behavior and why; the laws surrounding this relatively recent phenomenon; and, finally, the steps to consider should someone find themselves in the unfortunate situation as the victim of a cyberstalker.

Robert Lloyd-Goldstein, MD, JD, in his contribution to the aforementioned anthology states: "Unsurprisingly, the growth of new technologies, such as the proliferation of computers and the ubiquity of the world wide web, has been accompanied by the emergence of electronic surveillance, email stalking and internet harassment, among other forms of online crime."

**Figure 26.1   Stalking opportunities abound.**

As Figure 26.1 demonstrates, the pervasive growth and ubiquity of technology presents increasing and omnipresent methods of electronic communication, each of which offers an avenue for cyberstalking.

*Cyberstalking*—the word alone conjures up visions of a creepy-looking, shifty-eyed, mal-intended marauder, roving about, preparing to molest or attack some unsuspecting, innocent victim.

In many ways, this is not too far from the truth.

Stalking, in its traditional sense, is the obsessive following, observing, or contacting of another person, or the obsessive attempt to engage in any of these activities. It's been around for as long as man could well stalk. Stalking victims broadly range from ordinary citizens such as Joan 6-pack to public figures such as John Lennon and Jodie Foster.

Cyberstalking, on the other hand, is a relatively new occurrence and incidents are rarely publicized, that is to say, cyberstalking is typically an anonymous crime.

## What Is Cyberstalking?

According to the U.S. Department of Justice, cyberstalking is

> "… the use of the Internet, e-mail, or other electronic communications devices to stalk another person. Stalking generally involves harassing or threatening behavior that an individual engages in repeatedly, such as following a person, appearing at a person's home or place of business, making harassing phone calls, leaving written messages or objects, or vandalizing a person's property. Most stalking laws require that the perpetrator make a credible threat of violence against the victim; others include threats against the victim's immediate family; and still others require only that the alleged stalker's course of conduct constitute an implied threat."[2]

Little statistical data has been compiled on cyberstalking incidents (e.g. see Figure 26.2) Nonetheless, what data does exist forecasts daunting news as shown in a report from the United States Department of Justice [2]:

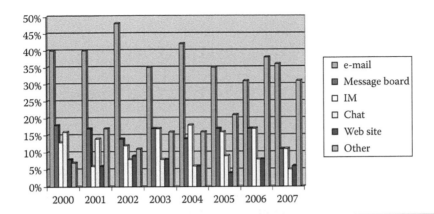

**Figure 26.2   Primary sources of cyberstalking. Other includes auctions, personals, online dating, virus, hacking, greeting cards, gaming, mailing list, Webcam, blogs, guestbook, spyware, trojans. (Courtesy of haltabuse.org)**

- There may be tens or even hundreds of thousands of cyberstalking victims in the United States
- Almost 25% of stalking incidents among college age women involved cyberstalking

The numbers are not surprising, given the decreasing expense and thereby increased availability of computers and online services. More and more individuals are purchasing computers and logging onto the Internet. Moreover, since cyberstalking is done behind the scenes, that is, anonymously, a veil of perceived safety protects the perpetrator.

## How Is It Done?

Cyberstalkers target their victims through chat rooms, message boards, discussion forums, and e-mail. Their behaviors take many forms including threatening or obscene e-mail; sending the victim a stream of spam or junk mail; live chat harassment or flaming; leaving improper messages on message boards; sending malware, e.g., viruses; sending unsolicited e-mail; tracing another person's computer and Internet activity; and electronic identity theft.

Similar to the effects of stalking off-line, victims of online stalking report it as a terrifying experience. Police reports indicate that many times, cyberstalking situations evolve into off-line stalking, and a victim may experience abusive and excessive phone calls, vandalism, threatening or obscene mail, trespassing, and physical assault.

## Who Cyberstalks?

As Figure 26.3 shows, anyone can be online stalker, although the majority are male and the majority of their victims are female.

Cyberstalking is often perpetrated by people that are known to the victim. In fact, as shown in Figure 26.4, almost 50% of the victims knew their stalker.

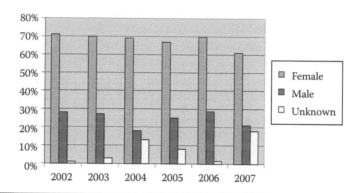

**Figure 26.3    Gender of victim. (Courtesy of haltabuse.org)**

They may be coworkers, former spouses, or frustrated suitors whose advances were ignored or rejected. They could also be fans or groupies, especially when a cyber-celebrity or well-known chat room or discussion board leader is involved.

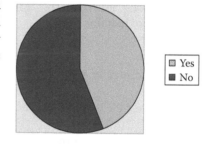

## Why Cyberstalk?

Bad people do bad things. There are just as many predators on the Web as there are in real life. The only difference is the manner in which the behavior is manifested. What is different is the methods they use to victimize. As in real life, a minority of predators

**Figure 26.4    Cyberstalker known to victim (2007). (Courtesy of haltabuse.org)**

are abusing technology to prey on the innocent. Electronic stalking behavior is really just a reflection of the world in which we live.

Cyberstalkers are often driven by revenge, hate, anger, jealousy, obsession, and mental illness. Sometimes, the perpetrator intends to teach the victim a lesson in netiquette. Often, the victim is merely in the wrong place at the wrong time, or has made a comment or expressed an opinion that the stalker dislikes.

Sitting alone behind a computer lends itself to a feeling of security, a sense of anonymity, which allows one to demonstrate behaviors not comfortably displayed face to face. Cyberstalkers can be rude, insensitive, angry, passionate, exuberant, etc. In fact, it can be said that the experience of online communications can be likened to the consumption of alcohol—the lowering of inhibitions and an increase in directness.

## Cyber-Behaviors

Cyberstalkers meet or target their victims by using a multitude of available technologies including search engines, online forums, bulletin and discussion boards, chat rooms, and very recent offerings such as MySpace, Facebook, or Friendster. These social networks are essentially online communities, which allow for the propagation (and potential abuse) of personal information. Victims of cyberstalking may not even know that they are being stalked.

Cyberstalkers oftentimes research individuals to feed their obsessions and curiosity as seen from the following excerpt from an article in the November 2008 *Marie Claire* magazine.

> My boyfriend's ex-wife is a 29 year old, 5-foot-9 costume designer and lover of whiskey, Hitchcock and Lena Horne. She's agnostic, wants children someday, and has a ruby-lipped smile. How do I know all this? I cyberstalked her. [3]

More commonly they will post defamatory or derogatory statements about their target on Web pages, message boards, and in guest books hoping to get a reaction or response from their victim, thereby initiating contact. Once they get a reaction from the victim, they will typically attempt to track or follow the victim's Internet activity.

Classic cyberstalking behavior includes the tracing of the victim's Internet address in an attempt to verify their home or place of employment. Online dating Web sites are another common way for cyberstalkers to "meet" their prey. All too often, however, "there is a false degree of safety assumed by women looking for love online," as reported in a 2007 study led by Paige Padgett from the University of Texas. [4]

Examining the choices women made when meeting men from online personal ads for friendships, love, and sex, Dr. Padgett concluded that the high frequency and intensity of e-mail communication, prior to meeting face to face, lent itself to an accelerated form of intimacy on behalf of her participants. Said Padgett, "This may have affected women's decisions to engage in risky sexual behavior."

## Cyberstalking and the Law

With personal information becoming readily available to an increasing number of people through the Internet and other advanced technology, state legislators are addressing the problem of stalkers who harass and threaten their victims over the Internet.

Although cyberstalking in the United States is addressed at the federal level (the current U.S. Federal Anti-Cyber-Stalking law (47 USC sec 223)), the predominance of regulation can be found at the state level. The Violence Against Women Act, passed in 2000, made cyberstalking a part of the federal interstate stalking statute. Still, there remains a lack of legislation at the federal level to specifically address cyberstalking, leaving the majority of legislative prohibitions against cyberstalking at the state level.

Most stalking laws require that the perpetrator make a credible threat of violence against the victim; others include threats against the victim's immediate family; and still others require the alleged stalker's course of conduct constitute an implied threat. While some conduct involving annoying or menacing behavior might fall short of illegal stalking, such behavior may be a prelude to stalking and violence and should be treated seriously.

Online identity stealth blurs the line on infringement of the rights of would-be victims to identify their perpetrators. There is a debate on how Internet use can be traced without infringing on protected civil liberties.

The first U.S. cyberstalking law went into effect in 1999 in California. Other states include prohibition against cyberstalking in their harassment or stalking legislation. In Florida, HB 479 was introduced in 2003 to ban cyberstalking. This was signed into law on October 2003.

Some states in the United States have begun to address the issue of cyberstalking (National Center for Victims of Crime):

- Alabama, Arizona, Connecticut, Hawaii, Illinois, New Hampshire, and New York have included prohibitions against harassing electronic, computer or e-mail communications in their harassment legislation.
- Alaska, Florida, Oklahoma, Wyoming, and California have incorporated electronically communicated statements as conduct constituting stalking in their anti-stalking laws.
- Texas enacted the *Stalking by Electronic Communications Act*, 2001.
- Missouri revised its state harassment statutes to include stalking and harassment by telephone and electronic communications (as well as cyber-bullying) after the Megan Meier suicide case of 2006. [5]
- A few states have both stalking and harassment statutes that criminalize threatening and unwanted electronic communications.
- Other states have laws other than harassment or anti-stalking statutes that prohibit misuse of computer communications and e-mail, while others have passed laws containing broad language that can be interpreted to include cyberstalking behaviors.

Most stalking statutes require that the perpetrator make a real or implied "credible threat" of violence against the victim or the victim's family. The laws are sufficiently disparate as the threat factors, which leads to some level of interpretation as to whether the cyberstalking is reportable. However, most agree that there are common factors, as shown in Table 26.1.

**Table 26.1   Common Factors in Cyberstalking**

| Key Factor | Description |
|---|---|
| False accusations | Posting false information about a person on public Web sites |
| Attempts to gather information about the victim | Monitoring the victim's online activities; tracing the victim's Internet address; and soliciting personal information about the victim from the victim's family, friends, or acquaintances |
| Encouraging others to harass the victim | Involving third parties in the harassment |
| False victimization | Claiming that the victim is actually doing the harassment |
| Attacks on data and equipment | Attempting to damage the victim's electronic equipment by, e.g., sending an e-mail message infected with malware |
| Ordering goods and services | Subscribing and sending goods to victim's home or workplace |
| Arranging to meet | Setting up in-person meetings with their victims (typically done with younger victims) |

*Source:* Courtesy of National Center for Victims of Crime, Washington, DC.

## Cyberstalking Laws in Other Countries

Other countries have begun to include online abuse in their anti-stalking legislation. In Australia, the Stalking Amendment Act (1999) includes the use of any form of technology to harass a target as forms of "criminal stalking." In the United Kingdom, the Malicious Communications Act (1998) classified cyberstalking as a criminal offense.

## How Can I Tell If I'm a Cyberstalking Victim?

When identifying cyberstalking "in the field," and particularly when considering whether to report it to any kind of legal authority, the following features or combination of features can be considered to characterize a true stalking situation:

- Malice
- Premeditation
- Repetition
- Distress
- Obsession
- Vendetta
- No legitimate purpose
- Personally directed
- Disregarded warnings to stop
- Harassment
- Threats

## How Can We Be on the Alert?

There are several good resources on the Internet that provide information in anti-stalking.
  Here are a few important pointers to help you understand how to thwart cyberstalking:

The following checklist gives you information on how to avoid becoming a victim

- Maintain vigilance over physical access to your computer and other Web-enabled devices. Cyberstalkers use software and hardware devices (sometimes attached to the back of your PC without your knowledge).
- Be sure you always log out of your computer programs when you step away from the computer and use a screensaver with a password. Your entire family should develop the same good habits.
- Make sure to practice good password management and security—never share your passwords with others. And be sure to change your passwords frequently!
- Use search engines such as "Google" to search for yourself and your family members now and then to check on what's available about you and your kids online. Don't be shy about searching social networks and be sure to remove anything private or inappropriate.
- Get rid of calendars or itineraries regarding your future travels from Web sites and social networks.

- If you suspect that someone is using spyware software to track your everyday activities, and you feel as if you're in danger, seek help.
- As always, use good, updated security software to prevent someone from getting spyware onto your computer via a phishing attack or an infected Web page.
- Limit the amount of personal information you provide for online resources such as social networks.

## Keeping Your Children Safe Online

- Keep the computer in a central family location, not in the child's room.
- Get to know your children's online friends.
- Screen e-mail with all younger children.
- Help your children keep computing online in balance.
- If you can't be home with them when they're online, use child protection software to help keep an eye on them.
- Make sure they understand that they should never meet anyone in real life that they met online without parents in attendance.

## What If I Think I'm a Victim?

1. In order to locate local victim service professionals who may be able to offer assistance, safety suggestions, and information and referrals, contact the Helpline of the National Center for Victims of Crime at *1-800-FYI-CALL*, 8:30 a.m.–8:30 p.m., Monday through Friday, Eastern Standard Time.
2. The Privacy Rights Clearinghouse
   3100 5th Avenue., Suite B
   San Diego, CA 92103
   (619) 298-3396
3. Resources on the Internet:
   a. National Center for Victims of Crime Stalking Resource Center
   b. National Network to End Domestic Violence (NNEDV)
   c. Working to Halt Online Abuse (WHOA)—whoa@haltabuse.org
   d. CyberAngels
   e. Safety Ed International
   f. Electronic Privacy Information Center (EPIC)
   g. Online Privacy Alliance
   h. Network Solutions WHOIS—helps determine contents of domain name registration
4. Your local prosecutor's office, law enforcement, or state Attorney General's office. Check in the Blue Pages of your local phone book under the appropriate section heading of either "Local Government," "County Government," or "State Government."
5. Consumer reports online: http://www.consumerreports.org/electronics-computers/resource-center/cyber-insecurity/cyber-insecurity-hub.htm (must be a subscriber of Consumer Reports)

# References

1. J. R. Meloy (ed.) (1998). *The Psychology of Stalking: Clinical and Forensic Perspectives*. Academic Press, San Diego, CA, ISBN 0124905617, 9780124905610, 327 pp.
2. U.S. Department of Justice (August 1999). Cyberstalking: A new challenge for law enforcement and industry, a report from the Attorney General to the Vice President. U.S. Department of Justice, Washington, DC, pp. 2, 6.
3. A. Whitefield-Madrano (2008). Confessions: Google stalking, *Marie Claire*, November 2008.
4. P. Padgett (2007). Personal safety and sexual safety for women using online personal ads, *Sexuality Research and Social Policy*, 4(2); 27–37.
5. S. Michels, Prosecutors bringing charges under law inspired by Megan Meir suicide, http://abcnews.go.com/TheLaw/story?id = 6520260&page=1, December 24, 2008. Accessed March 8, 2010.

# *Incident Handling*

# Chapter 27

# Is Software Write Blocking a Viable Alternative to Hardware Write Blocking in Computer Forensics?

Paul A. Henry

## Contents

Hardware write blockers have historically been the only choice in protecting the integrity of evidence in computer forensics. This chapter explores some of the increasing competitive issues and the often overlooked total cost of ownership considerations that are driving some within the industry to seek out software-based alternatives. Further, it explores the viability of using current generation software write blocking as an alternative to hardware write blocking by providing the details of the authors actual "hands-on" testing of a software write blocker to validate its forensic soundness.

## My Personal Observations

If you have been in computer forensics for any length of time you already have had to put together quite a collection of hardware write blocking devices for drive imaging and for knock-and-look events. But it never seems to be enough; first you have to deal with the issue of legacy drive interfaces that you may still run into today such as SCSI, IDE/ATA, and today's newer SATA drives. We have to consider the myriad of new small form factor laptop drives, the new solid state drives appearing in current generation laptops and let us not forget all of the external drives with their USB, IEEE1394, and eSATA interfaces. You are constantly buying new hardware write blockers in order to be able to simply keep up with the drives you are faced with imaging.

For a commercial forensic practice there is another consideration; you have to keep in mind that you are competing with other computer forensic service vendors that may have already upgraded to today's latest eSATA interface–based write blockers. You could very well find yourself priced out of competition because of your slower legacy acquisition speeds. So for anyone offering commercial forensic services, it is not just simply necessary to keep up with the evolution of hard drives themselves but also a matter of upgrading write blockers to take advantage of faster interface speed, or worst case, lowering one's billable imaging rates in order to remain competitive.

Evolution of drive acquisition speeds (actual not theoretical):

| USB 2.0 | 30 MB/s |
| --- | --- |
| Firewire 400 | 35 MB/s |
| Firewire 800 | 75 MB/s |
| eSATA-150 | 115 MB/s |

*For a small forensics shop, keeping up to date with hardware write blockers can get expensive. In order to be able to handle the common drive situations you will run into today, you actually need multiple hardware write blockers, and then there is the issue of the evolving interfaces to your PC and keeping your imaging services competitive.*

Buying used write blocking gear to try to keep your costs down is not necessarily a viable solution either. I recently purchased a hardware write blocker/high-speed imager myself on eBay. The particular device "new" (in the configuration I bought it in) was worth just under $5000 and I was able to pick it up for only $2000. I validated it against a handful of drives with known hashes—speed was great averaging around 3.6 GB/min and the hashes all matched (forensically sound) and all seemed well. However, the very first job I used it on just weeks later, it died—no available power for the target drive. I contacted the vendor and knowing it was out of the 1 year warranty I asked about a repair, and the price I was quoted was $600 regardless of what was wrong with it—I was told this was the company policy. What appeared to be nothing more than perhaps a $5 component was going to cost me $600 and if I opened the case and tried to repair it myself, I would be banished to "voided warranty land" forever—never then being able to resell the device.

## Exploring Software-Based Alternatives

For me, it seemed to be a good time to perhaps reconsider hardware write blockers in general as really being my only choice in producing forensically sound images. Looking at the constantly changing environment in drives and interfaces while also considering the investment I already have in lab and portable forensic servers, using a forensically sound software write blocker is beginning to look like a viable alternative. All of my forensic servers already have removable IDE—SATA drive trays and multiple USB—IEEE1394 and eSATA ports. I wondered if I could find a software write blocker solution that would work across literally anything I could connect to my forensic servers. I could reduce the costs associated with both maintaining my existing hardware write blockers and the cost of upgrading them to remain competitive from a performance perspective.

I spoke to peers and also to a few hardware acquisition/write blocker vendors. The big areas of push back they pointed out to me in considering moving to a software write blocker are performance, features, and forensic soundness. Well performance seemed easy enough to test, I only found one feature that a hardware product offered—the ability to search for keywords during an acquisition—a feature I have yet to have a client request, so all that remained was testing for forensic soundness, something that is already a best practice whenever you buy any new hardware write blocker or upgrade its firmware. So taking a closer look at software write blockers was now a high priority for me.

I read through the reports at NIST on software write blocker validation and it certainly seemed to me that software write blockers are perhaps coming of age. Further research on the Internet led me to SAFE Block XP 1.1 from Forensic Soft. I read the test results from the NIST write blocking suite on the Web site, looked at the price $219 and decided to take a closer look using their free trial offer (http://www.forensicsoft.com/catalog/index.php). I downloaded the install software and filled out the registration form so a temporary license key could be sent via e-mail. This was a simple process, and literally I was up and running in minutes ready to write block any IDE (PATA & SATA), SCSI, FC, SAS, USB, or IEEE1394 drive I could connect to my portable forensic server. I ran the SAFE Block software for a couple of weeks simply getting myself used to the GUI and its overall operation and to see if it had any negligible impact on my system—without relying upon it as a write blocker for any case-related forensic evidence.

## Taking a Software Write Blocker for a Test Drive

My first impression of the GUI was pretty good—all of my interfaces for not only my boot hard drive but all of my removable drives and my external ports could be quickly write protected, and just as importantly, I could password protect my configuration. I chose to set up my configuration to automatically block literally anything I could plug in to the machine by default but to also remember anything beyond the default that I had changed. That is, default block but then allow a particular USB drive to be written to—shut down, reboot, and have it come back to the previous state with access allowed to the USB drive I permitted earlier, but anything else I then plugged in was automatically write protected.

What about performance? I dropped a 250 GB SATA drive into one of my removable trays and decided to see how well it performed when imaging. Having lived in a world of imaging hard drives at rates that seem to range from as little as 1 MB/s to a best case of around 15 MB/s using a hardware write block and a USB connection, I was only expecting a marginal improvement. Using FTK Imager and with the software write block enabled for the physical drive in the SAFE Block XP GUI, I was able to image a 250 GB SATA drive in exactly 69 min. That works out to a rate of just under 60 MB/s—that is close to the 3.6 GB/min. I have only been averaging getting 3.6 from my dedicated "high-end" stand-alone acquisition hardware. You have to consider that the same drive would have taken me between 6 and 8 h to image using a USB connection with a hardware write blocker. I then tried to validate the image I created against the drive, the MD5 hash validation ran at over 90 MB/s as well—unheard of speed in a write block, USB, or even IEEE1394 world.

## But Is Software Write Blocking Really Forensically Sound?

Rather than simply accepting the vendor's claims, I decided to test it myself with a SATA drive. I used the NCFS five-step procedure for validating a write blocker outlined in the HELIX documentation and adjusted it for the specifics of the hardware configuration of my portable forensic workstation.

1. Prepare the media.
   a. Insert the drive into the removable drive tray.
   b. Wipe drive and validate.
   c. Format the drive.
   d. Copy data to the drive.
   e. Delete a portion of the data on the drive.
   f. Since all of my drives are configured to use write caching for performance, I added the extra step of flush the drive write cache using the MS SysInternals "Sync" program.
   g. Image and MD5 Hash the drive to a folder called "Step-1".
2. Test the media.
   a. Copy additional data to the drive.
   b. Delete a portion of the data that was written to the drive.
   c. Flush the drive cache.
   d. Image and MD5 Hash the drive to a folder called "Step-2".
   e. Compare the MD5 Hash for the drive in folder "Step-1" with the MD5 Hash for the image in folder "Step-2." The media had in fact been changed so the MD5 Hash values should be different.
3. Activate the write blocking device.
   a. Activate the software write block for the drive under test.
4. Test the write blocking device.
   a. Attempt to copy data to the drive.
   b. Attempt to delete data from the drive.
   c. Attempt to format the drive.
   d. Flush the drive cache.
   e. Image and MD5 Hash the drive to a folder called "Step-5".
5. Check for any changes in the media.
   a. Compare the MD5 Hash for the image in folder Step-2 and the MD5 Hash for the image contained in folder Step-5. If the write block is forensically sound the MD5 Hashes will match validating that the write block prevented any changes to the drive.

## Forensic Validation of SAFE Block XP Version 1.1

### Step 1: Prepare the Media

My portable forensic server uses removable drive trays, so I shut down and replaced the XP boot drive with my Fedora boot drive and booted into Fedora Linux (configured for "NOSMP"). I used SMART to wipe the drive with all "0" characters and verified via Hex view that the drive had been properly wiped. Rebooted to XP and formatted the drive for NTFS (Figure 27.1).

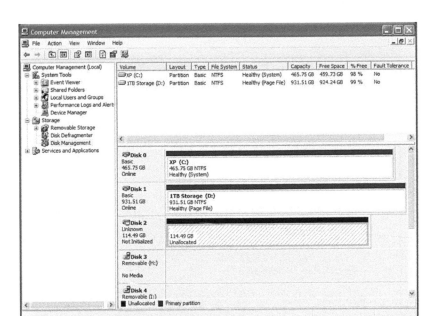

**Figure 27.1    Step 1 in forensic validation of SAFE Block XP Version 1.1 to prepare the media.**

I set the drive letter to F: and assigned the drive label as "SB_Test" (Figure 27.2).

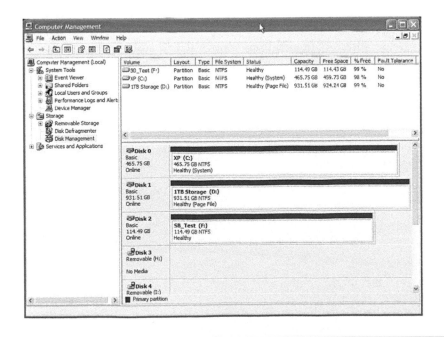

**Figure 27.2    The drive letter set to F: and assigned the drive label as "SB_Test".**

I then verified that software write block was not enabled for the drive under test (Figure 27.3).

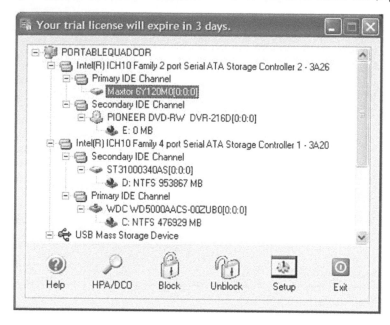

**Figure 27.3   Verification that software write block was not enabled for the drive under test.**

I copied the Program Files directory (folder) from the portable forensic workstation C: drive to the F: drive.

I copied the \system directory (folder) from the portable forensic workstation C: drive to the F: drive.

I then deleted the \system directory from drive F:

I ran the sync command from the DOS prompt on the F: drive (Figure 27.4).

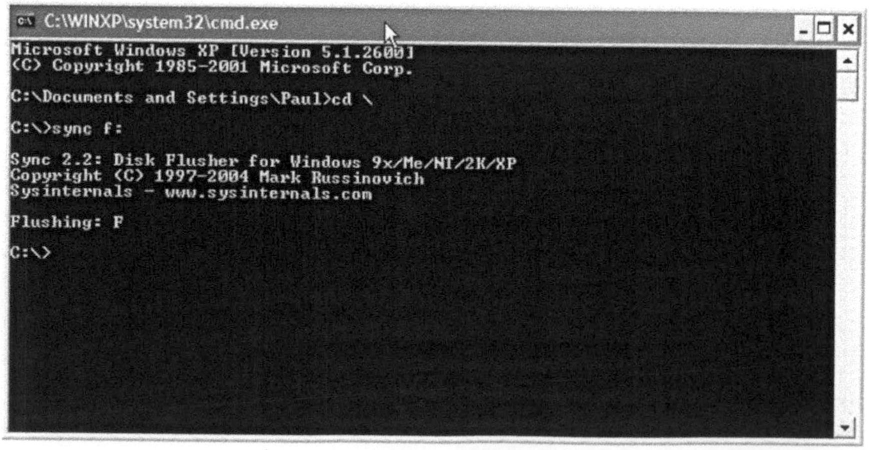

**Figure 27.4   The system after running the sync command from the DOS prompt on the F: drive.**

I then created a physical image (Figure 27.5) of the drive using FTK Imager and selected Raw (dd) image (Figure 27.6).

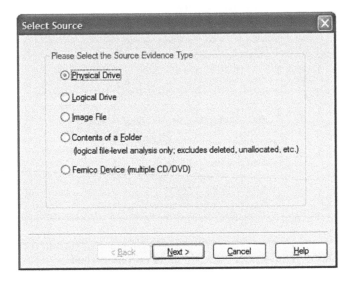

**Figure 27.5    Creation of a physical image of the drive using FTK Imager.**

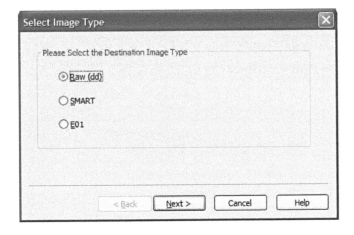

**Figure 27.6    Selection Raw (dd) image.**

I set the destination as folder "Step-1" and imaged drive F: (Figure 27.7).

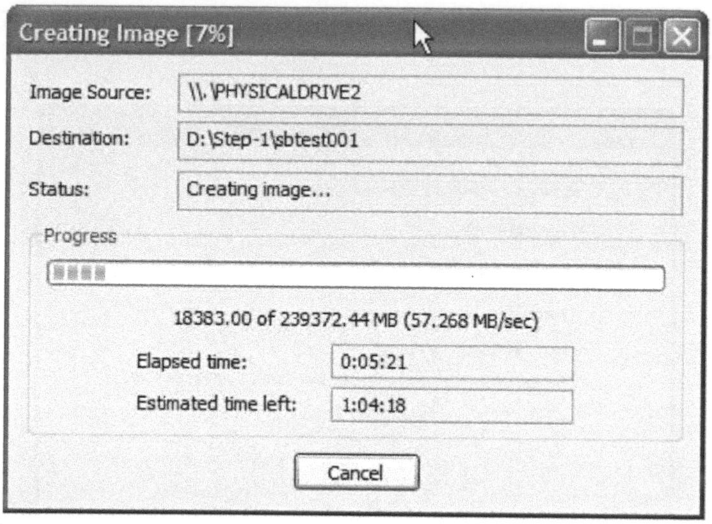

**Figure 27.7    Destination set as folder "Step-1" and F: drive imaged.**

Note the 57.268 MB/s speed.
Image complete for Step-1 and the MD5 Hash was recorded as:
2a2363a3640b57760e3bcbdcbf25fcd6

## Step 2: Test the Media

I added additional files to the F: drive (Figure 27.8).

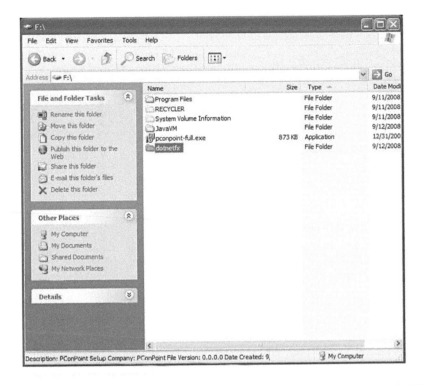

**Figure 27.8  Additional files added to the F: drive.**

I then deleted a portion of the files that I had just been added (Figure 27.9).

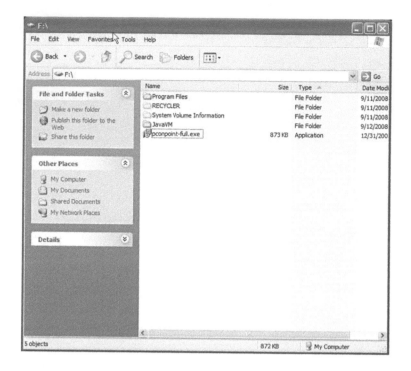

**Figure 27.9** **A portion of recently added files deleted.**

I flushed the drive cache (Figure 27.10).

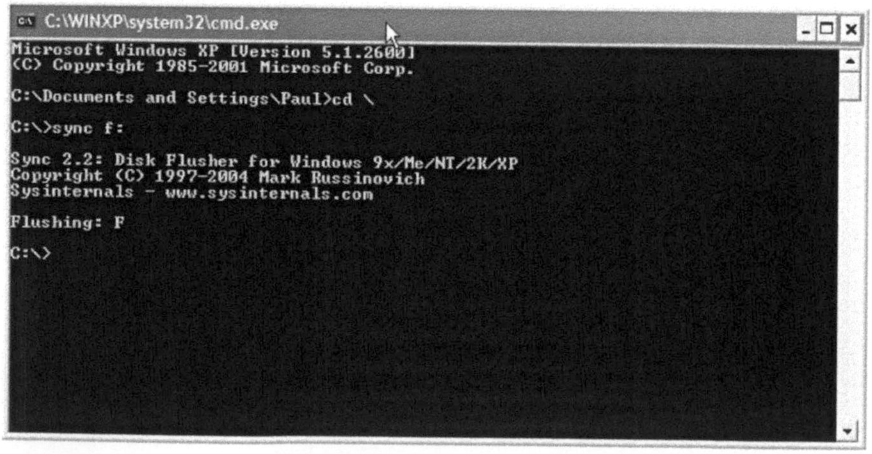

**Figure 27.10** **The drive cache flushed.**

I created a physical image (Figure 27.11) of the drive using FTK Imager and selected Raw (dd) image (Figure 27.12).

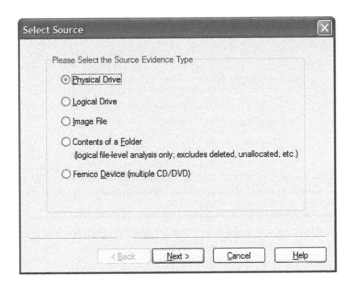

**Figure 27.11    FTK Imager used to create a physical image of the drive.**

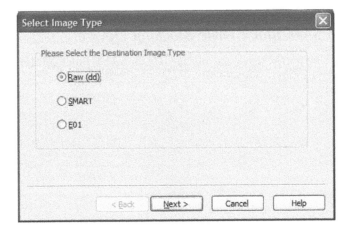

**Figure 27.12    Raw (dd) image selected.**

I set the destination as folder "Step-2" and imaged the F: drive (Figure 27.13).

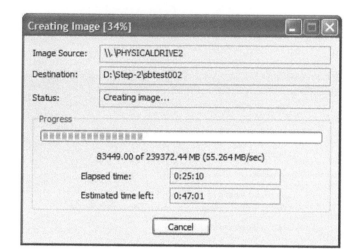

**Figure 27.13  The destination set as folder "Step-2" and the F: drive imaged.**

I recorded image MD5 Hash d1e2a8e6e99475eb53d9a3ca52600dc9
I then compared the MD5 hashes for the 2 images:
MD5 Hash from Folder Step-1 2a2363a3640b57760e3bcbdcbf25fcd6
MD5 Hash from Folder Step-2 d1e2a8e6e99475eb53d9a3ca52600dc9
As expected, the MD5 Hashes do not match as the drive had in fact been changed.

## Step 3: Activate SAFE Block Write Blocking Device

I enabled write blocking for the drive within the GUI for SAFE Block XP (Figure 27.14).

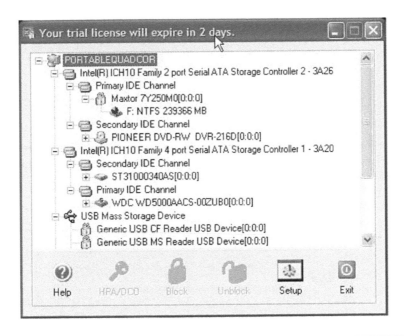

**Figure 27.14  Write blocking enabled for the drive within the GUI for SAFE Block XP.**

## Step 4: Test the Write Blocking Device

I attempted to copy the folder "Forensics" from the C: drive to the F: drive (Figure 27.15) and received the following error message:

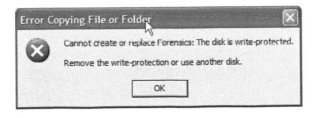

**Figure 27.15  Error message received after attempt to copy the folder "Forensics" from the C: drive to the F: drive.**

I attempted to drag and drop the Intel folder from the C: drive to the F: drive (Figure 27.16) and received the following error message:

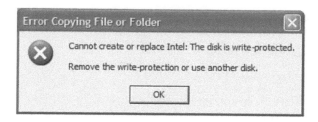

**Figure 27.16 Error message received after attempt to drag and drop the Intel folder from the C: drive to the F: drive.**

**Figure 27.17 Error message received after attempt to delete a file from the F: drive.**

Attempted to delete a file from the F: drive (Figure 27.17).

I then attempted to format the F: drive at the DOS prompt and DOS responded by informing me that the media was write protected. I then attempted to delete all files from the F: drive at the DOS prompt (Figure 27.18) and again DOS responded by informing me that the media is write protected.

```
C:\WINXP\system32\cmd.exe

F:\>dir
 Volume in drive F is SB_Test
 Volume Serial Number is 0861-7B16

 Directory of F:\

09/12/2008  09:28 AM    <DIR>          JavaVM
12/31/2005  11:20 PM           893,808 pconpoint-full.exe
09/11/2008  10:31 PM    <DIR>          Program Files
               1 File(s)        893,808 bytes
               2 Dir(s)  250,755,186,688 bytes free

F:\>del *.*
F:\*.*, Are you sure (Y/N)? y
F:\pconpoint-full.exe
The media is write protected.

F:\>
```

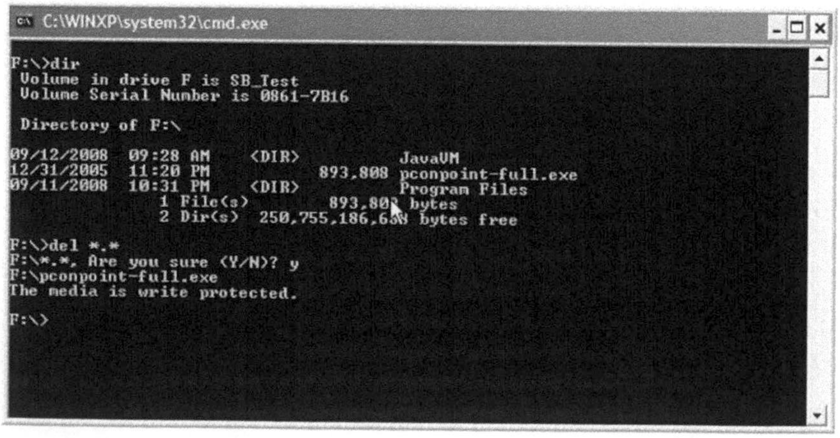

**Figure 27.18 Following an attempt to delete all files from the F: drive at the DOS prompt, DOS responded saying that the media is write protected.**

I flushed all data in the drive cache for drive F: (Figure 27.19)

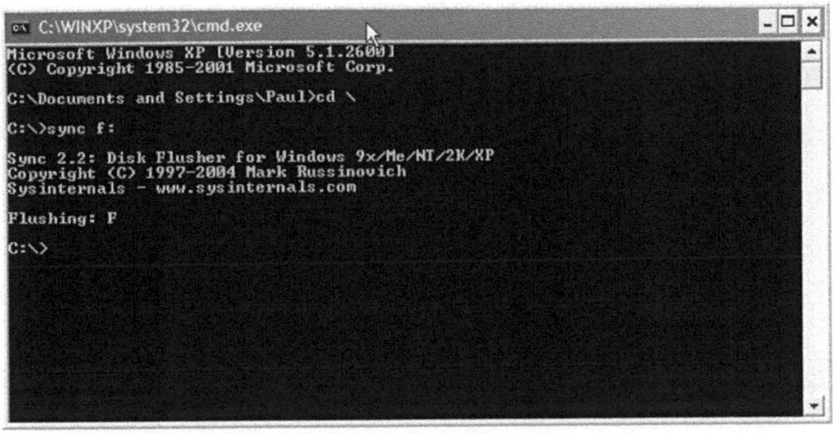

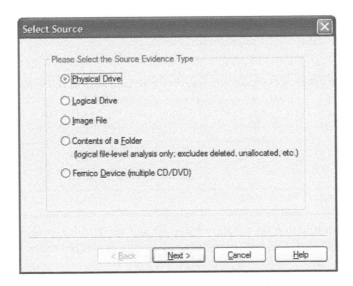

**Figure 27.19  All data in the drive cache for the F: drive flushed.**

I created a physical image (Figure 27.20) of the F: drive using FTK Imager and selected Raw (dd) image (Figure 27.21).

**Figure 27.20  A physical image of the F: drive created using FTK Imager.**

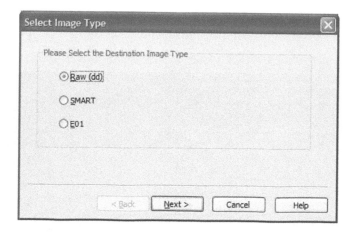

**Figure 27.21    Raw (dd) image selected.**

I set the destination as folder "Step-5" and imaged the F: drive (Figure 27.22). Note the acquisition speed of 53.969 MB/s while operating against a write protected drive. That works out to 3.23 GB/min.

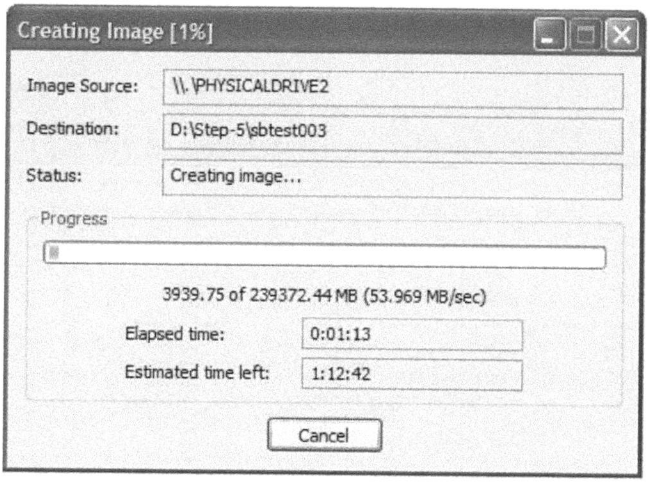

**Figure 27.22    The destination set as folder "Step-5" and the F: drive imaged. Note the acquisition speed of 53.969 MB/s while operating against a write protected drive, which works out to 3.23 GB/min.**

I recorded the image MD5 Hash d1e2a8e6e99475eb53d9a3ca52600dc9

## Step 5: Check for Any Changes in the Media

I then compared the MD5 Hash from the image in folder Step-2 with the image in folder Step-5:
MD5 Hash from Folder Step-2 d1e2a8e6e99475eb53d9a3ca52600dc9
MD5 Hash from Folder Step-5 d1e2a8e6e99475eb53d9a3ca52600dc9

*The Hashes match the drive and did not change—SAFE Block XP version 1.1 has been found to be forensically sound.*

I then removed the drive and imaged it with my hardware imager to see what the performance difference might be and to verify the drive MD5 Hash. I configured the imager to use the UDMA5 speed selection—it automatically then adjusts the speed to work best with the source and target drive. The target drive was a 3 GB/s 1 TB SATA drive. Note that the hardware imager was operating with an acquisition speed of 2.42 GB/min (Figure 27.23) and we previously attained an acquisition speed of 3.23 GB/min while imaging behind the software write block (Figure 27.22).

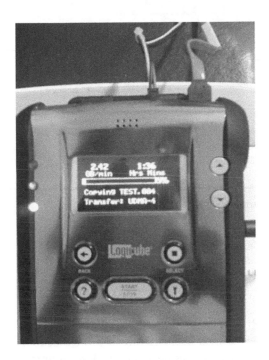

**Figure 27.23  The hardware imager was operating with an acquisition speed of 2.42 GB/min.**

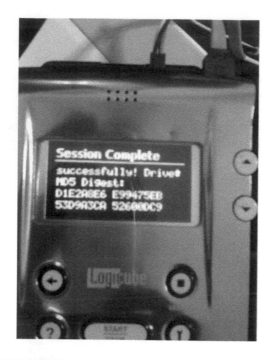

**Figure 27.24   Imaging completed.**

The MD5 Hash of the image of the drive produced behind the software write block matched that produced by the hardware imager (Figure 27.24).

## Conclusion

Software write blocking as presented in the testing of SAFEBlock XP 1.1 is a viable and forensically sound alternative to current hardware write blocking solutions. When one considers the total cost of ownership and ongoing maintenance and warranty costs of hardware write blocking devices, the dramatically reduced cost of software write blocking presents an undeniable business case for consideration.

*Complete acquisition report from folder Step 1*
Created By AccessData® FTK® Imager 2.5.4.16 080324
Case Information: Test of SAFE Block software write block
Case Number: sbtest001
Evidence Number: sbtest001
Unique Description:
Examiner: Paul A. Henry

*Notes*:
Information for D:\Step-1\sbtest001:
Physical Evidentiary Item (Source) Information:
[Drive Geometry]

Cylinders: 30,515
Tracks per Cylinder: 255
Sectors per Track: 63
Bytes per Sector: 512
Sector Count: 490,234,752
[Physical Drive Information]
Drive Model: Maxtor 7Y250M0
Drive Serial Number: 36593039374d45472020202020202020202020202020
Drive Interface Type: IDE
Source data size: 239372 MB
Sector count: 490234752
[Computed Hashes]
MD5 checksum: 2a2363a3640b57760e3bcbdcbf25fcd6
SHA1 checksum: d176fce35286a23059acbc5bd376ecac0b2f1a5c

*Image Information*:
Acquisition started: Thu Sep 11 23:17:31 2008
Acquisition finished: Fri Sep 12 00:44:25 2008

Segment list:
D:\Step-1\sbtest001.001

*Image Verification Results*:
Verification started: Fri Sep 12 00:44:26 2008
Verification finished: Fri Sep 12 01:25:26 2008
MD5 checksum: 2a2363a3640b57760e3bcbdcbf25fcd6: verified
SHA1 checksum: d176fce35286a23059acbc5bd376ecac0b2f1a5c: verified

*Complete acquisition report from folder Step-2*
Created By AccessData® FTK® Imager 2.5.4.16 080324
Case Information: Test of SAFE Block software write block
Case Number: sbtest002
Evidence Number: sbtest002
Unique Description:
Examiner: Paul A. Henry

*Notes*:
Information for D:\Step-2\sbtest002:
Physical Evidentiary Item (Source) Information:
[Drive Geometry]
Cylinders: 30,515
Tracks per Cylinder: 255
Sectors per Track: 63
Bytes per Sector: 512
Sector Count: 490,234,752
[Physical Drive Information]
Drive Model: Maxtor 7Y250M0
Drive Serial Number: 36593039374d45472020202020202020202020202020
Drive Interface Type: IDE

Source data size: 239372 MB
Sector count: 490234752
[Computed Hashes]
MD5 checksum: d1e2a8e6e99475eb53d9a3ca52600dc9
SHA1 checksum: dd4a1294cb768c1dad2235d30a6904c4ffc04d14

*Image Information*:
Acquisition started: Fri Sep 12 09:33:19 2008
Acquisition finished: Fri Sep 12 11:00:02 2008

Segment list:
D:\Step-2\sbtest002.001

*Image Verification Results*:
Verification started: Fri Sep 12 11:00:02 2008
Verification finished: Fri Sep 12 11:46:23 2008
MD5 checksum: d1e2a8e6e99475eb53d9a3ca52600dc9 : verified
SHA1 checksum: dd4a1294cb768c1dad2235d30a6904c4ffc04d14 : verified

*Complete acquisition report from folder Step-5*
Created By AccessData® FTK® Imager 2.5.4.16 080324
Case Information: Test of SAFE Block software write block
Case Number: sbtest003
Evidence Number: sbtest003
Unique Description:
Examiner: Paul A. Henry

*Notes*:
Information for D:\Step-5\sbtest003:
Physical Evidentiary Item (Source) Information:
[Drive Geometry]
Cylinders: 30,515
Tracks per Cylinder: 255
Sectors per Track: 63
Bytes per Sector: 512
Sector Count: 490,234,752
[Physical Drive Information]
Drive Model: Maxtor 7Y250M0
Drive Serial Number: 36593039374d45472020202020202020202020202020
Drive Interface Type: IDE
Source data size: 239372 MB
Sector count: 490234752
[Computed Hashes]
MD5 checksum: d1e2a8e6e99475eb53d9a3ca52600dc9
SHA1 checksum: dd4a1294cb768c1dad2235d30a6904c4ffc04d14

*Image Information*:
Acquisition started: Fri Sep 12 12:49:00 2008
Acquisition finished: Fri Sep 12 14:15:55 2008

Segment list:
D:\Step-5\sbtest003.001

*Image Verification Results*:
Verification started: Fri Sep 12 14:15:55 2008
Verification finished: Fri Sep 12 15:12:45 2008
MD5 checksum: d1e2a8e6e99475eb53d9a3ca52600dc9 : verified
SHA1 checksum: dd4a1294cb768c1dad2235d30a6904c4ffc04d14 : verified

## About the Author

**Paul A. Henry**, CISSP, MCP+I, MCSE, CCSA, CCSE, CFSA, CFSO, CISM, CISA, is senior vice president of CyberGuard Corporation, Deerfield Beach, Florida.

# PHYSICAL SECURITY

## *Elements of Physical Security*

# Chapter 28

# Protection of Sensitive Data

Sandy Bacik

## Contents

What constitutes sensitive data for an enterprise: paper copies of forms, faxes, employee data, insurance information, support contracts, intellectual property, or client data? How does the enterprise physically protect sensitive data in hard copy form or removable media? Locked closet, desk, or cabinet? Are there any environmental concerns with those areas? Many organizations are digitizing their hard copy files for more efficient and effective storage, but some regulations for records retention still require an organization to retain the hard copies. And many times, an enterprise will store electronic copies on removable media.

The amount of data that a staff member comes across daily can be enormous. It is not possible to protect all the data that a staff member can come across. The enterprise needs to document what constitutes sensitive data (data classification policy) and identify the level of protection required. This chapter discusses the physical (not logical through access control) protection of sensitive data and what to consider in the environment.

## Temperature

One of the main environmental threats to equipment and sensitive data is temperature. The generally accepted, ideal temperature is between 68°F and 74°F (20°C–24°C) for storage of electrical equipment

**449**

and paper. Excessive heat degrades network performance and causes downtime. As the temperature increases, a heat sink fan works harder to cool the central processing unit (CPU). Continuous overworking causes the fan to fail, leading to equipment overheating. A machine shuts down when it reaches an unsafe temperature in order to prevent permanent damage. When that happens, an administrator must then be located, day or night, go to the machine, and reboot it after it has cooled. Consequently, services hosted by a down machine are unavailable until it is restarted, which can take minutes or hours. If the services are critical, revenues can be lost, users cannot login, and communications are interrupted. If the equipment shutdown is not done properly, data can be lost.

Excessive heat and rapid temperature changes damage equipment. Together, heat and moisture accelerate the breakdown of materials used in microchips, motherboards, and hard drives, which ages equipment more rapidly. Heat-damaged equipment must be replaced, increasing the cost of network maintenance. Controlling temperature is becoming more important and more difficult because of changes in equipment design and greater use of network services. As old equipment is replaced with new equipment, that new equipment has more power and cooling requirements because it runs faster and hotter. New equipment also has smaller and more condensed circuit board, thus trapping heat in a smaller space. The smaller, more efficient, equipment is then packed tighter. The increased density increases the amount of heat dissipated within the rack and data center. Increased network usage also increases heat, so as usage levels change during the day, so does the temperature and the need for cooling. For networks that operate near capacity 24 h a day, every day of the year, there is little, if any, time for machines to cool down.

Strong temperature controls that include training, monitoring, and testing the temperature devices will ensure that equipment will have longevity in the production environment.

## Humidity

Another main environmental threat to network equipment and sensitive data is humidity. Temperature and humidity have been shown to be interdependent. Humidity, too much dampness or moisture in the air, can cause water damage to electronics, paper, and computer equipment. Humidity can be natural or man-made. Rapid temperature increases can increase humidity, while rapid drops can cause water in humid air to condense on equipment. Some causes for high humidity are a mixture of hot and cold air, leaky pipes, and an increase of water used in day-to-day activities. The relative humidity should be between 40% and 50%.

High humidity levels can produce condensation problems within a data center and other office storage areas. Condensation occurs when humidity levels are too high or when there is a rapid temperature drop and then the enterprise can potentially have water running along pipes. Condensation inside equipment can cause rust, short circuits, or deposits of dirt and minerals that ruin equipment.

Like a temperature control, a companion humidity control device that includes training, monitoring, and testing the temperature devices will help ensure that equipment will continue to have longevity in the production environment.

## Hard Copy Deterioration

Where there is moisture due to high humidity, there can be biological growths such as molds or fungi, insects and rodents infestations. Biological agents attack paper and other organic materials when both temperature and humidity are not regulated properly. Mold spores and fungi can remain suspended in the air until they find suitable conditions for their living habits. Mold and fungi can result in the staining and deterioration of organic materials. It is a common experience to note that mold and fungi growth can occur more readily on items that are tightly packed and have stagnant pockets of moist air, which favors mold and fungi growth.

In addition to high temperature and humidity, staff's cleaning negligence can favor mold and fungi, as well as the growth and proliferation of insects. This negligence can result in the following:

- Accumulations of dirt and dust from poor or careless housekeeping practices on materials and electronics
- Trails of foodstuff in storage and exhibit areas due to staff leaving items behind
- Opening or closing of air vents or poorly sealed windows and doors
- Poor ventilation in and around the materials and equipment

Rodents and insects can be some of the worst enemies of books and other organic materials. Insects are attracted to the proteins and carbohydrates in the form of paste, starches, or other organic substances. Damage can vary from a few markings and holes to complete destruction.

## Light

Another cause of deterioration of sensitive data can be light. The types of materials that are subject to damage by light are pigments and dyestuff, including inks, paper, and other cellulose materials, and various other organic materials holding copies of sensitive data. Inks and dyestuff fade when exposed to light. Unfortunately, coloring in pictures and forms fade selectively, some disappearing while others remain unchanged, which means that the color relationships of hard copies can be distorted.

Serious paper deterioration is caused by cellulose oxidation that comes through ultraviolet rays (like sunlight) and fluorescent light. Two changes affect hard copies: embrittlement and deterioration. Embrittlement is paper whitening and color fading of certain inks and paper. Deterioration is the oxygenation that occurs when paper reacts to the air and turns yellow or brownish, like old newspapers you might find in an attic or basement. One other thing with light damage, paper continues to degrade after the light source has been removed.

## Data-in-Motion and Data-at-Rest

With sensitive data there are two types of data that may need encryption: data-in-motion and data-at-rest. Data-in-motion is data that is in transit between two points or data in transmission. Data-in-motion comprises data moving over LANs, WANs, the Internet, etc. Data-in-motion can also be in motion when stored on removable media and being transported to another location. Data-at-rest is the data at the endpoints of transmission. This can be data stored in applications, databases, files, etc. One thing to remember is that the encryption of data-in-motion does not necessarily protect data-at-rest.

Where and when should sensitive data be encrypted? Possibly, all the time, depending upon the regulations and enterprise standards. When the decision to encrypt is made, the data owner and system owner need to decide where and how to implement encryption. While the author cannot recommend specific encryption software or methods, the enterprise, data owner, and system owner should document business requirements for encryption. Some of the business requirements should consider the following:

- Risks of sensitive data disclosure
- Amount of sensitive data
- Frequency of sensitive data changes
- Cost of the encryption and storage solution
- Burden of the maintenance of the encryption and storage on staff

## Destruction of Sensitive Data

When sensitive data has come to the end of its useful life, is in surplus, or needs to be destroyed per a records retention standard, methods and processes need to be in place. If the sensitive data is stored on media, then methods and processes need to be in place for media destruction or reuse.

The most common methods of destroying paper media are individual shredders, shred bins, and confidential destruction bins. Many times, individual departments will purchase shredders because they work with sensitive data on a daily basis. Should an enterprise determine the need for multiple shred and confidential destruction bins with contracted services, the enterprise needs to understand the use of the bins and contracted third parties need to meet the enterprise needs. If an enterprise contracts services for destruction of paper contained in bins, on at least an annual basis the enterprise should test or follow the contracted services to ensure the paper is stored and destroyed per contact requirements.

Many times, certain departments will store sensitive data on removable media. Removable media is one of the hardest things to control within an enterprise, because it can accidently disappear and never be found or it can walk off enterprise premises and be used for another enterprise's competitive advantage. Things like a USB drive can be reused many times, therefore, an enterprise needs to have standards on how to reuse removable media. Depending on the removable media, physical destruction can include crushing, shredding, incinerating, or otherwise rendering the physical media unusable. If the media is to be reused, then processes need to be in place to eliminate the original data from the removable media, such as low-level formatting or completely overwriting the data.

## Current Monitoring Practices

In a typical business, three groups monitor the environment: system and network administrators, security personnel, and facility maintenance employees. Network administrators often rely on a single thermometer and subjective notions about "comfort" to control the temperature of server rooms and data centers. In addition, security personnel and facility maintenance departments monitor areas outside of the server rooms and also check the environmental controls within the data center on a "regular basis." This "regular basis" should be at least daily, yet, many times, is only quarterly or when there is a reported problem. These three groups usually attempt to coordinate their efforts, but each maintain separate systems, practices, and habits. Ultimately, system and network administrators are primarily responsible for protecting hardware. This approach has the following weaknesses:

- Staff are not trained to recognize all threats—Damage caused by the environment can be subtle or attributed to other causes. Accelerated equipment aging due to heat or condensation occurs over years and is often written off as a natural process (i.e., "equipment just wears out"). Condensation, rust, and heat damage is usually hidden inside machines, out of sight.

■ Nonstandard (inconsistent) processes for all staff—The room thermometers are checked only when the environment feels too hot or cold. Unfortunately, the sense of a "comfortable" temperature and humidity level varies from person to person.

■ No 7 × 24 × 365 monitoring activities—Environmental threats can occur 24 h a day, every day of the year. Staff are not always in the data center, especially on nights and weekends. Depending on staffing levels and schedules, server room environments can be unmonitored up to 65% of the time during an average week.

■ It is not my job—Another gap can occur because of shared responsibilities. Facilities might be monitoring for water leaks and flooding, but they rely on system and network administrators and security personnel to review every time they enter the data center. Frequently, one person will not look, because they think someone else is doing it. Or someone will see something and report it to the wrong person. The vulnerabilities develop and potential problems are never investigated until it is too late.

■ No automated environmental tracking—Temperature and humidity levels constantly change. Without a condition logging, an administrator cannot identify changes through trending metrics. Therefore, these problems continue for days or months, while time and money is wasted investigating false causes and solutions.

■ Staff have so many daily duties, they only focus on catastrophes, not daily problems— Enterprises want to avoid catastrophes, but they do little to protect from threats that slowly damage hardware or promote preventative maintenance, such as detecting gradual temperature increases that indicate a need to clean fans or air filters.

An effective server environment monitoring system addresses the weaknesses in the current practice of having personnel monitor the environment. Enterprises need a combination of manual and automated monitoring to protect all sensitive data.

## Conclusion

Any changes to environmental conditions anywhere sensitive data is stored can impact its future use and cause potential damage to that sensitive data recovery. Environmental monitoring includes temperature, lighting, humidity, airflow, and cleanliness. To start, a sensitive data policy should be created that is similar to Exhibit 28.1. Regular controls for environmental conditions include

■ Changing filters
■ HVAC maintenance
■ UPS maintenance and testing
■ Maintenance and testing of environmental controls
■ Proper and thorough cleaning

Manual and automated environmental monitoring of sensitive data can provide the following benefits:

■ Control equipment maintenance costs: In a stable environment, equipment lasts longer, and less equipment is damaged and needs to be replaced. Sometimes, the savings from not having to replace equipment can pay for the cost of the monitoring system.

■ Longer lead time to fix a small problem: Early warnings permit staff to respond to an issue before it becomes a disaster.

- Reduced production downtime: Hardware used in good consistent environmental conditions operates more efficiently and effectively, reducing the number of outages.
- Environmental data logs for trending analysis: Reporting and monitoring the environmental log data ensures stable conditions and also makes available more data when an investigation is required.

**Exhibit 28.1**  Sensitive Data Policy

| Title | Sensitive Data Policy | | | | |
|---|---|---|---|---|---|
| Part Number: | PL00550 | Revision: | 1.0 | Effective: | 20050930 |
| Owner: | CSO | | | Last Review: | 20070501 |

*This electronic document supersedes all previous electronic and printed documents or oral statements regarding this policy.*
*MYC Policies are subject to change at the sole discretion of MYC management.*

*Scope*

This policy applies to any data that has been classified by MyCompany (MYC) as sensitive data and is stored on any media or medium.

*Purpose*

The purpose of this policy is to provide behavioral guidance to MYC staff or any party who is contractually bound to handle sensitive data produced by MYC, who produce, or have access to MYC sensitive data.

*Definitions*

See the information assurance glossary.

*Responsibility*

- Contracted parties: Must be provided with sufficient training and supporting reference materials to allow them to properly protect and otherwise manage MYC information.
- Department heads: Will be responsible for authorizing access to sensitive data and will perform regular access reviews against MYC sensitive data.
- Information security: Will perform regular risk and compliance reviews against MYC information and will coordinate any information incidents.
- Information technology: Will maintain the technology required for information assurance.
- Management: Must make sure that information is protected in a manner that is at least as secure as other organizations in the same industry handling the same type of information and as required by law.
- Staff: Must be provided with sufficient training and supporting reference materials to allow them to properly protect and otherwise manage MYC information.

*Policy*

For MYC departments, department heads are responsible for implementing additional precautions to be used by any individuals who have access to sensitive data. Parties that are contractually bound will be responsible for implementing additional precautions to be used by their staff. For contractually bound parties, additional precautions include

- Limited access (on-site): All areas that contain sensitive data should not be accessible to all staff. All areas that contain sensitive data must not provide unsupervised access to third parties. Department heads or their designee will work with information and physical security to control access to areas containing sensitive data. Areas that cannot be locked cannot be used to store sensitive data. Department heads or their designee will identify individuals who have a need to access these areas to perform their job function, and will communicate the names of these individuals and their required access to Information and Physical Security. When leaving their area containing sensitive data, staff, to the best of their ability, must properly put away and secure sensitive data.
- Limited access (remote): Non-MYC spaces used by contractually bound third parties should only be accessible by individuals the third party has approved to access the sensitive data. All areas that contain sensitive area must not provide unsupervised access to the third parties. Areas that cannot be locked cannot be used to store sensitive data. When leaving the area in which sensitive data is stored, staff, to the best of their ability, must properly put away and secure sensitive data.
- Maintenance and cleaning staff: For departments that contain sensitive data, the department head or their designee will determine if it is practical to request that the cleaning staff perform their duties during normal business hours, while the area is staffed. If none of the department employees are present, the cleaning staff will not clean that area that contains sensitive data at that time. If a department has stored sensitive data but receives cleaning services after hours, then the staff shall, to the best of their ability, properly put away and secure sensitive data before ending their workday. Cleaning staff will not have master keys for any areas that they clean during normal business hours.
- Copiers, printers, and fax machines: Department heads or their designee will work with information technology, and information and physical security to ensure that all printers and fax machines that output sensitive data will be in a limited access area. In areas where this is not possible, staff, to the best of their ability, will not leave printed or faxed sensitive data unattended.
- Shredding/confidential containers: For departments that handle sensitive data, the department head or their designee will work with Procurement to ensure that the department has access to a secured repository in which they can deposit sensitive data to be shredded.

*Questions about this policy*
If you have questions about this policy, please contact the Information or Physical Security teams.

*Violations*
Unauthorized access, disclosure, duplication, modification, diversion, destruction, loss, misuse, or theft of MYC information by staff, willingly and deliberately, may result in the loss of access to computer and/or network resources and may include termination and legal prosecution. Disciplinary measures are on a case-by-case basis.

/Name/, Chief Security Officer

# About the Author

**Sandy Bacik**, CISSP, ISSMP, CISM, CHS-III, has over 22 years experience in information security and various information technology positions.

# Chapter 29

# Water Leakage and Flooding

Sandy Bacik

## Contents

Mother Nature is always a force to be reckoned with.

1. December 26, 2004, an undersea Indian Ocean earthquake and the following tsunami ("Asian Tsunami" or "Boxing Day Tsunami") off the west coast of Sumatra, Indonesia, killed more than 225,000 people in 11 countries, and inundated coastal communities with waves up to 30 m (100 ft) high. Indonesia, Sri Lanka, India, and Thailand were hardest hit. The reconstruction and recovery would probably take between 5 and 10 years. Industrial fishery is the major economic activity that provides direct employment to about 250,000 people. The fishery industry is a dynamic export-oriented sector, generating substantial foreign exchange earnings. Preliminary estimates indicate that 66% of the fishing fleet and industrial infrastructure in coastal regions have been destroyed by the wave surges, which will have adverse economic effects both at local and national levels. How many enterprise infrastructures were never restored or totally recovered from flooding?

2. August 25–27, 2006, Hurricane Katrina hits Florida, the Gulf of Mexico, and Louisiana, and then returns to make a second landfall with more disastrous results and more repercussions in the months afterward. Whole infrastructures were destroyed. How many businesses never recovered and how many enterprises recovered and considered the recovery from flooding successful?

3. October 2007, Tropical Storm Noel turns into a hurricane and Grijalva River bursts its banks and floods the state capital of Villahermosa with up to 8 ft of muddy and foul

water. To make matters worse, the federal electric utility decided to release water from the lake behind the Penitas hydroelectric dam. At the height of the flooding four-fifths of Tabasco was submerged. Villahermosa was flooded for more than a week. With natural flooding, enterprises have time to activate their business continuity and disaster recovery plans. In this situation, the Red Cross, the Mexican armed forces, and private sector companies set up basic communication and other electronic systems to ensure communications were active. Companies still had their IT infrastructure destroyed by the floodwaters and were able to eventually recover after power and communications systems returned to normal.

Yet, man-made water disasters can be just as deadly for a business.

1. July 15, 2002, Walnut Creek, California, fire broke out in the corporate headquarters of WildPackets. Monthly backup tapes were stored offsite, but June's tapes were still onsite. Despite a fireproof safe, the tapes were not usable due to smoke and water damage. WildPackets had to use May's monthly backups to recover their systems. A week later WildPackets was in a new building and resuming shipments.
2. July 9, 2008, Lucas Oil Stadium had 20 roof drains break sending much water to the lower levels of the building just weeks before the grand opening. While damage was confined to less than 1% of the building, the lower building levels contained electrical boxes, telephone closets, and the data center. Recovery was completed and the opening on was held on August 16th as scheduled.

Water damage is one of the most problematic and commonly experienced forms of disaster damage. Causes of water damage include natural flooding, burst or leaky pipes, fire hoses, and humidity. To better protect an enterprise from water damage, it is necessary to know what it is and how it can occur. The recovery from water damage is varied depending upon how soon the incident was discovered. The main thing to remember with water damage is to act fast before it becomes a disaster. For example, your enterprise decided to expand (or contract), so larger (or smaller) areas are required to store electronic equipment and hard copy data. Let us say a new internal location is selected for the new server room. Now imagine, you find a large enough area with good ventilation; there exists dry pipes for extinguishing fires and the air-conditioning units do not have their drip pipes running over the network equipment. The floor is on a raised platform. Good considerations for an initial design. And the move of equipment starts. Oops! The pipes from the restrooms on the floors above run directly over the new server room and one of the pipes bursts due to a plumbing mistake. What type of activities or safety measures should be put in place? Was there anything in the design that would have prevented any water-carrying pipes from running directly over the new server room? IT and management need to understand and take into consideration water leakage and flooding because they do not need to live in a flood plan area to have a flood or water leak into their equipment rooms. Water leakage and flooding need to be addressed within an environmental safety policy and program. Water leaks and flooding are not an everyday occurrence and we know that water and electricity do not mix and can cause significant damages. We will discuss issues and possible resolutions for locating server rooms and critical computer equipment away from a water source or transport pipes and other water type issues within the environment.

# Types of Water Damage

In most environments, there are three classifications of water damage:

- Clean water: This type of water damage does not pose any health risk to humans and is really just annoying.
- Grey water: This type of water damage could eventually pose a health risk to humans and contains degrees of chemical, biological, or physical contaminants.
- Black water: This type of water damage (such as sewage) contains highly unsanitary agents and can impact human health.

Reviewing the pipe and hose systems within the enterprise can assist in limiting the risk of water damage.

# What Can Water Damage Do

Many times, network and system administrators focus on protecting network devices from logical security attacks and connectivity failures, often inadvertently missing the ever-present danger of environmental threats. These threats include temperature, humidity, and water leaks. Environmental issues can damage equipment, slow performance, and force hardware to shut down. The costs of water and environmental threats can include the following:

- Loss of revenues due to unavailable equipment
- Replacement of damaged equipment, including additional administrative time to investigate and fix problems
- Lower productivity due to downtime

When staff observe water leakage and flooding, staff should look in all directions within the data center (above, below, inside, and just outside) to determine if there is any potential source for the damage, instead of just what is in front of them. Some of the items we must look at are as follows:

- HVAC units
- Outside water sources (ponds, lakes, streams, water mains)
- Pipe entrance into the room or building and transport pipe locations
- Restrooms or cafeterias/cafes
- Fire hydrants
- Server room wet pipes

Sometimes, staff can create water type situations in the data center by

- Adjusting the heat or air conditioning while working in the server room and forgetting to reset it when they leave, making the HVAC and other ventilation equipment work harder.
- Placing boxes in front of vents "temporarily" and forgetting to move them, which blocks airflow, again making equipment work harder.
- Similarly, cleaning crews sometimes close or open doors that should be left open or closed for ventilation, making the HVAC and ventilation equipment work harder.

Proper planning moves equipment away from condensation, drip, and water pipes that might burst or leak. Blocked ventilation systems can cause condensation if they are overworked and the moist air is not removed quickly. If ventilation vents are located above or behind machines, condensation can form small water pools that no one may notice until it is too late. Small amounts of water near air intakes raise humidity levels and can fill servers with moisture. Depending on the angle of the pipe, water can travel long distances behind walls or over rooms for a long time before it is noticed and any action is taken. Cables and wires within the data center are often located beneath floor panels. The cords are generally kept safe from being unplugged, but monitoring the physical status is difficult. Water leaks may have happened for a long time before anyone lifts a floor tile. Besides possible power outages, this situation can also break down insulation and cause performance degradation.

## Humidity and Condensation

The main environmental threats to network equipment are temperature and humidity. The generally accepted ideal temperature is between 68°F and 74°F (20°C–24°C) for storage of electrical equipment and paper. When the temperature is normal, the relative humidity (i.e., the amount of water in the air) should be between 40% and 50%. High humidity levels can produce condensation problems within a data center. Condensation occurs when humidity levels are too high or when there is a rapid drop in temperature. Besides the potential of water running along pipes, condensation inside equipment causes rust, short circuits, or deposits of dirt and minerals that ruin equipment. There exist moisture-absorbing circuit boards that can expand and contract with changes in relative humidity levels, but constant expansion and contraction can break microelectronic circuits and edge connectors.

With high humidity levels (above 60%) and persistent high temperatures, the conditions are ideal for fungus growth. Besides affecting human health, fungus can also clog the machine's airflow and promote heat retention and condensation. Fungus retains moisture and promotes corrosion, which can damage circuits and motherboards.

To assist with humidity issues, there is humidity-measuring and -controlling equipment within the data centers, which can be adjusted according to one's requirements. This can be the humidity monitoring or cooling equipment, which has an integrated mechanism for humidity control. Current trends recommend having separate equipment for humidity control rather than letting air conditioners handle it on their own.

## Current Monitoring Practices

Like the current monitoring practices described in Chapter 28, water leaks and flooding need to be included in that monitoring with the humidity and water level sensors. Staff need to walk the entire data center on a daily basis, including lifting floor and ceiling tiles to check if there is any additional dampness or clogging. Enterprises need a combination of manual and automated monitoring to protect all sensitive data.

## Conclusion

In conclusion, the most common environmental monitoring practices include having staff just observe and report problems. This practice has some inherent weaknesses, such as changing conditions, not recognizing threats, not knowing how to track environmental threats, and focusing on major incidents and not daily threats that may damage equipment. Automated environmental monitoring systems help prevent the damages caused by environmental threats, such as temperature, humidity, and water leakage, that could destroy network components in a data center or network equipment room. Automated systems can send alerts through flashing lights, buzzers, and messages via SNMP traps, e-mail, and the system's Web-based administrative interface. Is there any way to stop all water-based risk within a server room environment? Probably not, but the enterprise needs to mitigate the water-based risk and have compensating controls in place just in case. Like the results of a combination of automated and manual monitoring documented in Chapter 28, water leaks and flooding need to be included in that monitoring with the humidity and water level sensors.

## About the Author

**Sandy Bacik**, CISSP, ISSMP, CISM, CHS-III, has over 22 years experience in information security and various information technology positions.

# Chapter 30

# Site Selection and Facility Design Considerations

Sandy Bacik

## Contents

Information technology (IT) has been complaining to facilities about additional power and air requirements needed for the server room within enterprise headquarters. IT has documented the current and future environmental requirements for production equipment. The business park, where headquarters is located, is having new construction being performed for other business expansions. The power company while digging a new trench cuts the power to the whole business park. No problem, the generator kicks on and the server room equipment is continuing merrily on the production processing schedule. The power company gets the power back on and the generator senses the power and switches back to regular power. Oops! The building uninterruptible power supply (UPS) breaker trips and the server room does not have an additional UPS in place and does not have a separate power source. All 200-plus network devices and servers hard crash, because the building breaker tripped and the generator did not come back on because it sensed the line power. IT needs 72 continuous hours to recover and bring all systems back online. Could this have been prevented? Were there simple items that should and could have been in place for business continuity and disaster recovery? While the answer is yes, there may have been communication problems between IT and facilities, or there might have been budget issues as to who should have paid for the upgrades.

This chapter will walk through checklists and discuss what-ifs on selecting a site and designing a facility to store the enterprise production and test equipment. It reviews what the ideal environmental conditions should be to ensure IT obtains the most productivity from equipment. At some time or the other, IT will need to discuss the movement of corporate equipment to a larger or smaller location due to budget, size, or support. Facilities may be the group who signs the contract for the location, but IT must be involved with documenting the business requirements for keeping the network and services up and running. Every enterprise, at some point in its history or in the future, will consider building its own server room or data center, or outsourcing the facility to a supplier. The enterprise might be outgrowing its existing internal facility, it may be reviewing to outsource the hosting, or it may be compressing the facility. When an enterprise starts looking for a site or a data center–hosting facility, it must look at where the site is going to be located and the facility design. This chapter also includes questions that need to be considered as the enterprise develops business requirements and items that need to be included when performing a facility audit, as well as issues that need to be taken into account when reviewing a site and facility to host its assets.

## Business Requirements and Threats

In recent years, trends have existed for data center expansion or consolidation and for going green. For many enterprises it does not make sense to have the enterprise headquarters in one geographic location and the data center in another. This is mostly because of the cost and logistics of doing business in another location, where the infrastructure and personnel costs might just exceed the value of the data center site location. If the business has a continuity and disaster recovery plan, then it may outsource to a co-location facility in another part of the country. Centralized data centers have assisted enterprises in achieving cost savings and effective and efficient production activities. When an enterprise determines that a new data center or server room location is required, it needs to look at the cost savings and business requirements as well as the vulnerabilities of that location, such as

- Population density and the amenities in the location
- Environmental concerns
- Proximity to possible hazardous events—natural or man-made
- Existence (or not) of early-warning systems and communication methods
- Readiness of emergency preparedness of the location
- Construction styles, building codes, and regulations of the location
- Cultural and support factors
- Business and government climate, volatility, and insurance
- Real estate and financial environment

Enterprise threats come in all shapes, sizes, durations, and forewarnings. If a data center becomes unavailable, direct and indirect losses can occur. Direct losses translate into additional costs and lost revenue. Indirect losses can include legal, contractual, regulatory, and customer obligations and costs. Threats can be regional, national, or international. When looking at a facility, most businesses think only about regional threats. Threats can be natural, unintentional, or intentional. Again, most businesses look at natural threats and potentials for an intentional threat. As the enterprise builds or expands a facility, it needs to think about implementing safeguards to reduce the likelihood or frequency of risks and threats to limit the damage level that could be sustained and survived. A pre-assessment and strong design against threats, risks, and vulnerabilities will be more cost effective than correcting any damage. When performing a review or building business requirements, the enterprise should focus on the inherent risks and threats to equipment and data. At a high level, it must determine the requirements for

1. Physical and material supplies—number of components, terminals, desks, chairs, containers, tapes, disks, paper supplies, waste, cabling, wiring, cabinets, and network equipment
2. Facility location—building, room(s), work space, storage area
3. Environmental—air conditioning and flow, fire suppression, electricity, communication, water, power, backup power, and lighting

For these three high-level requirements, the enterprise must review and determine which of the following six security essentials they have to accomplish to meet the requirements for site selection and facility design:

1. Demarcate by established defined borders to create a defendable space.
2. Prohibit entry and exit through a limited number of portals.
3. Deter threatening entities by ensuring the building appears strong and solid and deny easy access to keys, information, badges, windows, and doors.
4. Delay unauthorized entry by creating sound alarms.
5. Monitor detection systems in case an intruder gets past the physical barriers.
6. Communicate alarms immediately to an entity that is prepared to respond and react to an intrusion.

When an enterprise looks at a specific geographical location, it needs to look at the area and see that the considerations mentioned below meet the enterprise policy and culture, because this is a crucial decision that will impact efficiency, reliability, security, and service levels. Some of the items to consider as part of business requirements are as follows:

- Human resources and staff-related issues (culture and quality of life)
- Network connectivity and redundancy
- Utilities (availability, emergency shutoffs)
- Security and safety of equipment, data, and staff
- Business service availability in the community
- Real estate and business market conditions
- Real estate and building acquisition contractual requirements

## Build or Select an Existing Facility

Whether an enterprise is expanding/consolidating, the enterprise also needs to determine if it will be using the existing facility, relocating to another facility, or building its own facility. Later in the chapter, issues such as TIA-942, facility telecommunication, and cabling requirements that an enterprise must be aware of are discussed. This site must fit into current requirements and any future expansion/consolidation of the enterprise. Check with your current carriers for assistance to determine if they will continue to fit your needs. Before the enterprise decides to use an existing facility or build a new facility, it needs to document the following related to existing equipment:

- How much power is being used by the facility and equipment? http://www.formalogy.com/iphone.html
- How much equipment is being used or will be used for foot printing the space requirements?
- How much cooling and airflow equipment will be needed to ensure a controlled environment?
- How much bandwidth is being used and will be used for processing?
- Are there any special structural requirements for storing the equipment?
- How long would we need to and could go on generator power, similar to a business impact analysis?
- Is one of the company's mission statements to go toward a green enterprise environment?

Executive management should know the direction the business will be going toward in the future and they can provide hints toward expansion or consolidation. Can I recommend the use of an existing facility or building a new facility? No, because this decision will depend on the business requirements and the mission and vision of the enterprise.

## Physical and Material Supplies

IT staff must often remain in the data center for hours at a stretch performing work, and need an area to work and access the network. What is the function of the facility? Is it just going to host networking and production computer equipment? What are the types and number of assets that will be hosted in a data center facility? Assets can range from firewalls and other network devices to production servers containing the enterprise's most critical information. First and foremost, the enterprise must develop a list of assets that are going to be hosted and the environmental requirements of those assets. If staff are going to reside, even part-time, within the facility, work areas and supplies will need to be included in the facility requirements. Depending on the size of the facility, requirements for extra cabling, wiring, and hard drive space may be needed. Determining the square footage required for equipment, cabinets, and supplies ("foot printing") will assist the enterprise in selecting the size of the facility.

### Facility

Before getting into more detail, a physical site needs to be selected to host the equipment. When an enterprise evaluates a site or decides to use an internal facility, the following items need to be taken into consideration to limit the risk and threats to enterprise assets.

1. General construction:
   a. Can the structure withstand the regional disasters? What are the natural regional disasters? What are some regular man-made regional disasters?
   b. How many controlled and uncontrolled ingresses and egresses exist?
   c. Is the structure new or has it been retrofitted?

d. Does the construction company have an excellent reputation for service?
e. Is there a gated entrance and how is it controlled and monitored?
f. Can the exterior and interior doors be easily compromised? What are the alerts when this happens? What about the door frames?
g. What utility grid does the site reside in? Are there redundant utilities for the site, such as power generators?
h. How soundproof is the facility?
i. Is there much glass on the exterior? Are there many windows in the facility for unauthorized access or for viewing activity within the facility?
j. Does the facility contain raised floors? What about a manhole or underground opening to access the facility?
k. Does the facility contain signage: warning signs, exits, emergency lights?
l. What are the hazards of the facility?
m. What are the intrusion alerts and how can they be set off?
n. When the fire alarm goes off, do all the doors unlock within the building, including the data center or the enterprise cage? If so, what is the process for keeping the data center secure during a fire alarm incident?
o. Remember: Just because a building is built to code does not mean it is a good design for the enterprise assets.

2. Site vulnerabilities:
a. Is the site located in a high-crime area? Will the site feel safe when leaving after-hours?
b. Is the area outside well lit or hazardous when leaving after sunset? Does the outside lighting illuminate critical areas (fire escapes, ground-level windows and doors, alleyways)? Is there auxiliary power for the external lighting? Can the lighting be easily compromised?
c. Is the facility internally well lit during the day, as well as the night? Is there auxiliary power for the internal lighting?
d. How close are the emergency services (police, fire)?
e. Does the site attract unwanted attention?
f. Is the site marked as a hosting facility for random violence?
g. If the enterprise places their assets on the site, who can access the facility and can someone see and monitor activities of staff?
h. Can someone drive a truck through the wall of the site and damage internal assets?

3. Site protections:
a. Where are the security cameras located and how many are there? What are the closed-circuit television (CCTV) aspects of the facility? How are they being monitored?
b. Are the security cameras tape or digital? What is the retention for the video footage? Does it meet the enterprise record's retention requirements?
c. Are the rooms locked independently?
d. Do guards regularly walk the facility for unsecured areas?
e. Are there environmental controls: smoke detectors, fire detectors, fire suppression, and heat and humidity sensors?
f. Will tampering with any of the environmental controls create alerts to appropriate personnel?
g. What are the access controls? Biometrics? Mantraps? Proximity cards?
h. If badges are used, is it easy to distinguish a visitor from a staff member?
i. How are visitors and regular staff logged for entry and exit to the facility?

j. How is the enterprise alerted when there is a facility compromise?

k. Can the site perform regular maintenance without affecting the enterprise operations?

l. Does the facility have layered security controls: facility site, facility shell, data cages/rooms, work areas?

m. When a facility staff member is terminated or turns in their resignation, what controls are in place to ensure access is removed and passwords have been modified?

n. What is the screening method for facility staff members? Are the guards and staff rotated on a regular basis to ensure there are fresh eyes monitoring the environment?

o. Are facility staff members provided special training for firearms, CPR, first aid, fire safety, etc.?

4. Adjacent or nearby buildings:

a. How well maintained are the nearby buildings?

b. Can someone compromise an adjacent building and acquire access to the enterprise facility?

If a server room is going to be used instead of a hosting facility, the following requirements will need to be considered:

1. Does the room have full-height fireproof walls to close access through false ceiling tiles?

2. Does the server room have separate environmental controls from the enterprise building? Power, air, fire suppression?

3. Who maintains and controls the access to the room?

4. When the fire alarm goes off, do all the doors unlock within the building, including the data center? If so, what is the process for keeping the data center secure during a fire alarm incident?

## Environmental

After determining the physical and material supplies that will be housed in the facility, a list of the environmental requirements is needed:

1. Does the facility power meet the enterprise current and future equipment power needs?

2. Is the airflow and air conditioning sufficient for the current and future layout of the equipment?

3. Is the humidity for the current and future environment regulated and monitored?

4. Is the power supply sufficient for the current and future layout of the equipment?

5. Is the fire suppression spread throughout the facility and is it adequate to cover the enterprise equipment? Or are there automatic sprinklers for fire suppression and no protection for equipment when the sprinklers are activated?

6. What type of communication lines are in the place for the network devices and servers?

7. What about voice communications for staff who may be working at the facility?

8. What are the personal facilities and rest areas for staff working at the facility?

9. Is there backup power and environmental controls? Are they tested on a regular basis?

10. How does the facility respond to power spikes or brownouts?

11. Are there any static controls for the equipment?

## *Effective Physical Security*

This section is more of a listing of things to consider and question on the facility design when building a facility/data center or server, and even when using a hosting provider for the enterprise data center.

Whether the enterprise has regulatory requirements for auditing computing facilities or not, it should implement regular processes to perform its own facility auditing. Some facility auditing requirements are as follows:

1. If the facility is hosted, can the enterprise obtain an annual risk assessment or SAS70 Type II audit from the hosting facility?
2. Obtain and review a listing of authorized staff to the facility. Is it reviewed and approved on a regular basis? Who performs the authorization? Determine who is responsible for the enterprise staff access control and interview them to ensure they understand their responsibility.
3. Obtain and review a list of application software, operating system version, and hardware with their function and owner that reside in the facility. Assess the equipment maintenance, change management, and configuration management processes for the facility. This may include interviews with the enterprise staff responsible for the equipment.
4. Walk through the physical safeguards with the enterprise staff for accessing and maintaining the equipment in the facility. This would also include device and server console access and controls.
5. Obtain and review the standard operating procedures for the facility as performed by enterprise staff.
6. Obtain and review the business continuity and disaster recovery procedures for the enterprise staff operating the facility.
7. Review the facility installation and maintenance of the environmental controls.
8. Obtain and review the enterprise procedures for incident handling at the facility; also include the hosted facilities incident response procedures.
9. Obtain procedures for routine testing of environmental facility controls.
10. Walk through the facility; is there ease of, but secure, access to the facility? Can enterprise staff perform their functions within the facility easily and securely?
11. Remember the following for a basic checklist for a facility/data center/server room:
    a. Dedicated and secured space
    b. Reliable environment conditions
    c. Clean work area
    d. Limited access
    e. Active monitoring
    f. Operational procedures
    g. Trained staff

## *TIA-942*

For a generally accepted standard for facilities, please review TIA-942—a standard developed by the Telecommunications Industry Association (TIA) to define guidelines for planning and building facilities (http://www.tiaonline.org/standards/). The TIA-942 specification references data center requirements for applications and procedures such as

- Network architecture
- Electrical design
- File storage, backup, and archiving
- System redundancy
- Network access control and security
- Database management
- Web hosting
- Application hosting
- Content distribution
- Environmental control
- Protection against physical hazards (fire, flood, windstorm)
- Power management

The principal advantages of designing data centers in accordance with TIA-942 include standard nomenclature, fail-safe operation, protection against natural or man-made disasters, and long-term expandability and scalability.

## Conclusion

There are several things that need to be considered when selecting a site to support the enterprise. Documenting business requirements is a must before selecting a location for the data center. Most enterprise strategic plans only look ahead for up to three years, yet when looking for a data center site the enterprise needs to see much farther into the future. While the above are a sampling of questions to consider, you can also use something like the National Institute of Standards and Technology's Risk Management Guide for Information Technology Systems (SP 800–30). These documented requirements will then provide the enterprise with a site that will have efficient and effective productivity for a long period of time.

## About the Author

**Sandy Bacik**, CISSP, ISSMP, CISM, CHS-III, has over 22 years experience in information security and various information technology positions.

*Chapter 31*

# An Overview of IP-Based Video Surveillance

## Leo Kahng

## Contents

The information security industry has a long-standing history in Internet protocol (IP)–based tools, utilities, and communications, but this is not so much the case in the physical security realm, which is in the midst of a transition to IP. In 2007, Forrester Research stated in its report called "Trends 2007: Physical and Logical Security Convergence" that "…the physical security environment has been dominated by analog, stand-alone control systems with limited interconnectivity, digital communications, or integrated management capability." Physical security is often emphasized as one of the first layers of defense when addressing information systems, but it is a significant and critical element of security practices that can have a great impact on the networking foundation and information security architecture. In fact, it is significant enough that the certified information systems security professional (CISSP) examination identifies physical (environmental) security as one of its ten common body of knowledge (CBK) domains. This is then subdivided into layered physical defense and entry points, and site location principles.

Among the various physical security methods, such as physical facilities access, access control, and network admission control, one of the most traditional and widely used elements of physical security is that of video surveillance, which, until lately, has been largely based on analog technologies and site-based data-handling practices. This chapter covers key concepts and design considerations regarding video surveillance deployed over IP networks, as it realizes some unique benefits over previous surveillance systems, as well as new methods of data handling that IP transport enables. Leveraging the reach and flexibility of IP presents a range of advantages and enhancements that can increase responsiveness, reduce casualties and loss, and reduce the costs associated with the implementation of a robust and resilient surveillance solution.

## Challenges and Pain Points with Traditional Video Surveillance

Though we will not delve into the very origins of video surveillance, much of what is available today evolved from closed-circuit television (CCTV), which can arguably be dated as far back as 1942 when Siemens AG used such a system to remotely monitor the launching of V2 rockets to observe launch characteristics and any malfunctions or errant behavior. CCTV has since then managed to find its way into law enforcement organizations to fight crime, followed by a migration into the commercial sector, primarily in banks and retail, to monitor facilities access patterns and deter theft. In recent times, one of the most demanding applications for video surveillance is in the gaming industry where nonstop scrutiny in facilities such as casinos is of the highest priority for gaming houses to protect their interests from the less trustworthy. Additionally, in the past few years, a heightened awareness of physical security is steadily growing in the state and local government space, and especially in the K-12 and higher education environment. One such example is that of traffic monitoring cameras. However, one of the most widely covered tragic incidents of the recent past was the shooting at Virginia Tech, which unfortunately exposed a greater need for safety and security awareness in the education sector.

When we examine traditional video surveillance systems, several deficiencies are exposed that drive the need for a highly connected and converged solution that IP can bring forth.

- *Local access only*: The majority of existing legacy CCTV surveillance systems are almost entirely closed. The infrastructure, the video capture, camera management, and storage of the video feeds are all conducted locally, on-site. Remote access to these systems does not exist and the operation of these systems requires a skilled on-site staff to man an operations center or security office for as long as the surveillance is necessary. The transfer of information to and from the site is performed by manual means.
- *Low level of threat detection*: When security personnel have to observe the video streams that are being piped to monitors and recording systems, visual fatigue can set in very quickly. Studies have shown that up to a 95% decrease in event detection can occur after only 22 min of consecutive viewing. When events are missed, it is then up to review teams to evaluate hours of recorded material to identify and assess threats, which may have already damaged the integrity of a secure facility, or created a loss of assets.
- *Investigation delays*: With surveillance systems that rely on video tape or other removable media that is housed on-site, investigations of security incidents can be greatly delayed. For instance, the correct media has to be found (locate a tape in archive), then it has to be shipped to the reviewing party, then the media has to be reviewed and analyzed. Essentially, once the media is in the reviewers' hands, they have to watch as much video as was recorded and rely on their vision and alertness to detect the events that are in question.

- *Number of monitoring locations can be very limited*: Traditional surveillance systems require dedicated cabling plants. Often, these were expensive coaxial cable (most popular) or fiber-optic cable infrastructures. In order to place more cameras in strategically advantageous locations, cable needed to be pulled and back-hauled to the central command center for video monitoring.
- *Lacking ease of scalability*: In order to add more cameras, more matrix switching is required to handle the additional inputs and output streams, which often required a hardware upgrade or replacement.

Many other elements of traditional video surveillance can be pointed out, but the ones listed above represent some of the more popular pain points or challenges that are faced. One common theme that is present in the above-listed challenges is a very high degree of human interaction required to operate and manage traditional CCTV solutions.

# IP Video Surveillance Today

When we approach video surveillance from an IP standpoint, we immediately begin to incorporate features and utilities in the network infrastructure to augment the physical security enhancements that video monitoring enables. For instance,

- *Taking advantage of an existing infrastructure*: IP-based physical security leverages the network, which often already exists and provides a physical infrastructure that can be adapted and/or easily expanded to present more video camera coverage options.
- *Leverages network security features*: Use the authentication, authorization, and access control features native to the network security platforms in place. Monitor rogue device implantation in real time and implement policy-based countermeasures.
- *Enable the use of wired and wireless video surveillance cameras*: Anytime, anywhere coverage. Allows one to overcome the challenges associated with cabling where it is prohibitively difficult or costly to place a surveillance camera.
- *Digitally record video*: Provide immediate access to recorded events and enable real-time incident response, investigation, and resolution.
- *Monitoring and controls can be transferred to any point in the network*: No longer does one have to be physically colocated with the video surveillance infrastructure to manipulate and manage the video system. Provides true remote access to video streams, camera control, system management, and recorded video.
- *Ability to distribute management and recording of video*: Eliminates the "silo" effect and prevents systems from becoming a single point of failure.

One very innovative and important advent in the evolution of video surveillance is that of video content analysis (VCA), which is more commonly referred to today as video analytics. As mentioned earlier, in traditional video surveillance, the effectiveness of persons tasked with monitoring live video feeds, or reviewing recorded video footage, can dramatically decrease in as little as 22 min. Video analytics leverages automated algorithms and detection parameters to identify movement, anomalies, or behavior patterns within a particular field of view. For example, Figure 31.1 depicts an IP surveillance camera tracking movement within the field of view in a parking garage, where a person is spending time around a particular vehicle.

**Figure 31.1 Sample video analytics for motion or loitering.**

Using video analytics, human intervention can be greatly reduced, thus reducing the number of fatigue-related errors while allowing more efficient management of the video surveillance system. Video analytics enables real-time analysis and detection of security events from many different cameras, simultaneously, identifying events as they occur and providing tools to analyze the situation and even trigger responses, such as notifications, alerts, and alarms. Some of the most common algorithms and behavior detection scenarios are

- *Erratic/suspicious behavior*: Spending an unusual amount of time within one area or a repeating pattern of movement around vehicles in a parking garage.
- *Congestion detection*: Too many people in a particular space.
- *Motion detection*: An object, animal, or person crossing a particular field of view.
- *Abandoned object detection*: Parcels or luggage left unattended at an airport, for example.
- *Opposing flow*: Objects or persons moving opposite the normal direction of flow—a car going the wrong way down a one-way street.
- *Shape-based detection*: Automobile detection, detection of persons or animals, unusual size objects in the field of view.
- *Missing object detection*: Detection of something removed from a scene.
- *Video tripwire*: Alert based on detection of a breach of a defined boundary. This can be as simple as motion detection, or identifying movement or the presence of an entity in just a portion of the camera's field of view. Also, video tripwires can be utilized to trigger loitering alarms where a suspicious person may be lurking by a secure door waiting to enter a facility as someone from inside is leaving.

The current state of developments in the IP video surveillance realm negate the majority of the deficiencies encountered in traditional video surveillance systems, while reducing the level of human intervention and taking advantage of the IP network to provide real-time, anytime, anywhere monitoring for the betterment of physical security.

# Current Best Practices and Network Design Considerations for IP Video Surveillance

*Note*: In this section, we will examine several elements of consideration for design best practices. Though this is not a comprehensive overview, the topics of coverage are: the nature of video surveillance traffic, performance and storage considerations, multicast, quality of service and network design principles, and port-based security.

When considering the deployment of an IP-based video surveillance solution, many factors come into the picture that are not relevant to traditional surveillance topologies. One of the most obvious shifts in thought processes for design and best practices is the transport platform over which the video transmissions will traverse. We are now looking at an IP network to provide the communications infrastructure. With this in mind, some key best practices and network design considerations for IP video surveillance have been developed by Cisco Systems, which is beginning to challenge the traditional physical security brands by approaching this market from a networking perspective. Much of this segment, and those following immediately after, will be based on the design guidance set forth by Cisco Systems.

With a focus on the IP network, several factors come into consideration. Some of the most significant elements will be discussed in this section.

## The Nature of Video Surveillance Traffic

Surveillance traffic imposes demands on the networking infrastructure in the form of constant as well as variable bit-rate video, which have different implications for bandwidth utilization. Constant bit-rate video defines bandwidth for each video stream, which can be useful for capacity planning and storage, but can also occasionally waste bandwidth. Variable bit-rate video changes as differences in the video stream are captured. Typically, this results in lower overall bandwidth consumption, but traffic can be bursty, which makes it difficult to plan for capacity. To put this into perspective, let us examine Figure 31.2, which depicts constant bit-rate metrics based on video resolution.

To put video resolution into perspective, Figure 31.3 outlines respective resolution figures, represented as pixel measurements of width and height.

| Frame rate | Resolution | | |
|---|---|---|---|
| | CIF | 2 CIF | 4 CIF or D1 |
| 1.5 | 155,000 | 230,000 | 450,000 |
| 2 | 200,000 | 315,000 | 600,000 |
| 3 | 260,000 | 410,000 | 770,000 |
| 3.75 | 300,000 | 475,000 | 935,000 |
| 5 | 330,000 | 525,000 | 1,050,000 |
| 7.5 | 400,000 | 750,000 | 1,400,000 |
| 10 | 530,000 | 900,000 | 1,700,000 |
| 15 | 600,000 | 1,100,000 | 2,200,000 |
| 30 | 850,000 | 1,600,000 | 3,000,000 |

*Notes:* CBR rate guidelines by resolution and frame rate. Values in bits per second.

**Figure 31.2　Constant bit-rate bandwidth consumption guidelines.**

| Resolution | PAL | NTSC |
|---|---|---|
| QCIF | 176 × 144 | 176 × 120 |
| VGA | 640 × 480 | 640 × 480 |
| SVGA | 800 × 600 | 800 × 600 |
| XGA | 1024 × 768 | 1024 × 768 |
| CIF | 352 × 288 | 352 × 240 |
| 2 CIF | 704 × 288 | 704 × 240 |
| 4 CIF | 704 × 576 | 704 × 480 |
| D1 | 720 × 576 | 720 × 480 |

**Figure 31.3  Video resolution represented in pixels.**

Video is also categorized into live video as well as prerecorded video. Live video is clearly delay sensitive and quality of service (QoS) is very important in maintaining the integrity of live video streams. In most cases, transport is typically UDP (best effort). Recorded video is not adversely affected by delay, and reviews of the recorded video streams can be scheduled or ad hoc. Typically, transport is TCP based and the location of recording devices is of importance to understand where the information should be retrieved.

## Performance and Storage Considerations

When addressing video performance, parameters such as resolution and frame rate have a direct impact on both bandwidth and storage requirements. For instance, if we consider a video capture practice like dual-streaming, where live viewing locally and remotely need to be facilitated, one would be best served using high resolution and frame rates for local live viewing, while remote viewing can be adjusted to lower frame rates depending on available bandwidth. Also, especially for storage of captured video streams, the two leading methods are as follows:

- *Centrally located*: Centralized storage is typically deployed in a single environmentally controlled facility with close proximity to personnel who provide the technical support and management of the surveillance and storage systems. Often, these centralized storage models provide the advantage of potentially reducing operational costs due to only having a single location where the video is stored. However, in order to pass on video to other locations, or collect video from multiple locations in a central storage facility, there is likely more video (data) flowing across WAN links.
- *Distributed storage*: A distributed model for the storage of video surveillance streams positions storage to be located where events are happening, and within close proximity to local surveillance teams who can monitor and react to events in real time. Scalability can be achieved by using multiple smaller systems and there is not a single point of failure. Distributed storage also reduces the bandwidth requirements on the LAN and WAN links; however, there

are downsides like economies of scale—the cost per hour of storage with multiple smaller systems may be higher. Also, overall operational costs can be higher due to the required maintenance of more devices.

## Multicast: Just for a Quick Recap

- *Unicast*: Communications between one source address and one destination host address.
- *Broadcast*: Communication from one host address, typically to all hosts on a network segment or broadcast destination.
- *Multicast*: Communications where one host sends one copy of each packet being sent to a special address that is then used by several hosts interested in receiving this information. The receiving hosts are members of a designated multicast group and can join or leave the group dynamically, be members of one or multiple groups, and can be located anywhere on the network.

    Multicast is often desirable for IP video surveillance applications since increased efficiencies can be realized. For instance, lower CPU utilization is often observed since senders and receivers only receive requested data. Obviously, network utilization is optimal, when compared to replicating multiple streams. However, the nature of multicast relies on UDP, rather than TCP, for transport; thus drops can occur and are often expected since there is not a built-in receipt mechanism or congestion avoidance.

## Quality of Service and Network Design Principles

QoS is a critical technology that must be employed to maintain the integrity and efficacy of IP video surveillance. QoS when employed in IP networks allows a systems administrator to prioritize and protect video surveillance traffic from all other types of traffic that traverse the network. Also, proper deployment of QoS prevents the degradation of service events like packet loss, latency, and jitter, which represent the effects of mismanaged traffic congestion and will often result in poor video quality, sometimes a complete loss of video. Let us consider some of the impacts of these congestion events as they pertain to IP video surveillance.

- *Packet loss*—Video surveillance decoders may be able to tolerate some degree of packet loss, but the quality of the image will degrade. However, since surveillance video is often required to reconstruct critical information, there is not a specific amount of packet loss that can be deemed as "acceptable." IP video surveillance packet loss may represent itself as shown in Figure 31.4.
- *Latency*—This measure of delay represents the time required to encode, transmit, buffer, and decode the video. This delay sensitivity can be more critical for pan/tilt/zoom (PTZ) cameras due to their movement. A popular best-practice metric is to optimize total end-to-end delay to under 500 ms, with encoding and decoding best done under 250 ms, leaving 1–50 ms for LAN transport, and 100–150 ms for WAN transport.
- *Jitter*—Represented as delay variation, accounts for differences in the end-to-end delay for IP packets for a given video surveillance stream. Packets can over- or underrun the available buffer space, affecting the quality of playback. This effect can cause additional frames

**Figure 31.4   Examples of video surveillance packet loss.**

to be stored in the decoder's buffer, potentially reordering the frame sequence, introducing latency, and can result in dropped packets. Jitter is often recommended to be kept under 10 ms whenever possible.

Innovated by Cisco Systems, the hierarchical network design principle is often used in the deployment of IP video surveillance and leverages the advantages inherent to the core, distribution, and access layers design. A typical topology is shown in Figure 31.5.

QoS implementation for IP video surveillance traffic requires classification, marking, queuing, and scheduling provisions. The access layer defines the edge of the network, or the ingress point, where traffic must be classified and marked for further treatment in the architecture. The edge devices may be able to rely on configurable Differentiated Services Code Point (DiffServ Code Point, or DSCP) markings that originate from the end devices themselves, that is, video surveillance cameras. Access layer switches are then configured to trust these markings and preserve them upon ingress.

When looking at the actual classification and markings, the preferred methods for marking packets are for class of service (CoS), which is performed at Layer 2 of the OSI model, and DSCP marking, which is conducted at Layer 3. Let us briefly examine CoS marking at Layer 2 (Figure 31.6).

An Ethernet frame can be marked at Layer 2 (trunked) with their relative importance by setting the 802.1p user priority bits of the 802.1Q header. Since only three bits are available for 802.1p marking, eight COSs can be marked, 0–7.

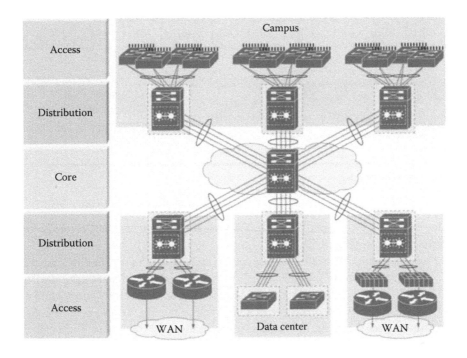

**Figure 31.5    Core-distribution-access design.**

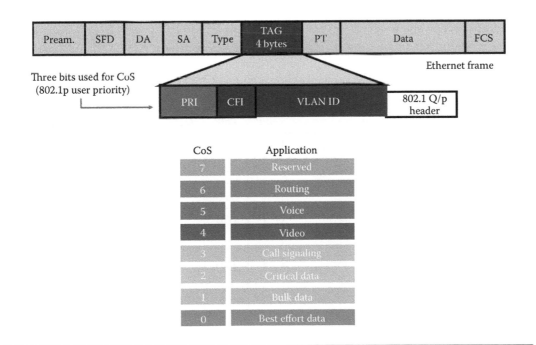

**Figure 31.6    CoS marking.**

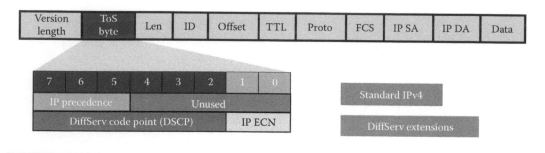

**Figure 31.7  IPP and DSCPs.**

If we now examine a DSCP marking at Layer 3, we see where several key pieces of information are coded into the packet (Figure 31.7).

Here we see information written into the type of service (ToS) byte. The three most significant bits of the ToS byte are called IP precedence (IPP). The six most significant bits of the ToS byte are called the DSCP, with the remaining two bits left for flow control. IPP values define eight levels of marking, which some find too restrictive and much prefer the 6-bit/64-value DSCP model. Figure 31.8 summarizes the recommendations for marking:

We must also consider the implications for WAN traffic. QoS for video surveillance across the wide-area network primarily accounts for queuing and scheduling. In particular, priority queue, or low latency queuing (LLQ) and class-based weighted fair queuing (CBWFQ). Priority or LLQ is employed to immediately service the highest priority traffic to minimize delay and prevent bandwidth starvation. CBWFQ will sort traffic based on markings and weighting them for servicing, while also providing traffic shaping for events like recorded video bursts across the WAN. For example, delay-, loss-, and jitter-sensitive traffic such as live video and audio surveillance and PTZ camera control will use a priority or LLQ algorithm.

| Layer 3 Classification | | | | |
|---|---|---|---|---|
| Traffic Type | IPP | PHB | DSCP | CoS |
| Live video surveillance | 4 | CS4 | 32 | 4 |
| Live audio surveillance | 4 | CS4 | 32 | 4 |
| PTZ/control | 4 | CS4 | 32 | 4 |
| Recorded video surveillance | 4 | AF41 | 34 | |
| Recorded audio surveillance | 4 | AF41 | 34 | 4 |
| System administration | 2 | CS2 | 16 | 2 |

**Figure 31.8  QoS baseline marking recommendations for IP video surveillance.**

Traffic that is more tolerant of fluctuations like recorded video and system administration can use CBWFQ algorithms.

With respect to network design for IP video surveillance, QoS, when implemented properly, can greatly increase efficiencies and the performance of surveillance systems, whether traffic is traversing the LAN and/or WAN. QoS is not a substitute for the proper provisioning of adequate link speeds but, conversely, provisioning a high level of bandwidth on a link is also not a replacement for properly configuring QoS on the network. When balanced in concert, these elements of networking work well together to provide optimal performance while not wasting bandwidth or network resources.

## Port-Based Security

Another best-practice focuses on port-level security where end devices such as the actual IP video surveillance cameras attach. IEEE 802.1x is a client-server based access control and authentication protocol that restricts unauthorized devices from connecting to a LAN through publicly accessible network ports. 802.1x provides this port-based network admission control for both wired and wireless endpoints. Used in conjunction with wireless network security, many security features are provided to protect wireless network access. Wireless security options include WEP, WPA, WPA2-PSK, and WPA2-Enterprise. Employing strict port-based security policies in addition to existing network security measures helps preserve the integrity of not only the network, but also the IP video surveillance cameras and what they are privy to viewing.

# Case Study: Retail

One the largest consumers of video surveillance technologies is the retail industry, which primarily uses surveillance to monitor theft patterns. In the 18th Annual Retail Theft Survey conducted in 2005, thieves stole over $5.8 billion from 24 surveyed retailers. This information was extracted from a survey that covered 13,313 stores with retail sales exceeding $519 billion that year. This shrinkage from theft accounts for about 2%–3% of revenues in most cases, and only 2%–3% of stolen merchandise is ever recovered. Using a combination of IP video surveillance, video stream storage, and video analytics, the retailer was able to respond much faster to real-time events and analyze events without personnel manning every video feed. Leveraging technologies like video analytics allowed security officers to concentrate on events to augment loss prevention, rather than scouring hours of video trying to locate a place in time where something happened. Additionally, employing tactics such as remote monitoring and operations of the surveillance system, and remote access to stored video greatly enhanced the productivity of the security staff. An example topology is represented in Figure 31.9.

In addition to the enhanced security and loss prevention, retailers have also discovered that surveillance systems are very effective in optimizing store operations and staff efficiency. For example, being able to monitor the number of open checkout stations as compared to the number of patrons standing in line allows the real-time analysis of operations efficiency and effectiveness. Should more staff be called in to speed up checkout, or should some staff be allocated to other departments when things are slow at the registers? These questions are easily answered in real time to optimize the efficiency of operations.

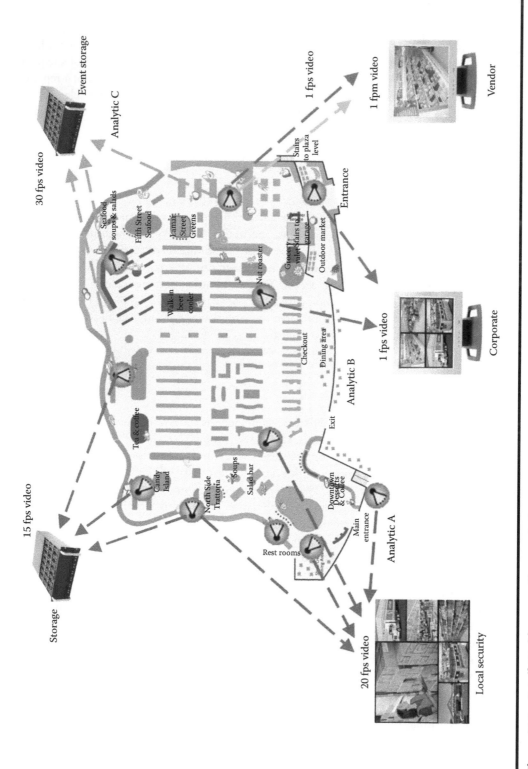

**Figure 31.9  Retail IP video surveillance solution.**

## Summary

In closing this overview of IP video surveillance, we are able to see some of the inherent advantages of deploying an IP-based surveillance system over traditional and/or analog solutions. We can also observe the efficiencies realized and potential cost savings when implementing an intelligent surveillance solution that leverages the existing network infrastructure. Also, when employing an IP video surveillance solution, we can clearly see that the system becomes a truly integral part of the overall networking platform and security practice, involving more than just video cameras and dedicated storage. As physical security endpoints are integrated into the network, the same diligence is required in properly managing security policies and integrity of the environment.

## About the Author

**Leo Kahng** is a consulting systems engineer for Cisco's U.S. Public Sector Sales theater, focusing on strategic business developments efforts in the education markets.

# Index

# Information Security Management Handbook, Sixth Edition: Comprehensive Table of Contents

**Domain 1    Access Control Systems**

(continued)

*(continued)*

## Domain 2 (continued)   Telecommunications and Network Security

**Domain 2 (continued)   Telecommunications and Network Security**

*(continued)*

**Domain 3 (continued)   Information Security and Risk Management**

(continued)

**Domain 3 (continued)  Information Security and Risk Management**

*(continued)*

**Domain 3 (continued)  Information Security and Risk Management**

*(continued)*

## Domain 4   Application Development Security

**Domain 4 (continued)   Application Development Security**

*(continued)*

## Domain 4 (continued)    Application Development Security

| Title | Volume 1 | Volume 2 | Volume 3 | Volume 4 |
|---|---|---|---|---|
| *Organized Crime and Malware,* Michael Pike | | | x | |
| *Net-Based Malware Detection: A Comparison with Intrusion Detection Models,* Robert M. Slade | | x | | |
| *Malware and Computer Viruses,* Robert M. Slade | x | | | |
| *An Introduction to Hostile Code and Its Control,* Jay Heiser | | x | | |
| *A Look at Java Security,* Ben Rothke | x | | | |
| **4.5 Methods of Attack** | | | | |
| *Hacking Methods,* Georges J. Jahchan | x | | | |
| *Enabling Safer Deployment of Internet Mobile Code Technologies,* Ron Moritz | x | | | |

## Domain 5    Cryptography

| Title | Volume 1 | Volume 2 | Volume 3 | Volume 4 |
|---|---|---|---|---|
| **5.1 Use of Cryptography** | | | | |
| *Auditing Cryptography: Assessing System Security,* Steve Stanek | x | | | |
| *Three New Models for the Application of Cryptography,* Jay Heiser | | x | | |
| **5.2 Cryptographic Concepts, Methodologies, and Practices** | | | | |
| *Cryptography: A Unifying Principle in Compliance Programs,* Ralph Spencer Poore | | | | x |
| *Cryptographic Transitions,* Ralph Spencer Poore | x | | | |
| *Blind Detection of Steganographic Content in Digital Images Using Cellular Automata,* Sasan Hamidi | x | | | |
| *An Overview of Quantum Cryptography,* Ben Rothke | x | | | |

**Domain 5 (continued) Cryptography**

*(continued)*

**Domain 5 (continued)   Cryptography**

**Domain 6   Security Architecture and Design**

## Domain 6 (continued)   Security Architecture and Design

## Domain 7   Operations Security

*(continued)*

**Domain 8 (continued)  Business Continuity and Disaster Recovery Planning**

*(continued)*

## Domain 8 (continued)    Business Continuity and Disaster Recovery Planning

| Title | Volume 1 | Volume 2 | Volume 3 | Volume 4 |
|---|---|---|---|---|
| *Business Continuity Planning: A Collaborative Approach*, Kevin Henry | x | | | |
| **Section 8.3 Elements of Business Continuity Planning** | | | | |
| *The Business Impact Assessment Process*, Carl B. Jackson | x | | | |

## Domain 9    Legal, Regulations, Compliance and Investigations

| Title | Volume 1 | Volume 2 | Volume 3 | Volume 4 |
|---|---|---|---|---|
| **Section 9.1 Information Law** | | | | |
| *Sarbanes–Oxley Compliance: A Technology Practitioner's Guide*, Bonnie A. Goins | x | | | |
| *Health Insurance Portability and Accountability Act Security Rule*, Lynda L. McGhie | x | | | |
| *Jurisdictional Issues in Global Transmissions*, Ralph Spencer Poore | x | | | |
| *An Emerging Information Security Minimum Standard of Due Care*, Robert Braun and Stan Stahl | x | | | |
| *ISPs and Accountability*, Lee Imrey | | x | | |
| *The Case for Privacy*, Michael J. Corby | x | | | |
| *Liability for Lax Computer Security in DDoS Attacks*, Dorsey Morrow | x | | | |
| *Compliance Assurance: Taming the Beast*, Todd Fitzgerald | | x | | |
| **Section 9.2 Investigations** | | | | |
| *Operational Forensics*, Michael J. Corby | x | | | |
| *Computer Crime Investigation and Computer Forensics*, Thomas Welch | x | | | |
| *What Happened?* Kelly J. Kuchta | x | | | |
| **Section 9.3 Major Categories of Computer Crime** | | | | |
| *Potential Cyber Terrorist Attacks*, Chris Hare | x | | | |

## Domain 9 (continued) Legal, Regulations, Compliance and Investigations

*(continued)*

Milton Keynes UK
Ingram Content Group UK Ltd.
UKHW052025071024
449327UK00027B/2433